A Jesuit Hacienda in Colonial Mexico

A Jesuit Hacienda in Colonial Mexico

 SANTA LUCÍA, 1576–1767

Herman W. Konrad

Stanford University Press

STANFORD, CALIFORNIA 1980

Stanford University Press
Stanford, California

© 1980 by the Board of Trustees of the
Leland Stanford Junior University

Printed in the United States of America

I S B N 0-8047-1050-3
L C 79-65518

Published with the assistance of the
Andrew W. Mellon Foundation

To the Mexican archivists
who make such studies possible

Acknowledgments

In the long and sometimes tedious investigation of records required to complete this study of latifundia, the unsung heroes of colonial research—the archivists—merit a special word of appreciation. J. Ignacio Rubio Mañé and his staff at the Archivo General de la Nación, in Mexico City, facilitated access to much of the documentation used, provided microfilms of key materials, and gave unstintingly of their time and interest. Father Daniel Olmedo, Director of the Biblioteca Mariano Cuevas, provided encouragement and microfilm at the early stages. The archivists at the Biblioteca Nacional were always helpful and provided microfilm copies of important documents. The family of the late Don Manuel Romero de Terreros, descendants of the post-Jesuit owner of Santa Lucía, generously allowed me into their home to examine hacienda records. Rolando Mellafe kindly microfilmed and sent materials from the Chilean National Archives. The library staff of the Washington State University at Pullman, in particular Adelle Knox, enabled me to make a thorough investigation of the Regla Collection and provided microfilm copies of large sections of it. The library staffs at the National Museum, Mexico City, the Library of Congress, Washington, D.C., and the University of Texas, Austin, provided assistance.

Much of the time needed for analyzing archival documents and writing the present version of this study was spent in Yucatán, Mexico. My knowledge and appreciation of Mexican colonial society has been immeasurably enhanced by the work and friendship of Don Alfredo Barrera Vásquez, Licenciado Victor Castillo Vales, and other Yucatecan scholars. Wilberth Herrera Pérez, Mario Martínez, and Beatriz Repetto provided valuable assistance in the transcription of microfilmed materials. My indebtedness to Candelaria Arceo de Konrad during the various stages of preparation of the study has increased in principle and in pleasure.

The original idea for the study emerged after reading Charles Gibson's *The Aztecs Under Spanish Rule: A History of the Indians of the*

Valley of Mexico, 1519–1810. Gibson's interest and encouragement helped translate the idea into reality. His patient persistence during the dissertation stage of the investigation was boundless. The tolerance of the University of Chicago and the University of Michigan in allowing meaningful interinstitutional collaboration warrants emulation. A special note of appreciation is due to Friedrich Katz, Enrique Florescano, Rodolfo Stavenhagen, Claude Morin, William Taylor, and Jean-Pierre Berthe for both direct and indirect stimulation. Finally, financial assistance by the University of Calgary for the preparation of the final version of the manuscript is gratefully acknowledged.

H.W. K.

Contents

Tables

Figures and Maps

A Jesuit Hacienda in Colonial Mexico

ONE 🔲 Introduction

Ignacio Loyola's black-robed followers came to New Spain in the 1570s, quietly, and in small groups. They encountered a situation where half a century of interaction between European and Indigenous peoples had already resulted in changes that were to persist throughout the colonial epoch.* The first group of fifteen Jesuits, arriving at New Spain's gulf port of Veracruz in 1572, were directly aided in their coming by the Spanish crown and had been commissioned by superiors in both Spain and Rome to assist in the dual task of civilizing and Christianizing the society being created in New Spain. They arrived eager to work with the natives, well prepared to interact harmoniously with Spanish institutions at all levels, and with special abilities to deal with those in high authority. Their arrival was accompanied by a minimum of fanfare.

Initially the Jesuits established themselves in the European population centers. Other mission orders—Augustinians, Dominicans, Franciscans, and to a lesser degree Carmelites—had already claimed as their jurisdiction the easily accessible remains of Aztec imperialism, thereby blocking immediate access to the Indigenous populations. Despite their eagerness to work with the native populations, the Jesuits' instructions and experience as educators dictated that they begin in the Spanish population centers. Here they were to lay the solid foundations for later frontier mission endeavor, creating at the same time the educational institutions that had such a profound impact upon the highest levels of Spanish society, as well as upon the rest of the colony.[1]

Conditions were most favorable when the Jesuits expanded their activities into New Spain. Since its institutionalization by papal authority in 1535, the order had achieved structural cohesion and a high degree of operational efficiency. Its educational successes in Europe, as the major Counter Reformation thrust, and its mission

---

*I use the term Indigenous as a synonym for the sectors of the New World society usually called Indian.

activities in the Philippines, Hispaniola, Florida, and Peru, had gained it many friends and admirers in church, state, and private sectors of both Spain and New Spain. As a new, elite intellectual and moral force, the Jesuits were still largely unaffected by the power struggles between church and state, and between the secular and regular clergy. Their special attachment to the papacy, symbolized by their fourth vow of obedience to the pope and their strategic command center in Rome, was complemented by their practical value to the Spanish crown. For Philip II, in his role as custodian of church affairs in Spain, the Jesuits represented a potentially powerful agency for implementing Spanish objectives in the colony's European population centers and on the Indigenous frontiers. The material cost to the crown would be limited. Its legal, moral, and political support was of greater importance, since the private sector was more than willing to provide material means. Offers of financial assistance to the Jesuits were so plentiful that the order's acceptance became a matter of choice, based on an evaluation of the short- and long-term implications of each gift. In addition, the Jesuits had already demonstrated an extraordinary ability to create and manage financial resources through astute investments in revenue-producing urban properties.[2]

The promise was quickly realized as the Jesuits established and consolidated their institutional presence in Mexico City, the capital of the thriving viceroyalty of New Spain. From there, the order's educational institutions spread rapidly into the other important Spanish urban centers, as did support from crown officials, the clergy, successful individuals, and all strata of the nascent society. Their missionary focus was most evident on the expanding northern frontiers, where they played a dominant role in the pacification and incorporation of hostile cultures. Individuals such as Andrés Pérez de Rivas and Francisco Kino exemplified these successes, which, though not so spectacular as those in Brazil, New France, and Paraguay, ensured a continuing positive image in the colonies as well as in Europe.[3]

At the same time, through direct and indirect assistance of royal officials and private individuals, a solid economic base was created in New Spain. This base, centered as it was in the utilization of rural properties, deviated from the accepted European practices of essentially urban-derived financing. The rural properties forming that base were the *haciendas*, producing cash crops, food crops, and livestock. The estates provided revenues for sustaining a constantly expanding sphere of Jesuit activity throughout the order's colonial experience. These economic activities, frequently located on the periphery of the Spanish urban centers, brought the Jesuits into unplanned and unanticipated contact and confrontation with the secular and material side of colonial society. Although the crown, as patron, was willing to overlook the implications of the competitiveness of Jesuit economic activities, the archbishops and bishops were not so inclined. The result was an ongoing, and growing, conflict over jurisdiction (rights and duties in the performance of ecclesiastical rites) and resources (the tithe and other church fees). Simultaneously, the increasing dominance of Jesuit estates in specific rural areas led the private and Indigenous sectors to view the Jesuits as economic competitors rather than ideological allies.

By the middle of the eighteenth century, the Jesuits were heavily involved in the material affairs of New Spain, but still highly respected and well supported in their educational and mission activities. Opposition to the Jesuits was much stronger in Europe. The events that led to the sudden expulsion of the order from the Spanish colonies and the expropriation of all their institutions, in 1767, did not originate in New Spain or the Indies, although developments there cannot be discounted. Economic, ideological, and political factors converged to produce, by papal decree in 1773, the extinction of the Company of Jesus, heralded two hundred years earlier as the outstanding moral force in the Roman Catholic world.

The Bourbon monarchy proved to be the driving force behind the Jesuits' demise. In Portugal, suppression took place in 1759, preceded by accusations of complicity in a plot against the crown. In France, a Jesuit economic maneuver provided the immediate pretext, although royal support for the Jansenist rather than the Jesuit side of ideological perspectives was more fundamental in the order's suppression, in 1764. In Spain, there were charges of complicity in political acts in opposition to royal authority. There were other factors: the determined opposition to a crown-supported canonization of the former Mexican nemesis, Archbishop Juan de Palafox y Mendoza; and certain reasons Charles III insisted on "keeping in his royal self."

On February 27, 1767, the Spanish king signed the order expelling the Jesuits from his dominions. Two days later, at night, the order was executed: all Jesuit possessions in Spain were occupied, and the Jesuits were placed under arrest. In New Spain, with equal suddenness, and under the cover of darkness, the order was implemented by the viceroy on June 25, 1767. Thus the Jesuit haciendas, along with all other Jesuit institutions in Mexico, became royal property. The public manifestations against this act, in Guanajuato, San Luis Potosí, Valladolid, Pátzcuaro, and other centers, were quickly suppressed, and the Jesuits themselves were shipped to Europe under arrest. The crown appointed administrators to run the ex-Jesuit haciendas, which were subsequently sold to private individuals of wealth and status.[4]

Chroniclers of Jesuit activities in the Americas have written extensively about mission activities and educational institutions.[5] Largely ignored, until recently, have been the Jesuit haciendas, developed to provide material support for the order's institutions in the cities and on the mission frontiers. François Chevalier's publication of the eighteenth-century Jesuit document *Instrucciones a los hermanos jesuitas administradores de haciendas,*[6] and his analysis of the society's haciendas as part of the emergence of the latifundium in colonial Mexico,[7] focused research in this area. Studies by McBride, Simpson, and Gibson, while outlining the general structure of rural economic development, reemphasized the need for specialized research on haciendas.[8] An increasing number of scholars are now focusing their attention upon this important aspect of colonial development.[9] Studies of regions and specific estates in New Spain, furthermore, have uncovered a greater diversity in the scope and function of haciendas than was suggested by earlier studies.[10] The publication of documents about Mexican Jesuits[11] and about hacienda administration in other areas of Latin America[12] also provides a fuller background for case studies. This case study, although regional in emphasis, provides an important vantage point for viewing the development of colonial society.

The focus of this study is Santa Lucía, the earliest of the Jesuit-created hacienda complexes in Central Mexico. Initiated in 1576 as the direct result of a monetary gift from a generous benefactor, and terminated as a Jesuit estate with the unceremonious expulsion of the order in 1767, Santa Lucía represents much more than an economic resource built by the disciples of Loyola. As one of the largest and most prosperous haciendas of its time, it reflects many facets of the larger institution of the latifundium, its development, growth, and function. Santa Lucía and *anexas,* as its holdings were usually called, were deliberately established, although with misgivings, as a means of supporting the Colegio de San Pedro y San Pablo in Mexico City. Unintentionally, and without misgivings on the part of the Jesuits, it became an institution in itself, with far-reaching consequences.

Although the process of colonial estate formation has been clearly outlined by Chevalier, detailed examples documenting it are largely lacking. Part I of this study (Chapters 2–4) has been designed to show the historical development of a major hacienda complex. As far as archival materials allow, it documents acquisition processes and details initial involvement, expansion, consolidation, and maximum extension, providing a Jesuit rationale for these activities. A chronological summary of each acquisition, including the background of each property prior to Jesuit ownership, has been provided in Appendix A. These materials demonstrate that hacienda growth and development continued throughout the colonial era. They suggest that large estates were a by-product of the constantly shifting economic fortunes of the colony, that they were consistently profit-oriented, and that success was directly related to the ability to adapt to local and regional market demands.

Success depended upon a dual strategy of specialization and diversification. A growing European community in the colony provided ready markets for food crops and livestock products, and, with the development of mining activities, these markets expanded. At the same time, demands external to the colony afforded markets for some livestock products (such as hides), sugar, and special items such as dye goods. Over time, changes in market demand, competition from other colonial areas, and the inability of Indigenous rural production to supply traditional crops—the last intensified by demographic decline and loss of control over resources—forced shifts in production emphasis. By the eighteenth century, sugar was of marginal importance, replaced largely by European and Indigenous cereal crops; as the dispossessed native sector recovered numerically, the production of *pulque* (maguey liquor) became central. The ability to specialize and compete by producing demand goods determined an individual estate's commercial success or failure. However, disease, drought, depression, and other factors causing fluctuations in the colonial economy meant that, during any given season, production failures could be anticipated. Having access to diverse crops and income offset short-term total losses, thereby maintaining the productivity of a particular estate. Thus, although commodity specialization was desired, success depended upon sufficient diversity to allow for adaptation. Small estates had neither the capacity nor the resources to adapt to changing conditions. Large estate complexes, such as Santa Lucía, proved more successful.

Throughout its almost two-hundred-year history, Santa Lucía

interacted with the society of New Spain in many ways and at many levels. Cities and mines were affected by the agricultural and livestock products that streamed from its many lands. Viceregal authorities aided its expansion in the face of legal restrictions. Judges of the *audiencia* (royal court) regulated differences between the owners of Santa Lucía and those who lived on its fringes. Secular ecclesiastical officials, such as Bishop Palafox, saw it as a symbol of the abuse of religious privileges and fought against it accordingly. Passing travelers, such as the Italian Gemelli Carreri, visited Santa Lucía and described it with great admiration.[13] And the Indigenous people who lived in the path of its expansion were slowly but irrevocably drawn into its sphere of transforming influences. Its management produced a hierarchy of efficient administrators, a model that *latifundistas* were largely unsuccessful in duplicating. The styles of operation developed on Santa Lucía were so well established and unquestioned that later non-Jesuit owners found it in their best interest to "deal with the property as did the fathers in their time."[14]

Apart from showing that the Jesuit haciendas can be seen as an extension of European economic principles being adapted to new geographic and human environments, the material presented in Part I of this study indicates how economic involvement in the New World affected the Society of Jesus. The long-term impact resulted in financial successes that made possible continual expansion of educational and mission endeavor and, at the same time, established conditions requiring increased involvement in secular aspects of colonial life. And the Jesuits, like their secular *hacendado* (hacienda owner) counterparts, exploited their elite status and close ties with royal authorities to further interests that conflicted with crown policy and administrative intent. The resolution of conflict, in most cases in favor of hacendado interests, aided in the frustration of humanitarian impulses guiding royal legislation. By the middle of the eighteenth century, the status of Santa Lucía as a major producer of pulque—a means of supporting the rampant alcoholism within the Indian sectors struggling to come to terms with their unfavorable social and economic conditions[15]—indicates the degree to which the Jesuit estates had become part and parcel of an economic system that functioned to support a colonial aristocracy at the expense of the less powerful Indigenous, African, European, and miscegenated lower classes. In the end, Santa Lucía's very success helped to undermine royal confidence in its owners, and indirectly helped set the stage for the dramatic expulsion of the Jesuits from the Spanish colonies.

Part II (Chapters 5–8) examines administrative structure, management strategies and their impact, and hacienda production and revenues. Linkages between Europe and the colony, between Mexico City (the viceregal capital) and the countryside, between the hacienda's production nerve-center (the Santa Lucía residence) and its dependent units, and between the hacienda and the Indigenous rural communities are examined. These chapters demonstrate how the rural estates were not only tied to, but dependent upon, the interests and demands of the urban centers. Jesuit principles of hierarchical organization, formulated to control and direct an expanding cadre of ideological entrepreneurs, proved applicable to missions, educational institutions, and commercial enterprises. The key role of an efficient communication system, the importance of record-keeping, and, above all, the usefulness of maintaining close working relationships with the political and social elites are reflected in the day-to-day activities of Jesuit haciendas. Their development and growth coincided with an ongoing battle between the Jesuits and civil and Indigenous authorities, in a lawyers' war of "mine and thine."[16]

In Part III (Chapters 9–11), the emphasis shifts to a more detailed examination of the impact of the hacienda upon the lives and activities of the men, women, and children who worked on the estate. The account records of Santa Lucía are rich in detail, allowing for a presentation of labor patterns, an examination of debt and credit mechanisms used to control and exploit available labor, and a reconstruction of daily, weekly, monthly, and annual work activities (Chapter 9). The available evidence suggests that debt peonage, although practiced, was not so oppressive a device as has been commonly thought.[17] When labor status is related to race and class distinctions accepted in colonial society, the evidence suggests that occupational status was more important than social distinctions. Santa Lucía's endurance helped to break down the existing stratification in society and to alter those in formation, providing direction to new cultural, economic, and social delineations among African, Indigenous, and European elements.

Examination of the role of slaves on the hacienda (Chapter 10) indicates that this source of labor played a vital role throughout most of the colonial period, and long after Mexico ceased to be a large-scale importer of African slaves. Of particular significance was the role of slaves in livestock production and the consequences of this involvement as a factor in the merging of slaves and ex-slaves with other racial groups in the rural areas. Comparative status of slaves working in different hacienda contexts also underlines the importance of occupational roles rather than legal or social distinctions, as status indicators.

In Chapter 11, attention focuses upon the impact of the hacienda on the life-style of hacienda workers and the peasant villages that provided the labor force. Although Santa Lucía's status as a corporate Jesuit enterprise produced unique configurations and fostered a somewhat somber dedication to economic production, its status as a large-scale, secular commercial activity overshadowed Jesuit influence. For the majority of workers, the life-style produced did not vary significantly from that experienced by individuals affected by non-Jesuit estates. An examination of a typical year of activities in the mid-eighteenth century provides insights into the nature of the annual economic cycle for a large hacienda complex. The yearly cycle of activities of shepherds, goatherds, and cowboys provides a glimpse into the experience of selected rural sectors of colonial society, and accounts of individual experience allow for a sampling of variation and individual differences. Finally, a comparison of the situation of hacienda workers to that of village residents provides a rough gauge for contrasting the relative well-being associated with regular hacienda employment with the marginal well-being experienced in the *pueblos* (villages).

In Part IV (Chapters 12 and 13), Santa Lucía is compared to other haciendas in colonial Mexico. This allows for a broader treatment of questions relating to the nature, role, and function of haciendas in colonial society. Production strategies, management structures, acquisition patterns and their consequences, utilization and control of labor, residence patterns, and general impact are compared. In addition, an attempt is made to assess the larger role of haciendas as an institution introduced and controlled by Europeans and how it affected basic social, political, economic, and historical processes.

The term *hacienda*, as used in this study, has been deliberately chosen. It indicates rural-based productive economic activities as well as urban influences and activities. Its colonial usage, in the first instance, referred to liquid assets, including real and movable property. In sixteenth-century Mexican usage, *hacienda* referred to both rural and urban contexts, encompassing a broad spectrum of economic activities. Colonial haciendas were not distinct from what contemporary writers refer to as *plantations*, defined as agrarian, capital- and labor-intensive, export-oriented institutions of production. *Hacienda*, the generic Hispanic term for a wide range of economic activities, and *plantation*, the Anglo-Saxon term for specialized agrarian activities in tropical latitudes, were variations of a single phenomenon in colonial times.[18]

The Jesuits maintained a sixteenth-century usage of the term throughout the colonial period. But they did qualify it when referring to specific activities and estates within their economic empire. Terms such as *hacienda de ganado mayor* (ranch for cattle, horses, or mules), *hacienda de ganado menor* (ranch for sheep, goats, or hogs), *hacienda de ovejas* (sheep ranch), *hacienda de cabras* (goat ranch), *hacienda de caballar* (horse ranch), *hacienda de azúcar* (cane fields), *hacienda de pan* (wheat fields), *hacienda de pulque* (maguey plantings), *hacienda de labor* (crop lands), *hacienda de matanza* (slaughtering and processing facilities), *hacienda de astilleros* (woodlands and lumber mills), *hacienda de minas* (mines), and *hacienda de molino* (milling facilities) were common in the eighteenth century. Other terms, such as *rancho, estancia, sitio, hato, labor, trapiche,* and *ingenio* were also employed, with or without reference to specific properties.[19] The exclusive association of the term *hacienda* with only the rural dimensions of agrarian production was never a feature of colonial Mexican usage. The term, at the same time, was maintained as the primary referent for the crown, or state, treasury. The term *hacendado* came to mean the owner of rural properties.[20] The individual hacendado, however, almost always maintained urban connections.

Although this study focuses upon Santa Lucía, my primary objective is to analyze the colonial institution of the hacienda. This was essentially an urban-controlled, rural-based economic institution dedicated to producing livestock, food crops, and cash crops, or any combination thereof. As used throughout, such categories refer to production strategies rather than precise, mutually exclusive types of activities. All activities on the Jesuit estates were geared to producing cash revenues, and in this sense they were all oriented to cash crops. But each type of activity had distinctive features.[21] Livestock production involved extensive use of land, with pasture and water resources often widely dispersed. It was a new feature introduced into the colony by Europeans, and it played a significant role in sustaining the conquest society while transforming the conquered Indigenous sectors. Food-crop production involved intensive use of land and water resources within more rigidly defined geographical areas during the crop cycles. It involved the introduction of new European crops and the maintenance of traditional native crops, serving the needs of both sectors while facilitating their integration. Cash-crop production frequently included food crops, so no clear distinction between the two categories can be made in terms of type of crop, although the emphasis of cash-crop production was primarily on external sales (regional or export), calling for labor-intensive strategies. It accentuated the division between the European and Indigenous sectors and encouraged the introduction of foreign labor—primarily African slaves—into the colonies.

All three strategies involved direct input from the hacienda owners, who provided investment capital and management direction, and who expected to gain profits and prestige. They all included the use of rural land, pasture, water, and other resources (for example, woodlands and building materials), plus an administrative residence and storage, processing, and service facilities. In most cases they involved a mixture of resident and seasonal labor. These features of the hacienda—an institution that grew up between the Spanish city and the rural countryside—should not be confused with the variables related to location, market conditions, and types of ownership (corporate versus private). Among these variables are size, utility of resource base, stability of ownership, administrative efficiency, type and source of labor (including debt or credit status), residence status (or access to hacienda resources), degree of self-sufficiency, and type of product. Productivity, or the success or failure of individual estates, might be best explained in terms of these variables, representing assets or restraints in carrying out objectives.

The details that occupy most of the pages of this book should be seen as incomplete, but key, bits of evidence, gathered to reconstruct the outlines of an institution within a specific historical context. Only attention to detail from specific cases can establish a basis for a clearer picture of the range of variation found within the larger institution. A systematic clarification of nomenclature as used throughout the colonial period in distinct regions is still required. When produced, it will add significant details while clarifying basic issues and processes.[22] Santa Lucía represents but one expression of the larger institution. It was a hacienda shaped by location, market conditions, and ownership. It reflects many of the changes occurring through time. The concept of the hacienda had more than one meaning in colonial society, as it does in this study. It refers to the larger economic institution; it refers to a particular estate complex such as Santa Lucía; and it refers to the components within the particular complex—its dependent ranches, farms, and facilities.

To appreciate and understand the factors affecting Santa Lucía, it is important to keep in mind the larger cultural, economic, political, and ideological influences that were shaping European society and the colonies in the Americas. Although past scholarship has emphasized such factors in the exploration of the nature and significance of colonial society, it has frequently done so at the expense of what was actually taking place in the local context and, in most cases, has overlooked what was taking place on the haciendas. It is here, in the specific, local context, that this study concentrates most heavily, providing details and insights for recasting views about the nature of haciendas and society in the Spanish colonies.

PART ONE

The Acquisition of Properties

TWO 🈯 *The Beginnings, 1576-1586*

The willingness of the Jesuit academician to take the advice of a
secular friend led to the establishment of one of the most productive latifundium complexes in colonial Mexico. In December 1576,
the Reverend Doctor Pedro Sánchez, father provincial of the Jesuit
province of New Spain, purchased a collection of partly developed
rural estates near Mexico City and named them Santa Lucía, in
honor of the purchase-date's patron saint.[1] The order spent 17,000
precious pesos* to buy land, some deteriorated buildings, 16,800
sheep, 1,400 goats, 125 mares, a few stallions, mules, donkeys, and
dogs, 8 African slaves, and ranch and farm tools.[2] The source of
the funds was a wealthy Spanish admirer, Don Alonso de Villaseca. In making the purchase, Sánchez committed Loyola's disciples in New Spain to a type of economic activity in which they
had no experience or training. A few months earlier, Villaseca had
given the Jesuit order 40,000 pesos in endowment funds to establish in Mexico City its administrative and intellectual center, the
Colegio de San Pedro y San Pablo.[3] Sánchez planned to invest part
of the endowment in urban properties, including a tile factory, in
order to produce fixed rents. Villaseca, however, suggested that in
New Spain greater revenues could be realized by purchasing inexpensive rural estates, which, if given the careful attention of the
industrious Jesuits, would quickly prosper.[4] On his own initiative,
the provincial took Don Alonso's advice rather than follow accepted procedures and in so doing took the first step in a process
that—despite the initial protests of fellow Jesuits and opposition at
the highest levels of the order's hierarchy—resulted in the Jesuits'
owning many prosperous agricultural and livestock estates in New
Spain. At the moment of purchase, Sánchez was not concerned
about the policy implications of his innovative step. His primary
purpose was to establish his order firmly in a new province, with

*Throughout this study, the term peso refers to a peso of 8 reales, unless other-
wise indicated.

sufficient economic support to sustain ambitious educational and missionary objectives.[5]

Finding the Proper Patron

The first Jesuits to arrive in Mexico were educators, their expenses paid from the treasury of Philip II of Spain.[6] Beginning in 1547, prominent personalities in New Spain, including the viceroy, the bishops of Chiapas and Michoacán, members of the audiencia, members of the Mexico City *cabildo* (municipal council), and wealthy individuals such as Villaseca had been petitioning the Spanish crown and the Jesuit father general in Rome to send Jesuits to Mexico.[7] In 1571, Francisco de Borja, as father general, decided the time had come to establish the Jesuit presence in Mexico. He chose two experienced educators, Pedro Sánchez and Diego López, to lead a group of fifteen Jesuits to New Spain.[8] The eight fathers and seven brothers left Cádiz on June 13, 1572, and arrived in San Juan de Ulúa (Veracruz) on September 19. They hurried from the Gulf Coast to the Highlands and established themselves in the modest surroundings of the Hospital de Nuestra Señora in Mexico City. Here the black-robed clerics immediately found themselves the object of attention of wealthy and influential personages eager to be accepted as patrons, or as founders of the college the newcomers had been directed to establish.[9]

The choice of a patron was a delicate matter, for Jesuit temporal needs and ideological goals had to be matched with the resources of the donor. The choice would set the tone for Jesuit interaction with the society of New Spain. The many candidates were quickly reduced to three: the viceroy, Don Martín Enríquez de Almansa; the secretary of the Mexico City cabildo, Don Francisco Michón Rodríguez; and Don Alonso de Villaseca, a wealthy private citizen. The viceroy offered the Jesuits a location near the central plaza of the city, which was thought to be too conspicuous. The cabildo secretary, in an exaggerated display of piety, prostrated himself before the Jesuit leaders and offered his haciendas, his properties in the city, and himself to the order, insisting he would not arise until accepted. But such public display and the impact of an open alliance with government officials did not find favor with the independent-minded Jesuits.[10]

Villaseca, who preferred to do his good works as secretly as possible,[11] chose the opposite approach. First, he sent a modest monetary gift to the temporary Jesuit quarters to help pay daily expenses. Seeing this gift favorably received, he sent two trusted members of his household to talk to Sánchez and López secretly, and to offer the order a modest residential site—a city block composed of five separate lots with some walled-in structures in poor condition—beside his own residence. The Jesuits agreed to inspect the property at night and under these circumstances made their first direct contact with Villaseca. Sánchez, as provincial of the new province and rector of the future college, consulted with the other Jesuits and decided to accept this studied but secretive offer of patronage.[12] They took formal possession of the residential site thirty-nine days after arriving in Mexico City and in December 1572 moved there from their temporary hospital quarters, thereby becoming the neighbors of one of the wealthiest and most influential individuals in the viceroyalty.[13] Thus, Don Alonso won the struggle among the colony's leading residents to become patron of the highly regarded newcomers.

Villaseca was devoted, powerful, rich, and shrewd, although not necessarily in that order. He shared the well-trained austerity and devotion of Loyola's followers which, when put into practice in the management of material goods, produced almost miraculous results. Villaseca had come to the New World to search for opportunities not available in Spain. He arrived in Mexico at the beginning of the 1540s, too late to claim any of the honors of conquest, but within twenty years he was considered one of the richest men in New Spain.[14] Aided by his marriage to Francisca Morón,[15] the daughter of a wealthy hacendado, he rapidly accumulated rural and urban properties. By the 1570s he controlled a small empire, including holdings in what are now the Mexican states of Hidalgo, Guanajuato, Mexico, Veracruz, and Zacatecas. His business ventures included livestock-raising, mining, agriculture, and real estate. His business accounts between 1542 and 1580 show he was engaged in producing cereal grains, meat, and woolen and leather goods for the rapidly expanding urban and mining centers. He bought rural and urban properties when prices were low and sold them when prices rose. He rented properties and lent money at fixed rates, as well as operating mines.[16]

With Villaseca as patron, the Jesuits came into close contact with an individual who shared many of their own views about austerity and ostentation, sacrifice and success. In terms of material wealth, business experience, and political influence, Villaseca was the best possible contact for a new organization wishing to establish itself quickly in New Spain without becoming enmeshed in political and economic conflicts, for Don Alonso had managed to achieve his wealth while making many friends and few enemies—a rare combination. What Don Alonso did not have was a son, a minor calamity in his time and culture, and a fact immediately recognized by the Jesuits as propitious for their access to his wealth, but which complicated relations with his heirs.[17] Lacking a son of his own to inherit the family name and fortune, Don Alonso chose the many sons of the Society of Jesus to receive his wealth and advice.

The Patron's Gifts

Documents drawn up to legalize the transfer of property from Villaseca to the Jesuits detail the order's introduction to legal conditions in New Spain.[18] A letter of donation dated November 6, 1572, stated that Villaseca, a resident of Mexico, seeing that the Jesuits had no place to build their college and wishing to assist them in serving the Lord, made a "free, perfect, irrevocable" donation of five lots to the society to do with as they pleased. The properties were declared to be free from debts or encumbrances. Conditions were added: the Jesuits were to use the donation as the site for a college to be named in honor of Villaseca's patron saints, Peter and Paul, and if the named college were not built on the specified site, the donation would become void.[19]

The contradictions—on the one hand, indicating an irrevocable gift without restrictions and, on the other hand, canceling the donation if a specifically named college was not constructed—reflected the interests of both parties and the legalistic framework within which they functioned. Jesuit activities were carefully regulated by the statutes of the society, which insisted that all donations be subject to terms set by the order.[20] Gifts must be unconditional and irrevocable. These conditions were stated in the document, which then listed the conditions set by the patron. Both parties in fact agreed on the use of the property, but Villaseca, by now an old man looking ahead to the time when his presence would no longer prevent someone else from usurping his patronage role, added legal documentation. The Jesuits' acceptance of Villaseca's conditions was based, in part, upon Sánchez's wish to respond positively to the donations of a trusted friend and upon the practical reality that in a new mission province the intent of the order's statutes might take precedence over a literal interpretation.

A formal act of possession concluded the property transaction. Such notarized possession acts completed the legal process while formally recognizing the new owners. Included were symbolic rites of introducing the new owner to physical properties—including inspection of land, buildings, and other goods; a symbolic expulsion of the previous owner; and symbolic acts of possession such as opening and closing doors or gates, pulling up grass or plants, and throwing stones within the property.[21] The ritual varied according to the type of property involved, but it was designed to provide one last opportunity for an interested third party to raise objections. Such an objection had to be dealt with before the transfer could be completed. These legal safeguards, in theory designed to protect the rights of Indians or Spaniards, in practice frequently failed, for influential Spaniards usually found ways of either suppressing or ignoring last-minute Indigenous claims.[22] In this case there were no objections, and the Jesuit fathers peacefully became urban property holders. Such rites of possession were to be repeated many times, documenting the acquisition of types of wealth not envisioned by the Jesuit statutes, while at the same time drawing the order into secular activity in New Spain. The Jesuits quickly became very skillful in adapting Spanish practices to their new situation.

Having easily acquired a sponsor and a building site, the Jesuits anticipated similar success in finding resources to build their main college, or Colegio Máximo.[23] Villaseca's unsuccessful rivals, and the Jesuits themselves, assumed that Don Alonso would provide such financing in short order.[24] Villaseca, however, waited almost four years before manifesting his intentions. Much of the time he was away from Mexico City, at his rural hacienda residence in Ixmiquilpan. He gave continued evidence of his patronage through monetary and material assistance, buying up and donating lots adjacent to the Jesuit residence, but no substantial donation funding the college. His contact with the Jesuit provincial remained firm, but as far as the rest of the order was concerned he was aloof and, as one member recalled later, "dry and strange."[25]

For their part, the Jesuits plunged into the task of ministering to all levels of Mexico City society, their residence becoming the administrative center for teaching and preaching functions.[26] Funds from a variety of sources enabled them to begin building a church and to establish a school for the "sons of the most noble." The black-robed fathers quickly became a familiar sight to all levels of society—among the slave and servant sectors, where they established programs to teach children, and among the wealthy Spanish and poor Indian sectors, where they preached and administered spiritual comforts.[27] Within three years of their arrival, they were established in major Spanish urban centers such as Antequera (Oaxaca), Guadalajara, Michoacán, Valladolid (Morelia), and Zacatecas. By early 1576 the original group of fifteen had increased to forty-seven.[28]

The Jesuits were quickly inundated with gifts and offers of gifts of both money and property. They accepted numerous urban properties—houses and lots—which they rented out at fixed rates, following Jesuit tradition.[29] The first rural property was accepted in 1574, when a royal notary, Antonio de Contreras, donated land near Tepotzotlán for their college. Since usufruct rights were maintained for the lifetime of the donor, no immediate benefits accrued to the Jesuits.[30] The next year a Spanish farmer (*labrador*), Lorente López, donated a highland, wooded property roughly twelve kilometers west of the growing viceregal capital.[31] The Jesuits converted this gift into a rural rest and recreation base for their members, giving it the name of Jesús del Monte. By means of a rental agreement, the wheat production of this estate produced revenues for the society, and the property provided firewood (*leña*), lumber, and other agricultural products for the residence in Mexico City.[32] Still, the proposed Colegio Máximo, which was to coordinate all Jesuit activities in New Spain and the Philippines, remained unfunded and unstarted.

This all changed in the summer of 1576, when Sánchez received word that Don Alonso wished to see him at Ixmiquilpan. Sánchez traveled the 150 kilometers from Mexico City as quickly as possible to hear the long-awaited news—a formal proposal to fund the Jesuit college. Villaseca reminded Sánchez that it had always been his intention to fund the college, in preparation for which he had donated properties in Mexico City and provided an annual subsidy of 2,000 pesos. Now he was offering an endowment and further gifts for the acquisition of lands to meet other requirements. The provincial immediately returned to Mexico City to confer with his colleagues (the father general had agreed in principle to accept Villaseca as the founder of the Colegio Máximo as early as 1573) and quickly returned to Ixmiquilpan with witnesses and a notary.[33] A contract was drawn up and signed on August 29, 1576, specifying that 40,000 pesos were being given to establish resources, "buying for the said effect land possessions of planted grains, or other things that would seem best to them [the Jesuits], and to ensure a certain income."[34] The reference to rural properties reflected the interests of the patron rather than the Jesuits. The father general, upon receiving a copy of the contract, tried unsuccessfully to have a new contract drawn up which would be more in accord with Jesuit statutes for establishing colleges.[35] Villaseca was to receive benefits, including special masses said on his behalf and for his heirs in all perpetuity. Villaseca inserted an extra provision for three special annual masses not normally included in such patronage contracts. He also transferred to the society two outstanding credits worth 5,150 pesos, funds designated to cover the cost of his burial in the center of the chapel of the Colegio Máximo.[36]

The formal agreement indicates the degree to which a powerful and resourceful individual such as Villaseca was able to influence the Jesuits.[37] Despite instructions from the new Jesuit father general (Everardo Mercurian) that no founding contract be drawn up until he had received a report on local conditions by a society *visitador* (inspector), an agreement was made and signed at the time and location determined by Villaseca.[38] Don Alonso's advanced age and illness, plus the take-it-or-leave-it nature of his offer, forced Sánchez to act decisively or run the risk of missing the gift he and the society had been anticipating for four years.

News of the agreement reached the father general before Sánchez's formal report. Mercurian immediately wrote to his provincial (June 1577) and later (March 1578) sent Sánchez instructions to draw up another agreement with Villaseca, more in keeping with society statutes. At the same time, a letter was written to Villaseca, welcoming him as the college founder. The father general tactfully suggested that, since this was the first such agreement made in the New World, it would be a model for all subsequent agreements between the society and its patrons and that therefore a new agreement must be drawn up. A second set of detailed instructions was issued to Sánchez (January 1579), who was either unable or unwilling to convince Don Alonso, since no changes were ever made.[39] When Villaseca died in 1580, the issue was laid to rest. Thereafter, the society took great pains to accord to their benefactor only the highest praise.[40]

The dealings of Provincial Sánchez with Villaseca can be seen as a paradigm of Jesuit accommodation to the new conditions in the Indies—the coming together of an experienced cleric whose previous activities had been largely confined to the administration of educational institutions in Spain, and the secular businessman who had achieved great financial success in New Spain. By the time the actual agreements were signed, they had observed each other closely for four years. This was ample time for Don Alonso to be able to demonstrate that, in the economic climate of New Spain,

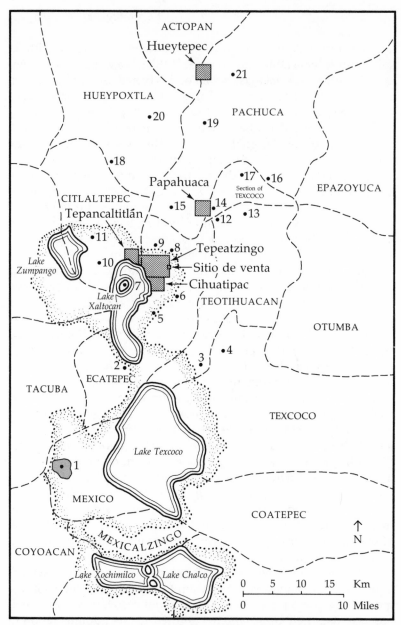

MAP 1. Original Santa Lucía purchase, 1576. The dotted lines show the
pre-Conquest lake levels; the dashed lines show the corregimiento boundaries. 1, Mexico City. 2, Ecatepec. 3, Tepexpan. 4, Acolman. 5, Ozumbilla. 6, Tecama. 7, Xaltocan. 8, Los Reyes. 9, Xoloc. 10, Xaltenco. 11, Zumpango. 12, Temascalapa. 13, Atocpan. 14, Chiapa. 15, Tizayuca. 16, Tezontepec. 17, Ixtlahuaca. 18, Hueypoxtla. 19, Tolcayuca. 20, Tezontlalpa.
21, Acayuca.

entrepreneurial initiative paid handsome dividends. Sánchez's colleagues in Mexico and his superiors in Rome, however, wished to adhere to the society's previous experience and norms. This forced the provincial to make decisions that he was convinced would serve the long-term interests of the order, despite criticism and opposition. Sánchez's decision to purchase Santa Lucía and to have the society administer the hacienda was made in this context. The decision to manage the properties much as Villaseca managed his own estates represented a radical change in Jesuit economic policy.[41] It is unlikely that the provincial was aware that this new orientation, designed to meet immediate economic needs, would have profound implications.

The Santa Lucía purchase consisted of pasture lands adjacent to and north of Lake Xaltocan, falling within the jurisdictional limits of the districts of Citlatepec (Zumpango), Ecatepec, and Pachuca (see Map 1).[42] The owner was a hacendado and land speculator of Portuguese origin, Alonso González, who had purchased the properties, plus livestock and equipment, in the 1560s. Wishing to maintain a low profile in temporal affairs, the Jesuits used an agent by the name of Juan de Monsalve Cabeza de Vaca to make the purchase. He functioned as buyer, to gain legal title to the hacienda, and then donated it to the Jesuits. The purchase was made on December 4, 1576, and the donation on December 23.[43]

Early Hacienda Formation: Historical Context and Procedures

According to their titles, the Jesuits had acquired five *estancias de ganado menor* and one *sitio de venta*, although one of the estancias had earlier been classified as being for *ganado mayor*. The term *estancia*, frequently used interchangeably with *sitio*, referred to a grant of pasture land whose dimensions were established in 1536 by the viceroy of New Spain, Antonio de Mendoza. The classification of *ganado mayor* referred to grants for raising cattle, horses, mules, and donkeys, the area of which was 1 square league, or 17.56 square kilometers (6.78 square miles). Those for *ganado menor* were for raising sheep, goats, and hogs, with an area of 0.44 square leagues, or 7.79 square kilometers (3.01 square miles). A *sitio de venta* was a much smaller land unit, measuring 0.36 hectares (0.86 acres), designated for residences, mills, or post houses.[44] Legally, the total area of Santa Lucía—using the *ganado mayor* dimension for one of the estancias—should have been 48.8 square kilometers. Its actual area was 70 square kilometers.[45] The discrepancy has two explanations. First, it was customary to include in the formal boundaries only land considered usable for pasture, which would indicate that some 20 square kilometers consisted of ravines, rocky slopes, or otherwise unproductive terrain. Second, using the pretense of unusable terrain, land purchases often exceeded their stated legal limits. In short, the amount of land to which hacendados claimed title had its extralegal dimension, depending to a large degree upon who did the measuring.

The physical and cultural milieu to which the Jesuits were committing themselves had already undergone a series of traumatic upheavals.[46] The area, in the northern part of the Valley of Mexico, when conquered by Cortés, was inhabited by Otomí, Tepaneca, Ocolhuaque, and Chichimeca peoples reduced to subject status by Aztec imperialism. Spanish imperialism intensified the subjection of northern valley communities to urban centers through *encomienda* (tribute and labor) obligations, although the physical presence of Europeans in the countryside remained prohibited (except for missionaries) until the emergence of royal officials (*corregidores*) pledged to protect native and crown interests. But even the best humanitarian and legal intentions of Spanish legislators, exemplified by the New Laws of 1542, failed to produce a tolerable accommodation by local residents to new economic and political realities. Native authorities, eager to achieve status within Spanish spheres of influence, cooperated in the exploitation of their own communities. They acted initially as intermediaries, then as subsidiaries, as the audiencia and the viceroy began the formal process of transferring land ownership to Spanish hands after 1542. At the same time (1545–1548), two additional transforming powers were introduced with frightening intensity: epidemic disease and massive herds of livestock. The first severely decreased the population, weakening its ability to defend cultural and political institutions and, above all, to continue agricultural production. The second severely disrupted agriculture and, simultaneously and cumulatively, destroyed much of its fertile foundations built up over past centuries.

By the 1570s, Spanish institutions were already having a visible impact in the countryside, although European rural residence was still minimal. Ecclesiastical structures, built with local labor, dominated plazas previously occupied by pyramids serving local and imperial deities. The role of Indigenous leadership had been redirected to suit the interests and institutions of the conquerors.[47]

The traditional means of social mobility, related to warfare and religion, had been eliminated, and economic roles in commerce and trade had been greatly curtailed. Regional demographic developments, despite our imprecise knowledge of many local details, provide overwhelming evidence of the cumulative impact of half a century of life under Spanish rule. Texcoco, which had 100,000 tributaries shortly after the Conquest, by 1570 counted less than one-fifth that number.[48] In the other corregimiento jurisdictions central to this study, the following totals were reported: Ecatepec, 2,600; Pachuca, 6,233; Tetepango-Hueypoxtla, 21,450; and Zumpango, 6,600.[49] The changing complexion of the jurisdictions during the transition from encomienda to corregimiento (1530s to 1560s) and imprecise population figures prevent an accurate count, but Gibson estimates a decline of between 75 and 88 percent.[50] What is clear, in retrospect, is that Indigenous societal structures that had provided vitality in earlier times were largely incapacitated and relatively helpless to defend the northern valley populations against the intrusions of haciendas.

At the time of the first Jesuit involvement, the processes of upheaval and change were not so obvious as they now are. Jesuit records provide considerable evidence of reluctance to become involved in rural haciendas, but not because of anticipated impact upon the rural sectors. The Jesuit academicians were probably unaware of actual rural conditions. Their direct contacts were Spanish individuals and officials who had already established rural property claims. Santa Lucía lands had passed from native to Spanish ownership between 1542 and 1565. In Spain there seems to have been a more profound understanding of what was taking place, amply documented by the stream of royal *cédulas* (orders) attempting to enforce more favorable terms for the king's "Indian children." The Indians themselves were too preoccupied with immediate survival needs to perceive the implications of the development of rural haciendas. The purchase of Santa Lucía also coincided with the epidemic known as the "great cocoliztli" (1576–1581),[51] which dealt an additional blow to staggering rural societal structures.

All five estancias of Santa Lucía were nominally under the control of the Indian towns until 1542, although much of the area had been subject to the tribute, labor, and other demands of Juan González Ponce de León, to whom Cortés had ceded encomienda rights after the Conquest.[52] His son, Juan Ponce de León, inherited the encomienda only to find that the implementation of the New Laws would result in his losing the inheritance. To maintain at least part of the area, he applied for a royal grant of ownership (*merced*) for the estancia known as Tepeatzingo.[53] The viceroy approved the merced in May 1542, transferring ownership to land previously within his encomienda of Tecama, consisting of a small rocky hilltop surrounded by marshlands and rich pasture lands adjacent to the *pueblo* lands of Xoloc and Axoloapán.[54]

According to royal instructions, such grants were to be clearly designated as to size, type, and obligations, which normally consisted of having to populate the lands with at least a set number of livestock within one year and a prohibition of resale within four years.[55] The Tepeatzingo grant did not contain any of these specifications. Ponce de León's close connections with the audiencia—he was the son-in-law of Hernando de Herrera, *relator* (court reporter) of the audiencia—may have been a factor behind the loose wording of the merced, which in effect meant that he could continue to do almost as he pleased with the human and land resources of his encomienda.[56] The grant did stipulate that his heirs and their successors would maintain the land. Sale or donation of Tepeatzingo to church, monastery, hospital, or any other religious entity was prohibited. Another condition was that the grant would not prejudice the crown in any way, or the rights and privileges of Indians living adjacent to it. These were standard clauses in most royal grants.[57]

Seven years after receiving title to Tepeatzingo, Ponce de León became embroiled in a dispute with the Tecamans and Xaltocans regarding the damages his livestock was doing to native crops. The Tecamans complained, the audiencia investigated, and Ponce de León was ordered to remove all but one hundred head of livestock from the estancia and to pay a 100-peso fine. The livestock that remained did so under the condition that guards and corrals would prevent recurrence of encroachment upon crop lands. Ponce de León complied with the order: he removed his cattle and legitimated his raising of horses by getting permission to keep brood mares on the estancia. He also used part of his property to raise sheep and cereal crops. The administration of the estate was in the hands of a *mayordomo* (custodian) while Ponce de León resided in the viceregal capital.[58]

Ponce de León was murdered in 1552, raising the problem of how to divide Tepeatzingo among his children, all minors. The manager of the estate, as guardian, petitioned the audiencia for permission to divide the estancia and to reintroduce large numbers of cattle and horses the family kept on other properties. The audiencia ruled that all the Ponce de León properties should be sold, including Tepeatzingo, its corrals, and its 2,500 sheep. An agent for one of the daughters, Doña Ana Ponce de León, finally bought the estancia and its sheep in 1554. The treasurer of the audiencia, Don Fernando de Portugal, had designs upon the estate and influenced the audiencia ruling of a forced sale. He finally acquired the estate in 1556, paying the same price as the Ponce de León agent had two years earlier: 937 pesos, 4 *reales* for the estancia which now included 600 sheep, 30 mares, 1 donkey stallion, 4 mules, and an unspecified amount of seeded and cultivated land. Portugal then received permission formally to include as part of Tepeatzingo a small complex of buildings and corrals adjacent to the royal road running between Mexico City and the mining center of Pachuca. Portugal also requested a clarification from the audiencia of boundary lands with Tecama and Xaltocan. At this time, Tepeatzingo was technically declared to be for *ganado menor*. Portugal owned the estate for twelve years before selling it to Alonso González, who, in turn, sold it to the Jesuit agent.[59]

With Tepeatzingo, the Jesuits received the legal title, which included copies of all petitions, disputes, decisions of the audiencia, previous sales, and records of possessions covering twenty-four years.[60] These documents clearly demonstrate the ability of the Spaniards to influence decisions to their own advantage. Despite protective legislation, we see a steady encroachment upon Indigenous rights and property. In the case of Juan Ponce de León, the crown was able to stem excessive exploitation by terminating encomienda privileges in the 1550s. The designation of Tepeatzingo for *ganado menor* in 1556 was an attempt to protect, or at least to define, native jurisdictions. Nevertheless, with the transfer of property ownership into Spanish hands, little could be done to prevent the pasture grant from being used for all manner of livestock, for agriculture, or for the addition of a residence complex. The Indian town attempting to invoke Spanish protective legislation on its behalf discovered that the representatives of the crown charged with implementation, such as Fernando de Portugal, were themselves the encroachers.

Papahuaca, the second of the five estancias, was clearly defined as being for *ganado menor*. It was located to the south of Temascalapa and named after a hill known as the "place of avocados."[61] The formal description noted that it fell within the jurisdictions of the pueblos of Tecama, Tepexpan, Tizayuca, and San Miguel, bordering on an Indian estancia called Santa Ana, pertaining to Tepexpan. Portugal received title to Papahuaca through merced in

1559. Although formal possession was not taken until 1562, Portugal was using the area as early as 1556. This pasture grant, in contrast to the one for Tepeatzingo, included the standard clauses regarding size, resale, and utilization.[62]

Portugal used Papahuaca and Tepeatzingo for raising sheep but kept his eyes open for other means of making a profit. He decided to take advantage of the strategic location of his properties—adjacent to the royal highway leading to Zacatecas and the north, and midway between the mining center of Pachuca and Mexico City— to establish an inn or post house. Permission for this venture was received in October 1567 by means of a grant for a *sitio de venta*,[63] which specified that the post house was to include four upper and four lower chambers. The contents of such a post house indicated accommodations suitable for people of varying importance. Of the six beds required, one was to have two mattresses, two sheets, two pillows and two blankets, while the other five were to have two sheets, one pillow and one blanket. The inn was to have on hand sufficient provisions for guests or travelers. The grant prohibited resale within four years, or sale to ecclesiastical institutions. Portugal had an agent take formal possession of the *sitio de venta* in November 1567. He requested the merced as a prelude to selling to Alonso González in January 1568. González, who had made a down payment in 1567, wanted clear title to his purchases. Portugal's request for the post house was accompanied by a petition for another *estancia de ganado menor* called Tepancaltitlán, to which he did not receive title until after González had taken possession of his purchases on January 22, 1568.[64]

Tepancaltitlán bordered Tepeatzingo on the west, along the edges of Lake Xaltocan and within the jurisdictional boundaries of Xaltocan and Zumpango. The residents of these towns previously used the area as a source of roots, grasses, and salt, and for hunting ducks and geese. The March 1568 grant to Portugal stated that these local privileges were not to be infringed upon when the land passed to Spanish ownership.[65] Portugal transferred this title to González, who had taken over the properties in January of the same year. The audiencia's tolerance of manipulation of the law is evident in these proceedings. Portugal operated an inn without permit and sold land to which he did not have title, all in clear violation of the stipulation against resale for four years in the royal grants.

Alonso González was a sheep rancher (*ovejero*) who owned other properties in the area and wished to enlarge them.[66] He offered

Portugal 11,500 pesos for the three estancias, including 13,500 sheep, houses, corrals, horses, dogs, 7 slaves, tools, farm and ranch equipment, and 200 *fanegas* of maize.* By May 1570, González still owed Portugal 3,500 pesos for the purchase. In the meantime, the audiencia treasurer, in another business deal, had transferred collection rights to a Mexico City resident, Juan Guerrero. Guerrero and his son Agustín—the son-in-law of Don Alonso de Villaseca—finally collected the remaining debt from González in January 1571.[67]

González already owned the two other estancias pertaining to the original Santa Lucía purchase. One was located northwest of Acayuca, although in the jurisdiction of the pueblo of Tezontlalpa. It was known as Hueytepec, or the place of the large hill.[68] Most of it actually was a flat plain. Antonio de Nava, while serving as crown administrative officer, or *alcalde mayor*,† in Tenayuca, claimed title to this estancia through merced in July 1563. The grant allowed for resale earlier than the normal four years, and Antonio de Nava did just that, selling the estancia to a Mexico City merchant, Juan de la Mesa, in February 1564, for 196 pesos. The next year this merchant sold Hueytepec to González for 4,400 pesos, but it now included 5,000 sheep, 5 Negro slaves, and ranching equipment.[69]

In 1566, González purchased the last of the estancias, known as Cihuatipac, located halfway between Tecama and Xaltocan.[70] A minor audiencia official, Juan Rodríguez Camarra,[71] made a petition for this land in 1564, only to have the *encomendero* of Xaltocan, Alonso Avila Alvarado, strongly oppose such a merced. The audiencia instructed the *alcalde mayor* of Xaltocan, plus eight members of its town council, to investigate and report on the status of the area. Avila Alvarado, with his vested encomienda interests,

---

*LB, pp. 461–68. A fanega is a dry measure, equaling roughly 1.5 bushels when referring to maize, Gibson, *Aztecs,* p. 601. This is the figure used throughout the study, although Carrera Stampa, p. 15, equates 1 fanega to 3.58 U.S. bushels of maize. *Fanega* was a term also applied to designate the area of seeded or seedable land. Such units, equaling the amount of land required to sow a fanega of seed, were called *fanegas de sembradura.* This land unit varied according to the terrain, as did the density of seed per area.

†The alcalde mayor was the official crown representative, or officer, in an administrative district. Although the term *corregidor* was frequently used to designate the same office, and is most appropriate when discussing corregimiento, I have chosen to use the term *alcalde mayor.* For a detailed discussion, see Gibson, *Aztecs,* pp. 81–97. His table for the jurisdictions of the Valley of Mexico (p. 87) suggests a definite preference for the term *alcalde mayor* throughout the colonial period. This also holds true for the documentation consulted for this study.

claimed that the Indians of Xaltocan had very little land as it was, and none available for agriculture and grazing. Rodríguez, however, claimed that the property was not being used and that his ownership would not prejudice Spanish or Indian interests.

The investigation on behalf of the audiencia took place in January 1565, and a report summarized the findings as follows:

Most powerful Lords, in compliance with your command I went to the place and location shown to me by Juan Rodríguez Camarra, the site for the *estancia de ganado menor* he is requesting from your Highness through merced. And I walked and surveyed all the area, which has no plantings, no worked land, no fruit trees, and no magueys. It is waste and pasture land, uninhabited, and in the lake. The officials of the pueblo of Xaltocan presented themselves and agree to the conditions as stated. They consent and see as good that your Highness make a grant of the *estancia de ganado menor* to Juan Rodríguez Camarra. The estancia can be given in merced without prejudice and for useful purposes. The above is sworn before God and this cross, in accordance with the obligations of my position.[72]

The *alcalde mayor* added that the people of Xaltocan favored the merced because they considered Rodríguez a good friend held in high esteem. Ten days later the merced was approved. It included all the standard clauses regarding resale and the requirement to have 2,000 sheep on the estancia within one year. Eight months later, Rodríguez sold Cihuatipac for 230 pesos to a fellow Mexico City resident, Juan Bautista Figueroa. Bautista Figueroa turned around and sold Cihuatipac to Alonso González for the same price six months later, in March 1566. González, however, could not take possession because of Xaltocan claims of irregularities in the original merced.

Contrary to the contents of the report to the audiencia, the Xaltocan officials did not favor allowing their lands to pass into Spanish ownership. They did not sign the report to the audiencia (that is, mark their cross on the statement under the supervision of a royal notary who vouched that they knew the contents), nor did they participate at the official transfer of the property to Rodríguez. The formal statement of possession noted the absence of representatives from Xaltocan, indicating that Rodríguez, accompanied by two Spanish friends and a notary, had taken possession without opposition in 1565. But in 1566, when González wished to take possession, Xaltocan made a formal objection. This was promptly quashed by a special order from the audiencia instructing the *alcalde mayor* to hand over Cihuatipac to González. Still, Juan Rodríguez's violation of the resale clause technically invalidated the merced. In 1567, González petitioned the viceroy, as president of the audiencia, to rectify this defect. The viceroy responded in 1573, noting that, although both Rodríguez and Bautista Figueroa had sold the estancia before the prescribed four years, González had populated it with the required number of sheep within one year and was therefore entitled to clear title.[73]

Spanish acquisition procedures for the five original Santa Lucía properties show the inability of Indian pueblos to maintain control over their traditional lands. Both the viceroy and officers of the audiencia were callous toward Indian rights and Spanish law, while aiding fellow Spaniards to gain legal title to Indian land. Apart from Tepeatzingo, these lands—dry grasslands, wet marshlands, rocky hillsides—were still under Indigenous legal control as late as 1559, despite the incursions of Spanish livestock and agriculture. Within a decade, crown officials (Portugal, Rodríguez, de Nava) acquired legal title through merced and almost immediately sold the estancias to fellow Spaniards. The representatives of the crown used their considerable influence to move the law in their favor, while less influential residents, such as Alonso González, had to take far greater precautions in fulfilling the formal requirements of Spanish law.

The pre-Jesuit history of the Santa Lucía estancias suggests definite sequences within the general transfer of land ownership from Indian to Spanish hands. In the first phase, those closest to the seat of power—the viceroy and the audiencia—acquired legal title through merced. They, in turn, sold the properties to private entrepreneurs such as Alonso González.[74] His use of the estancias suggests that he was an estate speculator who bought up properties but whose primary interest was not ranching. A comparison of inventories of goods and livestock he accumulated in the 1560s and those listed when he sold to the Jesuits in 1576 indicates that he did nothing to improve the properties. The lists of tools and equipment are identical, apart from the addition of a chicken coop and the deterioration of some of the livestock equipment. Between 1565 and 1568, González bought 18,500 sheep, and he sold 16,800 to the Jesuit agent. The price paid for the five estancias, plus slaves, livestock, and equipment, was 16,130 pesos, and the sale of basically the same entities brought him 17,000 pesos. Changes included the addition of horses, and donkeys and a variation in slaves bought and sold. Of the 12 slaves bought, 3 were among the 8 sold in 1576.[75] In the course of his speculative dealings, González borrowed funds from the Dominican convent and monastery at Coyoacán, thereby adding encumbrances or liens to the properties, a feature common in the period. Debts attached to property deeds would then be transferred to the new owners.[76] González represented the entrepreneurial impulse of the times, as did Villaseca. But González, in contrast to Villaseca—who knew how to manage his estates effectively—did not accumulate a huge fortune nor great prestige among his contemporaries.

The Jesuits Become Hacienda Owners

The official Jesuit version of how they came across the Santa Lucía properties was that Sánchez, relying upon divine guidance, had ridden out one afternoon, discovered the estates, and bought them on December 13, 1576.[77] A more plausible version is that Villaseca, who knew of the estates by virtue of his son-in-law's direct financial involvement and who passed them every time he traveled between Mexico City and Ixmiquilpan, arranged for Juan de Monsalve Cabeza de Vaca to act as the purchasing agent for the Jesuits. Monsalve purchased the estates on December 4, nine days before the day of Santa Lucía.

In the sale contract, González claimed the estancias were free from any outstanding claims, but if such arose, he would resolve them at his own expense. On December 23, Monsalve transferred ownership to the college of the Jesuits in Mexico City as a "free, perfect, and irrevocable" donation. The donation to the Jesuits stated that they could sell, donate, give, change, or dispose of all or part of the estates according to their pleasure, and that Monsalve would not be held responsible for any disputes, problems, or debts the new owners might encounter. Included with the donation statement, in a separate notarized document, was a declaration by Monsalve that he had acted on behalf of Sánchez and Díaz, "therefore the college can enjoy and utilize the named properties as their very own, they having been purchased with their own money."[78]

As soon as they received the property deeds the Jesuit leaders carefully revised them to eliminate any defects that might jeopardize the transactions at a later date. They discovered that Alonso González's wife, María de Aguilar, was listed as the co-owner in earlier documents but was not listed as a participant in the sale to Monsalve. This omission could have resulted in claims against the properties by María de Aguilar. To prevent this, a second sale contract, specifying her agreement and participation, was drawn up between González and Monsalve. This contract, it was noted, "was not to be seen as changing any of the conditions of the first, only adding force to the sale and eliminating a defect." Another possible claim against the estancias was removed when Monsalve was called upon by the Jesuits to pay the outstanding 2,000 peso encumbrance resulting from González's loan from the Dominican convent and monastery at Coyoacán.[79]

Despite precautions to ensure the orderliness of documentary details of ownership, the Jesuit legal position remained questionable. Each of the estancia titles carried a clause, under the signature of the viceroy, prohibiting sale to or ownership by an ecclesiastical body. Although this article of Spanish law was generally ignored in New Spain at the time, the Jesuit provincial directed discreet inquiries to the viceroy regarding the matter, only to be advised to go ahead and make the purchase. The viceroy had his instructions from the king to assist the Jesuits in becoming established in New Spain.[80] This he was willing to do because it was the will of the king, laws to the contrary notwithstanding. In this instance, as was to happen frequently in the coming years, the Jesuits discovered that having the support of those in the highest positions of power was far more important than fulfilling the letter of the law.

The Jesuits were now faced with the practical problem of management. Cihuatipac, Hueytepec, Papahuaca, Tepancaltitlán, and Tepeatzingo, under Indian or secular Spanish ownership, had never been integrated into a single, functioning, economic unit. Before the Spanish Conquest, these lands had been used primarily for agriculture. After the Conquest, large-scale livestock production had been introduced during the encomienda period. In the era of secular Spanish ownership, the estancias had been sporadically exploited for cattle, horses, sheep, and goats, with segments coming under the influence of Spanish agriculture. Alonso González was the first individual to have owed all five at one time, using them primarily for sheep-raising and making no effort to create a single hacienda out of the three distinct geographical areas. González had managed his sheep flocks from his residence in Tecama.[81] His shepherds were slaves who may have been housed in the rudimentary facilities on the properties. The post house established by Portugal, if it functioned at all, was not a going concern under González's management. Without previous experience, the Jesuit officials in Mexico City were unsure of how to get started.

Santa Lucía, in December 1576, was representative of many of the rural properties in the early stages of hacienda development in colonial Mexico. It consisted of:

1. *Land:* roughly 70 square kilometers, of which 48.7 were legally designated as pasture for *ganado menor.* Along with the land itself went the control of entrances and exits, rights to ponds, springs, watering holes, grass, and everything pertaining to the properties. The Indians of Xaltocan and Zumpango retained rights to ducks, geese, salt, roots, and grasses from Tepancaltitlán.[82]

2. *Buildings and corrals:* rudimentary dwellings and corrals at the *sitio de venta* and at Tepeatzingo.

3. *Livestock:* 16,800 sheep, 1,400 goats, 125 brood mares and colts, 1 stallion, 1 saddle horse, 2 donkey mares, and 2 donkey stallions kept for breeding three-year-old mares in order to produce mules.

4. *Slaves:* eight Negro slaves under restraint (*enfrenado*), including six adult males, one female, and her infant mulatto son.[83]

5. *Equipment and tools:* one chicken shelter, two iron rings and cramp-irons (from collars used by animals pulling carts), two hay boxes, one small saw, one forged iron hoe, one chisel, one pickaxe, one hoe, one whetstone with an iron attachment, two iron wedges, one forged iron shovel, one small iron bar, one iron axe, one iron spoon, one perforated copper pot, one large copper cauldron, one clay water pot, one small table with its benches, four wooden cups, one old wooden bed, one wooden bench used as a seat, one lock with its key, four stones (*metates*) for hand-grinding maize, two wooden molds for making adobe blocks, nine molds for making cheese, one press to make cheese with eight cups and two large pots, one iron restraint for Negroes, one set of handcuffs, two doors with their locks and keys, two doors without keys, two doors in the maize-storage building with lock loops, seventy-two fanegas of maize, branding irons, and dogs used for sheep-herding.[84]

6. *Privileges:* the right to operate a post house and the use of González's brand for sheep.[85]

Pedro Sánchez quickly discovered that buying Santa Lucía was much simpler than managing it. Most of his Jesuit colleagues were frankly opposed to the idea of the society operating a livestock estate and suggested that their provincial follow institutional custom and lease the property at a fixed annual rent. When the father general heard about his provincial's intentions, he too advised against engaging in such secular activities. Quickly the Jesuits in Mexico City found themselves involved in their first crisis of conscience in

New Spain. Had it not been for the delay in the exchange of communications and instructions between Mexico City and Rome—at least a year, and frequently two years or more, depending upon the operations of the royal fleet*—Sánchez's determination to follow the advice of Don Alonso would have been blocked. As it was, the time gained while communications were in transit allowed for a thorough local debate regarding rural estates. During this debate, which dominated the first decade of Jesuit ownership of Santa Lucía, the hacienda became very profitable and the Jesuit college grew dependent upon its resources.

When Sánchez reported his purchase to Rome, he included both his reasons for the acquisition—essentially those offered by Villaseca—and the dissatisfactions expressed by his brethren.[86] The father general, still attempting to get Sánchez to renegotiate the founding contract with Don Alonso, decided it was time to establish guidelines for the economic administration of the Mexican province. Mercurian acknowledged that the techniques applicable to Europe might not render the same results in New Spain, but, he pointed out, even more problems would be created by livestock-raising activities. Practical as well as legal issues were involved. On the practical side, besides actual hacienda administration, were probable rumors and unfavorable reactions against the order. The question of the legality of ownership of such properties also concerned the father general. He indicated that the society's attorney general would consult with the Council of the Indies about Jesuit properties and endowments in the Indies. To help clarify local economic matters he was appointing brother Alonso Pérez, who had arrived in New Spain in 1576, as provincial economic adviser and spokesman. He added instructions that further local steps should not be taken before larger issues affecting the order as a whole were dealt with.[87]

In Mexico, the dispute came to a head during the society's first Provincial Congregation, held October 5–15, 1577. At such meetings, all the members of a Jesuit province met to evaluate past events, to plan future work, and to draw up a general progress report for the father general.[88] The meetings allowed for the emergence, within a specific province, of diverse opinions upon which

---

*It took Pedro Sánchez and his successors in Mexico in the 1570s and 1580s at least a year to receive replies from Rome, and frequently much longer. Such mail traveled with the Spanish royal fleet to Spain, whence it was sent to Rome. About two years for an exchange of correspondence was normal, from letters published in MM, vols. 1 and 2. Regarding mail movements of the period, see Bose, *Los orígenes.*

the head of the society passed judgment and issued instructions. Congregation reports show that Sánchez was immediately challenged regarding the propriety of administering Santa Lucía. He, in turn, defended his actions by pointing out that in New Spain, in contrast to Europe, there were no convenient ecclesiastical incomes from rentals because such rents or annuities (*casos o censos*) were of the worst type: they were dangerous and risky in New Spain because of fraud, so that each successful collection also made an enemy; and such rents did not increase in value, but decreased. Therefore, argued the provincial, here "it is judged that the best method is to have lands for wheat and ranches for livestock." And, he pointed out, Santa Lucía now had 20,000 sheep and was visited from time to time by one of the brothers from the city, the hacienda having its own shepherds and Negroes to take care of the flocks. The annual profit expected was 1,500 pesos.[89]

This argument was not accepted by the congregation, and Sánchez was challenged for a second time during a debate about provincial methods of providing economic resources. The provincial attempted to convince his critics by outlining the overall financial problems faced by the society in New Spain.[90] He pointed out that, since the Colegio Máximo in Mexico City was to be the central training institution for all of New Spain and the Philippines, it was of utmost importance to have a strong economic base such as rural estates would provide. He suggested that the province would be well advised to enlarge its rural holdings rather than to curtail them. He pointed out that Jesús del Monte would produce more revenues through direct Jesuit administration than through the current rental agreement. Surpluses generated from the haciendas should be sold, and the college would be financed by such profits. A special dispensation from the father general would be required, however, in order to sell surpluses for profit.[91]

Mercurian's response was phrased so as not to contradict the steps taken by his provincial. Selling surpluses for profit, he indicated, was not against the regulations of the order. But, he suggested, it would be preferable not to invest in livestock. In the future, economic investments should be sought which would be "more secure" and "less embarrassing," and involve "fewer distractions." To clarify the issue he was sending a visitador, the Reverend Doctor Juan de la Plaza, a former provincial of the Jesuit Spanish province of Andalucía.[92] Mercurian's real uneasiness was clearly expressed in his instructions to the visitador:

Look into this matter of livestock estancias and agricultural lands, accompanied by such an uproar and being of such a secular nature. Determine why some persons, acting completely outside our regulations, have made economic partnerships with others by giving money for commercial contracts [*compañía*]. Why was this carried out, without taking the advice of practical persons, such as the case of the expenditure of 17,000 pesos for livestock?[93]

The father general was concerned about secular economic activities. He believed, mistakenly, that Villaseca had gone into a commercial partnership with the order[94] and, since the purchase of Santa Lucía, had learned of two related disputes involving secular authorities. When the Colegio Máximo took over Santa Lucía, one of the Spanish hacendados owning property on its borders decided to press his claim and, he hoped, his advantage over the recently arrived friars. He had buildings and corrals on land claimed by previous Tepeatzingo owners and now claimed the mislocation of Jesuit property boundaries rather than the mislocation of his facilities. When the audiencia was presented with the formal version of the conflict, not wishing to offend either the esteemed newly arrived Jesuits or the well-connected hacendado, it passed the matter on to the Council of the Indies. The matter was eventually resolved by the king, in favor of the Jesuits.[95] The second dispute, also quickly passed on to higher authorities by the local audiencia, was with the office of the Mexican archbishop over whether produce from Jesuit rural estates was exempt from ecclesiastical taxation (tithe), as claimed by the Jesuits.[96]

Mercurian had every reason to be concerned about what was going on in Mexico. As a seasoned administrator he was sensitive to the distance separating Mexico and Rome and the possibility that the man chosen for his proven competence, Sánchez, might be acting on sound principles. Thus he cautioned restraint to his provincial, instructed his visitador to make a thorough investigation, sent word to Villaseca confirming his status as a college founder, and instructed his *procurador general* (consul general) to justify Mexican economic activities before the royal court in Spain.[97]

This strategy sought to minimize internal discord and maximize external support, and it proved very successful. Within a few months, Philip II wrote to his viceroy that the Royal Council of the Indies had dealt with a Jesuit case concerning some properties with corrals, lands for pasturing livestock and planting maize and wheat, and rights for milling grains. Royal instructions were that the Jesuits be allowed to proceed without interference. Orders would be forthcoming regarding details.[98] And in Mexico the close friendship between Villaseca and Pedro Sánchez continued. Sánchez or Alonso Pérez, the appointed economic spokesman, made frequent visits to the crusty old Don Alonso at Ixmiquilpan. Villaseca continued to make donations to the Jesuits, including a fund of 6,458 pesos, 6 reales, to cover burial and posthumous honors on his own behalf. Between 1572 and Don Alonso's death in September 1580, Sánchez signed twenty-five agreements with Villaseca resulting in the transfer of over 123,000 pesos to the Jesuits.[99]

Juan de la Plaza arrived in Mexico as visitador in February 1580. His views on economic administration differed from those of Sánchez, who, having served as provincial for eight years, requested and was granted retirement from administrative duties. He devoted his remaining thirty years in New Spain to teaching and ministering to the sick and dying. Plaza took over as provincial in November 1580, determined to redirect economic policies, but once in office, he found the established train of events difficult to reverse.[100] One of his early actions regarding Santa Lucía was to have Monsalve, the agent who originally donated the properties, draw up a new document of donation which included the revised sale document signed by Alonso González and his wife, thereby safeguarding the legality of the acquisition.[101] Early in 1582 college officials requested, and were given, permission by the viceroy to make some alterations at Hueytepec by moving a house they owned closer to available water sources. The issue here involved royal legislation concerning the distance between established Indian residences and new Spanish residences in the countryside. In this case, the proposed location of the Jesuit house contravened legal statutes. The viceregal solution was to order the movement of the Indian residents into a nearby pueblo, thereby allowing the Jesuits to improve their property without violating royal statutes.[102]

Arrangements were made with an attorney of the audiencia, Cristóbal Pérez, in 1582, to acquire two additional *sitios de ganado menor* for the growing sheep flocks of Santa Lucía. These were flat grasslands in the northern jurisdiction of the pueblo of Acolman and its subject pueblo, Santa María. The attorney requested these estancias, in merced, for himself in February and May, and in July of the same year donated them to the Collegio de San Pedro y San Pablo. The Jesuit economic spokesman, Alonso Pérez, was directly involved in the transactions, having been granted power of attorney to claim possession of one of the estancias. The titles of these grasslands indicated that they were to be populated with 2,000 *ganado menor* within one year, could not be resold within four years, and were not to be sold or transferred to an ecclesiastical entity.[103]

Other donations were being accepted by Jesuit colleges from leading citizens in numerous Mexican centers. In Pátzcuaro the society accepted a ranch with 4,000 head of cattle in 1583, and in Colima it was offered estancias including 700 horses, 400 goats, 100 hogs, 100 sheep, Negro slaves, and a cacao orchard with 10,000 boxes of cacao. Despite Jesuit reservations about administering rural properties, these offers were not turned away. The reason was the rapid expansion of Jesuit colleges in urban centers and a growing need for economic resources. By 1582 the Colegio Máximo had expanded to include seventy active clerics and novices, seventy students in its seminary program, and three hundred students in seven university classes. Economic support in New Spain was lagging to such a degree that the Mexican province requested permission to import 2,000 ducats annually to sustain college growth. The society needed all the resources it could muster.[104]

Still, the internal opposition to Santa Lucía persisted, and Plaza was determined to rid the Colegio Máximo of the hacienda. In a memorandum to the father general dated May 24, 1583, he proposed the sale of Santa Lucía, claiming support from all the members of the society in Mexico except Pedro Sánchez. Plaza emphasized his predecessor's vigorous opposition but insisted that the sale of the hacienda should take place, even if it meant taking a loss on the original investment. A change of provincial in Mexico—Plaza being replaced by the Reverend Antonio de Mendoza—and of father general in Rome intervened, and no immediate action was taken on the proposal.[105]

The new father general, Claudio Aquaviva, filled a lengthy term (1581–1615) during which the issues surrounding Santa Lucía were carefully studied, clarified, and finally settled. During his administration, the Jesuits stressed close cooperation with crown officials in the viceroyalty, an avoidance of Jesuit involvement in secular reform among Spanish society in New Spain, and greater involvement in a spiritual ministry to Indians and African slaves within its spheres of influence. His term of office coincided with great expansion of Jesuit educational institutions in urban centers and involvement with unpacified Indian groups on the northern frontiers, activities which required constant, growing financial support.[106]

Resolving Conflict and Establishing Administrative Policy

Meanwhile, the debate about economic policies shifted from the type of resources best suited to meet economic needs to the manner of involvement of individual Jesuits in the administration of economic resources. The reason for the shift was that the upper ranks of the Jesuit hierarchy—upon determining that civil and crown officials were not opposed to their owning rural estates[107]— decided to support the policies implemented by the first provincial. The second provincial, despite local support, had not been able to reverse such policies. Mendoza, whose term lasted from 1584 to 1590, had the task of finding long-range solutions that would serve the practical needs of his order and eliminate the moral doubts of his fellow priests. He had been chosen by the father general for this task and instructed accordingly.

One of the problems central to managing Santa Lucía was that Jesuits were reluctant actually to stay at the estate, whose activities, being commercial and secular, were not easily related to Jesuit concepts of missionary service. Individuals attempted to communicate this directly to their father general, as did Diego García, who had arrived in Mexico with Plaza. He complained that Jesuits sent to rural estates suffered from isolation and ran the risk of inviting scandal. He suggested hiring secular administrators,[108] a solution that was current practice for most urban-based hacendados. The father general, however, had already ruled out this option. He had been informed of the neglect of the spiritual welfare of Santa Lucía slaves—no baptisms having taken place for two years, one slave having died without baptism—and issued a strongly worded directive to the Mexican province to care for all the souls under their influence.[109] Mendoza's solution was to send an older Jesuit father, who was familiar with the native language but too old to work on the mission frontiers, to live on the hacienda. His function was twofold: to provide company for the Jesuits managing the hacienda, and to attend to the spiritual needs of Indian and Negro workers.[110]

But the internal dissent, described by the provincial as "demands and replies and many differences in opinion,"[111] lingered. When Jesuit direct management of Jesús del Monte was initiated, additional pressure developed to sell Santa Lucía and again rent out Jesús del Monte. By 1585 a consensus had been reached and was reported to the father general. In this report, Mendoza outlined the opposing positions of his predecessors and explained how he and others within the province had come to change their minds in favor of the policies of Pedro Sánchez:

Although initially all were of the judgment that it [Santa Lucía] should be sold, by the time I became provincial they had already changed their minds, excepting Father Plaza. The reason for the change in judgments by the fathers, in part, was the changed circumstances. Remedies had been discovered to remove the mentioned inconveniences without letting go the grazing lands. Also, through Father Plaza's attempts to make a sale, it was clearly seen that they would be getting only one-third as much revenue from the original investment as they were receiving, if that, seeing that grazing lands in the Indies are a sure investment. For these reasons they asked me to suspend the business of selling it until you could be informed of the actual state of affairs we are in now, and to be informed of your reactions.[112]

Mendoza had just visited Santa Lucía, which he described as one of the finest estancias of all of New Spain, since it had good pastures to sustain up to 50,000 sheep if necessary. During the dry season, when pasture in other areas was scarce, the marshy areas surrounding the buildings could support all the livestock of the college. Furthermore, it had a plain rich in salt (*salitre*), which all the cattlemen in the area used. Owning such rich land meant that the college needs could be provided for. Other attractive features were the hacienda's proximity to Mexico City, facilitating administration and providing easy access for its meat and wool products to the Mexico City markets. The value of Santa Lucía, Mendoza insisted, was twice as great as that of any similar hacienda in the entire viceroyalty.[113]

The provincial's optimism about Santa Lucía was directly related to the growing revenues it produced. From 1,500 pesos in 1577, hacienda income had more than doubled by 1582, to 3,423 pesos, and continued increasing in 1583 (4,418 pesos) and 1584 (5,349 pesos).[114] The hacienda was now meeting the expectations of Villaseca and Pedro Sánchez, and promised to continue to prosper. Prices for wool had recently more than doubled, from 4 reales per *arroba* (twenty-five-pound unit) to 8.5 and 9 reales per arroba, and meat prices for cattle had risen to 5.5 reales per yearling.[115] The rise in wool and meat prices was related to changed conditions in the viceroyalty. The great epidemic of 1576–1581 had adversely affected agricultural production, resulting in serious food and labor shortages. The opening of profitable mining enterprises in northern New Spain increased demands for livestock products and attracted growing numbers of Europeans to the viceregal capital.[116] The combination of endemic misfortune and new economic opportunities placed a well-located and well-managed hacienda in fortunate circumstances.

Steps had also been taken to solve the internal problems of hacienda administration. Initially, college officials adopted the management structure of Santa Lucía's previous owner, consisting of a resident mayordomo who supervised the African slaves and hired Indian workers from nearby pueblos to tend the flocks and take care of other agricultural tasks.[117] Alonso González's mayordomo, Pedro Nieto, had been retained and incorporated into the Jesuit order. Nieto, in recapturing an escaped African shepherd, had struck the slave in the face, resulting in the slave's loss of one eye. The incident so upset Nieto that he "repented" and requested permission to join the order. After serving his novitiate year, he was returned to Santa Lucía to resume his previous responsibilities, this time as a *hermano coadjutor* devoted to the society.* Another *hermano coadjutor* with agricultural experience, Marcos García, was sent to the hacienda to supervise the rural activities.[118]

By 1585, most of the administrative difficulties had been resolved. Complaints about isolation and unhappiness regarding work tasks were solved by a careful choice of brothers and by having at least two Jesuits on the hacienda at all times. The intention was to have one father present who would concern himself with the spiritual welfare of workers, but this was not always possible in view of these priests' preference for other mission work. Even priests too old to remain active on the mission frontiers resisted hacienda placement. The solution worked out for Santa Lucía, and applied to other college haciendas, was to have a father on the hacienda if possible, and always at least two brothers.[119] Their conduct was carefully regulated to avoid criticism from the secular world. A special permit (*licencia*) was required in order to travel, write letters, or carry goods from one place to another. A daily schedule was stipulated as follows: arise at 4:00 A.M., midday meal at 11:00 A.M., supper at 7:00 P.M., and bedtime at 9:00 P.M.[120]

During the first decade of Jesuit ownership of Santa Lucía, the order was forced to adapt to the practical realities of New Spain.

*A *hermano coadjutor* was a brother "co-helper," a member who took novitiate training and then assisted in the temporal affairs of the society. Those working in the frontier mission often also filled religious teaching roles. See Chapter 6 for a fuller discussion of coadjutor positions among the Jesuits. Nieto's biography can be seen in DBCJM 10: 503–13.

Letters between the Mexican provincials and the father general are a reliable guide to the nature of the problems faced and the solutions chosen. Increasing direct involvement in the local economy is indicated by permission to sell firewood, lime, and agricultural and livestock surpluses.[121] The provincials never took steps before consulting with local authorities. Pedro Sánchez had consulted with crown and civil spokesmen before taking his bold initiative.[122] Mendoza consulted with the judge of the municipal high court of Mexico City and high officials of the secular clergy regarding the issue of propriety. He was told that Santa Lucía would be less troublesome than almost any other rural estate in the viceroyalty. All religious groups had this type of asset because urban property rentals were not a sound investment: collection of rentals created a flood of legal disputes in the Mexico City courts, and houses were a bad investment since repair costs were high and Mexico City was subject to heavy rains and earthquakes. At one point, the viceroy had suggested to Sánchez that he invest endowment funds in annuities (*juros*) in Spain, but quickly changed his mind when Sánchez pointed out the negative repercussions this might have in the royal court. In view of the alternatives, since mining and merchant activities were equally unacceptable for the Jesuits, landed estates were simply the least troublesome investment available. Privately Sánchez had been advised, "When in Rome, do as the Romans do," which he did.[123]

Plaza, however, attempted to extricate the province from previous commitments. The best offer he received for Santa Lucía and its lands, livestock, slaves, and equipment was 24,000 pesos. The prospective buyer admitted to a higher value of 27,000 pesos, and the provincial was asking 30,000 pesos. In exchange, the buyer offered houses worth 14,000 pesos, at the time renting for 400 to 500 pesos per annum; letters of credit which produced 500 pesos annually; the remainder in cash, to be paid over several years. The conditions of the offer were such that expected annual income from selling Santa Lucía would amount to 1,500 pesos, of which only 900 pesos was assured. When Mendoza reevaluated the experiences of his predecessor and contrasted this with the over 5,000 pesos earned by Santa Lucía in 1584, plus the 3,000 expected from Jesús del Monte, he became a firm supporter of Sánchez's policies. By 1585 the annual cash commitments of the Colegio Máximo were 10,000 pesos, plus other debts of 17,000 pesos. At best, 2,200 pesos per year could be expected from selling Santa Lucía and renting out Jesús del Monte.[124] Economic necessities by now outweighed moral and other reservations within the province about owning and managing rural estates.

The membership took longer to convince than the provincial. One casualty was the Colegio Máximo's rector (1580–1585), Father Pedro Díaz, who was pressured to resign his post despite his insistence that the college had sufficient funds to eat, dress, and build, thanks to the income produced by the rural estates.[125] Argument about the propriety of owning Negro slaves also continued despite the father general's earlier instructions that the services of slaves should be effectively used. The concerns of Jesuit provincial members were expressed in a January special report and in a November congregation report in 1585.[126] The Second Provincial Congregation (November 1585), in contrast to the first such meeting, concluded in favor of retaining rural haciendas.[127]

In 1586 the father general issued instructions to clarify secular involvements in Mexico.[128] He prohibited the order to take offices in municipal governments (*alcaldía*) as chief justices, civil administrators, or royal magistrates; to fill secretarial or notary positions (*escribanía*); to grant special favors in exchange for benefices; to act as marriage brokers; to become involved in the election of aldermen or mayors; to act as attorneys for non-Jesuit businesses; to become involved in others' debts; or to send money to Spain with others without a license from superiors. Such rules favorably impressed those local brethren who were anxious about secular influences in the province. About Santa Lucía, the instructions were brief—it was now clear that the hacienda should not be sold, and that "no brother is to stay there alone and there are not to be any women. And this order will be written in the book in Rome along with the rest."[129] A new position was being created to handle secular, economic, and legal matters. This was the office of provincial attorney (*procurador de la provincia*). Until this point, the Jesuit attorney in Andalucía had been responsible for the provinces in Mexico and Peru. The next step was to create the office of the college attorney (*procurador del Colegio Máximo*), where Jesuits with special business talents dealt with Santa Lucía and the rest of the college's administrative problems.[130]

Steps taken by upper-level Jesuit officers and changing conditions in Mexico put an end to the decade of discord over rural estates. Soon the troublesome issues were forgotten. When Sánchez described the acquisition, a few years later, it was in the following terms:

The results have demonstrated that he [Villaseca] was guided by our Lord because this estate [Santa Lucía] has been the support for the studies that continue in this kingdom: from which come many outstanding individuals occupying themselves in the conversion of the gentiles of this kingdom and of the Philippines, and for the benefit of all religions; it has produced the outstanding persons in letters and religion, and the prelates of the churches have the ministers and the curates they wish, and the cathedrals have doctors, and those taking doctorates are increasing; and for the building of the college, as it is today and is expected in the future—all of which is sustained by the estate of Santa Lucía![131]

By 1587 the Jesuits not only had successfully adapted to the economic opportunities but had firmly established their society to allow it to carry out the functions it had been sent to fulfill. Educational institutions in most larger Spanish urban centers provided intellectual direction and were training future leaders of the viceroyalty. Missionary activity had begun near urban centers and on the northern frontiers. Basic management principles had been worked out to deal with power structures, and administrative policies had been developed to control rural properties. The adaptation had been achieved through a series of rational decisions based on a combination of sound local advice and experience. The internal debates allowed the Jesuit ideological framework to incorporate a new situation. Such successes, however, were not entirely due to acts initiated by the followers of Loyola. Crown officials and influential individuals lent more than a helping hand. A strong element of chance was also involved. Santa Lucía, after all, was not a productive economic venture when it was acquired by the Jesuits. Epidemic disaster, an expansion of Spanish entrepreneurial initiative in mining, and the rapid growth of Mexico City vastly improved prices and demands for hacienda produce.

THREE 🔹 *Building Santa Lucía,*
1586-1646

Financial returns from Santa Lucía during its first decade of operation as a corporate Jesuit estate convinced the order's officials of the utility of developing and operating rural haciendas. As each new college was founded, it invested in rural estates to produce revenues and supplies. The more important the college, the greater the number and variety of properties under its jurisdiction. The larger colleges, at Tepotzotlán, Puebla, Valladolid, and Mexico City, soon controlled an imposing number of haciendas; more modest colleges, at Mérida, Pátzcuaro, Oaxaca, and Veracruz, controlled fewer and smaller rural estates. As the needs of these teaching and training centers grew or shifted, the officials of the order (from provincial to father general) encouraged the college administrators (rectors and procuradores) to redistribute resources so that economic needs could be met uniformly throughout the province. Local hacienda administrators—usually *hermanos coadjutores* assigned to specific colleges—had little say in policy beyond their influence upon their college superiors, who were under constant economic pressure to improve and expand profitable hacienda operations. This expansion was not for the sake of temporal aggrandizement, as claimed by opponents of the Jesuits, but to keep up with continually expanding financial demands resulting from ambitious building, mission, and teaching programs.[1]

During the province's internal crisis of conscience over secular influences (1576–1586), little initiative was taken to increase Santa Lucía, despite Pedro Sánchez's suggestions that this be done.[2] A practical impediment was the immediacy of the "great cocoliztli" epidemic in the countryside (1576–1581). After its main impact had passed, by 1582, the two *sitios de ganado menor* acquired through the audiencia attorney increased the area accessible to Santa Lucía's growing sheep flocks. By 1585 these included 30,000 sheep, whose areas of forage appear to have been confined to the Valley of Mexico but not to area owned by the Jesuits.[3] This, however, was not a particularly large sheep ranch by contemporary standards. Chevalier's study shows haciendas with over 100,000 sheep during the period, and Alonso González, using basically the same properties, had had up to 26,000 sheep in the late 1560s.[4] But the owners of Santa Lucía, noting an annual net increase of 1,000 pesos during the early 1580s,[5] were convinced of its potential and acted accordingly.

A major development program for Santa Lucía was begun in the late 1580s, when work was started on a large residence complex (*casa principal*). This included the construction of offices and a residence for the Jesuit administrators, storage facilities for equipment and produce, corrals, sheds, and shearing facilities for the livestock, residences for slaves, and a chapel to serve the spiritual needs of all those associated with the hacienda. The site chosen for the *casa principal* was the rocky knoll from which Tepeatzingo took its name, located in the center of the large, flat plain on the northeast corner of Lake Xaltocan. Here an austere and monastic-looking stone structure arose, built with Indian labor. In essence the complex was a series of vaulted rooms with interior corridors lined with arches, located around interior patios. Besides a main patio, it contained a series of smaller sheep-shearing patios or enclosures. Numerous subterranean storage rooms were located beneath the interior corridors. The main entrance faced west, flanked on each side by a row of wall niches containing statues of saints. A simple chapel topped with a façade to house three bells was built in the northwest corner of the actual residence. The 1592 date above the exterior entrance to the chapel indicated termination of the main residence construction.[6]

The Santa Lucía residence was strategically located. It was close to Lake Xaltocan, a source of water and the maritime transportation network still serving Mexico City and lakeside communities in the valley. The Indian pueblos of Xoloc and Los Reyes, on which the hacienda was to draw heavily for its labor needs, were only a short distance to the north. The royal road connecting important mining centers at Pachuca and the viceregal capital was close by. The former lake-bottom lands surrounded the entire complex, providing year-round pasture.[7] This area increased as the northern valley lake system was systematically drained, although in times of heavy rains and raised water levels it turned into a swamp. In contrast to most of the native pueblos in the Valley of Mexico, which were located on slopes and hilltops, the Santa Lucía residence complex was located in the midst of a valley plain. Its walls were massive, over a meter thick, built of stone and mortar, reaching heights of five meters. The entire structure reflected stability and permanence, in keeping with the intentions of the institution that built it.[8]

The Jesuits were now disposed to accept donations of rural properties from admirers. In December 1586, the owner of one of the largest entails in New Spain and son of the conqueror of Florida, Don Carlos de Luna y Arellano, donated one *sitio de ganado menor* and two plots of agricultural land, or *caballerías,** to the Colegio Máximo. These lands were located in Toluca Valley, between the Río Hondo and the main road between Mexico City and Toluca, bordering the pueblo lands of Ocoyoacán and Capulhuac.[9] Despite their location—roughly ninety-five kilometers from Santa Lucía itself—these grasslands and farmlands were added to the holdings of the hacienda. The eighty-five hectares of farmland probably were not initially used for agricultural crops, as their titles stipulated they must be, but the pastures may have been. These were located near the pasture lands of Ocuila, which were later extensively exploited for Santa Lucía flocks.

The addition of properties located a considerable distance from the hacienda residence, and the incorporation of agricultural lands, signified a broadening of hacienda activities. Santa Lucía, although emphasizing sheep production, was soon expanded to include the total range of livestock and agricultural production common to the established hacienda complexes of central highland Mexico.[10] The nucleus of this type of estate had been created by Alonso González. Previously the college administrators had relied upon Jesús del Monte as a source for agricultural crops. They now adopted a policy of creating a series of haciendas that specialized in the production of cash crops such as sugar, food crops such as wheat (*trigo*), barley (*cebada*), oats (*avena*), beans (*frijol, habas*), chick-peas (*alverjón*), and maize (*maíz*), or livestock (sheep, goats, cattle,

---

*The *caballería,* which in Spain originally meant a unit of agricultural land granted to a horseman (or *caballero*) in exchange for services rendered to the crown, in New Spain became a standardized unit of measurement, equal to 46.75 hectares (105 acres). Originally the size of the unit varied, and it included provisions for irrigated land, nonirrigated land, and grasslands for small numbers of livestock. By the time the Jesuits became involved in landholding, the legislative dimensions had become established, although in practice they were not rigidly adhered to. See Galván Rivera, *Ordenanzas,* pp. 105–6; Chevalier, *La formación,* pp. 46–51; and Gibson, *Aztecs,* p. 276.

horses, mules, and hogs). Santa Lucía combined livestock and food-crop production with its own slaughterhouses (*matanzas*), mills (*molinos*), and textile factory (*obraje*).

College officials quickly recognized the need for greatly increased pasture and agricultural land and saw that a passive role, as a recipient of donations, would not allow the building of the type of hacienda desired. Properties individuals might wish to donate to the society, regardless of good intentions, might be of poor quality or located in areas difficult to exploit effectively. As of the late 1580s, the Jesuits adopted a policy of active land acquisition, and between 1587 and 1646 they acquired at least 350 square kilometers of pasture land and 3,642 hectares of farmland for Santa Lucía (see Appendix A for a chronological listing). A closer examination of these acquisitions demonstrates the astute management practiced by the Jesuits in building their hacienda into a massive, diversified enterprise.

In the chronological analysis of these acquisitions, three main phases become evident. First, between 1586 and 1598, pasture and farmlands were increased close to the original purchases, roughly within a triangle bounded by the pueblos of Acayuca, Tepexpan, and Zumpango. Second, between 1605 and 1620, there was increased expansion in the same area, also between Acayuca and Pachuca, plus the acquisition of large tracts of summer pasture lands outside the Valley of Mexico—at Ocuila close to Cuernavaca, near Chilpancingo in the present state of Guerrero, and on the Chichimec frontier west of Guadalajara in the jurisdiction of Izatlán. Third, between 1621 and 1646, fewer properties were acquired, mostly carefully selected land adjacent to properties already a part of Santa Lucía.

1586–1598: Nearby Farmlands and Distant Pastures

College officials acquired fifteen properties for Santa Lucía from 1586 to 1598 (see Appendix A), including 93.5 square kilometers of pasture (twelve *sitios de ganado menor*), 1,022 hectares of farmland (twenty-four *caballerías*), and some small plots. Direct purchase accounted for slightly less than half the area, with the rest received from friends who described their gifts as charity or alms (*limosna*) in honor of the "love of God."[11] A closer look at the donations, however, suggests the donors acted as agents in most cases, acquiring through merced legal title to lands specified by the Jesuits and whose property deeds soon found their way into the hands of the college administrators. In some cases the land in question was already being used by the expanding hacienda. The followers of Loyola, it appears, quickly adopted the current practice of Spanish hacendados who requested, in merced, lands they were already using, thereby buttressing de facto possession with de jure ownership.[12]

In 1589, Baltasar de Herrera, a resident of Mexico who owned haciendas in Chalco and Xilotepec, donated one *estancia de ganado menor*. This was likely a genuine donation. The estancia was located twenty-five kilometers north of Tula, near the pueblo of Chapantongo, and was of poor quality, consisting of rocky slopes with dry gullies.[13] Its distance from Santa Lucía, its poor quality, and the fact that the original grant's clause against resale within four years was respected suggest that the Jesuits had no direct hand in the acquisition. They never did integrate it into Santa Lucía.

In August of the same year, a direct purchase was made of two caballerías close to the pueblo of San Mateo Ixtlahuaca. This was good farmland, with access to water, and adjacent to the two estancias the college had acquired through Cristóbal Pérez in 1582. The purchase cost 140 pesos and indicates an interest in cultivating agricultural crops.[14] Further evidence of this trend is suggested by a 1591 donation of a mill site, or *herido de molino*, from the pueblo of San Mateo Xoloc.[15] At the same time, the college began to extend its control over grasslands distant from the Valley of Mexico in order to provide summer pasture for growing sheep flocks. A *sitio de ganado menor* was purchased for 400 pesos from the Colegio de Santo Tomás in Guadalajara in 1594.[16] This acquisition and subsequent additions within a few years of grasslands in the jurisdictions of Izatlán, west of Guadalajara, indicate that Santa Lucía sheep were already making the long annual treks to distant pastures. Such pastures were common, and vital for large-scale sheep operations. The area had recently been devastated by European diseases that sharply reduced the native populations, facilitating takeover of lands by ranching interests.[17]

In 1595 more agricultural land was purchased, this time from the Indians of Zumpango. These *pedazos*, or plots, bordering the Santa Lucía pastures between Xoloc and Zumpango, were already being cultivated prior to purchase. The purchase was from the Indian aristocracy (*indios principales*) of Zumpango, who received permission from the royal authorities for the sale eleven months after title had actually been transferred. This transaction indicates that the Jesuits had by then adopted another secular Spanish habit, that of encroaching upon neighboring native land through usage and subsequently gaining legal ownership through a voluntary or coerced purchase.[18]

Further encroachment on the lands of Indian neighbors to the north of Santa Lucía took place in 1596, when a *sitio de ganado menor* and ten caballerías were accepted as donations. This land was located within the triangle formed by the pueblos of Tizayuca, Xoloc, and Zumpango. Four caballerías were accepted from Alonso Pardo and an equal number from Hernando Vázquez, both residents of Mexico City. They had their ownership of the lands confirmed through merced a few months before the donations, suggesting either that they were acting as agents for the Jesuits or that they were clarifying their titles before making genuine donations. A third donor was listed as a resident of Xoloc, Juan Turrado, whose formal claim to ownership of one sitio of pasture land and two caballerías had been confirmed in February, five months before his donation.[19] This was a clear case of legal maneuvering to gain land title, since Turrado had been working for the Jesuit hacienda for over a decade. The same lands had been formally ceded to the Indians of Xoloc in 1572, after a dispute with the native leaders in Tlaltelolco, who claimed the land and to which Xoloc was a subject pueblo. The Xoloqueños disputed the Jesuit ownership claim and succeeded in having the audiencia reaffirm Xoloc ownership in 1599. Although the Jesuits later made a payment for the lands, they remained an issue of dispute throughout the colonial period. The Jesuits, despite being at times legally prevented from using the lands, considered them part of Santa Lucía as of Juan Turrado's 1596 donation.[20]

A fourth donation, this time of two *sitios de ganado menor* in the northern part of the valley, was accepted in 1596. Francisco Pacho, a successful petitioner for lands in various parts of the Valley of Mexico since 1594, held legal title to these properties, located near the pueblos of Tezontlalpa and Tlacuitlapilco. Pacho's activity in land accumulation and previous experience as an agent for a third party suggest that he was acting on behalf of the Jesuits.[21] In the same year, two purchases were made in widely separate areas. The first added one *sitio de ganado menor* and two caballerías of farmland to the holdings in Izatlán at a cost of 300 pesos. The second was a major investment of 12,000 pesos for an estate similar to the original Santa Lucía purchase, but smaller and only partly developed. This estate, it turned out, had also been owned by Alonso González and willed to his wife and daughters.[22] When the wife died the estate was sold at public auction in 1593 to a resident of Texcoco, Pedro de Dueñas.[23] Three years later, Dueñas sold the greater part of his purchase to the Colegio Máximo. Included were three *sitios de ganado menor,* four caballerías, 12,000 sheep, 12 oxen for plowing, 6 plows, 30 horses, 40 cattle, some goats, dogs, a forty-five-year-old Negro slave, 30 pairs of sheep shears, 1 large metal cauldron for dyeing wool, and 1 cart.[24]

These lands had formerly belonged to the Indians of Acayuca and Tizayuca. González had acquired most of the land through mercedes, the latest dated 1586. The agricultural land had been purchased directly from the natives of Tizayuca, who were forced to sell it to pay their tribute obligations.[25] When the trustees of González's daughters attempted to sell the estate, a dispute arose over what would be a fair selling price. The audiencia finally stepped in and ordered a public sale at 5 reales "per head." This price, although referring to a set price for each "head" of sheep, covered the other animals (including the slave, who was listed as part of the livestock resources), land, equipment, and facilities. This was the accepted standard for sales of this nature. Dueñas bought at 5 reales per head in 1593 and three years later sold to the Jesuits at 8 reales, or 1 peso, per head.[26]

On the surface it appears that Dueñas was doing very well at the expense of the Jesuits, but a closer examination of the conditions of sale shows otherwise. The sale contract specified that the total price of the estate was to be paid in cash, and Dueñas promised to pay an outstanding 2,000 peso mortgage within three years to clear the titles of all encumbrances. The Jesuits made an initial cash payment of 3,000 pesos in July 1596 and made the following agreement for paying the outstanding 9,000 pesos:

1. At the end of August 1596, the college would sell Dueñas 4,000 arrobas of wool at 9 reales per arroba, for which they would be credited 4,000 pesos against the purchase, and Dueñas would pay them 500 pesos in cash.

2. At the end of August 1597, the college would sell Dueñas another 3,000 arrobas of wool at 9 reales, for which they would be credited 3,000 pesos against the purchase, and Dueñas would pay them 375 pesos in cash.

3. The remaining 2,000 pesos would be paid in cash within three years.

4. Delivery of the wool would take place at the main residence of the Santa Lucía hacienda.[27]

In effect, the college administrators bought the estate, incorporated it into Santa Lucía, and used its products as payment. They paid a total of only 5,000 pesos (actually an expenditure of only 4,125 pesos if the payments made by Dueñas to the Jesuits are to be taken into consideration) over a period of five years while selling 7,000 arrobas (approximately 175,000 pounds) of wool on terms and conditions entirely to their advantage. The final 2,000 peso payment was made in 1601.[28] This property was converted into a center for the production of cattle, horses, and mules. It became known as Santa María de las Pintas and was considered an anexa, or auxiliary hacienda, of Santa Lucía.

Before the end of the sixteenth century, three additional acquisitions provided two *sitios de ganado menor,* four caballerías, and one pedazo to Santa Lucía's growing terrains. A Spanish friend of the Jesuits, Alonso de Castañeda, donated one sitio and two caballerías in 1597. The properties were located in the northern jurisdictions of the Valley of Mexico, consisting of lands formerly controlled by the pueblo of Temascalapa.[29] The small plot was rich farmland sufficient for planting half a fanega of maize (1.78 hectares) located between Coyoacán and Tlalpan (San Agustín de las Cuevas). It had been owned by an Indian couple who sold the land, plus a house and a thatched hut, to the Jesuits in 1598.[30] The third acquisition was also a purchase, consisting of pasture and agricultural land in the distant summer grazing area in the jurisdiction of Izatlán.[31] The three additions clearly indicate the hacienda's trend of development through the accumulation of land in an expanding perimeter of influence, and an expansion of livestock and food-crop activities.

By the end of its first quarter-century of activity, Santa Lucía was producing an annual income of 17,000 pesos for the Colegio Máximo. The income resulted from an admitted investment of slightly more than 30,000 pesos for 179 square kilometers of pasture land, 1,020 hectares of designated farmland, and over 50,000 head of livestock (see Appendix A). The main source of profits was the sheep, by now numbering 50,000 and complemented by growing herds of cattle, horses, and goats.[32] The cattle, horses, and goats were largely confined to the northern jurisdictions of the Valley of Mexico, but the sheep ranged far beyond the limits of the valley. Food crops were being produced nearer to the main residence at Tepeatzingo with the establishment of the *labor,* or agricultural farmlands, of San Juan, west and north of Xoloc. The main food crops grown were barley and maize, with a lesser production of wheat, beans, and peas. San Juan had its complement of oxen and horses for tilling the soil and threshing the grains, plus a herd of hogs that produced meat for hacienda and college consumption. The hacienda's early successes under Jesuit management were a measure of the order's ability to adapt its human resources to new tasks in new circumstances. They had surpassed the entrepreneurial rural production style exhibited by individuals such as Alonso González, whose attempts at building a rural economic base failed to survive a generation, and were rapidly approaching the success exemplified by people such as Alonso de Villaseca. The Jesuits had absorbed the adaptation of Spanish agricultural practices to the Mexican setting and had quickly learned the subtleties of exploiting the natural resources of fertile land and a docile labor force.[33] Such accomplishments were greatly facilitated by having many influential friends in positions of authority, and few antagonists.

Friends and Concessions

Friends providing direct assistance included crown officials in New Spain and, more important, the favorable disposition of the king himself. Philip II, as the initial sponsor of the order's activities in Mexico, had an interest in granting special concessions to the Jesuits to further their work in Mexico. Jesuit exemption from paying *diezmo* (the ecclesiastical tithe) was perhaps the most important, since it meant an increase in profits—an advantage not allowed the secular hacendados. The tithe issue, aside from direct economic importance, also involved questions of royal authority and jurisdiction in church-state relations.

Diezmo became a problem almost immediately after the Jesuits acquired rural estates, when Alonso Flores, who had harvested 600 fanegas of wheat on lands rented from Jesús del Monte in 1577, was threatened with prison by the royal tithe collector for not paying the ecclesiastical tax. The Jesuits stepped in immediately, and their attorney, Brother Juan de Salcedo, took the case before the judge (*alcalde ordinario*) of the Mexico City town council, arguing that "the Jesuits and their properties were exempt from all types of papal tithes" by virtue of concessions granted by the pope. Salcedo pointed out that diezmo could not be collected from Flores since, "if it was, he would have to subtract it from his rent and thus it would be collected indirectly from the Jesuits whose privileges would be frustrated, resulting in an absurd and intolerable inconvenience." The *alcalde ordinario* transferred the case to the audiencia but ruled that Flores should pay the tithe while a final decision was arrived at by the audiencia and the Royal Council of the Indies in Spain.[34]

The importance of the diezmo issue and the ability of the Jesuits to make direct representation to the crown are underlined by the efforts taken to ensure a favorable response. In 1578, Father Pedro Díaz was sent from Mexico to Spain to see royal officials about tithes and other Jesuit privileges. From Spain, Díaz continued to Rome, where he consulted with the father general, and returned to Spain to continue discussions with the Royal Council of the Indies and the king. As a result, the crown committed itself to support the Jesuits in Mexico with annual subsidies to assist in the construction of a church and residence.[35] Under such circumstances, concessions that would enhance the financial situation of the Jesuits reduced the demands upon the royal treasury. In August 1582, the audiencia revoked the ruling of the *alcalde ordinario*, arguing that, in the case of the Jesuits, failure to pay the levy would not violate royal patrimony, as argued by town council representatives. In this ruling, the audiencia was upholding the right of the pope to extend tithe exemptions to the Jesuits, the latest such concession having been made by Pope Pius V in 1572. In November 1583, the audiencia reaffirmed this ruling.[36]

The secular clergy in Mexico, who would benefit from the tithe levies, were not happy with the outcome of this or any other case that confirmed the economic advantage of the regular clergy. Despite their common religious objectives and ideological goals in New Spain, when it came to political and economic power, the regular and secular elements were more adversaries than friends. This case placed the Jesuits in the role of defenders of regular privileges. The issue of tithe exemptions had been solved only temporarily. It was to keep reemerging throughout the Jesuits' stay in Mexico, with Santa Lucía becoming the central target of attack by members of the secular clergy.[37]

Special viceregal concessions directly aided the growth of Santa Lucía. When the plague of 1576–1581 produced a shortage of Indian labor, sheep owners protested to the audiencia. The viceroy responded with a series of instructions to *alcaldes mayores* stipulating that Indians adjacent to estancias were to be made available for Spanish use. In June 1578, these instructions were applied to Santa Lucía at the request of Jesuit officials. In the same month, the corregidor of the pueblo of Chiconautla received instructions from the viceroy that the hacienda's sheep were to be allowed access to the salt licks of Chiconautla and Tecama. The viceroy rejected pueblo arguments that their rights of protection against Spanish livestock intrusions were being violated. He instructed the Indians to build sheepwalks so flocks could make bimonthly trips to salt licks on Indian lands. Native agricultural lands would have to be enclosed if necessary, but a proviso was added that the shepherds were not to allow the sheep to leave the sheepwalks. Similar instructions were issued to Zumpango.[38] Another royal privilege granted to secular sheep owners, and extended to Jesuit flocks, concerned access to pueblo common pastures and barren or unapportioned lands (*tierras realengas y baldías*).[39] Salcedo obtained this right for the Jesuits in 1589, which allowed Jesuit shepherds to bed down their flocks where they wished in the stipulated areas. This privilege was confirmed and reapproved by the viceroy in 1596 after a request by the Colegio Máximo's attorney.[40]

Although crown officials were easily persuaded to grant privileges to Jesuit haciendas, secular Spanish ranchers were less favorably disposed toward Jesuit flocks. Disputes over pasture were common on drives between summer and winter pastures. One incident, in Querétaro, where a Francisco de Medina, "with his servants and other Spaniards," assaulted and threatened to kill an Indian shepherd accompanying Jesuit flocks from Santa Lucía, served as a test case. The Jesuit attorney protested, first to viceregal authorities, and then in 1595 to the king. Philip II intervened and instructed his viceroy to make sure that rights conceded to the Jesuits in 1589 were complied with. People who opposed the Jesuits, such as Francisco de Medina, were to be held responsible for damages and be fined 100 pesos.[41] Another intervention in favor of Santa Lucía occurred in 1601, when the viceroy ordered one Juan de Carranza to remove his cattle from Jesuit pastures near Actopan. Carranza protested that he had been forced by the slaughterhouses of Cuautitlán to bring his livestock into Jesuit pastures, but he was nevertheless fined 100 pesos.[42]

Early favorable governmental action on behalf of Jesuit haciendas helped offset the order's lack of experience in ranching and agriculture. In hacendado-pueblo conflicts the crown was inclined to favor its Indian wards, whereas in the Jesuit cases pro-Jesuit decisions reflected the privileged status of the order. The case where the audiencia forced movement of Indians near Tolcayuca in 1582, allowing the Jesuits to move a residence to a more convenient location, is a case in point.[43] In another case the Jesuits got permission to pay three-month rather than one-month salary advances to Indian workers to ensure adequate labor supplies for their college's building program.[44] The Jesuits were careful to obtain signed copies of their privileges. Such documents, besides their direct usefulness when Jesuit activities were questioned, served to remind the questioner of the special relationship between the order and crown officials.

A seven-year hiatus in land procurement began in 1598, coinciding with significant political changes. At this time (1598–1606), the crown implemented its program of civil congregation, designed to regroup the scattered remains of Indian communities so they could be more easily administered by royal officials. As Cline's study shows, "at a single stroke . . . the policy erased hundreds of minor settlements," including communities bordering on Santa Lucía.[45] Although the intent of this program was to protect the Indigenous sector, the opposite occurred. The pueblos lost control over traditional resources and what remained of local political and social organization. Civil congregation became a preliminary step to a further cycle of land appropriation by Spaniards, and by the Jesuits for the expansion of Santa Lucía. Such trends were further facilitated by recurring epidemics during the first decade of the seventeenth century.[46]

1605–1620: More Farmlands and Pastures

Between 1605 and 1620, twenty-six acquisitions were negotiated for Santa Lucía. Involvement by college officials is indicated by sixteen direct purchases versus ten donations, whereas in the 1586–1598 period, donations and purchases were almost equal. Involved were twenty-seven *sitios de ganado menor,* sixty-two caballerías, and thirteen pedazos of land, representing 210.5 square kilometers of pasture and 2,635 hectares of farmland (see Appendix A for the complete list). These fifteen years were the most intensive period of purchase in terms of number of transactions. They more than doubled Santa Lucía's pastures and tripled its farmlands. These acquisitions show intensification of Jesuit exercise of choice and less dependence upon friendly crown officials to facilitate land transfers.

The first priority, when purchases were resumed in 1605, was more farmland for the *labor* of San Juan, near Santa Lucía. Eight caballerías (340 hectares) of a flat, dark-soiled plain lying between the communities of San Sebastián, Zumpango, and Xoloc were bought for 1,300 pesos from the secretary of the audiencia, Martín

López de Gaona. The secretary was either doing the Jesuits a favor by acting as their agent—he had acquired the properties the year before as royal grants—or he was using his strategic political station to prosper from land speculation. In either case, the Jesuits got title to land they needed for producing barley, wheat, and maize close to the main Santa Lucía residence.[47] The secretary sold an additional four caballerías to the Jesuits in the same area in 1615, this time at a lower price of 100 pesos per caballería.[48] Two additional caballerías in the same area were bought in 1608 from a native governor of Zumpango, Don Juan Valiente. How Valiente acquired the right to sell the land and the price he obtained are not known. What is known is that the land had earlier (in 1583) been granted in merced to another member of the Zumpango aristocracy and had been disputed by the Zumpangueños and a Spaniard after San Sebastián became depopulated as the result of civil congregation. The audiencia ruled that Zumpango had a more legitimate claim, and pueblo representatives took formal possession in 1607, only to lose it the next year when Valiente sold it to the Jesuits.[49]

For Santa Lucía, these additions became the resources with which to develop San Juan into an important food-crop center. In short order they built a solid but imposing granary (*troje*), a small residence with a chapel, a series of enclosures for guarding the livestock, and implements required for agricultural production. Located within two kilometers of the Tepeatzingo administrative center, and one kilometer from the pueblo of Xoloc, San Juan was well situated, close to adequate supervision and adjacent to labor from communities which had lost their land and identity (San Sebastián) or had their lands greatly curtailed (Xoloc and Zumpango).[50]

In 1609, the Jesuits spent 3,607 pesos to establish another hacienda for Santa Lucía. This was another one of those partly developed estates owned by Mexico City hacendados who were happy to get a reasonable price for rural properties in which they had no long-range interest. It was located southeast of Tolcayuca, adjacent to the royal road leading to the Pachuca mining district, and thirty kilometers from Santa Lucía. This estate, developed in the late sixteenth century, was owned by Eugenio Vargas and his wife, Doña Julia de Salazar. Included, besides the land (one *sitio de ganado mayor* and six caballerías), were houses, corrals, livestock, and agricultural equipment.[51] It was quickly developed into an important multipurpose center called San Francisco de Xavier, later referred to as San Xavier or La Matanza, referring to its slaughtering activities. San Xavier was later to rival and, at times, surpass in importance the main residence of Santa Lucía. It produced food crops and livestock, and its buildings later included residences for administrators, slaves, and workers, shearing and slaughterhouse facilities, storage buildings, corrals, gardens, and a chapel. Like the structures at Tepeatzingo and San Juan, those at San Xavier were located in the midst of a large plain.

Tolcayuca, whose lands San Xavier absorbed and whose residents were to provide an important source of labor, was perched on mountain slopes five kilometers to the west. Zapotlán, which was also to be an important source of labor, was slightly more distant, to the north, straddling hilltops of a ridge which provided a stream of water later channeled into the reservoirs of San Xavier. Ixtlahuaca and Tezontepec, two other native communities important for Santa Lucía's development, lay to the southeast, but on the flat plain, ten and fifteen kilometers from San Xavier.[52]

Ixtlahuaca, which in pre-Spanish times had the advantage of rich agricultural lands and an adequate water supply, gradually lost all but the land on which the heart of the community was located.[53] The Jesuits had already taken over two sitios and two caballerías of its lands in 1582 and 1589. They continued their acquisitions there in 1609 and 1612. Four caballerías were acquired through the services of Juan Turrado, who requested a merced and, when it was received on October 14, 1609, immediately made the formal donation.[54] Three years later, four additional caballerías were bought directly from one of the local community leaders (*indios principales*) of Ixtlahuaca, Juan de la Cruz, and his wife, Luisa de los Angeles. The title to these lands, located near Zapotlán, had been gained through merced less than a year before the sale, which brought the couple 400 pesos. Other property transactions, in which Juan de la Cruz was involved indicate his active role in land speculation at the expense of Indian communities.[55]

The northward march of Santa Lucía continued with a series of acquisitions within the jurisdictions of the pueblo of Acayuca. If the Jesuits were operating as other hacendados did, and all indications are that they had adopted many contemporary practices, much of the land acquired was already being encroached upon by Santa Lucía livestock. In 1610, four caballerías were bought for 900 pesos from Juan Francisco Marroquín, who had obtained title to them between 1603 and 1606.[56] In 1612 the college attorneys completed negotiations for yet another partially developed estate located just north of the valley along a road leading to Acayuca. Included were three estancias, houses, corrals, and equipment formerly owned by one Antonio Machado, who had run afoul of the Inquisition. In 1607 the *alcalde mayor* of Pachuca was instructed by the Inquisition judges to seize the Machado properties and to announce their public sale by placing notices on the doors of churches. Apparently no satisfactory bids were received until the Jesuit offer of 520 pesos, made in February 1612. Three months later a public proclamation was made in Mexico City indicating that Machado's property had been offered for sale at public auction and sold to the highest bidder. The next day Father Martín, the Jesuit attorney, paid 320 pesos to the Inquisition treasury and ten days later the outstanding 200 pesos.[57] The estate, known as Hueytepec, became another one of the important anexas of Santa Lucía and was used primarily as a goat and horse ranch.

During 1614 and 1615, the Jesuits concentrated on increasing land areas where they already had established haciendas. A resident of Tolcayuca, Francisco Díaz de Velasco, donated four recently acquired caballerías in the jurisdiction of Acayuca, suggesting his role as an agent, and the expenditure of 100 pesos acquired another *sitio de ganado menor* in the same area, from a Mexico City resident, Baltasar de la Cadena.[58] Don Juan de Morada, also of Mexico City, sold them one estancia and four caballerías adjacent to the 1576 purchase of Papahuaca, land that once belonged to the pueblos of Chiapa and Temascalapa.[59] A further donation of three caballerías in the same area was made by a Captain Sebastián de la Barrera.[60] Further south, along the perimeters of Lake Xaltocan, the Jesuits bought two *sitios de ganado menor* and seven caballerías from a former royal official at Tepotzotlán, Gabriel Hortigosa.[61] And still further south, in the Coyoacán area, the Jesuits received a donation of thirteen small plots (varying in size from sixty by twenty to ten by five *brazas;* one braza equals two varas) from an Indian named Juan González. González had purchased these lots between 1600 and 1604 from eleven other Indians. His motive for making the donation was not given, but the circumstances surrounding the transactions suggest the formal donation was merely a legal procedure to disguise other dealings.[62] Finally there was a donation from an unexpected quarter, from one of their own members, Gaspar de Villerías. Villerías, as the eldest son of a hacendado who owned land west of Lake Xaltocan, received his inheritance—one estancia and two caballerías—after joining the order. As a Jesuit he could not own property, and the titles were promptly transferred to the Colegio Máximo.[63] These 1614–1615 acquisitions clearly indicate a broad-based source of property with donors reflecting diverse social and economic backgrounds.

Steps were also taken in 1614 to expand summer pastures relatively near the Valley of Mexico. As early as 1586, a donation in the jurisdiction of Metepec had brought to the attention of the hacienda administrators the location of well-watered grasslands on the lower southwestern slopes of the ring of mountains surrounding the Valley of Mexico. Some of the hacienda sheep had been sent to graze in the area during the summer, as allowed by laws governing pastures. With the general rush for titles going on, the Jesuits arranged to gain access to grasslands for summer pasture in the jurisdiction of Malinalco. Three *sitios de ganado menor* and four caballerías were received in donation from Doña Juana de Cuadra, lands which had been claimed in merced by two well-connected Spaniards between 1575 and 1585.[64] Two additional sitios were obtained in the same area (within the former jurisdictions of the pueblos of Malinalco, Ocuila, Santa Mónica, and Xoquinzingo) in 1618, with a Martín Hernández serving as middleman.[65] These summer pastures became known as Xoloc or Ocuila and played an important role in Santa Lucía sheep production over the next 150 years. Their proximity to the main hacienda winter pastures (one hundred kilometers) added to their attractiveness.

Another *sitio de ganado menor* close to the main Santa Lucía residence was purchased in 1616 for the very high price of 2,000 pesos.[66] In the last quarter of the sixteenth century, sitios acquired for the hacienda cost between 80 and 350 pesos. In the first two decades of the seventeenth century, the price had risen to 100 to 600 per sitio, the average cost being 441 pesos. The price varied largely according to the location and quality of the pasture in question.[67] The elevated cost of this sitio, sold to the Jesuits by Don Jerónimo de la Ricavilla, was a case of an offer he could not refuse. The Jesuits' inflated purchase offer was soundly based. The lands in question would extend Santa Lucía's control of the western banks of Lake Xaltocan as far south as Ozumbilla and provide additional fresh-water springs and natural salt deposits for sheep during their winter stay near the main hacienda.[68] With this purchase, Santa Lucía extended its ownership to virtually all pastures bordering Lake Xaltocan, from Ozumbilla on the eastern side to the Xaltocan causeway on the west. Elevated costs of individual sitios were a small price to pay for ensuring the control of such vast resources.

The remaining acquisitions until 1620 represented a Jesuit response to the increasing need for summer pastures for expanding flocks. The administrators of Santa Lucía had gradually increased these flocks to 100,000 sheep.[69] The summer pastures in the Izatlán area were no longer sufficient, even disregarding their great distance from the main residence. The location chosen for new summer pastures was the Chilpancingo area, 300 kilometers south of Santa Lucía. The initial properties, three *sitios de ganado menor*, were obtained through the services of agents. Diego Alonso de Alfaro, who acted as one of the agents in 1617, testified two years later that "the costs and expenses" of obtaining the merced had been paid "with funds of the college."[70] The college administrators quickly added 54 square kilometers of pasture and 170 hectares of farmland through purchase at a cost of 2,450 pesos. The properties were all located roughly within the area bounded by the settlements of Apango, Chilapa, Mochtitlán, and Tixtla and were referred to as Santa María.[71]

These pastures were designated as *estancias para agostadero*, to be used solely as seasonal pasture from a few days before Christmas until the end of May, "the period during which it is supposed that the local native inhabitants [*naturales*] will have already harvested their seasonal plantings."* The previous owners were a clergyman, a Spanish hacendado, and a member of the Chilapa native aristocracy. The negotiation surrounding the sale by the hacendado, Pedro Alonso Redondo, provides additional evidence of circumvention of legal demands in that the sale to the Jesuits was made over two months prior to Redondo's receipt of title. The *alcalde mayor* of Chilapa took formal possession of the properties in the name of the Jesuits. In one of the rare times they voluntarily disposed of property, the Jesuits turned around and sold one and a half estancias for the handsome sum of 1,000 pesos. The acquisitions in the Chilpancingo area, as in the Malinalco area, were taking place where local native populations had been sharply reduced during the preceding decades and, equally significant, were still in a state of decline.[72]

Jesuit selection of properties for Santa Lucía in strategic locations and their direct participation in the acquisitions during the first two decades of the seventeenth century demonstrate their successful adaptation to secular affairs in Mexico. Illegality of ownership by religious entities was no longer an issue, the practice being wide-

---

*PCRVP 1: 474r. The term *agostadero* derived from peninsular usage, referring to summer pastures as opposed to *invernaderos*, or winter pastures. In New Spain the winter-pasture term did not gain popularity; see Bishko, "The Peninsular Background," p. 508.

spread in New Spain as well as the rest of the Indies. Another legal technicality, this one occasionally prosecuted, concerned the clause forbidding sale within four years in most of the titles obtained through merced. By 1620 this seems to have become another legal technicality that could be ignored with impunity. In most of their acquisitions for Santa Lucía, the Jesuits were in violation of this clause. Actually, the officials of the order were only following the example of other religious organizations and current practice.[73]

That illegalities existed was essentially a reflection of the gap between Spanish law-making and the ability of the crown to have its representatives enforce the law in New Spain. The astute Jesuit fathers were thus able to use royal contacts to their advantage. The office of the viceroy made many of the decisions affecting the economic interests of all hacienda owners; and all hacendados took advantage of whatever favorable contact with this powerful office they could muster to further their interests. The Jesuits were well served by the viceroy during the early decades of the seventeenth century. When the *alcalde mayor* of Tolcayuca complained about Jesuit use of sheep and goat pastures for horses, the viceroy asked the Colegio Máximo to respond. A college attorney informed the viceroy that cereal crop lands near Zumpango required horses for threshing, and therefore 300 such threshing horses were kept near Tolcayuca, at Hueytepec. The practice had been going on for twenty years. At the same time, the attorney requested permission to continue as before, adding that the horses would be guarded and damages to neighboring crops would be paid for. This request was granted in 1609, and in 1613 the Jesuits got the official designation of the pasture for *ganado menor* changed to *ganado mayor.*[74] In 1619, another college attorney got the viceroy's signature on a special order preventing access to Santa Lucía by governmental representatives concerned with proper use of rural estates.[75] Also in 1619, the viceroy granted a request allowing Santa Lucía to have twenty native overseers (*capitanejos*) mounted on horseback, with saddles, bridles, and spurs. The rationale given for allowing these Indians privileges not shared by other Indigenous people was the "well-being of Santa Lucía."[76]

External Contacts and Internal Developments

Special concessions and routine favors granted to the Jesuits by viceregal authorities were reciprocated. The Jesuits were serving the interests of royal administrators in a variety of ways apart from their teaching and mission functions. Individual Jesuits assisted in engineering public works designed to eliminate flooding in Mexico City. During 1607 and 1608 at least three Jesuits, including the administrator of Santa Lucía, Bartolomé Santos, aided royal engineers with the drainage canal (*desagüe*) project. A group of Jesuits headed by the provincial assisted the viceroy in the official opening ceremonies of 1608.[77] Another Santa Lucía administrator, Juan de Alcázar, greatly aided the production of European crops through his introduction of improved agricultural techniques.[78] Viceregal authorities called upon another Jesuit, Juan Laurencio, to accompany the expeditionary force sent out to pacify the *marrón* (runaway slave) guerrilla band headed by the famous Yanga, and Jesuit advice contributed to the relatively peaceful and permanent solution achieved in 1609.[79] As a special concession to a viceregal request, the Jesuits accepted *doctrina* (mission district) responsibilities at Tepotzotlán under conditions that deviated from established norms of the order.[80] The positive interplay of interests between Jesuits and royal officials was strong during the early decades of the seventeenth century. The burst of acquisition activity between 1510 and 1516 cannot be detached from the viceroyship of an archbishop with a secular bent, such as García Guerra, or the fact that a former viceroy of New Spain and friend of the Jesuits, Luis de Velasco, became president of the Royal Council of the Indies in 1611.[81]

Close ties with the private sector also had their reciprocal aspects. The case of Juan Turrado is enlightening. He was an ardent admirer of the Jesuits who, after the death of his wife, began to work for the order as a volunteer in 1583. He used his agricultural skills to help develop cereal grain production at Jesús del Monte and then at Santa Lucía, where he was placed in charge of San Juan. One of his sons joined the order, and Turrado himself, although not a member, lived according to the Jesuit rule as it applied to *hermanos coadjutores*. Turrado had acted as an agent for the Jesuits in getting property grants for the expansion of the farmlands of San Juan in 1596. He was so well thought of by the Jesuits that he spent his last year at the Colegio Máximo preparing for death, a few hours before which he was formally admitted to the order—by special concession—as a *hermano coadjutor*. His death followed eighteen years of service, most of it at Santa Lucía. Eight years later, in 1609, a son by the same name acted as the Jesuit agent for acquiring property near Ixtlahuaca.[82]

The Colegio Máximo officials, aside from their efforts on behalf of Santa Lucía, were establishing other haciendas. The size of Jesús del Monte had been increased through a combination of donations and purchases. Its main function continued to be a combination of food-crop production, retreat residence, source of firewood and timber, and limited livestock production. Two other haciendas, located south of the Valley of Mexico, were also being developed. One was Xalmolonga, just south of the town of Malinalco, which was turned into a productive sugar hacienda. The second was Chicomocelo, another seventy-five kilometers to the east, near Zacualpa, also devoted to sugar production. These haciendas were acquired through donations and purchases, then increased in the size the same way Santa Lucía was.[83]

What was happening with the Colegio Máximo was being repeated many times at the other colleges throughout New Spain. The resources for all this expansion were not generated by the estates themselves but were largely the result of a constant flow of gifts to the society from wealthy and influential friends, such as Don Juan de Rivera, who with his wife provided 50,000 pesos for the founding of the residence of Jesuits, the Casa Profesa. In the early decades of the seventeenth century, the popularity of the black-robed disciples of Loyola was high among all sectors of society.[84]

The prosperity and well-being achieved by the Jesuits in Mexico was amply displayed in 1610 on the occasion of the inauguration of their Casa Profesa in Mexico City and the canonization of the order's founder, Ignacio Loyola. Mexico City was lit up with special decorations, lights, and fires for the eight-day Jesuit celebration. The elite of the city, including members of the audiencia, cabildo, and offices of the archbishop and viceroy, took part in special competitions, displays, parades, and religious services. The adornments of the statue of the new St. Ignacio alone were reputed to have cost 400,000 pesos. The conspicuous display of wealth was so great that even the order's own historiographer, Francisco Javier Alegre, commented that "the magnificence and great care with which the event was solemnized were incredible."[85] This demonstration of material wealth, however, was not consistent with Jesuit policy and practice in Mexico. The order's colleges and residences, although well constructed, were more austere than those of the Franciscans or Dominicans. The individual Jesuits remained closer to their vows of poverty than most of their contemporary colleagues in the other orders.[86] Secular Spaniards and the secular clergy were noted for their opulence, which contrasted sharply with the ordinary solemn decorum of the Society of Jesus.

By 1620, Santa Lucía also reflected prosperity. It had over 100,000 sheep and goats grazing on strategically located hacienda pastures.[87] The sheep alternated between Tepeatzingo in the valley, Ocuila and Santa María to the south, and Izatlán in the north; the goats were largely confined to the northern parts of the valley, near Hueytepec. Santa Lucía and San Xavier had slaughtering and shearing facilities to process the livestock, and granaries and storage sheds to hold the produce for better prices in easily accessible markets. Food crops were being produced at San Juan and San Xavier. Horses, cattle, and mules were increasing at Pintas and Hueytepec. Within the previous two decades, the pastures and farmlands of the hacienda had more than doubled, now including at least 380 square kilometers of grasslands and 3,655 hectares of farmland. The cost of these properties cannot be accurately determined, since not all purchase prices are available and most donations were disguised purchases. Using average values from transactions with indicated prices for sitios and caballerías, the total value, and probable cost, of the acquisitions since 1685 comes to 20,000 pesos,[88] or slightly more than a single year's income from Santa Lucía at the turn of the century. Unfortunately, the sums invested by the college for improvements, buildings, and equipment have not been discovered, nor have figures on the income produced in the early decades of the seventeenth century. In terms of its size and cost, in relation to productivity and profit, Santa Lucía appears to have reached a high point that would not be maintained in the shifting economic climate of New Spain.

1621–1646: Strategic Additions

Over the next three decades the rhythm of buying slackened, and attention seems to have shifted to management and internal development of the hacienda complex. This is clearly reflected in the few acquisitions made—only eight (listed in Appendix A)—which on closer analysis turn out to be additions to round off selected properties or negotiations calculated to avoid disputes with neighboring population centers. In 1621 a *sitio de ganado menor* was purchased for an undetermined price from the order's own college at Tepotzotlán. The pasture was adjacent to the 1616 purchase near Ozumbilla, at the place called Ojo de Agua, signifying the location of a freshwater spring. This factor, and access to the drainage canal from Lake Texcoco to improve transportation to Mexico City by canoe for Santa Lucía products, seem to have been the reasons behind the transfer of the property from one college to another within the order.[89] It is also interesting that transactions between Jesuit colleges were handled in the same manner as transactions between the Colegio Máximo and non-Jesuit entities.

The two transactions in 1624 were actually settlements related to earlier acquisitions. The first involved a lime deposit and facilities for producing lime used in construction. An encomendero of Tlapanaloya, Melchor de Cháves, had given the college use of these properties in exchange for some mules and oxen. His son, Luis de Cháves Villavicencio, argued that the Jesuits did not own them. The settlement reached called for Luis de Cháves to renounce all claims to the deposits in exchange for twelve mules.[90] In the second case, Don Antonio Domínguez used a legal ploy to increase the price of pasture (7.7 square kilometers) and farmland (170.1 hectares) in the Chilpancingo area. The Jesuits paid 400 pesos for the properties in 1619. Three years later Domínguez's agent convinced authorities that the titles were not clear. When the Jesuits countered with an offer of 650 pesos in 1624, all objections to the deal were dropped.[91]

Only three properties were acquired between 1627 and 1636. Two were *sitios de ganado menor* in the Valley of Mexico, near Tolcayuca and Tepexpan.[92] The third was in the Chalco jurisdiction, where Santa Lucía did not own land, but which was desirable for summer pasture. The properties were on the southern lower slopes of Mt. Popocatépetl, at approximately the same altitude as the Ocuila pastures. The land had been owned by Don Martín de Guzmán, an Indian leader from San Miguel Atlauhcan. Don Martín got permission to sell some of his land (located about five miles from Atlauhcan) because it was too far away from his residence, because wild boars destroyed the crops, and because he had enough other land to meet his needs. A public auction was called, and Juan de Salazar bought one sitio and two caballerías for 45 pesos. Salazar, at the same time, requested title to the properties as a royal grant. By the time he was given his merced (sixteen years later), the property had passed through the hands of another hacendado and its value had risen to 300 pesos. This area was later to be used for summer pasture.[93]

A 1639 purchase of additional farmland for San Juan involved the questionable Turrado donation of 1596. As indicated previously, the Xoloqueños managed to regain title to this land in 1602, but now, almost four decades later, decided to give up the title in exchange for 400 pesos.[94] A further purchase of summer pasture

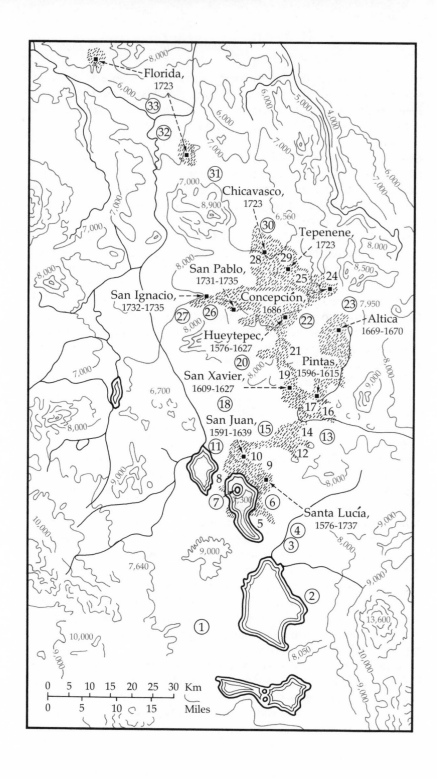

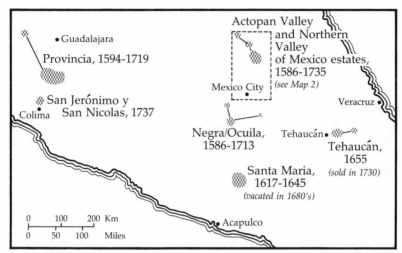

MAP 3. Santa Lucía acquisitions outside the Valley of Mexico and the Actopan Valley, 1586–1737.

lands was made in the Chilpancingo area in 1645, involving 5.5 *sitios de ganado menor*. This transaction is of special interest since it involved the 1.5 sitios the Jesuits had sold to Don Andrés Pérez de Higuera for 1,000 pesos in 1620. He and his wife subsequently accumulated another 3 sitios, which they sold to Pedro de Sagastibarría in 1632.[95] College officials paid 2,000 pesos for the lot, suggesting either a decline in value of pasture land in the area or shrewd bargaining.

By the middle of the seventeenth century, Santa Lucía was an outstanding hacienda in its own right and probably one of the largest in the central plateau of New Spain. Maps 2 and 3 show the location of acquisitions and later additions to hacienda properties. Individual properties cannot be located exactly because of imprecise boundary designations in the title documents and because of the scattered nature of individual estancias and caballerías. Few

MAP 2. Santa Lucía acquisitions in the Valley of Mexico and the Actopan Valley, 1576–1737. 1, Mexico City. 2, Texcoco. 3, Tepexpan. 4, Acolman. 5, Ozumbilla. 6, Tecama. 7, Xaltocan. 8, Xaltenco. 9, Los Reyes. 10, Xoloc. 11, Zumpango. 12, Temascalapa. 13, Atocpan. 14, Chiapa. 15, Tizayuca. 16, Tezontepec. 17, Ixtlahuaca. 18, Hueypoxtla. 19, Tolcayuca. 20, Tezontlalpa. 21, Zapotlán. 22, Acayuca. 23, Pachuca. 24, Tilcuatla. 25, Tornacostla. 26, Ajacuba. 27, Tetepango. 28, Chicavasco. 29, Tepenene. 30, Actopan. 31, Xolotepec. 32, Ixmiquilpan. 33, Tlacintla.

properties of any great size were integral blocks of land. Both in pre-Spanish times and after the Conquest, landholdings were normally scattered. The generally dispersed nature of Santa Lucía's holdings did have a rationale apart from customary tradition in that each unit was located where productivity was calculated to be favorable. Not all the caballerías were dedicated to agriculture, and not all pasture lands were devoted to livestock. Royal permits for access to *tierras realengas* and the wandering pragmatics of livestock herders meant that Santa Lucía stock greatly exceeded pastures to which the Jesuits held title. The property titles themselves were better as indicators of influence than as precise indicators of ownership of resources.

Royal Demands: Composición de Tierras

These same questions of ownership and influence were being raised by the king in his ongoing attempts to raise funds for royal coffers and to keep a check on power being accumulated by residents of New Spain. Even throughout the period when colonial officials were using their positions to gain land titles—in the latter decades of the sixteenth century and the early decades of the seventeenth century—the crown attempted to have all land titles in New Spain regularized, or composed (*composiciones de tierras*). One of the immediate aims of the land-regularization policy, first enunciated by Philip II in 1591, was to raise funds to help defray the costs of protecting the royal fleet which plied between Europe and the Caribbean ports. As Chevalier has pointed out, this levy imposed by the crown upon the landowners of New Spain turned out to be more advantageous for the landowners than for the crown.[96] However, the Spaniards being asked to present their land titles for inspection and approval, for a price, did not agree, and officials in New Spain managed to avoid pressing the issue until forced to do so. Between 1591 and 1639, only sporadic efforts were made to enforce the royal will despite repeated cédulas which had not previously included the Jesuit properties. In a cédula dated January 14, 1639, the king instructed his viceroy to demand *composiciones de tierras* from Jesuit holdings. He wrote: "It is my understanding that they [the Jesuits] possess, without title, many estancias and agricultural lands. In getting them legalized it should be possible to obtain a considerable return. And in executing the order you will give them the necessary titles, they being obligated to present their property deeds for confirmation."[97]

By early 1643, the crown surveyors were measuring Santa Lucía's properties while other royal officials were negotiating the price of putting all property deeds in legal order. The crown was demanding 5,000 pesos for water rights plus an undetermined sum to verify all titles to pastures and farmlands. Father Rojas, acting as attorney general for the Jesuit province, countered with an offer of 2,000 pesos for water rights and 3,000 pesos to verify all land titles for the order in Mexico.[98] Once negotiations were in progress, the viceroy issued instructions to the land surveyors to "cease their measurements and return all land titles presented to them," making specific reference to "the hacienda called Santa Lucía and its lands, waters, plots, ranches, farms, summer pastures, and everything else pertaining to the Colegio de San Pedro y San Pablo."[99]

The Jesuits, always anxious to keep their affairs in proper legal order, cooperated with royal officials as soon as it became clear that the levy would be implemented. They understood the advantage of having all claimed properties legitimated to protect their interests in case of disputes with native communities or other hacendados. The special relationship of the order with the crown also tempered the demands made by royal officials who, in meeting to discuss the case, agreed that the Jesuits would be able to continue the dispute indefinitely on terms favorable to their interests.[100] An agreement was reached in September 1643, whereby the Jesuits were to pay a fee of 3,500 pesos for water rights and an additional 3,500 pesos for legitimation of all their land titles, including land they claimed to own but for which they did not have titles. This did not include identifiable properties of Santa Lucía, but it did include 1,004 square kilometers of pasture and 6,880 hectares of farmland claimed by eight colleges of the order with questionable titles.[101] This bargain provides an insight into the extent of Jesuit landholding throughout the province, suggesting at the same time that colleges removed from the viceregal capital paid less attention to land titles than did the Colegio Máximo.

The Secular Clergy's Response: Palafox's Challenge

While property titles were being legalized under duress, the Reverend Juan de Palafox y Mendoza, bishop of Puebla—later archbishop of Mexico and interim viceroy (February 8–November 23, 1642)—confronted the Jesuits with the issue of wealth, power, and influence from another quarter, that of the secular clergy.[102] This quarrel had local, petty origins in Puebla, which boasted the presence of an influential Jesuit college. The issues, however, were real and concerned regular versus secular ecclesiastical jurisdiction and the question of excessive temporal income. According to Palafox, Jesuit annual income from haciendas in New Spain amounted to 400,000 pesos. He estimated their rural holdings to be worth 2,119,900 pesos.[103] He argued that, if current conditions continued, the secular clergy would end up becoming "chaplains of the Jesuits . . . and the other regulars reduced to requesting alms at their doors." The Jesuit performance of the sacraments for Indians on their estates, Palafox claimed, robbed the secular clergy of funds and violated the norms established by the Council of Trent. He also listed a series of specific charges: confessing of secular individuals without a permit from the bishop's office; performing sacraments and marriages outside their residences; withholding tithes from the church; failing to show proof of privileges; using legal methods against the ecclesiastical will; using compromised secular judges; and encouraging the pious not to comply with their ecclesiastical duties. In short, the Jesuits were excessively powerful and rich and should now be forced at least to pay diezmo.[104] Palafox made public his charges and attempted to force the issue.

This challenge forced the Jesuits in Mexico to justify and defend their rural estates, particularly Santa Lucía, which was given as the prime example of opulence. Economic means and policies were again being questioned. There is a parallel here to the situation during Santa Lucía's first decade, when justification for haciendas was hammered out within the order and tithe exemptions were confirmed during the test case involving Alonso Flores.[105] In the 1640s, however, the questions were being raised from outside the order, which now not only possessed a large number of flourishing haciendas but also was irrevocably committed to defending them.[106]

Palafox's actions were a continuation of attempts by the secular clergy in Mexico to overturn the 1583 ruling of the audiencia in favor of tithe exemptions. As early as 1614, the Council of the Indies had ruled that diezmo might be collected from the regular clergy in Mexico,[107] but no action was taken in view of an ongoing legal battle between the regular and secular clergy in New Spain. In 1639, the Puebla bishop became the official spokesman for the secular clergy's view, and as viceroy he attempted to force the Jesuits to pay the tithe. His singling out of the disciples of Loyola as affluent despoilers of the royal patrimony caused an uproar over the exact extent of Jesuit temporal wealth. The result was an intense and bitter conflict between Jesuit officials and Palafox. Each side sent a stream of testimony to the crown in Spain and to the pope in Rome. By 1648 the Jesuits had clearly won the battle, when King Philip IV sent a series of cédulas censuring the viceroy, the archbishop, and officers of the audiencia for allowing the conflict with the Jesuits to emerge in the first place. At the same time, Palafox was specifically instructed to favor the Jesuits in his diocese.[108] In the end, the Jesuits lost the war and within two decades were compelled to pay the tithe on the production of their rural estates.[109] The king's decision in 1648, nevertheless, demonstrated the influence and good standing the order enjoyed with the crown in Spain. In New Spain this high esteem was less secure.

There was a sharp discrepancy between 1645 figures presented by Palafox regarding the income of the Colegio Máximo from its rural estates and 1644 figures reported by the Jesuit provincial to the father general in Rome. According to Palafox, the profit amounted to 50,000 pesos per annum; according to the Jesuits, Santa Lucía and anexas, plus the sugar estates and other haciendas pertaining to the college, produced only 25,000 pesos.[110] In fact, the debts of the Colegio Máximo were increasing very rapidly during the attack by Palafox. The internal records of the college showed total debts of 39,552 pesos for 1639, which a decade later had increased to 230,000 pesos.[111] Ironically, the Jesuits were being attacked for having excessive income at the very time when productivity and income from haciendas were rapidly declining.

The debate between the Jesuits and secular or clerical detractors over special economic privileges—diezmo and sales taxes (*alcabala*)—intensified during the remainder of Jesuit colonial residence in Mexico. Each side chose and manipulated economic statistics best suited to support its arguments. The Jesuits were quick to point out that Palafox's figures were exaggerated, aside from failing to take into account the services being provided in educational and mission work or the order's privileges based on royal and papal concessions. When the Jesuits added their debts, incurred by the opening of new colleges, residences, and frontier missions, the order's financial situation was made to seem precarious and in need of assistance. In contrast, their opponents ignored debts and services, choosing to emphasize the gross value of temporal properties and haciendas such as Santa Lucía. Most of the time, the crown's decisions on specific issues favored the Jesuits, because it approved of the work being done and recognized that to lessen the resources available for the functions of the order would only increase pressure upon crown resources for direct financial assistance. Having unhappy archbishops was preferable to having to release pesos from royal coffers to meet Jesuit needs.

Temporal wealth was also viewed differently by Loyola's followers than by civil and secular ecclesiastical authorities in New Spain. This, in a sense, was the real issue. The Jesuits, when assessing their temporal holdings, always had in mind their spiritual and educational objectives. The needs of the Sinaloa and Sonora missions, the opening of California as the latest frontier, the consolidation of colleges in Mérida and Guatemala, the lack of sufficient funds to found colleges at Pátzcuaro, Tehuacán, and Veracruz, and the current building programs in Mexico City and Puebla[112]—these were weights on the debit counter during the 1640s, against which income and resources at hand had to be measured. And invariably the means were insufficient. The provincial's report to Rome showed income during 1644 for the Colegio Máximo to be 25,000 pesos, with debts amounting to 150,000 pesos. For the province as a whole, income was calculated at 117,000 pesos and debts at 438,520 pesos.[113] Material possessions in themselves had little meaning except as sources of income which, in turn, had to be measured against debts and needs.

FOUR ⊞ *Maximum Expansion and Development, 1647–1767*

By the middle of the seventeenth century, much of the best land in the Mexican Central Highlands had been claimed by Spanish hacendados building entails for their heirs, business interests concerned with farming, mining, and ranching, the dwindling remains of the Indian aristocracy, or religious entities (colleges, hospitals, monasteries, convents, and seminaries).[1] Land still retained by native pueblos was now regulated by registered property deeds that were zealously defended. The native loss of land and the demographic tragedy imposed upon Mexico by Spanish stimuli occurred simultaneously. By 1650, Indian population had reached its low point and began a slow, painful demographic recovery.[2] Table 1 provides a breakdown of the general trends in the jurisdictions where Santa Lucía properties were located. These figures indicate an overall reduction of 87.24 percent between 1570 and 1643, and a subsequent 18 percent increase by the 1680s. The population by the 1680s nevertheless was still only 15 percent of the 1570 total. In the Valley of Mexico jurisdictions central to Santa Lucía expansion, such as Ecatepec, Pachuca, and Zumpango, the reduction between 1570 and 1643 was 92 percent, the increase between 1643 and the 1680s was 11.7 percent, and the increase between the 1680s and 1743 was 69.9 percent. By 1743, overall demographic recovery was pronounced—an increase of 57 percent from 1680—and the struggle over land control became intense, at times resulting in violent confrontation. Even in areas where native retention was significant (such as the valleys of Metztitlán and Oaxaca), much of the land was of limited value or in the hands of *caciques* (local Indian rulers) who were directly or indirectly controlled by Spanish interests. Whatever land the pueblos still retained became subject to increasing subsistence demands of growing Indigenous and Mexican (mestizo, mulatto) populations in the century after 1650.[3] A decrease in the availability of *tierras realen-*

TABLE 1

Indian Tributaries in Selected Jurisdictions, 1570–1743

Jurisdiction	1570	1643	1680s	1743[a]	Page in GHGNS
Actopan	12,000	1,092	1,509	2,391	45
Chilapa	7,440	1,480	2,000[b]	2,169	113
Cuautitlán	10,600	1,193	1,866	1,940	128
Ecatepec	2,600	443	284	890	227
Ixmiquilpán	5,400	790	1,521	2,076	155
Malinalco	6,985	1,405	1,667	2,310	171
Metztitlán	15,800	3,570	2,190	4,746	185
Pachuca	6,233	136	322	417	210
Tetepango-Hueypoxtla	21,450	1,236	1,421	2,068	278
Texcoco	18,851	1,565	2,295	5,142	313
Tixtla	2,950	1,350[c]	1,760[b]	2,468	317
Zumpango	6,600	662	781	1,049	402
TOTAL	116,909	14,922	17,616	27,666	

SOURCE: GHGNS.

[a]Figures in GHGNS refer to families, here converted to tributaries using the conversion ratio of 1.15:1 provided by Cook and Borah I: 278–99.

[b]Refers to 1700.

[c]Refers to 1626.

gas, and royal restraints upon the breaking up of established *mayorazgos* (entails), further limited hacienda territorial expansion.[4] The net result was increasing tension between hacendados and the pueblos over access to rural resources which, besides land, included access to water, wood, and other products of the soil. Such was the context in which Santa Lucía achieved its maximum size and development.[5]

Balancing Debts and Profits

Conditions after 1647 changed rather than halted Jesuit expansion of Santa Lucía. Although an occasional pasture or farm plot was separately acquired through purchase or donation, the strategy now adopted by college officials was to purchase rural estates of considerable size. They began to accumulate the entails of families whose need for ready cash was stronger than their will to leave property to their children. In surveying the continued growth of Santa Lucía until the Jesuit expulsion in 1767, the focus of attention shifts from the details surrounding estancias and caballerías to the contexts surrounding the less frequent Jesuit additions to Santa

Lucía and the manner in which the hacienda's lands were used (for a listing of such acquisitions see Appendix A). There were fewer additions, but they were larger in area. The continuing accumulation of lands by the Jesuit college was a response to expanding financial needs and increasing debts of the Colegio Máximo. Jesuit expansion outstripped economic growth. Although income from rural estates remained more or less static, despite careful management, debts and financial needs continued to grow. The incomes derived from Santa Lucía and other estates were never sufficient to meet the needs of the colleges to which they were attached.

During the second half of the seventeenth century, the father general was constantly having to remind the administrators of the central college in Mexico to control debts which, nevertheless, rose steadily as a result of building programs and teaching activities. The period is marked by a decrease in the rate of increase of revenues expected from Santa Lucía and its anexas. In part, this resulted from the less favorable competitive position of Jesuit estates resulting from the loss of their diezmo exemption. The general economic situation in New Spain had changed as well, and rural estates of all types no longer were so profitable as they had been during the first half of the century.[6] Santa Lucía's development in the second half of the seventeenth century was a direct Jesuit response to specific as well as general economic conditions of the period.

Indebtedness of the Colegio Máximo increased after the 1640s, reaching a high point in the early 1680s, and declined thereafter. Between 1651 and 1685, the Colegio Máximo administrators spent 380,000 pesos to pay off 176 loans, mortgages, and accompanying legal fees while, at the same time, new debts were being created to outfit additions to rural estates.[7] The college's total debt and annual debt payments caused the fathers general in Rome to become concerned about its financial state.* In 1647 Vicente Carafa became upset over types of expenditures in Mexico, as when Provincial Francisco Calderón spent 14,000 pesos to build retirement quarters for himself in the Casa Profesa "richly adorned with new books, chairs, images, and curtains." The provincial received a letter from the father general stating unequivocally that such expenditures represented a gross violation of the poverty principle of the order.

*The increase of Colegio Máximo debts was pronounced between 1644, when total debts were 150,000 pesos, and 1681, when they had risen to 474,158 pesos, after which they gradually declined. Annual debt payments in the 1670s and 1680s were slightly over 20,000 pesos. AGNAHH 285, 33; Alegre, 3: 343; DBCJM 4: 212; 5: 433–40.

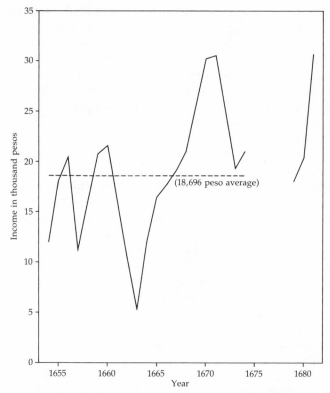

FIGURE 1. Santa Lucía income, 1654–1681. Source: AGNAHH 285, 33.

The funds had been taken out of income from the college's lucra-
tive sugar estate, Xochimancas. The colleges, it was suggested, had
other important needs for which these funds could be spent.[8]
Twelve years later the father general again issued instructions to
apply income received from Xochimancas, inheritances, and alms
to reducing college debts.[9]

Income from Santa Lucía varied considerably from year to year
between 1654 and 1674, averaging 18,696 pesos net revenue per annum (Figure 1), and reaching 30,919 pesos by 1681. Annual fluctuations in income, ranging from 13,000 pesos below and above the
average, created additional problems for college administrators interested in rational economic planning. Such fluctuations suggest
that hacienda incomes were generally unpredictable, being dependent upon weather-related crop failures and sudden changes in
prices for hacienda produce. The sharp rises and falls of income lev-

els between 1654 and 1664 can be related to serious droughts in the Valley of Mexico in 1653 and 1662–1663.[10] Jesuits reported that 1661 had been a "sterile" year for Santa Lucía and had requested permission to borrow 6,000 pesos. Specific evidence for the other fluctuations was not shown in available documents. The financial burden of the college was complicated in 1664 when one of its creditors, the Convent de Nuestra Señora de la Concepción, started legal action to recover an outstanding debt of 50,000 pesos.[11]

Santa Lucía profit margins were closely tied to the sale of livestock (goats, mules, sheep), livestock products (meat, hides, tallow, wool), and cereal grains. Monthly accounts between September 1646 and December 1648 also show an active movement of other sale items, including finished textile products such as blankets and clothing (hats, shirts, dresses, expensive outfits for hacienda overseers); foodstuffs (bread, fruits, chocolate, sugar, fish); and equipment (axes, sheep shears, wool cards, machetes). These items were sold to neighboring pueblos and passing merchants but without significantly increasing profits. The accounts listing these sales, excluding major sales of sheep and goats, showed an overall deficit of 629 pesos during a twenty-eight month period in 1646 to 1648.[12]

1655–1687: Buying Out Unsuccessful Competitors

Three developed haciendas were purchased between 1655 and 1687 to increase net revenues. Two of the estates, San Juan de Altica and Concepción, were located on the northern extremes of the Valley of Mexico and west of Pachuca; the third, Tehuacán de Cabras, was in the Tehuacán Valley. These moves represented a greater emphasis upon livestock such as goats, cattle, mules, and horses. Other purchases south of the Valley of Mexico being made by the Colegio Máximo during the same period, but not aggregated into Santa Lucía, emphasized cash crops, particularly sugar. Diversification and expansion were the policies adopted in the late seventeenth century to solve the fiscal problems of mounting debts and uneven income.

Tehuacán de Cabras was a hacienda in southern Veracruz Vieja and Tehuacán, acquired in 1655.[13] Its owner, Juan de Castillo, aspired to become a college founder in Tehuacán, located in his administrative jurisdiction. He had been *alguacil mayor* (chief constable) in Tehuacán in the 1620s, when he made his original offer to the Colegio Máximo, but the Jesuits were not then considering college expansion in the area. The hacienda itself had been built up by Alfonso Díaz Manzano in the late sixteenth century by accumulating diverse mercedes through agents and purchases. Information about the hacienda is somewhat limited, as its property titles (Appendix, no. 52) were transferred when the Jesuit college in Puebla bought the estate in 1730. By purchasing Tehuacán de Cabras, rather than accepting it as a donated endowment property, the Jesuits avoided compromise—to found another college. With this acquisition they sought to enhance cash income from a proven hacienda, including livestock (40,000 goats and limited numbers of horses, mules, and cattle), irrigated farmlands, residence, and slaves. The 1655 price of 29,724 pesos bought a property encompassing some 400 square kilometers (fifty-one *sitios de ganado menor* and *mayor,* thirty caballerías) and a problem in administrative control: although incorporated under Santa Lucía's administrative umbrella as an anexa, Tehuacán de Cabras was roughly three hundred kilometers from Tepeatzingo and Mexico City.

Jesuit administrators were never able to manage this estate effectively. Agricultural production, the Jesuits discovered, could not be conducted successfully at a distance. The meat and hides produced were marketed regionally. The goats and goatherds were not brought annually to the Valley of Mexico to allow annual adjustments of wages, accounts, and overall accountability. When the hacienda was sold to the Jesuit Colegio del Espíritu Santo in Puebla, the reason given was that administrative problems related to distance prevented the investment from realizing its potential. The Jesuits received 31,000 pesos for the hacienda and its livestock. The Puebla college administrators had much greater success with the same hacienda, as they had more effective control. Santa Lucía's administrators, however, quickly realized that any larger estates to be incorporated into their operation should be more suitably located.[14]

Such was the case with Altica, a hacienda owned by the Rivadeneira family.[15] Altica's lands, scattered between Tezontepec and Tornacostla, were located in the jurisdictions of Epazoyuca, Hueypoxtla, and Pachuca. Santa Lucía administrators found the Altica properties attractive for a number of reasons: they were adjacent to lands already under Jesuit management, their passage into Jesuit hands assured virtual domination of the area by Santa Lucía, and since it was valley and hillside slopes, the land could be used for livestock and farming, activities that currently were producing excellent revenues.[16] Negotiations were completed in 1669, and Altica became Jesuit property in 1670. Although the purchase supposedly involved 8 *sitios de ganado menor,* 16 caballerías, and some houses, the actual land titles indicated less pasture (only 6 sitios) and substantially more farmland (27.5 caballerías).[17]

The history of Altica is similar to that of other estates developed by private hacendados in central Mexico. Don Gaspar de Rivadeneira, the owner, had become wealthy from his mines in the Pachuca district and had used this income to found a number of haciendas as a means of establishing for himself and his heirs a niche in the emerging Mexican landed aristocracy. Don Gaspar began founding haciendas in 1598. He initially accumulated properties through a series of royal grants negotiated by agents. Additional properties were purchased from fellow Spaniards engaged in land speculation. A residence was built at Altica, and the scattered properties were managed by mayordomos who supervised the production of livestock and cereal crops. Altica's main development took place in the first two decades of the seventeenth century. The *composiciones de tierras* proceedings in 1643 confirmed legal title for a token contribution of 150 pesos to the royal coffers. By the late 1660s, Don Gaspar's heirs decided to sell Altica, one of their least impressive haciendas, while keeping the entails of Estanzuela and Estrada-Carbajal, which became prosperous.[18]

Under Jesuit ownership, Altica became San Juan de Altica and was turned into a cattle and horse ranch. In 1679 Santa Lucía's branded cattle numbered 3,000 and horses, 640. Three years later these numbers had increased to 4,000 and 1,640, thanks to the increased pastures of Altica.[19] Most of the horses were brood mares for producing mules, which Colegio Máximo officials considered to be one of the most profitable business ventures in New Spain at the time. Herds of mares, called *manadas,* averaging forty per herd, each with its donkey stallion, formed the majority of the horse population.[20] The legal status of these properties, prohibiting their utilization for cattle and horses, had long been violated. The Jesuits merely followed local custom, and their reintroduction of large-scale cattle- and horse-ranching in the northern perimeters of the Valley of Mexico more than a century after the crown had made concerted efforts to halt such negative impact upon native agriculture met little opposition. But by the 1670s, conditions had been greatly altered. Many of the original communities had long since disappeared, through demographic decline and congregation policies, or their residents had been absorbed into the nearby mining labor forces, as indicated by the number of tributaries in the jurisdictions of Pachuca (Table 1). Furthermore, the accumulated impact of grazing, desiccation, and deforestation had so decreased the productivity of the soil that much more land was needed per animal than a century earlier.[21]

By 1681 Santa Lucía livestock operations had expanded significantly, as had the demand for livestock products. During this year the hacienda counted 110,504 sheep, 53,343 goats, 4,000 branded cattle, 1,640 mares, 400 horses, 40 donkeys, 25 mules, and 60 hogs. Despite the size of the sheep flocks, from 1679 to 1681 it was necessary to buy 18,670 sheep to meet Pachuca slaughterhouse demands. Meat, transport animals, and other products such as hides, leather, tallow, and woolen goods, produced at Tepeatzingo, San Xavier, Hueytepec, Pintas, and Altica, played an important role in supplying the nearby Pachuca mining needs. Income reached almost 31,000 pesos in 1681, the bulk of it from livestock operations.[22] Agricultural food crops were valued at 4,000 pesos and still largely confined to San Juan, whose capacity included 180 hectares of barley, 120 hectares of wheat, 50 hectares of maize, 20 hectares of chick-peas (alverjón), and 12 hectares of beans (habas).[23] Aggregate totals of livestock had now reached 170,000, plus 400 hectares devoted to food crops.[24]

The policy's success encouraged its continuation. Therefore, when an opportunity presented itself in 1685, negotiations were entered into for the purchase of another hacienda complex, located west and northwest of Pachuca, in the jurisdictions of Actopan, Pachuca, and Tetepango.[25] This hacienda, known as Carrión, or Concepción, was a mayorazgo created for the descendants of the conquistador Juan de Soto Cabezón. His heirs, Cristóbal and Pedro de Soto Cabezón, built up Carrión between 1585 and 1622. It was sold in 1651 and, after passing through the hands of five subsequent owners, in 1685 it came into the possession of a Pachuca resident, Andrés Fuertes.[26] Fuertes bought seventeen *sitios de ganado menor* and ten caballerías, which pertained to Carrión, plus two additional estancias and four caballerías, from two Pachuca residents and one Mexico City resident. He intended to raise goats, cattle, and mares, but no sooner had he taken possession of his hacienda, adjacent to Altica properties, then he became involved in a dispute with the Jesuits over boundaries. Fuertes attempted to have the previous owners settle the dispute out of court so he could have clear title. The net result was an intensification of the conflict, terminating in a petition to the audiencia to annul the sale.[27]

In the meantime, one of the mayordomos from Santa Lucía demolished a number of cattle-guard huts on the disputed properties, for which he was incarcerated in the public jail in Pachuca. The Jesuits in charge of Santa Lucía now entered the legal fray, claiming Fuertes's ranch hands had destroyed goats belonging to Altica. The Jesuits then decided to resolve the whole issue, "in the interest of peace and friendship," by offering to buy the Fuertes properties. Fuertes agreed to drop the dispute and sell to the Jesuits for the same price he had paid the year before. The Fuertes properties consisted of nineteen estancias, fourteen caballerías, a large, well-built residence, recently developed agricultural land, a goat range with large corrals, 43 mares, 40 plow oxen, farm and ranch equipment, and a license permitting 300 cows to be kept on the properties designated for sheep and goats.[28]

The Colegio Máximo agreed to pay 6,500 pesos in cash on March 8, 1687, in exchange for all the hacienda's papers and titles. Besides the cash payment, the new owners agreed to pay two outstanding debts of 1,000 pesos each to the Augustine College of San Pablo in Mexico City and the Augustine convent in the pueblo of Epazoyuca. Francisco de Monroy, a Spaniard who had been living on the properties in his own house, and his first male heir were granted permission to live there through their lifetimes. Fuertes received 2,500 pesos from college officials in January 1687, and they took formal possession in March of the same year, one week before they paid a cash balance of 4,000 pesos.[29]

The *casco* (main residence) of Concepción, like those of most of the residences on the Santa Lucía estates, was located on a flat plain facing the lands associated with it.[30] The Indian town of Tilcuautla straddled the lower slopes of the mountain range to the north, 1.5 kilometers away. Most of the land was west of Pachuca, crossed by a road leading to the northern mines of San Luis Potosí and Zacatecas and lesser routes leading to Pachuca, Tornacostla, Tetepango, and Actopan. Some of the land was suited for agriculture (Fuertes had 170 hectares of maize and other food crops in production) but some was dry, rocky, and uneven, better suited for goats and maguey. The estate had lands bordering those of Altica and Hueytepec which, in turn, bordered those of San Xavier.

Concepción, like Altica, had been marginally productive prior to Jesuit ownership, devoted to livestock and food-crop production. Unlike Altica, Concepción was not quickly integrated into Santa Lucía's scheme of production. A limited amount of maize was produced and livestock grazed on some of its pasture land, but, for the most part, hacienda administrators seemed content to rent out much of it to residents of nearby communities and small-scale mestizo farmers and ranchers. This use pattern may have been related to unproductive soils, but more likely it had to do with the land's numerous maguey plants, important for pulque production. During the seventeenth century, the Jesuits were still the viceroy-alty's staunchest opponents of the sale and consumption of that once sacred, traditional intoxicating beverage of the Aztecs, now the poor man's booze. Later, when the Jesuits became producers of pulque themselves, Concepción received much closer administrative attention.[31]

By the end of the seventeenth century, the adjustments made in Santa Lucía, plus the bolstering of sugar production at Chicomo-celo, Xalmolonga, and the recently acquired Cuatepec haciendas, resulted in the hoped-for changes in the Colegio Máximo's balance sheets. Revenues went up and debts began to come down. A letter from the Jesuit father general in 1695 expressed satisfaction with recent debt reductions. By 1696 the college was only having to spend 17,000 pesos annually to retire debts, 6,000 pesos less than had been the case fourteen years earlier.[32] In the meantime, Santa Lucía sheep flocks had been reduced, averaging slightly fewer than 68,000 during the 1690s, while other types of livestock increased.[33]

It was on March 20, 1697, that the well-traveled Italian writer, Juan Francisco Gemelli Carreri, made a visit to Santa Lucía resulting in a description that made a great impression upon European readers, unaccustomed to the scale of hacienda operations in New Spain.[34] Gemelli Carreri, in traveling from Pachuca to Mexico City, passed through parts of the anexas of Hueytepec, Altica, San Xavier, Las Pintas, and San Juan and stayed overnight at the main residence at Santa Lucía. The Italian also likely spoke to the general administrator of the hacienda at the residence, Bartolomé González. Gemelli Carreri claimed Santa Lucía had 140,000 sheep and goats, 10,000 cattle and oxen, and 5,000 horses and mares. He also claimed the Jesuits kept over 100 married Negro slaves in cabins, suggesting their main function was to breed offspring which brought the Jesuits 300 or 400 pesos per slave. This was a misrepresentation of Jesuit slave-holding practices. The Santa Lucía slaves were kept as field and ranch hands or domestics, and for working in the textile factory. The Jesuits allowed family life, even encouraged it, but there was never a policy of breeding slaves as a commercial activity. The Italian traveler's accuracy in reporting is further questionable in that he says Santa Lucía belonged to the Jesuit novitiate at Tepotzotlán.[35] Despite these shortcomings, the Gemelli report did clearly point out that Santa Lucía was one of the largest and most impressive haciendas to be found in Mexico at the end of the seventeenth century.

Protecting and Expanding Sheep Pastures

Maintaining sufficient pasture for up to 100,000 sheep presented a constant challenge. Since 1589, when access to vacant or unapportioned land had been established by royal cédula, these types of land had played an important role in sheep-raising. The pastures acquired in Izatlán in the late sixteenth century and in the Chilpancingo area in the early seventeenth century were used as summer pastures but do not represent the full extent of pastures used by the sheep flocks. Equally important were the smaller pastures owned at Atlauhtla and Ocuila. They were not large enough to be significant, but they became the centers from which the surrounding vacant lands could be exploited. In the early years, the flocks of the Colegio Máximo, as well as those of Tepotzotlán and the other Jesuit institutions in the Valley of Mexico, relied upon the distant summer pastures in the Guadalajara and Colima regions. Crown lands and the seasonal availability of native lands between crop cycles (roughly between late December and May) provided additional pastures.[36] The lands owned in and near the Valley of Mexico were never sufficient for the year-round maintenance of Santa Lucía flocks.

From the outset the sheep were separated into two main flocks according to color (black morenos and white morenos), and these large units were broken down into smaller units, or manadas, varying in size from a few hundred to 4,000 to 6,000 animals under the care of supervisory shepherds (*vacieros, manaderos*), their assistants (*pastores*), and dogs.[37] The main flocks of Santa Lucía, under the charge of a mayordomo, increased from two to four and were called Negra, Ocuila, Provincia, and Xoloc. Although listed in the administrative records as belonging to individual haciendas, these flocks were not identified with fixed geographical entities, as were goats, cattle, horses, and cereal crops. Negra, Ocuila, and Xoloc were the flocks using pastures south of the Valley of Mexico on the western slopes of the *mesa central*, in the jurisdictions of Cuautla Amilpas, Cuernavaca, and Malinalco. The Xoloc flocks got their name from the pueblo close to Santa Lucía, adjacent to which the shepherds kept the animals during their April–November annual stay in the Valley of Mexico. Along

with Ocuila and Negra, they were the flocks that spent July
through November in the rich pastures near Santa Lucía and the
rest of the year in the southern pastures. Provincia referred to the
flocks pasturing in the distant northern jurisdictions of Izatlán,
Amula, Autlan, Tuspa, and Xiquilpa.[38]

In 1692 this area was further extended into Nueva Galicia when
the Colegio Máximo took over, from its sister college in Mexico
City, San Gregorio, the rental of a *hacienda de ganado mayor* named
San Nicolás, near the town of Tequila. San Gregorio held a nine-
year rental contract (1687–1696) at 100 pesos per year, which the
Santa Lucía administrators now took over to increase pastures for
the Provincia flocks. These sheep, at least in a later period, left the
summer pastures toward the end of June and must have stayed
only briefly at Santa Lucía, since they left early in September.[39] In
the eighteenth century, control of pastures here was consolidated
by additional purchases.

Disputes with pueblos and other hacendados over pasture and
grazing rights were common, and the Jesuits were always ready to
defend the privileges granted to them by royal authorities. One
such case, in 1673, involved residents of Amecameca who, claimed
Gaspar de Silva, the administrator of Santa Lucía, were impeding
access of the hacienda's sheep to public and royal lands (tierras realengas, baldías, y sementeras). Armed with a directive from the
viceroy's office, the administrator served notice on the *alcalde mayor*
of Chalco, the residents of Amecameca, and the *alcalde mayor* of
Xochimilco to comply with the royal will and desist from impeding
Santa Lucía livestock. The people in question promised to obey the
directive although, in point of fact, it was the Jesuit flocks that were
the intruders, at times on land still unharvested.[40]

In 1675, in another incident, the shoe was on the other foot, as
Cuautepec was being invaded by neighboring cattle, horses, mules,
and oxen. The protective stone fences of Cuautepec were being deliberately breached by the residents of the pueblos of Huasculco, Temoaque, and Zacualpa. It was a serious conflict: the native cane-
field guard working for the Jesuits was threatened and assaulted,
and the Jesuits were claiming damage to their crops and pastures.
Here, again, the Jesuit administrators were quickly supplied by college attorneys with a legal writ to ensure the protection of Jesuit economic interests. Public announcements of the royal orders were
made at Temoaque on the market day, and an original copy of the
order, signed by the *alcalde mayor* of Cuautla de Amilpas, was retained by the Jesuits for future reference.[41]

The increasing competition for access to pastures prompted the Jesuits to increase their holdings of lands at Ocuila early in the eighteenth century. They acquired two *sitios de ganado mayor*, one *sitio de ganado menor*, ten caballerías, and two pedazos from the Augustine convent at Ocuila (see the Appendix for a fuller description). The convent had owned the properties prior to 1634, after which it had sold title to them to individual Spaniards on three occasions, for 2,000 pesos, on the condition that it could reclaim ownership upon repayment. The Jesuits entered into such an agreement with the convent shortly after the properties had been reclaimed in 1703. Their lawyers then made a formal legal claim for permanent ownership, based on the argument that they had bought the lands outright for 2,000 pesos. Their claim was supported in court, and on February 7, 1713, the Jesuit college took formal possession of these Ocuila lands.[42] A few additional acquisitions were made in the same area, but the dates of the titles are not clear. Later records indicate holdings of over 89 square kilometers of pasture and some 800 hectares of farmland.[43] From the beginning of the seventeenth century the Jesuits also were granted legal, continuous access to pasture land owned by one of the order's admirers, Baltasar de la Cadena.[44]

An accurate tabulation of all land actually used by Santa Lucía flocks at any given time would not be possible because it included both public and private property. It also seems clear that the pasture land actually a part of Santa Lucía could not have sustained existing livestock. For example, in 1681, when total livestock numbers were at least 170,000, the amount of land per animal comes to 0.56 hectares.[45] Since 45 percent of this land was the arid Tehuacán goat ranch, and the pastures on the northern perimeters of the Valley of Mexico were also arid, available land per animal was much less. In order to compete successfully for adequate pasture resources, the Jesuits were constantly making adjustments—frequently at the expense of native communities and carried out with the assistance of influential friends.

This was the case when Provincia pastures were formally extended by an additional 1,088 square kilometers, between 1716 and 1719, thanks to the timely intervention of a highly placed royal official. These pastures were located between Guadalajara and Colima and had been used by the Santa Lucía flocks with no problem during periods of local population decline. Don Joseph Miranda Villaysan, *oidor* (judge) of the Guadalajara audiencia and officially in charge of regulating land and water rights, was the principal actor in getting this enormous area transferred into Jesuit hands. He used his political post to great advantage for personally acquiring the largest estate in all New Galicia. In 1716 he arranged for the Colegio Máximo to claim sixty-two *sitios de ganado mayor* in return for 1,800 pesos for the royal coffers.[46] Within three days after these arrangements, the merced was confirmed by the audiencia in Guadalajara. Titles were issued and permission to take official possession of the lands was dispatched to the Jesuits. The towns whose lands were being infringed upon—Atemaxac, Ataco, Tapalpa, and Xonacatlán in the Sayula jurisdiction and others in Zapotlán—resisted.* Despite official threats of 200 lashes to each person resisting, the pueblos refused Santa Lucía livestock access to the pastures. The case went all the way to the Council of the Indies. The Indian communities were attempting to halt a century-old process of land loss now that increasing local populations had greater need of traditional rural resources. The Jesuits, for their part, were attempting to establish legal claims to areas they had already been using for some time. On May 22, 1719, a royal writ was issued confirming Jesuit ownership.[47]

1714–1738: Incorporation of Additional Unproductive Estates

The upturn of Jesuit economic fortunes visible in the last decade of the seventeenth century had encouraged expansion of rural estates by Jesuit colleges throughout the Mexican province. Because sugar estates, which had produced handsome profits in the late seventeenth century, became less important owing to the depressed sugar market in New Spain in the early eighteenth century,[48] the Jesuits became interested in increasing livestock production and reemphasizing cereal cash crops. Thus, when a prominent Mexico City resident, Don Juan Félix Ramírez, died in 1714, the Colegio Máximo was pleased to inherit one of his haciendas in the Chalco jurisdiction, called San Joseph de Chalco.[49] It included four auxiliary ranches used in the past for growing maize and wheat. The Jesuits spent 25,000 pesos developing San Joseph, clearing forested lands for wheat production and converting parts of the Chicomocelo sugar hacienda to cereal grain production.[50] Although not aggregated into Santa Lucía, the Chalco hacienda became an important estate of

*Sayula population was reduced by 87 percent between the mid-sixteenth and mid-seventeenth centuries, according to tribute lists. By 1700 the number of tributaries increased slowly, but the rate of increase rose quickly, with a doubling of population by the mid-eighteenth century, GHGNS, pp. 239–42, 338–40.

the Colegio Máximo. The other colleges in Mexico City (San Andrés, San Gregorio) and the provincial administrative offices (whose jurisdiction included the California missions) all acquired additional rural properties in or near the Valley of Mexico during the first quarter of the eighteenth century.[51]

Purchase of three haciendas on the periphery of the rich Actopan Valley was undertaken in 1723 to increase livestock production. The purchase of these haciendas, called Chicavasco, Florida, and Tepenene, involved an outlay of 25,000 pesos.[52] They were located west and north of Pachuca, between Ixquintlapilco and Ixmiquilpan, although an auxiliary ranch of Florida extended northward almost to Zimapán (see Map 2). Later justification for these purchases, made in 1735 and 1739, was the sale of the goat ranch (Tehuacán) located too far from the administrative center of Santa Lucía. Haciendas nearer to Santa Lucía would be easier to administer and at the same time would allow for an expansion of goat production and other livestock activities.[53]

Under previous ownership by the royal accountant, Don Melchor de Miranda y Solís, Chicavasco, Florida, and Tepenene had not been productive haciendas. Descriptions of the land in 1711 (for the purpose of *composiciones de tierras*) show substantial portions to be mountainous, rocky, and barren, considered "useless, without water or pastures." Don Melchor's widow paid 150 pesos to legalize the titles in 1712. Included were 3.25 *sitios de ganado mayor*, 14 *sitios de ganado menor*, and 6 caballerías previously legalized in 1695, plus 3.25 *sitios de ganado mayor*, 3 *sitios de ganado menor*, and 6 caballerías for which clear title could not be demonstrated. When Don Melchor died (between 1705 and 1711), an administrator continued the livestock operations (cattle and horses) for over a decade in the name of his wife, Doña Manuela Calderón, and the estate heirs who were still minors.[54] A portion of the land appears to have been sold prior to the Jesuit purchase. Improvements to the haciendas during this period had been minimal, and the Jesuits found it necessary to spend funds and effort to establish productivity.

The history and development of the three haciendas are similar to those of Altica and Concepción (see Appendix A). Between 1557 and 1620 most of the property titles moved into Spanish possession, through purchase or merced, and always in units not exceeding two estancias or two to three caballerías. By 1643 the haciendas were more or less established, and ownership was confirmed by the *composiciones de tierras* proceedings. Thereafter, the individual haciendas passed through a number of owners by inheritance or purchase. Along the way, the hacienda titles picked up encumbrances. Chicavasco and Tepenene titles had liens held by a religious brotherhood (*cofradía*) of Actopan, La Nuestra Señora del Rosario, and Florida and Tepenene encumbrances included obligations to pay for special masses (*capellanía de misas*) worth 4,000 pesos and 5,000 pesos respectively.[55] This pattern of instability of ownership, marginal productivity, encumbrances, and general disrepair was the norm for almost all the estates acquired for the expansion of Santa Lucía in the eighteenth century.

The Jesuits took formal possession of Florida's titles in February 1723. The properties were located within the jurisdictions of Actopan, Ixmiquilpan, Tlacintla, and Zimapán, and the hacienda was described as forming a large oval surrounded by mountainous terrain. The Colegio Máximo paid 7,748 pesos for the properties, 4,000 pesos of which went to pay outstanding religious obligations. This price included, besides the land and "some equipment and cattle," an additional ranch called San Pablo, located north of Ixmiquilpan. San Pablo consisted of another 54.4 square kilometers of pasture and 85 hectares of "irrigated and partly irrigated" farmland. It had previously been used as a horse ranch.[56]

By November 1725 the hacienda, now known as Santa Rosa de la Florida, had been converted into a livestock center with 1,116 brood mares, a small herd of donkey mares and stallions, 455 cattle, and 40 oxen used for agricultural activities. Farm equipment included plows, yokes, hoes, scythes, axes, rakes, branding irons, and saddles. No buildings of consequence existed other than the crude thatched huts used to shelter equipment and caretakers. Within a few years a simple residence and small chapel were constructed to house a mayordomo and to meet the religious needs of the labor force.[57]

The 5,000 pesos paid for the Tepenene hacienda, acquired in June 1723, were equal to the outstanding encumbrances for pious works. Included were 38.8 square kilometers of pasture and 46.7 hectares of farmland located mostly between Actopan and Tornacostla. The discontinuous nature of the individual estancias is evident, as Tepenene lands fell within the former jurisdictions of the pueblos of Actopan, Chicavasco, Ixquintlapilco, Tecazique, Tetitlán, and Tornacostla. In addition to the pasture lands the Jesuits received some equipment, twenty oxen, and fewer than one hundred horses. During the first year after purchase, approximately 70 acres were planted in maize. By 1725, however, the planting activities, along with the oxen and farm equipment, were transferred to Chicavasco. Under Jesuit management, San José de Tepenene was converted into a large-scale goat and horse ranch.[58]

The pueblo of Tepenene, located on a hilltop less than a kilometer from the hacienda residence, had all but ceased to function as a community by the time the Jesuits bought the property. The Tepenene residence, to which the Jesuits quickly added a large granary, a modest residence, and a small chapel, all enclosed behind stout stone walls, was on a flat plain and controlled the waters of a stream originating in the mountainous area to the north. The hacienda, therefore, had land and water for agriculture close by despite the arid character of most of the surrounding area. The road connecting Pachuca and Actopan (nine kilometers to the northwest) passed by the Tepenene residence, providing convenient access to nearby market centers and to the Santa Lucía main administrative center sixty-five kilometers to the south.[59]

Chicavasco, the third hacienda purchased in 1723, cost 12,200 pesos, of which 10,700 pesos went to pay off encumbrances.[60] Most of the estancias were grouped around the Indian pueblo called Chicavasco, located on a hilltop bordering the mountains that formed part of the southwestern boundaries of the Actopan Valley, nine kilometers from Actopan itself. According to the hacienda titles, it consisted of 56.5 square kilometers of pastures and 85 hectares of farmland. Parts of these lands were scattered over an extended area within the jurisdictions of Actopan and Tetepango-Hueypoxtla. As in the case of Tepenene, the pueblo had shrunk to a few residences, its lands having been absorbed by the expansion of haciendas over one and a half centuries.[61] The Chicavasco hacienda residence was located below the pueblo, to the north, sitting on the edge of a river draining into the Actopan Valley. With wooded slopes behind it, river-bottom lands in front of it, and hilly slopes close by, Chicavasco had the natural resources needed for improvement.[62]

The Jesuits developed Chicavasco into a center for farming and for raising and processing livestock. The existing buildings were gradually rebuilt and improved to include slaughterhouses, an enormous granary, barns, corrals, and a residence. Since it was only seven kilometers from Tepenene, to the east, it became the processing center for animals raised there and in other Santa Lucía anexas the Jesuits later acquired in the area.[63]

The purchase and incorporation of these three haciendas in 1723 continued Santa Lucía's expansion into the valley systems extending northwest of Pachuca. Their location along the communication and transportation corridors leading to Pachuca and other mining centers in the north was undoubtedly a factor the Jesuits had in mind when buying these estates which Spanish hacendados had been able to exploit only marginally during the seventeenth century and the early decades of the eighteenth. The area later became an important center for pulque production.[64]

Jesuit interest in this northern expansion continued, as demonstrated in 1729, when Santa Lucía's owners were willing to accept, through donation, three haciendas belonging to the wealthy Mexico City hacendado, Licenciado Don Juan Luzón de Ahumada. Don Juan presented the estates, located in the Tulanzingo jurisdiction, to the Jesuits to allow them to found a college at Pachuca. However, the debts of the haciendas, which they were to make good within seven years, proved to be too great, and the properties were sold to pay these debts, amounting to 76,000 pesos.[65] The college at Pachuca was never established, but the Colegio Máximo's rural resources did expand during the first third of the eighteenth century. Apart from significant mission expansion in northern Mexico and California, new colleges and seminaries were being founded at Puebla (1701), Guadalajara (1715), Havana (1722), León in Michoacán (1731), and Guanajuato (1732). Each new teaching center acquired extensive rural estates to support its development and activities. Secular ecclesiastics, crown officials, and wealthy individuals encouraged such expansion through donations and offers of patronage as founders.[66] The aggressive expansion policies of Joaquín Donazar, the Colegio Máximo attorney in charge of Santa Lucía operations (1723–1740), complemented this general trend.

During the 1730s, Jesuit college officials acquired more land, this time property claimed as part of the entailed estates of the hacendado Don Francisco Peralta y Murilla (see Appendix A). On December 6, 1731, the procurador for the Colegio Máximo presented a writ to the royal land court stating that the Jesuits had learned that official measurement of the Peralta y Murilla mayorazgo—accumulated by Don Jerónimo López de Peralta y Murilla between 1562 and 1620—showed it to contain seven *sitios de ganado menor* in excess of legal titles held. Since they already owned haciendas near the area in question (called San Ignacio and bordering San Francisco de Chicavasco), the Jesuits formally claimed these lands to be unapportioned and therefore available (*denuncia por realengas*). While this claim made its way through legal channels, other negotiations were initiated to purchase the mayorazgo itself, the bulk of

which was located between Tepenene and Chicavasco, in the jurisdictions of Actopan and Tetepango. It consisted of eighty kilometers of pastures and sixty-four hectares of farmland, and was
known as the hacienda of San Pablo, or Tulancalco y Punta del
Garambullo.[67]

The audiencia responded favorably and formally declared San
Ignacio as realengas, at the same time ordering it to be sold at public auction. This auction took place on February 28, 1733, and the
Jesuits emerged as the purchasers. The price was 1,000 pesos plus
30 pesos (3 percent) to cover legal costs. Formal possession took
place in 1735, consisting of an inspection of the boundary markers
by the procurador of the college and a judge from Tetepango. At
each marker—either a natural landmark or a mortar and stone construction located on hilltops, in gullies, and where the properties
intersected with more than one neighbor—the existing one was
confirmed or a new one erected. The proceedings gained formal
status by virtue of the symbolic acts of possession that accompanied property transfers. In all, thirty-two markers were either
confirmed or erected. During such traditional legal proceedings
there were always—in theory at least—opportunities to resolve minor differences over the exact location of boundary markers or the
ownership of specific terrain. A mulatto slave of a Doña Mecela
Mellado interrupted proceedings by claiming the boundaries were
usurping some lands belonging to his mistress, but without success. The Indians of the pueblo of Tecomate, in another interrup-
tion, were successful in having a marker relocated in their favor.[68]

The date of transfer of San Pablo is unclear. Documents show
that Peralta y Murilla received crown permission to sell the entail in
July 1735, and the Jesuits were using the properties as early as
1732. Since ex post facto legalization of property transactions was
common, it is reasonable to assume that the Jesuits were in possession of the lands long before legal procedures were completed. The
total expense of acquiring San Pablo and San Ignacio was 13,567
pesos. A decade later (1744–1745), 3,180 pesos were recouped
when three sitios were sold to other hacendados.[69]

A number of names were used for this latest anexa of Santa
Lucía, including San Ignacio, San Pablo, San Pablo y San Ignacio,
and San Ignacio de Punta. It became a center for sheep-raising,
starting with a flock of 7,000 known as the *chinchorro de ovejas de
Mesquital*. Improvements made to the properties included ponds
near pastures used for fattening livestock prior to slaughtering,
corrals, storage facilities, and a residence for the mayordomo.[70]

As with other purchases, the Jesuits carefully examined the titles for San Pablo and San Ignacio. They discovered the deeds to be in complete disorder. No titles could be found for 4 sitios and 4.5 caballerías; for another 4 sitios and 3.5 caballerías, although titles existed, the properties in question were not those belonging to the Murilla entail. In establishing boundaries with the neighboring hacienda, Xalpa, owned by Don Melchor de las Cámeras Morato, other irregularities came to light. The Jesuits, according to titles in hand, owned the property in front of the main residence of Xalpa, and Don Melchor held title to properties being used by the Jesuits. The documentary disorganization was carefully sorted out, some titles were exchanged with their neighbor, and an amicable agreement was reached in the establishment of boundary markers.[71]

The type of disorder encountered in the Murilla mayorazgo titles does not appear to have been uncommon in the area. In contrast, the Jesuits were always meticulous about the documentation of their properties. The difference in attitude and practice between Jesuit and secular hacendados reflects both interest and the managerial skills that each applied to these estates. Under secular management, productivity was limited and the haciendas were weighed down by liens and religious obligations. Under Jesuit management, the same estates were quickly improved, liens were eliminated, documents were brought into order, and the haciendas became productive.

Further expansion for Santa Lucía was also being pursued in the distant Provincia area. In 1737 a hacienda called San Jerónimo was purchased by the Colegio Máximo for 19,000 pesos. It included sixteen *sitios de ganado menor* and nine caballerías of farmland, known as the *labor* of San Nicolás.[72] The pastures had previously been rented and used as a lambing place for Provincia flocks. The impulse for purchase arose when the owner, Don Bartolomé de Sozoaga, died and left the properties to a nephew who decided to move to Spain. To maintain access to the pasture and prevent another buyer from acquiring the estate, the order bought it, including the *labor*, over 100 oxen and cows, and 700 horses. By 1739, payment of 8,000 pesos had been made and the rest was expected to come from sale of the farmlands, a sale that was never realized. Instead, goats were introduced at San Nicolás and cereal grains were produced to complement Provincia operations.[73]

The series of haciendas purchased during the 1720s and 1730s increased Santa Lucía pastures northwest of Pachuca by 313 square kilometers and confirmed access to another 125 square kilometers near Colima. Farmlands increased by 680 and 382.5 hectares in the respective areas. The exploitation and development of these lands demonstrated adaptation to changing conditions and a continued emphasis upon livestock and food-crop production. Traditional sheep and goat production was increased, now with new flocks much closer to administrative headquarters. Cattle, horses, and mules were emphasized on a greater number of anexas. Food crops, particularly maize, were being stressed. Besides the addition of functioning farmlands at the new anexas, an additional maize-production center, called Atlantepec, was started at San Xavier. One of the significant shifts at Santa Lucía, which had been in progress at the other Colegio Máximo haciendas devoted mostly to cash crops,[74] was the production of maize for sale at regional markets in addition to its use and distribution within Santa Lucía or other haciendas of the Colegio Máximo (principally as rations and for sale to the hacienda work force).

Santa Lucía's productivity, by 1738, can be assessed on the basis of statistics derived from internal records of the hacienda. Food-crop production was 3,912 fanegas of maize, 470 *cargas* (a load, usually 2 fanegas) of barley, 15 fanegas of alverjón, 75 fanegas of frijol, and 15 fanegas of habas. Livestock production included 17,400 lambs, 6,410 young goats, 576 colts, over 60 mules, and 355 calves.[75] These numbers represent only the aspect of production on which the hacienda was paying tithe. Based on values for the year, this production (which does not include wool, hides, tallow, or adult animals for meat) comes to a total of 20,880 pesos.[76] Hacienda and related income for the Colegio Máximo for 1738 was listed as 98,071 pesos.[77] This figure includes income from Jesús del Monte, Xalmolonga, Chalco, Chicomocelo, and Cuautepec, the last three being at this time devoted largely to maize and wheat production. Livestock owned by the Colegio Máximo in 1739, according to a report of its administrator in charge of rural estates, included 148,000 sheep, 35,000 goats, 9,890 horses, 6,500 cattle, 3,200 oxen, and 1,160 mules.[78] Most of this pertained to Santa Lucía, and most of it—apart from the livestock associated with San Jerónimo and the sheep flocks in distant pastures—was close to the viceregal capital.

Maximum Expansion and Its Limitations

Such continuing expansion of the Jesuit rural domain did not go unnoticed by the secular clergy. An opportunity to confront the

Jesuits was presented while Colegio Máximo officials were occupied in expanding their haciendas. The archbishop of Mexico, Juan Antonio Vizarrón, in an action similar to that taken by Palafox almost a century earlier, accused the Jesuits of holding excessive rural properties and of improprieties in tithe contributions. He argued that in 1734 the Jesuits had seventy-nine separate estates from which, in three bishoprics alone (Mexico, Puebla, Valladolid), they had an annual income of one million pesos. A formal charge of withholding the diezmo was made against the college administrator, Joaquín Donazar, backed by documents and witnesses, and resulting in an ecclesiastical court ruling of guilt and formal excommunication. When Vizarrón was named viceroy in 1734, an office he held until 1740, the Jesuits found that their customary ally in New Spain was now their accuser and opponent. Among the demands made against the Jesuits was a crown prohibition against further purchases of haciendas, plus over 8,000 pesos in back payment of tithes.[79]

The Jesuits rallied to defend their interests, their haciendas, and their good name, taking the case directly to the Council of the Indies and the crown. Only in 1750 did they get the favorable royal response overturning decisions against them in the lower courts.[80] The bitter struggle had side effects and left casualties, not the least of which was the prestige of the Jesuits. Attention and blame focused on Joaquín Donazar, the central administrator of the college concerned with hacienda expansion. Donazar had gained the Jesuits two powerful enemies with influence in Mexico City. One was the Peralta y Murilla family, to whose lands Donazar first got access because of faulty property deeds, resulting in Jesuit acquisition of San Ignacio and San Pablo. The second was the Marqués de Guardiola, with whom Donazar inherited (from Jean Nicolás, his predecessor) a legal suit during an attempt to buy another hacienda. As a result, instead of only the secular clergy writing to Spain and making public in New Spain charges against the Jesuits, part of the local landed aristocracy was also involved. Inquiries and reprimands were not long in coming from the office of the father general in Rome.[81]

The controversy brought to public attention the Jesuits' rapid expansion of their haciendas and the difference in understanding over how tithes were to be calculated. Within the province it became known that the Colegio Máximo, despite an average annual income of 81,683 pesos, was spending 6,500 pesos more than this each year. During seventeen years as college administrator, Donazar had increased debts by over 111,000 pesos. He attempted to justify the negative balance to the father general by explaining the need for capital investment to improve the performance and capacity of college haciendas, insisting that the properties he bought had already quadrupled in value.[82] To no avail. In 1740 Donazar was expelled from the order, and college officials were thenceforth more cautious.*

This was quite evident in the handling of the disposition of an immense sheep ranch known as the Hacienda de Ovejas de Gruñidora. Involved here were a casco and 1,316 square kilometers of pasture (75 *sitios de ganado mayor*) in the Zacatecas area bought by Donazar in 1736 at a cost of 26,983 pesos.[83] It was stocked with sheep from Santa Lucía and placed under the hacienda's jurisdiction until 1743, leading to the same administrative problems experienced with the Tehuacán goat ranch—too great distance and no control over profitability. For the next nine years it was under a separate administration and lost 14,000 pesos. Lacking a buyer because of its negative performance, Gruñidora was rented out, minus its sheep, for 500 to 600 pesos a year over the next decade. Finally, a sister college in Zacatecas offered to buy the hacienda for 22,000 pesos, making annual 3 percent interest payments while paying off the purchase price at a rate of 1,100 pesos per year. The sale to the sister Jesuit college was welcomed on two counts: getting rid of an unproductive estate, and avoiding public sale of haciendas. "Among ourselves," wrote one of Donazar's successors, "things can be done privately without public instruments" (that is, documentation).[84]

Gruñidora is not being considered as part of Santa Lucía, because it was never functionally integrated as an anexa. Some of its sheep were pastured there in the 1740s, and some of its livestock was processed at Chicavasco. It must be considered more as a bad investment that the Jesuits recognized and disposed of as soon as practical. Another smaller hacienda (five *sitios de ganado mayor* and ten caballerías) in the Zacatecas region, called San Diego de los Altos or La Trasquila, had been purchased by Donazar for 13,000 pesos. For a time its facilities were used for shearing some of the

*Besides the tithe and public image questions regarding Donazar's term of office, his superiors had reason to be concerned about his financial handling of college affairs. During his period of office (1723–1739), college debts more than doubled, whereas under Juan Nicolás (1686–1723) the average annual income exceeded expenditures by 2,458 pesos, and the college debt had been reduced from 396,440 pesos to 121,225 pesos. See J. Riley, "Management," p. 22.

Santa Lucía flocks from Provincia, but it never became one of the anexas mentioned in inventory-transfer lists drawn up and signed by incoming and outgoing Santa Lucía administrators. In all, between 1723 and 1750, the Colegio Máximo made ten purchases of estates at a cost of 125,000 pesos.[85] After the conflict with viceregal and ecclesiastical authorities in the 1730s, buying diminished to a few selected acquisitions for haciendas not forming part of Santa Lucía.

Aside from the lands formally aggregated to Santa Lucía and other haciendas of the Colegio Máximo, the Jesuits acquired an odd assortment of properties that did not fit into their scheme of development. Orchards, urban lots and houses, ranches in areas where they could not be effectively used, even an occasional mining property arrived as gifts, usually through the wills of admirers. Many such unplanned acquisitions were sold for cash. Juan Nicolás, for example, left a 1723 list of outstanding debts to be collected by Donazar from such sales. Included was an orchard in Chapultepec, ranches in Tacuba, Sacamilpa, Iguala, and Coaxomulco, a mining property in Taxco, lots in Mexico City, a quarry, and a number of pasture lands. They had been sold for 24,135 pesos, but by 1739 Donazar still had not been able to collect,[86] suggesting that many such minor transactions contributed little to overall financing. Their continued existence, however, complicates any attempt to unravel in precise detail property acquisition and disposal relating to Santa Lucía.

Rental Strategies

Santa Lucía administrators found there were times when they could not, or did not want to, acquire ownership. In these cases, they rented. Mayorazgos could be rented even if they were not supposed to be sold. The earliest rental encountered took place in 1677, when the De Loreto ranch, part of the Guerrero[87] mayorazgo in the Chalco jurisdiction, was temporarily added to Santa Lucía at a cost of 400 pesos per year. Other parts of the same mayorazgo, near Ixmiquilpan, were rented in the 1740s; the hacienda of San Nicolás, in the Tequila jurisdiction, was leased in 1692; and San Jerónimo y San Nicolás, near Colima, was rented in the 1720s and 1730s.[88]

Rentals of pueblo land also appear to have been frequent, although the area in question and the use of the land were less important than other objectives. In 1737, land was rented from Atapa, in the Xiquilpa jurisdiction, in order to gain access to the pueblo's year-round water supply.[89] Xoloc, Provincia, and Santa Lucía used pueblo lands rented by the hacienda's administrators in the 1720s and 1730s. The rental contracts could last anywhere from two to nine years, with the greater part of the fees paid in advance to ensure the renter a return from his property.[90] At times the shoe was on the other foot, as in 1745, when the Jesuits rented four *sitios de ganado mayor* from Chichicastla in order to reduce the pueblo's debts to Santa Lucía. For good measure, the Colegio Máximo lawyers arranged to have the pueblo's lands surveyed, to have their boundaries marked, and to have them properly legalized before the audiencia. After five years, Chichicastla's debt of 356 pesos was reduced to 106 pesos, and Santa Lucía goats were provided with an additional seventy square kilometers of pastures.[91]

In the case of Xante, adjacent to the Actopan Valley estates, the properties were part of the entail created by the son-in-law of Don Alonso de Villaseca, the sixteenth-century patron of the Colegio de San Pedro y San Pablo. Doña Josepha Manuela de Monroy Guerrero Villaseca y Luyando, eighteenth-century heir to the estates, was having financial problems. The hacienda was so unproductive that its tenant in 1746, one Pascal Ochoa, could not pay his rent and deserted the property. The Jesuits rented the estate for two years starting December 1, 1747, with the following conditions:

1. An advance payment of 550 pesos would be made.

2. During the period of the contract, the owners would not sell or try to sell the property, or at least they would not conclude such an agreement before expiration of the present contract.

3. The renters, for their part, were obligated to occupy the estate and to pay the rent even if they decided to quit the estate. The renters were not allowed to make any repairs or improvements, so they could not claim the costs of such repairs in lieu of rent. At the termination of the rent period, the renters were obligated to return the properties without putting forth any claims.[92]

The Jesuits' takeover of the Guerrero mayorazgo, aside from the immediate question of further expansion of Santa Lucía holdings, represents the complete change in status and relationships between Jesuit and Spanish hacendado during the years between 1576 and 1747. In 1576, when Don Alonso arranged for the buying of the partly developed estate that became Santa Lucía, the figures dominating the Mexican rural estates were rich entrepreneurs such as Villaseca. The Jesuits were landless, penniless educators whose strength lay in intellectual resources best applied to the urban milieu. Now, 171 years later, it was the Jesuits who controlled the rural estates, who had ready cash and the managerial skills to exploit the current situation. And the descendants of Don Alonso were now the ones without money, becoming progressively more landless and unable to function in the countryside!

The Jesuits were always adjusting to changing circumstances. Between 1720 and 1740, Santa Lucía and other Jesuit haciendas were plagued by a seemingly endless series of clashes with neighboring Indian pueblos over access to pastures, farmlands, and other natural resources such as wood and water.[93] By 1743 they had rented sections of Altica, Concepción, San Xavier, Florida, Tepenene, Chicavasco, San Ignacio and San Pablo, Ocuila, and Xante to more than 600 renters. Parts of San Juan, Hueytepec, and Pintas were also rented, in this case largely to small-scale pulque producers who rented land, equipment, and facilities at fixed annual rates.[94] Such moves had two practical purposes: to increase revenues under changing conditions, and to establish peace along the borders of Santa Lucía, avoiding litigation and the public spectacle of conflict.[95]

Santa Lucía's production emphasis during the 1740s and 1750s included livestock, food crops, and cash crops. Livestock numbers were kept high, necessitating greater numbers of cowboys, herdsmen, shepherds, and other workers. Increased maize output was required for rations and to meet demands of increasing rural Indigenous populations as well as growing urban centers. The Actopan Valley properties became the focus of attention as facilities and production capacities were improved, particularly at Chicavasco and San Pablo, where enormous granaries, new slaughtering facilities, and increased farming became evident. The cash crop was pulque, produced with small investments and rendering large profits. Much of the land too arid or rocky to support livestock, or in a deteriorated state because of overgrazing, was just right for the hardy maguey plant.[96]

1751–1767: Secular Administration and Pulque Production

In 1751 the administration of the entire hacienda was placed, for the first and only time, in the hands of a non-Jesuit, Don Pedro Villaverde, an experienced hacendado with close ties to Colegio Máximo officials. He later signed a contract stipulating that his own income would be 50 percent of the annual profits of Santa Lucía above 30,000 pesos. This type of administration represented

a dramatic change in policy that lasted until 1764. During Villaverde's administration, the emphasis at Santa Lucía continued as it
had in the previous decade, combining livestock, food crops, and
cash crops. When income levels declined during the late 1750s and
early 1760s, Villaverde was dismissed and Jesuit administrators
again took control.[97]

The expulsion of the Jesuits from New Spain in 1767 and the resulting expropriation of all their properties just three years after direct management had been asserted abruptly terminated their association with Santa Lucía. Their activities and policies during the
three years prior to expulsion show important shifts. Livestock
production became a less important source of revenue, and this
was reflected in smaller flocks of sheep, goats, cattle, and horses.
On the other hand, direct Jesuit management of pulque production
began, and income from this cash crop rose to 32,000 pesos per annum. Cereal crops continued to be produced, but the source of income from Santa Lucía had undergone a transformation. During
the last years of Jesuit ownership, pulque produced 80 percent of
Santa Lucía's revenues. Santa Lucía had been converted into a
pulque hacienda.

Santa Lucía's internal adjustments to accommodate large-scale
production of pulque were in many ways the most significant, final
hacienda readjustment made by the Jesuits in New Spain. Included were ethical, management, and labor decisions of far-
reaching significance. Loyola's disciples moved from staunch opposition, to tolerance and indirect participation, to wholehearted
involvement. By 1764, private voices were suggesting to the viceroy that he support a move to brand the production and sale of
pulque a "mortal sin," beyond the realm of "sacramental absolu-
tion."[98] Had the crown not expelled the Jesuits when it did, their
pulque activities would have provided the secular clergy (who
were involved themselves) with ammunition for another round of
confrontation over monetary matters.

Since their arrival in New Spain, the Jesuits had been staunch
activitists against intoxication and social disorders blamed on
pulque consumption. At their haciendas, vigilance had always
been exercised to prevent access to pulque. But since the maguey
plant was indigenous to much of the area of Santa Lucía (particularly from Tepeatzingo to Florida), and pulque elaboration requires
little skill or effort,[99] Jesuit opposition probably had only limited
impact on their labor force. When the viceroy decided to attempt
the total suppression of pulque sales in Mexico City in 1692, on the

heels of the famous *tumulto* (uprising of the dispossessed),[100] he got just the type of justification he wished—from none other than the Colegio Máximo and other esteemed Jesuits in Mexico City. The viceroy was advised "to extend himself, prohibit and prevent—using all means possible—that anyone gain benefit from, or sell throughout the viceroyalty, this noxious and scandalous liquor."[101] But his legislation against pulque in Mexico City was as ineffectual as it was temporary. Authorized taverns in Mexico City gradually increased, from twelve in the sixteenth century to forty-five in the eighteenth century. The scale of increase rather than the numbers is important, since there were always more unauthorized than authorized outlets, both in the city and in the countryside pueblos.* It was this expanding local market (rapid spoilage prevented pulque distribution in other than local markets) that large sections of Santa Lucía became dedicated to supplying.

Conversion of Santa Lucía to large-scale pulque production had its greatest push in the 1730s and 1740s, but the beginnings were much earlier. Concepción, acquired in 1686, marks the formal start of pulque income. This hacienda became the private business of renters, who paid fixed annual fees for access to firewood, charcoal, *nopales* (edible cactus), pasture, small plots of farmland, and the ubiquitous maguey. By 1723 income from pulque was a nominal 400 to 500 pesos per year. By the late 1730s, this had tripled. During Araujo's term as administrator of Santa Lucía (1726–1743), steps were taken to increase pulque-derived income through large-scale planting of maguey. Although the Jesuits supervised the development of pulque production and invested funds and labor to convert worsening pastures to maguey plots, they left the actual production and marketing of pulque to renters, at fixed annual rates. By 1743 pulque income had increased to 18,000 pesos and, by 1746, 70,000 new plants had been added to locations at San Juan, San Xavier, Hueytepec, and Chicavasco. Additional plots were soon established at Florida, Tepenene, Altica, and San Ignacio y San Pablo. During Villaverde's term as administrator, the pulque cash-crop activity of the hacienda was sublet to an experienced pulque producer who, in turn, sublet to others, always at fixed an-

---

*Gibson, *Aztecs*, p. 396. The actual number of taverns in the Valley of Mexico, or in the Highlands, has not been determined, but in the Valley of Oaxaca, where Indigenous dislocation and cultural disruption were less pronounced, a 1726 survey of Indian drinking houses showed 1 for every 7.9 tributaries; Taylor, *Landlord*, pp. 32, 82. This is based on 513 public and private taverns and the 1726 tributary population figure of 4,026.

nual rates. It was only during the final three years (1764–1767) that the Jesuits directly supervised all aspects of pulque production.[102]

By 1767 Santa Lucía's owners had invested considerable sums in the construction of small-scale pulque farms, with buildings, fermenting vats, equipment, and mule trains for transport. Labor costs related to maguey plantings, including over 10,000 hectares of the high-quality maguey *manso* (tame or domesticated), must have been high. Just the stone fences enclosing many of the plots were valued at 12,012 pesos. On the widely scattered properties of Altica, the cattle and horse anexa, the Jesuits had 43,696 *varas* (36.7 kilometers) of stone (*piedra y cal*) maguey fences. The 32,000 peso annual income of the last years represented only the beginnings of profits of a hacienda recently converted to pulque production.[103]

The great value of Santa Lucía at the time of its expropriation and subsequent sale to the Conde de Regla family was largely due to the recent and extensive increase in maguey plantings. Most of the profits of Santa Lucía in the years immediately after expropriation derived directly from its pulque production. In 1769 San Xavier (which at this point included Altica, Concepción, Hueytepec, and Pintas), the center of administration for the extensive maguey plantings developed under Jesuit ownership, showed a net profit of 45,777 pesos, 234 pesos more than the net profit of the entire Santa Lucía operation for that year. Under management of administrators appointed by crown officials, who were less competent than the Jesuits, profits initially continued to rise, but then declined. Between 1769 and 1773, at least 83 percent of the net profit came from San Xavier, reflecting the degree to which the Jesuits, in their last years, had again adapted their rural estates to the most productive economic activity of the period.[104]

The willingness of the Conde de Regla family to pay a fortune for Santa Lucía and other ex-Jesuit college haciendas was directly related to their profitability. Secular hacendados, or those who had made fortunes and wished the status of large-scale landowners, always preferred to acquire productive haciendas. These, through time, frequently lost their productivity, became neglected, and changed owners. In contrast, the Jesuits acquired run-down estates and successfully converted them to producing for contemporary demand. Herein lies one of the essential differences between the long-term, successful, corporate Jesuit estates and their privately owned secular counterparts, which were characterized by instability and lower productivity.[105]

Conclusions on Acquisitions

The materials presented in Part I of this study indicate that the transfer of land from Indigenous control, through the crown, into the hands of hacendados, and eventually into Jesuit control was an unabating process. The studies of Chevalier, Colmenares, Macera, and Gracía provide additional evidence of the same phenomena in the viceroyalties of New Spain, New Granada, Peru, and La Plata.[106] For Mexico as a whole, much detail remains to be investigated; nevertheless, the case of Santa Lucía documents important aspects of the larger picture. This single hacienda—more precisely, this complex administrative unit—amassed ownership titles to at least 2,727 square kilometers of land on which livestock, cash crops, and food crops were produced for the express purpose of maximizing revenues for a Jesuit academic institution located in Mexico City. If consideration is taken of all lands to which Santa Lucía had access, its maximum dimensions would roughly equal those of the Valley of Mexico.[107]

Table 2 provides a breakdown of the amount and type of land, purchase costs, and number of acquisitions from 1576 to 1750. These data show the progressive accumulation of properties throughout the colonial period. During the first century of Santa Lucía's development, the trend of numerous smaller acquisitions coincided with the general pattern of hacienda development in the private sector. During the following century the number of acquisitions was reduced, but size and cost of individual units increased significantly. The total cost of the land to the Colegio de San Pedro y San Pablo cannot be precisely determined since in some cases purchase costs included livestock and facilities, and not all purchase prices could be determined from the documentation. Available evidence suggests the land costs to have been between 150,000

TABLE 2

Santa Lucía Property Acquisitions, 1576–1750

Period	Pasture land (kilometers^2)	Agricultural land (hectares)	Cost (pesos)	Number of acquisitions
1576–1600	157.88	1,020	30,290	17
1601–1650	296.24	2,953	16,457	34
1651–1700	606.08	2,550	38,224	3
1701–1750	1,584.37	1,530	61,315	8
TOTAL	2,644.57	8,053	146,286	62

and 160,000 pesos.[108] Most of the total area acquired was pasture land.

Although Santa Lucía was located almost on the periphery of Mexico City, the bulk of its lands (69 percent of pastures and 25 percent of agricultural land)[109] were actually at great distances from the Tepeatzingo casco and were not consistently used. The lands most intensively exploited were closest to the viceregal capital, extending roughly between Cuernavaca and Ixmiquilpan. Here were concentrated most of the agricultural land (75 percent) and a significant but smaller portion of the pasture land (31 percent). Compared to most other haciendas in the *mesa central* and those of the south (including Oaxaca, Guatemala, and Yucatán), Santa Lucía was enormous.[110] Compared to the haciendas of the north (such as Coahuila), it was small.[111] But areal dimensions in themselves are not useful indicators of productivity or significance. The northern Sánchez Navarro haciendas, twenty to thirty times the areal dimensions of Santa Lucía, never approached its productivity, and the southern haciendas had negligible production.[112] It was types and locations of properties rather than dimensions that allowed the shrewd Jesuit businessmen to make continuous adjustments to maintain profitability. For example, by the 1760s, although the total area devoted to pulque production was only 4.4 percent of the total area acquired for Santa Lucía, income from this source represented more than 80 percent of annual profits.[113]

Such adjustments had to take into account changing markets as well as ecological shifts affecting the quality of soils and human population sizes. Santa Lucía began with European-introduced livestock, shifted to a combination of livestock and food crops, and terminated as essentially a cash-crop hacienda. Along the way, the bureaucratic distinctions between pasture and farmland were taken seriously only during requests for the actual properties. In the northern parts of the Valley of Mexico—where agriculture had flourished before Cortés, and where European livestock had helped destroy fertility and supportive land capacities—the Jesuits, once populations were recovering and social unrest was brewing, ended up producing a by-product of the indigenous maguey, on soils not fit for either livestock or agriculture, for a growing, insatiable market. Xochitl, that seemingly innocent Toltec seductress, mother of Meconetzin (son of maguey and origin of fortunate love affairs), still stalked the land.[114]

It is clear that many sectors of colonial society in Mexico greatly aided the Jesuits in their accumulation of vast rural estates. The crown, viceroys, the audiencia, members of the secular clergy, lay Spaniards, and members of the Indian aristocracy—despite the strong opposition of individuals such as Palafox—encouraged the Jesuits in the expansion of their academic and religious institutions and, at the same time, opened avenues which allowed the followers of Loyola to increase their holdings. Like their secular hacendado counterparts, the Jesuits quickly mastered and utilized power and position in their direct assault upon native lands during the years between 1576 and 1651, and in the early eighteenth century near Guadalajara. Overall, however, most of their acquisitions came directly from the Spanish hacendados, whom the Jesuits quickly surpassed as ranchers and farmers. The most intensive acquisition occurred during the first two decades of the seventeenth century and the first four decades of the eighteenth century, both periods coinciding with major institutional and mission expansion of the order in New Spain. The general Spanish assault upon native natural resources was greatly facilitated by the demographic cataclysm that weakened both the will and the ability of rural peoples to defend ownership claims.

PART TWO

Administration and Management

When Loyola developed the basic structure of the Jesuit order he did not anticipate its future rural estates, but the systematic procedures he set forth allowed for the incorporation of such secular aspects into the society. These procedures took into account the practical requirements for building and sustaining institutions, for fostering individual capacities and skills, and for coming to terms with the realities of power in economics, politics, and religion. The structure involved a hierarchy founded on principles of discipline, obedience, and individual poverty. The Jesuit order was militaristic in inspiration and organization, under the command of a father general and a chain of lesser officers. All individuals were responsible to superiors, and each Jesuit was taught to believe that his work played an important part in carrying out the directives of the order's commander-in-chief, Christ, who had established as his representative on earth the office of pope.[1] The day-to-day management of a hacienda such as Santa Lucía involved the lowest levels of the Jesuit hierarchy, the *hermanos coadjutores*. The conduct of its administrators and the products of their labor directly concerned the material welfare of higher levels and primary goals, and consequently were of direct interest to the father general.

The hierarchical command structure that linked the lowliest lay brother at Santa Lucía with the command center in Rome was based on a military model, but the actual functioning of the order was another matter.[2] Provincials, visitadores, procuradores, rectors, missionaries, and coadjutores worked and traveled as individuals in Mexico, although invariably accompanied—for reasons of need or propriety—by at least one other male, who might be another Jesuit, a secretary, a servant, or a slave. In view of the order's extensive territorial and material possessions in New Spain, not to mention the educational institutions, missions, and population under direct Jesuit control, there were strikingly few Jesuits involved—fewer than 700 in the province of Mexico in 1767, and fewer than 2,000 for all of South America.* The overall picture was one of widely scattered individuals and small groups, rather than the concentration of forces in defensible positions characteristic of the military. Within the ranks of the Jesuits, as the debate over the initial management of Santa Lucía clearly demonstrated, there were provisions for disagreement, individual initiative, and majority consensus not characteristic of the military model. No military organization provides a helpful parallel of such an extensive empire, created, expanded, and controlled over such long periods of time with so few people. Although Loyola's military experiences provided part of the background for Jesuit organization, and he used military metaphors widely in his writings, his day-to-day experiences during his spiritual formation (1521–1539) provide a better key for understanding Jesuit success.[3] These resulted in a particular system of authority, obedience, communication, and delegation of powers.

Figure 2 outlines the various levels of command and the administrative positions within the Jesuit hierarchy as they existed during the seventeenth and eighteenth centuries. At each level there was a central administrative office with jurisdiction over all activities at lower levels. It was subject to periodic review and received advice from a congregation or council. It was guided by constitutional documents that codified principles and rules of conduct. And it was assisted by a *procuraduría,* or office of legal and temporal affairs. The administrative structures created to incorporate Santa Lucía into the Jesuit system elaborated existing patterns. The basic elements had already been fully articulated in the Constitution drawn up by Loyola.

The model for management was the office of the father general itself. In theory this office was governed by the Constitutions and was subject to the will of the General Congregation, but since the father general interpreted the Constitutions and actually decided when, and if, the General Congregation was to meet, his office dominated. The father general was aided by a secretarial staff to handle clerical matters and by a legal staff, headed by a *procurador general,* to handle business matters. The office of the *procurador general* provided the expertise for handling business affairs, legal problems such as law suits, or whatever "necessary aids" were re-

*For Mexico, Zelis, "Catálogo," pp. 231–93, the total was 678. For South America, in 1748, the total was 1,913 Jesuits, including novices and students preparing to become Jesuits; in *Catalogus universite,* cited by Popescu, *El sistema económico,* p. 76.

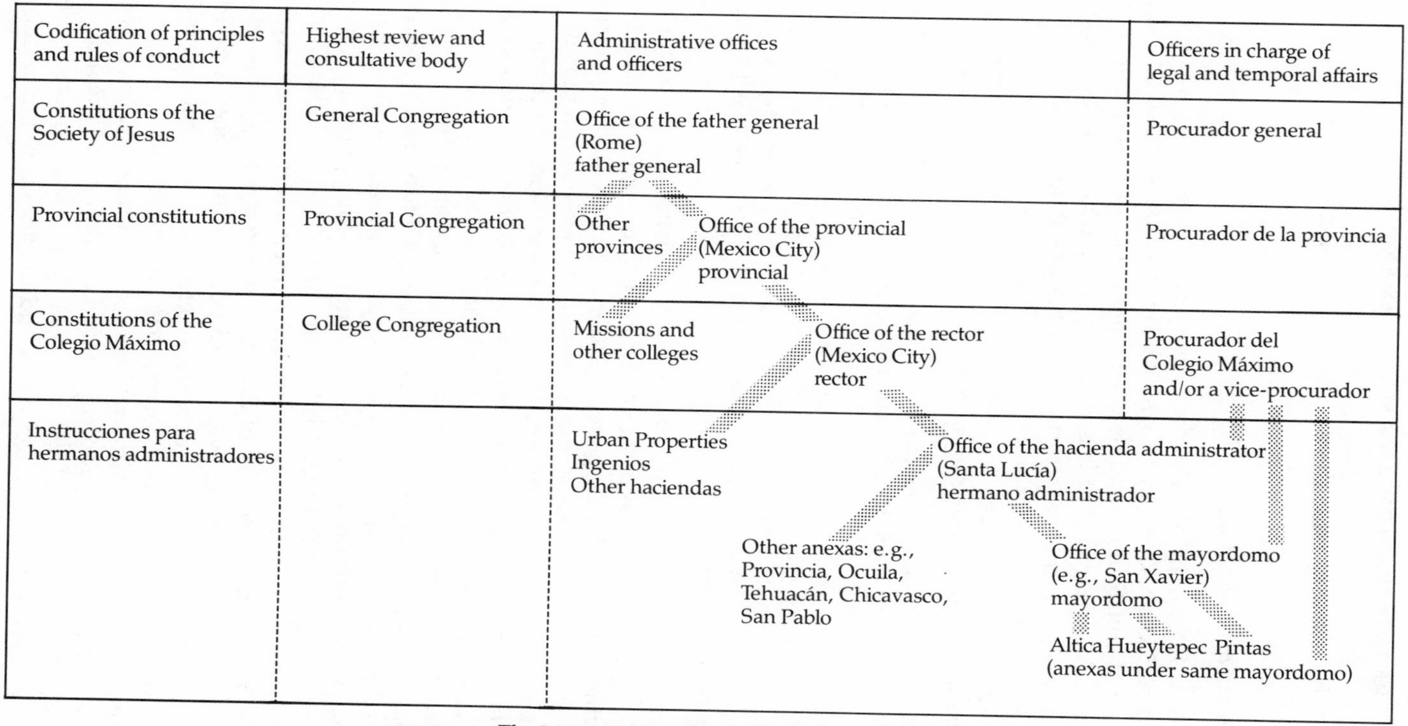

Codification of principles and rules of conduct	Highest review and consultative body	Administrative offices and officers	Officers in charge of legal and temporal affairs
Constitutions of the Society of Jesus	General Congregation	Office of the father general (Rome) father general	Procurador general
Provincial constitutions	Provincial Congregation	Office of the provincial (Mexico City) provincial — Other provinces	Procurador de la provincia
Constitutions of the Colegio Máximo	College Congregation	Office of the rector (Mexico City) rector — Missions and other colleges	Procurador del Colegio Máximo and/or a vice-procurador
Instrucciones para hermanos administradores		Office of the hacienda administrator (Santa Lucía) hermano administrador — Urban Properties, Ingenios, Other haciendas — Other anexas: e.g., Provincia, Ocuila, Tehuacán, Chicavasco, San Pablo — Office of the mayordomo (e.g., San Xavier) mayordomo — Altica Hueytepec Pintas (anexas under same mayordomo)	

FIGURE 2. The Jesuit administrative hierarchy and Santa Lucía.

quired for dealing with the secular world, including the secular clergy.[4]

Provincial and College Ties

In New Spain, the office of the provincial in Mexico City was subject to periodic reviews by provincial congregations. It had its own provincial constitution and its own chief legal counsel (*procurador general de la provincia*). At the level of the Colegio Máximo, the rector was aided by a college attorney and his assistants. The rector's duties were outlined by the college constitutions, and his activities were reviewed by college congregations. The rector's role in managing temporal goods was clearly defined by the Constitutions:

The society will take possession of the colleges with the temporal goods which pertains to them. It will appoint a rector who has more appropriate talent for that work. He will take charge of maintaining and administering their temporal goods, providing for the necessities both of the material buildings and of the scholastics who are dwelling in the colleges or of those who are preparing themselves. . . . The rector should keep account of the entire establishment so that he can give it at any time to whomever the general may ask him to do.[5]

Santa Lucía was directly under the jurisdiction of the rector of the Colegio Máximo and indirectly under the supervision of the provincial and the father general. During the first quarter-century of Santa Lucía's existence, the roles of the provincial and the father general were very important. With the expansion of the college system in Mexico, the father general became less involved in the business details and acted directly in matters affecting policy.[6]

During the seventeenth century, the provincial's office dominated policy affecting haciendas. By the eighteenth century, the office of the rector dominated. When problems arose, however, experienced administrators suggested solutions, acting upon the advice of trusted secular friends. Visitadores conducted periodic checks and made recommendations—usually written instructions carrying the approval and authority of the office of the father general—that standardized procedures within and between provinces. Routine decisions affecting Santa Lucía were delegated to the hacienda administrator by the college attorney, or to his assistant.

The hacienda administrator supervised the mayordomos, who implemented decisions and supervised operations on the individual anexas or ranches of the hacienda. There was no one-to-one relationship between mayordomos and the anexas of Santa Lucía.

Depending upon the activities at a given estate, taking San Xavier as an example, one mayordomo might handle livestock and another the slaughtering facilities and agricultural production. At the Actopan Valley estates, during the 1740s, there were separate mayordomos concerned with goats, sheep, cattle, horses, pulque, and the fattening and slaughtering activities at Chicavasco, without necessarily being associated with one anexa. The mayordomo in charge of the goat herds usually associated with Tepenene after the 1730s was, at different times, also identified with San Pablo or Florida, depending upon the location of the goats at the time of reference or taking of inventory. The main sheep flocks were consistently associated with specified areas and mayordomos until the 1720s, after which the Xoloc flocks became integrated with those of Provincia, and Negra and Ocuila were merged into one large flock called either Negra or Ocuila but under a single mayordomo. The farming operations at San Juan were directed by a mayordomo who resided at Santa Lucía.[7]

Although the mayordomos were directly responsible to the Santa Lucía administrator, they had frequent direct contact with the procurador or other representatives of the rector's office. Care was exercised, however, not to contravene the constitutional injunction telling rectors to take "care that no one interferes in the business of another." The rector was cautioned also to appoint only as many officials as were necessary and only those fit for their office.[8] The Santa Lucía management structure suggests that, in this respect, practice and theory were closely matched.

The office of hacienda administrator, including the brother who served with him on the hacienda, was the lowest rank filled by Jesuits. The mayordomos were not subject to the same vows of poverty, chastity, and obedience as their supervisors and represent the first layer in the overall hierarchical structure that was not in ideological conformity with Jesuit standards. The Jesuit sense of hierarchical order, however, penetrated further down in the structure of Santa Lucía's operations than the offices filled by Jesuits. The mayordomos had clerical and administrative assistants (*escribanos, ayudantes*) who kept accounts and helped implement administrative decisions. Beneath them were other overseers with limited decision-making powers, such as *sobresalientes, capitanes,* and *caporales*.[9]

A clearly defined hierarchy incorporated all members of the working force of Santa Lucía, extending from the lowest rank, occupied by children working as shepherds or in the fields, to the level of the mayordomos. The greatest numbers of individuals involved with Santa Lucía were at the bottom of the pyramid, receiving the lowest income of any paid worker and having least access to power and prestige. This type of organization was, of course, characteristic of most labor in Mexico and elsewhere in New Spain. One of the reasons Spain was successful in incorporating the native societies into its economic and political structures was precisely that there were parallels in the structures of both societies. The Jesuit organizational structure reflected European society. Santa Lucía's organization reflected the European incorporation of Mexican sociopolitical organizations. Between the Jesuits, who owned the hacienda, and the basically Indian labor force, which did most of the work on the hacienda, we find Spaniards, mestizos, mulattoes, and people of direct African origin.

Corporate Controls: Systems of Obedience and Communication

Jesuit success in utilizing vast human resources through their method of administration was largely the result of an efficient system of obedience and communication.[10] This applied to the order itself and to all levels of Santa Lucía. Within the order, every individual was bound by his vows to obey all superiors above him, and the Jesuits would have liked similar obedience from all those in their employment. The lay brothers in charge of administering temporal matters took vows binding them, not to the pope (as did the priests), but to the father general and to the Constitutions, understood as representing the essence of the Divine Imperative. They placed themselves at the disposal of the father general, or his representative, for whatever time he saw fit to employ them in temporal service. The Constitutions stressed that superiors should command rather than request subordinates to obey instructions.[11] The institutionalization of this sense of obedience to superiors enabled the Jesuits to function more efficiently than other religious orders in most endeavors.

The concept of obedience also included accepting one's station or assignment, or, phrased in biblical terms, being "content with the lot of Martha."[12] Individual ambition and aspiration to higher ranks was discouraged. Thus, the Jesuit lay brother assigned to rural estates, rather than the more desirable mission frontiers, was "ready to be employed in low and humble offices and to spend all the days of his life for the benefit and aid of the society, meanwhile believing that by serving it he is serving his Lord and Creator."[13]

The greatest posthumous praise within the order was reserved for individuals who reveled in humble tasks and showed no inclination to fill higher-status roles for which they were well qualified.[14] However, "penances, hair shirts and other torments of the flesh" were discouraged to avoid physical impediments or excuses, as Loyola aptly stated, "for not carrying out what we have set before ourselves."[15] It was entirely within the discretion of superiors to decide where individuals would work and when they should be moved.[16] This concept, when successfully implemented on haciendas such as Santa Lucía, largely prevented the emergence of personal and conflicting interests on the part of lay brothers administering the estates.

The lines of communication within the Jesuit system coincided with its hierarchical structure. The father general, in principle, had complete information about all the activities of the society, the provincial about all the activities in Mexico, the rector about all the activities of the Colegio Máximo, the hacienda administrator about all the activities of Santa Lucía, and the mayordomo about all the activities of his particular farming anexa. One of the functions of a superior was to use more complete information about activities below him to detect problems and correct defects.[17]

To maintain this type of supervision, the father general's office had on hand copies of all the concessions, favors, and privileges of the society, plus summaries of them "and likewise a list of all the houses and colleges with their revenues; and another of all the persons who are in each province."[18] These lists were renewed annually and updated. Parallel lists and copies of documents were maintained by provincials, rectors, and hacienda administrators. Santa Lucía administrators had on hand copies of most legal documents pertaining to the hacienda, copies of privileges granted by the crown, and even copies of matters of general legal interest, such as the four-volume *Recopilación de las leyes de Indias.*[19]

The Jesuit system of communication included provisions for regular reports to superiors. Local superiors and rectors submitted written weekly reports to provincials, who reported monthly to the father general. In addition, local superiors submitted comprehensive reports to provincials every four months, sending copies to the father general.[20] Explicit in this system of communication was the idea of mutual assistance. The exchange of letters and reports between subjects and superiors kept all parties informed of what was taking place in other areas. This created an "arrangement through which each region can learn from the other whatever promotes mutual consolation and edification."[21] The result was a vast amount of written material and rich documentary sources for studying Jesuit estates, in comparison to the meager corpus of materials concerning secular estates.

Written instructions were of great importance. When superiors issued instructions or sent someone to accomplish specific tasks, they did so in writing. Instructions included specific details about "the manner of proceedings, and the means . . . to be used for the end sought."[22] Rectors, for example, set times for almost every activity under their jurisdiction and insisted that the schedules be carried out to the letter. Care was taken, however, to provide for local circumstances and seasonal changes, and local superiors were instructed to make adjustments corresponding to local conditions.[23] Implementation, nevertheless, was less than perfect.

One of the key functions of the hacienda administrator was to produce written communications. These are described in detail in the next section of the chapter. Mayordomos working for the Jesuits represented the lowest level of office producing records. No formal records or accounts were either required or expected from supervisory personnel beneath the mayordomo level.[24] Few individuals occupying offices beneath that level could either read or write Spanish, and they were not required to make significant independent decisions. They reported orally to the mayordomos, who were responsible for actions taken. Disputes between Jesuits and secular overseers were handled by a formal administrative system, with a strong degree of accountability on both sides. Differences between those in lower levels of the hacienda work hierarchy (from the shepherd supervisors down) and the mayordomos were resolved informally, without the same restraints against arbitrary action. Thus, the Jesuit system of communication extended one level beyond the offices filled by members of the order. Success in establishing this administrative bridge between themselves, a religious order, and the hacienda, a secular economic enterprise, was a central factor in the continued profitability of a hacienda such as Santa Lucía.

The Jesuit Instructions: An Operational Handbook

Very early in Santa Lucía's history, the office of the father general began to codify instructions applicable to haciendas. By the eighteenth century, the Jesuits had an extensive and detailed operations guide which served as a reference manual for Santa Lucía.[25] It can also be seen as a codification of rules applying to haciendas in New Spain in the same way that the Constitutions represent a codification of rules applying to the order as a whole. The internal structure of the Instrucciones was similar to that of the formal codes (the Constitutions) governing the order, provinces, or colleges. They all give systematic expression to rules governing the establishment, general management, and day-to-day administration of Jesuit institutions. All equally emphasize the order's provisions for temporal possessions, the hierarchy of order and authority, the need for qualified, tested, and experienced people to fill specified roles, and the demands of obedience, chastity, and poverty.

Like the other formal codes, the Instrucciones is broken down into topics, chapters, and subpoints. Eight topics are covered by twenty chapters and three hundred subpoints. Five chapters deal directly with religious duties and people concerned in spiritual matters; three chapters outline relationships with those living off the haciendas; three chapters deal with life on the hacienda and the care to be taken with equipment and facilities; three chapters outline the care of livestock and pastures; two chapters concern themselves with the production of cereal crops; two chapters outline the type of accounts required and manner of communication to be employed; one chapter gives instructions about how slaves are to be treated; and one chapter deals with sugar haciendas and sugar mills. The final instruction commands the administrator to read twelve chapters of the instructions every month, at the rate of three chapters a week, leaving the other eight to be read two or three times a year. Santa Lucía administrators were obligated to follow these instructions, and the review of communications by superiors would quickly identify lapses.

The internal accounting system applied to Santa Lucía was articulated in detail by the Instrucciones, but it has not been possible to date accurately the point in the hacienda's history when the eight sets of accounts stipulated became operational. The extensive documentation about Santa Lucía now housed in the Mexican National Archives, specifically the sections (*ramos*) Temporalidades and the Archivo Histórico de Hacienda, indicates very close adherence to the Instrucciones as of the 1730s. The documentation in the Regla Collection suggests that certain aspects related to legal documents were operational from the outset. Lack of documentation on daily, weekly, monthly, and annual hacienda accounts for the sixteenth and seventeenth centuries prevents precise dating.

Santa Lucía's business records during most of the eighteenth century were produced according to the Instrucciones. These eight types of accounts were central to the hacienda's management:

1. *Libro borrador:* an account daybook divided into two sections, the first for noting income, the second for expenses. The entries were to be divided by month, and at the end of the year the income and expense totals would be balanced. A new list would start with the new year.

2. *Libro de caja:* a cash account divided into two sections like the borrador, where the monthly totals from the borrador would be entered. This was the account inspected by the provincial during his visits to the hacienda. When the administrator went to Mexico City for his yearly spiritual exercises, he took this account book with him, to be audited by the college superiors.

3. *Libro de siembras y cosechas:* a record of plantings and harvests during the year. Daily and weekly entries were made of work accomplished and amounts planted or harvested, and entries on total plantings and harvests were included. In addition, this account noted the distribution of harvested products, listing day, month, and destination of goods leaving the hacienda. No products were to be moved without authorization by the college procurador, the rector, or another superior.

4. *Libro del asiento de los sirvientes:* a record book of people employed on the livestock ranches. They were listed by name, occupation, salary (by month), and rations (by week). Included would be an annual list of credits or debits, facilitating collection of debts or payment of salaries. After each accounting, or adjustment, new lists were made.

5. *Libro de inventario general:* a record of all assets of the hacienda, including an inventory of equipment and fixed goods as well as of livestock and supplies. This account was made every time there was a change in hacienda administration and was also used by procuradores, rectors, and provincials.

6. *Libro de mercedes de tierras y aguas:* a record of land grants and water rights of the hacienda. These records provided the basis for identifying all boundaries and was referred to whenever neighboring pueblos or individuals attempted to encroach upon hacienda jurisdictions.

7. *Cuaderno de las deudas sueltas:* a record of miscellaneous debts and credits of the hacienda, itemized according to each transaction resulting in either a credit or a debit.

8. *Cuaderno de la raya de los gañanes:* accounts of hacienda laborers, both those living on the hacienda and those coming for special

work (*peones*). The names of all individuals were entered, with margins on either side of the names. In the left margin, money earned was recorded in pesos, half-pesos, reales, and half-reales. In the righthand margin were noted numbers of days or half-days worked. Weekly balances of credits and debits of individuals and work gangs were noted, as were weekly and total labor costs for a given task.[26]

Apart from these standard accounts, the Santa Lucía administrators kept sets of documents such as letters, special instructions, contracts, and records of commercial dealings with people outside the college and the hacienda. First, there were letters between the administrator and the superiors in Mexico City. These letters were arranged according to dates and separated according to year, and were kept under lock and key. Second, there were letters from subordinates, such as mayordomos, regarding the business of the hacienda. Third, there were receipts generated by commercial activities with people outside the college and its haciendas (receipts from people within the college system were filed with the letters in the first category). And fourth, there were other documents and papers, such as letters of credit (*vales*) and letters of payment (*cartas de pago*), all of which were to be stored under lock and key in the administrator's office. In addition, copies of maps of the anexas were kept at the main hacienda residences such as Santa Lucía, San Xavier, and Chicavasco.[27]

The Instrucciones stipulated that the administrator of the hacienda must send monthly accounts of income and expenses to the college business offices, through which he also made all requests for supplies and funds. Requests for ordinary supplies normally were for cash, textiles not produced by the hacienda's mill, equipment required for ranching or farming, foodstuffs either not produced or out of stock, and even indulgences (*bulas*) which were sold to the labor force. An extraordinary request might be for special adornments for the hacienda chapel during a visit from dignitaries, or a request for cash to cover unexpected emergencies. Even when purchases were made in local pueblos, itemized lists were forwarded to the college administrators. Regular progress reports accompanied the accounts, and great emphasis was placed on the need to report, immediately, any damage to hacienda crops or property, or any threat that might result in litigation.[28]

The Instrucciones governing hacienda administration were not unique. Parallel instructions have been uncovered concerning the Colegio Máximo's sugar estates, as have detailed instructions concerning the cultivation of maguey.[29] Chevalier pointed out that the Instrucciones were regionally oriented, and as further research on Jesuit haciendas in other geographical areas is conducted, other comprehensive sets of instructions will be uncovered.[30] Detailed, formal, written instructions were a part of Jesuit management at all levels of administration. The educational institutions and the missions were subject to the same type of administrative system.

One of the key reasons for adopting a rigid internal accounting system was the necessity to pay the tithe, which proved to be a mixed blessing. On the one hand, the college lost a percentage of its revenue from the rural estates because production was taxed.[31] On the other hand, having to pay the tax stimulated the maintenance of a much tighter system of accounting and control to make sure that the ecclesiastical tax collectors were not paid 1 peso more than required. The net effect in the long run, as far as Santa Lucía and other haciendas were concerned, was a more efficient accounting of hacienda affairs, resulting in closer supervision of production. The increased effectiveness of administration allowed the hacienda to expand and continue producing revenues rather than stagnating, as would an estate with a less rigorous accounting system.

Because of the Jesuit hierarchy, the hacienda's system of administration suffered less from the inconsistencies and conflicts of interest on the part of lower-level administrators characteristic of the Spanish colonial government. The practical accommodation to unreasonable or impossible demands, symbolized by the expression *obedezco pero no cumplo*, did not develop within the formal structure of Jesuit administration. Whether or not it did occur in relations between mayordomos and hacienda workers is difficult to determine because of the lack of a formal record-keeping system at this level. Despite the great distance between administrative centers and actual activities, and the few Jesuit supervisors involved, the administrative system not only remained intact but was able to encompass massive territorial expansion without increasing greatly the number of administrators. The history of Santa Lucía demonstrates the effectiveness of management practices which could adapt to different types of production without alteration of the management structure.

Delegation of Authority and Management Flexibility

The key to the long-term success of Jesuit management was its system of delegating power, enabling those closest to the actual decision to provide accurate information or make the relevant decisions. Superiors removed from the scene where decisions were being made seldom acted blindly, since they relied upon the informed judgments of subordinates. The founding of the Colegio Máximo, the purchasing of Santa Lucía, the acquisition, rental, or sale of properties, and many key administrative decisions, in the first instance, were local decisions based on delegated authority. Constitutionally, such decisions were the responsibility of the father general, not the Jesuits in Mexico:

In the superior general is vested all the authority to make contracts for the purchase or sale of any moveable temporal goods whatsoever of the colleges and the houses of the society, and to demand or repay any annual taxes whatsoever on their immoveable goods, for the utility and benefit of the same colleges, and the right of being able to free himself from the debt by restoring the money which was given. . . . The general may sell, or retain, or apply what he thinks wise to one place or another, as he perceives to be conducive to the greater glory.[32]

Loyola's practical experiences as pilgrim and soldier, however, had convinced him that local circumstances often required immediate decisions based on local knowledge. Provisions for delegating authority to trusted persons was provided for, as follows: "The provincial superiors, the local superiors, the rectors, and the general's other commissioners will have the part of this authority which the general communicates to them. They will not be obliged to assemble their associates to perform acts of this nature collectively."[33] This power to act, without waiting for confirmation from superiors who were far away and unfamiliar with local conditions, provided a degree of flexibility within the administrative system and allowed it to function efficiently. The royal administrative system, in principle, demanded compliance with the royal will, expressed through cédulas, in local circumstances, where compliance was frequently against the interests of local officials and power blocs (encomenderos, hacendados, audiencias, cabildos), resulting in a frustration of the design and intent of royal administration.[34] In the Jesuit system such inconsistencies could be avoided. In the original purchase of Santa Lucía and the decision to manage rural estates, Pedro Sánchez was acting with authority vested in him before arriving in New Spain. As provincial he had the greatest authority in Mexico, although the Provincial Congregation could, and did, question his decisions. The debates about Santa Lucía management and the use of African slaves, during the first decade, were by-products of the Jesuit system. And in the end it was the father general who confirmed the decisions taken, based on a thorough evaluation of local circumstances.[35]

With the creation of the Colegio Máximo's business office (procuraduría), authority for making business decisions was delegated by the rector to the procurador. This was always done in writing so that there would be no confusion regarding which decisions could be taken independently and which required prior consultation with superiors. During the accumulation of the Santa Lucía properties, there were many occasions on which the rector authorized the procurador to make purchases, or in which the procurador delegated this authority to the hacienda administrator or others. As a result, non-Jesuits became authorized to make purchases, to tender petitions for grants of land through merced, or to receive lands on behalf of the college. When the alcalde mayor and justicia of Chilapa took possession of lands for the college in 1617 and 1619, they did so on the basis of a formal power of attorney from Jesuit officials.[36] Even the activities of the Jesuit agents who acquired properties on behalf of the Colegio Máximo were not taken outside the provisions of the Jesuit system. Such delegated authority, since it was transmitted through a notarized statement of power of attorney, was recognized as valid by Spanish government officials while, at the same time, it represented the delegated authority that ultimately resided in the Jesuit father general.[37]

By the end of the seventeenth century, authority over most temporal affairs had been delegated to superiors below the level of the office of the provincial. A few copies of such statements of powers by delegated authority were found in the hacienda papers of Santa Lucía. The original rental of the hacienda of San Nicolás in 1687 can be used to illustrate what powers were being delegated, and how. In this case, the rector of the Colegio Máximo, in his capacity as vice-provincial during the provincial's absence, formally delegated authority to the rectors of colleges "to take any action regarding the purchase, sale, rental, and defense" of the haciendas pertaining to these colleges "subject, of course, to the ratification of the provincial."[38] Furthermore, authority was given to defend the haciendas and their livestock and servants against all judges and tribunals of the crown or any ecclesiastical courts. The statement goes on for several pages, outlining in detail what actions could be taken regarding improvement of properties, purchase and sale of livestock and lands, and initiation of law suits in defense of Jesuit privileges and properties. In addition, authority was granted to delegate further "all, or part, of the powers" and to name individuals for specific or general administrative tasks.[39]

By the middle of the eighteenth century, most of these powers were being delegated directly to the administrator of Santa Lucía. When Joaquín Padilla took charge of the hacienda in 1746, the college rector formally transferred to him authority to handle all disputes, lawsuits, civil and ecclesiastical negotiations, and executive and ordinary business presently pending or that might arise in the future. Padilla was empowered to deal with the audiencia, with tribunals, and with civil and ecclesiastical courts. He could make demands on behalf of the hacienda and respond to any demands made against it, legal or otherwise.[40] Since Padilla was a *padre* (having undergone rigorous training) rather than a hermano (with limited formal training), such delegation of powers was retained by an individual whose education and experience as a Jesuit were more apt to conform to the order's standards than those of a coadjutor. Coadjutores working as administrators on the haciendas were not granted the degree of authority that was given to the padres.[41]

Similarly, Pedro Villaverde, the secular administrator in the 1750s, was not granted similar powers. When he started functioning as hacienda administrator, he had authority to make only minor business decisions and no authority in legal matters. The contract he signed to run the hacienda on a profit-sharing basis with the college allowed him almost complete control over business decisions but very little power in making decisions that affected the Colegio Máximo. Villaverde was never given significant authority in handling legal matters.[42] During his term of office, there was always a padre assigned to Santa Lucía to assist, or check, his administration.

Written instructions implied both the authority and the duty to act. When Santa Lucía administrators wrote instructions to mayordomos, the authority and duty to act were inherent in the instructions, but only as defined by the instructions. Bernardo Tomás de Miers, administrator of Santa Lucía from 1743 to 1746, wrote to his mayordomos and told them how they were to handle anyone who inquired about the hacienda: "Tell them to ask me and do not tell them anything, nor give them lodgings, nor give them anything even if they claim they have been sent by me."[43] All written instructions between the various levels of command within the Jesuit administrative system implied the authority to act and the command to act in the specified manner. Delegation of authority to mayordomos invariably took the form of written instructions, implying limited powers, whereas the administrators maintained more sweeping powers.

The Jesuit Style

Simplicity and austerity were hallmarks of the Jesuit management style that lent themselves to efficient control of resources. Even the physical evidence, such as their documentation, reflects this. The quality of paper used in day-to-day record-keeping, the size of sheets or folios used in letters, even the quality of penmanship was illustrative. The typical correspondence of a mayordomo to an administrator or procurador consisted of a piece of paper of ten by twenty centimeters, both sides filled with laboriously noted detail about the weather, crops, compliance with earlier requests, or accounting of livestock and harvests. Little space went untouched by the quill of a literate mayordomo or his secretary (more common for the sheep-flock mayordomos). The Jesuit administrators corresponded more widely, with the college procuradores and rector, fellow administrators associated with the same college, secular business contacts, and, on occasion, higher Jesuit authorities such as the provincial. The size of sheets used tended to be twice that of the mayordomos, with more empty space, better penmanship, and a range of topics beyond weather and crops, encompassing strategy, problems, and policy. An element of justification for actions, aside from detail-reporting, is evident here, and even more so among the writings of the procuradores. These dealt with a wider range of both secular and Jesuit sectors, sometimes having to account directly to the father general in Rome, but more frequently to the provincial, fellow procuradores in other colleges, merchants, members of the royal bureaucracy, and private citizens. Here the folio appears more frequently, as do exterior seals, addresses, and a more liberal use of paper and rhetorical phrases. The correspondence of rectors, provincials, visitadores, and the father general, for the most part, was straightforward and parsimonious. Customary non-Jesuit style, including extensive rhetorical introductory and closing passages—frequently with little of consequence between—was not entirely neglected, depending upon the rank of the recipient and the nature of the topic. Business matters could be simple and to the point, whereas problems of political import invariably required more space and eloquence. In contrast to the large, expensive folio with the interior of one page containing an aristocratic lady's expression of religious devotion and appreciation of some aspect of the order's work[44] one can place the crisp note of the college rector inviting the viceroy to a college religious activity.[45] These two pieces of correspondence, in their physical nature, content, origins, and destinations, help place the Jesuits in perspective in eighteenth-century New Spain.

Jesuit policies governing management were clearly established by Loyola and elaborated upon by his successors. These policies were based on an ideology that firmly held to a highly structured hierarchy whose proper functioning depended upon complete obedience by all subordinates. The incorporation and maintenance of temporal estates such as Santa Lucía did not necessitate a re-structuring of Jesuit ideology as long as these temporal estates were clearly the property of the order rather than of an individual, and as long as they served the purpose of furthering the spiritual objectives expressed by the Constitutions. The prototype of Jesuit order was celestial, explained by Loyola as follows: "Even in the angels theirs is the subordination of one hierarchy to another; and in the heavens, and all bodies that are moved, the lowest by the highest, and the highest, in their turn unto the Supreme mover of all."[46]

Insofar as the Jesuits played a role in structuring the activities of Santa Lucía, it was within this ideological framework. Insofar as Santa Lucía was an integral part of Jesuit activities in Mexico, it was also within management structures developed to implement this ideology. Poverty, obedience, and chastity differentiated the Je-suits from their secular hacendado counterparts and provided built-in advantages in maintaining efficient rural estates. The aspect of obedience to superiors was of paramount importance, ensuring that orders given would be carried out. This alone would not have guaranteed Santa Lucía's long-term success, since superiors were frequently far from the hacienda and preoccupied with the spirit-ual concerns of the order. This problem was solved by their system of delegation of powers to the level where the person most compe-tent to make the proper decisions had the authority to act in re-sponse to the changing challenges faced by rural estates. Without a workable system of delegation of powers, Santa Lucía would never have developed or flourished as it did.

SIX 🏛 *Administrators*

"Others extract the profits while owners are left to report the losses when rural estates are left under the sole control of mayordomos."[1] This statement, made by a college administrator, sums up the Jesuit view of the management practices prevailing on many secular estates. In their role as hacendados, the Jesuits placed administrators in control of the activities of mayordomos and other subordinate hacienda administrative personnel. Little is known about administrative roles in colonial society because the topic has been largely overlooked. Chevalier suggests that the masters of the haciendas and their mayordomos were the primary agents of administration but does not provide details.[2] Taylor's portrayal of developments in the Valley of Oaxaca indicates hacienda owners staying at the main residence during planting and harvest, with the mayordomos looking after administrative details the rest of the year.[3] Gibson's study, which deals only marginally with haciendas, identifies the key role played by mayordomos in labor supervision and agricultural crop production.[4] Barrett's analysis of the sugar estates of the Marqueses del Valle, however, indicates the importance of an administrative office between the actual owner and the mayordomos engaged in day-to-day supervision of hacienda activity. At the Cortés estates, the administrators based their authority on delegated powers of attorney.[5] The studies of Bazant and Harris identify the administrator's role more clearly. In the case of the Sánchez Navarro estates, members of the family owning the haciendas resided on the rural properties and directly administered them.

The Jesuit distinction between mayordomo and administrator was important: mayordomos had limited delegated authority, and administrators had significant delegated authority. Barrett's study and the case of Pedro de Villaverde at Santa Lucía suggest that the office of administrator was much more common in colonial Mexico than indicated by present studies.[6] By the latter part of the seventeenth century, many owners of the mayorazgos in central Mexico preferred the pleasures of urban life or were too busy attending to other civic and economic interests to spend much time on their rural haciendas. They required the services of someone with more authority than a mayordomo. The magnitude of the diverse holdings of individual families, furthermore, suggests that the owners needed professional managers to supervise the activities of mayordomos who coordinated the actual activities on the haciendas.

The hacienda administrator was very important for Santa Lucía and other Jesuit haciendas. The mayordomos were a secular element in the total administrative structure of the Jesuits who were bound, by the policies of their order, to concern themselves primarily with educational and mission matters. The hacienda administrator's office allowed the Jesuits to incorporate secular skills and experience without losing control over the spirituality of those directing secular matters. For the most part the administrators were *hermanos coadjutores,* although in the eighteenth century, especially on estates with large number of slaves, padres filled such roles.[7]

Having a corporate network of contacts and communications built around the men staffing college offices proved advantageous for the Jesuits in New Spain. The coadjutor in Veracruz reported regularly to Mexico City on the arrival of ships, the latest prices, the types and quantities of goods entering the port, and useful information about the activities of government officials.[8] Coadjutores in Puebla, León, Guadalajara, Querétaro, Oaxaca, Havana, Valladolid, and other centers reported regularly on local matters. If it was cheaper to buy equipment or textiles in Veracruz, they were bought in Veracruz. If buying in Veracruz, followed by shipment by mule train to Mexico City, helped to avoid paying the sales tax, this was done. The price and quality of the cacao consumed by the Jesuits at Santa Lucía,[9] or the axes used for trimming timber, depended upon the information that was regularly collected by the Mexico City procurador and the instructions issued on the basis of this information. The Jesuit administrators knew their prices and the state of the market, and they insisted on the best.

Administrators in the Formative Stage

A separate office of hacienda administrator emerged gradually at Santa Lucía. In the early years the Jesuits incorporated the mayordomo role, thanks to the services of two individuals with considerable New World experience in livestock and farming operations.

The first was Pedro Nieto, Tepeatzingo's pre-Jesuit mayordomo, who was retained as a paid employee until the 1583 incident resulting in his joining the order. Nieto (1548–1637) came from Asturias, where, in his early youth, he gained agricultural experience. At the age of nineteen he became a soldier and left for New Spain to seek his fortune. He took part in the 1566–1567 Florida expedition but quickly learned, as did the majority of youths of humble origin who came to the New World with great expectations, that fame and fortune were reserved for the few having necessary connections with expeditionary leaders or the crown. In New Spain he turned to the more secure and familiar occupation of working on rural estates. After becoming a *hermano coadjutor,* he returned to Santa Lucía to serve his order faithfully for twenty years in their livestock enterprises, after which he became a doorman at their College of San Ildefonso.[10]

Juan Turrado's contributions were in agriculture. He began working at Santa Lucía in 1583 and was in charge of establishing the *labor* of San Juan. The Jesuits claimed he was worth two well-paid workers, a man "of great skill in business," able to get along well with Indians whose "coarseness of behavior and laziness" resulted in many conflicts. He would arise before dawn and ride to Xoloc to collect workers for agricultural tasks. He lived according to the Jesuit rule although not a member, and ate the same food as the workers. He ate poorly. Help given in time of sickness, as surgeon for those suffering injuries, gained Turrado the respect and affection of the native labor force. The Jesuits claimed the Indians' esteem for him was so great that, during a shortage of male workers, women in the pueblo offered their services for agricultural tasks. After eighteen years of service he died, in 1601, at the age of eighty-four and was given the honor of deathbed admittance to the society and burial in the Colegio Máximo.[11]

Two others who had a great impact upon the rural estates were Juan Crox (1551–1614) and Marcos García (1552–1606).[12] Both joined the order in Spain, where they served in agricultural tasks as coadjutores before being sent to Mexico. García had been a vassal of a duke from Toledo before joining the Jesuits, after which he worked as caretaker of mules (*mozo de mulas*). He was sent to New Spain in 1576 and spent the next thirty years working for the Colegio Máximo and Colegio del Espíritu Santo at Puebla. He is credited with having founded two haciendas for the Colegio Máximo, probably Santa Lucía and San Juan, and two more for the Puebla college. García was the first Jesuit acting as an administrator, although the office was not formally recognized until the 1590s. He dressed poorly, ate badly, and slept many nights under ox carts. He rose two hours before dawn to do his spiritual exercises and never initiated any step without permission from superiors. His austerity and self-deprivation resulted in blindness, and he spent the last nine years of his life at the Puebla college.[13]

Juan Crox came from Valencia, where he joined the order in 1568 and worked fourteen years at the Jesuit college. After coming to New Spain (1582) he worked twenty years at Santa Lucía and other recently established haciendas. Like García, he impressed his superiors with his humble attire, virtue, and great efficiency in managing rural estates. His skill at curing the illnesses of Indian laborers earned him local respect and devotion. Like his colleague, he suffered from physical afflictions, in his case severe asthma. The number of years he was associated with the Colegio Máximo is not indicated. He probably worked longer at the Puebla college, where he spent his last year in serious illness.[14]

These four individuals played key roles in the formative years of Jesuit hacienda development in Mexico. Their prior agricultural experience in Spain was used to good effect on the Jesuit haciendas. The descriptions of their lives indicate that conditions on the rural estates were harsh, that the native labor force was subject to constant disease and poor food, but that they responded positively when concern for their personal welfare was shown by hacienda supervisors. The actual tasks performed by these individuals, described as the "most humble work of the field," also suggests that, by the late sixteenth century, the Indian pueblos were still adapting to Spanish food-crop and livestock production. Personal example, rather than instruction, was necessary for efficient rural production. The personal virtues of the early hacienda managers, if Jesuit reports can be relied upon, were beyond question.

The office of hacienda administrator was formalized during the period of Juan de Aldana and Juan de Alcázar.[15] They came to New Spain in 1585 while in the employ of the Marqués de Villamanrique. They were in their twenties and had experience with Spanish agriculture. Shortly after arriving in Mexico, they left their employer, who served as viceroy (1585–1590), to become Jesuit coadjutores. After serving in domestic tasks at the Colegio Máximo, they were placed in charge of running the new haciendas. As skilled agriculturalists, they became part of the bridge over which Old World agriculture was successfully transferred to Mexico.

Alcázar can be seen as a prototype of Santa Lucía's early administrators. He spent over twenty years working with the rural estates being created by the Colegio Máximo. In the words of his biographer, he "guarded zealously the temporal matters of the haciendas as if they were haciendas of Christ and his family."[16] His achievements were later described as follows:

Besides being an example for the farmers, he was also an authority for all the hacendados because of his great knowledge of agriculture. It was he who improved the plow and other farming equipment, he improved the storage granaries, he improved the organization of work methods in planting to the extent that he can be called the "father of agriculture" in our country.[17]

Alcázar initiated the preparation of a hacienda administrator's handbook in which he recorded information on local farming practices and outlined the types of seasonal variations affecting agriculture in Mexico.[18] Like García, he was content with the Indian diet of tortillas and tamales and was known to go to considerable lengths to ensure that the native labor force was supplied with sufficient maize. His twenty-three years as Santa Lucía's administrator were marked by greatly increased revenues and the consolidation of numerous properties into a highly efficient hacienda complex.

Aldana's technical knowledge of agriculture was not so scientific as that of Alcázar. During periods of drought he would supplement his prayers for rain with "cruel self-flagellations." His knowledge of herbal medicine was widely recognized and in demand by hacienda workers, Jesuits, and non-Jesuits. He kept a stock of roots and plants to effect cures and demonstrated religious concern for the African slaves employed on the haciendas, spending his evenings teaching them how to confess and to sing Christian songs. Aldana's usefulness in administering rural estates was widely recognized. Besides his work at Santa Lucía and the Colegio Máximo (1590–1595), he worked for thirty years for Jesuit colleges at Puebla, Oaxaca, Guadalajara, Valladolid, Guatemala, and Nicaragua.[19]

As hacienda administration became more routine and formal, greater powers were granted to the brethren filling these roles. Bartolomé Santos, for one, started as a Santa Lucía administrator in the 1580s.[20] By 1595 he had been promoted to procurador with powers to make purchases, receive possessions, and handle the legal affairs of the hacienda. Santos' recognized technical skills were also drafted into the service of the viceroy in 1607, to assist in planning the canal of the Valley of Mexico. At this time Santos was administering Santa Lucía, whose Tepeatzingo properties bordering the lake were subject to floods. A solution for Mexico City's problem with floods therefore also served Jesuit purposes.[21]

Cristóbal Cerezo was one of the early hacienda administrators who was granted sweeping powers. He served both as hacienda manager and, at least till 1630, as procurador of the Colegio Máximo. It is not clear whether he moved from the office on the hacienda to the college business office, or whether he temporarily took over the college office responsibilities for the purpose of transacting the legal steps in property transactions.[22] The earlier case of Santos and the later case of Juan Nicolás indicate that the rector and provincial moved their more capable administrators from one office to the other, delegating to them whatever powers were required to further the economic welfare of the college.[23]

The Role of the Hermano Coadjutor

Table 3 identifies the individuals who managed Santa Lucía's affairs while it was a Jesuit hacienda. The first column includes the hacienda administrators and their assistants who lived at the main residence of the estate. The third column identifies the college procuradores and their assistants who managed the college business offices that were centrally concerned with Santa Lucía. They occasionally visited the hacienda and its anexas but resided in Mexico City. Both offices were, for the most part, filled by laymen rather than priests. The length of the terms of office of the hacienda administrators, in comparison with the length of terms served by provincials and rectors, suggests that the administration of the province and the Colegio Máximo was routinized to the extent that good administrators could take over for short periods of time, whereas taking over the management of haciendas required special qualities. Good administrators of the estates were left in their jobs for long periods.* The formal religious training of the coadjutores who became business managers consisted of a two-year term at the Tepotzotlán novice training center before taking on their more secular occupations. This period, depending upon the progress of

---

*The average length of term in office for provincials was 2.8 years, covering the period between 1572 and 1767. For rectors the term was apparently the same, although the sample here is not complete. Alegre, vols.1–4; DBCJM, vols. 1–10; MM, vols. 1–5. Santa Lucía administrators averaged 13 years of service, while college procuradores for whom starting and terminating dates could be determined averaged slightly over 14 years of service. Not included in these calculations are those men in office at the time of the Jesuit expulsion.

TABLE 3

Santa Lucía Administrators, 1576–1767

Hacienda office[a]	Term	Colegio Máximo office	Term
Pedro Nieto[b]	1576–1583	H Bartolomé Larias	1572–1583
H Marcos García	1576–158?	H Juan de Salcedo	1578–1583
H Juan Crox	1582–?	H Alonso Pérez	1578–1585
Juan Turrado[b]	1583–1601	H Andrés Juan	1579–1589
		H Cristóbal Pérez	1581–1627
H Pedro Nieto*	1584–1608	H Martín González	1585–1600
H Bartolomé Santos	1585–1610	H Juan López de Arbaisa	1588–1597
H Juan de Aldana	1590–1595	H Bartolomé Santos	1595–?
H Gregorio Montes	1596–?	H Francisco Juárez	1605–1627
H Juan de Alcázar	1601–1623	P Pedro de Cabrera	1607–?
		H Francisco de las Casas	1615–?
		H Gabriel de Tapia	1616–?
		H Hernando de la Cruz	1617–1620
H Esteban Gómez	1620–1626	H Toribio Gómez	1621–1639
H Cristóbal Cerezo	1626–1653	H Cristóbal Cerezo	1626–163?
		H Alonso de Rojas	1640s
H Gaspar de Silva	1654–1674	H Luis de Peña	1640s
H Jorge Fernández*	1650s–?	H Luis Sánchez	1660s
		H Alonso Alvarado	1660s
		P Bartolomé Cuellar	1667–1671
		H Toribio Gutiérrez	1667
H Diego Lozano	1675–1677	? Juan Vallejo	1670s
H Diego de Río Frío	1678–1684	? Antonio de Mendaria	1670s
		H Fabián Ruiz	1677–1680
H Bartolomé González	1684–1722	H Miguel de Novas	1680–1685
		P Bernabé Gutiérrez	1680–1681
H Antonio López*	1692–?	H Juan Nicolás	1686–1723
		H Sebastián Vázquez	1687–1712
H Joseph García*	1704–1722	H Justica Nicolás	1707–?
H Lázaro Pérez*	1720s	H Ignacio Núñez	1707–1716
H Pablo de Araujo*	1712–1726	H Joaquín Donazar	1718–1740
H Joseph García	1722–1726	H Jorge Tellado	1719–?
H Diego de Arias*	1723–1737	H Pedro de Beristáin	1723–1740
H Pablo de Araujo	1726–1743	H Martín Amazorráin	1730–1735
H Thadeo Joseph Rosales*	1743–1745	H Francisco Antonio de Yarza	1730–1740
P Bernardo Tomás de Miers	1743–1746	P Miguel Quijano	1740–1755
		P Diego Verdugo	1740s
H Miguel de San Martín*	1746–1747	H Ignacio Gradilla	1742–1764
P Joaquín de Padilla	1746–1751	H Martín de Montejano	1742–1767
H Joseph Pamplona*	1747–1748	H Miguel de San Martín	1744–1747
Pedro Villaverde[b]	1751–1764	H Santiago Viug	1745–1751
H Francisco Acosta*	1752–1758	P Juan Francisco López	1757–?
P Miguel Fernández*	1752–1754	H Francisco Xavier de Yarza	1760s
P Ignacio Inviar*	1756		

TABLE 3 *(continued)*

Hacienda office[a]	Term	Colegio Máximo office	Term
P Salvador Bustamente*	1758–1759		
P Joseph Rincón*	1760–1762		
H Miguel Sabel	1764		
P Xavier Rivera*	1764–1765		
H Santiago Coronel	1764–1766		
P Manuel Peralta	1765–1767		

NOTE: Although the Jesuits clearly distinguished between the status of hermano and padre, the general public apparently did not. All workers and the mayordomos on the haciendas usually referred to hermanos as padres, as did secular business contacts and the crown documents concerning disputes or property titles. Thus, much of the documentation refers to padres when the individuals in question were actually hermanos coadjutores.
[a]H = hermano coadjutor; P = padre; * = assistant to the administrator.
[b]Not members of the Jesuit order.

the individual, was frequently reduced to one year during the seventeenth and eighteenth centuries. These laymen did not take the fourth vow of obedience to the pope. In contrast, the training of a priest, who completed his four vows, might last fifteen years.[24]

Any study of the economic activities of the Jesuits in Mexico must focus upon the laymen who managed the temporal business of the order. Who were they, where did they come from, and how did they function in the expansion of Jesuit involvement in the economic life of Mexico? An overall sketch aimed at answering these questions will be presented before taking a closer look at individuals who directed the destiny of Santa Lucía.

An analysis of biographical data for sixty-six coadjutores in Mexico between 1572 and the 1650s shows that the majority (66 percent) came from Spain as youths to seek their fortunes in New Spain.[25] Whether they failed to fulfill their expectations in the secular world, or were attracted to the prestige of the Jesuits, is unclear. What is known is that 80 percent joined the society while in their twenties or older and then served the rest of their lives in a secular capacity. Roughly 50 percent worked on rural estates, primarily in agriculture, while those in the cities served as carpenters, masons, tailors, shoemakers, launderers, bakers, cooks, nurses (*enfermeros*), custodians, purchasers, attorneys, administrators, and occasionally teachers (*doctrineros*) or sacristans. Most of these laymen served the order faithfully until death. Thirty percent served for 50 years or longer. The average length of service was 28.6 years, a figure that includes the roughly 20 percent who had to be dismissed from the society by order of the father general for failing to live according to the rule.[26] The Colegio Máximo had a larger proportion of the coadjutores working for it than any other college. In the sample mentioned, 62.5 percent spent at least a short period working there, and of these, 75 percent worked in some capacity with rural estates. In 1581 there were thirty-four coadjutores in Mexico, and fifteen were working for the central college. This was when large-scale construction was going on. During the 1620s, between fifteen and twenty-two coadjutores were with the college, and these numbers remained relatively stable until the Jesuit expulsion.[27]

The popularity of the Jesuits during the first half of the seventeenth century is reflected by the number of laymen who joined the order. This caused concern in the office of the father general, who issued a constant stream of instructions aimed at controlling activities that might give the society the appearance of becoming secular. It was during this period that a special book of instruction concerning coadjutores was started. Among the instructions sent to provincials and rectors were reminders not to accept anyone under the age of eighteen from New Spain, or persons of illegitimate birth. Permission to learn to read and write was restricted to special cases, and only under special circumstances were hacienda administrators to be given permission to buy and sell hacienda products or goods without prior authorization.[28]

In the 1640s, Palafox charged that the large numbers of coadjutores in the society were a bad influence. He claimed they never took solemn vows, remained in secular clothes, and were free to leave at any time, even to marry when they left.[29] Critics within the society, such as Father Juan de Mariana, echoed such views. Mariana complained to the father general that the coadjutores were lowering the standards and reputation of the order. Among reasons listed by Mariana for the deteriorating economic situation were the following relating to the laymen:

1. They spent too much money on expensive clothes, paper, books, and maintenance.

2. They were too numerous, since they had to be fully supported, and they insisted on traveling like "the sons of counts."

3. They were not coordinated in their administration of temporal goods, since one would build while the other would tear down, one would plant and the other would uproot.

4. They had too much control over the ordinary finances and failed to observe proper bookkeeping procedures.

5. They became involved in countless disputes which cost the order up to 50,000 ducados per year.[30]

One of the by-products of these complaints was a general tightening of administrative procedures and the implementation of policies that decreased the number of coadjutores in Mexico. By the time the Jesuits were evicted from Mexico in 1767, only 148 of the 678 members were coadjutores, a reduction from 42.4 percent of the total membership in the mid-seventeenth century to 21.8 percent in the mid-eighteenth century. The composition of membership had also changed during the years. Before the mid-seventeenth century, only 14.3 percent of the coadjutores had been born in New Spain. By 1767, 43.2 percent were from New Spain, 30 percent from Spain, and the rest from other parts of Europe or other areas within the Spanish empire.[31]

Biographical information about Santa Lucía's administrators before the eighteenth century is limited largely to materials written by the Jesuits. The panegyric nature of these materials makes it difficult to reconstruct an objective picture. For the last decades of Jesuit residence in Mexico, however, correspondence and other hacienda records allow a more candid view.

Available records do indicate that the college administrators listed in Table 3 were highly skilled. The men filling the office of procurador in Mexico City during the early years were builders. Bartolomé Larias was skilled in architecture and construction and served as building master for the college. He appears to have drawn up the plans for the main residence of Santa Lucía.[32] Juan López de Arbaisa was another master builder who probably supervised construction when he was in charge of the Colegio Máximo building program after 1585. His skills were widely recognized, and he was called upon by the viceroy in 1607 to divert threatening floodwaters by means of drainage canals.[33] Some procuradores were entrusted with other important responsibilities. Juan de Salcedo made at least two trips to Madrid on behalf of the economic interests of the Jesuits in Mexico and appeared personally before the Royal Council of the Indies.[34] Martín González got the viceroy to permit Santa Lucía's flocks access to crown lands and also traveled to Rome on an unspecified mission.[35] Alonso Pérez was the officially appointed economic spokesman for the Jesuits during their first years in Mexico. His close associations with Alonso de Villaseca enabled the Jesuits to gain valuable insights into the economics of New Spain.[36] Andrés Juan set up records to keep track of property titles in 1583.[37] The procuradores moved from Mexico City to other centers, according to where their services were most urgently required. Their activities were not restricted to the college or Santa Lucía, but were directed to the general welfare of the order as a whole.

Change and Stability in the Seventeenth Century

Hacienda administration entered a long period of stability after the beginning of the seventeenth century. This was facilitated by having administrators spend lengthy terms at Santa Lucía. For the most part the men on the haciendas concerned themselves with ranching and farming, while the college procuradores handled purchases, sales, and legal contracts. As business managers for the Colegio Máximo, their activities transcended the concerns of Santa Lucía, encompassing all the rural estates of the college. Pedro de Cabrera, Francisco de las Casas, Hernando de la Cruz, and Gabriel de Tapia fit into this category.[38] Others, such as Francisco Juárez, Toribio Gómez, Alonso de Rojas, and Bartolomé Cuellar were concerned with even broader issues since they also served as procuradores of the entire Jesuit province, handling cases arising from the hacienda that could not be solved at lower levels of authority.[39]

These men had had diverse backgrounds. Juárez, for example, had been a merchant specializing in trade with the Philippines before joining the order in 1599. His first assignment as a coadjutor was that of cook; from this he moved to *procurador general de la provincia* (1605) and later spent over twenty years as procurador of the Colegio Máximo (1606–1627).[40] Cuellar, one of the few priests who held such offices, had worked as a missionary in the north (1648, 1655–1659) and Oaxaca (1661–1667); he was then procurador at the Colegio Máximo (1667–1671) and later procurador for the province (1671–1677), after which he served as rector in Zacatecas and Puebla.[41]

The high rate of turnover, in terms of length of office and type of individual occupying the office in the Colegio Máximo's business administration, contributed to the college's increasing debts between 1620 and the 1680s. It was only after the emergence of a single, dominant individual over a long period that the drift of the college's financial ship was arrested and it was brought back on a course that pleased the higher Jesuit superiors.[42] This individual was Juan Nicolás, in whose term college finances took a definite turn for the better.

Santa Lucía operations, in contrast, had achieved administrative stability at the beginning of the seventeenth century. This stability was reflected in the steady profits produced by the hacienda. During Gaspar de Silva's term (1654–1674), despite the fluctuations caused by factors largely outside his control and having to come to terms with paying tithes, annual profits averaged roughly 19,000 pesos. Silva exercised a great deal of authority. He personally handled the disputes with neighboring pueblos and played the key role in transacting the Altica purchase.[43] Much of the buying and selling, normally done by the procurador, were done by him. Accounts in his possession at the time of his death indicate he had business dealings with a wide range of buyers of Santa Lucía products. Authority delegated to Silva included handling legal issues involving audiencia officials, sales, purchases of hacienda produce, and hacienda relations with the secular clergy.[44]

For the next decade, Diego Lozano and Diego de Río Frío were in command and significantly increased the hacienda's production of cattle, goats, horses, and mules. Records detailing monthly income and expenses handled by the administrator between January 1679 and March 1681 show that he paid out 73,575 pesos, 6 reales, and took in 69,785 pesos, 3 reales. These figures do not represent total income, as the profits from 1679–1680 totaled 39,267 pesos. The discrepancy between the total funds received by the administrator and the profits reported for the hacienda is explained by the fact that the college business office took in most of the funds derived from sales of agricultural products, livestock, and wool. Average monthly expenditures on the hacienda, during the twenty-seven-month period, were 2,725 pesos.[45]

Model Administrators

With the emergence of Juan Nicolás as college procurador in 1686, the productivity which had become characteristic of the hacienda began to be felt in the college. Bartolomé González was now the hacienda administrator. With his friend Juan Nicolás also in office—they had served their novitiate together—both the college and the hacienda were under the supervision of competent, dedicated laymen. They established a record of longevity in office that was not surpassed during the history of the hacienda and the college. Nicolás was later praised by his fellow Jesuits as having been the perfect example of pious devotion matched to business efficiency. They collected a series of statements honoring Nicolás after his death entitled "In Praise of a Dead Administrator."[46] Such statements, expressing as they did the sentiments of his friends and associates of long standing, need to be examined in the light of his administrative record.

This record was most impressive, showing Nicolás to have been a pragmatic, cautious, and realistic businessman. He reorganized the policies of the temporal affairs office and greatly reduced the college debts which had been accumulating under his predecessors during the previous half-century. When Juan Nicolás entered the order, the Colegio Máximo's debts amounted to over 468,000 pesos. At the time of his death, some forty years later, those debts had been reduced by more than half,[47] and in the meantime the rural estates of the college, including Santa Lucía, had been substantially increased (see Appendix A).

Nicolás's first job at the college had been to take care of the store and warehouse for the sugar produced by the ingenios. Here he demonstrated a special ability to deal with demanding merchants, and his supervisors placed him in charge of all the college's estates in 1686. Shortly after taking over the procurador's office, Nicolás began to bring order into the record-keeping system, which had fallen into disarray. The many papers the college had been collecting over the past hundred years—copies of titles, cédulas, court cases, privileges, and so on—were deteriorating. Titles dating back to the 1540s were no longer legible, so Nicolás asked and received permission from crown authorities to have new, notarized copies made of the originals.[48] Prior to Nicolás's term in office, the record-keeping procedures and storage of documents relating to temporal affairs were subject to the preferences of the numerous individuals holding the office of procurador. After Nicolás's term, the documentation followed very closely the procedures outlined in the Instrucciones, suggesting that perhaps Juan Nicolás was the author of that document.[49]

During Nicolás's term, most of Santa Lucía's business was directed by González, but the procurador did make frequent trips to the hacienda. His schedule seldom varied. He always got up very early for personal prayers, then heard mass, had breakfast, and mounted his horse to visit the various hacienda operations, ill health and inclement weather notwithstanding. Nicolás's relations with mayordomos, hacienda laborers, slaves, and administrators were excellent. They looked forward to his visits, partly because of his reputation for being able to solve difficult problems. He responded with equal serenity to news of disputes, livestock disaster, or good news, stating only, "As God wills, by whose reckoning we operate." González made these comments, adding that Nicolás had always been punctual in sending supplies and operating funds to the hacienda, thereby allowing the estate to prosper. During the last year of Nicolás's term, he personally took over the management of the college sugar estate which had been attacked and burnt by hostile neighbors. At intervals he also functioned as *procurador de la provincia*.[50]

Relations between Santa Lucía and the college were harmonious, as González and the procurador complemented each other in skill and efficiency. Under González's guidance the hacienda prospered, although the latter part of his term was marked by numerous disputes with neighboring pueblos. González personally handled many of the legal details during such confrontations. In 1684 his official title was *administrador general* of Santa Lucía. In 1714 he gained the additional status of *procurador general* of the hacienda and its anexas.[51] He was assisted by a number of coadjutores, one of whom, Joseph García, took over as administrator when González's lengthy tenure in office terminated. García had spent eighteen years assisting González, so when he took over in 1722 he was completely familiar with the responsibilities of the job. This sort of apprenticeship appears to have been the norm in Santa Lucía management.

The Immodest Administrator

If the administration of González and Nicolás represented cautious but sound management, that of their successors (Joseph García and Pablo de Araujo at Santa Lucía and Joaquín Donazar at the college offices) was much more daring. Joaquín Donazar, after serving as vice-procurador for five years, took over in 1723. He was contentious, abrasive, secular, and entrepreneurial, much to the dismay of some of his superiors. During his term, Santa Lucía entered its greatest era of territorial expansion. Donazar bought and sold properties with reckless abandon in comparison to the other Jesuits. He supervised the purchase of a large portion of the Actopan Valley, attempted to create a self-sufficient hacienda out of Provincia in the Guadalajara-Colima jurisdictions, and sold the goat ranch in the Tehuacán Valley.[52] Donazar involved the Jesuits in serious conflicts with neighboring pueblos and earned the distrust and suspicion of secular ecclesiastical as well as crown officials. Eventually he was excommunicated by the archbishop of Mexico and ended his career on a dismal note when, by order of the father general, he was dismissed from the order in 1740.

Donazar's life-style was more in keeping with that of his secular contemporaries than with that of his predecessor. When he traveled from Mexico City to Santa Lucía he went by carriage and complained about the roughness of the roads.[53] Once at the hacienda he switched to horseback for his rounds of hacienda activities. He disliked all the letter-writing and record-keeping required during his forced exile on Santa Lucía and the anexas. His requests for cigars, wine, beer, and news of political consequence—for example, whether Havana had anything new to report about an incoming viceroy—indicate indulgence in personal comforts. This contrasted sharply with Brother Nicolás, who had hardly allowed himself his ration of chocolate in the mornings. Donazar did keep up a steady stream of correspondence with fellow coadjutores in Valladolid, Veracruz, and Mexico City. He sought to have them intercede on his behalf with his superiors, the audiencia, and the secular clergy, so that he could return to Mexico City. Donazar considered the censure imposed upon him to be "ridiculous" and the church officials who initiated it "ignorant doctors." He admitted ignoring the ecclesiastical orders that he refrain from engaging in public commerce, and continued "selling and buying behind the curtain."[54] One of his business ventures involved supplying secular friends in Mexico City with suitable young, female domestic slaves from the haciendas. Although he followed the Jesuit rule in terms of confessions and annual spiritual exercises, Donazar was very much a man of the secular world.[55]

And it was Donazar's lack of public display of somber humility that contrasted so sharply with the demeanor of his predecessor, Juan Nicolás. The one was expelled from the order the other idealized. Nicolás was credited with the saintliness associated with hermanos of the late sixteenth and early seventeenth centuries; Donazar was associated with the worldliness the Society of Jesus fought to keep at a distance. But the real difference between the two was more of form than content. During his long administration, Nicolás engaged in many of the same activities held against Donazar, such as large-scale expansion of rural estates, becoming involved in contentious litigation, and engaging in questionable business practices. Nicolás had more problems with neighboring pueblos than did Donazar, including physical attacks. Nicolás attempted to buy the office of alcalde mayor at Malinalco and Tetepango by providing funds for friends seeking the office. The last two decades of his term of office were anything but peaceful.[56] In any case, the acts of both men were based on the consent of supervisors. "Nothing has been done without the direction of the supervisors and the advice of prudent, practical, and experienced men," was Donazar's summation of his own administration.[57] Nicolás could have made the same statement. The difference between the individuals was in personal style: Nicolás was somber, Donazar flamboyant. As administrators, they did their job as they thought best for the college and the haciendas. Donazar managed to attract the opposition of the secular clergy and important members of the local aristocracy, and the result was an embarrassing public quarrel with repercussions in Madrid and Rome. Nicolás attracted the opposition of lesser officials and native pueblos, matters which were handled within Mexico or quietly within the courts, without public scandal. Within the Jesuit administrative system there was a tolerance for problems and difficult solutions, provided that solemn decorum was preserved, but there was no room for damage to the public image of the order.

The Restructuring Administrators

The significant structural changes taking place in Santa Lucía during the 1720s and 1730s were largely implemented by Pablo de Araujo, assisted by Diego de Arias. It was Araujo who integrated the new purchases into the overall operation of the hacienda. He supervised the beginning of a new goat-raising rancho centered at Tepenene and established a second center for cattle production at Chicavasco. After the main Xoloc flocks were sent to the Provincia pastures, he started a new sheep-raising center at San Pablo and San Ignacio. A new maize-production area called Atlantepec was opened on lands pertaining to San Xavier. In addition, a large-scale building program was started at Chicavasco, which became a new center for fattening and slaughtering livestock of all types. Despite such accomplishments, Araujo's term (1726–1743) was more important in the history of the hacienda as the beginning of large-scale pulque production.* Araujo was well equipped to run the hacienda, having spent a fourteen-year apprenticeship as assistant before taking over as administrator.

Araujo's many projects left him little time to spend at the main residence of Santa Lucía. He was constantly engaged in what Donazar referred to as "making the rounds" (*hacer correrías*). Throughout his lengthy residence at Santa Lucía in 1737, Donazar

---

*Annual income increased tenfold, from 500 pesos to almost 6,000 pesos, by 1742; PCRVP 1: 522v–524v.

made numerous requests for supplies and operating funds on Araujo's behalf. A noteworthy deviation from normal requests was one for beer, because Araujo was constantly nagging for it (*"me mata para cerveza"*), to which Donazar added that it had a salutary effect on the administrator.[58] Araujo either did not have the time or did not see the necessity for maintaining the rigorous bookkeeping practices required by the Instrucciones. His successor was to complain about a lack of receipts and orderly accounts.[59] Araujo was well liked by hacienda workers and mayordomos, some of whom took advantage of his good nature and lack of record-keeping rigor to divert large amounts of hacienda produce from normal channels and pocket the profits. Araujo died in office, and his assistant, Thadeo Rosales, filled in as acting administrator from June 1 to July 20, 1743, when his successor was appointed.

Bernardo Tomás de Miers, who took over from Rosales, was the first of a number of priests rather than brothers who became associated with Santa Lucía administration during this period. The naming of priests to hacienda posts was not new for the Colegio Máximo itself. As of the late seventeenth century, they occasionally occupied the position of procurador, and on the cash-crop haciendas (Chicomocelo, Cuautepec, Chalco, and Xalmolonga), which employed large numbers of African slaves, they served regularly as of the early eighteenth century.[60] Their function on the cash-crop estates was directly related to the attempt to select more highly trained individuals to deal with complex relations with neighbors and to handle the religious dimension of master-slave relations. The increasing prominence of the padres in the eighteenth century may also be seen as an indication of absorption of secular influences by the order itself. With the increased expansion of territorial domain, more administrators were required, but now there were not enough hermanos coadjutores to fill these positions. To what degree this shift in use of Jesuit personnel can be attributed to practical necessity or a waning of spiritual zeal is a question warranting further study. It is clear that direct involvement increased, and at Santa Lucía, starting with Miers, there was usually at least one padre involved.

When Miers took over in 1743, he immediately set out to reestablish bookkeeping order and to plug the many holes through which the hacienda's profits were being siphoned off. The most notable culprit was Nicolás López Lascano, the manager of Santa Lucía's pulque production since 1727. Lascano and his relatives, according to Miers's calculations, had defrauded the hacienda of 100,000 pesos over seventeen years.[61] He discovered that mayordomos and renters were robbing the college at every opportunity. Mayordomos were collecting rents and not reporting them. Renters were pasturing far more livestock and planting more maize and barley than their rental agreements called for. Rather than protecting hacienda boundaries, they were aiding nonrenters in gaining access to hacienda lands, thus robbing Santa Lucía flocks of needed pastures. Or they were stealing and selling the livestock in collusion with shepherds and mayordomos. At Ocuila, for example, six *sitios de ganado mayor* and seven caballerías of land were being used by at least 300 people, although only 106 were paying rent. Other people were denuding the forests, stealing sheep, and engaging in private business with the shepherds and pasture guards. And, to make matters worse, the paltry 412 pesos collected as rent was being spent by the mayordomos on trinkets (*pitas y flautas*). Miers detailed similar conditions at San Ignacio, San Pablo, and Xante.[62]

During his three years as administrator, Miers asserted tight control over all aspects of hacienda activities. Special emphasis was placed on increasing the maguey plantings for pulque production. The harvesting of the sweet sap of the maguey (*aquamiel*) was let out to a trustworthy individual, Don Manuel de Orruño. Miers did not interfere with the production of pulque, but he did keep a close watch over Orruño's activities. He was satisfied when, at the end of his term, this aspect of hacienda activity was returning 18,500 pesos annually.[63] As long as the pulque manager produced this income, the hacienda administrator left him to his own devices. The projects started by Araujo in the Actopan Valley estates were pursued with diligence.

Relations with the labor force of Santa Lucía were much harsher under Miers than they had been under Araujo. During the three years, the number of slave desertions from Santa Lucía increased, and slaves considered troublesome were sold.* Miers believed in treating Indians harshly, instructing his mayordomos to give "seven good lashes" to any individual who cut leaves from freshly planted maguey plants, to fine ox keepers two reales for every plant damaged by the oxen, and to prevent resident laborers from having any business contact or communication with neighboring pueblos. Pasture guards were specifically forbidden to visit pueblos or other ranchos, or to become involved in godparent relation-

---

*BNM 1058, 1. When Miers started his term, Santa Lucía had 284 slaves. Three years later this number had been reduced by 64: 26 slaves had fled, 23 had been sold, and 15 had died.

ships with people from them.[64] Miers left his post in 1746, when the provincial instructed him to do so. The impact of his reforms was temporary rather than long-term. Under Joaquín de Padilla, his successor, the hacienda again became more strongly influenced by policies uncharacteristic of the Jesuit sense of order.

The administrations of García, Araujo, Miers, and Padilla represented a period where non-Jesuit influences were strengthened. The type of control and influence exercised by González and Nicolás was never reestablished. Donazar's more secular approach to business and his administration can be seen as a basic turning point in Santa Lucía's relations with the secular world. Neither Donazar nor any of his successors in the procurador's office managed to dominate the affairs of Santa Lucía. Perhaps the hacienda's operations had become so extensive that this was not possible. Francisco Antonio de Yarza took over most of the policy-making decisions when Donazar was forced into his involuntary exile on the estates. The rest of the procuradores to follow, Miguel Quijano, Ignacio Gradilla, and Miguel de San Martín, attempted to reassert control over Santa Lucía's, affairs, but this became visible only during the final three years before the Jesuit expulsion.

Padilla's term (1746–1751) can be seen as a period in which secular influences took precedence over Jesuit influences. Although he had been delegated almost complete authority over all business and legal affairs, he turned more direct management control into the hands of non-Jesuits. Besides the pulque production, other parts of the hacienda were now being rented out for fixed incomes. San Juan, along with 120 oxen and its equipment, was rented to a Bachiller Don Fulgencio Vega y Vica for 500 pesos per annum.[65] Part of Pintas was rented to a Bachiller Julián González for 150 pesos a year.[66] This still left Padilla with a very large, complex hacienda to administer. His major areas of interest were the recently acquired anexas in the north. San Xavier, Chicavasco, and San Pablo began to become more dominant as centers of administrative direction. In August 1751, Padilla was asked to turn administrative control over to the procurador, Ignacio Gradilla. A decision had been made to place Santa Lucía under the administrative control of Don Pedro Villaverde.

The Secular Administrator

Villaverde's takeover represented the culmination of tendencies evident for the last two decades. The negative publicity resulting from the dispute over the tithe convinced the Jesuits to withdraw from direct involvement in hacienda management. The sheer size of the operation, coupled with the decline of available coadjutores to manage temporal affairs, suggested attempting something new. Hiring a proven secular manager would lessen direct involvement while revenues would continue. Renting or subletting businesses for fixed annual returns was, after all, a common practice among secular and ecclesiastical hacendados. In order to ensure a Jesuit presence on the hacienda, however, four different padres were assigned to Santa Lucía during Villaverde's tenure (see Table 3).

Villaverde was chosen by Gradilla. The circumstances of the appointment provide further evidence of the growing impact of secular business practices. Don Pedro's contacts with Santa Lucía were of long standing. He owned two haciendas in the Actopan Valley and at times used Santa Lucía pastures for his livestock. In 1746 Miers passed on a request to his superiors, from Villaverde, to allow his brood mares to use the hacienda's pasture. Miers recommended acceptance on the condition that Don Pedro's cowboys maintain strict vigilance over the animals. He had just intervened with one of Santa Lucía's pasture guards who was about to drive Villaverde's horses to the Pachuca impoundment corrals, thereby saving the owner a 500 peso fine.[67]

Such lenient treatment by Miers, normally a rigorous custodian of Jesuit rights and privileges, was due to Villaverde's connections with superiors. Don Pedro was a close friend of Gradilla, who was a godparent (*padrino*) of at least one of his sons. The frequent personal notes in Don Pedro's business correspondence with Gradilla and other procuradores during his term confirm that his interaction with the Jesuits was more than purely a business relationship. Gradilla was procurador during all of Villaverde's term. A nephew of his, Don Bernardo Tamariz y Gradilla, later became involved in the business affairs of Santa Lucía. Although the Instrucciones clearly discouraged any commercial dealings with relatives of the order, here was a clear case of involvement of kinsmen.[68] Dependence upon kinsmen to fill offices of trust was very much a feature of colonial Spanish society. The policies of Gradilla and the involvement of Villaverde underscore the degree to which secular influences were taking hold in the style of Jesuit operations.[69]

Villaverde started working for the Jesuits with nothing more than an oral agreement between himself and Gradilla. During his first six months he was referred to as acting administrator (*suplente*), after which time the college administrators agreed to give him full responsibility along with the title of *administrador general*. Both parties agreed that his salary would consist of one-half the annual profits above 30,000 pesos. In addition, he would be responsible for supervising the pulque operations, from which the college expected to receive 20,100 pesos per year. At the end of every third year there would be a general audit to determine income and profits. If production fell below the expected levels and profits were less than the agreed-upon sums, and if it could be demonstrated that external factors (disease, drought) were to blame, Don Pedro would not be responsible for making up deficits. However, if production sagged as a result of his administration, he remained accountable for the full 50,100 pesos. Strange as it may seem, in view of established policies of documenting all business contracts, no formal agreement was drawn up until 1759. At this time Gradilla and Villaverde signed a formal agreement stipulating procedures which had been in effect during the last eight years. In 1762 this formal agreement was reaffirmed with additional clauses providing that, after his term, Villaverde and the Jesuits would come to an agreement on the increased value of the hacienda, of which Don Pedro was to receive a one-half share.[70]

Don Pedro and his family moved into the Santa Lucía residence after his trial period. For the first time in the hacienda's history it had a resident mistress, Doña Francisca Xaviera, and children to contend with.[71] In the past, mayordomos had lived at Santa Lucía with their wives and families, but never as masters of the residence itself. This undoubtedly influenced hacienda living patterns and brought additional secular influences to bear on the residence that had previously been more protected against outside contacts. One notable change in the hacienda inventory after Villaverde's departure in 1764 was the existence of a "viceroy's room," indicating that the viceroy stayed at Santa Lucía on occasion.[72]

Under Villaverde the system of management did not change noticeably. The college procuradores continued to transact negotiations for purchases and sales. Record-keeping procedures remained as they had been, and Villaverde dutifully reported all actual and potential conflicts with neighbors or government officials. Don Pedro kept Orruño as manager of the pulque operations. He spent many days away from the main residence supervising the activities on the anexas and continued a voluminous correspondence with the college administrators. With Gradilla as procurador, the business transactions between hacienda administrator and college procurador remained largely confined to friends and confidants.[73]

Gradually, as Don Pedro became more familiar with all the in-
tricacies of Santa Lucía activities, his personal influence increased.
He took over more responsibilities and made many of the decisions
regarding production and sale of hacienda produce. But he never
had delegated to him the type of sweeping powers the college superiors had vested in their own administrators such as Padilla. Decisions concerning policy were still being made by the college.

The extant correspondence of Villaverde provides a useful for-
mat for analyzing how the Santa Lucía administrator functioned.[74]
The detail, volume, and regularity of this correspondence suggest
that policies previously established were adhered to. The Jesuit
system of communication between college administrators, hacienda administrator, and mayordomos did not change with the introduction of a secular administrator. During 1754, for example, Villaverde wrote at least eighty letters to Gradilla. An almost equal
number were sent to Martín de Montejano, the assistant procurador in charge of sales and purchases for Santa Lucía. This meant an
average of three letters per week from the hacienda administrator.
Since all correspondence was promptly answered, an equal number of letters were coming to Santa Lucía from Mexico City each
week with comments, instructions, and advice. Don Pedro also
received regular reports from his mayordomos. Pedro Rosales, the
mayordomo of San Xavier, sent Villaverde fifty-seven items of correspondence during the six months between February and July.
Other reports, although not so frequent, came from mayordomos
at Chicavasco, Florida, and San Pablo. The contents of the mayordomos' reports were included in Villaverde's reports to the college
officials. In addition, Villaverde kept close contact with Thadeo
Rosales, who was now administrator of another Colegio Máximo
hacienda in the Chalco jurisdiction,[75] and with the activities at
Jesús del Monte. He also corresponded with the tithe collector
from Texcoco, businessmen from Pachuca, Puebla, and Actopan,
and representatives of a Franciscan college in Mexico City called
San Fernando.

Since each of Villaverde's letters has both date and location of origin, it is possible to reconstruct the administrator's movements
throughout the year. In 1754 he wrote most of his letters from Santa
Lucía itself but was making frequent trips to his own hacienda near
Tetepango. Anexas of Santa Lucía most frequently visited were
Chicavasco, San Pablo, and San Xavier. From October to December,
most of his letters were being written from San Pablo and Chicavasco. By 1757 his trips to his own estates were less frequent, and

the next year he was delegating much of the local administrative supervision to his sons while he traveled to Provincia.[76]

In the early years of his administration, Don Pedro's efforts pleased the Jesuits. After the first three-year audit, profits from Santa Lucía stood at 95,978 pesos, 2 reales, apart from the pulque income. The second accounting, in 1757, showed 90,003 pesos, 6 reales, profit from livestock and agricultural production in addition to pulque returns. In the rest of his term, however, profits decreased: during the 1757–1760 period, annual profits averaged 24,840 pesos, 3 reales, while in the 1760–1763 period they dropped to 18,817 pesos, 5 reales. College officials became very concerned about falling revenues, since livestock numbers and agricultural harvests had been increasing.[77]

The Jesuits Reestablish Administrative Control

As this trend appeared to be continuing, the Jesuit superiors decided to take action. In 1764 the provincial abruptly instructed Don Pedro to hand over his administration to the college procurador. At the same time, Gradilla was transferred to another job. Gradilla protested privately to the provincial about the manner in which Villaverde was being dismissed. He reminded his superior of an understanding with Don Pedro that, if and when the Jesuits felt dissatisfied with their administrator, they would let him know privately, allowing him to terminate his employment "with decorum, not with dishonor as was now the case."[78]

Don Pedro joined the protest to the provincial, stating that the declining rates of income from Santa Lucía could not be blamed on his administration, and that a depressed market value for pulque was at fault. Revenues from pulque had indeed dropped, and Orruño deserted his contractual obligations to Don Pedro when this income fell to 14,000 pesos a year. What appears to have happened was a repetition of the situation encountered by Miers when he took over in 1746: hacienda supervisors were lining their own pockets at the Jesuits' expense. The extent to which Villaverde may have engaged in private business with the hacienda's resources is difficult to specify. Orruño certainly must have been doing what Lascano had done before him. When Villaverde was forced to leave, he suggested to the Jesuit superiors that he be allowed to keep the pulque operations, offering to pay the college 25,000 pesos per year rather than the lower figure accepted earlier. But the Jesuits showed no interest in keeping him on.[79]

Villaverde settled his accounts with the college and left quietly, but no sooner had the order been expelled from New Spain, in 1767, than he filed a claim against the now ex-Jesuit estates for almost 80,000 pesos. This case dragged on for twenty years with the sums gradually shrinking, first to 30,000 pesos and then to 20,000 pesos. Both Don Pedro and his lawyer died before a settlement was reached in 1785. The properties and assets left by Villaverde to his children, according to his will, were not extensive, suggesting that he did not profit excessively from his tenure.[80]

With the dismissal of Villaverde, three Jesuits took over all of the Santa Lucía operations. Miguel Sabel, who had served as administrator for two decades at Chicomocelo, was moved temporarily to Santa Lucía to straighten out problems in pulque production. Santiago Coronel had been sent to the hacienda as an assistant a year before Villaverde's departure and now was made hacienda administrator. In addition, Padre Xavier Rivera, who had moved to the hacienda with Coronel, assisted in running the estate, although his primary role may have been that of chaplain. Sabel returned to Chicomocelo after a year at Santa Lucía to be replaced by Padre Manuel Peralta. At the Colegio Máximo, Martín de Montejano, Gradilla's former assistant, took over the procurador position.[81] These were the administrators who supervised the reduction of hacienda livestock and final reshaping of Santa Lucía for emphasis upon pulque cash-crop production. Pulque income quickly more than doubled, from 14,000 pesos per year during the last years of Villaverde's administration to 32,000 pesos per year during 1765–1766. The Jesuits had reestablished administrative authority over Santa Lucía, their most important hacienda. Having experimented with non-Jesuit management, they now rediscovered what Alonso de Villaseca had insisted upon in 1576—there was no substitute for the hard work, care, and industry of the Jesuits themselves when it came to managing temporal affairs.[82]

Although circumstances had changed vastly during the nearly two centuries of Santa Lucía ownership, the administrative structure operational at the time of Jesuit expulsion was essentially the same as the one that had been carefully developed during the sixteenth century. The early administrators had been individuals of Spanish origin and experience. The men filling the same roles in the mid-eighteenth century were from Oaxaca (Miers), Guatemala (García), Hispaniola (Sabel), Havana (Acosta), and Mexico (Gradilla, Padilla, Coronel, Quijano), with a broad background of experience in New World business affairs.[83] There were still a considerable number of padres and hermanos of European origin associated with the Colegio Máximo, but the center of orientation and direction was definitely that of New Spain. So was the administrative system of Santa Lucía: conceived in Europe, tested, adapted, and successfully implemented on a sustained basis in Mexico.

SEVEN

Conflicts and Disputes

Large-scale hacienda complexes, whether owned corporately or privately, frequently became embroiled in conflict. As one of the largest and most prosperous estates, attached to the Jesuits' central college in Mexico, Santa Lucía was seen by contemporary critics as symbolizing Jesuit involvement in secular affairs, despite the fact that its owners developed it to meet economic needs and not to become integrated into the colonial economy. Nevertheless, its acquisition became the first of many steps that merged Jesuit institutions into the economic and political structures of Spanish society in New Spain. Becoming large-scale hacendados identified the Jesuits with the interests of the conquerors—cultural, economic, political, and social—despite the fact that their ideology, and frequently their corporate sympathy, identified with the interests of the conquered. Where Jesuit missions had almost complete jurisdictional control, as in the northern missions, they could, and did, reshape local life-styles differently than was the case in areas controlled by the crown.[1] Nevertheless, the location of the Santa Lucía estates in areas under jurisdiction of secular powers, and the purely economic rather than religious involvement of the Jesuits, resulted in Santa Lucía's becoming embroiled in the same type of conflicts faced by any other hacienda. The solutions arrived at and the methods used to achieve them differed substantially from those of other hacendados, however.

Santa Lucía's owners had distinct advantages in resolving conflicts. Having the crown as official patron and sponsor during the early years resulted in favorable treatment from viceroys and the audiencia. Recognition as highly esteemed educators and missionaries resulted in gifts and assistance from many individuals of great wealth and influence. Above all, having at their disposal the considerable intellectual, legal, organizational, and economic resources of the order itself meant that the owners of Santa Lucía were well equipped to deal with confrontation regardless of its origin. In a real sense, the Colegio Máximo was using Santa Lucía to compete with all levels of colonial society—government, civilians, and the native communities—for the same economic resources.

The Jesuits were remarkably successful competitors. A chronological list of eighty-five disputes involving Santa Lucía appears in Appendix B.* Actual disputes were more frequent than those listed because many conflicts involving the hacienda were settled quietly and peacefully, without litigation or documentation. The Jesuits frequently complained about this endemic "plague" of New Spain. Many cases involving land claims and tithe payments kept resurfacing throughout the colonial period. The legal issues surrounding land acquisitions and the disputes accompanying many property transfers were discussed in Part I. The greater number of disputes listed for the eighteenth century merely indicates that this period is better documented than the sixteenth and seventeenth centuries, not that there were fewer conflicts during the earlier period.

Six arenas of conflict have been identified and will be discussed in turn. All involved the non-Jesuit sectors of society and are being identified as follows:

1. Secular civil authorities: essentially crown officials at all levels

2. Secular ecclesiastical authorities: a range of persons from the pueblo *cura* (parish priest) to the pope

3. Regular clerical authorities: members of the other religious orders

4. Hacendados: owners of other rural estates

5. Indigenous communities and pueblos: groups ranging in size from small ranchos to larger centers such as Zumpango

6. Individuals: persons dealt with as individuals rather than as members of the other sectors mentioned

In many instances of conflict, practically all sectors were involved in some manner or at least affected, as, for example, in major disputes over possession of properties. In other instances, the same individuals functioned in multiple roles and sectors, as, for example, the cura who acted as both crown and ecclesiastical official, owned estates, lived in a native community, and engaged in private business.

*The numbers in the following discussion refer to numbered items in the appendix, which provides the essential details.

Resolving Differences with the King's Representatives

Santa Lucía conflicts, in most cases, involved the Jesuits with Spanish governmental officials. Of the five branches concerned with colonial administration—*gobierno, justicia, militar, hacienda,* and *eclesiástico*—the Jesuits dealt most frequently with the first two. Posts in these two branches, as Gerhard points out, were often filled by the same individual.[2] The crown saw the Jesuits in Mexico primarily as educators and missionaries, only secondarily as hacendados, and allowed them advantages in addition to those enjoyed by other hacendados. The royal eye was discreetly closed to its own legislation directed against ecclesiastical hacendados. Royal decisions openly favored Santa Lucía, starting with the 1579 cédula ordering the destruction of the neighboring hacendado's buildings on lands claimed as part of the Jesuit holdings.[3]

The Jesuit administrators found themselves in direct confrontation with crown officials during the 1639–1643 (no. 17) and 1754–1757 (no. 79) proceedings concerned with the registration of land titles (composiciones). In both instances the settlements reached proved beneficial to the Colegio Máximo in that the ownership claims were confirmed. And in both cases the royal authorities, from the audiencia downward, made financial as well as property concessions to the Jesuits, recognizing that, if they pushed their demands, the college's lawyers would only appeal to higher authority. The Jesuits always seemed to be able to appeal to higher authority if the lower courts proved difficult. They had the contacts and legal competence to take almost any case all the way to the Royal Council of the Indies, or to the crown itself. This power was used judiciously and effectively.

There were occasions, however, where determined opposition was met at lower levels of royal authority. One case of special note was the 1712 dispute with Zumpango (no. 37) over land ownership. The antagonist here was the *alcalde mayor* of Zumpango, Don Bernabé Pando Terreros, who was both willing and able to fight the Jesuits to a standstill. Don Bernabé violently opposed Santa Lucía's occupation of lands claimed by Zumpango. In question was a piece of property lying between the hacienda and the pueblo for which both parties held titles. The Jesuit claim was based on their 1608 purchase of two caballerías from Zumpango officials, that of Zumpango on a 1583 merced to the pueblo. After their purchase in 1608, the Jesuits occupied the area (no. 12), then Zumpango gradually repossessed it, only to have it legally restored to Santa Lucía in the 1680s (no. 27), after which it was again gradually taken over by Zumpango. The Jesuits sought to reassert possession by constructing buildings in 1712, at which point the *alcalde mayor* moved in with an armed force. He imprisoned and beat Santa Lucía personnel, impounded and mistreated hacienda livestock, and threatened the lives of the hacienda's *gañanes* (laborers), mayordomos, administrators, and anyone else attempting to take over actual possession of the land. Faced by such opposition, the Jesuits immediately resorted to legal means of settling the dispute, producing testimony from thirty witnesses—including people from Ozumbilla, Pachuca, Tecama, and Tizayuca—supporting claims of having been violently wronged.

Despite the open support of the royal official collecting evidence (who resided at the hacienda during the proceedings and kept Juan Nicolás, the college procurador, informed about them), the *alcalde mayor* refused to back down. He claimed that both the witnesses and the investigating officials were openly prejudiced and working in concert with the Jesuits. The fine of 500 pesos levied against Don Bernabé for his excesses only intensified his anger. Cooler heads finally prevailed as the college rector instructed his procuradores to seek reconciliation rather than pursue the legal case, which the Jesuits were almost certain to win in the end. The crown appointed the curas of Tolcayuca and Xaltocan, plus a drainage-canal official, as conciliators. A compromise signed by both parties stipulated common access to the area in question. Zumpango formally recognized the Colegio Máximo's legal claims to ownership.[4] But neither the pueblo nor the hacienda would be allowed to cultivate crops on the land, and both parties would share the costs of maintaining wells and boundaries. A fine of 1,000 pesos was to be imposed on either side breaking the agreement. The Jesuits could have easily afforded to lose the land, which at the time was marginal to Santa Lucía's needs. Zumpango had much greater need for it. The Jesuits established legal ownership as a matter of principle, confident of being able to gain complete access to the land at a later date should this be desirable.

Had it not been for the personal involvement of the Zumpango *alcalde mayor*, this dispute would have been quickly settled in favor of Santa Lucía. Don Bernabé's own contacts with higher officials in Mexico City, which he used to back up his more boisterous claims of intending to send Bartolomé González and other hacienda officials to China on donkeys and in chains, or to hang them from the nearest prickly-pear tree, presented the Jesuits with a threat they had to handle cautiously. One of the by-products of the dispute was a series of Jesuit-initiated boundary realignments with other Santa Lucía neighbors (nos. 38, 39, 41, and 43). The Jesuits were armed to handle legal cases but quick to seek reconciliation when faced by hostile crown officials.

On the whole, Santa Lucía administrators managed to maintain friendly working relations with royal officials at all levels. The Jesuit hierarchy interacted with the secular administrative bureaucracy in New Spain as well as in Spain. Personal contacts and good will at higher levels inevitably affected decisions at lower levels. Although difficult to document in detail in relation to specific minor disputes, informal influence must have been great. The role of the private Jesuit confessor with the king, the permanent position of a Jesuit general attorney in the royal court to handle cases before the Royal Council of the Indies, the proximity of the audiencia and the Colegio Máximo in Mexico City, plus the fact that many crown officials had received their training in Jesuit institutions—all provided avenues of influence above and beyond the legal framework applied to actual cases.[5] Santa Lucía administrators maintained sleeping quarters for the viceroy when he traveled in the area. Royal officials, even when investigating cases involving Santa Lucía (no. 37), were known to stay there and keep the Jesuits informed.[6] In view of such access to official power, it is not surprising that college officials could get the audiencia involved almost at will (83.5 percent of the cases in Appendix B), or that seemingly local conflicts over boundaries, crop damage, pastures, rentals, or money payments would end up being discussed in the Royal Council of the Indies (nos. 1, 2, 4, 40 , 47, 58, 71). Not all cases resulted in a clear-cut victory for the Jesuits, but the simple knowledge that they could take almost any case as far up the court system as they wished restrained most opponents, including royal officials. The recorded consensus of the 1643 Crown Commission enforcing property-title regulation summed up the situation: the Jesuits could continue disputes indefinitely on terms favorable to their interests.[7]

To ensure a positive disposition by local authorities at the *alcalde mayor* level, college officials also attempted to buy offices. Such practices became evident in the eighteenth century, when conflict over access to rural resources between hacendados and local pueblos became more intense. In 1722, for example, Juan Nicolás paid Don Joseph de Echeverría 6,372 pesos to assist him in buying the Malinalco *alcaldía mayor*. Nicolás provided 12,000 pesos to another friend, Don Juan Antonio de Trasviña, to get him out of a financial mess. Donazar, in 1736, mentions a payment of 2,500 pesos to Don Juan Domingo Antón to buy the *alcaldía mayor* of Tetepango. In such cases, funds were invested in direct attempts to solve conflicts between college haciendas and local populations. The correspondence describing these transactions makes it clear that they were undertaken with the approval of the Jesuit provincial. The incidence of conflict with the Indigenous sectors in Malinalco and Tetepango had increased in tempo and intensity. Litigation was costly, time-consuming, and publicly embarrassing. Controlling the local oficios would "eliminate a thousand disputes with anticipation."[8]

The Secular Clergy

In dealings with the secular clergy, the Santa Lucía operations were part of an ongoing conflict. Decisions went against the Jesuits when the clerical officials also held secular administrative offices. The tithe was the single most important point of conflict, and the issue was plainly money. Either the archibishop or the Colegio Máximo would substantially benefit, depending on whether the Jesuits were forced to pay the "tenth" as did their secular hacendado contemporaries. When this issue first emerged in 1577 (no. 2), the king intervened in favor of the regular clergy. The secular clergy fought this decision and in 1605 managed to get the papacy to agree that the diezmo, at a lower rate, might be collected from some of the business ventures of the regular orders (no. 11). In 1614 the Royal Council of the Indies ruled that such taxes should be collected (no. 13), but appeals by the Jesuits and other orders prevented implementation during the early part of the seventeenth century. The actions taken by Palafox in attempting to force collection were initially thwarted, when the crown again intervened in favor of the Jesuits, but eventually successful in that the order was forced to comply in the 1660s (no. 16).

Numerous disputes arose between Santa Lucía administrators and the officials of the various bishoprics in which the tithe was being paid. The most serious took place in the early 1730s, when Joaquín Donazar was formally accused and declared guilty of withholding payments (no. 57). On at least three occasions (in the 1640s, 1660s, and 1730s) the diezmo conflict resulted in strong criticism by the Mexican clerics of the Jesuits, criticism to which the Jesuits were forced to respond. This led to widespread unfavorable publicity about Jesuit rural estates. It is noteworthy that the individuals who were able to force the Jesuits to defend their interests were bishops who subsequently were named viceroys.[9]

In defending their economic activities, the Jesuits had to justify their rural estates, particularly Santa Lucía, because they symbolized the order's temporal wealth. The arguments brought forward by the Jesuits remained the same throughout, having been first articulated to the father general in the internal crisis of 1576–1587: rentals were insufficient and unreliable; other methods of financing educational and mission work had been found, after experimentation, to be impractical. In the eighteenth century the archbishop complained to the king that the Jesuits were so wealthy that their residences and colleges were plated with silver gained from the wealth of the rural estates. This elicited a counterthrust on the part of the Jesuit spokesmen, who described the individual Jesuit as being true to his vows of poverty and having only enough to provide modest food and clothing, whereas the holders of ecclesiastical prebends paraded ostentation in their churches, in their persons, and with many lackeys, servants, carriages, and fancy horses. Such conspicuous consumption, argued the Jesuits, was gained at the "cost of the fatigue of miserable Spanish and Indian farmers who are particularly vexed, being so helpless and defenseless."[10]

Although they paid the diezmo for a century, the Jesuits never wavered from their conviction that the money they were thus contributing to the secular clergy would have been better spent in support of their own activities. In 1750, in response to Jesuit pressure, the crown once again came to their assistance and issued a cédula greatly reducing the amount of tithe they had to pay. The 10 percent levy on farm and livestock production was reduced to 3.33 percent. The rate for pulque was reduced to 1.33 percent, and the rate for milk and cheese was set at 1.66 percent. These rates remained in effect until June 1767, when the crown reestablished the earlier rates of 10 percent.[11] Neither achieving these reductions nor later losing them, however, seems to have been accompanied by extraordinary conflict between the two branches of the clergy.

Apart from the tithe issue itself, disputes frequently arose regarding the time and form of payment on Santa Lucía's production. Such problems were handled locally, between the college procurador and the tax collectors. Most of the Santa Lucía tithes were paid at the Texcoco collection center, administered by tax farmers who contracted directly with the bishopric or who sublet collection rights to a third party. The far-flung nature of the hacienda's enterprises called for the payment of portions of the tithe in the bishoprics of Tlaxcala, Michoacán, and Guadalajara.* Tlaxcala collected from the production of the goat ranch, Tehuacán de Cabras, and a portion of the sheep flocks using the Chilpancingo pastures. Provincia production, for tithe purposes, was taxable in Guadalajara (25 percent), Michoacán (25 percent), and Mexico (50 percent). In the Mexico bishopric, payments were also made to collection centers at Cuautitlán and Ixmiquilpan.

Extant tithe receipts and statements covering 1702 to 1767 show that Santa Lucía administrators occasionally were a few years behind in making payments and that they had minor differences with the local tax collectors.[12] The procedures for determining payable amounts made evasion possible. The hacienda administrator, first of all, made an annual audit of hacienda production and prepared, for the tax collectors, a notarized formal statement. The diezmo was based on actual production rather than profits, encouraging conservative estimates on the part of the administrators. The procurador came to an agreement with tithe officials regarding the type of payment—in kind or in cash—and when and where it was to take place. The collectors then made requests for delivery, frequently sending representatives to the main Santa Lucía residence or to the anexas to claim the produce or its cash equivalent. On other occasions the administrators sent the agreed-upon tax to the collection center. All these transactions were documented, and any movement of commodities or cash involved signed receipts. One-tenth of the yearling sheep, goats, hogs, branded calves and colts (mules and horses), of the harvested maize, barley, wheat, frijol, European beans, and chick-peas, and of the shorn wool went under the description of *diezmo de semillas, lanas, y ganados*. The tithes for pulque production were handled between the pulque contractor and tax collectors, not the Jesuits. Disagreements over weights and measures were common, a matter the provincial's business office attempted to remedy by issuing formulas for measuring products and paying the tithe.[13] All matters of dispute or uncertainty were to be referred to the college superiors. Under no circumstances were tax collectors to be permitted to see Santa Lucía's actual account books.[14]

Overall, the regional tax collectors appear to have had great con-

*Names and jurisdictions of the bishoprics changed throughout the period under discussion; see GHGNS, pp. 17–22. The eighteenth-century classifications are being followed here. Locations cited on the diezmo receipts were also inconsistent; e.g., Michoacán and Valladolid were used interchangeably, and at times the distinction between Guadalajara and Valladolid is not clear; AGNAHH 293, 2.

fidence in the integrity of Santa Lucía accounts. The contents of 213 statements on tithes in the eighteenth century indicate harmonious relations between the mayordomos and administrators who dealt directly with the tax collectors. If serious conflicts emerged, they were handled in Mexico City or at higher levels. On the hacienda itself, last year's production was paid regularly in July, sometimes in kind and sometimes in cash. In 1728, for example, Santa Lucía diezmo consisted of 412 pesos, plus 108 arrobas of wool, 37 colts, 8 calves, 15 mules, 6 hogs, 184 fanegas of maize, 18 cargas of barley, and 6 cargas of chick-peas. In 1737 it consisted of a cash payment of 3,113 pesos, 6 reales.[15]

Parish priests (*curas beneficiados*) and ecclesiastical judges were frequently parties in disputes concerning Santa Lucía. The Jesuit chaplain at the main residence could give religious instruction, hear confessions, and say mass, but he did not have the right to perform baptisms, marriages, or burials. This meant either that curas came to the hacienda residences to perform such ceremonies or that the people of Santa Lucía went to the curas in the pueblos. To avoid conflicts, hacienda administrators were cautioned not to act as intermediaries between gañanes, sirvientes (livestock-ranch employees), and curas. Secular clerical officials in the countryside were to be treated correctly but formally. If they made requests from the hacienda, such matters had to be referred to the college officials.[16] Jesuit officials were interested in keeping local disputes with the secular clergy at a low profile in view of their ongoing conflict with the bishop's office regarding the tithe. Palafox, in the 1640s, and later clerics, in the 1730s, accused the Jesuits of stepping outside their jurisdictional bounds in matters such as performing sacraments on hacienda properties within secular jurisdiction. Technically, although much of Santa Lucía's labor force came from parishes controlled by other regular orders (Franciscan, Dominican, Augustinian)—in the Valley of Mexico, for example, secular parishes were in the minority—all parishes were subject to claims and counterclaims within the context of parochial disputes between secular and regular factions.[17] The Jesuit strategy was to avoid such disputes wherever possible. Santa Lucía administrators and chaplains were instructed to defer to parochial curas regarding administration of sacraments. Resident and part-time workers were instructed to comply with ecclesiastical obligations in home parishes.[18]

Through the years, standardized arrangements were made between Jesuits and curas. Santa Lucía and San Juan were in the parish of the Tizayucan cura. They paid him a regular biannual stipend for his religious services rather than for each time he baptized, married, or buried hacienda residents. Between 1713 and 1738, he received 150 pesos a year; during the 1740s, 130 pesos a year; during the 1750s, 80 pesos a year; and during the 1760s, 50 pesos. The reductions signified diminished resident populations at Santa Lucía rather than changes in rates. San Xavier and Hueytepec came under the jurisdiction of the Tolcayucan cura, who was paid 50 pesos a year, either in cash or in livestock. The Tezontepec cura was regularly paid with sheep or tallow. The hacienda administrator made the payments, except during Villaverde's term, when such potentially complicating transactions were handled by the office of the procurador.[19]

Conflicts with curas revolved around two basic issues. First, there were questions about services to the hacienda and payments for these activities. Second, the activities of the cura within his own parish, his personal financial interests aside from his pastoral interest, frequently conflicted with the economic interests of Santa Lucía.

In 1717 a dispute with the cura of Tizayuca (no. 45) concerned pastures, land, and relations between Santa Lucía and the pueblos in his parish. The cura, Antonio Blanco Palomares, actively encouraged the Indians to encroach upon hacienda lands. As a result, he was removed from the parish until matters settled down. Jesuit influence with the archbishop brought about the temporary removal. They accused the cura of being a troublemaker, an initiator of disputes between the hacienda and the pueblos.[20]

In a 1745 dispute (no. 69), the central protagonists were the hacienda administrator and the cura of Tolcayuca, Licenciado Don Luis Antonio Terreros y Valcárzel. Miers claimed the cura owed the hacienda 578 pesos, based on advances of 1,131 pesos made to the cura since 1740, minus payment for services rendered and goods received. The cura was accused of charging outrageous additional fees to San Xavier personnel and defaulting on payment for purchases of livestock, maize, straw, and textiles, and on rental of maguey plantings. Terreros declared that the itemized statements accompanying Miers's letters were full of falsifications, which he was keeping as evidence to frustrate any attempt by the college to pursue the conflict "with ink and without blood."[21] Since the Jesuits were not prepared to make a legal case of the matter, they quietly accepted a loss.

Curas played a central role in conflicts between the hacienda and pueblos because they were frequently the only individuals in the pueblos (aside from the *alcalde mayor* if one was in residence) who had the training, experience, and contacts at higher levels to counter Jesuit claims. Curas were considered more as adversaries than as friends,[22] and their business interests in the rural areas conflicted with those of the Jesuits on many occasions.

The Regular Clergy

Relations with members of other regular orders were less antagonistic. The intense jurisidictional battles fought between the Jesuits and other orders—for example, the continuous conflict between the Jesuits and the Franciscans in Yucatan[23]—were not reflected in Santa Lucía affairs. Although the Augustinians, Dominicans, and Franciscans had the initial clerical jurisdiction in the areas where Santa Lucía had property, and even though these orders had numerous convents and monasteries in these jurisdictions, the contacts with Santa Lucía were largely restricted to business involving such things as loans, property transactions, and the purchase of hacienda products. Hacienda administrators were instructed to provide hospitality for traveling members of the other orders if they requested lodgings. Alms gatherers were to be accommodated, but the procurador's office stipulated the amounts and kinds of gifts to be given to these almoners. Such gifts were only to be given if they went to convents and hospitals within the bishopric of the hacienda.[24]

Disputes with other orders over control of religious funds produced by property also occurred (no. 63). During the acquisition of lands, numerous conflicts had to be resolved with convents and institutions that either owned lands or held encumbrances on the estates purchased from private families. The Jesuits had always been careful to have their titles immediately cleared of such encumbrances and in so doing eliminated cause for countless disputes between themselves and the other orders. When litigation between the Colegio Máximo and another institution did take place, the costs soared, since both parties had the legal skills and influence required to keep the cases active. The clerical costs of creating the legal documents in a relatively minor dispute with the Convent of San Sebastián in 1743 (no. 63) amounted to 270 pesos.[25] Such costs could not easily be absorbed by individuals, pueblos, or hacendados with limited means, in contrast to large institutions. Legal confrontations with other regular orders were carefully avoided.

Other Hacendados

As one of the most powerful hacendados in the Valley of Mexico, the Colegio Máximo more than held its own in disputes with other hacendados. Santa Lucía involved the Jesuits in many confrontations over access to pasture and water resources, most frequently expressed in disagreements over the location of boundaries (nos. 1, 7, 18, 28, 32, 36, 41, 43, 48, 55, 58, 65, 81, and 85). In the more densely populated areas, stone fences and rows of maguey plants could be used to enclose pastures and agricultural plots, so as to keep out non-hacienda livestock and clearly identify ownership. But the Santa Lucía holdings were too scattered and extensive for such means to be used in most areas. The day-to-day protection and control of the hacienda's natural resources were in the hands of the labor force supervised by the mayordomos or the administrator. This left a great deal of latitude for attempted and actual possession of lands owned by Santa Lucía. Many boundaries were unclear and unstable, consisting of configurations of the landscape or trees that could easily be cut down. Adding to the confusion was the fact that, although legal owners might be clear as to what lands they owned by virtue of the boundaries agreed upon during possession proceedings, such knowledge—and the documents and maps that recorded it—were not available to pasture guards, shepherds, cowboys, or their immediate superiors. Regulations of the Mesta (Stockman's Association) favoring livestock owners and the access privileges to crown lands only added to the confusion, making the documented boundaries useless as protective devices.

Conflict between hacendados and Santa Lucía's owners was, in a restricted sense, a continuation of the competition between encomenderos that began in the early sixteenth century. By the middle of the seventeenth century, the hacendados and the Jesuits were competing for property titles, each attempting to maximize their holdings or the profits they could derive from them. By the eighteenth century, the Jesuits had clearly emerged as the dominating force, having bought out their weaker competitors and established a lasting presence with Santa Lucía and its anexas. The legal conflicts themselves, as individual cases, were minor skirmishes in the larger battle for control over rural resources. Reaffirmed or reestablished boundaries with other hacendados had a minor influence upon the general trends. These were more directly affected by the power and influence Santa Lucía's owners had with royal officials.

Within the private hacendado sector, however, there were individuals whose political power enabled them to thwart Jesuit plans in specific instances and to mount an attack against their hacienda system. Juan Nicolás's attempt to increase sheep pastures in the early eighteenth century resulted in initiatives to acquire a mayorazgo owned by Don Manuel de Urrutia y Estrada, a hacienda called Melilla reputed to be one of the best and valued at 110,000 pesos. Its encumbrances and unresolved legal problems prevented Nicolás from acquiring the Melilla titles. When Donazar became administrator, he pushed hard to buy the hacienda. One result was that the Marqués de Casafuerte and the Marqués de Guardiola, both of whom had interests in the properties, joined ranks against the Jesuits. Their influence in court proved to be a key force in audiencia and bishopric sanctions against Donazar in 1734. Eventually, after the case reached royal and ecclesiastical courts in Spain, the Jesuits could claim a legal victory of sorts, but the damage to their prestige in New Spain was considerable. They failed to acquire Melilla and instead purchased the unproductive Gruñidora hacienda. Of the sixteen major disputes Donazar claims to have successfully resolved during his tenure as Colegio Máximo procurador, he called this dispute the most vicious, "a bloody attack against the Company."[26]

Indian Pueblos and the Exercise of Powerful Persuasion

The most important arena of conflict involved Santa Lucía and the Indian communities. Forty-seven of the eighty-five disputes in Appendix B were with pueblos located on Santa Lucía's borders or entirely surrounded by the hacienda and its anexas. In a broad sense, these were skirmishes in a much larger battle between the Indigenous populations and the representatives of Spanish civilization. The native communities were attempting to retain and, as their populations gradually increased in the late seventeenth century and early eighteenth century, to regain their agrarian patrimony. As conquered peoples with little hope of reestablishing their autonomy, they nevertheless continued to use available means of defending what they believed to be their rights. They understood and accepted their "legal" rights, as articulated by Spanish law, differently than the crown and its officials. Crown officials, in turn, had a different understanding of native rights than the forces behind the latifundium system spreading throughout New Spain.[27]

None of the conflicts with Santa Lucía or its owners was directed

against the Jesuits as Jesuits. Rather, they were directed against the
hacienda as part of an alien cultural and economic system which
had usurped native lands and which depended upon pueblo labor
to ensure its continued dominance. The native struggle was expressed in many ways. On the one hand, there was passive resistance to linguistic, religious, and cultural integration. This was
made possible by crown policies insisting that Indian communities
had certain limited territorial rights—the 600 vara limit as a minimum—and that individuals could retain their language and their
communities. Restrictions against Spanish residence in the pueblos helped to ensure that local communities continued to have a
cultural and territorial basis of identity. The large-scale response of
excessive drinking and drunkenness can be seen as a type of passive resistance of pueblo inhabitants.[28]

On the other hand, the native resistance was active in its consistent challenge of hacienda claims to lands formerly owned by the
pueblos. When the conflicts came to the courts, the pueblos had all
the disadvantages, having to deal with Spanish courts in a legal
and cultural context they failed to comprehend, and having to face
an adversary who had all the legal skills and political connections.
Most of these cases ended in clear-cut victory for the Jesuits (nos.
3, 12, 21, 23, 24, 26, 27, 31, 33, 35, 44, 50, 54, 62, 64, 68, 72, 77, 80,
and 82) or in compromises that did little more than establish the
status quo. Since the Jesuits were careful to keep their claims and
demands in conformity with legal requirements, the overall effect
of the court cases was merely to reaffirm Jesuit superiority in this
type of confrontation. Even when stalemates or compromises were
achieved, they were the result of the advocacy of the local cura or
alcalde mayor who, because of his own interests in exploiting the
pueblos, usually represented a greater threat to the communities
than did Santa Lucía. In the twenty cases just listed, the Jesuits received favorable judgments in all but one at the level of the audiencia or through the intervention of the viceroy. These were levels of
colonial administration where their influence exceeded by far that
of representatives of the pueblos. In the one case where the Royal
Council of the Indies became involved (no. 44), it was at the request of the Jesuits, resulting in the transfer of sixty-two sitios de
ganado mayor of pueblo lands for little more than a token fee.

Disputes over land ownership with Ixtlahuaca (no. 33) clearly
demonstrate the inability of pueblos in the Valley of Mexico to retain land the Jesuits claimed for Santa Lucía. Ixtlahuaca had lost
most of its traditional land to Spaniards in the late sixteenth cen-

tury, when local populations were in sharp decline and royal land grants were being freely distributed. The Jesuits subsequently acquired the land and first used it for grazing sheep and goats, but by the beginning of the eighteenth century it was part of the Pintas anexa devoted largely to horses. This meant that only a small hacienda labor force patrolled the area. Under these circumstances, the now expanding pueblo population began to use what it still considered its traditional lands for its own livestock and maize crops. When Santa Lucía administrators became aware of this, they attempted to force the Ixtlahuacans back into the 600 vara pueblo limit allotted by law. The Ixtlahuacans, in turn, with the aid of the justicia of Texcoco, attempted to have local courts rule that the land belonged to the pueblo. The Jesuits entered the legal battle in 1709, when a court order was issued restricting non-pueblo access to four *sitios de ganado menor* and fifteen caballerías of land. The Jesuit lawyers took the case before the audiencia. They presented their legal titles and the argument that essential lands of Santa Lucía had been usurped and damaged by overgrazing. The pueblo, the lawyers pointed out, was restricting free movement of hacienda livestock by putting up corrals and enclosures, which would inevitably result in increased pasture costs for the hacienda. Since Ixtlahuaca was not even a pueblo—lacking a minister and Holy Sacrament—but merely a barrio of Acolman, it should not even be allowed the 600 varas. Besides, it was pointed out, no opposition had been registered when the Jesuits had occupied the land.[29]

Faced with the Jesuit titles and arguments, the audiencia went through the procedures of formal investigation and then ruled against Ixtlahuaca. The pueblo, however, was given permission to collect *tuna* (prickly-pear fruit) and to use maguey plants on the land. Once the legal issues were settled to their satisfaction, Santa Lucía administrators found themselves in possession of a considerable area that the pueblo residents had converted to maize production. This was integrated into San Xavier's farmlands as Atlantepec. Ixtlahuaca residents, left without sufficient land to meet local needs, were forced to rent parcels of land from Santa Lucía. Conditions for rental included agreement to provide labor during periods of high demand (planting, weeding, harvest) at San Xavier. Apart from minor incidents of continued conflict with individuals from the pueblo, the Jesuits maintained territorial dominance, at the same time assuring themselves of an ongoing labor source. After the expulsion of the order, further attempts were made by the Ixtlahuacans to reclaim these lands.[30]

The condition of other valley pueblos adjacent to Santa Lucía was similar. Xoloc, for example, by 1639 found that 20.7 square kilometers (two *sitios de ganado menor* and twelve caballerías) of land they had owned was occupied by Santa Lucía and its San Juan anexa. This effectively blocked access to land south and west of the pueblo. To the north, which consisted largely of rocky, barren hillsides, the situation was even less promising. And 1 kilometer to the east was the neighboring pueblo of Los Reyes. Ever since the establishment of Santa Lucía, the residents of Xoloc had been a principal source of labor, as shepherds and as seasonal workers at San Juan. In 1710 members of the Indigenous aristocracy of a barrio of Xoloc, San Lucas, attempted to dispute land ownership with the Jesuits (no. 35). They claimed one *sitio de ganado menor* and two caballerías as having been donated "in perpetuity" to them, whereas the Jesuits could demonstrate legal titles, in proper order, and payment for the land. One of the outcomes of this dispute was a rectification of boundaries and the discovery that Santa Lucía lands extended to within 300 varas of the Xoloc church. The Jesuits had no trouble winning the suit but were pressured into donating 300 varas to the pueblo in order to conform to minimum legal ownership standards.[31] In 1758 the Xoloc livestock owners were hard-pressed even to maintain agreed-upon grazing access to some of the marshland of Santa Lucía (no. 82).

What held true for Ixtlahuaca and Xoloc also held true for many of the pueblos adjacent to Santa Lucía estates, although not necessarily to the same degree. The expansion of San Xavier meant that much of the former agricultural lands used by Tolcayuca and Zapotlán was no longer available for subsistence needs, and legal attempts to challenge Jesuit officials only reaffirmed the pueblos' marginal access to land resources (no. 21). Within the jurisdictions of Ecatepec and Pachuca, Santa Lucía controlled at least 194 square kilometers as early as 1670 (see Appendix A). The audiencia sided with Jesuit authorities in cases of dispute (nos. 22 and 23). Zumpango, despite assistance from local Spanish officials,[32] was unable to make long-term or significant inroads into Jesuit claims (nos. 27 and 37). The eighteenth-century disputes with Xaltocan (no. 52), Acayuca (no. 53), Temascalapa (nos. 56 and 72), Tecama (no. 61), Metztitlán (no. 62), Anajac (no. 77), Tepenene (no. 78), and Tecomate (no. 80) resulted in formal reassertions of Jesuit control over land, water, forest, and grassland resources, and pueblos more vulnerable to hacendado external control. Tezontepec's modest victory in 1751 (no. 75) was only a formal restatement of royal legislation allowing limited, seasonal access to former resources. Since the successful hacendado also served as a model the pueblo caciques and local Indian aristocracy wished to emulate, they attempted to create their own livestock herds, succeeding only in building up miniature herds whose marginal access to land further limited pueblo agricultural production.*

Having little success with the weapons and arena of combat chosen by the hacienda owners, the pueblos nevertheless attempted to use some of the tricks they learned from associating with representatives of Spanish culture. This involved the use of forged documents, agreements, or titles. A common ruse attempted with new owners of property who still lacked detailed knowledge of the local situation was to present them with claims of privileges or rights based on falsified documents. When the Conde de Regla took over Santa Lucía, he was approached by representatives of Los Reyes who claimed they had long-established rights of access to the *ciénega* (marshland) pastures in the dry season, in exchange for allowing hacienda livestock to graze their stubble fields after harvest. The Jesuits had made such an agreement with Xoloc, Xaltocan, and Temascalapa, but never with Los Reyes. Its officials used a copy of an agreement with Xoloc and falsified it to show that they were included. With the Jesuits, whose papers were in better order than anyone else's, such ploys usually failed. Judging from the consistency and perseverance of the practice, success with other hacendados must have been much greater.[33]

Although the pueblos consistently lost the battles in court, they were more successful with practical methods—namely, the occupation and use of hacienda land wherever and whenever possible. Santa Lucía officials quickly discovered that their boundaries were frequently ignored by Indians who pastured their small quantities of livestock or made their *milpas* (maize plantings) on hacienda property. Already in the early seventeenth century, when most of Santa Lucía's activities were still centered around the main residence, its managers discovered that Hueytepec and Pintas lands were consistently reoccupied by pueblos nearby. Seasonal occupation of the anexas, as happened with sheep- and goat-ranching, meant seasonal absence of the legal owners, and this was an open invitation for former owners to move onto the land. The Jesuits annually

---

*Diego Millan, possibly the richest of the Ixtlahuacans, managed to accumulate 300 sheep and goats, 40 cattle, and 16 horses by 1744. He became a renter of a rancho in the Altica anexa; PCRVP 1: 544r–545v. For a further discussion of pueblo land-access problems in relation to the large haciendas, see Chapter 12.

found themselves having to force the Indians off the land when the flocks returned, accompanied by annual hassles over boundaries, jurisdictions, and rights. The Jesuits claimed these annual transgressions created such a proliferation of legal suits with pueblos that the cost of resolving them and getting favorable judgments in the courts was greater than the value of the properties. Their solution was to populate these areas with permanent residents faithful to them, thus ensuring year-round occupation and avoiding both the encroachment and the disputes.[34]

Effective occupation of land ensured continued ownership less expensively than did legal procedures. This motive, coupled with increased expansion of ranching activities, explains the progressive Santa Lucía expansion northward from the main residence. It was also a factor in the attempt to build Provincia into a self-sufficient hacienda complex in the eighteenth century. The strategy of permanent occupation as a means of solving boundary-maintenance problems was most successful when the pueblos were suffering severe demographic losses. But when the hacienda continued to expand, and the pueblos recovered their demographic strength, these measures no longer proved effective.[35]

Violence and tactics of intimidation became frequent along Santa Lucía's borders, as they did at the other estates owned by the Colegio Máximo. The people of Malinalco in 1721 carried actions one step further than the Zumpangueños in 1712 (no. 37), attacking and burning the Xalmolonga estate. In 1717 the cura of Tizayuca was being blamed by the Jesuits for encroachments by pueblos (no. 45). In 1718 a confrontation resulted in a Provincia shepherd burning down a rancho where he was pasturing Santa Lucía flocks (no. 48). By the 1730s matters had so deteriorated that officials of the Colegio Máximo appealed to the Royal Council of the Indies and received through it a royal directive calling on all their haciendas' neighbors to refrain from damaging hacienda pastures and farmlands and to stop leaving their own livestock unattended, or suffer a 200 peso fine (no. 58). In the 1740s there were still frequent clashes between Santa Lucía supervisors and the pueblos in the jurisdictions of Actopan, Metztitlán, and Tetepango-Hueypoxtla (nos. 62 and 66). Pueblos were intimidating San Xavier caretakers openly in 1746 (no. 70). In the last case the hacienda worker was imprisoned on a trumped-up charge, beaten, and threatened with death because he insisted on fulfilling his obligations as a pasture guard. He requested that his Jesuit superiors move him to another occupation because of the beatings and threats.[36]

Pueblo pressure on Santa Lucía grasslands was particularly intense in the Malinalco and Ocuila jurisdictions. Major legal confrontations either failed to solve the conflicts (nos. 30, 40, 51, and 67) or resulted in legal victories (nos. 68 and 71) that were not enforceable. Frequently the Jesuits resisted even the seasonal intrusions by pueblo residents attempting to pasture livestock or harvest forest products. The pueblos claimed this as a right or denied that they had transgressed the (for practical purposes) nonexistent hacienda borders. Ad hoc attempts to catch transgressors in the act may have resulted in imprisonment of individuals but never proved to be a long-term solution. During Villaverde's administration this was still being attempted with Chicavasco and Tepenene pueblo residents, but with limited success, since the instigators were pueblo leaders who were difficult to catch in actual acts.[37]

Direct physical confrontation was also attempted by having hacienda *labor* residents run off intruders or kill livestock caught within Jesuit boundaries. But any case of physical force invited an equal response, as demonstrated by a 1710 encounter at Jesús del Monte. Here pueblo residents of Tecamachalco were poaching firewood and lumber and continued to do so after the audiencia had publicly threatened lashings and forced labor in the textile mill. The Jesuit mayordomo, aided by royal officers (*tenientes*), attempted to catch the culprits, but they hid in the pueblo. When the mayordomo succeeded in apprehending twenty cargas of firewood, his own life was threatened by friends of the poachers who forcibly relieved him of the evidence. When the audiencia finally managed to imprison three individuals, they were unable to pay the 500 peso fine levied against them. They attempted to launch a counterclaim against college officials, arguing that their women and children were naked and hungry and they were suffering in prison for crimes they had not committed in the first place.[38] The Jesuits also knew that desperate, poor people were capable of desperate acts.

Since it proved impossible to keep neighbors from encroaching upon hacienda lands, either through costly legal means or by vigilance, the Jesuits attempted a compromise solution—renting. Individuals and pueblos were permitted limited, controlled access to Santa Lucía lands for grazing livestock, planting crops, cutting wood, and making charcoal, provided that they promised to keep others off and to pay rental fees. This procedure, calculated to produce revenue for the college and solve the boundary-maintenance problem, was clearly articulated by Donazar: "To take away from the Indians all opportunities for new intrusions, various renters were placed on the most distant borders in order to contribute a little and to defend a great deal."[39] In areas where pueblos had once been located but had been depopulated through congregation policies or demographic disaster—the focus of many disputes by pueblos over land possession—the Jesuits allowed selected renters to establish cattle and horse ranches of considerable dimensions. This policy, Donazar indicated to his superiors, resulted in the effective occupation of most of the abandoned pueblos as well as the protection of hacienda lands.[40]

Increasingly, Santa Lucía accumulated renters, or *arrendatarios*. During Pablo de Araujo's term as administrator (1726–1743), this policy was implemented on a large scale. The administrator or a designated mayordomo would make formal, written rental agreements with neighboring pueblo residents. Individuals were allowed to build modest residences and to take over ranchos—some of considerable size—on land they formally recognized as belonging to the college, which they promised to defend against the predations of their countrymen. When Miers took over from Araujo, he made a detailed inventory of the renter situation. His tally showed at least 600 renters with agreements at the following anexas: Altica, San Xavier, Concepción, Florida, Chicavasco, Tepenene, San Ignacio and San Pablo, Ocuila, and Xante (which was rented in the first place). The renters were planting approximately 170 fanegas of maize (607.5 hectares), at least 80 cargas of barley, frijoles, and other crops. Maguey plantings were being harvested at six of the anexas; at four, renters had permits to harvest and sell *tuna*. Firewood, charcoal, and lumber were then being taken at six anexas, and on parts of Florida, along the Río Totonicapa, renters had banana and sugar-cane plantings. Total rent, per annum, amounted to 5,713 pesos and involved, besides the activities just mentioned, pasture for 25,000 sheep and goats, 1,250 cattle, and 1,750 horses, mules, and donkeys.[41]

In making his inventory, Miers also discovered the degree to which both the letter and the intent of the formal agreements were being scorned. At Altica, where much of the land was enclosed, renters left gates open, allowing strange livestock to enter instead of protecting the hacienda's pastures. They corralled and mistreated the hacienda's mares, saddled its horses, and conducted private commerce with the cowboys and the mayordomo. At San Xavier the situation was better, although the Indian gobernadores of Hauquilpa and Tolcayuca were not living up to their agreements to provide the anexa with a steady supply of agricultural labor. At Xante the Santa Lucía goats were being denied pasture while the neighboring Indians had taken over pasture on the equivalent of one *sitio de ganado menor* more than stipulated, and the yearly rental paid was 250 pesos less than it should have been. Tecomate residents were defrauding San Ignacio of both livestock and firewood. But the worst situation was at Concepción, where Lascano and his friends were systematically diverting pulque income into their own pockets.[42]

Miers instituted a wholesale housecleaning, terminating the rental contracts of many individuals engaged in fraud and replacing them with clients who he hoped would be more reliable. Lascano and others like him were sent packing. This administrative vigor had its immediate impact, but the effects were short-lived, since all the available renters, and the hacienda workers at levels below that of the administrator, were susceptible to the pressures of conducting private business at Santa Lucía's expense. Orruño, who took over from Lascano, served the college's interests well for a time but, as pointed out earlier, his period of administrative integrity could be measured when profits rose and remained high. When he started to look after his own interests and this began to be questioned, he did not wait to be dismissed.

What happened at such high administrative levels must surely also have happened at lower levels. The sheer size of Santa Lucía, and the few Jesuits involved in its administration, created a situation in which it was impossible for administrators to keep as close control as vigilance demanded. Since their primary focus was upon hacienda production rather than renter activities, they were forced to accept the losses as the price of relative peace along Santa Lucía's borders. This was less costly than either litigation or physical confrontation, and eminently more successful for dealing with the larger issues of dispute over agrarian resources.

Another area of conflict with Indian communities centered around the sheer size of the hacienda. By controlling such a large portion of the Valley of Mexico, the Jesuits became a convenient scapegoat for disasters, man-made or otherwise. If the rains were exceptionally heavy and flooded the pueblos, as happened in 1714 and 1723, the Jesuits were blamed—in the first place for not having built a proper dam to control floodwaters, and in the second place because their dam broke. Tizayuca and Zumpango, led by the cura of Tizayuca, initiated a suit against Santa Lucía's owners in 1723 (no. 50) for flood damages. They blamed a faulty dam owned by the hacienda at Pintas. The audiencia sent out its investigators, who quickly exonerated the accused. Engineers brought forward by the Colegio Máximo praised the strength, structure, and usefulness of the hacienda's dam, casting the blame for flooding upon the pueblos for not having cleared the silt and debris from their own drainage channels.[43]

Private Citizens

Legal confrontations with individuals usually involved financial matters. Five of seven disputes with private citizens listed in Appendix B had to do with money being claimed by the Jesuits as outstanding, or the right to certain funds (nos. 4, 15, 59, 83, and 84). The other two cases were disputes over land (nos. 34 and 49). In all but one case the other party was a Spaniard and the conflicts were resolved through financial settlements. The Jesuits took such cases to the courts without hesitation, to establish clearly that they would not allow themselves to be taken advantage of from any secular business quarter. The one case involving a non-Spaniard concerned a cacique from Actopan who insisted on claiming part of the land included in the Chicavasco purchase in 1723 (no. 49). Rather than fight the issue, the Jesuits found it less expensive to pay his son 150 pesos in exchange for formal recognition of ownership. In the other land case (no. 34), Francisco de Monroy attempted to claim lands as realengas based on falsified documentation. The Colegio Máximo attorneys had little problem in having Monroy convicted of lying and creating false documents, and fined.

Finally, there were ample opportunities for disputes within the hacienda itself—that is, between the college and the hacienda, or among the anexas of the hacienda. The very structure of Jesuit administration militated against such conflict. The principle of obedience to superiors ensured that problems which might develop into serious conflicts on rural estates, or with the various branches of governmental service, remained merely differences of opinion to be resolved by superiors and accepted by subordinates. A coadjutor might disagree with the judgment of his superior at the college, or with a priest, and he was free to express this or to make suggestions to superiors, but he was not free to disobey commands and instructions. Even the more secular personalities, such as Donazar and Araujo, whose administration caused problems with secular authorities, obeyed superiors. Donanzar complained, but he complied with his instructions, and when he was dismissed he left quietly and with remorse.

Between administrator and mayordomos, possibilities for dispute were always present. The mayordomos of Santa Lucía, however, were not known to countermand administrative orders, or to challenge instructions. Mayordomos engaged in activities against the wishes of hacienda administrators, but they did so secretly, knowing that exposure would automatically result in reports to superiors, and punishment. Administrators tolerated noncompliance with policies at certain levels, or mayordomos on the sheep ranchos pursuing their own business on the side would not have stayed as long as they did. Although tolerated, deviation from policy was never officially condoned, and mayordomos faced the constant possibility of dismissal. On secular estates, the role of the mayordomo tended to become hereditary, with the office passing from father to son. At Santa Lucía, this was much less likely to happen. The structure of administration was geared to the placement of the most capable individual for a particular task, to be moved at the discretion of the superior. This in itself reduced opportunities for conflict. Having the separate anexas of Santa Lucía administered by the same man prevented conflicts of interest from developing on the hacienda. For example, all the sheep flocks did not arrive at the shearing pens at the same time because the administrator coordinated the activities of all the sheep ranches. There were, or course, countless minor incidents of conflict and dispute within Santa Lucía's labor force.[44]

What needs to be underscored, in conclusion, is that in all arenas of conflict involving Santa Lucía the Jesuits employed a variety of approaches to resolving conflict, each depending upon the order's great resources and each adapted to the exigencies of the situation. Individuals and groups opposing the Jesuits found that, in addition to the specifics of the dispute in question, they were up against the experienced professional lawyers within the order. Of the eighty-five conflicts listed in Appendix B, eighty, or 94 percent, came to the attention of the Colegio Máximo legal department, which possessed a formidable array of documents, experience, finances, and contacts. Santa Lucía administrators were involved in sixty-five cases (76.5 percent), but never without the assistance of their superiors. Anexa personnel were kept out of the formal disputes as much as possible—they were involved in only 40 percent of the cases—representing as they did a non-Jesuit element. The system was so successful that the Jesuit provincials had to become involved in only ten (12 percent) of the disputes. The result was that the decisions arrived at and solutions achieved, in most cases, benefited the Jesuits. As Donazar pointed out to the father general in his own futile defense, decisions made at the level of the procurador's office were always based on the advice of knowledgeable and experienced people and the consent of local superiors.[45]

EIGHT ▦ *Production and Revenues*

In defending Santa Lucía, the Jesuits always came up with the same justification: the hacienda produced revenues needed to support the activities of the Colegio Máximo. What the college officials were never forced to do was document the economic efficiency of the estate in any detail. Superiors and other officials received only summations and interpretations of actual production. The administrators guarded closely the documentation of economic performance from the eyes of anyone except immediate superiors with direct responsibilities.[1] This chapter examines the economic performance of Santa Lucía. Were the Jesuits justified in making the claims they did about their hacienda? How did they go about producing the enormous quantities of livestock and agricultural crops, and the products derived from them? Apart from being larger than most haciendas, was Santa Lucía distinctive in its manner of operation? Answers to such questions require a detailed analysis of the components of the hacienda's production.

Sheep

From its beginnings, Santa Lucía was essentially a sheep ranch, purchased because of the current demand for wool and mutton. The production of these commodities in the 1570s was actively encouraged by the colonial government. Sheep-ranching in New Spain remains largely unexplored and unexplained. Despite the documentation of the privileges and powers of the Mesta in Spain and New Spain, and Chevalier's overview of the importance of livestock development in the economy of Mexico,[2] we lack studies of individual ranches or even a structural analysis of all the components of sheep-ranching. This means there are no standards against which to judge the sheep-raising activities of the Jesuits. The focus here, therefore, will be upon the importance of sheep-raising in the development and prosperity of Santa Lucía.

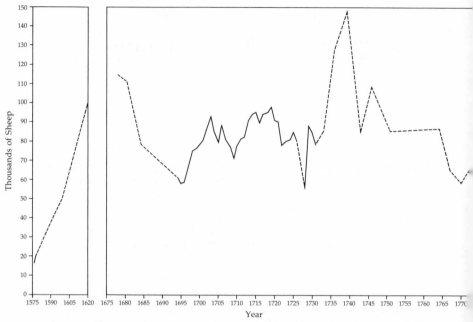

FIGURE 3. Santa Lucía sheep populations, 1576–1772. Source: AGNAHH, 285, 286, 288, 293, 297, 299, 312, 313; AGNTe 83, 205; BNM 1085; PCR.

The hacienda was shaped by its sheep-ranching. The quest for pastures led to property acquisitions in areas far from the Valley of Mexico, for as pastures became exhausted in one area, access to additional pastures had to be arranged. One of the primary concerns of Santa Lucía's managers was the adequacy of pastures, water, and salt. This concern brought about actions that resulted in numerous contacts and conflicts with native communities, other hacendados, and crown officials. By far the largest area of Santa Lucía was devoted to the needs of the sheep flocks.[3]

The number of sheep involved was great. Figure 3 presents available data on total flock sizes, showing a considerable fluctuation. Santa Lucía had highs of over 150,000 sheep, with lows of slightly fewer than 60,000 after the initial flock buildup in the sixteenth century. Details for the sixteenth and most of the seventeenth centuries consist of scattered references, but for the eighteenth century information is more plentiful. Sheep flocks were subject to periodic diseases that could dramatically and quickly reduce flock sizes. Figure 4 shows these fluctuations for the individual flocks. It is interesting

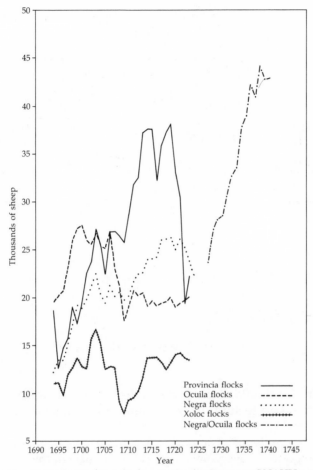

FIGURE 4. Santa Lucía sheep flocks, 1694–1740. Source: AGNAHH 313, 17.

that the increases in flock size were frequently as sudden as the declines, suggesting that, although the hacienda owners may have been relatively helpless to prevent periodic declines, the Jesuits were adept at overcoming these losses and did not suffer severe economic setbacks over extended periods.[4]

Between 1694 and 1767 the records of sheep-ranching at Santa Lucía provide sufficient details to present a coherent picture. Despite the different locations and sizes of the flocks, they all made the annual trek to the main hacienda residence for shearing, culling, and flock redistribution. Apart from attempts tó eliminate this

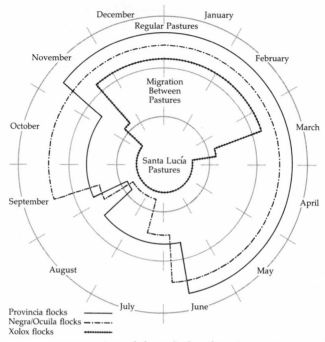

FIGURE 5. Annual sheep-flock cycles, 1694–1740.

necessity for the Provincia flocks in the late 1730s and 1740s, this was a standard feature. Figure 5 shows the annual cycles of the various flocks.

Sheep were classified according to age, sex, and condition. Common categories in everyday usage at Santa Lucía in the eighteenth century are presented in Table 4, along with values assigned to each classification as of 1764.

For purposes of management, the main flocks were broken down into smaller units. Each sheep ranch had a mayordomo who supervised a number of smaller flocks (*vaciadas* and manadas) under the direction of vacieros and manaderos. A vaciada contained between 3,000 and 5,900 animals and a manada, from 1,500 to 3,000 animals. There were smaller units of 1,000 to 1,500 sheep called *media* (half) *manadas,* and if the number was fewer than 1,000 it was usually referred to as an *atajo,* or sometimes a *chinchorrito.* *

---

*The term *vaciada,* in its technical sense, referred to a flock of infertile ewes, and the term *manada* referred to fertile ewes. Although this may have been the practice in Iberia, where the terms originated, at Santa Lucía the terms merely indicated

TABLE 4

Classifications and Values of Sheep, 1764

Classification	Description	Value (reales)
Borregos	Lambs, 8–12 months	11
Borregos de arredro	Lambs separated from flock of birth	10–11
Borregos capados	Lambs, castrated	11–15
Borregos primales	Lambs, yearlings	11–15
Carneros	Sheep for slaughter	14
Carneros añejos, viejos	Sheep for slaughter, old	2–15
Carneros capados	Sheep, castrated	11–15
Carneros padres	Rams for breeding	4
Carneros primales	Sheep, yearlings	15
Carneros sanchos		
Cojos y mancos	Sheep, lame or injured	2
Corderos	Lambs, less than 8 months,	2
Corderitos	Lambs, just born	0.5
Ovejas	Ewes	4
Ovejas de toda brosa	Ewes, all types	4
Ovejas de vientre	Ewes, fertile	4
Ovejas partidas	Ewes, having lambed	4
Ovejas preñadas	Ewes, pregnant	4
Ovejas viejas	Ewes, old (for slaughter)	4–5

SOURCE: AGNTe 83, 3.

NOTE: 8 reales per peso. The standard market value per head when assessing entire flocks was 4 reales.

The total number of sheep at a particular ranch determined the number of smaller flocks. For the period 1694 to 1723, Xoloc, for example, had four to six manadas and vaciadas for a sheep population varying between 7,932 and 16,814 animals, while at Provincia during the same period there were between four and ten manadas and vaciadas for a total sheep population varying between 12,572 and 38,176 animals.[5] The size of each individual subunit also varied, depending upon the total number of sheep in the main flock. At Xoloc the subunits were smaller than they were at Negra and Provincia.[6]

Provincia, because of its distance from main hacienda facilities, presented special problems. Pregnant ewes and those with young lambs were not taken on the long, arduous drives to the Valley of Mexico. This meant that shearing equipment had to be sent to this

flock sizes. For Iberian practices, see Bisko, "Peninsular Background"; and J. Klein, *The Mesta.*

anexa, and day-to-day supervision was never as thorough as the Jesuit administrators would have liked. The annual migration left Zapotitlán (in the jurisdiction of Amula) after mid-June and arrived at Santa Lucía almost two months later. Here the adult sheep were shorn of their wool, and the lambs were separated and transferred to Ocuila or sold. The old ewes and rams were culled and sent to the slaughterhouses at San Xavier or Chicavasco, as were the animals that suffered lameness or injuries en route. The actual shearing was done quickly at the special facilities at Santa Lucía's main residence. An Indian crew of seventy-six could handle the large Provincia flocks in ten working days.[7] By the end of August or early September, the shepherds had settled their accounts with the hacienda, the mayordomo had taken on provisions from the hacienda stores, and the flocks, after a short recuperation in Santa Lucía pastures, began the long trek back to Provincia before mid-September.[8]

Although they left behind the old, the maimed, most of the lambs, and the portion of the annual lamb crop claimed by the tithe collectors, the flocks leaving for the Provincia pastures were the same size as when they arrived. The difference was made up by adding young ewes from the Negra flocks. Male lambs were produced for sale and slaughter, whereas the young ewes were used to keep up the size of the flocks. Since only three rams were required for every hundred ewes, having an abundance of ewes was important. Next year's lamb crop depended upon the number of fertile ewes available during any given year. Young ewes were added to the outgoing flocks, and young lambs were kept at Ocuila, where they would be closer to the market represented by Mexico City. The flocks returning to Ocuila were between 13 and 21 percent smaller than arrivals.[9] The Jesuits used their total sheep resources so that flock sizes in all areas could be controlled. If one ranch suffered declines through disease, the addition of ewes from another ranch allowed a rapid buildup of the sheep population.

Profits earned in any given year depended upon the number of animals sold, on the hoof or slaughtered, and the amount of wool sold. Already in the sixteenth century, Santa Lucía administrators demonstrated a willingness to deviate from the standard local practices of selling by means of contracts and according to the accepted price. The Jesuits began selling without contracts and at lower rates—one-half a *real* less than the going rate—in order to sell both wool and mutton for cash and in a single sale. Such volume selling, besides providing immediate usable income for the

college, avoided the risk of having to collect payments on contracts. It was a sound business practice in view of the economic climate in Mexico at the time, although one of the Jesuit provincials
complained that his brethren were becoming hagglers over prices
and causing scandal.[10] These policies took advantage of the high
rates of reproduction noted for the sixteenth century, when sheep
flocks doubled in size in a year or less. Jesuit documents detailing
annual lamb crops, however, indicate more modest increases. One
of the flocks the Jesuits acquired showed 70 percent of the ewes
with lambs in 1568.[11]

By the eighteenth century, rates of reproduction had declined.
Tithe records, based on the number of lambs and other animals
(aged, lamed) sold annually, serve as a convenient guide to the
productivity of the sheep ranches. Xoloc consistently produced a
higher percentage of lambs than did the other ranches. This was
likely the result of a combination of better pastures, shorter distances between summer and winter pastures, and better control
over shepherds whose activities were closest to Santa Lucía itself.
Data for the four ranches between 1694 and 1723 show that Provincia and Negra were less productive than Ocuila and Xoloc. Annual
sales from Xoloc averaged 16.24 percent of flock totals; from Ocuila
the average was 11.67 percent; from Negra it was 9.5 percent; and
from Provincia, only 8.5 percent.[12] When Ocuila and Negra were
integrated into a single flock, as of 1727, its rates of production
increased. From 1727 to 1740, annual rates of flock-size increase
fluctuated between 20.3 and 40.9 percent, averaging out at 30.4
percent.[13] The Jesuits claimed they annually lost at least 10 percent
of the lambs because of disease or theft. Shepherds, furthermore,
were allowed to claim a percentage of the annual lamb crop as
incentive bonuses.[14] Other losses were incurred during the annual
drives, since lambs were paid out en route as pasture and bridge-
crossing fees. To this must be added the losses from injuries during
the drives between summer and winter pastures. For Provincia
(1694–1723), an average of 1 percent of the total flock was used to
make fee payments en route and an additional 1.38 percent became
injured.[15] Losses to predators—human and otherwise—were also
probably high, although the responsible shepherds, not the hacienda, made up such losses. Available data from the eighteenth
century indicate that during the most productive years 70 percent
of the ewes had lambs, whereas in adverse years a mere 35 percent
lambed. On the average, the expectation would be for 50 percent,
based on the normal ewe population (two-thirds of the total

flock).[16] Assuming that Santa Lucía was more productive and better managed than most secularly owned haciendas, the evidence suggests a general decline in productivity of sheep ranches in New Spain over a period of two centuries.

Labor requirements were not uniform on the sheep ranches. A comparison of man-to-sheep ratios from 1739 to 1751 shows that Negra required only one man per 600 sheep, whereas the ratio at Provincia was 1:400 and at San Ignacio 1:200.* Such discrepancies relate to conditions peculiar to each ranch. Negra relied upon richer pastures concentrated in a smaller area and thus required fewer men than Provincia, whose flocks had to be more closely guarded during the long annual drives and pastured for much of the year in extensive, poorer pastures. Both ranches relied heavily upon mounted shepherds who were much more mobile than those at San Ignacio, where most of the shepherds were on foot, taking care of smaller flocks in an area where there was greater competition for pasture resources from the surrounding pueblos. To what extent sheepdogs were being used in the eighteenth century is unclear. Hacienda inventory lists mention sheepdogs during the sixteenth century, but not for the later periods.

Wool

Wool played an important role in the overall economics of sheep-ranching, as it did in the configuration of Santa Lucía itself. Without the necessity of annually cropping the wool from the sheep, the yearly migrations would have revolved only around pasture needs. The residence complex and the obraje were designed to take advantage of annual wool growth on the moreno sheep. The value of wool was determined by its color, either white or black, and length, either long or short. The amount of wool per animal at any given shearing was not great. Using as a guide information about Provincia in 1751 that roughly two-thirds of any given flock on the drive was shorn, and the tithe reports on total weight pro-

---

*These calculations are based on known flock sizes during years for which numbers of workers at the ranches were available. A larger sample would be desirable to check for fluctuations and trends. The sheep figures for Negra and Provincia may be somewhat low, since the worker lists used included both dismissals and replacements during given accounting periods; AGNAHH 299, 1, 7, and 15; 313, 4, 11, and 17; AGNTe 20, 30. Dusenberry reports a 1:200 ratio for manadas in Spain in *The Mexican Mesta*, p. 10. For sheep drives between California and Idaho in 1865, actual ratios of 1:740 were recorded; sheepmen figured 1 man and 1 dog per 1,000 sheep. See Wentworth, "Trailing Sheep."

duced per year, we find that, for Santa Lucía from 1713 to 1736, the average annual yield per sheep amounted to 0.58 pounds.[17] Because tithe statistics were based on the amount of wool calculated as the annual production rather than the amount actually cut, upward adjustments of this low yield are necessary. Based on a 1677 ruling of the Royal Council of the Indies, the Jesuits, being regulars engaged in mission and educational activities, could deduct prior to diezmo calculations the portion used for their own sustenance.[18] This included the wool processed at the Santa Lucía obraje. Processed woolen goods either found their way back into the internal economy of the hacienda, through distribution to slaves or advances to paid workers, or were sold to buyers outside the hacienda. The percentage of wool processed appears to have been two-thirds of annual production during the eighteenth century. This means the annual yield per animal was three times the 0.58 pounds, or 1.74 pounds. This figure corresponds more closely to yield ratios Brading has noted for the Bajío area early in the eighteenth century.[19] The wool yield was low in any case, and substantially lower than the 2.65 pounds per animal calculated for Santa Lucía during 1596 to 1597.[20]

Income from wool sales was substantial, although the price for wool changed with the times. During the late sixteenth century the Jesuits were getting 9 reales per arroba.[21] In the eighteenth century an arroba sold for between 26 and 32 reales, depending upon the type, quality, and scarcity of the product. Average values, according to the tithe records, were roughly 24 reales per arroba.[22] For the period between 1713 and 1736, wool revenues represented 41.6 percent of the combined value of wool and sheep sales.[23] Annual production during the eighteenth century for lambs and wool is indicated in Table 5. By using the average values for lambs (5 reales per head) and wool (24 reales per arroba), income from these products for the Colegio Máximo can be determined. Income during the poorest year, 1728, would have been 7,056 pesos, 2 reales, and for the best year, 1736, the income would have been 17,926 pesos.[24]

These figures, however, cannot be projected backward and applied to the seventeenth century. Prices differed, and income from the sheep ranches during the earlier period appears to have been higher than it was in the eighteenth century. In 1600, for example, when Santa Lucía was still primarily a sheep ranch with 50,000 animals, it had a reported income of 17,000 pesos.[25] The limited information available about sheep production in the seventeenth cen-

TABLE 5

Santa Lucía Annual Lamb and Wool Production, 1713–1767

Year	Number of lambs, 8–12 months[a]	Wool (arrobas)[b]	Year	Number of lambs 8–12 months[a]	Wool (arrobas)[b]
1713	10,830	1,440	1726	6,564	1,260
1714	10,822	1,420	1728	6,106	1,080
1715	10,671	1,400	1729	—	1,370
1716	9,716	1,430	1730	—	1,320
1717	9,828	1,400	1731	—	1,210
1718	9,734	1,400	1733	—	1,740
1719	9,832	1,410	1734	—	1,500
1720	9,780	1,400	1736	16,970	2,440
1721	9,710	1,390	1738	17,400	—
1722	9,355	1,370	1745	9,146	1,476
1723	9,193	1,350	1751	8,251	—
1724	8,760	1,350	1764	14,000	—
1725	9,020	1,370	1767	—	494

SOURCES: AGNAHH 293, 2; 313, 17; BNM 1058, 1: 117–206.
  [a]These were *borregos de arredro*, whose taxable (tithe purpose) value fluctuated between 8 and 14 reales a pair. The most common value quoted was 10 reales a pair, signifying one male and one female.
  [b]At 25 pounds per arroba.

tury suggests a higher ratio of annual lamb production and better returns from sheep-ranching than for the eighteenth century, but lower than for the sixteenth century.[26]

Goats

In terms of the number of animals involved, goats were the second most important product of Santa Lucía. The original purchase included 1,400 goats pastured in the northern part of the Valley of Mexico, using Hueytepec as a center. The omission of any mention of goats in the documentation until the 1670s suggests that goat-raising remained modest at Santa Lucía until that time. In 1676 there were 9,000 goats at the hacienda, still centered at Hueytepec. Just what prompted the Jesuits suddenly to expand goat production, other than as an attempt to reverse the deteriorating economic situation of the Colegio Máximo, remains open to speculation. In 1655 the goat ranch in the Tehuacán Valley was purchased, and shortly afterward the flocks at Hueytepec were expanded. By 1678 the total goat population of the hacienda stood at 38,592 animals, and three years later the number of goats had increased to 53,343. This was the highest figure for goats encountered in the hacienda's records, and it is doubtful that the 1681 figure was ever surpassed.[27] The amount of pasture available for the Tehuacán ranch was limited, and the flocks at Hueytepec were significantly expanded only after the land purchases of the 1720s and 1730s. When the Tehuacán ranch was sold, the total population stood at slightly more than 9,000. Numbers increased again in the 1730s with the opening of new goat pastures at Tepenene and San Pablo. By the mid-1740s the goat population was up to 40,000, and during the last decade an additional goat-raising area was being established at Provincia.

Table 6 presents available figures on annual goat production and total goat populations. These data indicate that the ratio of annual production to total goat population was lower than for sheep at certain times (9.2 percent in 1719 and 6.4 percent in 1726) and higher at other periods (18.2 percent in 1746 and 20.8 percent in 1751). In 1747 the year's production of goats was 7,370, and 9,530 animals were slaughtered at Chicavasco. The number slaughtered included both kids and the old animals culled from the flocks. The values assigned by the diezmo officials varied less for goats during the eighteenth century than they did for sheep. Between 1721 and 1747, pairs of goats were valued at from 7 to 9 reales. The average would be 8 reales, or half a peso per animal. If the entire flock was being taken into consideration, the value was 3.5 reales per animal.[28]

Goats, like sheep, were classified according to age, sex, and condition.* The breakdown of the goat ranch into vaciadas, manadas, and atajos followed the same pattern as for the sheep ranches. The classifications for the goatherds, including salary levels and ration allotments, were also practically identical to those of the shepherds. The parallel extended also to the number of goatherds used. Tepenene, in the 1740s, had between 96 and 112 goatherds listed on the hacienda accounts, suggesting a ratio of 1 man to 200 or 250 goats. Although this was much lower than the ratios at Negra and Provincia, it was much like that of San Ignacio, located in the same general area. One noticeable difference on the goat ranches was the existence of the position of cheesemaker, an office that could be filled by either a male or a female. Income from goat cheese amounted to 35 to 70 pesos per year from 1715 to 1732.[29] Goats were valued for their meat and hides. During a productive year,

---

*The common classifications for goats were *chivatos*, 6 to 12 months, valued at 3.5 reales; *chivos primales*, yearling goats valued at 7–8 reales; *chivos añejos para matanza*, goats fattened for slaughter valued at 9 reales; *cabras de vientre*, fertile female goats valued at 3.5 reales; *chivos padres*, billy goats for breeding valued at 3.5 reales; and *chivos viejos*, old goats ready for slaughter valued at 5 reales. AGNAHH 293, 2.

TABLE 6

Santa Lucía Annual Goat Production and Total Goat
Populations, 1576–1767

Year	Number of goats, 6–12 months	Number of goats slaughtered	Total goat population	
1576	—		1,400	
1676	—		8,000	
1678	—		38,592	(13,232)
1679	—		48,600	
1681	—	4,743	53,343	(20,600)
1684	—	5,716	42,178	(16,118)
1713	(720)			
1714	(700)			
1715	(720)			
1716	(730)			
1717	(750)			
1718	(700)			
1719	(720)			
1720	(700)			
1721	(720)	3,870	35,331	(7,820)
1722	(745)			
1723	(690)			
1724	(690)			
1725	(650)	3,759		
1726	(570)		36,641	(8,922)
1727	(580)			
1728	(721)			
1729	(620)			
1730	(520)			
1731	(600)			
1732	(600)			
1735	—	3,500		
1736	5,100			
1737	2,470			
1738	6,410			
1739	5,280			
1740	6,302			
1743	—		30,053	
1744	—	6,056		
1745	7,750	6,726		
1747	7,370	9,530	39,963	
1748	5,200			
1751	—	5,313	25,483	
1754	2,050			
1755	2,300			

TABLE 6 *(continued)*

Year	Number of goats, 6–12 months	Number of goats slaughtered	Total goat population
1756	2,350		
1757	2,390		
1758	2,070		
1764	—		35,616
1767	—		8,045

SOURCES: AGNAHH 285, 33; 293, 2; AGNT 1560; BNM 1058, 1: 99–206.
NOTE: The figures in parentheses refer to Hueytepec alone.

such as 1747, the income to be expected from the slaughter of 9,530 goats amounted to 11,912.5 pesos.[30] Goat meat seems to have been a basic consumption item at the mines in the Pachuca area. Goatskins were popular not only for the leather but also as containers for transportable liquids, such as the raw sap of the maguey plant (aguamiel) and pulque.

Horses, Mules, and Donkeys

Like all large livestock haciendas in colonial Mexico, Santa Lucía had its complement of horses, mules, and donkeys. The original land purchase had included 125 brood mares and colts, 4 donkey mares and stallions, 1 saddle horse, and 1 stallion. From this modest beginning the Jesuits eventually built up a population of up to 11,000 animals. Since mules are sterile, being a hybrid between the horse and the donkey, the haciendas, if they were to produce mules, required droves of brood mares and donkey stallions. The normal practice, followed by the Jesuits throughout, was to have a portion of the hacienda's three-year-old mares, kept in manadas of roughly 40 animals, pastured with donkey stallions.[31]

Santa Lucía produced horses, mules, and donkeys at all times, although during the first century the objective was primarily to supply the internal needs of the hacienda and the college. The horses were kept in the northern part of the Valley of Mexico, at Hueytepec and Pintas. After the 1670s production was substantially increased as a means of enhancing college revenues, and additional centers of horse production were started at Altica, Florida, San Nicolás (Provincia), and San Pablo. A limited number of reproductive, unbroken animals were kept at the main administrative centers of Santa Lucía and San Xavier, usually one manada of threshing horses. Such animals were used, not only for threshing, but also as a reservoir from which animals for other purposes could be drawn.

Horses and mules were used extensively for carrying people and goods. The supervisory personnel of Santa Lucía, from procurador down to chief shepherd, rode either horses or mules. The Jesuits themselves, even in Mexico City, seemed to prefer traveling mounted to using carriages. Carriage travel, of course, was largely restricted to parts of the *mesa central* where roads could easily be built and maintained. Any long journey was made either on foot or in a saddle. In Mexico City itself there was a great deal of carriage travel by the affluent sectors of society. Commentators such as Gage and Gemelli Carreri were impressed by the ostentation displayed in luxurious carriages and fine teams of horses and mules. This may be one of the reasons the Jesuits tended to shun this means of transport, although in the middle decades of the eighteenth century they did have carriages. The correspondence between the procuradores and Villaverde contains numerous requests by the procurador or rector for the hacienda administrator either to send the college carriage to Mexico City or to put it at the disposal of an important visitor.[32]

Most of Santa Lucía's produce was moved by pack trains consisting of mules and, to a lesser degree, horses. A weekly mule train traveled between Santa Lucía and the Colegio Máximo, carrying goods, supplies, and equipment. Regular movement of maize rations for the sheep and goat ranches necessitated the use of pack animals. During the harvest seasons, pack animals brought the cereal grains to the storage granaries at the main residence if the fields were distant. If fields were close, ox-drawn carts were used. The large sheep ranches (Negra and Provincia) had their own pack train that carried the supplies controlled by the mayordomo.

The mule was the most important source of animal power in Spanish colonial society. Good mules were worth three times as much as horses and twice as much as oxen. During the last quarter of the seventeenth century, the market for mules increased as sugar-producing estates began to shift from water power (ingenios) to animal power (trapiches), consisting primarily of mules.[33] This shift increased the demand for mules and may have been what prompted the Jesuits to increase production in the 1670s. Earlier Santa Lucía's production was hardly sufficient to meet the internal requirements of the hacienda.[34] For the next century the hacienda produced mules for sale to other buyers, while continuing to supply the increased internal needs brought about by expansion. During the course of any given year, mules and horses were sold. There were also times when, despite the hacienda's own production, mules and horses were purchased from outside the hacienda. In 1739, the horse, mule, and donkey population of Santa Lucía was at its height. Values of animals, types of classifications, and numbers presented in Table 7 provide an overview of this aspect of hacienda production for 1764.

Production of horses and mules was carefully regulated. Each manada of *yeguas de vientre* (untamed or brood mares) was identifiable by name, and a careful record was kept of the number of colts of all ages in every manada. In roughly half the droves some of the mares were bred by jack donkeys, the rest by the young stallions in the manada. Mares were considered productive after their third year, by which time they had been cut from the drove of origin, or were reclassified as *yeguas* (mares) rather than *potrancas* (female colts). The *potros* (colts) were left with the manada until they were three or four years old. Stallions kept specifically for breeding receive very limited mention in the hacienda's records, except for the jack donkeys. The female mule colts stayed with the herd until they were three years of age, but the male mules were separated after two years. The colts appear to have been branded when cut from the herd. Mesta regulations stated that horses should be branded only after reaching two years.[35] The low value assigned to branded colts (other times referred to as animals *de marca*) suggests earlier branding so that underage animals could be sold. Besides the Mesta regulations there were good reasons for delaying the branding of colts, since tithe did not have to be paid prior to branding. By delaying branding, the losses from infant mortality or other causes would be sustained prior to branding, thus reducing the amount of tax payable.

Tithe records provide information on annual production for horses and mules. Throughout the eighteenth century, Santa Lucía's production of these animals was markedly more stable than the sheep and goat operations. Table 8 presents annual production figures for horses and mules between 1713 and 1764 in the jurisdiction of the bishopric of Mexico. The exceptionally low production figures for 1739 and the high figures for the following year require an explanation. In the fall of 1738, a combination of drought and disease had greatly reduced hacienda production and seriously weakened its labor force. Many of the animals branded in September 1738 had already died by the next July, when the tithe payments for them became due. The Jesuits appear to have had difficulty in getting the tithe officials to recognize their plight. Thus, in 1739, in the expectation that high mortality rates would increase, very few animals were branded. The high figures for 1740 indicate

TABLE 7
Classifications and Values of Donkeys, Horses, and Mules, 1764

Classification	Description	Number	Value (pesos)
Donkeys			
Burras mansas	Tame mares, pack animals		4
Burras de vientre	Brood mares		4–5
Burros oficiales	Jack donkeys, to breed with horses	52	20
Burros ahijados	Young colts		5
Burros de 1 año	Yearling colts		2
Burros de 2 años	2-year-old colts		5
Burritos de herradero	Branded colts		1
All others		84	
TOTAL		136	
Horses			
Yeguas mansas	Tame mares, saddle or pack		5
Yeguas de vientre	Untame mares, brood mares	3,673	2.5–3
Yeguas mancornadas	Tame brood mares		5
Garañones	Stallions		
Caballos mansos	Horses broken in for work	1,038	8
Caballos cerreros	Unbroken horses		
Potros	Male colts		
Potrancas	Female or filly colts		
Potros de 1 año	Yearling colts	776	2.12
Potros de 2 años	2-year-old colts	401	3
Potros de 3 años	3-year-old colts	360	5
Potros de 4 años	4-year-old colts		6
Potros ahijados de burras	Orphaned colts with donkey mare		1.5
Potros de herradero	Branded colts	1,101	1.12
TOTAL		7,349	
Mules			
Machos	Male mules		
Mulas	Female mules		
Mulas aparejos (de carga)	Pack animals		18
Mulas de silla	Saddle animals		18
Mulas de volanteras	Carriage animals		25
Machos y mulas mansos	Working mules, all types	658	
Machos/mulas de 1 año	1-year-old colts	146	6.5
Machos/mulas de 2 años	2-year-old colts	224	12.25
Machos/mulas de 3 años	3-year-old colts	301	13.5
Mulas de 4 años	4-year-old females		
Muletos de herradero	Branded colts		5
TOTAL		1,329	

SOURCES: Inventory taken at Villaverde's departure, BNM 1058, 1: 197–206; AGNTe 83, 3.

TABLE 8

Santa Lucía Annual Horse and Mule Production, 1713–1764

Year	Number of horses branded	Number of mules branded	Total value (pesos)
1713	135	52	402.75
1714	123	39	329.25
1715	138	32	316.50
1716	122	40	332.50
1717	126	41	342.00
1718	136	42	359.00
1719	140	43	368.50
1720	150	44	385.50
1721	136	46	377.00
1722	125	36	348.75
1723	214	57	552.50
1724	217	66	601.25
1725	104[a]	34[a]	
1726	219	77	658.75
1727	?	100	
1728	376	80	870.00
1737	394	63[a]	807.50
1738	576	61[a]	1,025.00
1739	132	28	365.00
1740	756	67	1,280.00
1747	471	85	971.25
1748	599	27[a]	870.25
1757	735	84	1,338.75
1764	795	91	1,448.75

SOURCE: AGNAHH 293, 2.
NOTE: Value refers to taxable value for tithe purposes.
[a]Incomplete data.

that such pessimism was unfounded, and they include many of the animals that would normally have been branded a year earlier.[36]

Income produced annually from this source is more difficult to determine, since few animals were sold as unbroken colts. Part of the annual revenues came from sale of animals within the hacienda itself, which was not subject to the tithe. During 1741 and 1742, the distribution of animals from one of the horse-raising centers (Hueytepec) amounted to eighty mules (sixty-two broken and eighteen unbroken) and forty-six horses (twenty-nine broken and seventeen unbroken). The total value of these animals, using the prices listed in Table 7 as a guide, would amount to 1,676 pesos.[37] Most of these animals were sold to the mayordomos, ayudantes, and vacieros on various livestock ranches of Santa Lucía. The mayordomos and ayudantes at Chicavasco, Hueytepec, Negra, and San Pablo bought 46.8 percent of the animals; 14.3 percent were bought by the vacieros and manaderos at Negra and San Pablo; and only 5 percent of the animals were sold to buyers not associated with the Colegio Máximo estates. The remaining 34 percent were sent to Jesús del Monte and Chicavasco to await further distribution. The mayordomos showed a preference for animals already trained, whereas the vacieros and manaderos preferred unbroken animals, which they used either as saddle or pack animals.[38] Hueytepec was the main center from which animals were distributed. Resident at Hueytepec were a number of wranglers who broke in the animals sold as *quebrantados*.

Cattle

Cattle were the fourth major component of Santa Lucía's livestock activities. The production of beef for consumption in a society with strong tastes for mutton and kid was not dominant. Equally important was the need for a steady supply of oxen—the primary power source for European-introduced agricultural technology—and for hides to supply the technological needs of an age dominated by leather. The original purchase in 1576 did not include either oxen or plows, but these were quickly adopted by the Jesuits when they established the San Juan farming anexa. At exactly what point Santa Lucía began breeding its own oxen remains unclear. The earliest reference to raising cattle was in 1596, when the second of Alonso González's estates was purchased. Throughout the sixteenth century cattle had been an endless source of conflict between hacendados and native communities in the Valley of Mexico, a factor that may have restrained the Jesuits from attempting to build up a cattle population in the early decades, when their properties were mostly located in the valley. Another factor militating against cattle-ranching in the Valley of Mexico was the legal technicality of having most of their property designated for the production of sheep and goats.[39]

Much of the technology surrounding cattle-ranching, as well as management practice, was of Iberian origin. The use of cowboys who hired themselves out for a year at a time and received wages paid in cash, a percentage of calves, or a combination of these, was a medieval tradition transplanted to New Spain. These cowboys, including a foreman and three or more hands, were liable for lost stock and when an animal died had to produce the hide and demonstrate the loss to have been caused by predators or disease. The use of saddles, bridles, stirrups, spurs, leather or fiber ropes and also the technique of throwing animals to the ground from horseback by grasping the tail and jerking the animal off its feet had been developed in Europe. The Peninsular herds had been of two types; those in *estantes* or local pastures, and the *transhumantes*, which might be driven between summer and winter pastures in widely separated locations.[40] In New Spain, royal legislation had restricted much of the long-range movement of cattle in the central Mexican plateau, largely because of the early havoc created by large herds of cattle upon Indian agricultural lands.[41] The cattle raised at Santa Lucía were confined to local pastures associated with the anexas (Altica, Hueytepec, Florida, and San Ignacio), under the supervision of vaqueros. Smaller herds were maintained at the farming anexas (San Juan, San Xavier, Chicavasco, and San Jerónimo y San Nicolás) to provide oxen and a limited number of dairy animals.

Information about Santa Lucía cattle production during the seventeenth century is limited. The purchase of Altica in 1670 provided the hacienda with a base for raising cattle. By 1678, 3,000 cattle were in evidence, a figure which was quickly increased to 4,000 by 1681, followed by a decline to 2,628 by 1684.[42] Lack of information for the next forty years (other than Gemelli Carreri's report of 10,000 cattle and oxen in 1696, which cannot be trusted) prevents a detailed plotting of cattle populations until early in the eighteenth century. Beginning with 1713, annual figures are available on the number of calves branded in the Mexico bishopric. These figures and occasional references to total cattle populations during the eighteenth century are presented in Table 9. This information suggests that cattle operations had reached their high point in 1740, at 6,500 cattle, with a reduction to 5,658 head by 1764, when Villaverde was relieved of his administrative responsibilities.

Starting with the late 1720s, cattle were in evidence at an increasing number of the anexas, a pattern that was at variance with the type of specialization characteristic of Jesuit administration. Two reasons can be identified for the changing patterns. First, herds were already in existence at the properties purchased, and the hacienda was by now so extensive that maintaining a high degree of specialization became increasingly difficult. Second, with increased agricultural production at the anexas in the Actopan Valley, herds were established to supply the oxen, beef, and rawhide needed in daily operations. Such internal distribution, besides be-

TABLE 9

Santa Lucía Annual Calf Production and Total Cattle Populations, 1713–1767

Year	Number of calves branded	Total cattle population	Year	Number of calves branded	Total cattle Population
1713	62		1731	150	
1714	60		1732	170	
1715	55		1735	110ᵃ	
1716	61		1736	315	
1717	65		1738	355	
1718	64		1739	29	
1719	66		1740	421	6,500
1720	67		1742	165	
1721	65		1743		1,819ᵃ
1722	65	1,319	1745	117ᵃ	
1723	59		1746	137	1,940ᵃ
1724	60		1747	186	
1725	70		1748	202	
1726	133	2,231	1751		1,965ᵃ
1727	120		1755	230	
1728	144		1757	249	
1729	160		1764	372	5,658
1730	90		1767		3,518

SOURCES: AGNAHH 293, 2; BNM 1058, 1: 99–206.
ᵃIncomplete data.

ing exempt from the tithe, lessened the amount of cash required for distribution to the labor force.

Like all other types of livestock, cattle were classified according to age, sex, and function. A breakdown of classifications and cattle populations at the various anexas is presented in Table 10. Cattle, unlike horses, were not kept in small separate herds but were separated according to age and function. The cows, calves up to two years of age, and breeding bulls made up the cattle herd. Each fall there was a roundup, after which the calves were branded. Young bulls selected to become oxen were castrated in their third year and as four-year-olds were trained to become plow oxen or cart oxen. Santa Lucía supplied most of the oxen required by its anexas, although on occasion such animals were purchased from other suppliers.[43] Working oxen were always kept apart from the other cattle. Special corrals were built near the fields so that time would not be lost in driving the oxen to and from their work. Each anexa with oxen had its own oxherd who was resposible for maintaining these draft animals. A team of oxen was worth 18 pesos.

TABLE 10
Santa Lucía Cattle Populations, 1764

Description	Location								Total	Value (pesos)
	Altica	Chicavaso and Tepenene	Florida	Hueytepec	San Juan	San Nicolás	San Pablo	San Xavier		
Vacas de vientre (breeding cows)	601	183	312	241	38	441	493	62	2,371	6.00
Becerros de 1 año (calves, 1 yr old)	204	13	97	56	—	181	82	48	681	2.50–3.25
Becerros de 2 años (calves, 2 yr old)	—	51	—	—	—	—	—	—	51	3.25–4.75
Terneras (heifers)	—	—	—	—	8	—	—	—	—	—
Terneras de 2 años (heifers, 2 yr old)	—	—	—	—	8	—	—	—	8	4.00–4.75
Novillos y toritos (bulls over 2 yrs)	—	—	—	—	10	115	—	—	125	7.25
Toros (bulls over 3 yrs)	197	—	116	55	—	85	195	—	648	6.25–6.50
Toros padres (breeding bulls)	—	—	—	—	—	—	—	—	—	6.25–6.50
Becerros de herradero (branded calves)	254	61	160	120	28	214	309	—	1,146	2.50
Bueyes (oxen)	—	76	26	—	103	150	64	209	628	9.00
Ganado vacuno (all types of cattle)	1,256	384	711	472	187	1,186	1,143	319	5,658	

sources: AGNte 83, 3; BNM 1058, 1: 197–206.

The number of oxen required by all of Santa Lucía depended upon the acreage being farmed. A steadily increasing number of oxen listed in the periodic inventories after the 1720s reflected the hacienda's increased emphasis on agricultural production.[44]

If branding records represent true patterns, the annual production of calves was not high. On the average, 6 percent of the cattle population was branded each year during the eighteenth century. Annual calf crops in the same period varied between 20 and 40 percent of the breeding cows. This means that only three of ten cows produced a calf that survived the first year. Since the breeding-cow population represented roughly 40 percent of the total cattle population, there should have been an annual increase of 12 percent. In other words, only half the calves born in any given year were actually branded, because the rest were lost to predators or were slaughtered for hacienda use, or they were branded but not reported. In view of Miers's reports of extensive theft of hacienda produce by renters, neighbors, and employees,[45] the discrepancies between known rates of reproduction and reported annual production for cattle, and perhaps for all other types of livestock as well, can be explained as losses suffered by Santa Lucía through neighbors' malfeasance. A limited number of cows were tamed and kept near the main residences to provide dairy products, particularly cheese. But, as the Florida mayordomo complained to the hacienda administrator in 1754, "such cows give very little milk."[46]

Hogs

Hogs were also raised at a few of the anexas. Suckling pigs were regularly sent as supplies to the Colegio Máximo from either Santa Lucía or San Xavier, each of which kept a swine drove. Two types of hogs were raised, the one being more or less confined and fed barley (*cerdo de cebada*), and the other (*cerdo de sabana*) left to forage in the fields under the watchful eye of a young male slave.[47] Besides meeting the table needs of the Jesuits in Mexico City, hogs were raised for their meat and the *chicharrón* (fried pork rinds) that were part of the rations received by the herdsmen working for Santa Lucía in the Actopan Valley anexas.

The maximum hog population encountered in the hacienda's documentation was 906, in 1726. A limited number of hogs were raised at Santa Lucía and San Xavier throughout the entire history of the estates. In the late 1670s the hacienda administrator attempted to improve the quality of the hogs by getting sows of good quality. At the time, the hacienda had two droves and a total of 50 or 60 animals. By 1722 the total population had risen to 492. During the first quarter of the eighteenth century, over 100 hogs were being branded annually.[48] The entire hog population was wiped out during the 1736–1739 epidemic, but by 1743 new stock had been bought, and 112 hogs were branded that year. By 1747 Pintas had become another location for hogs. Sales for that year totaled 69 animals at prices ranging from 20 to 27 reales for adult hogs. Branded young hogs were worth 4 to 5 reales.

Cultivated Field Crops

Maize and barley were the most important agricultural crops harvested at Santa Lucía. Maize, the stable consumable commodity of the Indigenous populations for centuries before the Spanish invasion, remained just that—the staff of life for the vast majority of those employed on the haciendas. Barley, the European-introduced cereal, was an important consumable for the mules and oxen used as a labor resource and for hogs being fattened for the table. Other native crops grown regularly were beans (frijoles), squash, sage, chile, amaranth, and tomatoes. Additional European crops included oats, wheat, broad beans (habas), and chick-peas. Maize, barley, and, to a lesser degree, frijoles were being cultivated at San Juan in the sixteenth century and later at San Xavier. With the expansion of hacienda holdings in the eighteenth century there was a proliferation of sites of agricultural production. During its final three decades as a Jesuit estate, Santa Lucía was producing maize, barley, and frijoles at all its anexas in the Actopan Valley. Increased demand for cereal grains to supply hacienda needs encouraged stepped-up production. Cereal crops were not raised at the sheep ranches, although renters there frequently made milpas and paid part of the rental in maize.

For agricultural production, in contrast to livestock production, studies such as those of Gibson, Florescano, and Moreno Toscano have detailed trends and developments for the Valley of Mexico.[49] They provide a contextual background for the specific case of Santa Lucía. From these studies we know that the production of maize was subject to the vicissitudes of climate, that production was uneven from year to year and location to location, and that prices were subject to substantial seasonal and cyclical variations. The instability surrounding production, coupled with the necessity of having a constant supply of maize to provide rations for the labor force, meant that the Jesuits could either buy maize, and be subject to unstable market fluctuations, or produce it to meet their own needs. Florescano's contention that maize played a key role in determining the well-being or misery of most of Mexican colonial society warrants serious attention. Maize was the central commodity in both rations and salary payments for all of Santa Lucía's labor force. When the maize crops were plentiful, storage barns guarded part of the payments for the workers in agricultural production and hacienda maintenance. Production of maize had a definite bearing on the annual profits of all the anexas. When crops were bad, maize had to be purchased at high prices, lessening potential profits considerably. Maize on hand eliminated the need for paying with cash or other commodities during most years. It could be easily stored and kept in reserve for up to three years; it was easy to handle and transport. Above all, it was always available on demand.

As pointed out in Part I, much of the land acquired for Santa Lucía was officially designated for farming. Exactly how much was under cultivation at any given time can be calculated only imprecisely. For the first hundred years, even information on fanegas planted is lacking. The periodic inventory lists drawn up when there were changes of administrators provide helpful clues, since they mention the number of oxen and plows owned by the hacienda. The existence of these draft animals and equipment indicates farming activity utilizing Spanish technology and methods. By 1700 they were in evidence at Concepción and Tehuacán as well as Santa Lucía, San Juan, and San Xavier. Apart from Altica, Hueytepec, and Pintas, they were at all the anexas by the late 1730s. The extent to which traditional indigenous technology was being employed to raise agricultural crops is difficult to specify. Jesuit experience and policy favored European methods, but the numerous renters undoubtedly still relied upon more traditional practices. Little mention is made in hacienda records of the procedures involved in growing such things as chile, squash, and sage.

San Juan remained the main center of agricultural production for at least a century. In 1681 the hacienda administrator reported having recently increased this anexa's capacity for growing maize and complained that, although it was also suitable for growing wheat, barley, oats, frijoles, habas, and alverjon, these crops were not sufficiently exploited because of labor shortages. With the 150 oxen he now had on hand, he felt that agricultural production of San Juan could be stepped up to such an extent that 3,000 or 4,000 pesos could be earned annually.[50] The estimated capacity for San Juan at

TABLE 11

Agricultural Production Capacities of San Juan and San Xavier, 1678–1764

Year	San Juan			San Xavier	
	Plows	Oxen	Mules	Plows	Oxen
1678	—	60	—	—	—
1681	—	150	—	—	—
1684	25	150	—	—	—
1722	30	108	34	32	130
1726	39	140	25	24	122
1743	25	102	—	20	157
1746	15	83	—	29	101
1751ᵃ	—	120	—	36	113
1764	20	103	—	34	209

SOURCES: BNM 1058, 1: 99–206.
ᵃSan Juan was rented out during this period; at San Xavier the following crops were sown: maize (30 fanegas), barley (128 fanegas), alverjón (11 fanegas), habas (2 fanegas), potatoes (42 quartillos), frijoles (18 quartillos).

the time was roughly 405 hectares.* Three years later (1684), 150 oxen and 25 plows were used in planting 20 fanegas of maize, 300 fanegas of barley, and other unspecified crops.[51] Mules were also used as plow animals at San Juan. Production capacities at the two main centers of agricultural production remained constant between the 1720s and the early 1740s, after which they briefly declined there but were expanded at the other anexas. Table 11 provides an overview of the production capacities of San Juan and San Xavier over almost a century. The existence of 628 oxen, listed in a Santa Lucía inventory for 1764, indicates a considerably larger overall capacity.

Information on annual maize production for the hacienda as a whole is supplied by the tithe records, which list annual production from 1713 to 1766. These records indicate that there were years when frosts and droughts seriously affected production. Table 12 presents available information for the major agricultural harvests of Santa Lucía in the eighteenth century. Despite the gaps in information, the picture demonstrates the inconsistency of returns from farming endeavors. During years of plenty, as in 1756, Santa Lucía produced surpluses of maize that were sold at a handsome profit. Annual needs for rations paid to the hacienda workers, at least

*Including the following crops: 14 fanegas of maize; 200 fanegas of wheat; 300 fanegas of barley; 10 fanegas of alverjón; 6 fanegas of frijol. AGNAHH 285, 33; BNM 1058, 1:117.

TABLE 12
Santa Lucía Harvests of Farm Crops, 1713–1766

Year	Maize (fanegas)	Maize (costales)[a]	Barley (cargas)	Alberjón (fanegas)	Frijoles (fanegas)	Habas (cargas)
1713	—	800	200	—	—	
1714	1,000		250	—	—	
1715	1,620		320	—	—	
1716	700		225	—	—	
1717	1,020		310	55	50	
1718	1,000		300	52	55	
1719	1,200		310	53	52	
1720	1,250		312	54	42	
1721	800		140	55	60	
1722	1,340		350	30	117	
1723	1,100		220	17	95	
1724	890		296	20	110	
1725	380		270	0	0	
1726	790		147.5	0	30	
1727	1,250		120	30	120	
1728	1,845		194	60	0	
1729	1,200		200	70	100	
1730	270		150	20	0	
1731	1,620		170	30	20	
1732	2,080		130	40	50	
1735	260	70	19[b]	—	—	
1736	2,870		490	30	168	
1737	—	52[b]	0	—	—	
1738	3,912		470	15	75	15
1739	2,173		672	35	30	2
1740	—	736	190	—	—	
1742	—	2,477	586	11	—	
1743	3,300		1,100	—	—	
1745	1,886		—	—	495	
1746	3,429		—	—	580	
1747	5,250		608	—	—	180
1753	—	1,640	362	13	22.5	100
1754	5,200		450	15	137	50
1755	—	1,590	85	—	—	
1756	—	12,151	—	—	—	
1760	—	1,085[b]	133	—	—	
1764	—	3,345	910	27	—	
1765	—	1,870[b]	190[b]	—	—	
1766	—	2,085[b]	360[b]	—	—	

SOURCE: AGNAHH 293, 2.
[a]Maize was sometimes measured in *costales de masorca*, or sacks of unhusked maize. The actual volume of maize involved depended upon the quality of the ears, varying between 0.5 and 0.75 fanega per costal.
[b]Incomplete data.

during the 1740s, were between 4,000 and 4,400 fanegas.[52] This represented a significant portion of the annual labor costs, depending upon the price of maize during a given year. During 1747, at the San Ignacio ranch, maize rations constituted 34.4 percent of the total labor costs.[53] The value of maize fluctuated, but the monthly salary schedules remained more or less constant. The value of the maize rations in 1750, for example, represented 49 percent of the labor costs.

Control of maize resources placed the Jesuits in a strong position to control labor. The Tolcayucans, who provided most of the labor for San Xavier agriculture and whose own ability to produce maize had been greatly reduced by the Jesuits' acquisition of the lands surrounding the pueblo, found themselves having to work for the Jesuits—who either had reserves or could buy maize not available to the Indians—in order to get maize. The weekly labor accounts for 1730 and 1736 show that, from late March to September (the period when pueblo maize supplies were lowest), the Tolcayucan laborers worked largely for maize, and to pay their pasture rentals. In other years (1732–1733, 1737) they received the bulk of their wages in cash.*

Costs of maize production varied from year to year depending, in part, upon the value of the maize expended in salaries. If the Jesuits could use their own surpluses, costs of producing the next year's crop were reduced. In 1732 the labor cost of producing 500 fanegas of maize at Atlantepec was 772.25 pesos, or 1.54 pesos per fanega. In the following year only 521.4 pesos were spent on labor resulting in 783.7 fanegas, with each fanega having cost 0.66 peso. The costs just quoted included preparing the land, planting, weeding and cultivating, guarding the fields, harvesting, and cutting and stacking the maize stalks to be used as animal fodder.[54] Agricultural schedules for the main agricultural crops are shown in Table 13. In the 1760s, the cost of preparing land for 1 fanega of maize (8.8 acres) was being calculated at 22 pesos, while for 1 fanega of barley (1.5 acres) the cost was 22 reales. Unharvested maize in the field was valued at 55 to 66 pesos per fanega, and growing barley was rated at 5.5 pesos per carga (slightly more than 3 acres).[55] Late spring frosts, droughts, and early fall frosts affected

---

*AGNAHH 313, 18. Between March and September 1730, San Xavier had from eleven to eighty-four agricultural laborers. In twelve of the sixteen weeks all the labor costs were paid in maize or credited to pasture rentals. In 1736 maize made up 25 percent of the wages, with the rest in the form of rent and cash. During the other years the weekly payments were mostly in cash.

TABLE 13
Santa Lucia Agricultural Schedules, 1700–1767

Month	Regular maize	Irrigated maize	Regular wheat	Irrigated wheat	Regular barley	Irrigated barley	Beans (frijoles)
January	Harvesting, storing		Harvesting, winnowing	Irrigating	Harvesting	Irrigating	
February	Harvesting, storing		Winnowing	Irrigating		Harvesting	
March		Plowing, sowing	Plowing	Irrigating		Harvesting	
April	Plowing, sowing	Sowing	Plowing, sowing	Harvesting	Plowing, sowing	Harvesting	
May	Sowing, first weeding	Weeding, irrigating	Sowing	Harvesting	Sowing		
June	First weeding, second weeding	Weeding, irrigating	Sowing, weeding	Winnowing	Sowing, weeding		Sowing
July	Second weeding		Weeding	Winnowing	Weeding		Sowing
August	Other weeding, mounding						
September	Mounding			Plowing		Plowing	
October	Guarding	Harvesting	Harvesting	Sowing	Harvesting	Sowing, irrigating	Harvesting
November	Guarding, harvesting	Harvesting	Harvesting	Sowing	Harvesting	Sowing, irrigating	Harvesting
December	Harvesting		Harvesting	Irrigating	Harvesting	Sowing, irrigating	

SOURCE: Gibson, *Aztecs*, p. 330.

both the labor costs and the volume of the harvest. Available data suggest that crop yields were very inconsistent. This factor, rather than labor costs, largely determined the eventual production cost per fanega in any given year.

Maguey Plantings and Pulque

Extensive exploitation of the maguey plant began early in Mexico. Pulque, its alcoholic by-product, was strictly controlled by cultural and religious norms in Aztec times. During the colonial period, Aztec norms were replaced by Christian and Spanish norms, and the Indigenous populations grasped at pulque as a crutch to help support them during the difficult period of stress and accommodation.[56] Pulque was the only alcoholic beverage accessible to the Indigenous population, which could not afford and did not use European-introduced beverages. The commercial production of pulque was well developed long before the Jesuits became involved. Even the crown was late in attempting to tax it. Taxation policies, dating back to 1663, sought to augment royal income and provide more accurate information on production and sale of pulque. Data published by Payno (1864) show royal income—based on a tax of 12 reales per carga of pulque entering Mexico City—at 66,000 pesos a year in 1669; by 1674, at 92,000 pesos; by the end of the seventeenth century, at over 100,000 pesos; and by the 1740s and 1750s, at 128,000 pesos. In 1764, the year the Jesuits took direct control of Santa Lucía pulque production, royal income from taxes on pulque entering Mexico City legally had reached 269,000 pesos. This sum represented some 179,000 cargas, or over 53 million pounds, of pulque.[57] And tax collectors were never able to exercise vigilance over all pulque brought into the viceregal capital by canoe, mule train, wagon, and donkey, and in assorted containers carried by humans. By the middle of the eighteenth century, pulque revenues for producers, distributors, and even royal coffers were more important than almost any other source of income.[58] Santa Lucía was producing, by 1754, 12,000 to 14,000 cargas (at 300 pounds per carga) of pulque annually. This was 12 to 14.4 percent of the taxed pulque annually entering Mexico City.[59] The portion of Santa Lucía pulque that may have been sold in the flourishing black market could not be determined, nor could the total volume of "illegal" pulque sold, although for a later period the clandestine commerce has been estimated at more than double the regulated sales.[60]

The Spanish Conquest provided new equipment for the manufacture of pulque—such as metal knives and rasps for preparing the maguey plant and stimulating the flow of aguamiel, sheep and goat skins used as receptacles for transporting and storing fermented and unfermented sap, oxhide fermenting vats and horsehair sieves for eliminating impurities, and donkeys, mules, and wagons for transporting the product—but little else. Payno notes that the Aztecs distinguished over twenty types of sap-producing magueys, and used and regulated wild and domesticated varieties extensively. The use of a long, hollow gourd (calabash) for withdrawing the liquid from the plant, flat stones for covering the collection cavity, and pottery and wooden containers was retained throughout the colonial period. There was no alteration in native procedures of removing the seed stalks of mature plants (castration), scraping the cavity to induce continuous sap flow, withdrawing sap twice daily by suction during the maguey's period of production, and adding roots and small quantities of ripe pulque to speed up fermentation (taking as little as twenty-four hours, or up to three or four days). The new dimension added to pulque production was its large-scale commercialization, resulting in the conversion of significant portions of the present Mexican states of Hidalgo, Mexico, Tlaxcala, and the Federal District to pulque production. This conversion took place, initially, on non-Jesuit estates. When the Jesuits joined the general trend, they incorporated existing technology and procedures, adding an efficient system of administration. Santa Lucía was strategically located to take advantage of expanding markets and established production methods.

The maguey, unlike maize, was relatively unaffected by frosts, droughts, and unseasonal rains, and required little attention. It had many uses, apart from pulque, which had long been part of the material requirements of the local populations: as a source of fiber for mats, carrying containers, cords, threads, and textiles; as a construction material for building and furnishing homes; as a hedge or fence to mark boundaries or enclose agricultural fields; and as a source of the sweet unfermented liquid (aguamiel) for its nutritional and medicinal value.[61] The native communities associated with Santa Lucía continued to depend upon the many products of the maguey plant throughout the colonial period, and the Jesuits allowed the Indians access to the maguey plants on their lands in the early years. The order became interested in exploiting the pulque market during the administration of Donazar, but never had a commercial interest in the other by-products of the maguey. Prior to the administration of Araujo (1726–1743), maguey cultivation was insignificant in the hacienda's economy.

Concepción became the first Santa Lucía center to engage in large-scale pulque production while it was being rented out. Native exploitation of the maguey at Concepción certainly preceded Jesuit ownership, but the collection of rentals, based on the number of plants and their pulque capacities, was established by Araujo. Plantings were measured either linearly, in leagues or fractios thereof, or in estancias, ranchos, and sitios. These latter measurements were borrowed from the livestock ranches and referred to rights of access to the plants on lands designated for livestock. Concentrated plantings of the maguey were referred to as *sitios de magueyales,* and the terms *medio sitio* and *pedazo* were also used. The productivity of plants was differentiated as competent or copious. Rental rates were low initially. A gobernador of Ticuatla paid 42 pesos annually for use of one *sitio de ganado mayor de magueyal* in the early 1740s. The alcalde of another pueblo paid 8 pesos annually for use of a *pedazo de magueyal* with a production capacity of four to six cargas of pulque per week.*

When Miers took over Santa Lucía, he placed pulque production on a rational footing more in line with the other economic aspects of the hacienda. A few individuals were still encouraged to make linear plantings in the interests of delineating hacienda boundaries. Most previous renters lost their privileges as central planning and administration became established. Starting with 1744–1745, other agricultural activities between August and September 20 became subordinate to the maguey planting at San Xavier and other anexas. Only good land (*tierra floja*) was used, and the mayordomos who planted magueys in infertile land (*tepetate*) did so at the risk of personally paying the labor costs.[62]

Maguey plants were classified according to type and age. A combination of Nahuatl and Spanish terminology was maintained in the nomenclature. Three types of maguey of Nahuatl origin were common at Santa Lucía: the *mexoxoctle* (also *metlocoztli*), or yellow maguey; the *mechichiles* (also *mechichitl*), or black maguey; and the *mexoxtle* (also *mexocotl*), or plum maguey. In addition there was a series of species referred to by Spanish names, such as the maguey *manso* (tame), *cimarrón, cimarrón chino, chino legítimo,* and *cimarrón*

*The Jesuit measurement was the same used by others, consisting of a carga of 12 arrobas, weighing 300 pounds; PCRVP 1: 521.

TABLE 14
Types and Values of Santa Lucía Maguey Plantings,
1767–1775

Type	Market value (pesos per caballería)
Manso superior	3,000
Manso bueno	2,500
Manso de menos calidad	2,000
Manso, todas calidades	1,600
Manso de menor calidad	1,500
Cimarrón grande	1,300
Cimarrón pequeño	800
Cimarrón chino	1,000
Cimarrón chino, inferior	800
Revueltos	800
Mechichitl	600

SOURCE: Private papers, Don Manuel Romero de Terreros.

blanco. An indication of respective productivity can be seen from values assigned to caballerías of plantings (Table 14).[63]

Most species of maguey, before sprouting seed stalks, produce a series of young plants that grow around the base of the plant. At two to three years of age, such young plants were dug up with an iron bar and trimmed back to three leaves plus the stalk. These plants were left exposed for two or three months prior to planting. If other agricultural plants (mostly barley) were being produced in the same soils, the maguey were planted in rows 44 feet (16 varas) apart.[64] The Jesuits, however, preferred more intensive plantings, with the young plants set in holes of half a vara in depth and width, in straight rows, with 11 feet (4 varas) between plants. Some plants were started in seed beds and transplanted to the fields after reaching a height of roughly 12 to 18 inches. These plantings were carted to the fields and planted in a check pattern. The individual maguey fields were increased, but initially they were not extensive.[65] With each plant requiring 16 square varas, a caballería of land had room for 4,608 magueys. To have 70,000 maguey plants in production in any given year, as was the case in the 1750s, and taking into consideration a maturation period of seven to ten years, Santa Lucía required plantings of 106.3 to 151.9 caballerías. This represented a total of 45.3 to 64.7 square kilometers of maguey. By the time the Jesuits were expelled in 1767, their maguey plantings had more than doubled. Many of the fields were enclosed by stone walls to prevent unauthorized access.[66]

Labor used in preparing the maguey fields for pulque production was highly organized. An adult male, in order to fulfill his daily quota, was expected to dig 125 holes or plant 200 young magueys. Cleaning the maguey consisted of trimming back all the leaves but three and the growth center, or heart, of the plant. This, according to Miers's instructions, was to be done annually. The quota set for cleaning maguey varied, depending upon whether the plants were scattered or in set patterns, and upon the size of the plants. The daily quota for plants over three feet in the concentrated fields was 130, in scattered fields, 100. For plants one vara in height, called *chicos*, the quotas were 200 and 150; for plants of half a vara, 350 and 250 per day. This was the quota expected in exchange for the 2 reales earned by field laborers. The mayordomos were instructed to check, twice a day, the quantity and quality of the work done.[67]

The Jesuits supervised the planting of the maguey fields but avoided direct administration of the activities connected with the production of pulque. This was perhaps a concession to the moral position of the society against the intoxicant which they identified as the cause of evil in native society. The hacienda, removed as it was from the mainstream of Jesuit activity, and essential to the economic welfare of the Colegio Máximo, apparently could engage in activities that might be inconsistent with the thinking of the superiors. Indirect involvement permitted both the economic benefits and avoidance of direct production of a substance identified as morally degrading. No record was encountered in the hacienda documentation of any great debate about getting involved in pulque production. Coming as it did during the administration of Donazar, it may be that the matter was never discussed. Once established, it remained unquestioned.

Don Manuel de Orruño contracted the pulque production for Santa Lucía for most of the time of Jesuit involvement. His predecessor had proved unreliable and was dismissed when Miers took over. Orruño was retained by Villaverde, and although the Jesuits kept a watchful eye on the economic returns, they avoided direct involvement until the dismissal of Villaverde. When Orruño started, 18,500 pesos were expected annually from pulque production. This figure increased to 20,100 pesos when Villaverde became administrator in 1751. In 1754 Villaverde estimated Santa Lucía had a potential of producing between 600 and 800 cargas of pulque a week, over five to six months. Actual production seems to have been around 600 cargas per week, indicating an annual production of between 1,800 and 2,160 tons of pulque. The college administrators apparently had suggested increasing weekly production to 800 cargas. This, Villaverde argued, could only be done by scraping the plants too early and too intensively, causing harm to the plants and eventually producing a lower yield.[68]

Although the maguey sap-flow cycles are seasonal, the pulque producers developed means of having year-round production. This may have been accomplished by knowingly accepting lower yields during certain seasons and "forcing" production. Monthly income from pulque at San Xavier over a three-year period (1740–1742) averaged out to 270.5 pesos per month. The mean monthly high for the period was 330.25 pesos (July), with a low of 224.9 pesos (March).[69] The prospect of a steady year-round source of revenue, in contrast to the seasonal returns from other activities, increased the value of pulque operations for the hacienda and the college.

Since pulque production was not directly controlled by the Jesuits until 1764, the records were either kept apart or remained with the contractors. Documentation on details of production and distribution are fragmentary. The contractor, not the Jesuits, paid the tithe on pulque. Whether these men made great profits or marginal profits is also difficult to determine accurately. Lascano padded his own pockets, but the degree to which Orruño followed suit can only be surmised. By the time Orruño "took off" in the early 1760s, income from pulque had dropped to less than 14,000 pesos a year. Villaverde then took over and attempted to restore higher levels of income. When dismissed, he offered to continue the contract for pulque at an annual rate of 25,000 pesos. The college administrators declined the offer, having decided to terminate their experiments with secular managers, as they put it, "in order that the products, and income, whether great or small, would be for the college."[70] Within two years the pulque income had climbed to 32,000 pesos a year.[71]

Hacienda Manufacture: The Obraje

Santa Lucía's obraje played an important role. Its primary functions were to convert wool into textiles that could be given to the labor force in lieu of money, and to produce blankets and a variety of textiles and yarns for sale to buyers not associated with the hacienda. The Jesuits established this obraje late in the sixteenth century or early in the seventeenth century. By the 1640s it was contributing significantly to the hacienda's income. Records of sales at Santa Lucía over twenty-eight months beginning with September 1646 show average monthly sales of 42 blankets (*frezadas*), 240 to 360 varas of a coarse woolen sackcloth (*sayal*), 18 varas of a fine woolen cloth (*paño*), 96 varas of a blue woolen cloth (*palmillas*), and linens made from hemp (*bramante*) and saffron (*brin*).[72] During the early years the obraje produced primarily frezadas, sayal, and paño.[73] As Santa Lucía grew, its activities were expanded, so that by 1751 the obraje was producing, besides the articles just mentioned, a coarse woolen cloth (*jerga*), another finer woolen cloth (*ruan*), and petticoats (*naguas*) and skirts (*huipiles*) commonly worn by Indian women.[74]

Obraje labor consisted largely of Negro slaves, mainly women and children. The Santa Lucía obraje was outside the crown-designated areas where obrajes could employ Indians.[75] The source of the ill repute of these sweatshops[76] was in evidence at Santa Lucía, where chains and leg irons were considered standard equipment. Throughout the eighteenth century, the obraje had between ten and twenty-one pairs of these *grillos*.[77] Some of the spinning wheels used to make yarn were equipped with their own chains to prevent the worker from absconding. Obraje activities included all the steps of converting the wool from the hacienda's shearing pens into finished products. First the wool was washed and dyed, then carded and spun, and finally woven into finished, salable items. Year-to-year records of obraje production could not be located except for a short period in the seventeenth century. The inventory of equipment of the obraje, however, can be used as a guide to production capacities (see Table 15).

Under Villaverde's administration, the costs of running the obraje outstripped the value of its production, and the Jesuits ordered it terminated and the slaves transferred to the college's sugar estate at Xalmolonga.* Besides the textiles, the obraje produced a wide vareity of threads and yarns used for the weaving. During the last years of operation some cotton was being spun and woven.[78] The common dyes used at the mill were alum (*alumbre*), copper and zinc sulphate (*caparrosa*), and brazilwood—which were imported—and native dyes such as indigo (*añil*), and the vegetable

*Seventy-nine slaves were employed at the obraje when Villaverde took over Santa Lucía; BNM 1058, 1: 197.

TABLE 15
Santa Lucía Obraje Equipment, 1678–1764

Year	Looms	Pairs of cards	Spinning wheels
1678	3	—	—
1684	3	—	—
1722	5	12	44
1726	7	—	44
1743	10	42	70
1746	14	32	81
1751	29	24	56
1764	0	0	0

SOURCE: BNM 1058, 1: 99–206.

dyes *cascalote* and *sacatlascale*. Quantities of threads were sold to the wives of hacienda workers or outside buyers. The most popular item was the plain woolen blanket, made in a variety of sizes. For a number of years in the 1750s the obraje supplied frezadas valued at 3,400 pesos for the Augustinian estate called San Nicolás.[79]

But the bulk of the obraje's products remained within the sphere of Santa Lucía activities, making up a significant portion of wages paid to herdsmen and resident workers. Obraje production does not appear to have been taxed by the ecclesiastical authorities. It had served the interests of the hacienda well until the termination of its activities. In the immediate post-Jesuit period, one of the first things the state-appointed administrator of Santa Lucía did was re-establish the obraje, claiming it proved to be "an advantageous saving for the hacienda."[80]

Overview of Hacienda Production

The Jesuits consistently attempted to maximize all available means of creating revenues. They required a great deal of organization to make the system work. The Jesuits were successful in establishing a rational system of organizing agricultural and livestock activities. They were not particularly innovative or different from their peers in the secular world, because they were specifically instructed not to attempt to be different. The Instrucciones suggested sticking to tried and proven methods.[81] Where the Jesuits excelled was in the organization and implementation of rural productive technology widely used in the region. The primary task of the administrators was to coordinate all facets of hacienda activities to serve the common goal of producing revenues for the College. Any single aspect of production rose to dominance only when it demonstrated a capacity to contribute accordingly. Jesuit administrators allowed sufficient flexibility for the hacienda to adapt to the changing market trends in Mexico during the colonial era. At all times they emphasized the type of productive activities calculated to produce maximum revenues.

Santa Lucía records report net annual income for the Colegio Máximo but do not distinguish clearly between capital expenditures (land acquisition, construction and improvement of facilities, and conversion of specific anexas from one activity to another) and labor expenditures involved in annual production. This makes it difficult to present a balance sheet of expenditures and income for specific years. An overall picture of the productive system employed at a hacienda such as Santa Lucía, however, is less difficult to detail. Involved was the internal versus the external economy of the hacienda, the relations between the anexas and the administrative center, and the role of Santa Lucía in the economy of the Colegio Máximo.

The internal economy of Santa Lucía was designed to minimize cash expenditures for goods and services originating outside the hacienda. Whenever possible, hacienda produce from individual anexas (livestock, food crops, manufactured obraje goods) was used as partial payment for the labor force, or to supply livestock and other consumption needs of individual units. Such internal transfers meant movement of items within the hacienda complex to ensure overall efficiency, under the supervision of administrators who could anticipate short-term needs at the specific units and who made adjustments to ensure harmony with long-term planning. Use of the hacienda's own communication and transport systems also decreased dependence upon external services and expertise and costs related to such services. In addition, these internal activities reduced taxation (alcabala, diezmo), since such transfers were considered necessary for the maintenance of the estate and therefore not taxable. If Santa Lucía and its anexas could not supply the goods and services—for example, during bad food-crop years or when skilled personnel was lacking—these would, if possible, be acquired from the other haciendas owned by the Colegio Máximo and under the administrative control of the same college officials in charge of Santa Lucía. The net result was a condition of internal mutual dependency and self-sufficiency geared, not to minimum market participation, as has been the traditional explanation for colonial haciendas, but to maximum participation and cash returns from the external, albeit regional, market.

It was from the external market that hacienda profits derived, through the sale of livestock, food crops (provided there were sufficient surpluses), cash crops, or processed goods (meat, hides, tallow, and textile products). This external aspect of hacienda economic design was implemented by administrative officials who had the contacts and experience to make deals resulting in maximum cash returns. Colegio Máximo receipts and bills of sale pertaining to Santa Lucía (1720s to 1740s) show transactions with merchants in Mexico City, Pátzcuaro, Guadalajara, Pachuca, Toluca, Sacala, Actopan, Xiquilpan, Zamora, Otumba, Ecatepec, Zapotlán, and other urban centers in the Central Highlands. Included were purchases as well as sales, particularly for maize during years of crop failure. Even when internal food-crop supplies were sufficient, external purchases might be made for purposes of speculation.[82] Since maize crops were generally erratic, shortages could always be expected. But with massive storage facilities at Chicavasco, Tepenene, and San Xavier, hacienda officials could buy cheaply during years of plenty and sell dearly during years of scarcity, or at least have relatively inexpensive stores for internal use during periods of high prices. Little information was found regarding the Jesuit sale and distribution of pulque during the few years they directly managed this aspect of Santa Lucía activity. The dramatic rise in income from this source during 1765–1766, and the restructuring of most hacienda activities to take advantage of increased demand, suggest that the Jesuits, had they not been expelled, would have achieved very substantial profits from Santa Lucía during the last third of the eighteenth century. The Colegio Máximo management design was ideally suited to such ends.

Reported annual profits (Table 16) during the 191 years of Jesuit control of Santa Lucía varied a great deal, reflecting the vicissitudes of disease, weather, and market conditions. The Jesuits were consistent in their insistence that Santa Lucía was the primary source of income for the Colegio Máximo and the activities it supported, even during years when the college reported net losses. For example, during 1724–1726, 1728–1729, and 1733, college deficits totaled 49,000 pesos, whereas Santa Lucía profits totaled 99,698 pesos.[83] Although the cumulative profits of the hacienda complex during the entire period of Jesuit ownership cannot be precisely documented, they can be estimated. For the 53 years for which annual profit figures could be located, the yearly average works out

TABLE 16
Santa Lucía Net Revenues, 1582–1767

Year	Revenue	Year	Revenue Hacienda[a]	Pulque[b]
1582	3,423	1680	30,920	
1583	4,418	1724	15,987	
1584	5,349	1725	13,142	
1585	7,000	1726	1,269	
1586	3,000	1727	22,271	
1600	17,000	1728	28,966	
1654	12,000	1729	17,744	
1655	18,000	1733	22,559	
1656	20,500	1740	—	5,883
1657	11,234	1741	21,912	5,883
1658	16,072	1742	21,912	5,883
1659	20,734	1743	21,912	—
1660	21,521	1745	—	18,500
1661	16,000	1752	31,993	20,100
1662	10,450	1753	31,993	20,100
1663	5,386	1754	31,993	20,100
1664	12,153	1755	30,001	20,100
1665	16,468	1756	30,001	20,100
1666	17,853	1757	30,001	20,100
1667	19,136	1758	24,840	—
1668	21,087	1759	24,840	—
1669	25,728	1760	24,840	—
1670	30,130	1761	18,818	—
1671	30,400	1762	18,818	—
1672	25,254	1763	18,818	—
1673	19,379	1764	—	—
1674	21,003	1765	8,000	32,000
1679	20,424	1766	8,000	32,000

NOTE: All amounts are expressed in pesos.
[a]Includes livestock and farming activities. Three consecutive equal amounts indicate combined three-year totals divided by three to obtain yearly average.
[b]The 1740–1742 figures are derived from a combined three-year total. The 1745–1757 figures were sums agreed upon by contract. Between 1757 and 1765 revenue declined to less than 14,000 before rising again to the 1765 figure. The 1765–1766 figures represented total profits, since the Jesuits were now directly administering the pulque production.

to 18,918 pesos. Projecting this average figure over 191 years gives a total of 3,613,338 pesos produced for the Colegio Máximo by Santa Lucía and its anexas from livestock and agricultural production. In addition, available information for 13 years of pulque income shows a yearly average profit of 18,058 pesos. Projected over the 27 years of known pulque production on the Santa Lucía anexas, the total comes to 487,566 pesos. The aggregate total for

Santa Lucía as a Jesuit hacienda, if these figures are indicative, would have been 4,100,904 pesos.

The value of Santa Lucía and its anexas (excluding the northern estates of Provincia and San Jerónimo y San Nicolás) was established by royal assessors after the expulsion of the Jesuits. It came to 1,172,010 pesos, the greater part of which was attributed to land converted to maguey plantings.[84] Ignoring for the moment the rapidly increasing value of such land during the latter part of the 1760s, and taking into consideration the profit figure of 40,000 pesos for 1766, the hacienda profit represented 3.4 percent of its assessed value.[85] This figure, however, needs to be adjusted upward, based on two factors: that the assessed value was much too high (the Conde de Regla eventually bought Santa Lucía and these anexas, plus a number of large haciendas previously owned by the Jesuit Tepotzotlán college, for 1,020,000 pesos in 1776),[86] and that the Jesuits were still not receiving all possible profits in view of the recent conversion to pulque and insufficient time to implement full administrative control. The increased profit from Santa Lucía immeditely after the expulsion, while under the less efficient management of crown-appointed administrators, bears out the importance of the second factor. The ratio of profit to value for Santa Lucía at the time of expropriation, therefore, might well have been twice the given percentage. Taking into consideration the material goods supplied to the Colegio Máximo, plus its revenues, the Jesuits appear to have had sound justification for their claims about Santa Lucía. Although very similar to other haciendas in terms of what was produced and the technologies of production employed, Santa Lucía had the benefit of a management structure designed to produce continuing profits. And despite the shifts and insecurities of crops and markets, the hacienda always managed to turn a profit.[87]

PART THREE

Hacienda Life

NINE ✠ Occupation and Status

The Jesuits' records on individuals working on their estates were for the most part restricted to economic data. Most workers were identified by their given Christian names, which were Spanish, without distinguishing cultural origins or social status. The Jesuits recorded data on occupations, salaries, rations, time worked, debts, credits, and performance on the job. This contrasts sharply with the documentation created by Spanish officials, which also identified individuals by their Christian names, but almost always qualified them by reference to racial classification, marital status, age, occupation, and residence jurisdiction. This documentary fact suggests that the Jesuits were less concerned with societal or legal distinctions of class* than were the governmental officials, and that performance rather than social status was the key factor determining promotion and social mobility on the Jesuit hacienda. People who lived at the hacienda or who came to work for it, whether for long or short durations, invariably did so in specified occupations. The list of occupations at Santa Lucía during the eighteenth century was very long. If such classifications can be taken at full value, occupational specialization was one of the dominating characteristics of labor organization in colonial Mexican society.

Each type of activity at Santa Lucía, whether concerned with livestock, agriculture, or the residences, required occupational skills that can be ranked. Criteria determining rank involved at least the following aspects:

1. Degree of supervision of other workers
2. Knowledge or special skills required
3. Involvement with funds or resources exchangeable for funds.

The higher the rank of an occupation, the greater the salary (calculated annually, monthly, or daily), the greater the rations (calcu-

---

*The Iberian usage of the term *casta*, referring to social-status differentiation, is implied here rather than suggesting caste differentiation. See Mörner, *Race Mixture*, pp. 53–74; and Wolf, *Sons*, pp. 235–39.

lated in most cases weekly and measured in fanegas of maize or fractions thereof, or in cash or meat), and the greater the potential for fringe benefits. Such fringe benefits included those gained with the knowledge of the Jesuits, such as incentive payments for production, as well as those gained secretly, at the expense of the Jesuits. In the latter case, keeping the secret—since theft or fraud was usually involved—was most important, as discovery usually meant dismissal or demotion.

Livestock-Ranching Occupations

Four levels of occupations can be identified in the livestock operations of Santa Lucía, as shown in Tables 17–19. At the highest level, directly beneath that of the Jesuits themselves, were the supervisors or managers of the individual cattle, goat, horse, and sheep ranches. Besides the mayordomo, who was in charge, there was frequently a substitute (sobresaliente) and an additional assistant (ayudante). In the absence of either mayordomo or sobresaliente, the ayudante was in charge. Salaries and rations depended upon the importance of the post. The range of income noted for this level indicates that the Jesuits did not have a set rate for each classification. Rather, they determined rates according to the importance attached to the position at a specific time. Mayordomos kept records and distributed rations and advances to workers. They usually had their own clerical assistant (escribano) and might have had additional personal servants not on the hacienda payroll. The occupations in level I were considered ongoing positions, with annual salaries.

Immediately beneath the mayordomo were people supervising activities of individual sections of a ranch. These were the chief herdsmen (vacieros, manaderos) and cowboys (caporales, vaqueros) who commanded the shepherds or cowboys taking care of individual flocks or herds. Their salaries were reckoned monthly, indicating less permanence and the possibility of more rapid turnover. During certain periods of the year, as during the annual sheep drives, additional help was required. Throughout any year the number of chief herdsmen and cowboys fluctuated. If herd sizes increased or decreased from year to year, this was reflected in the number of persons occupied at level II.

The third level contains people with special skills required at important periods in the annual livestock cycles—such as lambing (preñaderos, ahijadores), roundups (recojeros), and branding (herrade-

TABLE 17
Salaries of Occupations Involved in Sheep-Ranching, 1739–1751

Occupation	Salary (pesos per month)[a]		Rations (quantities of maize per week)[b]	
	Standard	Range	Standard	Range
Level I				
Mayordomo	—	25–41.7	48	—
Sobresaliente	—	8–25	24	—
Ayudante	—	8–12.5	24	—
Escribano	4	—	12	—
Level II				
Borreguero	8	8–10	12	12–14
Vaciero	6	4–10	12	—
Manadero	4	—	12	—
Capitán	—	3.5–6	12	—
Viejero	3	—	—	6–12
Atajero	2	1.5–2	6	—
Level III				
Ahijador	—	4–7	12	—
Boyero	6	3–6	12	—
Caballerango	—	3–5	12	—
Preñadero	4	3–4	12	—
Ranchero	—	4–5	12	—
Guarda-tierra	4	—	12	—
Arriero	3	—	12	—
Recojero	3	—	12	—
Maestro de muchachos	3	—	12	—
Trasquilador	c			
Level IV				
Pastor	3	3–4	12	8–12
Pastor de pie	2.5	2–3	—	6–12
Pastor (muchacho)	—	1.5–2.5	6	6–10

SOURCES: AGNAHH 299 and 313; AGNTe 83 and 205.
[a]Mayordomos were paid by the year, sobresalientes and ayudantes sometimes by the year and sometimes by the month. All figures here are monthly.
[b]Quartillos, at 48 per fanega.
[c]2 reales per day and no rations.

ros)—and people responsible for special tasks—such as caring for the pack train (*arrieros*), for the horses used as mounts (*caballerangos*), or for the oxen used in raising limited crops in outlying areas (*boyeros*), and guarding boundaries (*guarda-tierras*) or pastures (*guarda-pastos*). Such employment might be seasonal or year-round. Salaries were reckoned monthly and might be as high as those for people in level II. As a rule, these specialists did not have

TABLE 18

Salaries of Occupations Involved in Goat-Ranching, 1739–1751

Occupation	Salary (pesos per month)[a]		Rations (quantities of maize per week)[b]	
	Standard	Range	Standard	Range
Level I				
Mayordomo	—	10–46	48	—
Sobresaliente	—	8–12.5	—	12–48
Ayudante	—	6–8	—	12–24
Level II				
Vaciero	6	—	9	18–24
Level III				
Ahijador	4	3–5	—	6–18
Caballerango	4	—	12	—
Capitán	4	—	12	—
Guarda-pasto	3	—	12	—
Guarda-tierra	4	—	12	—
Ranchero	4	—	12	12–18
Arastrador	3	—	10	—
Maestro de muchachos	1.5	—	6	—
Quesero	1.5	—	6	—
Level IV				
Pastor	3	3–3.5	10	10–16
Pastor de pie	3	2.5–3.5	10	10–12
Pastor coleador	2	—	6	—
Pastor (muchacho)	1.5	1–1.5	6	5–8
Sabanero	1.5	1.5–2	6	6–9

SOURCES: AGNAHH 299 and 313; AGNTe 83 and 205.
  [a]Mayordomos were paid by the year, sobresalientes and ayudantes sometimes by the year and sometimes by the month. All figures here are monthly.
  [b]Quartillos, at 48 per fanega.

others working under their supervision except perhaps a young assistant (*muchacho*).

The fourth level of occupation involved the greatest number of workers. They received the lowest salaries, and their jobs required the least skill. These were shepherds, goatherds, and cowboys who cared for livestock under the direct supervision of others. On goat and sheep ranches they were normally on foot (*pastores de pie*) and represented between 40 percent (on the sheep ranches) and 75 percent (on the goat ranches) of the personnel. On cattle and horse ranches, people at this level were normally mounted and represented roughly 75 percent of the herdsmen. The number of cowboys employed at cattle ranches was much lower than for the

TABLE 19

Salaries of Occupations Involved in Cattle- and Horse-Ranching, 1739–1751

Occupation	Salary (pesos per month)[a]		Rations (quantities of maize per week)[b]	
	Standard	Range	Standard	Range
Level I				
Mayordomo	—	8–16.7	48	—
Sobresaliente	—	7–15	48	—
Ayudante	—	6–14.2	48	—
Level II				
Caporal	5	4–6	48	—
Vaquero	4	4–5	48	—
Level III				
Guarda-pasto	4	4–5	12	—
Guarda-tierra	3	3–4	12	—
Arriero	3	—	12	—
Caballerango	—	3–4	12	—
Milpero	2	—	8	—
Leñero	1.5	—	—	5–6
Boyero	—	1.5–3	—	6–12
Ordeñador	—	1–3	—	6–12
Level IV				
Sabanero	—	3–4	12	—
Yeguero	2	—	6	—
Vaquero	—	1.5–3	—	5–12
Becerrero	1.5	—	6	—

SOURCES: AGNAHH 299 and 313; AGNTe 83 and 205.

[a]Mayordomos were paid by the year, sobresalientes and ayudantes sometimes by the year and sometimes by the month, and herraderos (Level III) by the day. All figures here are monthly.

[b]Quartillos, at 48 per fanega.

sheep and goat ranches. Salaries at this level were also reckoned monthly and varied according to age and experience. A youth (muchacho) usually received half the salary of an adult. Muchachos were frequently sons, younger brothers, or nephews of adult herdsmen in levels II and III.

The personnel records of the livestock ranches also mentioned other occupations peripherally related to livestock care but essential to overall operations. The position of instructor of boys (*maestro de muchachos*) was one of these, indicating an adult paid to provide the youths with religious instruction. Such a position was normally associated with the residences of the hacienda, but it was also common at Provincia and Ocuila apart from a residence complex. The jobs of milker (*ordeñador*) and cheese maker (*quesero*) were restricted to the goat and cattle ranches. Female tortilla makers (*molenderas*) were employed for slaves working as herdsmen and paid by the hacienda. They were employed by herdsmen as well, at least periodically everywhere, but not paid by the hacienda. The sheep shearers (*trasquiladores*) worked primarily at Santa Lucía but also at Provincia, when shears were sent out to the pasture areas and gangs of trasquiladores were employed.

All workers associated with livestock ranches were classified as sirvientes, a term that requires clarification. At times the Jesuits used the term *sirvientes* to signify almost anyone working for them, including the gañanes and peones, titles usually used to refer to resident labor or unskilled day labor.[1] The term was also used to signify people employed as personal servants or engaged in domestic tasks at the Santa Lucía residences. The Instrucciones used the term *sirvientes del campo* to refer to workers on the livestock ranches.[2] Many of these sirvientes were in fact resident on hacienda lands, as they were permitted to build their own houses, to keep livestock, and to plant crops. This was particularly the case with the sheep ranches. Xoloc, for example, received its name from the fact that the shepherds established their residences near the pueblo of that name.[3] Provincia and Negra employees in the upper-level occupations were allowed to build their residences at the sheep pastures. This served the Jesuit interest in that such residents acted as custodians of hacienda property and protected boundaries against potential encroachers.[4]

Hacienda Residence Occupations

The residence centers of Santa Lucía used a wider variety of occupational skills than either the farming anexas or the livestock ranches. Each major residence had associated with it auxiliary activities calling for special labor skills. Santa Lucía had its textile mill and shearing facilities; San Xavier, and later Chicavasco, had slaughterhouses. In addition, each kept sufficient livestock close by to meet local needs. Chicavasco became a center for fattening livestock prior to slaughter in the 1740s and became identified by an alias, *la engorda*. These residences, and San Pablo after the 1750s, had, in addition to the occupations listed in Tables 17–19, most of the occupations listed in Table 20.

Occupational levels identified for the hacienda residences were similar to those for the livestock ranches. The mayordomo's position was less important because one of the Jesuit administrators (either the general hacienda administrator, his assistant, or one of

TABLE 20

Salaries of Agriculture and Residence Occupations, 1739–1751

Occupation	Salary (pesos per month except Level IV)[a]		Rations (quantities of maize per week)[b]	
	Standard	Range	Standard	Range
Level I				
Mayordomo	—	5–16.7	—	24–48
Sobresaliente	—	5–10	—	24–36
Ayudante	—	5–8	—	12–24
Level II				
Capitán	—	4–6	—	12–24
Caporal	—	4–6	—	12–24
Maestro	c			
Level III[d]				
Boyero	4	—	12	—
Guarda-milpa	4	—	12	—
Guarda-pasto	4	—	12	—
Milpero	4	—	12	—
Arriero	3	—	12	—
Mulero	3	—	12	—
Doctrinero	2	—	6	—
Leñero	1.5	—	—	5–8
Ordeñador	—	1.5–3	—	6–12
Quesero	—	1.5–3	—	6–12
Level IV				
Peón	2 rls.	1.5–2 rls.		
Muchacho	1 rl.			
Mujer	1 rl.			
Molendera		2–3 rls.		

SOURCES: AGNAHH 299 and 313; AGNTe 83 and 205.

[a]Mayordomos were paid by the year, sobresalientes and ayudantes sometimes by the year and sometimes by the month. Their salaries here are monthly. In Level IV peónes, muchachos, and mujeres were paid by the day, and molenderas were paid by the week. No rations were given to this category of worker.

[b]Quartillos, at 48 per fanega.

[c]Paid on piece-work basis, without rations.

[d]Other Level III occupations without fixed salaries or rations were albañil, adobero, cajonero, caponero, carpintero, carretero, cubero, herrador, herrador, herrero, ladrillero, maderero, noriero, puerquero, sillero, tejador, trasquilador, and criada de la casa.

the college procuradores) was usually present to supervise important activities such as construction, shearing, branding, slaughtering, storage of harvests, or sale and purchase of produce. The level I overseers at the residences worked under the direct supervision of Jesuits, so they were less independent than their peers on the livestock ranches. This was reflected in their lower salaries.

The level II supervisors were in charge of types of work activity rather than a section of the residence complex. *Maestros* here were master craftsmen who supervised the construction of buildings, corrals, and storage barns. At times these contractors came to the residence with their own labor crews, the members of which were called *albañiles* regardless of the type of construction being carried out. Capitanes and caporales were the foremen of labor crews used for building water ponds (*jagueyes*) or irrigation ditches, or they might be in charge of a group of specialists such as the trasquiladores.

Specialists at level III filled a great variety of occupations. They frequently had their own assistants or apprentices. At Chicavasco and San Pablo, where the Jesuits initiated large-scale building programs in the 1740s and 1750s, numerous carpenters and timber makers (*madereros*) were employed. Tile makers (*ladrilleros*), adobe brick makers (*adoberos*), box makers (*cajoneros*), firewood suppliers (*leñeros*), teamsters (*carreteros*), castrators (*caponeros*), smiths (*herreros*), branders (*herraderos*), farriers (*herradores*), saddlers (*silleros*), mule keepers (*muleros*), muleteers (*arrieros*), coopers (*cuberos*), drawwell operators (*norieros*), cheese makers (*queseros*), and dairymen (*ordeñadores*) either came to the residences for specific periods or lived there because their skills were in constant demand. They might draw a monthly salary or be paid on the basis of piecework.

At level IV there was a distinction between those working as domestics (*criadas de la casa*) and the unskilled peones doing outside work. Both types were common. Included also were women whose husbands had died or had abandoned them (*viudas, mujeres casadas abandonadas*) and unmarried women, including those who had never formally recognized the fathers of their children (*solteras*). They were not identified according to their occupational categories, although they worked in the fields, as domestics for married overseers, in the textile mill, in the slaughterhouses, or as tortilla makers (molenderas). The pay they received was equal to, or less than, that of male youths, although they might be given rations to enable them to support their children. Finally, in the interests of the spiritual welfare of the children, if a residence did not have a resident chaplain, someone was employed to give religious instruction. Both males and females could fill this role, referred to as doctrinero or *maestro de muchachos*. San Xavier may have had a regular school since, in 1744, reference was made to a *maestro de la escuela*, in addition to a doctrinero.[5]

Residence workers were frequently referred to as gañanes. The Jesuits used the term broadly. It could mean skilled workers, such as carpenters or masons who lived on the hacienda, or it could refer to nonresident, unskilled day laborers (peones). The term did signify someone associated with labor in agriculture or at hacienda residences.

Gañanes were generally not given rations and were paid on the basis of days worked or, if skilled tradesmen, for items of work accomplished. The Instrucciones referred to workers living on the hacienda as *gañanes rancheados*.[6] Administrators kept a special record book listing the names of all people living at Santa Lucía, including the wives and children of the workers. Those listed were also referred to as *sirvientes de la tabla*, and included ranch hands, farmworkers, domestics, and renters.[7]

Agricultural and Field Labor

The structure of the agricultural labor force, apart from the residences, was different only at the specialist level. Mayordomos from Santa Lucía, San Xavier, Chicavasco, San Pablo, and other anexas directed all the agricultural work done by the resident labor force. Major differences, however, can be noted: agricultural labor was always seasonal and labor-intensive, requiring more workers for short periods than any other hacienda activity. The specialist level consisted of occupations directly related to farming. The heavy work in preparing the fields was done by oxen, necessitating an ox keeper (boyero). Once the crops were developing, someone (a *milpero* or *guarda-milpa*) was constantly on hand to protect them from livestock, birds, and neighbors. Teamsters and muleteers became involved in bringing in the harvest to the hacienda residence and storing and distributing crops.

The labor force involved in farming was drawn largely from adjacent pueblos, and these workers were referred to as peones. Wages for this type of work on Jesuit haciendas were the same as elsewhere. Gibson has outlined the wage structure for the Valley of Mexico throughout the colonial period, showing that wages for unskilled workers remained stable from approximately 1630 until the beginning of the nineteenth century.[8] Jesuit labor records listing the peones' names, rates of pay, days worked, and total cost for seasonal work at given farming areas agree with figures presented by Gibson. Adult males received a daily wage of 2 reales. A few received less, from 1 to 1.5 reales. Youths and women received 1 *real* per day. Women working as molenderas received between 1 and 3 reales per week.[9]

Records for agricultural production at San Xavier between 1730 and 1743 tell us a great deal about field labor and relationships with

TABLE 21
*Agricultural Labor Requirements
of San Xavier, 1730–1743*

Size of labor gang	Total number of weeks employed in five years	Average number of weeks employed per year
101–130	2	0.4
91–100	2	0.4
81–90	3	0.6
71–80	4	0.8
61–70	7	1.4
51–60	21	4.2
41–50	16	3.2
31–40	20	4.0
21–30	16	3.2
11–20	25	5.0
5–10	7	1.4

SOURCE: AGNAHH 313, 5 and 18.
NOTE: Years covered are 1730, 1732, 1733, 1736, and 1743.

the pueblo of Tolcayuca, which supplied many of the workers.[10] During planting, weeding, and harvesting, many workers were required; during the rest of the year, few or none at all. Very few worked more than a hundred days in any year. Since agricultural schedules were more or less the same for all the haciendas involved in agriculture, the greatest call for labor came at certain key points in the annual agricultural cycle. For much of the year workers from Tolcayuca, a pueblo that lost most of its lands during the expansion of Santa Lucía, would not be able to get work at San Xavier even if they wished to. At the same time, San Xavier would have had a critical labor shortage if unable to round up sufficient able-bodied workers during the month of planting, the approximately six weeks of cultivation and weeding, and the roughly three weeks of harvesting. During these periods every effort was made to finish the work as quickly as possible with as many workers as could be usefully employed. Table 21 shows lengths of employment, using data from over five different agricultural seasons. The figures indicate that only in exceptional circumstances were more than 100 workers employed at once, whereas labor gangs of 31 to 60 people worked at San Xavier during only four weeks on the average. Only 11 to 20 persons from Tolcayuca could expect San Xavier to provide seasonal agricultural work for as much as 25 weeks of the year over the five seasons analyzed, and this would be the case only if they were always also included in the larger gangs. For most of the Tolcayucans, San Xavier provided limited work opportunities.

The Jesuits used direct and indirect pressure to ensure an adequate labor force. One approach was to make agreements with pueblo officials to supply the hacienda with labor on demand. Tolcayucan gobernadores were paid for this purpose, or an agreement would be made with the local cura. The willingness of the Jesuits to advance the Tolcayucan cura substantial sums beyond payment for ecclesiastical services was tied to an understanding that he would exert his influence to make sure the Jesuits had labor when needed. Threatening to prevent pueblo animals access to hacienda pastures was another measure used.

In January 1746, Miers stated the Jesuit position very succinctly. He needed workers and instructed the Tolcayucan authorities to have fifty adult males with their scythes and harvest baskets at the San Xavier fields at dawn, adding that if they refused none of the pueblo inhabitants would be allowed to rent pasture for their livestock. Similar demands were made of two other neighboring pueblos: from San Pedro twenty workers were required, and from Zapotlán ten were requested.[11] In February of the same year, after the harvests were in but while fodder was still being cut, there was some disagreement regarding the type of work the Tolcayucans were to be doing. The fodder-cutting and storage were assigned to San Xavier's resident labor force. The Tolcayucans, if they wished to work, could dig irrigation ditches. This was much more difficult work and had daily quotas equated with a day's pay of 2 reales. "Otherwise," noted Miers, in reference to the Tolcayucans, if they chose not to work, "who else will accommodate them, who else will pay them?" Two weeks later there was still some disagreement and Miers rephrased the hacienda position: "As I have said repeatedly, they [the Tolcayucans] are only to work on the ditches, and whoever wishes to command in a strange house can go bark at the trees."[12]

Another means of overcoming labor shortfalls at key periods was to employ large numbers of women and children. Adult males earning 2 reales per day did most of the work in preparing the fields and sowing the crops. For the cultivation, weeding, and harvesting, women and children, earning 1 *real* per day, were extensively employed. A breakdown of percentages of male adults, women, and youths employed during five years in agricultural work (Table 22) shows the importance of women and children. The

TABLE 22
Proportions of San Xavier Labor Force
by Age and Sex, 1730–1743
(Percent)

Year	Adult males	Females (Women and girls)	Boys
1730	55%	—	45%
1732	71	—	29
1733	65	11%	24
1736	61	9	30
1743	53.5	23.4	23.1

SOURCE: AGNAHH 313, 5 and 18.

sample is too limited to distinguish clearly whether the Jesuits preferred using women and children because it was cheaper, or whether they employed them only during periodic shortages of adult male labor.

Payment for agricultural labor was made weekly and reckoned in cash, but the Jesuits consistently sought to minimize the amount of money paid out for labor. As pointed out in the previous chapter, the Tolcayucans were sold considerable quantities of maize, the cost of which was deducted from wages. If labor was being supplied by a gobernador who rented pastures from the Jesuits, the rental was deducted, leaving the official to find his own way of paying the workers. Payment was usually made directly to the crew foremen (capitanes de las cuadrillas) accompanying pueblo labor.

Workers from pueblos were expected to bring their own tools. If they used hacienda equipment and either lost or damaged it, this was deducted from their wages. Other wage deductions might include the cost of meat. In 1744 the carcasses of a cow, an ox, and a number of goats that had died at San Xavier were given to the agricultural laborers. The rather high value of 7 pesos charged for the cow, which had perished from no fault of the workers, suggests the mayordomo may have been forcing such commodities on the Indians at artificially high prices.[13]

The pueblos' labor gangs were carefully watched, although they had their own crew foremen. At night, during the harvest season, they were taken to the hacienda and locked in a storage shed. Tools belonging to the hacienda were taken in at night and redistributed in the morning.[14] Contact between the temporary laborers and the resident or nonagricultural laborers was regulated to prevent interaction. If holidays occurred during a busy harvest period (for example, December 12, Day of the Virgin of Guadalupe), pueblo labor crews were kept at the hacienda during the holiday to make sure the labor supply would not be adversely affected by fiesta activities in the pueblos.

Labor Relations

Procedures for admitting workers to the residences were detailed in the Instrucciones. The same rules applied to supervisors, specialists, and unskilled workers. Briefly stated, only reliable people were to be employed, and they were to be clearly instructed as to their duties, salaries, and privileges. Individuals who did not conform to expectations were to be dismissed forthwith. Everyone working for Santa Lucía was to be informed at the outset that salary advances could not be expected as a matter of course. The policy of the Jesuits was "Work accomplished, work paid for."[15]

The names of all workers were recorded, along with year, month, and day of commencement of employment. Advances could be given, but preference was to be shown to workers from nearby pueblos. A period of testing a worker's reliability preceded any substantial advance of goods or money. And when advances were made, the amounts were to be modest. Administrators were advised to "be cautious." Mayordomos and other persons in confidence were questioned as to how well new workers performed their duties.[16]

Administrators were told they had both the right and the responsibility to punish wrongdoing by Indians living on the hacienda "in moderation when it was necessary," but they were cautioned never to punish those from the pueblos. In such cases the administrator was to report serious offenses to the officials of the individual's pueblo, thereby avoiding any pretext for conflicts with non-hacienda authorities.[17] Accounts were to be settled regularly, according to the level and type of occupation involved. Records of each day's work were to be kept, and clear instructions regarding the next day's work were to be issued.[18] When it was necessary to work on holidays or Sundays, additional wages were to be paid. Vigilance was to be exercised so that resident workers regularly attended religious services and refrained from "drunkenness, disputes, and scandals."[19]

Hacienda records indicate that these formal instructions were functioning guides that were not adhered to equally by all administrators. According to the standards of the Instrucciones, Araujo was too lenient and Miers too harsh. Villaverde and the mayordomos, who were not bound by vows of obedience or poverty, were influenced by more secular contemporary practices in dealing with employees. Forcing workers to accept merchandise instead of cash was a widespread practice these hacienda supervisors followed.

An examination of labor relations between the hacienda and the workers at the residences shows that each laborer was treated as an individual. General procedures were uniform, as were basic policies, but the benefits and wages received, or the debts allowed, depended upon the particular case. A number of cases will be used to illustrate the range of practices.

One of the carpenters working at San Xavier between 1745 and 1747 was Juan Fernández Perete. He was paid on a piecework basis. When he started in December 1745, he received an advance of 5 pesos. As of March 1747, he had received additional cash and goods (goat hides) worth 16 pesos. When his account was settled, it showed he had earned 66.5 pesos for building doors, windows, a ladder, two small carts, and one large cart. He was paid 45.5 pesos in cash when he left.[20]

Joaquín Tiburcio de la Cruz began working on July 31, 1744, as an ayudante. He received a monthly salary of 6 pesos, 12 *quartillos* (0.25 fanega) of maize, plus an unspecified number of reales as a weekly food ration. During the next three months the following advances were charged against his account: August 25, 25 pesos in cash for his wife; September 1, 1 peso in cash; September 26, 6 pesos paid to a third party to cover a debt; October 19, 21 pesos for three colts. His account was settled on January 31, 1745, because he wished to leave. He had earned 36 pesos and received advances worth 105.75 pesos. By returning two colts and turning over to the hacienda two yearling bulls, he reduced his debt to 41.75 pesos. He was allowed to leave on the condition that his debt would be cleared within three months.[21]

Joseph Jurado worked at Hueytepec as branding-crew foreman. He was allowed to run up debts totaling 286 pesos. When his account was settled, he paid the hacienda administrator 140 pesos and provided receipts for services rendered for the remaining 146 pesos.[22]

Juan de la Cruz, an ox keeper and plowman, together with his son, started working at San Xavier on September 15, 1745. The father's monthly salary was 4 pesos and the son's 2 pesos, plus their maize and chile rations. Cruz had previously worked at Pintas, and a debt of 14 pesos he had acquired there was transferred with him. During eleven months at San Xavier, his account was debited with one ox (10 pesos), three blankets (4.5 pesos), a saddle (16 pesos), tribute money given to the gobernador of Tolcayuca on his behalf (2.5 pesos), textiles (12.75 pesos), indulgences (0.75 pesos), half an ox (5 pesos), and cash (8 pesos). His total debts at San Xavier equaled 59.5 pesos. The combined salary of father and son amounted to 66 pesos, producing a net credit of 6.5 pesos. After the first accounting, the joint salaries of father and son were increased by half a peso and advances worth 32.5 pesos were given in textiles, plus a 16 peso cash advance for the wedding of a daughter. At the second accounting, there were no debts on the account.[23]

Bartolomé de la Cruz worked as a pasture guard at San Xavier. His starting advance on June 2, 1746, consisted of 6 pesos paid on his behalf to get him out of the episcopal jail in Tolcayuca. His monthly salary was 4 pesos, 12 quartillos of maize, and 2 reales per week food rations. During his first month his account was debited 5 pesos, one saddle (12 pesos), maize (4 reales), and meat (2 pesos). When his account was adjusted on April 2, 1747, his advances totaled 42 pesos. His earnings for the ten months worked came to 40 pesos, leaving him with a 2 peso debt at the beginning of the next term. His duties were clearly spelled out. He was to impound the livestock of any pasture renters who failed to pay their rent, without making any exceptions. He collected water-usage fees from people with access to water stored by a hacienda dam. And he was to prevent non-hacienda cattle from grazing while crossing hacienda property en route to salt licks. The slightest lapse in fidelity would result in punishment and dismissal.[24] Duties of all pasture guards were spelled out in detail. At San Pablo, in 1745, Andrés de Aguilar served in this occupation, with the same salary but with a smaller maize ration (10 quartillos). He had written instructions "not to allow cattle or any beast on our lands; nor the cutting or taking of even a stick of wood under any pretext; not to allow anyone to sleep on, or pass through, the hacienda property—on the pain of not receiving his salary and being punished."[25]

It was common to have more than one member of a family employed. Jerónimo Roldán, an ayudante at San Xavier, and his two sons were typical. One son, Manuel, worked as a pasture guard at the same salary as Bartolomé de la Cruz. At the first adjustment he had earned 22 pesos and had received advances for 13.5 pesos. This left him with a credit of 8.5 pesos, which was not paid out to Manuel but transferred to his father's account. The other son, Nicolás, earned 2 pesos a month, plus weekly rations, for teaching doctrine and the rosary to Indian children. When his account was settled he owed 3 pesos, which was debited against his father's account. Whenever more than one member of a family was employed, the senior member served as guarantor (fiador) for sons, brothers, or nephews.[26]

The cases just described show the individualized nature of labor relations between hacienda administrators and the resident workers. Accounts, wages, rations, and obligations varied according to the specific case. Only workers who proved themselves reliable were allowed to accumulate debts; others had to have a guarantor to cover debts for them. Accounts were adjusted periodically, depending upon when the worker started and the type of work. When top administrative posts (such as mayordomo or administrator) changed, a general accounting was required so that the new man knew the exact financial situation of everyone under him.

The idea of debt dominated labor relations. It was basic to the Jesuit system of accounting, but the objective was to maintain a balance between credit and debit. At Santa Lucía, minimum debt levels varied with individual cases, but overall policy was to allow only those debts to accumulate that could be recouped within the period of the next accounting. Accounts of the resident labor force provide little evidence of deliberate attempts to ensure labor by forcing debts, and a great deal of evidence to the contrary. As long as Santa Lucía had a significant slave-labor force in residence, and reasonable access to nearby pueblo labor, its need for a resident labor force was not large and centered on specialists rather than unskilled workers. Hacienda records suggest that the Jesuits had less interest in having workers in debt than workers had in being in debt. A 1732 inventory of resident workers for Santa Lucía listed 186 people associated with the main residence and the anexas in the Valley of Mexico whose debts or advances had not been settled. The average debt amounted to 4 pesos,[27] and there were no indications that these debts continued. Most of the debts represented advances for marriages or funerals. In 1764 the debts of gañanes at San Xavier amounted to 789 pesos. As Villaverde's lawyers were to argue later, these debts only represented the status of accounts at a particular moment,[28] not a policy of allowing large, long-term indebtedness.

Labor Patterns

The majority of people working on a continuing basis for the hacienda were involved in ranching. Livestock required care throughout the year, so the fluctuations in labor needs characteristic of agricultural production and residence activities was not so pronounced on the livestock ranches. During the annual migrations of the sheep flocks, additional herdsmen were hired, however, and during round-ups of cattle and horses and periods of castration or branding, more help was required. For some of the tasks (branding, castration), specialists were frequently hired. In general, apart from short-term seasonal requirements for additional workers, sizes of flocks and herds determined labor needs. As animal populations increased or decreased, so did the number of workers employed. In addition, a certain number of individuals deserted their jobs, were dismissed for failing to live up to expectations, or left for personal or family reasons. Except for those who deserted—and they were replaced as quickly as possible—the hacienda administrators made every attempt to ensure that the accounts of the sirvientes were balanced before contact was severed.

Total numbers of sirvientes employed in ranching activities by Santa Lucía during the 1740s have been estimated, although figures for all the ranches in any given year were not located. Taking the maximum number at each ranch during the period from 1739 to 1751 indicates a total of 490 sirvientes; if the minimum figures are added, the total is 388 (see Table 23). These figures represent the total number of shepherds, cowboys, and their supervisors employed during the course of a single year rather than the total number employed at any one time.

Within a given year, fluctuations were significant. The starting and terminal dates listed in the account books for sirvientes show that fewer than half the shepherds (for sheep and goats) worked the entire accounting period. During the 1748–1749 working year at Negra, for example, only twenty-four of eighty-one shepherds (30 percent) worked a full twelve months. Of the remaining shepherds, twenty-four (30 percent) worked more than ten but less than twelve months, sixteen (20 percent) worked more than six but less than ten months, three (3.7 percent) worked more than three but less than six months, and thirteen (16.2 percent) worked less than three months.[29] At San Ignacio during the 1746–1747 season a similar situation prevailed. In this case only 20 percent worked the full twelve months, 22 percent worked six to ten months, 22 per-

TABLE 23
Sirvientes on Santa Lucía Livestock Ranches, 1739–1751

Ranch	1739–40	1740–41	1741–42	1742–43	1743–44	1744–45	1745–46	1746–47	1747–48	1748–49	1749–50	1750–51
Negra/Ocuila (sheep)	70	60	76	—	91	—	—	—	84	81	80	—
San Ignacio (sheep)	—	—	—	—	—	—	45	50	52	—	46	—
Provincia (sheep)	—	—	—	—	—	—	—	—	—	—	—	85
Chicavasco (sheep, goats, cattle)	—	—	—	—	—	30	30	56	—	—	—	—
Tepenene (goats)	—	—	—	—	—	—	—	—	113	106	96	—
Florida (cattle, horses, sheep)	—	—	—	12	—	20	—	—	—	—	—	—
Hueytepec (horses)	—	—	6	—	—	—	8	—	—	—	—	—
Pintas (horses)	—	6	—	—	—	—	—	—	—	—	—	—
Altica (cattle, horses)	—	—	—	—	—	—	14	—	—	—	—	—
San Pablo (cattle, goats, sheep)	—	34	34	43	—	—	45	44	—	—	—	—

SOURCES: AGNAHH 299, 4–18; 313, 4–21 passim; AGNTe 20, 3.

cent worked three to six months, and 28 percent worked less than three months.[30] At Chicavasco, during a seven-month accounting period in 1746, 28 percent of the sirvientes worked five to seven months, 44 percent worked two to five months, and 28 percent worked less than two months.[31]

These labor patterns do not indicate problems in keeping sirvientes on the job. On the contrary, they indicate just how successful the Jesuits were in continually adapting labor supply to ongoing needs. An examination of the actual starting and terminal dates shows clear patterns. At San Ignacio, 25 percent of the short-term help consisted of youths who started work during a three-week period in late November and early December, when the flocks needed extra attention because they were being moved. The starting dates in the accounts for Negra and Provincia consistently show the addition of two or three men or boys over two- or three-day intervals when the flocks were beginning their annual drive to Santa Lucía. The staggered dates reflect the nature of the drive. To avoid the congestion of having 30,000 sheep traveling together, each vaciada or manada left a day's breathing-space between it and the others. Depending upon the number of animals in the vaciadas and manadas, one to three additional shepherds were required. Most of the youths working at the sheep ranches were undoubtedly providing this type of short-term help.

Even apart from seasonal fluctuations there was a significant labor turnover. The 1743–1744 Negra accounts listed twenty-five individuals who had "died, left, or deserted." Between 1739–1740 and 1740–1741, at the same ranch, twenty herdsmen were dropped and ten new men were taken on. Of the seventy-six sirvientes listed for 1741–1742, only twenty-one were still at Negra in 1749–1750.[32] Of the goatherds at Tepenene during the 1748–1749 season, only 72 percent had been there the previous year. In the following season, only 62.5 percent of the workers had worked the year before.[33] The highest turnover encountered was at Chicavasco, in 1744, when 53 percent of the sirvientes failed to continue into the next season.[34]

These turnovers were the result of Jesuit decisions rather than voluntary mobility on the part of the shepherds. The majority of new names on next-season lists were hired as additional help long after the new accounting period had started. Those who failed to continue into the next season were, for the most part, individuals the administrators decided they did not need. All the evidence from the annual records suggests it was the hacienda administrators who decided who would be working the next year rather than the workers. Annual fluctuations and turnovers were thus largely the result of hiring and dismissal policies.

Salary Payment, Debts, and Advances

Payment of sirvientes on the livestock ranches was governed by the same principles in effect for agricultural labor and workers at the hacienda residences. Whenever possible, hacienda produce, in the form of livestock or hacienda-produced textiles, was given as payment rather than cash. The listing of payments broken down into categories of textiles (*ropas*) and cash was a standard feature of the sirviente accounts. Wages were paid to herdsmen in three ways: through advances at the beginning of the work season, through advances during the work season, and by balancing accounts at the end of adjustment periods. Initial advances were given only to workers who had already proven their reliability. The top-level supervisors and chief herdsmen had little difficulty in getting advances at the beginning of the work season unless they were newly hired. Small advances of cash, clothing, and equipment were issued in most instances to individuals requesting them.

But care was exercised with all sirvientes to ensure that their accumulated advances did not build up into large debts. Since the major annual adjustment took place at the main hacienda residence, when the sheep flocks were brought in, goods or cash advanced remained the responsibility of the hacienda administrator. He was responsible for the eventual balance of the sirviente's account as well as his own. The mayordomos were advanced quantities of goods and equipment during the same period, to be distributed during the season. But this was done with the understanding that they had the responsibility of accounting for all goods and cash advanced. Quantities of cash were sent out to the mayordomos as needed, as were shipments of maize for rations. The mayordomo could make routine advances to his shepherds during the year, but any significant amount had to be authorized by hacienda administrators.

Routine advances during the work season consisted of small amounts of cash (usually less than 4 pesos), blankets, sleeping mats (*petates*), tobacco, clothing, textiles, hides, meat, pork rinds (*chicharrón*), and extra allotments of maize. The time and type of cash advances during the season suggest a strong element of paternal custodial interest. Deliberate efforts were made to ensure participation in religious events, such as the Day of the Dead (*día del finado,* November 1), Christmas, and Easter, by advancing money for buying candles. Cash advances to the wives, mothers, and even in-laws of herdsmen were frequent, indicating a concern for the welfare of the family of the worker and, perhaps, a certain distrust of the worker himself. Large sums given as advances invariably were directly related to baptisms, marriages, and funerals.

The records for Provincia covering 1751 showed cash advances for six weddings, four funerals, and five baptisms. The amounts involved ranged from 5.75 pesos to 24.75 pesos. At San Ignacio during the 1746–1747 season, advances were given for three weddings and two funerals. In one case the father of a vaciero was given 60 pesos for the funeral of the vaciero's mother, the amount being debited against his account. An ahijador, however, was advanced only 4 pesos for the funeral of an infant son. Such advances required a written authorization from the Jesuit administrator or his designated representative.[35]

If these advances resulted in unbalanced accounts at the next adjustment, steps were taken to change this. Vicente Jiménez, a shepherd at Provincia, got married during the year and left with a debt of 43 pesos, 7 reales. His brother Nicolás was subsequently "obligated to work the time necessary to help to liquidate the debt." The amount outstanding was debited against the account of the brothers' father, a vaciero. In another case at Provincia during the same year, a sirviente owed 45 pesos and had to promise repayment within four months.[36]

At the livestock ranches, the presence or absence of workers' debts depended upon local conditions. After the August adjustment in 1751, the Provincia sirviente accounts showed debts totaling almost 1,500 pesos. Most of this amount consisted of textile advances drawn on next season's anticipated earnings. Forty-three of eighty-five herdsmen were involved.[37] A similar situation had existed at Negra during the 1740s.[38] At Florida, the cowboys took credit advances for the 1742–1743 season in the form of colts (horses and mules) and textiles. Records for the next two years showed that debts did not accumulate, although the cowboys who continued from one season to the next took additional advances of livestock.[39] Pintas cowboys took most of their advances in cash, but at the end of the season the hacienda owed them up to 50 percent of the year's earnings.[40] Shepherds at San Pablo took most of their advances in the form of blankets, textiles, hides, and chicharrón.[41] The goatherds at Tepenene took goats, cash, blankets, and textiles,[42] and at San Ignacio the advances consisted of cash, additional maize, textiles, and sheep.[43]

In all cases, goods used for advances were materials or produce supplied by the hacienda or produced at the ranch in question. By using readily available items for advances, the Jesuits accomplished two ends: reduction of cash payments and elimination of the need to transport goods. An element of coercion was involved in such advances. If textiles represented the clothing needs of the sirvientes and their families, it would seem logical that such items be acquired much nearer to where the families resided. Provincia, for example, was hundreds of miles from the Valley of Mexico, where the workers took their advances. During the roughly two months between receiving these advances and getting back to their home jurisdictions, there were ample opportunities to be relieved of the advances. Whether mayordomos and chief herdsmen found ways of defrauding the lesser shepherds during the migration back to the Guadalajara-Colima pastures is not mentioned in hacienda records. However, we do know that pueblo caciques frequently defrauded residents of lower status. The sirvientes may have quickly exchanged their advances for cash from traveling merchants or in pueblos en route. The cowboys on the horse and cattle ranches received more animals than they required and may have sold them to pueblo caciques. Villaverde's lawyers later argued that forcing goods upon workers was an accepted standard practice in hacienda administration.[44]

During Villaverde's term, practices current among other hacendados played a significant role at Santa Lucía. Jesuit policies were clear on the matter of maintaining carefully controlled accounts at all times. The question of debt peonage and the degree to which it was prevalent during the mid-eighteenth century in central Mexico cannot be answered from the data of one hacienda. Evidence from Santa Lucía shows both the use of debts as a means of ensuring labor and strong measures to control these debts. It shows the transference of debts between members of a family, but little evidence that such debts were not quickly settled. Before the larger question can be fully answered, more information is required on the exact nature of debts: Whose interest did they serve? When were they allowed to accumulate? What sectors of the labor force were involved? The ability of the Jesuits to maintain close control of their labor force, both in terms of who worked for them and for how long, suggests that Santa Lucía did not suffer from labor shortages on its livestock ranches.

Further evidence of Jesuit ability to control the activities of sirvientes can be seen from annual changes in salaries, rations, and occupational status. At Negra between 1739–1740 and 1740–1741, there were seven promotions and demotions affecting both occupational category and salary, and nine changes of salary within occupational categories. This meant that 28.3 percent of the herdsmen who continued from one season to the next had their occupational status or salary changed.[45] At Provincia in 1751 there were five promotions, affecting 6 percent of the shepherds.[46] At Tepenene 31.6 percent of the goatherds kept over from 1748–1749 had their status or income changed. Of the nineteen cases, seventeen involved changes in job, rations, or salary, and only two involved all three items simultaneously. This indicates that salaries and rations were not entirely fixed in relation to job classifications. Of the twelve individuals whose maize rations were changed, seven had them decreased and five gained increases, but those who received these increases did not necessarily receive promotions. Five individuals gained salary increases and two were assessed decreases, but only two cases involved a change of occupational status.[47] These types of adjustments help explain the ranges in salaries and rations presented in Table 18. They were indications of a system of selective reward and punishment for performance.

Unfortunately, little information is available about the eventual disposition of funds, livestock, equipment, clothes, and textiles distributed. During the sixteenth century, unscrupulous Spaniards had established the practice of forcing useless or unwanted European goods upon the Indigenous populations. Whether or not vestiges of this were engrained in hacienda exchange of goods for labor warrants serious investigation. Gemelli Carreri describes situations in highland pueblos where individuals were being forced to accept goods at highly inflated prices.[48] Hacienda exchange practices, regardless of their intent, reinforced the introduction and acceptance of European goods and livestock in Indian sectors.

Mayordomos, Sobresalientes, and Ayudantes

Successful implementation of labor policies depended upon the administrative vigor of the Jesuits' subordinates—the mayordomos, sobresalientes, and ayudantes. By and large the Jesuits hired rather than trained the men at this level. It was in their interest to employ only men who demonstrated the ability to implement policies set by administrators. Since these subordinates did not necessarily share Jesuit convictions, control over them was based on material rather than religious principles. Disloyal or dishonest mayordomos seriously affected hacienda operations and drastically reduced revenues. The mayordomo level was the bridge between the college, its administrators, and the day-to-day supervision of hacienda production, between the Jesuits and the native labor force. In addition, it was the bridge between European economic practice and the traditions of the Indigenous cultures. Jesuit planning and organization alone could not guarantee successful hacienda operations. Competent and reliable subordinates were essential.

The Instrucciones envisioned the role of the mayordomo as similar to that of the administrator, although more restricted. Mayordomos were responsible for the spiritual and material welfare of the Indians under their direct administrative jurisdiction. It was their duty to maintain economic as well as social order. In the absence of a Jesuit administrator, the mayordomos distributed rations and salaries and kept accounts. They were in charge of the care and maintenance of equipment and livestock. The mayordomo saw to it that, when the short-term agricultural labor crews stayed overnight at the hacienda residences during key work periods, they were locked in at night, that all equipment was accounted for each evening, and that both equipment and peones were on the job at the proper hour in the morning. During the day the mayordomos were personally responsible for inspecting work activities. They had greater authority on the sheep ranches than at the residences. They were not allowed to engage in private business on the side or have their own livestock in areas where hacienda livestock was supposed to be. Incentive arrangements were permitted, but these were always to be regulated and controlled by the Jesuit administrators.[49]

Salaries for mayordomos, and in most instances for sobresalientes and ayudantes, were calculated annually. Weekly maize rations were more generous than for other occupational categories, and a weekly food allowance made up of cash or meat rations in the form of livestock was usually included. The mayordomos had their own families and household staffs to take care of. Their income was geared to allow for adequate care of their families and, in theory at least, was sufficient to prevent the necessity of unauthorized ap-

TABLE 24

Mayordomo Salaries and Rations, 1764

Location (activities)	Annual salary (pesos)	Weekly rations	
		Maize (fanegas)	Cash or meat
Santa Lucía and San Juan (agriculture)	150	1.00	8 reales
San Xavier (agriculture)	200	0.75	10 reales
Altica (cattle, horses)	96	0.50	8 reales
Hueytepec (cattle, horses)	96	0.50	8 reales
Pintas (horses)	96	0.50	8 reales
Concepción (pulque)	260	1.00	8 reales
Chicavasco (agriculture)	200	1.00	8 reales
Florida (cattle, horses)	96	0.50	8 reales
Tepenene (agriculture, pulque)	60	0.25	2 reales
San Ignacio and San Pablo (agriculture, sheep, cattle, horses)	300	1.00	2 pesos, 1 sheep
Ocuila/Negra (sheep)	400	1.00	?
Provincia[a] (sheep)	500	1.00	1 sheep
Tepenene[b] (goats)	552	1.00	?

SOURCES: AGNAHH 299, 5 and 11; 307, 14; AGNTe 20, 3.
[a]1750–1751.
[b]1747–1749.

propriation of hacienda produce. The hacienda supplied the mayordomos with residences and may have provided them with hacienda riding stock. The extent to which the mayordomos drew upon hacienda-produced poultry and garden crops is not indicated in the records. The range of salaries and rations for the mayordomos at the various anexas of Santa Lucía in 1764 is indicated in Table 24.

At the large sheep and goat ranches, the annual salaries of the sobresalientes frequently exceeded those of the mayordomos at the residences and cattle and horse ranches. During the 1740s the sobresalientes at Negra and Tepenene were making up to 300 pesos a year, and the ayudantes were getting up to 144 pesos, plus weekly maize and food rations.[50] Rates for mayordomos changed according to the responsibilities involved. At Chicavasco the mayordomo received 120 pesos in 1743–1744,[51] and in 1764 the annual rate was increased to 200 pesos. At Florida the 1744 rate was 120 pesos,[52] 24 pesos higher than the rate in 1764. As in all other levels of occupation at Santa Lucía, we see here the Jesuit policy of adjusting income to the importance of the job.

The top-level supervisors were also shifted from one job to another as the administrators saw fit. Ignacio García de la Sierra started out as ayudante at San Juan in May 1744, earning 60 pesos a year, plus half a fanega of maize and 4 reales a week in rations. After three months he was moved to San Xavier, still as ayudante, but with a salary increase amounting to 2 pesos per month, on the conditon that he "do everything he was commanded, loyally and zealously, with love and fidelity, and would not have any commercial transactions with anyone—at the risk of losing everything."[53] Of the sixty-nine mayordomos identified with Santa Lucía administration between 1694 and 1764, fifteen (21.7 percent) were moved from one job to another by the Jesuits.

The Jesuits exercised exacting vigilance over the accounts of the mayordomos. All goods and supplies issued had to be accounted for, as did all the livestock under their care. The seasonal adjustment statements usually started with a list of the goods advanced to the mayordomo, followed by an accounting of maize sent to him for distribution. If he collected rents for pastures or used hacienda equipment, such items also had to be accounted for. In contrast to the other levels of occupation, the mayordomo was allowed to accumulate substantial debts. In fact, the bulk of the funds outstanding in Santa Lucía's labor accounts were debts charged against the mayordomos. When Villaverde settled his accounts in 1764, nine mayordomos had debts totaling 7,950 pesos.[54] Lesser amounts had accumulated under the Jesuit administrators. Two conclusions can be drawn from the existence of such debts: first, that Villaverde did not maintain Jesuit policies of keeping debts to a minimum, and second, that the mayordomos had a vested interest in maintaining debts as a source of job security. As long as they were in debt to the hacienda, its owners would be reluctant to dismiss them.

On secular haciendas the position of mayordomo tended to become hereditary, passing from father to son. In class-conscious colonial Mexico the institutionalization of occupational roles, and the transfer of these roles from generation to generation, had become a part of the social fabric. This had been a feature of European as well as Aztec society.[55] Jesuit economic institutions, although equally stratified in terms of occupational roles, used performance rather than kinship as the criterion for filling occupations. Biographical and genealogical information for Santa Lucía's Indian labor force is too fragmentary to distinguish intergenerational transfers of occupation clearly. We do know that the youths who worked on the livestock ranches were mostly the sons of adults already employed. At the sheep ranches of long duration, such as Negra and Provincia, many instances of kinship among workers can be identified, but lack of consistent records over long periods of time prevents an accurate assessment of whether sons eventually took over the occupational roles of their fathers.*

Information about mayordomos is more complete, as of the late seventeenth century, and shows lengthy terms of office at Santa Lucía and the involvement of members of the same family over more than one generation. A Sánchez de Mejorada family provided mayordomos for Provincia for almost half a century. A de los Angeles family had supplied mayordomos for the Florida estate for three decades before its purchase by the Jesuits[56] and continued to provide mayordomos for the Actopan Valley anexas until the 1760s. Three brothers of a Lucio family worked as mayordomos at Negra, Ocuila, and Xoloc for over twenty years before being dismissed for raising their own cattle on the sheep pastures and, as the Jesuits put it, "occupying the shepherds with their own livestock." When ordering their dismissal, the provincial added that they were not to be employed at any time in the future at any of the ranches of the Colegio Máximo.[57]

Dismissal after long years of service was not uncommon. The reasons usually centered around the mayordomos' inability to resist stealing from hacienda flocks, failure to account for supplies and livestock, and in general paying too much attention to their private business interests. The Jesuits felt they must be harsh in such cases, as a warning to others. Miguel Nieto, for example, had worked at Ocuila early in the eighteenth century and later was put in charge of the small sheep flock kept permanently near Santa Lucía. He and his sons were also renting a small rancho near Pin-

*Although the sirviente accounts do not consistently identify kinship, the frequency of clusters of names with the same patronym, even during consecutive years when labor turnover was high, indicates employment of more than one member of the same family. At Provincia, during the 1750–1751 season, one-third of the shepherds (twenty-eight) belonged to eleven families. AGNTe 20, 3.

tas. When Miers dismissed him in 1744 he wrote that Nieto, "being already over seventy years of age, no longer took care of the sheep but only lied, slept, and visited."[58] His rental agreement was also terminated.

Thadeo Rosales, a son of Pedro Rosales, a mayordomo at San Xavier during the 1750s, was accepted into the order. Thadeo underwent novitiate training and then went right back to work at Santa Lucía as a coadjutor. This was, however, the only such case encountered.

The greatest turnover of mayordomos took place when new men took over the general direction of Santa Lucía. New administrators attempted to weed out the subordinates who had not been performing satisfactorily, or to bring in new men of their own choosing. During his first years in office, Villaverde shifted or replaced most of the mayordomos working for the hacienda. He even installed his son-in-law as mayordomo of the textile mill so that his daughter could continue living at the main hacienda residence. Villaverde's sons also helped him in administration, but not as mayordomos.

One of the most serious administrative problems faced by the Jesuits appears to have been maintaining effective control over the activities of the hacienda mayordomos. They made consistent efforts to deviate from the traditional secular practice of allowing positions of trust to remain tied to family and kinship circles, but they were not altogether successful.

They were much more successful in controlling the other part of the labor force that played an important role in the hacienda's affairs, the slaves.[59] Slaves were important in almost every facet of economic activity at Santa Lucía. The eight slaves included in the original purchase constituted a small but vital controlled labor pool for the sheep ranch in 1576. Through time this resident force grew to a maximum number of slightly more than three hundred individuals. The slaves performed most of the domestic tasks at the main residence. They were an important labor source in agricultural production and at the livestock ranches. They dominated the work in the textile mill and filled positions of confidence and special trust. The slaves were the one body of labor that was not constantly being hired, dismissed, or manipulated by change of salary and rations. As chattel, they had no legal claim to any return for their labor and were listed as items (*piezas*) in the inventory lists, along with the equipment, furnishings, produce, and livestock. Yet the permanence of their presence, and the importance of the role they filled, shaped the style of the hacienda's operation. Without slaves, the Jesuits' dependence upon Indigenous labor would have been much greater. With slaves, that labor was kept less essential and more manipulable. A more detailed discussion of slave roles is presented in the following chapter.

Santa Lucía records, as pointed out at the beginning of this chapter, identified the people working on the hacienda according to occupational rank. The identifications used for all individuals, whether African slaves, Indian shepherds, or Spanish mayordomos, indicated Christian baptism, without reference to race or social status. Local status was clearly defined by occupational roles associated with levels of income and types of authority. Status was also associated with terms such as *sirviente, gañan,* and *peón,* but these were not tied to residence or type of work. Race was associated with occupation to the extent that people of African and Indigenous origin occupied the lowest levels of the hierarchy of occupations and seldom the highest. Individuals of mixed racial origins occupied the middle ranges in the hierarchy of occupations and seldom the highest or the lowest. Occupations of the middle range, however, were open to people of African, Indian, and Spanish origin. Race was not a primary factor in hiring or dismissing workers. Labor need, in accordance with the demand of economic production, was the single most important criterion in determining who worked for the hacienda and the occupational role filled.

TEN 🔲 *Slaves*

By the time the Jesuits became involved in hacienda activities, the use of African slaves had become established in New Spain. This was a tradition with which the first groups of Jesuits were not comfortable and was one of the points raised against operating rural estates. When the father general ruled in favor of Jesuit direct involvement, this included maintenance of current slave-owning practices, with the proviso that special attention be given to the slaves' spiritual needs.[1] Thereafter the Jesuits did not question the morality of their status as slave owners.

The role of African slaves in grafting Iberian animals, plants, and production techniques onto the New World setting is at times overlooked. In the first instance, the ranch hand, shepherd, plowman, orchard man, or gardener and his immediate superior were frequently black men already acculturated into Iberian society. They not only helped establish the agrarian economy but also taught the Indigenous workers skills and values needed for such activities.[2] Dusenberry's analysis of crown legislation in Mexico governing livestock production shows that Africans were considered more useful in ranching and European agriculture than Indians. By 1550 Negroes outnumbered Europeans in New Spain, and in 1575 they still outnumbered Europeans in most bishoprics. At this time the Spanish rural overseers (mayordomos) were mostly blacks, mulattoes, or mestizos. Mesta regulations stipulated that cattlemen (*estancieros*) must have four Negroes for every 2,000 head of cattle, or pay a fine of 28 pesos.[3] During the formative period of livestock-raising, it was not uncommon for encomenderos to have their African slaves care for their livestock. Many slaves were actually mulattoes of Iberian origin, already familiar with European modes of rural production. Another uninvestigated aspect of this phenomenon is that many slaves directly imported from Africa came from areas where cattle-raising was long established, whereas cattle, horses, and other livestock represented a new and frequently devastating threat to Indigenous agriculture.

The Sixteenth and Seventeenth Centuries

Santa Lucía's initial slave acquisitions included persons already acculturated to rural activities in Mexico. They were counted among the livestock purchased with partly developed estates. The Jesuits built up their slave population in much the same manner that they increased livestock populations. In the sixteenth century, they purchased 9 slaves as part of properties bought from Alonso González, including 7 adult males, 1 female, and 1 infant.[4] During the seventeenth century, the Colegio Máximo purchased or sold 500 slaves.[5] An examination of the records of purchase by Jesuit colleges of 175 slaves during the seventeenth century permits the sketching of an outline of slave purchases, although the records in question do not necessarily identify the slaves as going to Santa Lucía.[6]

Like other types of property, slaves had titles. These documents identified the slaves by name, sex, origin, and physical condition, and listed previous owners. The titles examined showed limited purchases of individual slaves during the first two decades of the seventeenth century. During the 1620s, fifty-eight slaves of both sexes were purchased, mostly in groups of two to twelve individuals per purchase. Thereafter, most of the purchases included only one or two slaves. The prices ranged from 150 to 200 pesos for children under twelve years of age to 250 to 400 pesos for adults between the ages of twenty and thirty-five. The highest recorded price was 450 pesos. The individual slaves were purchased from Spaniards in positions of power and wealth; the group purchases were made from slave merchants. All bills of sale indicated that the titles were free from encumbrances and assured the buyer that the described items were not given to theft, drunkenness, or flight, and were free of vices, physical defects, and sickness *(enfermedades públicas y secretas)*.[7] Some slaves were branded on the chest, usually with letters of a previous owner, or on the face with the brand of flight *(marca de fuego)*, if they had fled and had been apprehended. The provincial alone had the power to authorize either the sale or purchase of slaves, and all transactions referred to such permits.[8]

Apart from a 1684 report of 108 slaves of all ages, no detailed list of slaves at Santa Lucía in the seventeenth century has been located. However, information about slaves owned by the Colegio Máximo's sugar estate, Xochimancas, can be used to outline the condition of Jesuit slaves in 1653. Xochimancas was acquired by the college in 1639, at a cost of 82,000 pesos.[9] Fourteen years later its slave population numbered 174 adults and 73 children. A detailed inventory of this population provides insights into age, origin, family structure, occupation, and Jesuit utilization of this sector of the labor force.[10]

The importance of new slaves *(bozales)* from diverse African locations and the emerging dependence upon non–African-born, hispanized slaves *(criollos)* is evident. The majority of adults, 100 of 174, were of African origin, including 28 recent arrivals (bozales). The bozales were not identified by origin, only by age and Christian name. Of the slaves identified by tribal or regional origin, the greatest number came from West Africa—Angola (16), Oxade (16), Congo (13), and Malemba (12)—a few from the east coast—Mozambique (9)—and still fewer from Biafra (4), Cocade (1), and Ambuchi (1). Of 60 criollo adults, 9 were born on the estate, 4 came from Puebla, and 28 were listed simply as *criollos de México*. Lesser numbers came from Asia (5), Seville (2), the Canary Islands (1), Santo Domingo (2), and the South American mainland—Peru (2) and Maracaibo (1). Since most, if not all, of the children were born at Xochimancas, local origin would account for one-third of the total population. The even distribution of sexes, the relatively large number of children, and age distributions can be seen in Figure 6.

Demographic data included in the inventory provide useful detail. Three of the four adult males who died in 1653 (aged thirty-three, thirty-eight, and forty) were of African origin, and the only female death was caused by her bozal husband. In all there were eight deaths, including three children of five or younger. Two young criollo males, aged twenty-two and twenty-three—one from Seville—were considered to have criminal characters. Of the three adults who were runaways *(cimarrones)*—all criollos—two were female. Six slaves (three couples) were sold in 1653: one elderly couple went to Santa Lucía, and one young couple with an infant who subsequently died and a childless couple went to other hacendados. Of the eighty married couples, only thirty-nine had children: sixteen with one child, thirteen with two children, nine with three children, and one with four children. Since the childless couples were mostly in the fertile twenty-to-forty age group, a high degree of birth control must have been practiced, or infant mortality rates were staggering. Two slaves were married to partners from neighboring haciendas, and one male to a free Negro female. Only one female was classified as mulatto.

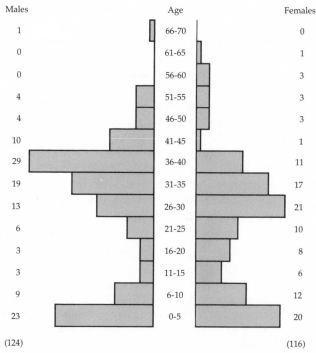

Males	Age	Females
1	66-70	0
0	61-65	1
0	56-60	3
4	51-55	3
4	46-50	3
10	41-45	1
29	36-40	11
19	31-35	17
13	26-30	21
6	21-25	10
3	16-20	8
3	11-15	6
9	6-10	12
23	0-5	20
(124)		(116)

FIGURE 6. Xochimancas slave populations, 1653. Source: BNM 83.

The sample is too small to be interpreted with any degree of certainty; nevertheless, it is suggestive. The criollos were better adapted to the environment. Their knowledge of Spanish and of local conditions increased their chances of becoming successful runaways, and they were more willing to challenge their conditions to the extent of being considered criminal. Slaves of African origin were less able to survive in the New World. Their death rate was higher, and they had fewer children. Occupations, listed for twenty males, suggest a high degree of specialization—carpenter, iron worker, herder, irrigator—and show that positions of responsibility and authority (sugar master, supervisor) were filled by slaves on Jesuit estates.

The data presented indicate a work context rigorously exploiting the labor of the slaves, limiting access to outside influences and to other ethnic sectors whenever possible. Xochimancas did employ considerable numbers of Indians as day laborers and seasonal workers. In a neighboring estate, in 1645, the workers were 22 percent Negro and 76 percent Indian,[11] yet no significant contact between slaves and the Indigenous sector is evident. The hacienda was administered by a Jesuit lay brother *(hermano coadjutor)* who was instructed to keep contact with Europeans to a minimum, and as a matter of principle mestizos and other Spaniards were not employed.

Instructions for managing Xochimancas, based on this period and issued in 1664, indicate that a regulated, controlled life-style was imposed on the slave.[12] Starting at 4:00 A.M. daily, tasks were detailed to ensure maximum activity of adults and children of both sexes. Slaves worked six days a week. On Sundays they received weekly rations, attended mass and religious instruction, and were obligated to put in short periods of field work. The latter was more in the interest of control than production, as is evident from the instructions:

This is to be done, not for the work itself, which should last three-quarters of an hour at most, but so that the father [Jesuit] knows they are all at home. This is always to be done on Sundays and holidays, because it prevents many offenses against God; since with laziness, some get themselves drunk, others of bad character go on the roads and rob the Indians; they go to other ingenios and don't return to the house in many months . . . all of which is avoided if they are kept occupied.[13]

The Jesuit writer apparently assumes that the better the control, the better the hacienda production, and that slaves are perpetual children, even if physically adult, and must have all aspects of their lives regulated.

For the situation at Santa Lucía in the 1650s, we have no comparable demographic data. Here, during the early years, the slaves worked as shepherds. As the Jesuits moved into the residences built at Santa Lucía, the slaves began to be employed as domestics also. As new slaves were purchased for the hacienda, they were initially put to work at tasks where they could be closely supervised. The early administrators, according to the Jesuit reports, maintained excellent relations with their slaves.[14]

With the establishment of the textile mill, the hacienda administrators found an economical way to occupy the female slaves year-round. The father general had forbidden the use of females in the residences to prevent any unnecessary contact between the coadjutores and the female slaves. Employing the women in the textile mill permanently attached them to the residence, a factor calculated to discourage their husbands involved in herding from taking flight. Since the weavers at the mill tended to be males, this may have been the place where the most recent arrivals became integrated into the hacienda's labor force. By the 1640s the mill was producing considerable quantities of blankets and textiles, and it can be assumed that the slave population was substantial by then.

Santa Lucía, including as it did a wide range of livestock and food-crop activities, provided less servile occupational opportunities for the majority of male slaves. There was less regimentation, less restrictive housing, greater access to Indian females, and greater contact with mestizos and mulattoes employed on the hacienda as carpenters, masons, muleteers, shepherds, and cowboys. The African population, furthermore, was not all concentrated in one location, since groups of slaves lived at the various estancias associated with Santa Lucía. Although they were under the general supervision of a Jesuit administrator, the immediate supervisors of most of the slaves were either Spanish or mestizo mayordomos. A greater degree of freedom was available for slaves at Santa Lucía than for those at Xochimancas. Symbolic of this basic condition was the fact that, at the sugar hacienda, all slaves lived in a slave compound; living quarters at Santa Lucía consisted of houses for individual families, and at San Xavier, part of the residence complex was devoted to rooms for slave families. In all three cases, slave residences were within the walled confines of the sprawling residence complexes.

Information about slaves at Santa Lucía during the seventeenth century, scattered as it is, suggests an early, heavy reliance upon this form of labor. Río Frío purchased at least 4 slaves during his term as administrator (1678–1684) and mentioned a total of 108 at the end of his term.[15] By 1696, according to Gemelli Carreri, that hacienda had over 100 married slaves living in their own residences (*cabañas*).[16]

The Eighteenth Century

For the eighteenth century, a more detailed picture of slave labor can be presented. In 1722, Santa Lucía had 291 slaves. Of these, 171 were at the main residence, working as domestics, as textile-mill laborers, or as shepherds. Of those remaining, 70 were at Provincia working in agriculture and herding, 13 were with the sheep flocks at Ocuila, 14 were at San Xavier involved in agriculture, and 23 were at the same anexa working as goatherds or in the slaughter-house. By 1743 the population had increased to 312.[17]

Within the next three years, 23 slaves were sold and 26 had deserted while the hacienda was under the rigorous administration of Miers. Increase by reproduction exceeded mortality, giving rise to a sustained population increase. From 1743 to 1746, there were 22 births and 15 deaths.[18] One of the differences noticeable on the slave inventories for the eighteenth century, in contrast to the seventeenth century, is the absence of references to new slaves (bozales) and place of origin, suggesting that most, if not all, were born in New Spain. Emphasized instead were characteristics related to work habits and docility or rebelliousness.[19]

During the final twenty years, the slave population decreased as a result of sales and the closing of the textile mill. When Miers restored the strong hand of Jesuit administrative control over Santa Lucía affairs, he identified 102 slaves whom he considered a burden because they were lazy, crafty, deceitful, sickly, careless, escapists, or incorrigible thieves. Miers received permission from the procurador of the college to have them sold because, as he put it, "the cost of what they steal, plus their food and clothes, is worth more than they are. All they do is destroy. They have to be forced to work and the work they do is badly done."[20] During 1750–1751, 51 slaves were sold to the Augustinians for 8,150 pesos, and another 55 were sold to a Spaniard for 7,800 pesos.[21] Under the circumstances, it is not surprising that there were numerous desertions during the first months of Villaverde's administration.[22] He also purchased 22 youths (18 males and 4 females) who, according to the current selling prices, would have been valued at 175 pesos each, making a total of 3,850 pesos.[23] With the closing of the textile mill in the early 1760s, an additional 79 slaves were moved from Santa Lucía to the Jesuit sugar estate at Xalmolonga.[24] These transfers reduced Santa Lucía's slave population by 207, so during the final few years Santa Lucía had to rely more heavily upon Indian labor.

Conditions and Occupations

While the Jesuits ran the haciendas, the slaves were used to meet the demands of the season. Those staying at the main residence were used for agricultural labor during the busy seasons. In 1746, during the first round of weeding and cultivation at San Xavier up to one-quarter of the field hands were slaves from the hacienda.[25] This reduced dependence upon pueblo labor and at the same time avoided paying out cash for wages. Occupational roles filled by slaves encompassed most of the jobs at Santa Lucía. The Instrucciones cautioned against placing too much trust in slaves, suggesting that they should not be made mayordomos, ayudantes, caporales, or guarda-pastos or be given other jobs requiring mounted travel. Administrators were advised, however, to use slaves as assistants in the distribution of rations and as supervisors over other slaves.[26] Hacienda records show that slaves worked in supervisory positions (vacieros, manaderos) at the sheep and goat ranches, as specialists (*carpinteros,* herraderos, arrieros) at the residences, and in positions of special trust. Supplies and funds were carried by slaves between Mexico City, Santa Lucía, and its anexas, and the personal assistant of the administrator was usually a slave. Such individuals were entrusted with the responsibility of passing on instructions to subordinates. Most of the household positions, during the later years, seemed to be filled by slaves. Despite the proscriptions of the father general's office against keeping females in the household, the cooks for the hacienda were female slaves. At other estates owned by the Colegio Máximo, slaves reached the positions of mayordomo, sobresaliente, and ayudante, but no such cases could be confirmed for Santa Lucía.[27]

Slaves owned by non-Jesuits also worked at Santa Lucía and received wages that were collected by their masters. Juan Nicolás, a slave of Agustín de Monroy, the mayordomo at Tepenene, was employed as a caporal at Altica in 1743. He drew regular rations, but his salary was paid directly to his master.[28] At Provincia the secretary (escribano) of the mayordomo was a slave named Eugenio. He drew a salary of 4 pesos a month that was credited to his master.[29] Upper-level supervisors hired by the hacienda used slaves as a means of gaining additional income.

Expenses for maintaining slaves during the eighteenth century were not high. They received weekly rations of maize and an annual allotment of new clothing. The annual clothing costs, judging from recorded distributions at San Pablo (1741–1742) and Negra (1746, 1749) amounted to 8 pesos per slave. Weekly maize rations were provided for slave shepherds at the same rates as other sirvientes. Women and children at San Pablo received maize rations of 3 to 6 quartillos, depending upon the age of the slave and the number of dependents.[30] The total cost of maintaining an adult male working as a manadero would have been 32 pesos a year.[31] The salary and ration costs for a sirviente at the same occupation would have amounted to 74 pesos a year.[32] Weekly slave rations, according to the Instrucciones, were to consist of maize, meat, salt, chile, tobacco, and honey, if available. To conform with Roman Catholic dietary proscriptions, substitutes of beans and fish were to be provided.[33] Other slave costs paid out by the hacienda included ecclesiastical fees for marriage permits and the expenses surrounding baptisms, marriages, and funerals. Slave shepherds were sometimes advanced small amounts of cash to hire their own molenderas. Indulgences sold through the archbishop's office were purchased periodically for all slaves over the age of twelve, as were personal rosaries.

Guidelines issued to the administrators stated that all slaves should be usefully employed. Boys above the age of eight were to be given work in keeping with their strength. Children, under the supervision of a female slave too old to do a full day's work, could collect stones, clean roads, weed fields, and clean up trash. Even children between the ages of five and eight were to accompany their mothers to the fields to take care of infants while the mothers worked. Children under the age of five, other than infants still nursing, were kept at the main hacienda residence under the watchful eye of an old woman. All children, as well as adults, regardless of age, were to be usefully employed. Leisure was a concept the Jesuits sought to suppress or even eliminate.[34]

Controlled separation of the sexes began early in the lives of the slaves at Santa Lucía. Girls from the age of five or six were kept apart from the boys and their activities closely supervised. Girls over the age of fifteen were considered old enough to have husbands. Many were mothers by the time they reached sixteen, and at least one twelve-year-old was already a mother.[35] Unmarried girls were put to work in the controlled setting of the textile mill. According to a report by Villaverde in 1751, he had all single females above the age of three in the mill and had them sleep apart from the other slaves.[36]

Demographic Profile and Nomenclature

A profile of the distribution of the slave population by age and sex (Figure 7) tells us a great deal about the 312 slaves belonging to Santa Lucía in the late 1740s. The distribution by sex shows an evenly balanced population, with 161 males and 151 females. Distribution by sex according to age groups indicates that, above the age of twenty-five, the females outnumbered the males, and the opposite was true for slaves under twenty-five. One of the reasons for this situation was that males were more apt to desert the hacienda

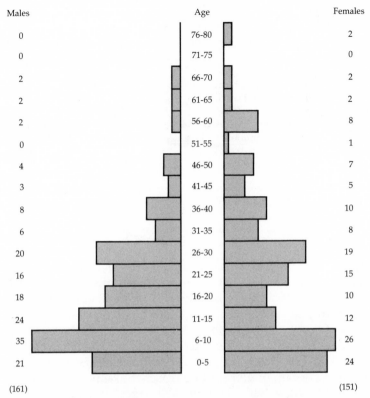

Males	Age	Females
0	76-80	2
0	71-75	0
2	66-70	2
2	61-65	2
2	56-60	8
0	51-55	1
4	46-50	7
3	41-45	5
8	36-40	10
6	31-35	8
20	26-30	19
16	21-25	15
18	16-20	10
24	11-15	12
35	6-10	26
21	0-5	24
(161)		(151)

FIGURE 7. Slave populations at Santa Lucía, 1740s.
Source: AGNAHH 329, 7–9.

than were females. According to the inventory of slaves, 7 males were absent and only 1 female.[37] In the eleven-to-twenty age group there were 42 males and only 22 females. This was the period in the lives of the females that caused the Jesuits their greatest concern.

The large number of children under the age of sixteen among the slaves (45.5 percent) indicates a population that more than reproduced itself. There was little need to buy slaves to keep up numbers. Over one-third of the slaves were children under the age of eleven, and 3.2 percent were above the age of sixty. This means that the active work force represented 62.7 percent of the total population. The low value assigned to children during their first few years suggests that infant mortality was high, or that the cost

TABLE 25
Santa Lucía Slaves and Family Units, 1745–1751

Type	Number of units	Total number of individuals
Both parents, with children	43	194
One parent, with children	21[a]	51
Couples, without children	13	26
Widows, without children	10	10
Widowers, without children	0	0
Married to nonslaves	11	19[b]
Orphans, single	12	12
TOTAL	110	312

SOURCE: AGNAHH 329, 8.
[a]Consists of 12 widows with children, 6 solteras with children, and 3 widows with grandchildren.
[b]Includes 8 children from female slaves married to nonslaves.

of raising the children was considered excessive. The value of an infant was the same as that of one carriage mule, 25 pesos.[38] The spacing of children among families with more than one child averages out to 3.02 years.*

Most of the slaves were members of families at the hacienda. The types of family units are indicated in Table 25. The largest families included six children, and the average for families with children was three per family unit. In three cases the families included unmarried daughters with children. The largest extended family encountered included twelve individuals.[39] Two of the families had twins, and one of these had two sets of twins. There were few widowers with children, because when a wife died, the husband quickly remarried an available female, usually a girl in her teens.

Despite their vigilance, the Jesuits were not successful in preventing intermarriage between slaves and nonslaves. Four female slaves were married to nonslaves, who were not identified, but their children were identified and included among the slaves, in accordance with the law. Of the seven males married to nonslaves, five had taken Indian wives, one a *mulata,* and one a *loba.* Of interest in these cases is the fact that, although the children of such unions were not slaves, and were not listed as such, the names of the mothers were included in the lists of slaves. This suggests that

*This figure would have to be adjusted to take into account infant mortality. Since the inventory lists mention deaths only if they occurred during the year of the inventory, it is not possible to know total infant deaths.

TABLE 26
Descriptive Nomenclature of Santa Lucía Slaves, 1751

Classification	Number	Percentage of all slaves (group total in parentheses)	
Negro (Negro)	19	20.9%	
Negro atezado (very black Negro)	11	12.0	
Atezado (very dark, or Black)	11	12.0	(44.9%)
Mulato (usually Negro and Spanish mix)	12	13.2	
Mulato blanco (light-skinned Mulatto)	5	5.5	
Mulato prieto (dark-skinned Mulatto)	16	17.6	(36.3%)
Lobo (usually Negro and Indian mix)	11	12.0	
Lobo prieto (dark Lobo)	1	1.1	
Alobado (with Indian physical characteristics)	5		5.5 (18.6%)

SOURCE: AGNAHH 329, 8. The list includes a representative cross-section of family units.

their life-style on the hacienda differed very little, if at all, from that of the slaves.

The nomenclature employed in describing slaves is of special interest as it provides valuable information on socioracial terminology, allowing for insights about degrees of miscegenation among Santa Lucía slaves. A 1751 sample of ninety-one slaves yields the classifications listed in Table 26. The terms emphasize descriptive categories related to physical color and type based, it appears, on visual inspection. The lists from which these data are drawn failed to include descriptive race-related classifications for all persons who had fled and were not physically present. The high percentage of mulatto and lobo slaves (55 percent) indicates the Jesuits were not successful in preventing either Spanish or Indian access to slave women. The constant presence of Spanish mayordomos and ayudantes may have helped produce the mulattoes. Hacienda documents do not mention any cases of transgressions by Jesuit administrators or chaplains. In one family unit, all the grandchildren of the mulatto parents were alobado. Included were unmarried daughters and a granddaughter with alobado infants, indicating Indian paternity. The term *zambo,* used elsewhere in colonial Latin America, was not employed by the Jesuits.[40] Marriage between males and females of the same classification group occurred approximately 50 percent of the time; the rest were between different groups. In another undated list kept by Santa Lucía officials that does not identify specific haciendas, 40 percent of the married couples had spouses who were not slaves. Such evidence, as well as the classification data, suggest that Jesuit ability to control miscegenation of slaves had become ineffective.

Mulattoes proved to be the least acquiescent of Santa Lucía's slaves. The adults on Miers's 1745 list of slaves who should be sold for reasons of thievery, drunkenness, and insubordination were principally mulattoes. Two-thirds of the undesirable slaves were from the mulatto group, which represented only one-third of the slave population. Only one lobo was on the list. The mulattoes, it seems, were more likely to challenge their masters and their own condition of slavery. They also identified more strongly than the Negroes and lobos with the white elements of colonial society. The Jesuits believed that if parents demonstrated undesirable characteristics, which they explained in terms of natural evil, their offspring would exhibit the same tendencies. This became a practical rationale for the sale of entire families.[41]

Control Strategies and Welfare Policies

Once a stable slave population had been established at Santa Lucía, natural reproduction created a more than sufficient labor supply, necessitating procedures to control numbers. Gemelli Carreri's observation that at Santa Lucía the Jesuits were breeding offspring for commercial purposes by the end of the seventeenth century correctly identifies the sale of slaves as a means of maintaining desired numbers. The Jesuit concern for the integrity of the slave family produced the policy of selling entire family units whenever possible. But this policy was operational mostly when adults were being sold. Individual children were either transferred to other haciendas or sold. The low number of females in the Santa Lucía population between the ages of eleven and twenty was the result of Jesuit policies rather than natural demographic patterns. Females who reached the age of puberty at Santa Lucía were frequently sold if they represented a threat to Jesuit standards of chastity. Unless a potential husband was on the immediate horizon, these girls became expendable. This is borne out by the correspondence between administrators and procuradores, which includes frequent references to young unmarried females who should or could be sold. Since the hacienda was not likely to keep slaves who could not be usefully employed, a certain number of young males also became expendable. Potential buyers were more inclined to purchase young slaves, as they were cheaper, trainable, and at the point in their lives when kinship ties were weakest. Among slaves, as in other segments of society, youth represented the most mobile period in the life-cycle of the individual.[42]

The movement of young, fertile, female slaves also served to prevent race-mixing. The Jesuits attempted to limit and, if possible, prevent the development of kinship ties between their slaves at Santa Lucía and other workers at the hacienda or from neighboring pueblos. Administrators were cautioned to seek godparents for slave children who were not freedmen or Indians. Even contact with kinsmen at other haciendas was discouraged, as when Villaverde refused the mother of a Santa Lucía slave permission to visit her daughter during Holy Week.[43] Baptismal padrinos were to be chosen from among a narrow circle of consanguineal kinsmen, for fewer problems in finding marriage partners at a later date would be encountered. (The Jesuits did not like to see individuals marry who were fictive kinsmen—that is, related through ties of compadrazgo—a position supported by church rules.)[44]

Success in preventing intermarriage between slaves and non-slaves was limited. In 1737 Donazar complained to other college officials about the large number of Santa Lucía slaves who were married to nonslaves. He suggested that permission should be sought from the provincial to allow the sale of ten to twelve slaves who had entered such unions.[45] The strongest argument in favor of permitting such unions, and likely the most frequent, was pregnancy, in which case ecclesiastical rituals were quickly called for to ratify sexual consummation—provided, of course, that the father was identified and single. There were also instances where slave girls formed open unions with Spaniards. One such case took place in the early eighteenth century, when the son of a wealthy neighboring hacendado married a hacienda slave girl. When he subsequently attempted to buy his wife from Santa Lucía, the administrator was displeased and demonstrated this by initially requesting the unreasonable price of 1,000 pesos. The price was subsequently reduced and the girl's freedom obtained, but under the condition that she never return to Santa Lucía, lest her success lead to imitation by other female slaves at the hacienda.[46]

Health care for the slaves was provided at the hacienda if possible. The Instrucciones stated that illnesses were to be treated with care and kindness. Rather than have slaves huddled in their huts with real or imagined illnesses, an infirmary was called for, to be attended by an old female slave working under the supervision of the chaplain. The nurse was to be chosen for her knowledge of ordinary cures and could be assisted by a younger female who would help out during epidemics. The popular medical guide, *Florilegio medicinal de todas las enfermedades,* served as the source of additional information.[47] The office of midwife was filled by a mature female slave. The chaplain gave her instructions on how to baptize infants in cases of emergency, for the Jesuits were concerned that all infants receive the rites of baptism, whether they survived or not.[48] Slaves suffering serious injuries were sometimes sent to the city to be treated by the college doctors, but generally medical care was left under the control of the chaplain.[49] Apart from isolated mentions of injury, hacienda correspondence provides few clues for assessing the degree of compliance with these official recommendations.

Slave life at Santa Lucía, except for those who worked at the textile mill, was less severe than at other Colegio Máximo estates, at least the sugar estates, and probably less severe than at most haciendas during the colonial epoch. The philosophy about slave care expressed in the Instrucciones reveals a practical concern for the material welfare of the slave as well as a strong concern for reinforcing Christian ideology. Shelter, food, and clothing were to be distributed fairly and adequately at all times. Sources of conflict and friction were to be eliminated, although not at the expense of productivity. Work tasks were to be clearly spelled out and planned to ensure the continued welfare of the college and the order.[50]

The strategy employed was to allow slaves who demonstrated acceptance of Jesuit standards to serve as agents for passing these values on to others. Work gangs of slaves were to be supervised by mature, loyal slaves who filled the position of *mandador* (instruction giver). Whenever possible, males supervised work being done by males, and females watched over the activities of females. The mandador assisted in the distribution of food and rations, issued everyday instructions, and, when necessary, became the agent through whom punishment was meted out.

The preoccupation of the Instrucciones with the question of how punishment should be administered suggests it was common. Moral suasion was advocated over physical punishment, and a distinction was made between contemporary secular practices of beatings and brutality and Jesuit forms of persuasion.[51] If punishment was to be administered, it was to be done immediately and effectively. The objective was to impress upon the transgressor the price of disobedience but always, at the same time, to hold out the possibility of pardon. Administrators were instructed to secretly ask friends of a slave being punished to intercede, giving the Jesuits an opportunity to respond charitably. The calculated effect, in serious cases where incarceration had been necessary, was "to give them freedom, doing it in such a manner that they would acknowledge gratefully their pardon and, at the same time, would be intimidated by the threat of greater punishment if they relapsed."[52] Or, as happened at Provincia in 1752, runaway slaves might be reintegrated into the work force without punishment, and given the same occupation as previously.[53] Greater vigor in administering punishment, however, appears to have been the rule. In 1754 at Santa Lucía, a recalcitrant slave was placed in irons and made to sleep in a cell, "as an example to others so they respond to reason."[54]

Since the Instrucciones defined policy rather than describing actual practice, the question arises of how successful the Santa Lucía administrators were in implementing the policies. The original group of slaves acquired with the purchases quickly adapted to the Jesuits for the most part. The curious case of Pedro Nieto becoming converted to the Jesuit life after an incident in which he injured a slave can be seen as an indication of the early impact of Jesuit influence. The good relations between early administrators and slaves and the concern the administrators expressed in providing instruction helped to integrate the new acquisitions into Santa Lucía's work force during the early seventeenth century.

Other evidence not directly concerned with Santa Lucía itself must also be taken into consideration. From the beginning the Jesuits became involved in teaching slaves the virtues of Christianity and Spanish civilization. In Veracruz, the entry point for most of the African slaves into New Spain, the Jesuits provided special attention for the Africans, and in Mexico City a similar situation prevailed.[55] Viceregal authorities quickly recognized the esteem the Jesuits had among the slaves. As noted earlier, two Jesuit priests were selected by the government to accompany the military expedition against the insurgent runaway-slave forces of Yanga in 1609. The result of this confrontation, in which the Jesuits served as advisors and participants, was, in Davidson's opinion, "the only known example of a successful attempt by slaves to secure their freedom *en masse* by revolt and negotiation and have it sanctioned and guaranteed by law."[56] Little evidence has been encountered suggesting that the hacienda administrators did not share the order's concern for the welfare of the slaves, although this concern was subordinated to production objectives. The Jesuits always kept their old slaves who had ceased to be useful, unlike many slave owners who found this a convenient time to grant freedom to slaves, thus eliminating further responsibility for their welfare.

Individual Welfare and Work

The question of slave welfare, however, was tied to more than the positive or negative dispositions of owners. The Jesuit system, after all, was designed to achieve maximum returns from the labor force, regardless of its social or legal status. The relative advantages or disadvantages for individual slaves were closely tied to the work they did—whether they were domestics, mill or obraje workers, field hands, herdsmen, muleteers, or persons in confidence entrusted with a great deal of liberty and responsibility. Cash-crop, food-crop, and livestock activities provided different contexts for slaves, even under the management of a single institution such as the Colegio Máximo. By examining the eighteenth-century slave inventories of Palapa-Xalmolonga, a cash-crop estate, plus Santa Lucía, devoted to a combination of food crops, livestock, and processing facilities, and Provincia, a subunit of Santa Lucía devoted primarily to livestock, the condition of slaves in various contexts can be explored. The demographic details are presented in Figures 8–10. Included in the sample are a total of 567 slaves, all subject to the supervision of the Colegio Máximo.

On the cash-crop estates, one finds basically the same conditions described for Xochimancas a century earlier as far as occupational position and other conditions of work are concerned. But if one compares Figures 8 and 9, one finds different patterns. The greater proportion of children to adults in the eighteenth century resulted from more couples having children as well as larger families. This, in turn, reflected a more stable population. Another difference was that in the eighteenth century all the slaves had been born in Mexico and acculturated into the slave system, whereas in the seventeenth century many were recent imports unaccustomed to slave conditions. The work conditions, however, had not changed substantially, and the day-to-day conditions of slave life remained constant. The slaves' access to alternatives remained limited.

At Santa Lucía (Figure 9), conditions had changed since a century earlier in that more males seemed to be working in the textile mill and the slave population was considerably larger. Occupa-

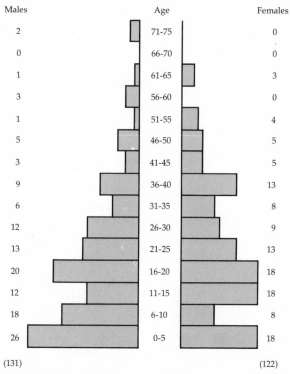

Males	Age	Females
2	71-75	0
0	66-70	0
1	61-65	3
3	56-60	0
1	51-55	4
5	46-50	5
3	41-45	5
9	36-40	13
6	31-35	8
12	26-30	9
13	21-25	13
20	16-20	18
12	11-15	18
18	6-10	8
26	0-5	18
(131)		(122)

FIGURE 8. Palapa-Xalmolonga slaves, 1750–1751. Source: AGNAHH 307, 9.

tional ranks did not include the high positions available on the sugar hacienda. These tended to be filled by Spaniards or mestizos. Groups from the main residence of Santa Lucía, usually family units or extended family units, were occasionally sent to other subunits of the hacienda to engage in agricultural labor, assist in construction, or provide domestic service for a Jesuit administrator. At Santa Lucía the picture shows less social stability and greater access to alternatives. Four slave females were married to freedmen. Seven adult males were cimarrones: six with their families, and one with a female and their infant son, leaving behind a wife with four other children. The large number of critical characterizations by Jesuit administrators—for example, slaves accused of being lazy, secretive, crafty, escapists, thieves, robbers, drunkards, and lacking in humility—indicate that a wider range of social and cultural alternatives was being exercised by the slave population.

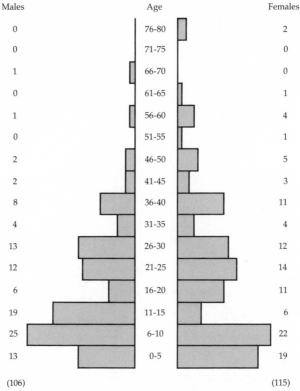

Males	Age	Females
0	76-80	2
0	71-75	0
1	66-70	0
0	61-65	1
1	56-60	4
0	51-55	1
2	46-50	5
2	41-45	3
8	36-40	11
4	31-35	4
13	26-30	12
12	21-25	14
6	16-20	11
19	11-15	6
25	6-10	22
13	0-5	19
(106)		(115)

FIGURE 9. Santa Lucía slaves, 1745. Source: AGNAHH 329, 8.

At Provincia (Figure 10), there were signs of stability and even greater access to alternatives affecting slave conditions. The large number of males aged fifteen to twenty reflects occupational needs. Youths from Santa Lucía became herdsmen at Provincia. The same figures are also distorted in that, in twenty-three married couples, seven males (30.4 percent) were married to Indian wives. Their children were not slaves, so there were fewer female slaves at certain ages. At the Provincia hacienda, one finds less critical characterization by Jesuits of slaves, and fewer absentees (only one couple, without children, were cimarrones). Most of the males at Provincia spent considerable time away from the residential base because of occupational demands. This meant a high degree of potential contact with non-African sectors. The ethnic composition of the population bears this out, as 53 percent of the individuals

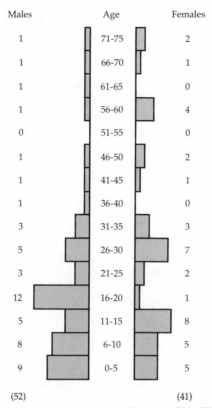

Males	Age	Females
1	71-75	2
1	66-70	1
1	61-65	0
1	56-60	4
0	51-55	0
1	46-50	2
1	41-45	1
1	36-40	0
3	31-35	3
5	26-30	7
3	21-25	2
12	16-20	1
5	11-15	8
8	6-10	5
9	0-5	5
(52)		(41)

FIGURE 10. Provincia slaves, 1751. Source: AGNAHH 329, 8.

were classified as either mulatto (35 percent) or lobo (18 percent). Slaves considered to be pure African ethnically—that is, Negro—represented 45 percent of the total. This high degree of miscegenation must have taken place primarily on the hacienda—the Jesuits started with basically African slaves and had been in operation since the early seventeenth century—despite Jesuit vigilance, suggesting greater access to alternatives based on decisions made by the slaves themselves. The Provincia slave population shows more marriages between male slaves and female Indians and ethnically mixed individuals, proportionately, than any of the other types of haciendas run by the Jesuits.

These data suggest that, within a stable system of Jesuit management, the individual slave's ability to exercise choices that affected long-term status and change was more dependent upon the specific work context than upon general changes of condition within the larger society. The food-crop and livestock estates allowed the slaves greater contact with other ethnic sectors and less oppressive working conditions. Within the narrow limits of choice allowed to them, the slaves exercised options that would change their slave conditions. The specific context allowing for greatest escape from control and regulation was the estate devoted to livestock. Thus, the conditions of the slaves on the cash-crop estates remained relatively unchanged, whereas on the livestock estates the differences between slave and nonslave lessened more rapidly. The slaves on the cash-crop estates were undoubtedly aware of this, although not able to change their condition as long as the Jesuit system remained intact.

After the Jesuits were expelled, the slaves responded accordingly. At Xalmolonga, for example, within three years of the loss of Jesuit control, the slaves had ceased to be compliant workers.[57] Of a total of 361 slaves on the Xalmolonga lists in 1770, only 70 (19.4 percent) were considered useful or obedient. Of the rest, 37 had fled (10.2 percent), 13 were in jail (3.6 percent), 12 of the women were in Mexico City (3.3 percent), and 68 were classified as rebels (18.8 percent) although still on the estate. The rest were classified as habitually ill, or too old or young to provide useful services. Once the Jesuits had been removed, so too were restraints that the new administrators were unable to reimpose.

The reaction of the Xalmolonga slaves provides a clue to why the Jesuits had more success with their slaves after 1750 than did their secular contemporaries. Their success was based on a highly efficient system of tolerable controls, consistently implemented. The slaves of the Jesuits knew what to expect, which was treatment seen to be less harsh and less arbitrary than they would get at the hands of private estate owners.

ELEVEN 🌀 *Days, Seasons, and Life-Styles*

The male-dominated Jesuit world was prepared to avoid the normal interactions of domestic life. The vocabulary of the Jesuits was rich in concepts of father, son, and brother, but lacking in concepts of mother, daughter, and sister, and in the dynamics that produced and reproduced both sets of concepts as part of a whole. It was the slaves who belied the monastic buildings and provided the primary context on the hacienda of society's most basic unit, the family. If Chevalier was right in his observation that the wealth of a hacienda could be gauged by its numbers of "relatives, retainers, gossips and familiars,"[1] then Santa Lucía would have to be seen as the epitome of failure. But the hacienda came closer to representing the epitome of success. In its production of livestock, food crops, and cash crops it was like many other haciendas, despite its distinctive life-style.

Distinctive Jesuit Features

The life-style at Santa Lucía was shaped by three dominating factors: the masculinity of its owners and administrators; the devotion of the Jesuits to obedience and the rule of the order; and the permanent presence of a substantial slave population. The combination of these factors caused the hacienda administration's preoccupation with production and led them to respond to the seasons with a carefully regulated plan of activities. Between 1576 and 1767 many things changed at Santa Lucía, particularly its size, influence, and emphases of production. But the basic nature of the life-style it supported changed only gradually.

The main residence of Santa Lucía symbolized everything that revolved around it. Perched on its rocky hillock, the somber, plain, but sturdy structure dominated its surroundings. Its interior patios were small, its living quarters austere and limited, serving the needs of privacy, work, and sleep. There were no large courtyards adorned with gardens, fountains, or other constructions suggesting a wealthy residence or a place to entertain friends, family, and associates. On the contrary, the structure was oriented to storing produce, housing equipment and supplies, and protecting the assets of the estate against the elements. The sundials in the interior patios were silent testimonials to the regulation of time and activities characteristic of the Jesuit work ethic.

The practical orientation to work was matched only by the orientation to devotion. Statues of saints filled a row of wall niches at the main entrance. The large chapel, plainly yet richly adorned, was the one place where all the residents met regularly to reassert their common concern for piety and obedience to a higher order. The three bells above the chapel rang their daily summons to morning and evening exercises of devotion. The interior and exterior entrances of the chapel admitted all who came voluntarily to the summons of the bells. Those who failed to come for reasons other than illness or absence quickly discovered the compelling nature of the Jesuit interpretation of the Divine Imperative: six to eight lashes administered by the resident overseer.[2]

The contents of the chapel, itemized in great detail in the inventory lists, mirror the world view the Jesuits hoped to impart to their slaves and all others who worked for them. Eight paintings of the life of Ignacio Loyola adorned the walls, as did another scene of Saint Ignacio with Saint Xavier (Francis Xavier) and still another showing the two with the Holy Virgin. Statues and paintings of Christ and the Holy Family dominated. Depictions of the sacred historical rites of passage—the Annunciation, Crucifixion, Resurrection, and Ascension of Christ—served both decorative and instructional purposes. Numerous representations of the Virgin of Guadalupe were in evidence, as were paintings and statues of all the patron saints of the hacienda and its anexas. As might be expected, Santa Lucía dominated the latter group. The adornments in the chapel were to serve as aids in instruction as well as guides to devotion.[3]

The hacienda's center of worship was also well provided with vestments, altar decorations, candle holders, curtains, and all the artifacts required by priests in the performance of their religious duties. This was the one place at Santa Lucía where gold, silver, and expensive cloths, such as Chinese silks and velvets, were in evidence. The chapel had an organ and also kept guitars and harps which provided the music during the religious fiestas. Throughout the chapel's history, chaplains and overseers came and went, but the Jesuits always insisted that one or more clerics attend to the religious needs of the people who used it. Employees of Santa Lucía who had occasion to come to the main residence for almost any reason probably entered the chapel. All employees and slaves who resided there did so regularly. In the early decades of the eighteenth century, when residence population was highest and most activities were still centered near Santa Lucía, well over 300 people attended special functions. As late as 1758, by which time the resident population had decreased substantially, more than 200 people took part in religious festivities honoring the Holy Virgin.[4]

The rhythm of daily life at Santa Lucía was governed by the performance of religious duties. One of the criticisms of the hacienda by the Jesuits from 1576 to 1587 was its lack of provision for the spiritual guidance of Africans and Indians working there. The father general quickly issued instructions that established routines affecting the lives of all residents.[5] Special attention was given to slaves and Jesuit administrators. For the slaves, the day began at dawn. The hacienda chaplain or a devoted elderly slave provided half an hour of religious instructions before mass in the chapel. Breakfast followed, after which the day's work began. Supper, at least for the Jesuits in residence, was at 8:00 P.M., followed by an accounting of the day's activities and the issuing of instructions for the next day's work. Before the slaves were enclosed in their quarters, which at Santa Lucía consisted of family dwellings rather than the slave compound characteristic of the sugar estates, a nightly chanting of the rosary took place. On Sundays and holidays the ritual was adjusted to provide additional religious instruction. At 3:00 P.M. the chaplain gathered everyone together to sing the Ave Maria, recite the catechism and the *doctrina cristiana*, and sing additional hymns. Participation in confession and communion was expected on Sundays and holidays. The hacienda observed the days prescribed by the Roman Catholic religious calendar, placing special emphasis upon the days of the Virgin of Guadalupe and of Santa Lucía (December 12 and 13).[6] The 1758 report on hacienda religious activities confirms that the schedules outlined in the Instrucciones were still being followed.[7]

Hacienda fiestas were essentially religious events accompanied by singing and processions. The bullfights, plays, games, and dances that became part of hacienda festivities throughout Mexico

during the colonial period were not permitted at Santa Lucía.*
Since the hacienda had a resident chaplain and received frequent
visits by other Jesuits from the Colegio Máximo, deviation from the
established norms would immediately have become known to college officials. At the anexas specializing in cattle- and horse-ranching, which were further removed and lacked the constant supervision of a Jesuit administrator, fiesta activities common to other
haciendas probably did take place. But as far as the slaves were
concerned, the Jesuits sought to make good Christians of them in
the expectation that they would be better servants for it.† Under
the administration of Villaverde, more secular activities may have
taken place. Hacienda documents, however, have very little to say
about social events.

The administrators normally rose before dawn. They attended to
their private prayers and then participated in the morning mass before being served their breakfast. Dinner was served at noon and
was followed by a midday examination of conscience. After the evening meal, hacienda workers with problems could approach the administrator in his office. Mayordomos or ayudantes received their
instructions and reported to the administrator after he finished
with the other workers. The day concluded with prayers in the
chapel.

The administrator confessed to the hacienda chaplain every Sunday morning before hearing mass. On Holy Thursday, the chaplain performed a special mass for the administrator. Twice a year
the administrator was to return to the college and renew his vows
to his superiors and participate in three days of religious exercises.
This activity could take place on the hacienda if permission was
granted by the college rector. If held on the hacienda, it included
special prayers, devotions, and a private renewal of vows in the
chapel. Once a year, during a slack period in the work schedule,
the administrator took his spiritual exercises away from the hacienda. These included a general confession on his part to the college
rector. At the same time, an audit was made of the hacienda financial accounts for the past year. At the hacienda the administrator
was the titular head of the household and the larger "family" of
hacienda workers. His participation in devotional activities was to
be an example for everyone else.[8] Equal devotion was not practiced

---

*"And they do not allow bullfights, or comedies, or games, or dances, which are
attractions for lazy folk." IHAH, p. 89.

†"Make good Christians of the slaves and you will make good *sirvientes*, and God
will give his blessing in everything." *Ibid.*, p. 83.

by all of Santa Lucía's administrators, which necessitated formal guides such as the Instrucciones. But even in the eighteenth century, when secular influences were strong, the administrators did comply at least with the formal demands of their position. The correspondence between administrators, mayordomos, and college officials includes frequent references to religious events or involvement in religious exercises.[9]

If the administrator showed signs of erring, the hacienda chaplain was there to make suggestions and give guidance in spiritual matters. Since these individuals were chosen for their weaknesses rather than their strengths—they worked at Santa Lucía as chaplains because they were unfit for service at the college in Mexico City—their influence upon the administrator was limited.[10] The repeated injunctions in the Instrucciones that administrators treat chaplains with proper charity and respect strongly suggest that this respect may have been lacking.[11] The jurisdiction of the chaplains was restricted to spiritual matters. Besides maintaining the chapel they operated a school for children of both slaves and other residents, but they were not to interfere with "the agriculture and temporal management of the hacienda."[12] And at Santa Lucía they did not. If the needs of production required that slaves and other residents work on Sundays and holidays, the administrator exercised his right to see that this took precedence over the set religious schedules. In one instance at least, the college procurador was informed of complaints by Santa Lucía slaves about abuses by their chaplain.[13]

Apart from the special emphasis on the saints' days of the hacienda, the religious obligations stressed at Santa Lucía did not differ from or conflict with the demands set by the curas for the pueblo residents. The Jesuits were concerned with preserving their ecclesiastical privileges on the hacienda but not in provoking conflicts with the non-Jesuit clergy. Thus, as mentioned earlier, hacienda chaplains were instructed not to perform baptisms, marriages, or burials in the hacienda chapel except in cases of extreme necessity. If slaves or workers died on the hacienda, they were not buried there. Only Jesuits were buried at the hacienda, and then only if it was not convenient to send the body to the college. The cura from Tizayuca performed the sacraments surrounding burial. Slaves were buried either at Xoloc or at Tizayuca, as were other hacienda workers from that parish. An attempt was made to allow the cura from the home parish of the individual worker to perform the rites of baptism and marriage as well. Hacienda chaplains could perform these ceremonies if permission was granted by the local cura. The guiding principle, set by the college officials, was to allow the local cura precedence in cases of conflict, for the sake of peace and tranquility.[14]

At the anexas of Santa Lucía, the provisions for compliance with religious duty were less elaborate than at the main residence. The chapels at San Juan and San Xavier were small, modestly adorned, but functional. San Juan's chapel, measuring barely four by six meters, contained a large, raised stone altar. The early morning sunlight illuminated a stained-glass window of Saint John, and the afternoon rays shone on a similar image of the Virgin of Guadalupe. At San Xavier the slightly larger chapel was windowless, the wall behind its altar graced with a large oil painting of its patron saint, with portraits of other saints on the side walls. These chapels served the devotional needs of the visiting or resident overseer, resident slaves, and workers. For special occasions the chapels were supplied with additional adornments from Santa Lucía, or special services for resident workers—including processions, patron saints, and the village cura—were brought to the estate from adjacent villages. This was standard practice at San Xavier, most of whose workers were from nearby Tolcayuca. The smallness of the structures underscores their limited function. Most of the people who worked for the hacienda were nonresident and performed their religious duties at pueblo churches, which were larger, more elaborate, and dominated by a church tower. At the anexas bought in the late seventeenth century and in the eighteenth century (Concepción, Tepenene, Chicavasco) the chapels were somewhat larger and more elaborate than at San Juan and San Xavier, but they seldom had resident chaplains except when the hacienda administrators used them as their residence. This was the case in the 1730s and 1740s, when Araujo, Miers, and Padilla spent much of their time at the northern anexas. The Jesuits saw no need to spend great sums on chapels, in contrast to the elaborate church structures attached to their colleges.[15]

The Jesuits expected their mayordomos to fulfill somewhat the same role of religious example and father figure as did the administrator at Santa Lucía. Such expectations, although consistent with the structural design of administration, were not realized. Concern for production took precedence over the demands of religious conformity. The individual mayordomo's religious convictions were most important in determining how well religious schedules were followed at his anexa. At the sheep and goat ranches, except the

San Nicolás residence at Provincia, there were no chapels. Provisions for religious instruction for the youths with the flocks were made by hiring doctrineros. Attempts to have the sirvientes fulfill their religious obligations during most of the year, when the flocks were in the pastures, consisted of cash advances for candles, debits for the purchase of indulgences, and advances to allow financing of festivities—in large part paying the religious fees—centered around baptism, marriage, and burial. In short, the Jesuits did attempt to encourage their herdsmen to fulfill their religious obligations but made no great effort to supervise or control this.

At Santa Lucía itself, resident sirvientes, gañanes, and peones followed much the same religious ritual as the slaves. Attendance at daily mass was not required of nonslaves, although it was encouraged. Sunday and holiday attendance on the part of the rancheados was enforced. The field crews of pueblo labor who stayed at the hacienda during busy periods were not punished for noncompliance in order to avoid problems with secular authorities. But these people were prevented from going to their own villages on holidays that fell in the midst of a busy work period.[16]

Religious instruction provided for the Indian population at the hacienda was to be given in the native language. A blind or elderly person knowledgeable in these matters was employed if the chaplain was not conversant with the languages in question. Since Jesuits, in order to become priests, had to know at least one Indian language, it was likely that most of Santa Lucía's chaplains were able to provide this service themselves.[17] During the afternoon sessions of religious instruction on Sundays and holidays, Indians were to participate in Spanish. Through this arrangement, and by teaching children Spanish in the hacienda school, the Jesuits participated in the process of providing native populations with some skills in the Spanish language. Before the beginning of Lent, all Indians were advised to fulfill their religious obligations in their home parishes to avoid being punished by the local curas. The parish curas, particularly in periods of conflict with Santa Lucía, used nonfulfillment of religious duties by the Indians employed at the hacienda as a pretext to beat and imprison them.[18] The Jesuit requirements for the workers on the hacienda paralleled the requirements set by the secular clergy.[19]

Yet the Jesuits did attempt to influence the ideological views of all Indians with whom they came in contact, on or off the hacienda. The Instrucciones advised chaplains to hear confession from individuals from neighboring pueblos who did not have a resident cura. The administrators were told to write to the rector at the beginning of every third year to request visits by teams of priests to preach to both hacienda and non-hacienda Indians.[20] Students and priests from the Colegio Máximo made frequent visits to Santa Lucía to vacation as well as to participate in religious instruction. The archbishop also commissioned Jesuit priests to make preaching tours (misiones circulares) of pueblos under secular jurisdiction. Such visits were being made to pueblos in the northern part of the Valley of Mexico as of the early seventeenth century.[21] Alegre reports on the successes of the 1732 visit, when many idols were burnt and innumerable scandals were eliminated by getting couples living together to submit to the Christian rites of marriage. The Jesuits pursued this mission with such vigor that a local cura was led to comment that in Pachuca the only people left to be married were the curas themselves.[22] In petitioning on behalf of the Santa Lucía chapel in 1758, local curas commented very favorably on the efficacy of Jesuit preaching.[23]

Little mention is made of the zeal of the chaplains attending the hacienda. Records of expenditures during the eighteenth century show purchases of supplies and payment of fees to the Tizayucan and Tolcayucan curas. Weekly rations for the Santa Lucía chaplain consisted of bread, cigars, and sweets (panelas y panochos). At times aguardiente (brandy or sugar cane spirits) and table wine were also sent along from Mexico City on the weekly trip of the mule train. When the hacienda was visited by priests from the college, special provisions, such as chickens and turkeys, were bought from nearby villages. During 1745 the average monthly expenses for the chaplain and related activities amounted to 5.3 pesos.[24] During the same year, pueblo curas were being paid 6 pesos for weddings and 12 pesos for funerals of hacienda workers, and costs for services provided by pueblo curas exceeded those to maintain the chaplain.

In discussing the relationships between hacienda owners and workers, writers such as Chevalier and Wolf have stressed the role of the owner as patron and father figure. This view emphasizes the personalization of relationships between patron and peón. As patron the hacienda owner filled the role of a severe and demanding father who looked after the temporal needs and security of his workers, provided they submitted to his will and supplied him with needed labor. To reinforce the unequal nature of the relationship, bonds of kinship were forged between the patron and peón, and among the peones.[25] The extent to which hacienda owners actually filled this role in colonial Mexican society, since the majority appear to have preferred their urban residences, requires investigation. It definitely was not the case at Santa Lucía, where the administrator, although he served as a father figure, avoided kinship ties of any sort. On other haciendas the residence of the master may have been the symbolic center in defining relationships between master and worker. At Santa Lucía that center remained the chapel, where slave, Indian, and Spaniard were encouraged to establish relationships that would ensure both temporal and eternal bonds of security. The Jesuits were prepared to look after the temporal necessities of only those workers who demonstrated loyalty and good service. They were never prepared to create bonds that looked out for the security of the next generation.

The substitution of the role of father as Jesuit for the role of father as progenitor of the future owner of the hacienda was, of course, a by-product of celibacy. Contact with women and participation in sexual activities were vital links in the chain between generations for everyone on the hacienda except its owners and administrators. Without this vital link, the role of patron at Santa Lucía remained sterile. For the Jesuits, women were a source of potential evil and temptation instead of a source of physiological and psychological comfort. Success in fulfilling the rule of the order was measured, in part, by how well the Jesuit came to terms with a world where women could be honored in religion but had to be shunned in the flesh. For the Jesuit, the ideal woman was a virgin. Mothers and sisters in their own lives had been rejected in favor of loyalty to religion. In the lives they supervised, the relations of females were governed accordingly. Throughout the history of Santa Lucía, the Jesuit view on these matters did not change. As early as 1578 the father general had expressed shock and dismay that female slaves were working in the Jesús del Monte vacation retreat: "I have marveled that you have not told me of this, being such a new thing and full of so many inconveniences, apart from the indecency which it brings. You will remedy this, taking away this work from the female slaves, for there can be no shortage of Negro males and whites to do this work."[26]

In 1754 the father general wrote to the provincial about the same topic in much the same tone: "In the haciendas of the colleges there is too much frankness in allowing women to work in household positions, allowing them to enter into the residences of the brothers who manage the haciendas. The dangers involved should be clearly recognized. Many tears are shed over this situation."[27]

One of the seven virtues of Juan Nicolás, the administrator held up as an example for all other administrators, was that he never looked into the face of a woman. When women were present he kept his eyes fixed on the ground, and his conversations with them were always edifying. His successor, Joaquín Donazar, did not share the same convictions, but he was concerned about the purity or lack thereof of female slaves in Mexico City acquired with his assistance. He described one girl as very neat in appearance but no longer a virgin. If the Doña in Mexico City wanted her, despite this defect, he would examine her to determine whether she was pregnant and would report on his findings.[28] All administrators had an ongoing concern about maintaining decorum in contacts with all females and about regulating the lives and purity of the hacienda's female slaves.

Constant companionship of another male served as the main protection against isolated contact between Jesuit males and the females at the hacienda. Proscriptions against employing females in household activities, although stipulated by the Instrucciones and reinforced by the letters of the father general, were not entirely adhered to, if the number of female slaves identified as skilled cooks can be taken as a true reflection of practice.[29] Hacienda administrators were to avoid entering any sirvientes' residences occupied by the wives if the husbands were not present. Special attention was paid to seeing that all women living with males at Santa Lucía were properly married. One of the qualifications for accepting Indian couples as rancheados was precisely their having been married according to the rituals of the church. If a couple came under conditions of common-law marriage they were to be sent to their local cura to have the situation rectified.[30] Failure to comply with Jesuit standards would result in refusal at the hacienda. Mayordomos were permitted to have their families with them but were discouraged from maintaining or establishing kinship or patronage bonds with workers. Despite the restrictions against compadrazgo and family ties between those who ran the hacienda and the workers, these were never successfully eliminated. But it was not part of the life-style envisioned by the Jesuits as central to their haciendas.

Resident Workers

Work-oriented austerity and sobriety were features the Jesuits were most successful in implementing at Santa Lucía itself rather than on all the anexas. Neither the location of the main residence nor its appearance was conducive to pleasure, gaiety, or, at times, good health. During the rainy season and during years of exceptionally heavy rains, the hacienda became surrounded by the rising waters from Lake Xaltocan. The nearby ciénegas, although beneficial for the livestock, served as a breeding ground for insects.[31] Whenever possible, administrators who became seriously ill were taken to the city, where better medical attention was available. The early administrators had extensive medical skills. Aldana and Alcázar applied their knowledge to both Jesuit and non-Jesuit. No mention is made of administrators with medical skills for the eighteenth century. Nonslave and non-Jesuit workers at Santa Lucía received less attention when ill. The Indians continued to rely upon proven methods of the past. Their herbalists served the needs of the pueblos despite curas' attempts to eradicate the supernatural beliefs that surrounded their botanical knowledge. Against the European-introduced diseases, the Indigenous populations remained almost helpless, as the demographic history of the colonial period amply demonstrates. If hacienda sirvientes became involved in conflicts that resulted in injuries, the guilty party was assessed the costs of restoring the injured party to health and the value of lost wages.[32] And if members of the labor force insisted on "scandals, hates, conflicts, wedlock outside the law, drunkenness, or disputes" such bad customs would have to be exercised in their own pueblos as they were not to be tolerated on the hacienda.[33]

Daily and seasonal activities of the hacienda resident workers varied, depending upon occupational status and seasonal demands. Female slaves working as cooks were the earliest risers, having to prepare the morning meals and the chocolate of the Jesuits before attending mass. Molenderas rose early to make fires, grind maize, and make tortillas, regardless of whom they served. At all times of year there were visitors at the hacienda. Shepherds accompanying the sheep flocks made their annual appearances between July and September, when gangs of trasquiladores were also present. For the household staff at Santa Lucía, there were few periods when things were quiet, regardless of whether the administrator was present or on his rounds. In his absence, the mayordomo and chaplain were in attendance to command attention and give instructions.

Textile workers led the most regimented lives. The separation of tasks into specialties (washing, dyeing, carding, spinning, and weaving) and the sheer monotony of the work produced unwilling workers. The necessity of using chains within the confines of the sweatshop suggests that compulsion was required and that the mill was used as a form of punishment. Miers reports placing one of the slaves he had on his list of useless slaves who should be sold—a thirty-five-year-old male described as a "malevolent thief"—in the mill on the orders of the procurador.[34] Different administrators supervising textile activities varied in their harshness, but work in the mill could be described as monotonous at best. In response to inferior products being produced by the mill in 1754, Villaverde placed one of the slaves in chains as an example to the other workers.[35]

Resident specialists such as carpenters, masons, and smiths worked at a variety of jobs depending upon the demands of the moment. During periods of labor shortage these men might find themselves assisting in the harvest, or they might be sent to other anexas to help in building programs. The ox keepers were expected to be on the job very early. In 1754 one of the mayordomos reported to Villaverde that, although he had given instructions that the oxen should be out of the corrals at 4:00 A.M., he had discovered them still in their enclosures at 7:00 A.M. The regular ox keeper had left them in the care of his brother, reason enough for being in danger of dismissal from the hacienda.[36]

Shepherds

For the Santa Lucía labor force engaged in livestock production, seasonal and daily rounds of activities were less subject to change, as they were geared to the needs of animal husbandry. Shepherds were among the least watched-over workers of the entire hacienda. Compliance with the type of performance expected by the Jesuits depended upon the vigilance of supervisors. While on sheep drives, pastores frequently slept under the stars. The most common advances en route were sleeping mats and blankets. Corrals and shepherd huts were standard features at the main pastures and were used when possible. At times shelters belonging to neighbors were used. The mayordomos traveled in greater comfort. The Provincia mayordomo, for example, traveled with a bed and a tent.[37] His tent served a dual purpose, providing shelter from the elements and protection for the goods and supplies he carried with him.

Mayordomos made the day-to-day decisions regarding movement of the flocks. They arranged for payment of bridge fees and pasturing fees, or the purchase of additional supplies such as maize and tobacco. Letters were sent regularly to either the hacienda administrator or the college procurador while en route, to keep him informed of problems and progress. The long periods of travel by Provincia sirvientes and their annual exposure to the Valley of Mexico must have had a profound impact on their lives, creating traditions and habits that differentiated them from the shepherds who spent only short periods of time on the sheep drives.

The annual cycle of events, even for the families of the Provincia shepherds, was strongly influenced by the annual migrations of the flocks. Available records indicate that most weddings and baptisms took place in April, May, or early June, prior to the beginning of the annual drives and the consequent absence of male members of the family. The hacienda allowed wives, sisters, and mothers to draw additional advances of textiles and cash immediately before the men's departure. We do know that Santa Lucía's shepherds, like all shepherds involved in such annual migrations, had to adapt their lives to the demands of their employment. The Jesuits attempted to maintain tight supervision over their workers. Vacieros, manaderos, and pastores who neglected their duties stayed with the hacienda only until they were found out.[38]

Most of the details about the daily life of shepherds, and the seasonal and generational changes, have yet to be studied for the seventeenth and eighteenth centuries. The accounting statements generated by the Jesuits, however, allow a reconstruction of the seasonal round of activities.[39] The anexa of Negra, after merging with Ocuila, became the largest of Santa Lucía's sheep-raising operations. By the late 1730s its sheep populations peaked at almost 50,000 animals and throughout the 1740s were held at somewhat lower levels. The labor force required to tend these flocks varied between sixty and ninety shepherds drawn from the Ocuila and Malinalco jurisdictions, where these flocks spent most of the year. The annual round of activities was governed by three main factors: the reproductive cycle of the sheep, the annual variations in rainfall and temperature which affected access to water and pasture, and the annual drive to Santa Lucía for shearing and culling of the flocks and settling of the sirvientes' accounts. The drive itself was initiated by Santa Lucía administrators, who had to coordinate the arrival of all flocks, and could vary from year to year. In 1735, for example, the shearing began on August 13 and was completed ten days later. That year, 38,764 sheep were involved, broken down into fourteen flocks ranging in size from 4,600 to 120. Always the first to arrive were a flock of old sheep that would not be returning. The mayordomo reported with them or the first vaciada. His concern, once the main residence was reached, was not the shearing, which was managed locally, as was the control of the flocks at the residence. The mayordomo's immediate obligation was to settle his own accounts for the past year and to prepare for the annual adjustment of the shepherds' accounts. The vaciadas and manadas arrived separately, each accompanied by three to five shepherds. The last flock to arrive was the smallest, made up of the injured, and destined for slaughter. If a flock was larger than 4,000, it would have at least two mounted attendants and probably up to three shepherds on foot. For them this accounting was often the most important event of the year. Besides learning what their balance was, how much cash or goods they could receive, they would be informed whether they would be kept on or not, and if so what their responsibilities would be. A steady shepherd's position with the Jesuits represented reasonable working conditions and a good income, two items of increasing scarcity in times of rapidly increasing pueblo populations.

Continuance in a shepherd position was by no means to be taken for granted. Of the seventy individuals employed during 1739 at Negra, only twenty-one were still on the job by 1750. Between 1739 and 1740, twenty shepherds were discontinued and ten were added. Of the sixteen shepherds in charge of individual flocks in 1739, only seven were in charge of flocks during the next season. Three were dropped from the rolls and ten others already employed were put in charge of flocks. By 1744 only three had maintained their supervisory positions. Not all changes, however, were made on the day of accounting. During the 1740–1741 season, fourteen shepherds left Negra. Five left with debts (totaling 24 pesos), indicating that they had abandoned their jobs, and the other nine had had their accounts balanced with the mayordomo, suggesting their departure was initiated by the hacienda administration. But the accounting came yearly, although the day shifted periodically. Between 1739 and 1743 it was August 1, then it was moved to October for 1745–1746, and between 1748 and 1750 it took place on September 1. Such shifts represented adjustments in the annual appearance of Negra flocks at Santa Lucía. Between 1728 and 1738, shearing commenced as early as July 12 or as late as August 29.

The annual drive into the Valley of Mexico had important repercussions in the lives of individual shepherds who spent the rest of the year much closer to their home communities. For shepherds whose service was considered reliable, the rewards were substantial. Despite the high turnover of Negra shepherds, ten of the eighteen who had flock responsibilities during 1739–1740 were still at the anexa in 1750.[40] One of the rewards for them was job security. One such individual was Joseph Antonio Rodríguez, who in 1739 held the position of vaciero, earning 10 pesos a month plus a weekly maize ration of 12 quartillos. During the twelve months following the accounting of August 1, 1739, he earned 113 pesos, 5 reales, based on time worked. He took a sanctioned absence from work from March 12 to April 1. His account for the year showed he had acquired one mule, one sheep, two salted hides, two large blankets, 20 pesos and 1 *real* in textiles, 6 pesos and 2 reales in cash, plus three indulgences worth 2 reales each. When he settled his account on August 1, 1740, Rodríguez received 41 pesos, 1 *real*, in cash and took 26 pesos worth of goods as an advance on the next year's wages. He again took a brief leave (twenty days in August) and during the season acquired roughly the same allotment of textiles as in the previous year, plus three blankets and three bulas. Since he did not acquire any livestock, his cash income at the August 1, 1741, accounting was higher (66 pesos, 1 *real*). During the 1741–1742 and 1742–1743 seasons, he did not miss any days and acquired roughly the same quantities of textiles, blankets, and bulas. At the August 1, 1743, accounting he was promoted to the position of ayudante and his salary increased by 2 pesos per month. This new status resulted, during the next accounting period, in greater cash advances, the acquisition of four blankets, four bulas, a fancy hat, two sheep, and a bridle, plus a greater quantity of textiles. He maintained this position until at least 1750, occasionally missing a few weeks of work and annually taking somewhat larger quantities of textiles. In 1747 he acquired a horse and had charged against his account the advances of his son Carlos (17 pesos, 3 reales), who began working as a foot shepherd. By the next year the son had his own separate account and his wages had been increased from 2 to 3 pesos per month. During the 1748–1749 and 1749–1750 seasons, Joseph Antonio received, in addition to the textiles, blankets, and bulas, cash settlements of 50 pesos per year.

The case of Rodríguez shows advancement in occupational status, increased wages, the addition of a member of the family to the Negra work force, and, above all, a steady pattern of acquisitions and income. What happened to the cash income and the eventual distribution of the textiles—whether they were used by the female members of the family or were resold in his own community—cannot be determined from the accounts. The case does present a

stable pattern of annual activity and very little variation in acquisitions from the hacienda stores. As ayudante, Joseph Antonio had
greater responsibility than as vaciero, when a single flock and its
small crew were his primary concern. As ayudante he would assist
in the supervision of other flocks and herdsmen in their daily and
seasonal tasks. The Negra flocks ranged over pastures covering at
least 576 square kilometers.[41] They were kept in separate flocks but
moved to pasture and water sources best suited to the season.
Periodic access to salt licks had to be arranged, or salt from stores
distributed when natural sources were not available. Special attention and additional help were required during the period of lambing, which seems to have varied for individual flocks. Pasture
guards had to be instructed or corrected when there were incursions by neighbors onto sheep pastures of the anexas. Corrals for
the nightly protection of flocks had to be maintained, as did the
shepherd huts associated with them. The ayudante had to be able
to conduct all the supervisory tasks of a sobresaliente, whose job
he might eventually take over. His direct responsibility over stores
(textiles, equipment) and maize for rations, was minimal except
during temporary absences of his own supervisors. He did not
keep accounts but did assist in the distribution of rations. But his
exposure to all the facets of sheep-pasturing activities could lead to
promotion to the level of mayordomo. More likely it might result in
a transfer to another of Santa Lucía's anexas. The Jesuits appear to
have been reluctant to place tributary Indians, the legal status of
Rodríguez, in mayordomo positions. The Jesuit records unfortunately do not provide any information about the status and function of people such as Rodríguez in their own communities.

   Mathías de Buendía, another tributary Indian, worked at Negra
during the same period as Rodríguez. He was a lambing specialist,
which meant that he moved from flock to flock to assist during the
lambing periods. His salary was 7 pesos per month plus maize rations, which remained constant between 1739 and 1749, when it
was increased to 8 pesos per month. His functions included more
than just the lambing, since he worked the entire year. During the
1740 sheep drive, for example, he was in charge of one of the
smaller flocks driven to Santa Lucía. His annual accounts show
great consistency. He hardly ever took cash advances during the
season, the greatest in any year being 8 pesos, 2 reales. The types
and quantities of textiles he acquired varied only slightly from year
to year and represented, on the average, 38 percent of his annual
salary. This left him with cash payments of roughly 50 pesos due

him at each accounting at the Santa Lucía hacienda. Since his occupation required riding stock and none was acquired through the hacienda, some of this cash would have been spent on mules or horses. The amount of tribute paid indicates he was married, and the presence of another Buendía on Negra's sirviente lists could mean other family members also worked at the anexa. During one year he paid for confessions, indicating these did not take place before the Jesuit chaplain at Santa Lucía. Except for such scattered bits of information, Buendía, like most shepherds at the anexas, remains little more than a work statistic on Jesuit records.

But there were minor differences between the anexas. This can be seen in comparing the 1749 status of Joseph Serón, a sobresaliente for the San Ignacio de la Punta sheep flocks,[42] with that of Rodríguez. Both men received 12 pesos a month plus rations, but Serón did not only acquire textiles in lieu of wages. He bought shoes, hats, sheep, hides, and chicharrón, the latter involving a weekly expenditure of 3 reales. He also started his new account on September 1 with a holdover debt of more than 34 pesos. During the previous season he had drawn almost biweekly cash advances, totaling 30 pesos. But at the end of the season he had a cash income of 54 pesos, 1 *real*, a figure very close to Rodríguez's cash income at the end of the same season. Although Rodríguez had lower expenses, he received a larger portion of his year-end settlement in the form of goods, whereas Serón received cash. The differences in the annual round of activities for both men would have been minimal. Dependence upon cash advances by shepherds in the Actopan Valley was greater than in the Malinalco-Ocuila jurisdictions, suggesting fewer alternatives open to them for meeting subsistence requirements for their families.

Goatherds

The annual round of activities for the goatherds was similar to that of the shepherds, although the structure of goat-ranching differed. In the late 1740s the Tepenene flocks numbered over 21,000 animals ranging over less productive areas in the Actopan Valley. Since goats forage well where other animals cannot survive, they ranged widely over the rocky slopes of the mountains in the less fertile southern parts of the valley. Tepenene maintained 50 saddle and pack mules to serve the goatherds, in addition to 19 horses. Goatherds at the higher occupational levels were mounted, but foot herders were always a necessity as the goats constantly were in terrain unsuited to riding stock. No long-range annual drives were necessary. Those animals annually slaughtered were first separated, then allowed to fatten in more lush pastures before being driven to Chicavasco for slaughter. The intensive work periods of the year included the time when the nanny goats gave birth, the castration of yearling billy goats not kept as breeding stock, the branding of yearlings, and the clipping of at least part of the flock. Tepenene equipment included twelve shears for clipping, but the use and disposition of the goat hair were not recorded.[43]

The goatherds, for the most part, were tributary Indians from the pueblos in the Actopan Valley. Annual accounts covering 1747 to 1750 provide insights about selected individuals.[44] Manuel Felipe held the post of vaciero, earning 6 pesos a month in addition to half a fanega of maize as a weekly ration. A close kinsman of his was the Tepenene sobresaliente. During the 1747–1748 season he acquired a saddle, sandals, three blankets, two hats, two goats, textiles worth 20 pesos, and cash advances of 13 pesos, 1 real. He missed nineteen days of work and at the September 8, 1748, accounting received 40 pesos in cash. During the next season his acquisitions were roughly the same, although he worked the entire year, but in the 1749–1750 season he purchased two mules and six goats. During this season his maize rations were reduced by one-quarter, and he received 11 pesos, 1 real, at the annual accounting, which seems to have taken place at Chicavasco.

Sebastián de la Cruz held the position of capitán, earning 4 pesos a month and a quarter-fanega as a weekly ration. He started the 1747–1748 season with a 10 peso deficit. During the year he missed two months and sixteen days because of illness, a period for which he was not paid. Since he acquired more goods (three goats, one blanket, one hat, maize, and textiles) and cash than his earnings, he still had a deficit of 16 pesos, 5 reales, at the 1748 accounting. During the following season he worked all year and, besides advances of cash and textiles, received candles and chicharrón. By the end of the third season, during which he missed two weeks, he had cleared up his deficit and wound up with 12 pesos in cash. During this season two of his sons had been temporarily employed by Tepenene, and their advances, a total of 7 pesos, 1 real, were charged against his account. Cruz's pattern of acquisitions was similar to those of Felipe, except that they did not include riding stock, but he received less cash at the accountings.

Zipriano Llano worked as a pastor at the goat ranch, earning 3 pesos a month plus 10 quartillos of maize each week. He missed one month because of illness during 1747–1748 and five weeks during the 1748–1749 season for the same reason, but kept his maize rations, and missed ten days during the 1749–1750 season. In September 1747 he had an outstanding debt of 25 pesos. This was reduced to 18 pesos the next year, then to 11 pesos the following year. By the September 1750 accounting he had eliminated his debts and received a cash settlement of 5.5 reales. His acquisitions from hacienda stores were similar to those of the capitán and vaciero, but in smaller quantities. During one of the seasons his brother-in-law received 8 pesos in cash.

These three cases indicate that Tepenene goatherds gained sufficient income from their employment to meet their needs, but that different occupational ranks resulted in various margins of well-being. The vaciero, at the end of a working season, received substantial cash payments; the capitán was able to eliminate his debts and have modest surpluses after three years; but the *pastor*, although he eliminated his debts, was not able to create cash surpluses. The *pastor* found it necessary to buy more maize than other goatherds and was ill more often, indicating that he was less well-off than his higher-ranking fellow workers. Tepenene goatherds working only a few months of the year, if they had no additional means of subsistence, were in a precarious situation.

Cowboys

For the cowboys associated with the raising of cattle, horses, and mules at Santa Lucía, life-styles were also largely shaped by occupational demands. Hueytepec had herds of horses and mules numbering slightly over 1,200 in the early 1740s. The range work involved relatively few cowboys—a foreman (caporal) and a crew of five to eight riders. Such a crew handled twenty-five to thirty droves (manadas) on the pasture ranges and were assisted by residence-associated cowboys in the special annual tasks during round-ups, branding, castration, and breaking-in. The range hands, besides being responsible for the water and pasture needs of the animals, acted as guardians of Hueytepec boundaries against non-hacienda residents and pueblo livestock. The dependence of cowboys upon hacienda resources rather than pueblo lands for subsistence needs is indicated by the structure of their wages. Cash income, per month, was lower than that of the mounted shepherds and goatherds, generally 4 pesos, but maize rations were higher, amounting to 1 fanega per week. In addition they received a weekly cash ration of 2 reales. Such weekly rations suggest almost complete reliance upon hacienda maize for domestic needs, with the cash rations used for buying other food and household necessities.[45]

Eugenio González's accounting records covering a four-year period (January 1741 to November 1744) indicate that the Hueytepec crew consisted of more than one member of a single family. His father was foreman in 1741 and another González was mayordomo. Although both supervisory positions were given to others during 1742, by 1743 the foreman position was again held by one of the Gonzálezes, and the eight-man crew included four González family members. The annual accountings were either in early January or early October. Every change in foreman necessitated an accounting. Range crews were selected by the foreman from among individuals he could trust (de su plena confianza). It was not uncommon for cowboys at Hueytepec and San Pablo to miss from two weeks to two months of work each year due to illness.[46] They seldom had significant cash surpluses at the accountings.

Cowboys tending Santa Lucía cattle worked under conditions similar to those at the horse ranches. One noticeable difference was a much smaller maize ration (12 quartillos) and only 3 pesos per month in wages. This was offset, however, by being allowed to have small private maize plantings (milpas) on hacienda lands. If livestock activities coincided with the periods of maize harvest, such a ranch hand might get a cash advance to pay someone else to do the harvesting. The cowboys at San Pablo frequently took small cash advances during the year to pay for domestic purchases. Such advances would be given directly to their wives, particularly if they were residents of neighboring pueblos. A cowboy might be in charge of up to two droves of cattle, but more frequently only one.[47] Like the goatherds in the northern regions of the Valley of Mexico and the Actopan Valley, the cowboys were not involved in annual long-distance drives. Whether they were resident sirvientes or not, they usually came from the towns of pueblos near the Jesuit estates.

The Jesuit Instrucciones outline criteria and conditions governing the ranch hands. Only experienced, intelligent hands were to be chosen, not "the very poor loaded down with useless [in terms of work ability] families, and whenever possible only those without any kinship or other close ties with the order." They were to be informed which day of the week they must come to the mayordomo (or his representative) to report on carrying out of responsibilities and to receive instructions. This could be on Sunday, when they received their weekly rations, or at least every first Sunday of the month. The hacienda administrator was to make periodic field checks on the vaqueros to confirm personally that their work was satisfactory. Workers derelict in their duties were to be warned at the first offense, threatened with dismissal on the second violation, and summarily dismissed, after settling their accounts, after the third misdemeanor. Special care was to be taken on paydays to prevent pressure upon the sirvientes to make contributions for special masses or fiestas. This was directed toward pressures coming from within their pueblos, especially from the local cura. Debts related to immediate family needs, such as baptisms, marriages, burials, and illness, would result in cash advances from the hacienda. But other debts, resulting from the worldly market, *alcalde mayores,* and curas in the pueblos, were not to be covered by advances. When paid at the annual accounting, the workers would be instructed to pay their debts immediately so the hacienda would not subsequently be inconvenienced.[48]

1754: A Year in the Life of a Hacienda

A typical year and its round of activities varied from anexa to anexa, according to location and the types of agricultural and livestock activities involved. However, a composite picture for the mid-eighteenth century, derived from the administrators' and mayordomos' correspondence, will be presented here.[49] This was 1754, when the emphasis was on livestock and food-crop production. January began with the harvest of maize, barley, and beans in progress at Chicavasco, San Pablo, San Xavier, and Tepenene. Maize-harvesting finished at San Xavier on January 1, yielding 2,500 fanegas. Nine days later, at San Pablo, 1,253 sacks of maize had been safely placed in the granary, and 88 cargas of frijoles had been harvested. To test the quality of the crop, 2 sacks of the maize were husked, allowing for an estimate of 935 fanegas and reassurance of a good yield. But at Chicavasco the yield was bad, and an 800 peso loss was calculated, based on a yield of only 800 fanegas and production costs of 2 pesos per carga. The maize harvest finished on January 15, and barley-harvesting was over five days later at San Xavier. At Tepenene better results could be reported by the 20th, when harvest activities had been completed, including two days of husking corn at the residence. This allowed for a projection of 8,758 fanegas at Tepenene. Overall, the maize crop had been plentiful, totaling almost 13,000 fanegas, sufficient to meet internal hacienda needs and to allow for sale of surpluses. Except for the poor yield at Chicavasco, the anexas' yield ratios (of fanegas per *costal*, or sack of ears) were good: 0.93 at San Xavier, 0.74 at San Pablo, and 0.87 at Tepenene. Husking activities would continue at the residences, carried out by the local labor force, whose live-stock-related work tasks were minimal during January. The cowboys were more active, since this was the dry season and water needs were pressing. Some cattle were driven to the swamplands of Santa Lucía, and others were closely supervised to ensure pasture and water supplies.

In February, non-hacienda labor was needed, but resident workers were kept busy storing and processing crops (husking maize, shelling frijoles) and performing maintenance tasks. Manufactured goods were moved from the textile mill (blankets, cloths), and small quantities of maize and frijoles were sold. Leather goods produced at Chicavasco (harnesses, ropes, containers) were transported to Santa Lucía. Mayordomos and administrators were getting their accounts related to food-crop production in order. In March more intensive agricultural activity commenced, including the preparation of fields and the planting of irrigated maize. The muleteers were kept busy moving supplies and some food crops to anexas where they were not produced but would be needed. Maintenance and building programs occupied the labor forces at most of the anexas.

During April, after a promising early rain, the planting of maize was intensified. Besides finishing the planting of irrigated maize, the workers planted the regular (unirrigated) variety. Gangs of Indian laborers from neighboring pueblos were used for much of this work, as well as for harvesting irrigated barley fields at Florida. At San Xavier and Chicavasco, the last of the previous crop of maize was being husked, and after the barley was brought in it was winnowed. Barley straw was also collected in the fields, transported, and stored at the appropriate anexas for local consumption or sale. Straw sales took place in Pachuca, to passing mule trains and even to pueblo curas who owned carriage and riding stock. In preparation for later sheep-shearing activities, surplus wool stocks not processed by the textile mill were sold off and the obraje supervisor made his annual accounts. The administrators lined up prospective buyers of sheep and wool, made diezmo payments for last year's production, and allowed small sales of sheep, cattle, mules, and hogs. In addition, over 3,000 sheep were moved to Ocuila for fattening. Stocks of maize and barley were moved to Santa Lucía in anticipation of later arrivals of the shepherds. April's early rain was followed by prolonged dry weather.

Scanty rainfall during the spring months meant more than usual irrigation activities during May at Chicavasco and Tepenene. In anticipation of a bad harvest, it was decided not to sell maize to Pachuca merchants. An added somber note was reported from Florida, where 300 goats were killed by a hailstorm and not even the hides were salvaged. In addition, 277 of the 3,946 yearly lambs being fattened at the ciénega at San Pablo became ill. Before matters got worse it was decided to sell the flock to a Puebla buyer, based on information provided by a Jesuit from the Puebla college regarding current shortages there. At the cattle ranches the calves were being branded. Blankets from the textile mill were transported to Mexico City, and a quantity of black wool was dispatched to a missionary father. Labor gangs from the pueblos made a brief appearance in May for the first weeding of the maize fields.

Because the drought continued throughout June, special masses were said to the patron saints of the affected anexas. The prospects for agricultural production looked glum for the coming year. Oats, frijoles, and alverjón were doing badly. Regular maize and barley plantings were never finished, and what was planted was expected to yield only meager returns. Thanks to irrigation possibilities at Chicavasco, San Xavier, and San Juan, there was still some hope for maize and barley plantings. On the livestock front, activity was increasing. The sheep flocks kept at San Pablo were brought to the residence for shearing—completed on June 21—and animals to be slaughtered were separated. Early in the month neighbors of Tepenene tried to gain access to lands belonging to the anexa and were interfering with its goatherds. The Jesuits attempted to get Actopan authorities to imprison the Indian leaders, but without success.

In July, Indian labor gangs were brought in for a second weeding of the maize plantings. The drought broke early in the month, prompting a more favorable crop outlook and temporarily eliminating irrigation at Tepenene, Chicavasco, San Pablo, and San Xavier. The first of the flocks from Provincia arrived at Santa Lucía, and shearing activities were started on the 23rd. Along with the flocks came news that 8,151 sheep had died during May and June, with another 151 dying en route. The hacienda administrator visited San Pablo in preparation for livestock sales and slaughter. The conflict with Tepenene neighbors continued, and attempts were made to force labor payments for Indian livestock intrusions. The

Indians launched a formal suit to reclaim land they felt belonged to the pueblo. Agricultural prospects improved in August as rains fell regularly at all the anexas. At Santa Lucía the shearing of Provincia flocks continued, and animals to be consumed at the college were brought to the city. Activities on the anexas were not intense, allowing for some construction at Altica and San Xavier. In addition, ongoing construction of ponds was reported.

The tempo of work picked up in September, when the shearing and separating of Ocuila flocks were completed. Shearing accounts were settled, including diezmo payments for sheep and wool from Ocuila, Provincia, and San Pablo. Expenditures of over 21,000 pesos were reported for remodeling water-storage and irrigation facilities, but the period during which the work was actually carried out was not indicated. Crop prospects at Chicavasco (maize) and Tepenene looked good, despite the small plantings. The locus of intense activities for September was Santa Lucía.

In October the emphasis shifted to San Xavier and San Pablo, where the Santa Lucía administrator spent most of the month. An intensive period of slaughtering was initiated at San Pablo, beginning on the 15th and lasting three weeks. Here the sheep that had been culled from the annual drives had been fattened and now were butchered. This resulted in large quantities of tallow, meat, and salted hides. Some of the tallow was sent to Santa Lucía and San Xavier, and there was correspondence and discussion regarding markets where top prices could be obtained, such as outlets in Pachuca, Puebla, and Mexico City. A limited amount of agricultural work was started at San Xavier, where plowing for the next seeding of irrigated barley commenced. Continuing rains were reported, and rents were collected from renters of hacienda land.

Livestock-processing continued into November, but heavy rains at the beginning of the month retarded meat-drying. The hacienda administrator remained at the anexa to be nearer the fall round-up and branding of horses and cattle. Immediately following the round-up, there were sales of colts, mules, and calves. Goats were slaughtered and goat hides sold. Agricultural activities included preparation of land and planting of irrigated barley. Sales included 7,096 goat hides, 2,500 cargas of tallow, 400 loins (lomos), and over 1,000 tongues. From the obraje, seventeen dozen hats plus blankets were shipped to Augustinian buyers. By-products of the processing, such as kidneys, dried smoked meats, and loins, accompanied distribution of sale goods as gifts to friends and business associates. Less charitable activities were directed against the Indians of Tepenene who were contesting land claims with the Jesuits. Having failed with persuasion, the mayordomos took matters into their own hands, forcefully ejecting Indian squatters and in the process destroying forty dwellings *(ranchitos)*. Besides complaining to the audiencia, the Tepenene Indians were expected to respond with force. To forestall this, Villaverde called together the mayordomo, sirvientes, and renters of the anexa, and armed them to resist any repercussions. When these did not appear to be forthcoming, the administrator returned to Santa Lucía.

Compared to the previous month, December was a sea of tranquility. The intensive phase of annual livestock production had been completed, although the distribution of products (hides, tallow, and livestock) continued. The late planting of barley and maize (unirrigated) resulted in later harvestings (normally begun in November) and, according to reports from Tepenene, the yields were reasonable although not copious. The Santa Lucía administrator had spent ten days at the Actopan Valley estates to supervise livestock and agricultural activities in the area. He was at San Xavier for three days later in the month, returning to his Santa Lucía residence on the 24th in order to spend the festive Christmas season with his family.

Overall, 1754 was a good year, with plentiful agricultural harvests at the beginning and steady livestock production throughout. The disputes with Indians at Tepenene had been troublesome, as was a conflict with the pueblo of Tolcayuca—led by the local cura—over the location of hacienda boundaries. Such conflicts could be expected in any year and did not interfere with overall productivity. Recorded profits for the year from food crops and livestock operations were approximately 30,000 pesos. In addition, the farmed-out pulque operations yielded 20,000 pesos. The Colegio Máximo officials had reason to be satisfied with the performance of Santa Lucía.

The year 1754 represents a specific point in Santa Lucía's history as a Jesuit estate, one where direct involvement was at a minimum. A century earlier, the seasonal round of activities, and most of the hacienda returns, had still been tied to livestock. The hacienda complex had been much smaller, its claim to former agricultural lands of Indian communities much less, and its dependence upon pueblo labor less important. In the mid-seventeenth century, the Santa Lucía and San Xavier residences had been the main centers of activity. Jesuit involvement had been greater and conflicts had related to access to pastures rather than the direct control of land.

And in 1754, secular influences dominated hacienda activities at Santa Lucía. The Jesuits of the previous century would not have approved of activities related to pulque production.

Hacienda-Pueblo Relations and Comparisons

Seasonal and economic factors largely defined the daily life of Santa Lucía's many workers. But the hacienda was only a temporary work experience for the great majority. They were bound by its conventions only as long as they were part of its apparatus of economic production. For the Indians from the neighboring pueblos, the hacienda imposed limitations on access to land for their own use while providing opportunities for employment. During these short periods of employment they might spend days, although seldom weeks, living at the hacienda residences. But their function was clearly defined and their access to other residents on the hacienda severely restricted. Relations between Santa Lucía and Xoloc, San Juan and Zumpango, or San Xavier and Tolcayuca were controlled and defined by the owners and managers of the hacienda, not by workers at the hacienda and their kinsmen in the pueblos. The hacienda did not attempt to define the relationships within the pueblos by intervening directly in family life or insisting upon conformity to social conventions.

The hacienda labor force and kinsmen in the numerous communities on its fringes had their life-style shaped by influences other than the hacienda. Constant demands from within the pueblos, by the state-appointed secular officials governing the communities, by the church-appointed religious officials governing religious conduct, and by the rural Indigenous aristocracy struggling to maintain its own position, may well have been more oppressive than the hacienda's impact.[50] In many ways the hacienda competed with such forces for the labor of the pueblos, for the eventual distribution of cash income of all pueblo residents, and for their loyalty. The idea that these were separate native communities, or *repúblicas de indios,* divorced from the day-to-day demands of the larger urban-based sectors of society and the largely urban-controlled rural haciendas, is based more on myth—albeit myth supported by legal intent—than on documented reality.[51] The conflict the Jesuits had with the Zumpango *alcalde mayor* in the early eighteenth century and many of the conflicts with pueblo curas were directly related to conflicting demands upon the resources of the pueblos.[52] Although Santa Lucía successfully exploited pueblo labor and land resources claimed by the pueblos, there was an element of reciprocity. Labor services were in most cases reasonably compensated, and in some cases well rewarded. The actions of Santa Lucía's competitors within the pueblos were not always so just.

Within the pueblos, the local caciques and curas frequently made demands upon the local population, including members working on the haciendas. Caciques attempted to monopolize available land resources for their crops and livestock and to exploit the labor of the villagers through their own arrangements with nearby haciendas. Curas, for example Don Luis Antonio Terreros y Valcarzel, who was in Tolcayuca during the 1740s, pressured villagers to make contributions for special masses and fiestas. His fees for religious services (masses, baptisms, marriages, and burials) placed a constant drain upon the cash income of those who worked at nearby San Xavier. He claimed that when these workers returned to their village it was often to beg for clothes and alms because of their poverty. The cause of such conditions, according to a Jesuit administrator, was his excessive demands upon the villagers. Upon learning that Bernardino Francisco, who worked at San Xavier, had gossiped that the cura was indiscreetly living with a mistress, Don Luis had him imprisoned and fined the equivalent of two months' wages (7.5 pesos). He collected the fine from the Jesuits, who charged the money against Bernardino's account.

Don Luis's life-style contrasted sharply with that of his parishioners. He owned flocks of sheep and operated fifteen pulque ranchos rented from the Jesuits. He refused to acknowledge large debts with the Jesuits (see Appendix B, no. 69) after having received numerous cash advances from them. He regularly purchased expensive clothes and textiles from Jesuit sources in order to provide gifts for relatives (his mother and brother) and his vicar. The cura traveled in style, using two types of carriages (*coche* and *volante*) drawn by mules and horses purchased from the Jesuits. His correspondence with the Jesuits gives evidence of business associations with Mexico City, influential political connections in high places, an attitude of superiority toward the Jesuits, and a paternalism bordering on contempt toward the peasant villagers of Tolcayuca.[53]

The extent to which differences between curas and hacienda workers from pueblos were normative for the period cannot be easily determined from hacienda records alone. Zorita's fact-finding report during the early stages of hacienda encroachments and studies by Gibson and Zavala and Miranda agree that conditions were difficult for most, if not all, pueblos.[54] The implications of this study indicate a gradual deterioration of conditions within the pueblos as they were gradually cut off from traditional resources and faced with impositions emanating from outside the communities. One way of comparing pueblo life-styles, such as that of Tolcayuca, and the life-style of Santa Lucía workers is to examine land and livestock holdings of pueblo residents. The extensive list of renters of Santa Lucía, drawn up by the hacienda administrator in the 1740s, provides specific data for individuals from numerous pueblos.[55]

In the Valley of Mexico, where the Jesuits had the lion's share of the land resources, individual Indians from pueblos still managed to raise livestock and plant crops. Diego Millán, from Ixtlahuaca, was considered an *indio rico* and planted 6 fanegas of maize, besides owning 300 sheep, 40 cattle, and 16 horses. He paid the Jesuits 90 pesos a year in rental fees. Of the twelve renters of Altica lands, which totally surrounded Ixtlahuaca, Millán was the best-off, yet the value of his livestock (467 pesos, 4 reales) was less than the annual salary of a top mayordomo of a Santa Lucía sheep or goat ranch, or the equivalent of slightly more than three years' income of a good sheep vaciero. His maize plantings might produce a substantial crop in a good year, but income from this source, in this location, was never certain. Three members of the Lucio family, from Tezontepec, were able to pay 39 pesos in rental, indicating their collective resources to be slightly less than half those of Millán. Another individual from Ixtlahuaca managed 12 horses worth 60 pesos, or less than the annual salary of a vaciero working for the Jesuits. For the individuals renting from Altica, on the average owning 139 head of livestock worth 166 pesos, the value of their livestock was slightly less than two years' income for a regular vaciero with the Jesuits.[56] A peón from the pueblo, if he worked 250 days a year at the standard 2 reales per day, would have earned 62 pesos, 4 reales, which comes to 37.6 percent of the value of the livestock of livestock-owning Indians considered well-off. The differential between the livestock owners and the peones, however, would be greater, since the pueblo peones seldom found year-round employment. However, the renters of hacienda lands and pastures could not be sure their privileges would be extended into the next year. Members of pueblos such as Ixtlahuaca and Tezonte-pec who were granted renting rights usually held community positions of authority (alcalde, gobernador) and reciprocated by ensuring that the Jesuits had labor from the pueblo on demand.[57]

The San Xavier renter lists included a number of Indians from the neighboring pueblos of Tolcayuca and Zapotlán.[58] Their livestock holdings were substantially smaller than those of the group renting from Altica. They owned between 18 and 150 sheep, between 2 and 14 horses, and no one paid more than 12 pesos annual rent. From a list of twenty-three individuals, six were associated with the hacienda itself and another four held positions of authority in the pueblos. At Tepenene the privilege of owning 100 goats or less, or planting between 1/16 and 1 fanega of maize, meant two days a week of labor service to the hacienda. At Chicavasco the livestock numbers and area of maize planted were only fractionally larger,[59] and at Florida the Indians on the list managed access to up to 1 fanega of maize plantings, an average of 144 sheep or goats, 4 cows, and 5 horses.[60] Maximum rental at Florida was 12 pesos a year; at Chicavasco, 20 pesos a year. At Ocuila, pueblo officials had access to forests from which they exploited lumber and charcoal. Small rental fees of up to 7 pesos a year were paid, but the work was conducted by pueblo carpenters and charcoal makers.[61]

Data from the renter lists do not indicate whether or not the hacienda lands were the only resource for pasturing livestock, planting maize, or extracting forest products. Yet the relative capacities of pueblo residents for private economic initiative are indicated. Such opportunities were both relatively meager and dependent upon good relations with the owners of adjacent haciendas. The economic returns for the sectors of power and prestige within the Indigenous communities (gobernadores, alcaldes) in given years appear not to be equivalent to annual wages of top-level hacienda employees. In most cases they appear to have been even less remunerative than annual incomes of vacieros and manaderos.[62] Furthermore, the types of activities pursued on the fringes of the Jesuit hacienda suggest that the livestock activities at the anexas served as an example people in the pueblo attempted to emulate. The diffusion of a livestock-oriented life-style into the pueblos themselves had a double impact beneficial to hacienda interests and detrimental to pueblo resources. On the one hand, the spread of knowledge about raising livestock meant a growing potential labor force that could be easily integrated into hacienda productive activities. On the other hand, such livestock exerted further pressure upon the agricultural lands traditionally devoted to pueblo subsistence.

Descriptions and values of buildings and residences occupied by hacienda workers and the Jesuits provide further clues for a comparative assessment of life-styles. The occupants of the lowest work categories did not have their own homes on hacienda property, but specialists and supervisors frequently did. At Tepenene the mayordomos and ayudantes who maintained their own ranchos lived in buildings worth between 18 and 45 pesos. The lesser value was for a stone-and-mud-walled house roughly twelve by fifteen feet with palm or thatch roofing. In addition they might have a thatch-roofed hut. The residence of one of the former mayordomos (Serrano) consisted of two structures of slightly larger dimensions, with plastered stone walls, plus three *jacales* (thatch and pole huts). The entire residence was valued at 45 pesos. An unidentified ayudante's house was described as consisting of one large room worth 32 pesos. The sirviente residences at Concepción were a continuous structure with a beamed ceiling, divided into units and owned by the hacienda.[63] San Xavier had eighty-four residences for its laborers, each valued at 8 pesos, 7 reales.[64]

The substantial residence complexes at Santa Lucía and its anexas were monumental structures in comparison to those of the workers.[65] At Tepenene the residence had two stories with enclosed patios, living and sleeping quarters, and a chapel. The external dimensions were thirty-one by thirty-three varas, and it was valued at 408 pesos. In addition, this anexa had a series of pulque residences valued at 606 pesos. Concepción's residence was larger, forty by forty-one varas, and included stables, storerooms, residence quarters, and a chapel, collectively valued at 1,240 pesos. Its pulque ranchos and water tanks, ponds, and a dam were worth an additional 2,860 pesos. Florida's residence and contents were valued at 1,007 pesos, and its water reservoirs were worth another 1,067 pesos. Altica's residence, plus corrals, equipment facilities, water works, and pulque facilities, had a value of 6,189 pesos. The same items at Hueytepec, plus its chapel, were worth 10,595 pesos. At San Pablo the complex, plus water works, came to 9,540 pesos apart from the San Ignacio facilities, worth 1,683 pesos.

But the largest residences were at San Xavier, Chicavasco, and Santa Lucía itself. At San Xavier, the residence complex and chapel alone had a value of 12,798 pesos. Its exterior dimensions measured 133 by 140 varas, with massive stone walls 6 varas high facing north and south; the side walls were a mere 4 varas high. This fortresslike complex had two large interior central patios flanked by two side patios, adjacent to which were the residences for Jesuit administrators and slaves. It also had an extensive network of corrals, a very large artificial water pond, smaller ponds, and an orchard, together worth another 7,734 pesos. The exterior dimensions of the residence complex were roughly equivalent to those of the cathedral in Mexico City.[66]

The dimensions of Chicavasco were even more impressive. Its residence complex, valued at 12,979 pesos, extended 180 by 120 varas and included an immense storage granary, stables, sheds, corrals, and water tanks. Its dominating feature was the granary, measuring 9 varas in height, 17 varas in width, and 60 varas in length. Its roof was supported by a center row of ten stone columns whose bases were 1 square meter in area. Its rows of windows were located high on the walls, allowing for ventilation but not unauthorized entry. This granary was built in the period of Jesuit hacienda development, when serious attention was being given to the production of cereal grains in the Actopan Valley. Its storage capacity indicates that the type of production the Jesuits had in mind by far exceeded internal needs of the hacienda.[67]

But compared to the main residence of Santa Lucía, the San Xavier and Chicavasco complexes would have to be seen as modest. As Don Alonso Villaseca had predicted, at Tepeatzingo the industrious Jesuits had built a most successful and substantial center of hacienda operations whose buildings, in 1767, were valued at 38,482 pesos. Most other structures erected during the colonial period in the pueblos of the northern part of the Valley of Mexico were modest by comparison. Most churches in the native communities, outside of Zumpango, Tezontepec, and Tizayuca, could have been placed inside the granary of Chicavasco, and only the tip of a single church tower would have been visible.[68] The hacienda of the Jesuits clearly differentiated itself, in function and style, from the life of its non-Jesuit dependents—and their dependents in the Indian pueblos.

But colonial life-style cannot be measured simply through material manifestations related to property, residence, and income. Less tangible aspects, concerning security, power, and influence, although more difficult to measure, also need to be taken into consideration. By the mid-eighteenth century the Jesuits and their haciendas presented the appearance of security, and their power and influence within the colony were questioned only by the wealthy (private estate owners) and the powerful (the secular clergy). Hacienda workers from the pueblos were forced to refocus their perspective, to exchange their identification and village loyalties for the new opportunities offered by the hacienda, to exchange traditional agrarian livelihood patterns for the privilege of full participation in the urban-directed economy. The pueblo residents, including kinsmen of the hacienda workers, and the majority of the rural inhabitants, however, lost security, power, and influence. What they retained was their identity as Indians, legally defined as wards of the crown, and treated by church and state as perpetual minors, without full rights of participation in the important decisions affecting their everyday affairs.

PART FOUR

Colonial Haciendas

TWELVE 🔲 *Santa Lucía in Colonial Mexico*

Santa Lucía represents Jesuit involvement in hacienda development in colonial Mexico. The Jesuits deliberately played down their role as hacendados because they considered Santa Lucía and other haciendas primarily as means of producing economic resources to sustain educational and missionary endeavors. Although investigators of colonial society in Latin America have long recognized the importance of Jesuit economic institutions, knowledge of the structure of such institutions and their impact upon the rest of society, let alone the availability of longitudinal case studies against which to test generalizations, has remained limited.[1] The potential usefulness of this study lies both in its analysis of the structure of a large-scale hacienda complex and in its recording of hacienda transformation, spanning more than three centuries. In the preceding chapters, specific details about Santa Lucía have been presented, keeping in mind the immediate agrarian context as well as the broader issues related to colonial institutions. This chapter attempts to distinguish between the unique and general characteristics of this hacienda within colonial Mexico.

The case of Santa Lucía raises a series of questions. Was it a unique corporate endeavor, in contrast to other corporate or private agrarian endeavors? If so, then its success can more narrowly be attributed to the genius of its Jesuit owners, and its relevance for understanding other colonial haciendas can be dismissed. Was it essentially like other haciendas, albeit more successful? If so, then its relevance cannot be dismissed, but its success might still be explained by special circumstances deriving from location—on the periphery of Mexico City—and access to markets, or by skills, political connections, and superior administration supplied through the Colegio Máximo. Or was Santa Lucía both unique, in its internal corporate ties, and similar to other haciendas, in its activities and impact? If this was the case, then impact upon other haciendas, by example, should not be overlooked, and greater attention can be directed to the larger question of the nature and impact of haciendas in colonial society. Recent publication of regional and case studies makes it possible to begin to make the necessary comparisons. Fortunately, such studies encompass central, northern, and southern regions of colonial Mexico, allowing for broad rather than localized comparison.

Santa Lucía Within a Jesuit Context

Santa Lucía was one hacienda complex owned by one college. By the middle of the eighteenth century there were twenty-seven different colleges in the six Mexican bishoprics, as well as 103 missions in the north.[2] Thanks to Tovar Pinzón's analysis of the global nature of Mexican Jesuit holdings (despite the incompleteness of the data), an indication of the larger Jesuit picture is available. Most of the Jesuit colleges and missions had rural haciendas. The values assigned to these estates immediately after Jesuit expulsion in 1767 suggest an important economic role. In the bishoprics of Guadalajara, Mexico, and Valladolid, Jesuit haciendas had an assessed value of over 4 million pesos. The total value of all Jesuit haciendas in colonial Mexico has been calculated at 8.5 million pesos.[*] Included were many haciendas, but the number is difficult to determine precisely. In 1734, Jesuit opponents claimed the order had seventy-nine haciendas within three bishoprics, whereas the Jesuits insisted there were only twenty-two, although admitting to twenty-four ranchos plus six sugar and lumber properties, for a total of fifty-two.[3] Thirty years later (1764), in the same area, the Jesuit figure had increased to forty-five haciendas, sixteen ranchos, and five sugar estates, for a total of sixty-six properties. Of the last total, the Santa Lucía complex represented six of the haciendas and seven of the ranchos.[4] For the six Mexican bishoprics and the missions, the hacienda total likely reached double the 1764 figure, as the assessed values of all Jesuit estates suggest.[5]

Santa Lucía's share of the total production of Jesuit haciendas was significant but subject to constant change in connection with shifts in production on the hacienda. According to Tovar Pinzón's

*Tovar Pinzón, "Elementos constitutivos," p. 136, lists haciendas valued at 3,765,288 pesos but does not include all the haciendas. J. Riley, "Wealth," pp. 247–48, estimates the value of capital in the haciendas as 8,568,640 pesos, based on a net annual profit of 428,432 pesos, calculated to represent 5 percent of capital worth.

data on thirty-four ex-Jesuit haciendas during the 1767–1768 season, the Santa Lucía percentages were as follows: cattle, 15.7 percent; horses and mules, 13.2 percent; sheep and goats, 21.7 percent; maize, 5.4 percent; wheat, none; and barley, 12.8 percent.[6] The actual percentages were much lower, as the sample did not take into account several other haciendas, including the important Puebla college hacienda of San Jerónimo, which in the mid-1760s had over 140,000 head of livestock.[7] Assuming the actual Santa Lucía percentages were less than half the figures just given, they were still substantial. Its share of the pulque production would have been much higher—since pulque was produced by Jesuit haciendas only in the Central Highlands and, as far as can be determined, only by the estates of the Colegio Máximo and the Tepotzotlán College—representing at least 50 percent of total Jesuit pulque production. Overall, Santa Lucía started out as the Jesuits' most important hacienda, a status it retained throughout the colonial period. It also served as model and pace-setter for other Jesuit haciendas. In this sense it can be considered unique in the Jesuit scheme of agrarian involvement. Keeping in mind the expansive nature of Jesuit economic activities throughout Central and South America, where colleges and missions used the same financing strategy, Santa Lucía can be seen as a small but representative part of a much larger landscape.

Within this larger picture, Santa Lucía's experience was representative in other ways. Patterns of land acquisition, continuous expansion and adaptation to local economies, management practices, techniques and types of production, utilization of labor, and policies of conflict resolution were equally applied at other Jesuit haciendas. The Colegio Máximo experience with Santa Lucía was duplicated many times over. Regardless of region, the process of land acquisition was continuous, as was hacienda expansion.[8] The sources of property, or funds for its purchase, were equally uniform. Throughout Mexico the Jesuits received donations from a wide range of admirers, including rich clerics, widows and widowers, Spanish landowners, and Indians. They used college endowments and profits from the estates to expand. Reliance upon borrowed funds for hacienda investment and the practice of renting to increase access to pasture, water, and other desired resources were also widespread.[9] Jesuit administration of rural properties, regardless of location, included the use of *hermanos coadjutores* and priests, and hired, non-Jesuit supervisors from the level of mayordomo downward. Reliance upon slave labor of African origin was common, as was the utilization of Indigenous labor. The Jesuits' system of accounting was standard in the eighteenth century on all their estates, although success in implementing these practices varied from region to region. Paying in cash, rations, textiles, and other hacienda products, and the use of credit advances to manipulate the labor force also fit into the general pattern.[10]

Productive activities on Jesuit haciendas did vary, depending upon region, local economy, markets, types of land, and rural conditions. Each college attempted to produce a wide range of items to take maximum advantage of available markets. Adjustments were constantly made to changing market conditions. Most colleges operated hacienda complexes specializing in sheep, goats, horses and mules, cattle, cereal crops, or combinations thereof. Localized land and labor-intensive activities (such as the cultivation of sugar cane, wheat fields, vineyards, and cacao orchards) were usually under separate administration, particularly if a large slave force was involved. If these operations did not have auxiliary ranches and farmlands, food and animal needs were met by other haciendas owned by the same college. The Jesuit strategy was designed to minimize the reliance of one college upon another college's resources and to maximize participation in the regional economy and absorption of short-term losses due to bad crops, poor prices, or rapidly changing demands. If changing economic conditions reduced the profitability of a specific crop, the estate would be adapted to a more productive alternative. The conversion of sugar-producing estates to cereal crops (for example, Chicomocelo, Xochimancas, and Chalco) and the shifting of Santa Lucía to pulque production were adjustments of this sort. Processing facilities such as obrajes, slaughterhouses, mills, and pulque-fermenting ranchos were emphasized or deemphasized depending upon local economic circumstances. Such facilities served internal needs of all units within a college's control and provided sale items for regional markets.[11]

There was an element of self-sufficiency in this strategy, but it was clearly geared to the productive activities of individual colleges rather than being narrowly applicable to specific haciendas. Within a hacienda complex such as Santa Lucía, this type of self-sufficiency was operational only to the extent that it enhanced profitability. And it was always tied to local and regional economic conditions. The Colegio Máximo economic activities were very similar to those of the Colegio del Espíritu Santo in Puebla or any of the other Mexican colleges. Details, scale of operation, types of prod-

ucts emphasized, and relative success did vary from region to region, both within Mexico and in other Jesuit provinces in South
America.

Similarity among the Jesuit operations generally was a result of a
management structure developed by the leaders of the order and
implemented within individual provinces. The Jesuit practice of
transferring rectors, provincials, and individual priests within and
among provinces ensured uniformity.[12] Thus, the similarity of
Santa Lucía operations to those of other Jesuit haciendas was a
normal consequence of overall Jesuit economic planning. Jesuit haciendas, from their beginnings in the sixteenth century, were essentially rural activities under the control and direction of urban
colleges and can be seen as an extension of urban control over resources in the countryside. They were never rural economic activities separable from the Spanish urban centers.

Chevalier observed that, by the end of the seventeenth century,
decentralization of authority had resulted in a transfer to the countryside of influence, power, decision-making, and economic development. He wrote: "Only one City, Mexico, broke the monotony
of an otherwise standard pattern; the capital was like a limit set to
the country-side's encroachment and a purchase point for a government that ran the risk of seeing the rest of the vast country slip
from its grasp."[13] Within the limits of Jesuit rural involvement,
such developments did not take place. The countryside remained
firmly under the control of urban centers. This was also the case in
the secular sector of the economy throughout the colonial period.

Secular Estate Development

Private Spanish ownership of rural resources began almost immediately after the conquest led by Cortés. Despite crown legislation prohibiting Spanish ownership of rural lands, individuals
such as Bernardino de Castillo and Antonio Serrano de Cardona
were inclined to acquire estates. In the area of the present State of
Morelos, M. Riley has found evidence of land seizure and forced
transfer through rental of considerable areas, quickly devoted to livestock production, cereal, cash crops (sugar, wine), and orchards.[14]
Despite concessions of specific areas to Cortés, official policy favored only limited access, governed by encomienda legislation.[15]
When the negative impact upon Indigenous sectors became clear,
the New Laws were passed to check abuses, but at the same time
they provided official approval of direct ownership of rural lands

by individuals. In the ensuing scramble for land, individual Spaniards with power and influence gained the upper hand and the best available lands. The process quickly became irreversible and continued well into the eighteenth century. Although Indian communities resisted the swelling encroachment upon their lands, and in specific localities managed to maintain considerable areas, they were caught between the pincers of internal community disintegration—largely by virtue of demographic catastrophe—and the externally imposed economic system that progressively weakened their hold upon rural resources. Much of their loss turned out to be the hacendados' gain.

In the Valley of Mexico, the initial assault was three-pronged, consisting of direct purchase from individuals, the exercise of encomienda and political privilege resulting in usurpation, and the use of the legal merced.[16] This set the stage for the establishment of the haciendas, whose numbers increased and whose sizes were constantly being adjusted. Gibson identifies "legal grants, consolidation, expansion, purchase, composición and denuncia" as the means by which 160 haciendas were established by the late eighteenth century.[17] Most started as collections of small numbers of caballerías and sitios, acquired by an emerging hacendado or his agents, later to be consolidated into a larger estate. This pattern was most pronounced between 1550 and 1625. Periodic composición demands between 1643 and the 1750s confirmed ownership, and additional purchases increased holdings and allowed the creation of hacienda complexes. Purchases and denuncia proceedings, many in the eighteenth century, eliminated many unsuccessful hacendados and enlarged the holdings of the successful. The establishment of mayorazgos, in principle designed to ensure the continuity of ownership within a family over succeeding generations, had little effect in preventing ownership transfer. Cumulative encumbrances, changing family fortunes, and the rise of individuals with new wealth resulted in the appearance of new hacendados and a greater concentration of land resources among people of wealth and political influence. These owners were almost always residents of Mexico City, holding interests in a variety of economic ventures.[18]

Farther south, in the Valley of Oaxaca, the land rush began later and lacked the intensity of hacienda activity in the Central Highlands. Between 1570 and 1643, forty-one haciendas became established, composed mostly of small numbers of caballerías and sitios acquired through merced, purchase, and usurpation. During the seventeenth century, through composición procedures, additional purchases, and rentals, much of the hacienda land became concentrated in the hands of fewer families, but maximum expansion of individual estates did not occur until well into the eighteenth century. Mayorazgos established in the seventeenth century seldom survived more than three generations in the same family. Leading hacendados were the prominent political figures. They resided in the new Spanish urban center of Antequera (City of Oaxaca) and dabbled in a wide range of business activities. In the Valley of Oaxaca, the Indigenous nobility copied the Spanish style successfully, achieving the status of hacendado in sufficient numbers to control a significant portion of rural resources. Here the Indian communities were also more successful in retaining land, confirmed by legal titles. Haciendas in Oaxaca were not so large or important as in the Valley of Mexico, but their establishment also coincided with local demographic decline.[19]

Similar conditions prevailed in the Actopan and Metztitlán valleys, to the northeast of the Valley of Mexico. Significant population decline preceded and accompanied hacienda formation. One of the successful early hacendados here was none other than the Jesuit advisor, Don Alonso de Villaseca. He exhibited the characteristics of his peers in the diversity of his economic enterprises, his political influence in high places, and his accumulation of many properties. Most grants of sitios and caballerías to Spaniards in the Metztitlán Valley were transacted between 1607 and 1615. Composición legalized the possession of additional lands, further increased through purchase, denuncia, and usurpation. By the middle of the eighteenth century the haciendas were concentrated in the hands of seven hacendados, essentially miners and merchants with business interests and residences in Pachuca and Mexico City. Native land retention was considerable, slightly more than 50 percent of the total area, but much of this land was marginal.[20] For the Actopan Valley, the property titles of estates acquired by the Jesuits in the eighteenth century (Chicavasco, Tepenene, San Ignacio, and San Pablo) provide background information. By 1616, sixteen individuals had been granted twenty-four mercedes of caballerías and sitios. Only one grant was given before 1550, eight took place between 1550 and 1575, four more by 1599, and eleven between 1602 and 1616. The grantees were people with status and connections in Mexico City, or agents acting on behalf of sponsors, and at least three members of the Indigenous nobility. By the first quarter of the seventeenth century, ownership was concentrated in the hands of six individuals. By 1643, composición confirmed control of the estates by three hacendados. By 1693, two mayorazgos held all the properties. Continuing encumbrances and shifting fortunes resulted in purchase of the lands by a corporate institution (the Colegio Máximo), aided by a denuncia claim, before the middle of the eighteenth century. Confiscation by the crown (1767) brought these estates, plus other haciendas in the area, into the hands of an individual of recent wealth and noble status, the Conde de Regla.[21]

The same family acquired much of the land in the Hueyapan Valley, to the north of Pachuca. Here, the early important encomendero, who was both a royal official and a cousin of Cortés, received mercedes, bought and usurped additional lands, and through agents acquired and enlarged his domain. The transfer of caballerías and sitios from Indian to Spanish hands was most intense between 1592 and 1615. In the seventeenth century, land changed hands and composición consolidated extraofficial acquisitions, allowing the emergence of few hacendado families. In the eighteenth century, Pedro Romero de Terrero—who arrived from Spain in 1733, started as a muleteer and prospered to the extent that he could "pave streets with silver" in honor of a son's christening—established new mayorazgos after buying out marginal haciendas. The events in the Hueyapan Valley indicate that attempts by Indigenous communities to halt the loss of most of their lands were matched by their failure to reclaim lands once they had become part of the haciendas.[22]

Hacienda formation in the Bajío district (Guanajuato and southern Querétaro) and the colonial diocese of Michoacán began late in the sixteenth century. Although Indian communities gained legal title to land, this did not prevent its eventual transfer into Spanish hands. In the seventeenth century, politically well-connected and economically powerful individuals laid claim to the best rural lands. The means were the same as elsewhere—merced, purchase, usurpation, composición, and denuncia. In the eighteenth century, successful miners and businessmen moved into the class of the "new rich" and demonstrated their status by buying and expanding haciendas. Morin provides a list of examples of property assemblages: in Celaya, twelve hacendados owned 44 haciendas; in Silao, three hacendados held 8 haciendas and 11 ranchos; in Dolores, three hacendados owned 10 haciendas. Fewer than twenty individuals controlled more than one-quarter of the best rural lands. The situation in Michoacán reflected the recently emerged aristocracy, including the Marqués de San Francisco, with 2 haciendas and 43 ranchos; the Countess of Miraville, with 7 haciendas and 21 ranchos; Francisco Xavier Paulín, with 6 haciendas and 57 ranchos; and José Matamoros, with 1 hacienda and 78 ranchos. Four individuals in the Zitácuaro district owned 198 of 276 ranchos.[23] By the end of the colonial period the landscape of colonial New Spain was dotted with 5 Spanish cities, 8 towns, 322 pueblos, 846 haciendas, and 1,788 ranchos. Many of the ranchos were anexas of haciendas owned by powerful, wealthy hacendado families who lived in the Spanish cities and engaged in a wide range of business activities.*

The picture for Northern Mexico shows progressive accumulation of the best lands by government officials and their relatives and retainers. Such powerful men, aided by hundreds of middlemen and agents, gradually built up large estate complexes in New Galicia, Nuevo León, and New Mexico. The owners of the large livestock estates were mostly rich men from Mexico City, Puebla, or Querétaro, or they were governors and miners from the north. They used the same methods of property acquisition as in other areas. In this area, however, there were few sedentary, agrarian Indigenous communities. Thus the haciendas frequently became new population centers, taking defensive postures against the area's nomadic, hostile Indian populations. Chevalier suggests a far greater degree of ownership stability for the north than has been found in central and southern Mexico. This was not necessarily the case. Most of the data cited by Chevalier concerned the sixteenth and early seventeenth centuries, predating periods of high turnover of ownership noted elsewhere. Harris's study of Coahuila indicates low levels of ownership stability throughout the seventeenth and eighteenth centuries.[24]

Apart from the regional studies, case studies reaffirm the consistent pattern. Hacienda case studies include research on San José de Coapa and José Antonio Uría, two haciendas in central Mexico; San Jerónimo, near Tehuacán; La Parada y San Diego and Bledos, near San Luis Potosí; and the Sánchez Navarro haciendas, in Coahuila. They varied in size—from San José de Coapa's 430 hectares (1778), through La Parada's 34,526 hectares (1767), to the 271,727 hectares of the Sánchez Navarro haciendas (1805)—but all started as collections of small properties acquired by numerous indi-

---

*Brading, *Miners*, p. 230, indicates that 1,046 of 1,406 (74.4 percent) of the ranchos in the Bajío district were anexas in 1793. See also his "Estructura."

viduals. Consolidation into larger haciendas, frequent transfer of ownership (by individuals, families, and institutions), and mixed success in exploiting local resources were common features. Productive activities covered lumbering, livestock, food crops, cash crops, and combinations thereof. The shape of the individual haciendas, by the second half of the eighteenth century, turned out to be collections of discontinuous properties of various sizes and locations, dedicated to activities best suited to local rural resources and available markets. In all cases, ownership and exploitation were firmly linked to the needs and demands of the Spanish urban centers.[25]

Regional and local patterns of hacienda formation in colonial Mexico show a consistent, monotonous pattern. The cast of characters was richly varied, and the scenery changed from one location to the next, but the same plots and actions were repeated. This was so because the script for the scenarios had a common origin— the prestige, power, and wealth of essentially urban individuals near the center of the governing Spanish influence. Jesuit participation, exemplified by Santa Lucía, added nothing new. This is not to suggest that the corporate Jesuit hacienda was indistinguishable from the private hacienda, or that all haciendas were equally successful. But it does suggest that there is little information currently available to justify placing Jesuit hacienda formation outside the mainstream of events.

Stability of Ownership

The stability of Jesuit ownership of Santa Lucía, until 1767, was never in doubt. Stability aided continuous growth and domination of local regions and provided a barrier against outside encroachment upon the hacienda. After the mid-seventeenth century, Santa Lucía's growth depended less upon Jesuit ability to encroach upon Indigenous lands than upon the ability to incorporate smaller and less stable estates.[26] Once Jesuit ownership was swept away, Santa Lucía and additional Jesuit estates were absorbed—after a decade of state control—by the enterprising Regla family. The Reglas and their descendants maintained control until the twentieth century, or as long as they remained a powerful political force in national affairs.[27] But relatively few haciendas duplicated the Santa Lucía pattern of only two owners over four centuries. Colonial institutions designed to enhance ownership stability, including mayorazgo and *cacicazgo* (cacique rule, including control of property)—as a study of the land titles of almost any of the eighteenth-century hacienda complexes amply demonstrates—ensured stability of ownership only as long as the hacendados maintained positions of wealth and power. Those families that fell behind in the ongoing scramble for wealth, or whose devotion to pious works overcame temporal objectives, found their haciendas burdened with encumbrances. Hacendados who lost their wealth became suddenly indebted, and their estates changed hands.

Ownership instability was a constant feature of the colonial history of rural properties. Between 1550 and 1650, sitios and caballerías granted in merced changed hands constantly as some entrepreneurial individuals trafficked in rural real estate while others built hacienda complexes. During the following century the developed estates continued to change hands. Taylor has documented such trends in the Valley of Oaxaca for ten haciendas with seventy-three ownership changes.[28] The titles of Jesuit properties in the valleys of Mexico, Actopan, and Metztitlán show the same pattern (see Appendix A). The studies of Brading, Harris, and Morin indicate similar transfers further to the north.[29] The trend continued well past the colonial period. Apart from a few magnates, the average northern hacendado did not hold onto his estates for more than three generations. This pattern was reinforced by miners and merchants who became wealthy enough to buy up haciendas as a base from which to gain titles and social respectability.[30]

Ecclesiastical institutions, including convents, hospitals, and Jesuit colleges, provided a degree of stability otherwise lacking. As beneficiaries of bequests, implementers of pious works, and money lenders, they gradually accumulated increased assets.[31] As early as 1712, in Tlaxcala, for example, roughly 25 percent of the value of 94 haciendas and 85 ranchos in private hands was dedicated to religious works.[32] Most of the haciendas in the Puebla area were controlled by religious institutions at the beginning of the nineteenth century.[33] Of the 4,945 haciendas and ranchos listed for New Spain in 1809, those without encumbrances were in the minority.[34]

The Role of Hacienda Residences

Hacienda owners preferred city residence and most visited their rural estates only periodically. Villaseca's preference for his Ixmiquilpan hacienda residence during the 1570s appears to have been an exception. But he did not neglect his Mexico City residence. Evidence available from Oaxaca, Tlaxcala, central Mexico, the

Bajío, Zacatecas, Michoacán, and northern Mexico confirms Brading's contention that "Mexican hacendados formed an absentee landlord class who relied upon their estates to yield an income sufficient to maintain an upper-class, town-dwelling family in style and comfort."[35] These hacendados did maintain rural residences which were secondary, in most cases, to their urban residences. The Marquis of Aguayo, the greatest of the Coahuila landowners in the late eighteenth century, owned not one but "four palatial residences in Mexico City." Even the Sánchez Navarros, although they preferred to reside in the midst of their growing rural empire, like Villaseca two hundred years earlier, took great pains to maintain a residence close to the center of power, Mexico City.[36] The Jesuit colleges in the urban centers filled similar roles. The hacienda residences were visited by superiors but inhabited only by the administrators.

The role and function of rural hacienda residences in the colonial period remain largely uninvestigated. Today the rural Mexican landscape is still dotted with the remains of enormous hacienda structures, many of which are empty shells or are being converted for commercial activities. A precise dating of the building booms that resulted in the erection of hacienda residences is lacking for all areas of Mexico. In the formative period of hacienda development, rural residences were modest, built of adobe and stone. This held true for the livestock and cereal-grain estates, although at the productive sugar estates impressive residences had already appeared in the sixteenth century. Descriptions of livestock and food-crop haciendas in the seventeenth century suggest only modest construction.[37] The Santa Lucía residences at Tepeatzingo and San Xavier appear to have been exceptional. In actuality they were designed primarily for production rather than residence. But by the mid-eighteenth century the Jesuit hacienda residences were impressive.[38] Most of them were built during periods of relative prosperity and when low-cost labor was available. The mining-boom periods in central and northern areas produced impressive hacienda buildings for temporary residence and other functions. Many of the great country residences in central Mexico appear to have been built in the eighteenth century, when food-crop production was profitable, labor was plentiful, and mining and pulque were booming. Fragmentary evidence prior to 1767 suggests a correlation between rural residence construction and periods of prosperity, coupled with a plentiful labor supply. In Yucatán the henequen boom brought forth a great number of impressive rural residences in the late nineteenth and early twentieth centuries. But the same hacendados had even more pompous Mérida residences which they occupied for most of the year.[39] One of the conclusions suggested may be that the idea of rural conspicuous consumption, demonstrated by nonutilitarian, palatial hacienda residences, was not a characteristic feature of most of the colonial period. Such structures appeared only after relatively few hacendados controlled the majority of the haciendas. The colonial hacendados, being largely urban residents, preferred to display their opulence in the city.

Administration and Management Patterns

Santa Lucía administration and management reflected patterns consistent with general practices. The encomienda period of the sixteenth century, when encomenderos had restricted access to rural communities, was influential in shaping administrative strategy for rural activities. Encomenderos relied upon men in their confidence to manage their rural interests. These might be acculturated African slaves or Spaniards of lesser status. Warren's analysis of correspondence (1533–1534) between a Mexico City encomendero and his mayordomo, located near Lake Pátzcuaro, identifies early patterns. The encomendero sent a steady stream of instructions to his mayordomo concerning livestock and cereal-crop production, the collection of tribute, and the movement of goods to Mexico City.[40] At the Cortés properties in Morelia (1522–1550), local administrators held delegated powers to supervise most aspects of production and related business.[41] Pedro Nieto operated in a similar manner for Alonso González during the period immediately prior to Jesuit acquisition of his properties. In effect, the logistics of rural management had been developed before the emergence of the hacienda.[42]

Once the haciendas became established, the roles of mayordomo and administrator took on increasing importance. If rural production was limited in quantity or restricted to a special type of activity (sheep, cattle, horses, hogs, wheat, or barley), one mayordomo could adequately supervise. As anexas were added and hacienda complexes emerged, administrators and a number of mayordomos were required. The pattern outlined for Santa Lucía in the eighteenth century, with an administrator, numerous mayordomos, ayudantes, sobresalientes, *capataces* (foremen), vacieros, and supervisors of lesser status, was normative for most large hacienda complexes. Mesta regulations incorporated hierarchical administration practices for livestock production. On small or marginal haciendas, like many in Oaxaca, a mayordomo might be granted wide-ranging delegated authority vested in the administrator on large estates. Whether the administrator was a member of the landowning family or was a professional working under contract depended upon local circumstances and preferences. In the case of the Jesuit estates and those of the Sánchez Navarro family, the top administrative role was normally filled by a member of the hacendado institution or family. In many other cases it was filled by a professional administrator under contract.[43]

The Spanish system of political administration can be seen as a model for hacienda management. The crown always had to rely upon appointed or delegated authority for implementation of policies. In politics, as in hacienda administration, there were differences in skills, loyalties, and abilities to please superiors. In both cases, documented regulations spelled out spheres of decision-making and degrees of delegated powers. And in both cases, the proprietary powers—in the person of viceroy, governor, captain general, archbishop, or hacendado—made periodic visits to inspect and supervise. The "rich men" of the north and the viceroys would always be accompanied by a retinue of friends, relatives, and lesser officials. Whether they came to their possessions "like Carolingian kings" or as austere proprietors depended upon taste, wealth, and local circumstance.[44]

Jesuit administrators, following the model of the order itself, were less pompous, more efficient, and governed college needs. Crown administration was also carefully spelled out in documents, but it was frequently framed to fit ideal standards rather than real situations, resulting in deceit, inefficiency, and unplanned results. The efficiency of eighteenth-century private hacienda administrators is a matter requiring further investigation. Those working for Santa Lucía exhibited tendencies to look after their personal interests whenever possible, despite the vigor of Jesuit supervision. The Jesuits attempted to use their own members to fill top positions, although they could and did—in the case of Villaverde—use professional administrators. Their mayordomos came and went, depending upon how well they fulfilled expectations. But their ability to work on Jesuit or non-Jesuit haciendas did not depend upon special training. Jesuit control over administrative personnel was superior to that of most competitors, but they added little that was new to current practice.[45]

Rental and Production Strategies

The Jesuit practice of renting out areas or activities, such as pulque production, was also in keeping with traditions of the larger society. Hacendados in distinct areas frequently rented out rural properties rather than manage them directly. The Mariscal de Castilla, in 1772, was receiving 21,820 pesos from three large haciendas rented out to 594 individuals.[46] Such rentals might well have represented a strategy of gaining a cash income rather than a granting of land access in exchange for labor and produce. In the Jesuit case, a boundary-maintenance function can be identified for rentals of smaller properties along the borders of their haciendas. The extent to which this was current practice requires further study.[47] The idea of living from rentals, in any case, was firmly engrained in Spanish economic affairs. Urban properties, mines, ecclesiastical properties, and crown revenues (taxes) were customarily contracted out to others at fixed annual rates. The renters attempted to profit beyond their contracts where they could. The implementation of commercial rentals in rural agriculture was consistent with other facets of colonial business practice.

Rental strategy was always conservative in the sense that a safe level of income was preferred to the higher risk and greater potential profit of direct involvement. Jesuit productive strategy was somewhat similar in that risks were minimized wherever possible. The Jesuits avoided capital-intensive high-risk ventures, such as mining activities (with minor exceptions), that might produce high, short-term returns but ran the risk of failure and resulting low returns or large losses. Reliable, steady income was preferred. Such a strategy was encouraged by the constant and expanding financial needs of colleges and missions, whose activities could not be jeopardized by sudden or great losses resulting from unnecessary risk. Santa Lucía can be seen as an implementation of such principles. As a multifaceted, diversified hacienda complex, it allowed for maximum participation in the regional economy. The same principles applied to all the estates owned by the Colegio Máximo. In the beginning, sheep production, most profitable at the time, was the main emphasis while complementary sugar estates were developed. In the seventeenth century, cereal grains were added and the range of livestock production was enlarged. With a promising and stable pulque market established by the mid-eighteenth century, this cash crop replaced sugar in the role it had played a century earlier. Throughout, a combination of cash crops, food crops, and livestock activities served complementary functions to ensure a constant, even if not spectacular, income.

Other Jesuit colleges followed the same strategies. The Puebla Colegio del Espíritu Santo controlled a variety of haciendas including San Jerónimo, which paralleled Santa Lucía in pursuing a mixed production of livestock and agricultural crops. San Jerónimo's annual net income during 1762 to 1766 averaged out to 15,000 pesos, an annual profit of 7.7 percent of the value of the hacienda at expulsion.* Throughout colonial Mexico, the Jesuit colleges became involved in producing most of the products important to the Spanish economy, including cacao, tobacco, wine, pulque, and even minerals. But mining was only pursued on a limited scale by the Zacatecas college in the eighteenth century. The college haciendas did not get involved in untried activities, preferring to follow the commercial trends of their regions. They invested in pulque and minerals only after these products had become established, proven commodities in reliable markets. This strategy of "playing safe" avoided the risk of entrepreneurial daring, relying upon superior management to produce steady income levels. This was in keeping with the desire of a large corporate institution to maintain a low profile in economic matters.[48]

But the idea of not utilizing their haciendas efficiently, of holding land for the sake of prestige or deliberately reducing production to a minimum in times of declining markets was foreign to Jesuit thinking.[49] Evidence from other eighteenth-century haciendas suggests that the Jesuits were not alone in holding such views. The secular hacendado may not always have been able to exploit all his rural holdings effectively, but the constant necessity to maintain his wealth, which could be translated into power and prestige, provided a powerful stimulus to do so. The risk involved in not attempting to maximize production was to lose ground to more successful competitors, examples of which were always at hand. The Jesuit strategy of attempting to have hacienda complexes, and total college resources, function so as to minimize dependence upon other estates or upon the resources of other colleges may also have much broader significance. What have been described as attempts to maintain hacienda self-sufficiency, of hacendados attempting to produce all required goods and services within their individual es-

---

*Ewald, *Estudios sobre la hacienda*, p. 135, lists the assessed value at 195,000 pesos. If the actual sale price (175,000 pesos) is taken as a base, the annual 15,000 peso profit represented 8.57 percent of its value.

tates, may well have been attempts to implement policies the Jesuits carried out successfully on a large scale.*

Hacienda practices demonstrated by the Jesuits were largely borrowed from the private sector. Cortés and the successful encomenderos of the early sixteenth century always attempted to maximize the range of productive options available to them.[50] The tycoons of the later sixteenth century, such as Villaseca and Melchor de Covarrubias, were even more successful in this. They served as models for their less successful peers. And it was precisely these individuals who became the founders of the important Jesuit colleges. They were the Jesuits' early economic advisors, whose very success served as an example.[51] As the colonial economy expanded into frontier areas during the seventeenth century, production was geared to regional, intercolonial, and foreign markets (Europe, Asia). The minerals, leather goods, sugar, dyestuffs, and other commodities were subject to market fluctuations, competition from other colonies (including non-Spanish colonies), and mercantilistic metropolitan policies.[52] The growth of colonial urban centers and increased rural populations, by the eighteenth century, resulted in hacienda production being increasingly geared to the demands of mining areas and urban centers in Mexico. The successful hacendados were those who were able to establish large complexes with diversified production. The majority who initially were granted lands, or who started smaller haciendas, failed to maintain possession over lengthy periods, or to establish diversified production practices.[53] The adage "Many are called but few are chosen" aptly describes the fate of colonial hacendados. The estates of those who fell by the wayside were absorbed by the successful. The survey of Jesuit acquisitions for Santa Lucía during the last century of the order's residence in Mexico documents this on a small scale, as does the development of colonial haciendas, on a larger scale. The Jesuits incorporated such estates and adapted production to suit current demands. By the mid-eighteenth century these demands increasingly included producing cereal grains for the expanded Indigenous sectors, in addition to supplying regional needs. The new tycoons of the second half of the eighteenth century, exem-

---

*The self-sufficiency thesis was proposed by Chevalier, *La formación*, p. 242, and later scholars have repeated the contention; for example, see Lockhart, "Encomienda and Hacienda," p. 424. Tannenbaum, *Ten Keys*, p. 81, goes so far as to insist that the aim of hacienda organization was to buy nothing, to raise and make everything within the limits of the hacienda itself.

plified by the Regla and Sánchez Navarro families, absorbed the ex-Jesuit haciendas without having to restructure production strategies or management principles.[54]

Hacienda Labor Relations

Similarity between Jesuit and non-Jesuit practice in utilization and control of hacienda labor can also be demonstrated. In order to examine this question, hacienda labor can be divided into two types: slaves and nonslaves. In the nonslave category, the distinction between Indigenous and non-Indigenous labor is important. Among the non-Indigenous sector, further subdivisions between Spaniards (peninsular and creole), genetically mixed sectors (mestizos, mulattoes, and alobados), and free blacks and mulattoes need to be made. The nature of Jesuit records, which seldom included racial identification of the mixed sector, plus very limited, detailed, labor-category breakdowns from other case studies, prevents a close comparison between Jesuit and non-Jesuit haciendas for factors associated with race. Consequently the emphasis here must be restricted to general patterns related to occupational roles and status.

The use of slaves of African ancestry was widespread and intensive during the sixteenth and seventeenth centuries but declined progressively during the eighteenth century.[55] The slave had an important role in year-round labor-intensive activities, such as those on sugar estates, in textile mills, and in domestic service. In areas where climate, disease, depopulation, or royal restraint limited access to Indigenous labor, Africans were imported to fill the breach. This held true for all of colonial Spanish America and not just Mexico. But the assumption that the role of the black or mulatto slave was largely restricted to cash-crop endeavors (sugar, cacao, dyestuffs, vineyards, coffee, and tobacco) warrants reexamination. Slaves were important in both the establishment and operation of livestock and cereal-grain estates. For the sixteenth century, the evidence is widespread. Lockhart indicates that practically all encomenderos in Peru used "slaves to care for land and livestock." Many of these early cattlemen and agriculturalists were Iberian mulattoes who worked in gangs of ten to twelve males accompanied by one or two female cooks.[56] The bills of sale of livestock estancias in Argentina, Colombia, Ecuador, Peru, and Mexico frequently included Negro and mulatto slaves.[57] Taylor's study of the Valley of Oaxaca indicates that this pattern held true even in areas where ranching was relatively unimportant.[58] The eyewitness accounts of Vásquez de

Espinosa early in the seventeenth century provide supporting evidence. His descriptions of livestock and cereal-grain production in Hispaniola, Jamaica, Guadalajara, Puerto Bello (Panamá), Bogotá, Zaragoza (Antioquía), Cuzco, and Santiago in each instance are accompanied by references to Negro slaves and mulattoes as the primary labor force.[59]

The important role of the African on the livestock frontier has been glossed over. When the plains of Venezuela were opened to livestock exploitation in the seventeenth century, it was the African slave who filled the role of capataz, and frequently vaquero.[60] This also held true, as is being belatedly discovered, for much of what is now southwestern North America and extended even to southern Canada (Alberta).[61] This oversight may stem from the fact that livestock activities were influenced but not dominated by the black man. An additional factor relates to the shared European values of many of the slaves and their masters. Mörner notes that "slaves could be of real use as cattlehands only if left some freedom of movement and given some trust."[62] Such trust, in turn, depended upon shared values and objectives, resulting in less restrictive working conditions than on the sugar estates and in the textile mills. When the Jesuits acquired Santa Lucía and its complement of African slaves, they opted to continue a firmly established labor practice.

Many of the new slaves acquired for Jesuit haciendas were bought during periods coinciding with expansion of cash-crop and food-crop activities, which were labor-intensive, with lesser numbers at the ranches. This was a general pattern, recognized by Mesta and other royal ordinances attempting to define Negro and mulatto activities and relationships with Indian communities.[63] Less strict supervison and control over slaves engaged in livestock and food-crop production provided opportunities for increased African interaction with neighboring Indigenous communities. Many of the sexual encounters between Indians and Africans, resulting in an emerging racially mixed rural population—classified as prietos, alobados, and lobos, but hardly ever as zambos[64]—derived from hacienda-pueblo contacts. At the same time, Spanish-African sexual unions increased the numbers of nonslaves with partial African parentage, the mulattoes. In addition, some of the Blacks who achieved freedom from slavery through legal or other means, such as successful flight, remained in the countryside.[65] In effect, the haciendas became a vehicle for bringing and keeping African elements in the rural areas.

Jesuit records do not identify free blacks and mulattoes working at Santa Lucía, suggesting a deliberate attempt to restrict their influence. This would have been in keeping with a policy of not providing slaves with direct contact with a role model other than the obedient, compliant worker. But, by the 1740s, 55 percent of Santa Lucía's slave population was classified as being other than Negro.[66] This indicates that a high degree of miscegenation did take place. Even the recorded classifications must have included an element of distortion, since the administrator or mayordomo reporting the birth of a slave child could never know with certainty who the father was. To have a child baptized as a Negro, if the mother was black, would fall in line with Jesuit aspirations to social control and might cover up sexual indiscretions by hacienda personnel or the failure of responsible supervisors to ensure correct sexual conduct on the hacienda.

The documented miscegenation taking place on a hacienda such as Santa Lucía was duplicated within the nearby pueblos. Here, however, documentation of miscegenation would be less evident. Civic and ecclesiastical restraints against race-mixing encouraged Indian women and their legal husbands to recognize and baptize offspring as their own regardless of actual non-Indigenous genetic input.[67] It can be reasonably assumed that the tempo of miscegenation, within both hacienda and pueblo populations, was greater than officially recognized by hacendado, church, or state.

Slaves continued as part of hacienda work populations in the eighteenth century despite the small numbers of African slaves being imported to colonial Mexico after the late seventeenth century.[68] The evidence from the Jesuit estates indicates that slave reproduction more than exceeded mortality and manumission rates. Santa Lucía's owners were consistently able to sell off surplus slaves. This may have held true also for other livestock and food-crop hacienda owners. The Mesta regulations continued to list fines and transgressions for Negroes and mulattoes in the eighteenth century.[69] After the Jesuit expulsion, slaves remained present on haciendas in Oaxaca, and many ancestors of the large numbers of free mulattoes and Negroes residing outside urban Antequera had worked on rural haciendas.[70] Numerous studies of colonial Mexico show a significant number of Blacks and people of partial African ancestry working on rural haciendas. This held true for distinct regions such as Coahuila, Michoacán, the Bajío, Zacatecas, and central Mexico.[71]

In the light of the regional studies, the Santa Lucía patterns of utilization of slave labor can be seen as consistent with wider trends and not unique. Although the majority of Negro and mulatto slaves owned by the Jesuits were subject to the more controlled, harsher working conditions of obraje, cane field, and sugar mill—or wheat fields when this grain replaced sugar as an important cash crop—a significant percentage held less oppressive positions, such as herdsman, labor supervisor, trade specialist, domestic, or person in confidence attached to the office of the administrator. At Santa Lucía in 1722, 25 to 40 percent of the total slave population were employed in the latter categories.[72] This type of pattern may have been duplicated on the secular haciendas. Chevalier has noted that it was normal for large haciendas to have 10 to 20 slaves. Large cattle and sheep estates in Nuevo León, in the seventeenth century, relied heavily upon black slaves.[73] Don José de Gallardo's 144 slaves spread over six sheep haciendas in 1683 exceeds the 108 slaves at Santa Lucía in 1680.[74] Gerhard's survey of all the jurisdictions of New Spain in the sixteenth and seventeenth centuries points to significant percentages of Negroes and mulattoes in most areas. By the late eighteenth century, slaves and the descendants of slaves constituted a sizable portion of the rural populations.* These data add weight to Aguirre Beltrán's point, made in 1952, about "the inconsistency of this myth . . . that, during the colonial period, the black slave was . . . only destined for work in sugar mills and haciendas of the Tierra Caliente, but was . . . brought in significant numbers to all areas of the Tierra Dentro, the *altiplano* and the altas sierras."[75] One of the important vehicles of that distribution was the livestock and food-crop hacienda.

Santa Lucía's nonslave labor force was also organized and administered according to norms common to other large haciendas. By the 1740s—the period on which the materials presented in Chapter 9 draw most heavily—the system of occupational rank, differentiated by amount of income (cash, rations, material goods, and available credit), degree of responsibility, and specialized skills, was a standard feature in colonial Mexico. It persisted throughout the second half of the eighteenth century and beyond, although constantly modified to suit local circumstances and types of production.[76] To what degree the Jesuits may have been influen-

*GHGNS provides many examples of early (sixteenth and seventeenth centuries) appearance of Negroes and mulattoes, along with hacienda establishment, and high population percentages, in the eighteenth century. For example, in the Colima jurisdiction, Africans appeared in the 1550s to work on haciendas. By the late eighteenth century, mulattoes constituted the largest element (43 percent) of the total population in an area dominated by twenty-four haciendas and thirty-eight ranchos; p. 82. See also pp. 45–402 *passim*.

tial in shaping this structure remains an open question. Detailed studies of special cases in the sixteenth and seventeenth centuries, plus a systematic analysis of the changing development of labor-organization practices on haciendas, remain challenges for the colonial investigator. It is known that much of the structure of labor organization related to livestock production was directly adapted from Iberian practice.[77] This may also have held true for cereal-crop production. It is also clear that within colonial Latin America the hierarchically oriented structure of civil and ecclesiastical administration provided a powerful stimulus for the labor systems developed on the haciendas.

For purposes of comparison, the hacienda nonslave labor force can be classified into three categories: residents, who tended to become part of a permanent community; conditional residents, whose physical presence depended upon occupational role and was conditioned upon fulfilling spelled-out, mutually agreed obligations; and nonresidents, who periodically worked on the hacienda but who came from adjacent pueblos, from the region, or elsewhere. These are not absolute categories that can always be clearly differentiated. There was overlap between residents and conditional residents, and movement from one category to the other took place almost continually. Nonresidents might become conditional or even permanent residents. Exact location of work and residence—whether at the hacienda residence or merely on hacienda-owned property—are additional factors in this typology, as is the length of time involved.

Santa Lucía's location near Indian pueblos and its economic functions were shaping influences on its resident labor force. Santa Lucía was a residence for administrators and slaves rather than the nonslave work force. Its modest chapel, coupled with the limited ecclesiastical jurisdiction of its chaplain within a diocese controlled by the secular clergy, suggests a working community rather than a permanent settlement with community functions paralleling those of nearby pueblos and towns.[78] Still, ongoing demands required a permanent work force of up to 300 people. This resident population was housed within the *casco principal* or was confined within the outer wall of Santa Lucía.[79] Similar patterns also took shape at San Juan, San Xavier, Tepenene, Chicavasco, and later at San Pablo, San Ignacio, and San Nicolás. Most of these premises were adjacent to pueblos, or only short distances from them. In the case of the livestock centers, such as Provincia, Negra/Ocuila, Altica, Pintas, Hueytepec, and Florida, the physical premises were modest and had a limited resident population, or, as in the case of the major sheep ranches, there were hardly any residence buildings at all. In effect, the Jesuits did not attempt to create new communities within which the nonslave workers fulfilled normal civic, religious social, and kinship obligations.[80]

This did not mean there was no continuity between succeeding generations of workers or that a substitute community to replace pueblo or town failed to develop. It did mean that the orientation of the hacienda did not exclude other communities. The Jesuits restricted ritual (compadrazgo) and consanguineal kinship activities within their sphere of control. Most hacienda workers, if they came from nearby pueblos, retained kinship, political, religious, and social ties with those communities. If they wished to engage in conduct not sanctioned by the Jesuits (such as drinking, bullfights, and other social amusements), they did so in their home communities. By the eighteenth century, with the emergence of a growing racially mixed sector without residence roots in pueblos, the Jesuit haciendas may have taken on features of permanent communities. Continuing presence on the hacienda, however, was always conditioned upon occupational demand and compliance with Jesuit norms.[81]

The type of community allowed by the Jesuits at Santa Lucía is at variance with the hacienda community generally portrayed for the colonial period.[82] The extent to which the Santa Lucía working-community type also held true for secular haciendas cannot be determined without detailed case studies of such haciendas. Since Jesuit modes of production, political and ecclesiastical jurisdictional restrictions, and other features were also operational for non-Jesuit haciendas, similar communities can be projected. It is doubtful that the same conditions, with merely differing ownership, would have produced entirely different hacienda communities. Regional location and demographic factors were likely stronger determining elements than ownership. In areas lacking adjacent pueblos, as in northern Mexico, and areas where local populations were transient rather than sedentary, the hacienda of necessity became a new population center that grew into a full-fledged community. Its early formation was conditioned by the presence of a considerable number of slaves and by the necessity of bringing into the area— which was in the process of being dominated by European mining, livestock, and farming activities—mestizos or people of European origin. This development took place, for the most part, at a later date and in areas removed from the Spanish urban centers. Haciendas close to Mexico City, for example the hacienda of San José de Coapa, had no residents other than the administrative staff.[83]

Conditional rather than permanent residence was a central feature of hacienda communities. The conditions were set by the owners and implemented by managerial staffs (administrators, mayordomos, ayudantes). At Santa Lucía, conditional residents included all four levels of occupations on the livestock and farming estates, as well as residence workers (see Tables 17–20, Chapter 9). Apart from the top-level supervisors, they were classified as sirvientes or gañanes. Their status, occupation, rate of payment, duties, and privileges were systematically recorded and periodically reviewed. Adjustments were made at the discretion of supervisors, governed by the wishes of the owners, and conditioned by seasonal, annual, and production trends. Occupational roles were more permanent than the individuals filling them.[84]

The location and type of housing for the conditional resident varied. Some lived within the walls of the hacienda casco, in quarters provided by the estate. Such employees minded the hacienda store, storage facilities, equipment, stables, and household. Part of the supervisory staff (mayordomos, ayudantes, sobresalientes) held the same privileges, although the demands of seasonal activities dictated constant movement between hacienda residence and anexas. Housing outside the casco walls, provided by the estate or built by the occupants, served as dwelling places for workers in charge of livestock (oxen, mules, hogs) or facilities (corrals, waterworks). Cowboys tending cattle and horses on the range temporarily occupied ranch huts and changed locations according to the movement of the livestock. The same applied to supervisory-status herdsmen of sheep and goat flocks, but on long-range drives they used tents. Pasture and field-crop guards lived in huts adjacent to fields or at strategic locations of potential incursions. For most of the herdsmen, huts adjacent to pasture corrals served as temporary or seasonal dwellings, at which the molenderas hired to prepare meals also resided. When the flocks were on the move, the herdsmen slept under the stars. Renters occupied simple dwellings on the fringes of hacienda property, or on ranchos located in the areas where they were cultivating crops or pasturing livestock. After the wholesale conversion of much of Santa Lucía to pulque production, the rancho pattern of residence became more pronounced. At Concepción, from as early as the late seventeenth century, dispersed dwellings with their pulque facilities were common. This pattern of rancho residence may have included the bulk of Santa Lucía conditional residents immediately prior to Jesuit expulsion.

Temporary residents, also frequently classified as gañanes, included many of the lower-status herdsmen on the sheep and goat estates, specialists contracted for construction of buildings, waterworks, and other facilities, and work gangs hired for seasonal tasks related to livestock (shearing, branding, butchering) and farming activities (plowing, planting, weeding, harvesting, preparing and maintaining irrigation works). The total number of workers in this category likely exceeded all other types of laborers during any given year, but they resided on the hacienda only as long as there was demand for their services. Work gangs assisting in cereal-grain production resided on the hacienda only during the height of demand, when they were prevented from returning at night to their pueblos. Work gangs from Xoloc, Tolcayuca, Zapotlán, and Tezontepec generally returned for the night to their communities. But on weekends or during fiesta periods falling within busy work schedules, they spent nights in temporarily empty granaries, storage sheds, or other facilities of the hacienda residence complex. Some of the temporary residents, such as young shepherds who worked only certain months of the year, might later become conditional residents who worked entire seasons; eventually, if they achieved positions of responsibility, they might become permanent residents. Specialists working on construction and maintenance projects, provided their work was good, might be rehired and come with their families to live on hacienda premises. They might eventually achieve a type of permanent-resident status, accompanied by the privilege of access to hacienda resources for private livestock and farming activities. Although the documentation is too scattered to present a clear picture, it is probable that many of the renters of parcels of land and pastures were individuals who had gained the confidence of hacienda supervisors while working as temporary residents.[85]

Since the Jesuits followed rather than led regional practice in production, these residence patterns were probably common, at least in areas of relatively high rural population. Jesuit hacienda development reached its peak in the eighteenth century. Between 1650 and 1750, Jesuit and non-Jesuit hacendados were integrating already developed haciendas, along with established labor and residence practices. Although adapted to Jesuit needs, such units were not radically reshaped in terms of relationships with the work force. Jesuit success was linked more closely to better financing, planning, and management. It was not the result of any new formulas. Had the Jesuit pattern been unique, it would quickly have been seized upon by secular hacendados who shared the same profit motives. The regional and case studies referred to in this chapter indicate similar rather than divergent resident patterns in Jesuit and non-Jesuit haciendas.

The Santa Lucía type of work context, as opposed to the permanent community fulfilling long-term social, religious, and political functions, was widely distributed but cannot be assumed throughout colonial Mexico. Jesuit patterns were generally consistent with current practice, and Jesuit haciendas, regardless of their location, were much like those of their neighbors, provided the jurisdictional (legal, ecclesiastical), demographic, and resource restraints were similar.[86] Since these restraints were similar in given regions, as were types of productive activities, there is little justification for assuming divergent rather than parallel work and residence patterns.

Debt Peonage

The question of debt servitude is closely related to the role of the labor force in hacienda production and administration. Jesuit accounting and bookkeeping procedures (see Chapters 5, 9, and 11) were guided by the principle of maintaining a balance between credit and debit. The balance was to favor the interests of the hacienda owners. Accounting statements, made at a specific point in the annual round of the production cycle, frequently showed hacienda workers with debts. The survival of such accounts from Jesuit and non-Jesuit haciendas encouraged investigators to interpret such data as indicative of a firmly entrenched system of debt peonage in the mid-eighteenth century. They may have been projecting backward in time conditions of the nineteenth and twentieth centuries.* Katz, after surveying labor conditions throughout

*Chevalier, La formación, pp. 219–26, said debt peonage was established during the seventeenth century and remained a standard feature. The idea that debt peonage was firmly established in the eighteenth century has been challenged by Brading, Miners; Gibson, Aztecs; Harris, Mexican Family Empire; Morin, "Croissance"; J. Riley, "Management"; Tutino, "Hacienda Social Relations;" and the majority of authors in Florescano, Haciendas. Taylor, in Landlord, pp. 147–49, 252, indicates that debt peonage was present in Oaxaca but not at significant levels. His data on 475 workers on fourteen haciendas show an average debt of 35.5 pesos. Workers with less than 30 pesos in debt represent 56.2 percent of the sample. A major problem with the figures presented by Taylor is their add-and-average character, without reference to individual cases—that is, occupation, wage-rate, full-time or part-time employment, and the exact context of the accounting statements. Taylor, however, does point out that the indicated debts may have reflected the strength of the bargaining position of the workers rather than a weak position.

rural colonial Mexico, concludes that "debt-peonage was of limited importance at the end of the colonial period."[87] Santa Lucía data bear this out, suggesting that relatively few workers were allowed to accumulate debts. Those who carried debts from the previous season—as opposed to taking on credit beyond the cash value of accumulated wages up to the day of accounting—were seldom workers of lower status (levels II–IV, Tables 17–20). Individuals with debts were usually those of greater status with responsible positions. For them, debt status might be seen as a form of job security, as the hacienda owners had a vested interest in continuing their employment to protect investments already made. Seasonal workers who periodically made their appearance in labor gangs were not allowed to accumulate debts or to receive credit advances.*

Credit-debit balances of workers were carefully regulated. Labor accounts of herdsmen and residence workers at Santa Lucía in the mid-eighteenth century demonstrate a low incidence of carryover debts from previous seasons. The highest incidence was encountered for the Provincia shepherds (1750–1751), when twenty of eighty-five workers (23.5 percent) had been advanced credit beyond their earnings. The total value of the debts was 371 pesos, 3 reales, or an average of 18.5 pesos per worker. Workers with debts, in most cases, were shepherds holding supervisory positions. After the settling of accounts, including advancement of material goods as credit for the next season, forty-three of eighty-five workers (50.6 percent) were indebted to the hacienda. The total credit advanced came to 1,487 pesos, 7 reales, an average of 34.6 pesos per worker. This level of credit was well below the expected annual earnings of the workers in the following accounting period. The credit advanced at the accounting period, therefore, still allowed for additional advances during the season while minimizing potential carryover debts between years.[88]

At most of the anexas of Santa Lucía, carryover debts and credit

*Tovar Pinzón, "Elementos constitutivos," pp. 176–78, observes that the Jesuits may have been deliberately withholding wages from workers as a means of creating working capital for the hacienda. This idea warrants further investigation. His data from one of the Puebla college estates (Ozumba), however, do not convincingly demonstrate this. Of the 243 workers in his sample, 77 (31.7 percent) had carryover debts averaging 8.6 pesos, and 166 workers held credit positions averaging 13.7 pesos. Such amounts would be no more than a few months' wages and would fall within the range of expected advances of goods and cash during the working season. Since the Jesuits bought at least some of the material goods advanced during the season, the relatively small amounts in question would not have produced any useful amount of working capital beyond supplying the workers in question.

advances were lower than at Provincia. Of the 46 shepherds at San Ignacio in the 1749–1750 season, only 13 (28.2 percent) were advanced credit, totaling only 41 pesos. At San Pablo (1744–1745), total credit advances for 45 shepherds amounted to 366.5 pesos, the equivalent of roughly two months' salaries and rations. The same situation held true at Ocuila (1743–1744), where 40 of 66 shepherds (60.6 percent) received credit valued at 842 pesos, representing less than the value of two months' salaries. At Tepenene (1747–1748), 59 of 133 goatherds (52.2 percent) received credit advances and, of these, 80 percent received material goods valued at less than 15 pesos. In 1740, at a cattle ranch, 5 of 6 cowboys received credit advances averaging 3 pesos, 1 *real*.[89] The Jesuit hacienda data indicate the existence of carryover debts at insignificant levels, including only small amounts. It shows that credit advances were common, but the amounts advanced usually equaled only a few months' wages, and such advances were not given to all workers. This practice of controlled debts and advances allowed the hacienda owners to lessen the amount of cash paid out in salaries and to use hacienda-produced goods to pay for labor. A system of institutionalized forced debts as a strategy for maintaining a captive labor force was not a feature at Santa Lucía.

Conditions described for Santa Lucía were not unique. Morin encountered similar practices in the bishopric of Michoacán during 1756 and 1757. He found that many workers on livestock estates failed to work full seasons, received wages in cash and material goods, and were advanced credit at accounting periods. The emphasis upon payment with material goods (91 percent of annual payment) rather than cash closely parallels conditions at Santa Lucía.[90] Barrett found similar credit and debt practices on the Cortés sugar hacienda, as did Taylor for livestock and food-crop estates in Oaxaca.[91] Practices used in accounting and payment of workers, like many other aspects of hacienda operation, appear to have been strongly influenced by Iberian practices, transplanted to colonial America. Procedures applied to the cash-crop haciendas were strongly influenced by the continuing presence of a captive labor force. Slavery and other forms of forced labor (encomienda and *repartimiento*, or labor drafts) provided hacendados with workers without resorting to debt peonage.

In areas without available Indigenous labor, particularly in northern Mexico, the coercive features of debt peonage were manifest much earlier. Chevalier noted that, in the north, hacendados found it in their interest to institutionalize forced means to maintain desired levels of available labor.[92] In Coahuila, by the 1760s, debt peonage appears to have been standard. Harris explains that, "because of sparse population and often hazardous working conditions in the provinces, labor was scarce and peonage constituted the most effective means of ensuring a continuing supply."[93]

Special local and regional circumstances, rather than any institutionalization of practices of debts, credits, and advances—symbolized by the *tienda de raya* (company store)—were the key factors leading to debt peonage. Important factors involved include the size of labor populations, hacienda labor demand, availability of agrarian resources (land, water, flora, and fauna), and the status (social, political, and economic) of involved individuals. Under conditions of limited access to agrarian resources and large labor supply—conditions prevailing in the Valley of Mexico and near other large Spanish urban centers in the eighteenth century—pueblo residents and the non-Indigenous sectors of lower socioeconomic status found it in their interest to become indebted to hacienda owners to increase the latter's vested interest in their continuing employment. The hacendados, however, attempted to restrict debts, thus enabling them to manipulate labor more effectively according to seasonal and production demands. Under such conditions, higher-status employees in positions of confidence and responsibility managed to accumulate debts as a form of job security. Under conditions of labor shortage and availability of agrarian resources to pueblos and non-pueblo rural populations, debt peonage was undesirable for the labor force but desired by the hacendados.

The degree to which either hacendado or worker managed to achieve his goals depended, at the same time, upon political factors. As a powerful elite, with close links to colonial government, hacendados could manipulate official labor policies regardless of royal legislation on behalf of the Indigenous sectors. Their influence upon caciques in pueblos—who were fighting a losing battle to maintain power and status within an increasingly hispanized society—and upon corregidores and *alcaldes mayores*—who were frequently hacendados, or at least had the same aspirations—resulted in pressures favoring the interests of the hacendados. Their administrators and mayordomos contracted directly with pueblo authorities, who frequently attempted to comply with hacendado demands. Hacendado powers of persuasion were strengthened to the extent that pueblo caciques and curas were granted favors and access to hacienda resources, such as pastures, farmlands, and water supplies. In areas where there was a great deal of non-hacienda land available, or local populations were minimal, hacendados influenced colonial officials to act in their interests. At times this consisted in not implementing labor legislation against their interests. The entrenchment of de facto debt peonage in northern Mexico came about under such circumstances.[94]

The larger question of colonial hacienda labor relations must be seen within the context of the Spanish Conquest and gradual domination of the rural economy. Residence patterns, credits and debits, accounting procedures, free labor versus debt labor, and control of land resources were vital elements in the process, but always subject to restraints and potentialities created by climate, geography, populations, and markets. Within the larger process of economic expansion, forced obligations were constantly being imposed upon the Indigenous sectors. In the sixteenth century, the lines of division between Spaniard and Indian were clearly drawn. Within the limits of encomienda, the principle of forced obligations was exercised by labor and tribute demands. With the progressive limitation of encomienda rights, and more direct crown involvement, repartimiento practices sustained forced labor on behalf of the private sectors—including the haciendas—while the crown had control over tributary and ecclesiastical levies. By the middle of the eighteenth century, the racial and cultural lines of division had become blurred and blended, resulting in a growing miscegenated sector. The haciendas developed, both geographically and temporally, between conqueror and conquered. While incorporating part of the miscegenated sector, the hacienda continued to force its demands upon a growing Indigenous population. In the countryside, agrarian resources and choices in residence, types of labor activities, income levels, and individual status and welfare were increasingly controlled by haciendas. Choices exercised by rural pueblo and non-pueblo residents became more restricted.[95]

Within the larger process of economic domination, and within the peculiarities of hacienda production and operation, Jesuit estates functioned like other haciendas. The range of difference within the Jesuit system of rural estates, taking into consideration distinct regions, was as great as the range of difference between Jesuit and non-Jesuit estates. Nevertheless, there remained a basic difference between Jesuit and non-Jesuit haciendas in terms of administrative structure. Jesuit haciendas were always linked directly to a corporate institution, the Jesuit order. This order produced and controlled its own administrators, who were not only highly skilled but also well connected with the most powerful decision makers in colonial society. Such institutional and societal connections were not duplicated in the private sector. Individual business magnates with extensive rural properties, despite their ties to the ruling elite, rose and fell with regularity, whereas Jesuit colleges, once established, remained and constantly expanded. Within colonial Mexico, the corporate institution and its business ventures proved to be more durable than individual private enterprise, at least until the crown intervened to strip the corporate institution of its economic assets.

THIRTEEN 🕮 *Conclusion*

Hacienda influences cannot be isolated or viewed apart from other colonial processes. The military aspects of political conquest and the missionary phase of ideological conversion usually preceded hacienda establishment. Representatives of church and state—cleric and corregidor—not only were present as custodians of official interests but were ever willing to compete with hacendados for economic benefits in areas where haciendas were located, and in the Indian sectors. On the frontiers of hacienda expansion, especially in the north, where single military encounters seldom settled political issues, the hacienda advance became part of the political conquest. And the haciendas suffered attacks, raids, and reprisals as a consequence. Continuous Indian raids in northern Mexico were not just incursions and depredations. They must be seen as consistent attempts at territorial defense or appropriation of new resources (livestock, food crops, and technology) found on traditional lands.[1] In the mission provinces of the regular orders—Franciscans in Yucatán, Chiapas, and Guatemala; Jesuits in northern Mexico—hacienda development either was thwarted or was limited to estancias, sitios, ranchos, or specialized cash-crop endeavors. Here, the church's interest in controlling all aspects of Indigenous welfare, including economics, was a restraint on hacienda development.[2] Frontier and mission restraints were complemented and reinforced by the absence of large, new Spanish urban centers to provide a market for hacienda products. Within the larger colonial picture, hacienda development matured after political and ideological conquest, during economic integration, and before cultural and social transformation of Indian sectors was completed.

The physical establishment of haciendas in the countryside meant a permanent imposition on Indigenous institutions. These had already been severely strained by the Conquest, missionary Catholicism, and encomienda. Paradoxically, just when the crown was attempting, through the New Laws, to implement its humanitarian impulses against the abuses of the conquering encomendero, plague and pestilence struck the Mexican Central Highlands (1545–1548). The impact of epidemic disease was twofold: it further damaged already weakened local economic, social, and political capacities; and it provided an opening wedge for European appropriation of land resources. Massive depopulation left unoccupied, or at least undefended, pastures and fields that could be permanently and for the most part, peacefully transferred to new owners. This process was sanctioned by the edicts written to defend crown and Indian interests, but implemented so as to have the opposite effect.[3] The countryside communities of the Valley of Mexico were forced to react to new conditions, as was much of the settled, agrarian sector of Indian society throughout the colony. Although the hacienda was not the only imposition, it was one of the most important, most direct, and longest lasting.

Thrust between new, growing urban centers and established, shrinking rural communities, haciendas helped to destroy and build, to transform and preserve. As vehicles of economic conquest, they destroyed much of the traditional Indigenous economic structure, replacing a balanced system of hoe and hydraulic cultivation with a system of plow and hoe cultivation progressively unbalanced by falling lake levels, deforestation, and massive livestock penetration. The new products of the haciendas, at the same time, provided food, technology (leather goods and metal tools), and trade goods for the builders of the "new" Spain. As it grew, the institution of the hacienda increasingly became the common meeting ground between what had been Aztec Mexico and what would become Spanish colonial Mexico. Once firmly established, the haciendas injected an element of stability into the countryside, allowing for a gradual transformation of the experiences, wants, and needs of Indigenous communities. Loss of identity and traditional resources was offset by potential new sources of sustenance (European crops and livestock), new labor demands, new contacts (Europeans and Africans), and new aspirations—of imitating the life-styles of the conquerors. But having been stopped short of eliminating the rural communities or encroaching upon all available rural resources, the haciendas left a territorial domain within which something could be preserved. Because Indian communities were left some breathing space, they maintained a base from which they attempted to preserve identities and customs, to recoup lost terrain, and to challenge the new order.

Prior to 1650, when haciendas such as Santa Lucía had become firmly established near the center of colonial society, the social structure of Aztec times had undergone dramatic change. By then it had been dismantled and reassembled along new lines.[4] The hereditary nobility (*tlatoani*) had been reduced in numbers and influence, and the nobles who remained were reduced to positions of limited authority over the remains of rural communities. The roles of traders and artisan specialists had been taken over by Europeans or emerging ethnically mixed elements. Warfare and religion, the avenues of mobility for the commoners (*macehualtin*), had been eliminated or restructured. Following the example of their nobles, who almost trampled over each other in the rush to accept the baptism of the new Deity, the commoners responded to the friars with enthusiasm. Since the destruction of central temples and their reconstruction in honor of victorious deities were an old tradition, the breakdown of Aztec and local temples was quickly accomplished without significant resistance. The sweeping out of the Indigenous clergy and of public ceremonies—particularly sacrifices— was at least tolerated. The crucifix and the sacraments, after all, also signified sacrifice. New churches were built on the sites and with the materials of the old temples. But access to the new Deity was less personal and less dramatic than earlier, and although the statues and saints became incorporated, more ancient deities were not entirely discarded—only adhered to with greater circumspection. Rites and beliefs relating to domestic and field activities were maintained.

Traditional class and status differences in rural communities became blurred. With the arrival of the encomenderos, who interpreted Spanish authority as a provision of unlimited personal opportunism, new obligations and political systems were imposed upon all elements of Aztec society. Agents (slaves, retainers) of the encomenderos were used to reduce most peasants to a static, oppressed condition. "They seized their goods, destroyed their agriculture, and took their women. . . . They took tribute and sold it back at exorbitant profits."[5] The introduction of new crops, livestock, and obligations did not completely destroy rural society, but it did weaken it and reshape the former subservience to Aztec imperialism and the city-states to serve the Spanish interests centered in Mexico City. Traditional agriculture became more marginal; occupational choices became forced. The impact, over time, resulted in deculturation and absolute loss of power, wealth, and prestige. Gibson has documented the ruthlessness of the assault in the sixteenth century when encomenderos "jailed them, killed them, beat them, set dogs on them." He also has noted "one of the earliest and most persistent individual responses," which was turning to drink.[6]

Royal authority penetrated the rural areas with a multitude of minor officials (judges, constables, deputies, scribes, and interpreters). With the establishment of corregimiento, the door was opened for permanent entry of the private landowner, whose arrival coincided with that of European- and African-introduced diseases. During the Conquest, the 1540s, the 1570s, and periodically thereafter, death swept through the countryside. By 1570 the population of the Valley of Mexico had been reduced to roughly one-fifth of its pre-Conquest size. By 1650, four-fifths of the 1570 population had been eliminated.[7] This demographic decline forced a radical restructuring of rural society, and it prevented any sustained resistance to hacienda encroachment. Gradually, definite patterns of consolidation of rural resources in the hands of hacendados emerged. The hacendados usually were people closest to royal power: crown officials, ex-encomenderos, wealthy families, and corporate institutions. The remains of the traditional Aztec aristocracy joined the conquerors, the successful becoming genetically and socially integrated into Spanish society. As a result, former rural communities disappeared, others were reshaped through civil congregation, and the rural landscape became dotted with haciendas.

The restructured peasantry was less dynamic, less differentiated, and tied to the new economic, political, and ideological order. Churches, monasteries, and civic administrative structures dominated the central plazas of the traditional communities. The ceremonial aspects of Roman Catholicism—baptisms, masses, parades, fiestas—became part of the experience of individuals and communities. Christian titles became attached to individuals and their communities. But the process of ideological conversion failed to replace many aspects of pre-Christian activities. As long as some traditional agriculture was practiced, so were the rites and beliefs associated with it. As long as the numbers of clerics and government officials resident in the rural communities remained few—and there were seldom more than half a dozen in even the larger towns—ancient beliefs surrounding rites of passage in the life-cycle, seasonal cycles, and crisis occasions continued in the privacy of the home, in the fields and forests, and even behind the altars in the churches themselves. Since the clerics frequently preached in the Indigenous language, and the crown officials used interpreters, local languages remained intact.[8]

Rural culture, in its public expression, incorporated forms dictated by the Conquest culture, but privately at least part of the traditional past could be preserved. The new peasantry, having tasted the bitter fruits of the "enlightenment" of the new order and found it wanting in comparison to the regulated but more consistent lifestyle of earlier times, chose not to give up that birthright, but also not to flaunt it. Such indiscretion only resulted in fines, whippings, imprisonment, and additional burdens upon scarce material and social resources. The Indian religious brotherhoods (cofradías) formed to finance public religious activities maintained a native character. This allowed for the fulfillment of the expectations of the official religion without too close an inspection of traditional belief systems. The rural context, despite the economic and other impositions of the Conquest, allowed for the retention of an ideological perspective linked to the past. This perspective is still a central feature of the Mesoamerican peasant.[9]

During the period after 1650, in contrast to earlier responses to political and ideological pressures, rural society was forced to adjust to the more direct economic impact of the hacienda. Once patterns of hacienda-pueblo interaction became established they changed slowly, according to shifts in economic activity. By controlling the rural areas, the haciendas also limited alternative urban influences, serving as a bridge between the city and the countryside communities. With limited access to hacienda lands, pueblo residents were forced to draw upon their own communities for strategies of survival, and to defend their own interests. Most of the permanent labor positions on the haciendas were filled by non-Indians—by slaves, mestizos, and Spaniards. Indians played more important roles in livestock production, where permanent employment meant a reasonable livelihood. Agricultural production employed large numbers of pueblo residents, but only for short periods, as few individuals worked more than six weeks on a hacienda during any given year. Special activities such as shearing, slaughtering, and round-ups provided employment for even shorter periods. Because the hacienda, being work-oriented rather than community-oriented, failed to provide alternative contexts for social, religious, and political participation, Indian pueblo residents were obliged to engage in such activities in their own communities. At the same time, they were provided limited opportunities to incorporate selectively new livestock and agricultural practices into the pueblo economy.[10]

Efforts by the crown to protect its Indian subjects prevented a wholesale violation of Indigenous rights and property, despite the circumvention of most royal legislation by hacendados.[11] The very fact that Santa Lucía officials were forced to resort to the courts, even if the pueblos lost most of the cases, served as a reminder that the letter of the law needed to be observed. Once the population crisis became stabilized and pueblos recovered their numerical strength, they took more initiative in exercising their rights. The hundred years after 1650 witnessed a dramatic turnabout in pueblo-hacienda relations. After a century of retreat and defeat in the face of hacienda expansion, pueblos began to hold their own. Initiatives were pursued to reclaim traditional agrarian resources and to increase access to hacienda resources. This attack was manifest in a variety of ways. Encroachment upon hacienda pastures and farmlands became frequent. Appropriation of hacienda livestock and products—malfeasance from the point of view of the hacendados—became so common that one could say it became institutionalized. Resorting to the royal courts with legitimate or falsified documents to reclaim land, or to establish rights of access to water, forest, and field resources, was another strategy. Utilization of kinsmen or hacienda personnel in order to trespass without being reported, to change boundary markers, or to divert hacienda production also became common. The pueblos also competed more directly with the hacienda, by duplicating its modes of livestock and agricultural production on a minor scale. Finally, pueblos increasingly began to express a willingness to resort to violence in confronting the hacienda.[12]

All these pueblo initiatives were resisted, but the haciendas were gradually forced to give ground. The granting of increased rental access to hacienda properties for livestock and food-crop production was one such response. This took place not only on the extensive borders of haciendas but also within the estates. In the eighteenth century, large sections of Santa Lucía and its anexas were rented to Indians. By the 1760s, when much of Santa Lucía had been converted to pulque production, the Indian communities were heavily involved. They were participating at a more significant level although never in control of decisions affecting the terms of their participation.

The attempts of pueblo residents to alter the terms of their integration into the colonial economy were unsuccessful, yet they did not merely withdraw or attempt to maintain communities apart from the rest of society. Demands of the church in areas of public conduct and fees, demands of the state for tribute and labor services, and demands of survival provided compelling reasons for active participation in the larger society, even under conditions of servile dependence. Although marginal to the larger economy, and limited in avenues leading to wealth, power, and prestige, Indian communities consistently sought to take part. The suggestion that such rural communities became closed and isolated because they retained their language, traditional crops, and elements of pre-Conquest political and social organization has not been convincingly demonstrated for the eighteenth century.[13] Royal legislation did postulate the idea of *repúblicas de indios,* which could function largely apart from the rest of colonial society, but in this matter, as in much of the corpus of laws issued from Spain, the legislation merely points to the existence of problems. It suggests a contrary reality, since the royal laws seldom become solutions.[14] What took place was a gradual and traumatic redefinition of pueblo terms of involvement. Indian communities remained rural and subservient to conditions imposed by urban centers. The result was marginal participation and dependency rather than autonomy accompanied by nonparticipation.

Hacienda impact upon peasant life-styles was twofold. First, the pre-Conquest rural community's more complex economy—which included producer, supervisor, and policy maker—was simplified. The hacienda, once entrenched, took over the major role of producer, supervisor, and policy maker in the rural economy. Pueblo participation became determined by cycles of annual production and governed by age, sex, and occupational role. Second, the economy within the pueblo was reduced to hoe and plow production. When individuals or work gangs produced for themselves, it was on this plane. Two work patterns developed, one applicable to the pueblo, the other to the hacienda. The dualism was further accentuated by participation in local market networks, which served family and pueblo needs, and participation in larger regional and colonial markets, which served the urban centers and the haciendas.[15]

The hacienda's domination of rural resources played a key role in shaping peasant options. Haciendas tended to control the largest pastures, the best agricultural lands, the main water resources (either directly or with dams and reservoirs), the important processing facilities (obrajes, matanzas, and molinos), the largest storage facilities (trojes and *bodegas,* or storehouses), and transport (mules, horses, oxen, and vehicles). Pueblos retained marginal land or only small areas, received water not needed by the large estates, had only limited processing facilities (restricted largely to cottage industry), could muster only small-scale storage facilities (backyard bins, pueblo trojes), and usually lacked significant numbers of transport animals. Hacienda technology and labor organization were more efficient than what was available to the pueblos. Haciendas were better able to control market prices and could respond to changing market conditions by regulating production. Pueblos still retained some access to rural resources, but under conditions set by the haciendas and the larger economy. This took the form of rental—for set fees, labor exchange, or a part of annual production—or special concessions under conditions set by the hacendados. The peasant condition of subsistence production, supplemented by periodic cash income derived from labor, was thus reinforced.

An alternative way of examining relationships between the pueblos and haciendas and the larger society is to focus upon factors affecting life-styles. An ethnographic, holistic approach to a particular culture necessitates consideration of geography, ecological adaptation, technology, residence patterns, economy, political and social organization, family and kinship, and ideology. These categories are not distinct in the sense of being unrelated. They are merely convenient perspectives for examining a chosen culture. Since detailed studies of individual pueblos are lacking, the data are drawn from regional studies and from the pueblos associated with Santa Lucía and selected anexas.[16] Valley pueblos being considered here include Xoloc, Los Reyes, Tolcayuca, Tezontepec, Ixtlahuaca, Tizayuca, Tecama, Temascalapa, Zapotlán, and Zumpango. The time period under consideration is from before the Conquest to the 1770s.

Both natural and human geography had been altered. There were significant changes in the size and location of pueblos. Depopulation was massive and affected all communities. With the implementation of civil congregation, many smaller pueblos disappeared, but new pueblos apart from hacienda communities were not established. What changed was the relationship between the communities and their environment. The lakeside communities of the early sixteenth century, many located on hilltops and mountain slopes, gradually became landlocked as lake levels dropped and former lake-bottom areas became pasture or farmland. Deforestation, loss of soil fertility, and depopulation of the upper valley slopes resulted in fewer communities, surrounded by a changed environment. The ethnic elements of human geography were altered as Tepaneca, Mexica, and Acolhua geopolitical boundaries were disturbed and previous orientations toward larger towns or cities—such as Zumpango, Texcoco, Teotihuacán, Acolman, Tepexpan, Otumba, Xaltocan, Cuautitlán, and Hueypoxtla—were channeled toward Mexico City, Pachuca, or the haciendas themselves. As the natural and human geography of the region was transformed, the Indian pueblos, although they retained their physical locations, became less urban and more rustic.

Patterns of ecological adaptation changed. In Aztec times the ecological strategy was one of balance and preservation of the total environment. Farming took place on fertile soils and in *chinampas* (aquatic gardens) along the edges of the lakes. Hunting, fishing, and the harvesting of indigenous flora and fauna were carried out in such a manner as to preserve the resource base. By the eighteenth century, great changes had taken place. The lakes had been partially drained, the forests had been largely eliminated, and the farmland and grasslands had been transformed by two centuries of onslaught by livestock and new crops. Animal hooves and plowshares had cut into the fertility of the soils. The landscape had been restructured with little thought of preservation or ecological balance. The pueblos were left to cope with a deteriorated resource base, which had been savagely attacked and relentlessly exploited. They tended to follow the example of new practices rather than preserve more ancient traditions of conservation.

Technological change was significant. Pre-Conquest rural technology revolved around implements made of wood, stone, clay (ceramics), and local plants such as the ubiquitous maguey. Copper knives were used, as were obsidian blades, flakes, and chips. The technology of war, trade, and artisan production relied upon vegetable, mineral, and animal (skins, bones) material used in a complex manner. As these activities were curtailed, much of the technology surrounding them was lost. New technology incorporated from the conquerors consisted almost entirely of items introduced by the Europeans. The availability of iron and steel implements, draft animals, leather, and woolen products resulted in greater reliance upon the new technology. This technology of the city and the hacienda, along with textiles, found its way into pueblos via herdsmen who received these items in lieu of wages. Metal and animal products, and the animals themselves (poultry and livestock), came to be considered necessities, although many traditional items (ceramics and plant materials) were retained. The laws restricting the use of guns, swords, and the riding of horses and mules indicate that pueblo populations attempted to utilize them. The native nobility and non-Indigenous residents in the pueblos had access to most of the new technology, which gradually filtered into local hands. The net result was an increasing reliance upon Hispanic technology, much of which was available in only limited quantities. By the eighteenth century, only the poor Indians were still using the traditional *coa* (digging stick) for local agricultural production.[17]

Residence patterns did not change greatly for the poor, or for families living outside the center of rural communities. But at the center of the pueblos, Hispanic structures and styles dominated. Churches, new buildings of wood and stone around central plazas, and animal corrals were symbolic of new styles in the pueblos. For the majority of the peasants, house construction remained unchanged and relied upon traditional materials (stone, lime, adobe, grass, and wooden poles). The most common residence consisted of a "one-roomed, rectangular hut with a small open doorway."[18] The monogamous household remained a feature of the commoner as it already conformed to Christian expectations, whereas the traditional polygamous household of the noble officially became monogamous. Domestic and labor services rendered by peasants meant periodic absences from their communities. Herdsmen attached to haciendas may have maintained their pueblo homes, but heads of households and male members would have been absent for extended periods. Information about residence and changing patterns is still too limited to provide a clear picture. The restrictive legislation against non-Indigenous sectors suggests a growing presence, a factor favoring change rather than stability.

The pueblo economy underwent drastic changes. With less communal land to draw upon, traditional agriculture became less important, as surpluses for a wider market could not be produced. Subsistence needs could be supplied by pueblos with adequate resources, but participation in the new colonial economy became a necessity. Labor service grew more important. The more fortunate found steady employment on the haciendas. The majority were given part-time seasonal employment under conditions set by hacienda administrators. Residents in the pueblos (curas, caciques, and government officials) frequently implemented and organized this type of labor. Repartimiento demands accented the coercive nature of labor participation in the larger economy. The haciendas usurped first resources and then economic roles. At the level of the individual family, civic and ecclesiastical demands (fees, tribute, and religious ceremonial ritual) exceeded local capacities to meet obligations. The consistent efforts made by pueblo residents to acquire and raise livestock, or to produce the new crops, must be seen as attempts—mostly with limited success, except for the fortunate of the cacique class—to take part in the new economic order. Traditional crops and other economic activities, by the mid-eighteenth century, were insufficient to meet even subsistence needs, and pueblos came to depend increasingly upon hacienda-produced maize.

Political and social organization took on new dimensions. The effect of over 200 years of colonial rule upon class and status differentiation within the pueblos, as Gibson has noted, "was to equalize and compress, to move all classes towards a single level and condition."[19] Indian leaders retained their titles, but their importance outside the pueblos steadily declined. Many caciques eventually became indistinguishable from the ordinary peasant. Those who retained positions of power did so because they were able to manage "their lands, rents, agricultural production, and mode of life after the manner of all hacendados."[20] As a class they became more ethnically and culturally integrated into the hispanized sectors of colonial society. For the majority, the former class distinctions were all but eliminated, although *calpulli* (clan) identification was retained to some degree. But this had little bearing upon actual status and was not an important factor taken into consideration by authorities implementing civic and ecclesiastical demands. Patron-client bonds, hacienda-peón relations, priest-parishioner obligations, and crown-vassal status became the ingredients of political and social organization, the links to status, wealth, and prestige.

All attempts to interfere with traditional Indigenous aspects of family and kinship practices were directly tied to moral, "Christian" concerns. But the results were mixed, demonstrating the tenacity of the traditional family unit, despite duress and high degrees of external compliance with imposed expectations. A double standard was evident in the private activities of the conquerors, whose public piety and adherence to ecclesiastical standards were matched by their ability to contradict such standards by personal example. The monogamous standard proclaimed by the secular and regular clergy was honored only in the breach, as many males on the hispanized side of colonial society maintained the custom of extramarital unions. Scattered evidence from pueblos with resident curas indicates that they shared this practice, despite their vows of celibacy representing marriage to the church. In Aztec society, polygyny was restricted to members of the nobility and, at a formal level, such practices were not sanctioned. The peasant standard of monogamy did not have to be altered to fit Hispanic ideals. Attempts to limit marriage between Indians and non-Indians were largely unsuccessful, judging from the repetitiveness of legislation restricting such unions.[21]

The church was successful in forcing formal compliance with public ritual surrounding family affairs such as baptism, confirmation, marriage, and burial. With the elimination of the Indigenous priesthood, the clerics supervised the public aspects of family life. Fictive or ritual kinship, symbolized by the institution of compadrazgo, became a standard feature of pueblo life. Degrees of continuity of Aztec family and kinship practices cannot be ascertained without detailed studies of specific communities. It is clear that new labor demands upon females for domestic service, and upon males, who spent lengthy periods away from their families, seriously disrupted family life. It has also been demonstrated that, among the cacique class, formal adherence to norms imposed by the Conquest was common, since property, inheritance, and rights of position were directly involved.[22] But as long as pueblo families kept traditional forms of productive activity, its organization along family and kinship lines seems likely to have been retained.

The dualism of development suggested in family practice was most evident in ideology, articulated largely through religion. At a formal level, conversion to the Christian ideology became a fait accompli with the Conquest, although several generations of missionary activity were required to accomplish the finer details and to institutionalize the presence of the new ideological order. Despite the waning of enthusiasm on the part of the converted and the convertors by the mid-sixteenth century, official conversion could be continued simply by administering the rites of baptism to all infants. By the eighteenth century, baptism and other sacred rituals of church life had become the accepted practice. Having fewer material benefits in life, by virtue of socioeconomic status, and more to gain from the promises of the afterlife, most pueblo residents had reason to demonstrate greater piety than even the curas and priests. Participation in religious activities, as they interrupted the harsh routine of everyday life and provided contexts for social activities—which included frequent drunkenness and a temporary escape from oppressive conditions—fulfilled important functions. The pueblo church became the locus of public social activities, including fiestas, fireworks, processions, feasting, and fellowship. Such events, at the same time, became a mask behind which important elements of more traditional values could be maintained. Indigenous beliefs surrounding ethnic deities and their roles in regulating life-cycles, crop cycles, man-made and natural disasters, diseases, and good fortune were retained. The major adjustment in the retention of traditional beliefs involved closing off access to their expression. The cyclical reality of a world view governed by polytheism and regulated by sacred and secular calendrical rounds had to be kept private, in the home, or hidden. The linear reality of a world view governed by monotheism and regulated by priests, royal officials, and the Christian calendar had to be publicly expressed.

Viewed from the perspective of the ethnographer, the picture of rural pueblos, by the mid-eighteenth century, demonstrates the basic feature of a subservient peasantry. Differentiation of class and status within the Indian community was less important than the differential relationships between the pueblo and the larger society. These were governed by forces residing in Mexico City but largely mediated through the haciendas, which set the terms of economic participation. Social and cultural separation allowed for greater retention of traditional features within the pueblos, but never in isolation from outside influences. The pueblo communities were neither closed nor corporate, despite legislative definitions or expressions of intent. By the criteria of the ethnographer, the pueblos were greatly transformed by Hispanic influences, and they were open to continuing transformation. They consistently desired to participate in the larger economy, to incorporate its technology, its modes of production, and even its life-style. That they were largely unsuccessful in accomplishing such objectives was a product of factors over which they had little control. Pueblos participated marginally because they had become effectively marginalized.

The study of postcolonial peasant pueblos in Mexico has resulted in a large corpus of materials from which generalizations have been made.[23] The distinction between corporate, or "closed," versus "open" types of peasant communities has gained wide acceptance. These two types—the one with an internally conceived "bounded social system with clear-cut limits, in relation to outsiders and insiders," and the other without internally conceived barriers between community members and the outside world—have been postulated as deriving from the presence or absence of certain pre-Conquest ethnic compositions and experience.[24] Areas in Mesoamerica—Nahuatl, Otomí, Maya, Mixtec, Zapotec, and Huastec—and the Andes—such as Quechua, Aymara, and Auracanian—became dominated by closed communities, whereas areas dominated by creole influence remained open. In effect, the *repúblicas de indios* became closed peasant communities. Although such distinctions have proved useful for understanding the dynamics of peasant interaction with the dominating society, they have not explained how closure took place.[25]

The colonial experience of the areas covered by this study shows that rural pueblos do not fit the "closed" corporate model. The initial Spanish incorporation of Indian rural communities resulted in restructuring and compression of status differences, but not in closure to outside influence. Their economic marginalization, however, established the conditions for later closure. As long as the Conquest forces that reshaped the pre-Conquest peasantry—the clerics, caciques, and colonial administrators—were physically present, the pueblos remained open to outside influences. With the loss of status and power of the cacique class, the loss of influence and departure of the clerics, and the declining presence or influence of the colonial official, local communities responded. The pueblos localized and reshaped the function of these offices. They defined the roles in terms of the cultural experience of the pueblos, filling offices that were more symbolic than real as far as outside influence was concerned. The functions of the offices were adapted to fill internal needs rather than external goals. The result was a hardening of community boundaries, a strengthening of community identity, a reaffirming of Indigenous ideology. This process was uneven, its tempo governed by local and regional experiences.

The hacienda economy controlled by urban centers and rural estates, such as Santa Lucía, played an important role in the closure process. The haciendas regulated the economic terms. Their stability over time allowed pueblo work patterns, geared to dual participation in the local and larger economies, to become institutionalized. But they did not alter the basic aspirations of individual pueblo members. Peasants in the closed community, like their counterparts in the open community, sought to participate in the larger world. In the case of the closed communities, the preservation of redefined Indigenous priorities became more important, as it still is. With industrialization of the Hispanic economy, serving urban and export interests, the distinctions between the two types of communities was reinforced. The open, creole-dominated communities have had greater success in incorporating new technology introduced by hacendados on their rural properties. For the closed communities, tied to traditional modes of production, with limited land resources and labor patterns organized around family and kinship patterns, industrial technology has been less meaningful and its integration more difficult.*

If the haciendas were instrumental in defining the social and economic aspects of life for the colonial peasantry, they had other influences as well. The Indigenous sectors were never merely passive actors in the political drama of the countryside. The redefinition of class and status within the pueblos, and between the pueblos and the Hispanic economy, was accompanied by a redefinition of power. With the passing of the New Laws, the king provided his Indian vassals with legal means of defending their limited rights. Insightful observers of early colonial events, such as Alonso de Zorita, described the consequences in terms of commoners rising up against their lords, attempting to overthrow them and to "stop giving the service and tribute they formerly gave." The result, according to Zorita, was the emergence of rebels who would revolt, not only against their caciques, but against the colonial conquerors themselves.[26] What Zorita did not foresee, as he was reporting events of the sixteenth century, was the emergence of an ongoing struggle over control of economic resources and the power they represented. This conflict, over time, was increasingly articulated along class lines, pitting peasant, peón, and pueblo in an unequal battle against the hacendado and the dominating colonial society.

The experience of Santa Lucía provides a regional example of how and why such conflict took place. During the first century of this hacienda's development, beginning in the 1570s, the advantages were all on the side of the hacendados as the pueblos were hard-pressed even to survive. They lost ground on all fronts, with diminishing numbers, resources, status, and power to defend themselves. Successful communal attempts to halt territorial encroachment by legal means, individual acts of reclaiming land and appropriating or killing livestock, and communal resistance to forced integration did little to alter the larger process of domination and marginalization.[27] During the following century, after demographic recovery, pueblo stabilization, and increased demands on

---

*June Nash provides a helpful alternative model for understanding the dynamics of economic and political interactions between Indian pueblos and the nonpeasant sectors of contemporary Latin America. Her use of the concept of a "moving equilibrium" suggests constant adaptations within the closed community, resulting in maintenance of differential status between the community and the state while preserving community integrity. This type of approach overcomes the traditional bias of researchers who insist peasants are basically backward-looking conservatives unwilling to improve local conditions, rather than talented innovators attempting to incorporate change in a meaningful manner.

limited resources, the conflict became increasingly intense, direct, frequent, and violent. There were always individuals in the pueblo who sided with the hacienda—those holding well-paid jobs (herdsmen, conditional residents, and renters) or having access to hacienda resources (pasture, water, and land) who opted to defend personal advantage regardless of communal disadvantage. But the greater majority were on the outside looking in.[28]

Consistent pueblo attempts to use legal means to confront hacienda initiatives resulted in the legal confrontations described in Chapter 7 of this study. But fighting fire with fire, the pueblos discovered, was more a matter of fighting paper with paper, with the Jesuits having almost a monopoly over the weapons—the lawyers, legal influence, and funds to finance the war of mine and thine. Documentation of more direct individual action is less plentiful but indicates a willingness on the part of both sides to resort to force, despite Jesuit policies of peaceful coexistence.* Unobserved or direct appropriation of livestock or other hacienda resources became standard practice. In the implementation of this "malfeasance strategy," the pueblos were able to co-opt relatives working for the hacienda as accomplices, a type of fifth column in the opponent's territory. Consistently low livestock yields in the eighteenth century may, in part, be attributable to pueblo successes. Hacienda practices of labor control resulting in high annual turnover were an effective countermeasure. The Jesuit response to territorial encroachment by the pueblos was to establish border, or front-line, zones of renters, thereby engaging pueblo members to defend hacienda property against members of their own or other communities. Each side had to adjust strategy constantly in the ongoing contest. One Jesuit advantage, used to great success, was their ability to use the cura, local pueblo official, or cacique as an agent for controlling pueblo activities. The pueblos had little success in controlling mayordomos on Jesuit haciendas. On occasion, the cura and cacique served pueblo interests, but on the whole, when they confronted the hacienda, it was to serve personal interests at the expense of the pueblos.

Resort to violence and physical confrontation became increasingly evident in the eighteenth century. Such measures usually fol-

---

*Jesuit reactions to physical threats may not have been so passive as was dictated by official policy. During the mid-1740s the Santa Lucía administrator kept seven guns (four shotguns, one musket, and two pistols) in his residence. This was a period of intense confrontation with Indian pueblos. At other times the administrator kept one or two shotguns, presumably for hunting. See BNM 1058, 1: 159, 175, 198.

lowed unsuccessful attempts to settle disputes over resources through legal means. Documented conflicts at Jesús del Monte (1710), Provincia (1715, 1718), Xalmolongo (1721, 1750s), Tepenene (1730s, 1750s), San Xavier (1740s), Florida (1742), Chicavasco (1740s–1750s), and Ocuila (1740s) included threats upon property and hacienda supervisors, physical confrontations, and bloodshed of man and beast.[29] The crown intervened by sending royal troops to put down pueblo uprisings in Malinalco and Ocuila in 1722.[30] This was not the first or the last military intervention on behalf of a hacienda, as pueblo violence increased during the late eighteenth century. Archer's recent study of the colonial army in Mexico (1760–1810) shows numerous pueblo insurrections predating the violent reactions led by Hidalgo and Morelos.[31] In southern Mexico, outbreaks are highlighted by activities in eastern Yucatán (1639–1655), the Chiapas Tzeltal-Tzotzil revolt (1712), and the rebellion led by Jacinto Canek (1761) in western Yucatán.[32] Throughout the colonial period violent pueblo reaction, although successfully contained, was always present. The nineteenth-century "caste wars" represent a continuation of a class struggle over resources and power between a dispossessed rural peasantry and the classes dominating economic resources.[33] Eventually that struggle reached center stage, during the Mexican Revolution. And over fifty years later, the same struggle continues.

Broad interpretations based on a case study run the same risk of distortion as do interpretations lacking careful observation of special cases encompassing lengthy time periods and distinct regions. This study has examined the question of land tenure from the perspective of what was actually taking place on rural haciendas during roughly two centuries of Mexican colonial history. Santa Lucía's Jesuit ownership imparted certain unique features, but its longevity, scope of activities, and broad extent—throughout central Mexico and beyond the eastern and western flanks of the Highlands—suggest that Santa Lucía was not merely a local or regional entity.[34] Throughout the colonial epoch, the hacienda's activities were conducted in no fewer than one-quarter of the political jurisdictions of New Spain.[35] And it was one of the largest and most successful haciendas of its time.

In attempting to interpret the significance of the hacienda, rather than merely describe it, this study raises as many questions as it provides answers. Without detailed, long-term studies of individual pueblos, the general outlines of pueblo adaptation suggested here remain open to question. Local and regional variations require documentation to clarify or modify what is known about general processes. The status and role of cacique, cleric, and crown official in the pueblos beg for investigation in order to establish patterns as well as variations. The mechanisms of opening pueblo communities to wider colonial influences, and their closure to establish the closed corporate pueblo, so visible in the ethnographic literature, demand attention. The role of the small rural estate, in contrast to the large hacienda complex focused upon in this study, requires further investigation. Such investigations may assist in the unlocking of secrets needed for a clearer understanding, not only of particular pueblos and regions, but, more important, of the shape and character of a colonial peasantry. These secrets, however, are no longer guarded within the confines of the communities themselves. Time and constant adjustment to the everyday demands of survival have altered both the traditions and the perspectives of the residents. Fortunately, regional and national archives are rich in documents, the details of which must be carefully and laboriously sifted.

Appendixes

APPENDIX A   *Santa Lucía Acquisitions, 1576–1767*

No. and Means of acquisition	Property acquired	Date	Price	General location and jurisdiction(s)	Adjacent pueblos and towns	History of property	Sources
1. Purchase, from Alonso González	5 sitios gm, 1 sitio de venta, livestock (16,800 sheep, 1,400 goats, 131 horses and donkeys), 8 Negro slaves (7 adults, including 6 males; 1 infant), equipment, tools, buildings, and corrals	Dec. 4, 1576	17,000 pesos	*Valley of Mexico:* Ecatepec, Zumpango, Pachuca	Tecama, Xoloc, Los Reyes, Axoloapan, Xaltocan, Tizayuca, Temascalapa, Tezontepec, Acayuca, Tezontlapa	TEPEATZINGO May 23, 1542, merced to Juan Ponce de León May 1579, use and type of property redefined 1554, sold in public auction to agent for daughter, Doña Ana Ponce de León 1556, bought by Fernando de Portugal 1568, bought by Alonso González PAPAHUACA Aug. 22, 1559, merced to Fernando de Portugal 1568, bought by Alonso González TEPANCALTITLÁN Mar. 3, 1568, merced to Fernando de Portugal Jan. 1568, bought by Alonso González HUEYTEPEC July 6, 1563, merced to Antonio de Nava Feb. 1564, bought by Juan de la Mesa 1565, bought by Alonso González	BNM 1087, 2. DBCJM 3; LB, pp. 95–104, 429–78. AGNM 9: 177. AGNHJ 3, 3. PCRMR 1–4

	Size	Date	Price	Location	Sitio	Sitio de Venta	Reference
						Rodríguez Camarra Sept. 1565, bought by Juan Bautista Figueroa Mar. 1566, bought by Alonso González **SITIO DE VENTA** Oct. 6, 1567, merced to Fernando de Portugal Jan. 1568, acquired by Alonso González	
2. Donation, by Cristóbal Pérez	2 sitios gm	July 13, 1582	—	*Valley of Mexico:* Acolman	Ixtlahuaca, Santa María	Feb. 9 and May 7, 1582, merced to Cristóbal Pérez	PCRMR 3–4, 5: 1r–8v, 11v–16r
3. Donation, by Don Carlos de Luna y Arellano	1 sitio gm, 2 caballerías	Dec. 11, 1586	—	*Valley of Toluca:* Metepec [Tenango del Valle]	Capulhuac, Ocoyoacac	June 1, 1566, merced to Doña María de Torquemada Date unknown, bought by Juan Vázquez de Herrera Nov. 2, 1572, bought by Capt. Antonio Ortiz Matience for 70 pesos May 23, 1577, bought by Carlos de Luna y Arellano	PCRVP 1: 480v–501r
4. Donation, by Baltasar de Herrera	1 sitio gm	Mar. 16, 1589	—	*Northeast of Valley of Mexico:* Xilotepec	Chapantongo	Apr. 12, 1585, merced to Baltasar de Herrera	LB, pp. 600–604
5. Purchase, from Julio Román Pastor	2 caballerías	Aug. 26, 1589	140 pesos	*Valley of Mexico:* Texcoco	Ixtlahuaca	1580, merced to Cristóbal Hernández Date unknown, bought by Juan Román	BNM 1087, 2. PCRVP 1: 246
6. Donation, by pueblo of Xoloc	1 herido de molino	1591	—	*Valley of Mexico:* Ecatepec	Xoloc	?	AGNM 17: 68v
7. Purchase, from Colegio de Santo Tomás, Guadalajara	1 sitio gm	Sept. 14, 1594	400 pesos	*West of Guadalajara:* Izatlán	Ahualulco	Date unknown, bought by Colegio de Santo Tomás from Agustín Plasencia and wife	BNM 1087, 2
8. Purchase, from pueblo of Zumpango	Size and number of pedazos unknown	Jan. 29, 1595	450 pesos	*Valley of Mexico:* Ecatepec	Xoloc, Zumpango, San Sebastián	?	BNM 1087, 2. DBCJM 3: 412
9. Donation, from Hernando Vázquez	4 caballerías	Jan. 13, 1596	—	*Valley of Mexico:* Citlaltepec [Zumpango]	Zumpango	1595–1596, merced to Hernando Vázquez	BNM 1087, 2
10. Donation, from Alonso Pardo	4 caballerías	Jan. 13, 1596	—	*Valley of Mexico:* Ecatepec	Xoloc	1595–1596, merced to Alonso Pardo	DBCJM 3: 412. BNM 1087, 2
11. Purchase, from Colegio de Santo Tomás, Guadalajara	1 sitio gm, 2 caballerías	June 2, 1596	300 pesos	*West of Guadalajara:* Izatlán	Ahualulco	Date unknown, donated to Colegio de San Joseph by Diego Nieto Maldonado in the name of Hernando Argones Colegio de Santo Tomás's means of acquisition unknown	BNM 1087, 2

APPENDIX A. *Santa Lucía Acquisitions (continued)*

No. and Means of acquisition	Property acquired	Date	Price	General location and jurisdiction(s)	Adjacent pueblos and towns	History of property	Sources
12. Donation, by Juan Turrado	1 sitio gm, 2 caballerías	July 2, 1596	—	*Valley of Mexico (north):* Ecatepec, Pachuca	Xoloc, Tizayuca	Feb. 4, 1596, merced to Juan Turrado	DBCJM 3: 412. BNM 1087, 2. PCRVP 2: 17
13. Purchase, from Pedro de Dueñas	3 sitios gm, 4 caballerías, livestock (12,000 sheep, 12 oxen, 30 mares, 40 cattle), 1 slave (Negro, 45-yr-old male), equipment, tools, buildings	July 29, 1596	12,000 pesos	*Valley of Mexico (north):* Pachuca	Acayuca, Tizayuca, Tolcayuca	1544, caballerías bought from Acayuca and Tizayuca. Nov. 30, 1586, merced of 1 sitio gm to Alonso González. Jan. 29, 1587, bought by Antonio Delgadillo. 1593, bought by Pedro de Dueñas	BNM 1087, 2. LB, pp. 631–33; PCRMR 3–4: 48–58, 203–14
14. Donation, by Francisco Pacho	2 sitios gm	Aug. 20, 1596	—	*Valley of Mexico/Actopan Valley:* Hueypoxtla [Tetepango]	Tezontlalpa, Tlacuitlapilco	June 23, 1594, merced to Francisco Pacho	BNM 1087, 2
15. Donation, by Alonso de Castañeda	1 sitio gm, 2 caballerías	July 7, 1597	—	*Valley of Mexico (northeast):* Otumba	Temascalapa	?	AGNT 2033, 1: 31
16. Purchase, from Diego Sánchez and wife, María Magdalena	1 pedazo (10 brazos by 5 brazos), house and thatched hut	Jan. 5, 1598	130 pesos	*Valley of Mexico (south):* Coyoacán	Coyoacán, Tlalpan [San Agustín de las Cuevas]	Nov. 24, 1597, bought by María Magdalena, wife of Diego Sánchez, from Miguel de San Juan	AGNT 2033, 1, BNM 1087, 2
17. Purchase, from Sebastián Velázquez	1 sitio gm, 2 caballerías	May 15, 1598	?	*West of Guadalajara:* Izatlán	Ahualulco	?	BNM 1087, 2
18. Purchase, from Martín López de Gaona	4 caballerías	July 4, 1605	700 pesos	*Valley of Mexico:* Citlaltepec [Zumpango]	Zumpango, San Sebastián	1604, merced to Martín López de Gaona	AGNM 24: 193. DBCJM 3: 412; 6: 609; 8: 271. PCRVP 1, 2: 266
19. Purchase, from Martín López de Gaona	4 caballerías	July 15, 1605	600 pesos	*Valley of Mexico:* Ecatepec	Xoloc	1603–1605, merced to Martín López de Gaona	BNM 1087, 2
20. Purchase, from Don Juan Valiente	2 caballerías	Aug. 19, 1608	?	*Valley of Mexico:* Citlaltepec [Zumpango]	Zumpango, San Sebastián	Nov. 11, 1583, merced to Gregorio Sánchez, *principal* of Zumpango. Juan Valiente's means of acquisition unknown	AGNM 13: 28. PCRVP 2: 156
21. Purchase, from Eugenio Vargas and wife, Doña Julia de Salazar	1 sitio gm, 6 caballerías, livestock, equipment, houses, and corrals	Apr. 8, 1609	3,607 pesos	*Valley of Mexico (north):* Pachuca	Tolcayuca	June 20, 1598, merced of 4 caballerías to Cristóbal Pérez. 1598, purchased by Eugenio de Vargas and wife, Doña Julia de	LB, pp. 635–36

Juan Turrado				Texcoco		Turrado	
23. Purchase, from Juan Francisco Marroquín	4 caballerías	Apr. 23, 1610	900 pesos	*Valley of Mexico (north):* Pachuca	Acayuca, Huahualpa	1603–1606, merced to Luis Barrientos / Date unknown, bought by Juan Francisco Marroquín	BNM 1087, 2. DBCJM 3: 412 / BNM 1087, 2
24. Purchase, from Juan de la Cruz and wife, Luisa de los Angeles	4 caballerías	Mar. 21, 1612	400 pesos	*Valley of Mexico (north):* Pachuca, Acolman [Texcoco]	Acayuca, Zapotlán	May 1611, merced to Juan de la Cruz and wife, Luisa de los Angeles	*Ibid.*
25. Purchase, from Inquisidor Gutiérrez Bernardo de Quirós	3 sitios gm	May 11, 1612	520 pesos	*Valley of Mexico (north):* Pachuca	Acayuca	Aug. 20, 1607, Inquisition office confiscated properties of Antonio Machado / Dec. 1607, public notice of auction of Machado properties / Feb. 17, 1612, Jesuit bid of 520 pesos accepted as best offer	BNM 1087, 2. PCRMR 3–4, 10: 127r–138v
26. Purchase, from Baltasar de la Cadena	1 sitio gm	June 23, 1614	100 pesos	*North of Valley of Mexico:* Pachuca	Acayuca	Oct. 22, 1569, merced to Baltasar de la Cadena	BNM 1087, 2
27. Donation, from Francisco Díaz de Velasco	4 caballerías	Aug. 30, 1614	—	*Valley of Mexico (north):* Pachuca	Acayuca	1612–1614, merced to Francisco Díaz de Velasco	*Ibid.*
28. Purchase, from Don Juan de Morada	1 sitio gm, 4 caballerías	Sept. 23, 1614	400 pesos	*Valley of Mexico:* Texcoco, Teotihuacán	Chiapa, Tezontepec, Temascalapa, Tepexpan	Oct. 21, 1613, merced to Juan de Morada	*Ibid.*
29. Donation, from Doña Juana de Cuadra	3 sitios gm, 4 caballerías	1614	—	*South of Valley of Mexico:* Malinalco, Ocuila	Ocuila, Santa María, Malinalco, Xoquinzingo	June 4, 1575, merced of 1 sitio gm and 2 caballerías to Pedro de Salazar / Sept. 16, 1580, merced of 1 sitio gm and 2 caballerías to Pedro de Salazar / June 22, 1585, merced of 1 sitio gm to Pedro de los Ríos / Date unknown, acquired by Doña Juana de Cuadra	AGNT 2033, 57; 2205, 1. PCRVP 1: 621–23
30. Donation, from Sebastián de la Barrera	3 caballerías	Jan. 21, 1615	—	*Valley of Mexico:* Teotihuacán	Santa María Zultapan, Temascalapa	Aug. 23, 1611, merced to Sebastián de la Barrera	BNM 1087, 2. DBCJM 3: 411; 4: 741
31. Donation, from Juan González	13 pedazos	Mar. 15, 1615	—	*Valley of Mexico (south):* Coyoacán, Xochimilco	Coyoacán, San Miguel, Xochimilco	Date unknown, Juan González bought 4 pedazos from Indians of Xochimilco / 1604, Juan González bought 1 pedazo from Julio González / 1600–1604, Juan González bought 8 pedazos from Indians of Xochimilco	AGNT 2033, 1: 35. BNM 1087, 2

APPENDIX A. *Santa Lucía Acquisitions (continued)*

No. and Means of acquisition	Property acquired	Date	Price	General location and jurisdiction(s)	Adjacent pueblos and towns	History of property	Sources
32. Purchase, from Martín López de Gaona	4 caballerías	July 11, 1615	400 pesos	*Valley of Mexico:* Citlaltepec [Zumpango], Ecatepec	San Sebastián, Xoloc	May 20, 1505, merced to Martín López de Gaona	BNM 1087, 2. PCRVP 2, 156
33. Purchase, from Gabriel Hortigosa	2 sitios gm, 7 caballerías	Aug. 11, 1615	800 pesos	*Valley of Mexico:* Citlaltepec [Zumpango], Cuauhtitlán	San Agustín, Xaltocan, Ecatepec, Zumpango	Aug. 9, 1585, merced of 1 sitio gm and 2 caballerías to Gabriel Hortigosa Sept. 17, 1585, merced of 1 sitio gm and 4 caballerías to Melchor Muñoz Oct. 17, 1585, Melchor Muñoz donated properties to Gabriel Hortigosa	AGNM 12: 140. BNM 1087, 2
34. Donation, from Gaspar de Villerías	1 sitio gm, 2 caballerías	Sept. 10, 1615	—	*Valley of Mexico:* Cuauhtitlán	Coatepec, San Bartolomé (estancia)	Date unknown, Gaspar de Villerías inherited properties from parents, Juan de Villerías and Beatriz de Poras	BNM 1087, 2
35. Purchase, from Don Jerónimo de la Ricavilla and wife, Jerónima de Herrera	1 sitio gm	Mar. 10, 1616	2,000 pesos	*Valley of Mexico:* Ecatepec	Chiconautla, Ozumbilla	Date unknown, merced to Juan de Valladolid Seller's means of acquisition unknown	*Ibid.*
36. Purchase, from presbítero canónigo of Guadalajara cathedral, Diego de Aguilar	1 sitio gm	Apr. 19, 1616	600 pesos	*West of Guadalajara:* Izatlán	Chapulimita	?	*Ibid.*
37. Donation, from Pedro Hernández de Villanueva	1 sitio gm, 2 caballerías	Aug. 29, 1616	—	*West of Guadalajara:* Izatlán	Izatlán (pueblo), San Juan (pueblo), Margarita (pueblo)	June 8, 1616, merced to Pedro Hernández de Villanueva	*Ibid.*
38. Donation, from Hernán Pérez de Luna	1 sitio gm	July 17, 1617	—	*Chilpancingo area [Guerrero]:* Chilapa (and Tixtla)	Chilapa, Mochtitlán	July 13, 1617, merced to Hernán Pérez de Luna	*Ibid.* PCRVP 1: 451r
39. Donation, from Diego Alonso de Alfaro	2 sitios gm	July 17, 1617	—	*Chilpancingo area [Guerrero]:* Chilapa (and Tixtla)	Chilapa, Azacaloya, Tixtla	July 13, 1617, merced to Diego Alonso de Alfaro	BNM 1087, 2. PCRVP 1: 452r–453v
40. Donation, from Martín Hernández	2 sitios gm	Mar. 5, 1618	—	*South of Valley of Mexico:* Malinalco	Ocuila, Malinalco	Feb. 20, 1618, merced to Martín Hernández	AGNM 33: 228. BNM 1087, 2
41. Purchase, from Pedro Alonso	5 sitios gm	Apr. 16, 1619	1,700 pesos	*Chilpancingo area [Guerrero]:* Chilapa	Acatlán, Azacaloya	Nov. 17, 1617, merced of 3 sitios gm to Pedro Alonso Redondo	BNM 1087, 2. PCRVP 1, 2¢

No.	Transaction	Property	Date	Price	Region	Location	History	Reference
42.	Purchase, from presbítero of Tixtla, Don Antonio Domínguez	1 sitio gm, 4 caballerías	Dec. 3, 1619	400 pesos	*Chilpancingo area* [*Guerrero*]: Chilapa (and Tixtla)	Apango, Chilapa, Tixtla	sitios gm to Don Andrés Pérez de Higuera for 1,000 pesos / Feb. 5, 1604, merced of 4 caballerías to Alonso de la Torre / Feb. 13, 1612, merced of 1 sitio gm to Alonso de la Torre and wife / Aug. 11, 1618, properties bought by Antonio Domínguez	BNM 1087, 2: PCRVP 1, 26: 450r–452r, 475r–476v
43.	Purchase from Don Joseph Moctezuma	1 sitio gm	Jan. 16, 1620	350 pesos	*Chilpancingo area* [*Guerrero*]: Chilapa (and Tixtla)	Chilapa	1620, Joseph de Moctezuma, vecino of Chilapa, won recognition of claim that his grandfather received sitio in merced, and that it was passed to him through his father	BNM 1087, 2: PCRVP 1, 26: 453r–v, 476v
44.	Purchase, from Colegio de Tepotzotlán	1 sitio gm	1621	?	*Valley of Mexico*: Ecatepec, Cuauhtitlán	Ojo de Agua, Ozumbilla	Date unknown, acquired by Diego Ruiz; inherited by Juan Ruiz and sister, Ana de León (wife of Juan Fernández Salgado) / 1567, merced to Sancho Martínez de Gamboa / 1595, bought by Colegio de Tepotzotlán from Juan Ruiz and Juan Fernández Salgado	AGNM 9: 190v. DBCJM 3: 411
45.	Purchase, from Luis de Cháves	1 sitio, 1 horno de cal (lime kiln)	Aug. 17, 1624	12 mules	?	—	Jan. 3, 1543, merced to Melchor de Cháves / Oct. 27, 1596, Colegio de San Pedro y San Pablo obtained use from Luis de Cháves in exchange for 12 mules / 1617, dispute between Luis de Cháves (son) and Colegio over conditions of use	PCRVP 1, 2: 279–83
46.	Purchase, from Don Antonio Domínguez	1 sitio gm, 4 caballerías	Sept. 4, 1624	650 pesos	*Chilpancingo area* [*Guerrero*]: Chilapa	Tixtla, Apango	Dec. 3, 1619, bought by Colegio de San Pedro y San Pablo / Aug. 2, 1622, agent of Antonio Domínguez declared property still belonged to Domínguez / Justicia upheld Domínguez claim	PCRVP 1: 475r–476v
47.	Purchase, from Tolcayucan parish priest, Pedro Juárez de Salazar	1 sitio gm	Oct. 13, 1627	?	*Valley of Mexico* (*north*): Pachuca	Acayuca, Tolcayuca	Jan. 12, 1608, merced to Indian governor of Tolcayuca, Don Pedro Sánchez; later inherited by Don Tomás de Aquino / Oct. 13, 1627, Tolcayucan parish priest, acting as agent of Tomás de Aquino, sold to Colegio de San Pedro y San Pablo.	PCRMR 3–4: 79r–85v

APPENDIX A. *Santa Lucía Acquisitions (continued)*

No. and Means of acquisition	Property acquired	Date	Price	General location and jurisdiction(s)	Adjacent pueblos and towns	History of property	Sources
48. Means of acquisition unknown	1 sitio gm	1630	?	*Valley of Mexico:* Ecatepec, Teotihuacán	Tecama, Tepexpan	1585, merced to Jerónimo Vaeza de Herrera	AGNM 12: 1420. DBCJM 2: 411; 5: 160
49. Purchase, from Francisco Martín	1 sitio gm, 1.5 caballerías	May 31, 1636	300 pesos	*Valley of Mexico (south):* Chalco	Atlauhcan, Chimalhuacán, Chalco	Oct. 6, 1605, Don Martín de Guzmán, *indio principal* of Atlauhcan, granted permission to sell properties / Oct. 10, 1605, bought by Juan de Salazar / Nov. 22, 1627, bought by Francisco Martín	PCRVP 3, 23: 1–28
50. Purchase, from pueblo of Xoloc	1 sitio gm, 2 caballerías	1639	400 pesos	*Valley of Mexico:* Ecatepec	Xoloc	Apr. 4, 1599, ownership of land by Xoloc pueblo reaffirmed by audiencia / Sept. 3, 1602, Xoloc pueblo took formal repossession of properties	DBCJM 3; 411; 5; 160–61. PCRVP 2, 17
51. Purchase, from Pedro de Sagastibarria	5.5 sitios gm	Sept. 2, 1645	2,000 pesos	*Chilpancingo area [Guerrero]:* Chilapa (and Tixtla)	Chilapa	Apr. 25, 1620, Andrés Pérez de Higuera bought 1.5 sitios gm from Colegio Máximo / June 26, 1623, merced to Antonio de Arraiza 3 sitios gm / May 8, 1630, Doña Francisca Díaz Matamoros, wife of Andrés Pérez de Higuera, bought the 3 sitios from Antonio de Arraiza / Aug. 7, 1632, Pedro de Sagastibarria bought the 4.5 sitios gm from Andrés Pérez de Higuera and wife	PCRVP 1: 453r–454v, 477r–477v
52. Purchase, from Juan de Castillo	51 sitios gm and GM, 30 caballerías, residence complex, trapiche, cane fields, water rights, livestock	1655	29,724 pesos	*Tehuacán Valley and extending into Veracruz Vieja*	Putla, Quecholac, San Juan de los Chochos, Santa María Caltepec, Tehuacán, Temachalco, Tequila, Zongolica	TEHUACÁN / 1591–1598, Alfonso Díaz Manzano acquired 42 sitios gm (2 purchased, 10 received directly in merced, and 30 via agents) / 1614–19, Alfonso's widow, Leonor Dávila Montemayor, took over properties / 1614, Leonor Dávila Montemayor sold 26 sitios gm to brother-in-law, increased holdings at expense of Indigenous lands / 1619, properties sold	AGNAHH 285, 33: 286, 44; 307, 14. BNM 1058, 1. Ewald, *Estudios sobre la hacienda*, pp. 103–9

No. Mode of acquisition	Holdings	Date	Location	Constituent properties	History	Source
53. Purchase, from Don Juan de Rivadeneira and wife	8 sitios gm, 16 caballerías, hacienda residence	1669–1670; ?	*Valley of Mexico (north) and Pachuca area:* Epazoyuca [Cempoala], Hueypoxtla [Tetepango Hueypoxtla], Pachuca	Acayuca, Atladlauca, Altica [San Juan], Tilcuautla, Nopalapa [San Miguel], Pachuca, Tezontepec, Tlaculpa, Zapotlán	...020, 25 sitios gm (plus 16,275 goats, 510 sheep, slaves) bought by Juan de Castillo 1629, Castillo increased properties, attempted to make donation to Jesuits on condition they establish college in Tehuacán 1655, Jesuits bought estate 1730, property sold to sister college for 30,000 pesos A L T I C A 1543–1614, 14 separate mercedes obtained by 10 individuals, four of whom were agents of Don Gaspar de Rivadeneira 1598–1620, Don Gaspar de Rivadeneira and wife acquired properties 1643, Juan de Rivadeneira, son and heir, paid composición fees to confirm ownership of 8 sitios gm and 16 caballerías 1669–1670, Colegio de San Pedro y San Pablo negotiated and purchased estate	AGNT 2033, 1: 29–39. PCRMR 2, 1: 1–54v
54. Purchase, from Andrés Fuertes	19 sitios gm, 14 caballerías, hacienda residence, large corrals for goats, farm and ranch equipment, 43 mares, 40 plow oxen, license for 300 cows	Oct. 2, 1686; 8,500 pesos	*North of Valley of Mexico and northwest of Pachuca:* Actopan, Pachuca, Tetepango [Tetepango Hueypoxtla]	Actopan, Acayuca, Hueypoxtla, Ixquincuitlapilco, Pachuca, Tepanaloya, Tilcuautla, Tornacostla	C O N C E P C I Ó N O R C A R R I Ó N 1562–1622, 14 separate mercedes obtained by 11 individuals, including 2 mercedes by Pedro de Soto, son of conqueror Juan de Soto Cabezón 1585–1622, Pedro de Soto and brothers acquired 17 sitios gm and 10 caballerías 1645–1651, estate became encumbered to Augustinian college in Mexico City and Augustinian convent in Tizayuca 1651, Juan Antonio Robles Viscaya acquired estate, which then passed through the hands of 4 other owners prior to being acquired by his stepchildren, Miguel and Bartholomé Moreno Ortiz 1685, Andrés Fuertes bought estate, plus 2 sitios gm and 4 caballerías, and began to rebuild main residence	AGNT 2033, 1: 10v–19v. PCRMR 1, 6: 26r–38v; 10: 2v–26v; 11: 1v–42r

359

APPENDIX A. *Santa Lucía Acquisitions (continued)*

No. and Means of acquisition	Property acquired	Date	Price	General location and jurisdiction(s)	Adjacent pueblos and towns	History of property	Sources
55. Purchase, from Augustinian convent of Ocuila	2 sitios GM, 1 sitio gm, 10 caballerías, 2 pedazos	1703–1713	2,000 pesos	*South of Valley of Mexico:* Malinalco, Ocuila [Malinalco]	Malinalco, Ocuila, Santa Mónica, Xoquinzingo	1686, Colegio de San Pedro y San Pablo bought Fuertes holdings after dispute over boundaries OCUILA 1564–1618, 6 individuals acquired properties in small units via merced 1620s, Augustinian convent of Ocuila acquired properties 1634, convent 1 sitio GM, 1 sitio gm, 6 caballerías, and 2 pedazos to Martín Fernández 1635–1703, convent recovered and resold properties to Cristóbal Martín Guadarama and Don Juan Jerónimo López de Peralta 1703, Colegio de San Pedro y San Pablo bought 2 sitios gm, 1 sitio GM, 10 caballerías, and 2 pedazos from convent, then claimed sale to be irrevocable 1713, Jesuit ownership confirmed by audiencia	AGNT 2033, 1: 56v–62r
56. Claim, from pueblos of Sayula and Tuxpa jurisdictions	62 sitios GM	1716–1719	—	*Between Colima and Guadalajara:* Sayula, Zapotlán, Tuxpa	Ataco, Atemaxac, Sayula, Tepalpa, Xonacatlán, Zapotlán	PROVINCIA PASTURELAND July 7, 1716, Don Joseph Miranda Villaysan, *oidor* of Guadalajara audiencia, arranged merced of 62 sitios GM for Colegio de San Pedro y San Pablo July 10, 1716, audiencia confirmed merced July 12, 1716, titles issued to Colegio Mar. 5, 1717, permission for possession issued to Colegio July 1717, native towns resisted possession and disputed Jesuit claim May 22, 1719, after series of appeals, royal cédula confirmed Jesuit claim	PCRVP, 1, 2: 26–62

		Location	Price	Date	History	Source
widow and children of Don Melchor de Miranda y Solís	5 sitios gm, San Pablo: 2.25 sitios GM, 2 sitios gm, 3–4 caballerías, equipment, livestock	Ixmiquilpan, Tlacintla [Ixmiquilpan], Zimapán			1623, Luis de Olvera y Ochoa bought 2 of Juan de Olvera's holdings to establish basis of Florida estate 1643, son and heir, Luis de Olvera, acquired 2 additional properties and paid composición fees to confirm ownership of Florida 1651–1702, 5 properties acquired by 4 individuals via merced and purchase, which were to become rancho of San Pablo 1660s, Capt. Don Juan de Echavarría y Solís bought holdings of Luis de Olvera from heirs 1680s, property expanded by additional purchases, then sold to Juan Pérez de Lara 1695, Pérez de Lara paid composición fee (25 pesos) 1702, Melchor de Miranda bought estate from Pérez de Lara 1704, Melchor de Miranda bought the 5 San Pablo rancho properties 1712, Melchor de Miranda's widow, Doña Manuela Calderón, and (minor) children paid composición fees (150 pesos) for Miranda's estates: Florida, San Pablo, Tepenene, and Chicavasco	1: 19v–44r. PCRVP 1, 2; 3, 18
58. Purchase, from widow and children of Don Melchor de Miranda y Solís	5 sitios gm, 2 caballerías, farm and ranch equipment, 20 oxen, 100 horses	Actopan Valley: Actopan, Tornacostla [Tetepango-Hueypoxtla]	5,000 pesos	1723	**TEPENENE** 1614–1620s, Francisco de Gómez Higuera received merced and bought other properties from 4 individuals (lands acquired 1557–1616) 1640s, these properties of Higuera's acquired by Juan de Padilla 1650s, estate became encumbered to Cofradía de Nuestra Señora del Rosario de Actopan 1660s, cofradía sold estate to Capt. Don Juan de Echavarría y Solís 1680s, Don Sancho de Miranda bought estate	*Ibid.*

Location (Tepenene): Actopan, Chicavasco, Ixquintlapilco, Tetitlán, Tecazique, Tornacostla

Location (top): Tlacintla, Zimapán

APPENDIX A. *Santa Lucía Acquisitions (continued)*

No. and Means of acquisition	Property acquired	Date	Price	General location and jurisdiction(s)	Adjacent pueblos and towns	History of property	Sources
						1695, Miranda paid composición fees (50 pesos) for both Tepenene and Chicavasco	
						1702, estate inherited by Melchor de Miranda	
						1712, Melchor de Miranda's widow, Doña Manuela Calderón, and (minor) children paid composición fees for Miranda's estates: Florida, San Pablo, Tepenene, and Chicavasco	
59. Purchase, from widow and children of Don Melchor de Miranda y Solís	1 sitio GM, 5 sitios gm, 2 caballerías, 1 pedazo	1723	12,200 pesos	*Actopan Valley:* Actopan, Tetepango-Hueypoxtla	Actopan, Chicavasco, Santa María, Tetitlán	CHICAVASCO	*Ibid.*
						1563–1623, Juan de Olvera and son Diego acquired 7 properties through purchase and merced	
						1643, Manuel de Olvera, heir of Juan de Olvera, paid composición fees to confirm ownership	
						1690s, property became encumbered to Cofradía de Nuestra Señora del Rosario de Actopan	
						1680s, properties purchased by Don Sancho de Miranda	
						1695, Miranda paid composición fees (50 pesos) for both Tepenene and Chicavasco	
						1702, estate inherited by Melchor de Miranda	
						1712, Melchor de Miranda's widow, Doña Manuela Calderón, and (minor) children paid composición fees: Florida, San Pablo, Tepenene, and Chicavasco	
60. Purchase, from crown	5.5 sitios gm, 2.5 caballerías, 1 *solar* (house lot)	1731–1735	1,030 pesos	*Actopan Valley:* Hueypoxtla, Tetepango	Ajacuba, Tecomate, Tetepango	SAN IGNACIO	AGNAHH 307, 8; 329, 6. AGNT 2033, 1: 44v–49v. PCRVP 1, 2: 294–99
						Used as part of Mayorazgo de Murilla, established by Don Jerónimo López de Peralta y Murilla early in 17th century (see details of the early history under Item 61)	

362

| 61. Purchase, from Don Francisco Peralta y Murilla | 8–10 sitios gm, 5.5–6.5 caballerías | 1732–1735 | 12,537 pesos | *Actopan Valley:* Actopan, Tetepango | Actopan, Ajacuba, Chicavasco, Tecazique, Temoaya, Tornacostla | 1731, Colegio de San Pedro y San Pablo presented claim of *denuncia de realengas;* audiencia ordered sale, by public auction, of 5.5 sitios gm, 2.33 caballerías, 1 *solar*

1733, Colegio accepted as buyer of properties, paying 1,030 pesos for legal and other fees

1735, Colegio ownership confirmed by royal cédula and possession of property granted

SAN PABLO, OR TULANCALCO Y PUNTA DEL GARAMBULLO

1562–1580, Jerónimo Lopéz de Peralta acquired 3 properties through merced

1612, his son and heir, Don Jerónimo Lopéz de Peralta y Murilla, acquired 2 properties through merced via an agent

1620s, Don Jerónimo Lopéz de Peralta y Murilla bought 3 properties from Don Juan Barba Coronada (2 of which dated back to merceds of 1544 and 1571, the third acquired through merced in 1515) and 2 properties from Doña Catarina de Mendoza (inherited properties dating back to mercedes of 1562) to establish the mayorazgo de Murilla

1643, mayorazgo owners paid composición fees (100 pesos) for property including 10 sitios gm and 1.5 caballerías

1643–1720s, mayorazgo passed through a number of owners, including Hernando Díaz and Capt. Don Juan de Echavarría y Solís, and ended up (with alterations in numbers of sitios and caballerías) in hands of mayorazgo heir, Francisco Peralta y Murilla

1732, Colegio de San Pedro y San Pablo negotiated purchase of mayorazgo, took over its | AGNAHH 307, 8; 329, 6. AGNT 2033, 1: 50v–56v. PCRVP, 1, 9; 3, 18 |

No. and Means of acquisition	Property acquired	Date	Price	General location and jurisdiction(s)	Adjacent pueblos and towns	History of property	Sources
62. Purchase, from Don Joseph de Muguértegui	San Jerónimo: 16 sitios gm; San Nicolás: 9 caballerías	1737	19,000 pesos	*Colima area*	—	management, and paid for the 16.6 sitios gm, 6.67 caballerías, and 1 solar claimed by the mayorazgo	AGNAHH 307, 8. BNM 1058, 1. AGNAHH 298, 1
						1735, royal cédula confirmed permission to sell mayorazgo to Jesuits, which proved to be smaller than previously claimed	
						1745, Jesuits sold 3 sitios gm for 3,180 pesos	
						S A N J E R Ó N I M O Y S A N N I C O L Á S	
						1720–1737, Colegio de San Pedro y San Pablo rented properties of Joseph de Muguértegui (date of acquisition unknown) to complement Provincia operations. Bought by Jesuits when Muguértegui decided to return to Spain	

APPENDIX B

Conflicts and Disputes Involving Santa Lucía, 1576–1767

No.	Date	Levels of Jesuit involvement[a]	Second party[b]	Issue	Levels of litigation[c]	Outcome	Sources
1.	1576–79	Pr, SPySP: Santa Lucía	Hacendado: Juan de Padilla	Boundaries	K, RCI, Aud, RLO	Js won case	PCRVP 1: 1–225
2.	1577–83	Pr, SPySP	Secular clergy and crown	Payment of tithe	K, RCI, Aud, RLO, P, AB	Js exempted from payment	AGNAHH 324, 1
3.	1578	SPySP: Santa Lucía	Pueblos: Tecama, Chiconautla (Ecatepec)	Access to pueblo salt licks by livestock	Aud, RLO	Js granted access	PCRRP, fols. 39r–v
4.	1580–86	Pr, SPySP	Individual: Agustín Guerrero de Luna	Payment of his father's promissory notes to the Jesuits	RCI, Aud	Guerrero de Luna ordered to pay 75% of amount	JHS 3, 3: 239–63
5.	1582	SPySP, SL: Hueytepec	Pueblo: Tolcayuca (Pachuca)	Movement of hacienda houses	Aud, RLO	Permission granted	PCRVP 3, 28
6.	1589–96	Pr, SPySP: Santa Lucía	Audiencia and livestock owners	Free access to crown lands for college livestock	Aud, RLO	Js granted access	PCRD, fols. 47r–48v
7.	1594–97	Pr, SPySP: Santa Lucía	Hacendado: Francisco de Medina, rancher near Querétaro	Access to crown pastures	K, RCI, Aud, RLO	Medina fined 100 ps	PCRD, fols. 49v–71
8.	1598	SPySP: Santa Lucía	Pueblo: Zumpango	Boundaries	Aud, RLO	New boundary measurements	DBCJM 7: 506–07
9.	1601	SPySP: Santa Lucía	Individual: Juan de Carranza	Trespassing on SL pastures	Aud	Carranza fined 100 ps	AGNAHH 314, 25
10.	1603–70	SPySP: Santa Lucía	Pueblos: San Mateo and Santo Tomás (Cempoala)	Property ownership	Aud	?	AGNT 2328, 1
11.	1605	Pr, SPySP	Secular clergy	Tithe payment	RCI, Aud, AB, RLO	Continued conflict	DBCJM 3: 414
12.	1608	SPySP: Santa Lucía	Pueblo: Zumpango	Property ownership	Aud	Js paid 80 ps	DBCJM 8: 271
13.	1614	Pr, SPySP	Secular clergy	Tithe payments	RCI, AB, RLO	Continued conflict	AGNAHH 322, 17
14.	1619	Pr, SPySP: Santa Lucía	RLO	Access by officials to measure hacienda lands	Aud, VR	Officials denied access to Js lands	PCRRP, fols. 100r–v
15.	1620	SPySP	Individual: Alonso Guerrero de Villaseca	Mayorazgo of Villaseca	Private	Js to get 50,000 ps	AGNAHH 258, 5

APPENDIX B. Conflicts and Disputes (continued)

No.	Date	Levels of Jesuit involvement[a]	Second party[b]	Issue	Levels of litigation[c]	Outcome	Sources
16.	1639–68	Js, Pr, SPySP: Santa Lucia	Secular clergy	Tithe payment	K, RCI, VR, RLO, P, AB	Js paid tithe for SL production	DBCJM 3: 414–18
17.	1639–43	Pr, SPySP: Santa Lucia	K, VR, Aud, RLO	Registration of all property titles	VR, Aud, RLO	Js paid 7,000 ps	AGNM 51: 5–24. PCRVP 1 and 2
18.	1642–1767	SPySP, SL: Ocuila and Negra	Hacendados: (Malinalco)	Rights to water from Río Amazinac	VP, Aud	Continued conflict	AGNT 2054–55
19.	1652	SPySP: Santa Lucia	Pueblo: Xoloc (Ecatepec)	Hacienda debt of 88 ps	RLO	Js paid	PCRVP 2, 17
20.	1666	Santa Lucia	Pueblo Indians: (Ecatepec)	Rental of land and 30 ps debts	Private	Pueblo's claim dismissed by administrator	DBCJM 5: 161
21.	1670	Santa Lucia	Pueblos: (Pachuca)	Land ownership	Aud	Js ownership confirmed	PCRMR 3–4: 79r–87v
22.	1670	SPySP, SL: Hueytepec	RLO (Ecatepec and Pachuca)	Access to SL pastures	Aud	RLO ordered to enforce protection	PCRVP 3: 203v–209r
23.	1670	SPySP: Altica	Pueblos: (Pachuca)	Possession of land	Aud, RLO	Js took possession	PCRVP 3–4: 127r–138v
24.	1673	SPySP: Santa Lucia	Pueblo: Tlalmanalco (Chalco)	Access to pastures	Aud, RLO	Js assured access	PCRD, fols. 70r–72v
25.	1674–1730	SPySP	Pueblos: (Chalco)	Purchase and sale of properties	Aud, RLO	Js rights confirmed	AGNT 1915, 2
26.	1675	SPySP: Santa Lucia	Pueblos: (Chalco)	Damage to SL property by livestock	Aud, RLO	Js rights affirmed; fine levied	PCRD, fols. 77r–9r
27.	1684	SPySP: Santa Lucia	Pueblo: Zumpango	Land ownership	VP, Aud, RLO	Js regained control	PCRVP 2, 156
28.	1685–86	SPySP, SL: San Xavier	Hacendado: Andrés Fuertes	Ownership of lands of Concepción	Aud	Js bought whole estate	PCRVP 1, 11
29.	1690–1731	SPySP: Santa Lucia	Pueblo: Tetepango (Tetepango Hueypoxtla)	Land ownership	Aud	Continued conflict	AGNT 1634, 1
30.	1695–1748	SPySP, SL: Ocuila	Pueblos: (Malinalco)	Land ownership	RCI, VR, Aud, RLO	Continued conflict	AGNT 2205–7, AGNAHH 312: 328–29
31.	1702	SPySP, SL: San Juan	Pueblo: Cuautlalpan (Ecatepec)	Land ownership titles	Aud, RLO	Pueblo ordered to produce titles or pay fine	PCRVP 3: 223r–224v
32.	1707	SPySP	Hacendado: Pedro Díaz de Villegas	Land ownership titles	Aud	Js claims confirmed	PCRVP 3–4: 148
33.	1707–92	SPySP, SL: Altica, Pintas, San Xavier	Pueblo: Ixtlahuaca (Texcoco)	Land ownership	VR, Aud, RLO	Js won legal cases; conflict continued	AGNT 238, 4. PCRVP 1, 2

(Ecatepec)

#	SPySP	Party	Issue	Parties	Outcome	Source
36.	1712	SPySP: Santa Lucía	Hacendado: Juan de Avila (Ecatepec)	Boundaries between haciendas	Aud, RLO	Boundaries marked	PCRVP 2, 16
37.	1712	SPySP: Santa Lucía	Pueblo: Zumpango	Land ownership	Vr, Aud, RLO	Compromise	PCRRP, fols. 101r–106v. PCRVP 2: 214r–312v
38.	1712	SPySP: Santa Lucía	Pueblo: Axoloapa and barrios (Ecatepec)	Boundaries between pueblos and SL	RLO	Boundaries marked	PCRVP 2, 21
39.	1712–18	SPySP, SL: San Juan	Pueblo: Cuautlalpan (Ecatepec)	Property boundaries	Aud, RLO	New boundaries created	AGNT, 1504, 1: 85–97. PCRVP 2, 17
40.	1712–49	SPySP, SL: Ocuila	Pueblo: Malinalco (Malinalco)	Land rentals	RCI, VP, Aud, RLO	Continued conflict	AGNT 2200, 1
41.	1712	SPySP: Santa Lucía	Hacendado: Jerónimo de la Redonda (Ecatepec)	Water rights	Aud	Js confirmed hacendado's rights	AGNT 2080, 4
42.	1713	SPySP, SL: Cabras de Tehuacán	Pueblos: Caltepec, Azumba (Tehuacán)	Land ownership	Aud	Js confirmed ownership	PCRVP 1: 237–41
43.	1715	SPySP: Santa Lucía	Hacendado: Jerónimo Carranza (Ecatepec)	Hacienda boundaries	RLO	Boundaries confirmed	PCRVP 2, 18
44.	1716–19	SPySP, SL: Provincia	Pueblos: (Zayula and Zapotlán)	Land ownership	RCI, Aud, RLO	Js ownership established	PCRVP 1: 260–62
45.	1717	SPySP, SL: Santa Lucía	Secular clergy: cura of Tizayuca	Cura causing disturbance among pueblos	Aud, AB	Cura temporarily removed	AGNAHH 306, 5
46.	1717–47	SPySP, SL: Provincia	Pueblos: (Zapotlán)	Access to water and salt	Aud	Concessions by Js	AGNAHH 862, 1
47.	1717–98	SPySP (later Conde de Regla family)	Crown officials: Temporalidades	Value of estates and their boundaries	RCI, Aud	Compromise	AGNT 2033–35
48.	1718	Provincia	Hacendado: Juan de Silva (Zapotlán)	Destruction of property by Provincia shepherd	RLO	Js ordered to pay damages	PCRVP 3: 16v–24v
49.	1723	SPySP, SL: Chicavasco	Individual: Agustín Cano (Actopan)	Land ownership	RLO	Js paid 150 ps	AGNT 2033, 1: 39v
50.	1723–24	SPySP, SL: Pintas and San Xavier	Pueblos: Tizayuca and Zumpango	Flood damage from break in SL dam	VR, Aud, RLO	Js exonerated	PCRVP 3: 28r–160r
51.	1723–92	SPySP, SL: Ocuila (later Regla family)	Pueblos: (Malinalco)	Land ownership and access	RCI, VR, Aud, RLO	Continued conflict	AGNT 2205, 1: 341 ff.
52.	1724–27	SPySP: Santa Lucía	Pueblo: Xaltocan	Hacienda boundaries	Aud, RLO	Boundaries marked	AGNT 1784, 1: 37–44
53.	1727–61	SPySP, SL: Concepción	Pueblo: Acayuca (Pachuca)	Land ownership	Aud	Continued conflict	AGNT 2356, 1
54.	1730s–1760s	SpySP: Santa Lucía	Pueblo: Los Reyes (Ecatepec)	Access to SL ciénegas for livestock	Aud	Pueblo access denied	AGNT 1672, 3: 1–28
55.	1730–35	SPySP	Hacendado: mayorazgo de Murilla (Actopan)	Land ownership	RCI, VR, Aud	Js ownership established	PCRRP, fols. 6v–22r. PCRVP 1: 263 ff.
56.	1731–48	SPySP:SL:San Xavier	Pueblo: Temascalapa (Teotihuacán)	Land ownership	Aud	Js ownership confirmed	AGNT 1660, 4: 140 ff.

APPENDIX B. *Conflicts and Disputes (concluded)*

No.	Date	Levels of Jesuit involvement[a]	Second party[b]	Issue	Levels of litigation[c]	Outcome	Sources
57.	1731–39	SPySP	Secular clergy	Tithe payments	K, RCI, VR, RLO, AB	Js paid outstanding tithes	AGNAHH 298, 1: 329, 6
58.	1733	SPySP: Santa Lucía	All neighboring live-stock owners	Damage to cultivated areas and pastures	RCI, Aud	Transgressors to be fined	PCRVP 3: 214r–21v
59.	1733	SPySP	Individual: Alonso de Ulibarri	Debt of 5,712 ps	Aud	Js collected debt	AGNAHH 312, 4
60.	1735	SPySP, SL: San Xavier	Pueblo: Tolcayuca (Pachuca)	Land ownership and boundaries	Aud, RLO	Boundaries defined	AGNT 1803, 1: 26–29
61.	1738–57	SPySP: Santa Lucía	Pueblo: Tecama (Ecatepec)	Hacienda boundaries	Aud	Boundaries defined	AGNT 1580, 1
62.	1742	SPySP, SL: Florida	Pueblo: Metztitlán (Metztitlán)	Land ownership	Aud	Js ownership confirmed	AGNT 2033
63.	1743	SPySP	Convent of San Sebastián	Control of religious (*capellanía*) funds	Aud	Js gained control	AGNAHH 258, 12
64.	1743	SPySP: Santa Lucía	Pueblo: Axoloapan and barrios (Ecatepec)	Hacienda boundaries	Aud	Js boundaries confirmed	AGNT 1476, 7: 28–33; 76–79
65.	1743	SPySP	Hacendado: Joseph de Monterde y Antillón	Land ownership and boundaries	Aud	Continued conflict	PCRVP 1: 264–65
66.	1744	SPySP, SL: Chicavasco	Pueblo: Cofradía de Santa María (Tetepango)	Pastures	Aud	Js ownership confirmed	PCRVP 1: 527v
67.	1740s	SPySP, SL: Ocuila	Pueblo: Ocuila (Malinalco)	Access to SPySP forests	Aud	Continued conflict	PCRVP 1: 273–74
68.	1745	SPySP, SL: Ocuila	Pueblos: (Malinalco)	Pastures	Aud	Js ownership confirmed	PCRVP 1: 543
69.	1745	SPySP	Secular clergy: cura of Tolcayuca	Payment for religious services on SL	Private	Continued conflict	AGNAHH 313, 18
70.	1746	San Xavier sirviente, Bartolomé de la Cruz	RLO: gobernador of Tezontepec	Pasture conflict and imprisonment of Cruz	Aud, RLO	Cruz released	AGNAHH 314, 27
71.	1746–56	SPySP, SL: Ocuila	Pueblos: (Malinalco)	Land ownership and boundaries	RCI, Aud, RLO	Boundaries redefined	AGNT 2207, 1: 209 ff.
72.	1748	SPySP, SL: Pintas	Pueblo: Temascalapa	Land ownership and water rights	VR, Aud, RLO	Js confirmed ownership and water rights	PCRVP 3: 1r–9r
73.	1751	SL: Provincia	Individual: San Bartolomé (Ecatepec)	Injury to San Bartolomé resident by Provincia shepherd, José Cristobal Jiménez	RLO	Jiménez fined 7 ps, 1 real	AGNTe 20, 1: 42
74.	1751	SPySP: Santa Lucía	Pueblo: Tezontepec	Land ownership	Aud	Continued conflict	PCRVP 2: 26r–27r

76.	1753	SPySP, SL	Pueblos: Actopan Valley	Land ownership and rents	Aud	Js rights asserted	AGNAHH 288, 1
77.	1753–57	SPySP, SL: Chicavasco	Pueblo: Santa María Anajac	Land ownership	Aud	Js ownership confirmed	AGNT 1687, 1
78.	1754–56	SPySP, SL: Tepenene	Pueblo: Tepenene	Land ownership	Aud	Compromise	AGNAHH 288, 1; 312, 13
79.	1754–57	SPySP	K, RCI, VR, Aud	Registration of properties acquired after 1700	VR, Aud, RLO	Js paid 150 ps	PCRVP 1: 283–343
80.	1756–58	SPySP, SL: Chicavasco and San Pablo	Pueblo: Tecomate (Tetepango-Hueypoxtla)	Boundaries and land use	Aud	Js ownership confirmed	PCRVP 1, 228
81.	1758	SPySP, SL: Ocuila	Hacendado: Juan de Acosta (Malinalco)	Hacienda boundaries	Private	Boundaries agreed upon	AGNT 2033, 61
82.	1758	SPySP: Santa Lucía	Pueblo: Xoloc	Access to ciénega pastures	Aud	Js rights confirmed	PCRVP 1, 2: 227r–227v
83.	1760–71	SPySP	Individuals: Juan and Pedro López	Debt of 4,000 ps	Aud, RLO	?	AGNT 2085, 17: 106
84.	1764–85	SPySP (later Crown officials)	Individual: Pedro Villaverde	Administrative wages while Villaverde managed SL	RCI, VR, Aud, RLO	Compromise in Js favor	AGNTe 20, 83 and 205
85.	1767	SPySP, SL: San Xavier	Hacendado: Clemente Romero	Boundaries	Private	Boundaries redefined	PCRVP 3, 12

ABBREVIATIONS:

AB	Archbishopric	K	King
Aud	Audiencia	P	Papacy
D	Diocese	Pr	Province
Js	Jesuits	RCI	Royal Council of the Indies

RLO	Regional and local crown officials
SL	Santa Lucía
SPySP	Colegio de San Pedro y San Pablo
VR	Viceroy

NOTE: Representative rather than comprehensive coverage has been attempted. Some cases kept resurfacing and are treated either as individual disputes, if so treated by the courts, or as ongoing disputes. Arrangement is by the first reference encountered, not the termination date. The sources shown do not cover all the documentation on litigation—this would require an extensive survey of archives in Spain and Rome and a much wider survey of documentation in Mexico than was needed for this study—but are restricted to references more narrowly concerned with Santa Lucía.

[a] An unabbreviated place name (usually following a colon) indicates where the conflict started. The levels are ranked in descending order from the highest level involved.

[b] The second parties to the conflicts are identified first by type (e.g., hacendado, pueblo, individual), and then by name if known. Political jurisdictions, if applicable, are given in parentheses.

[c] The decision-making levels involved are ranked in descending order from the highest level reached. In the few cases where both church and crown institutions or officials were involved, I have listed them as separate groups.

369

Notes

Notes

The bibliography provides full citations for printed materials referred to in short form in the notes. Abbreviations used in the notes are:

AGN   Archivo General de la Nación, Mexico City
AGNAHH   AGN Archivo Histórico de Hacienda
AGNHJ   AGN Ramo de Hospital de Jesús
AGNJ   AGN Ramo de Jesuitas
AGNM   AGN Ramo de Mercedes
AGNT   AGN Ramo de Tierras
AGNTe   AGN Ramo de Temporalidades
ANCJM   Archivo Nacional de Chile, Santiago; Ramo de Jesuitas—México
BMNM   Biblioteca del Museo Nacional de Antropología, Mexico City
BNM   Biblioteca Nacional de México, Mexico City
CDHH   *Colección de documentos para la historia de la formación social de Hispanoamérica, 1493–1810*, ed. Richard Konetzke. 2 vols. Madrid, 1958.
CSJ   *Saint Ignatius of Loyola: The Constitutions of the Society of Jesus,* trans. George E. Ganss. St. Louis, Mo., 1970.
DBCJM   *Diccionario bio-bibliográfico de la Compañía de Jesús en México,* ed. Francisco Zambrano. 10 vols. Mexico City, 1961–1970.
GHGNS   *A Guide to the Historical Geography of New Spain,* by Peter Gerhard. Cambridge Latin American Studies, no. 14. Cambridge, 1972.
IHAH   "Instrucciones a los hermanos jesuitas administradores de Haciendas," AGNAHH, leg. 258, exp. 9, in *Instrucciones a los hermanos jesuitas administradores de haciendas,* ed. François Chevalier. Mexico City, 1950.
LB   Libro Becerro, Biblioteca Mariano Cuevas, Mexico City
MM   *Monumenta mexicana,* comp. Félix Zubillaga, S.J. In *Monumenta historica Societatis Jesu.* Rome, 1956–1973. Vols. 77, 84, 97, 104, 106.
PCR   Papeles del Conde de Regla, Washington State University, Pullman
PCRD   PCR Diligencias de Posesión de la Hacienda de Javier

PCRMR   PCR Mayorazgo de Regla. Títulos Originales. 4 vols.
PCRRP   PCR Reales Provisiones, Despachos y Otros Papeles Anexas
        a las Haciendas de Sta. Lucía, Sn. Xavier, y Anexas
PCRVP   PCR Varios Papeles Judiciales Pertenecientes a las Haciendas
        de Sta. Lucía, Sn. Xavier, y Sus Anexas. 3 vols.

Citations in the notes are in condensed form. The numbers after the abbreviated forms refer to *tomos, legajos,* or volumes; those after the comma refer to *expedientes, documentos,* or *cuadernos* (as in the PCR), and those after the colon refer to pages or folios. Thus, AGNAHH 329, 12: 52r refers to Archivo General de la Nación, Archivo Histórico de Hacienda, legajo 329, expediente 12, folio 52 recto; AGNT 2033: 75v refers to Ramo de Tierras of the same archive, tomo 2033, folio 75 vuelta; ANCJM 264, 12, refers to Archivo Nacional de Chile, Ramo de Jesuitas—México, tomo 264, documento 12. When letters are cited, as in AGNAHH 288, l, date, sender, and receiver are included if identifiable.

Chapter 1

1. For contemporary accounts of the Jesuit entry into Mexico, see Sánchez Baquero, Villerías, DBCJM, and MM. For an overview of early non-Jesuit mission activity, see Ricard.

2. For an overview of Roman Catholic activities in the Spanish colonies, see Gibson, *Spain in America,* pp. 68–89; Greenleaf, *Roman Catholic Church;* and Haring, pp. 179–208. Regarding relations with the Spanish crown, see Parry, pp. 152–72. For the formation of the Jesuit order, see Brodrick, Foss, Ganss, and Olin.

3. Jesuit educational systems are described in Ganss, Hughes, and Jacobsen. For northern Mexican activities, see Bolton, "Mission" and *Rim of Christendom;* Burrus; and Pérez de Rivas. For Brazil see Leite; for New France, Thwaite; and for Paraguay, Charlevoix.

4. Regarding the Jesuit expulsion see *Documentos sobre la expulsión;* and Mörner, *The Expulsion* and "Los motivos."

5. The Jesuit order fostered a definite awareness of the historical role it played and produced many capable historians, such as Alegre, Astrain, Clavijero, Cuevas, Decorme, and Florencia. Twentieth-century scholars include Brodrick, Burrus, Dunne, Jacobsen, Zambrano, and Zubillaga.

6. AGNAHH 258, 9.

7. Chevalier, *La formación.*

8. McBride; Simpson, *Encomienda* and *Exploitation;* and Gibson, *Aztecs.*

9. The increase in interest in the hacienda has been of such magnitude that it is now possible to speak of an explosion of hacienda studies. Significant review articles dealing with the topic include: Gibson, "Writings"; Lockhart, "Social History"; Mörner, "Spanish American Hacienda"; and Taylor, "Landed Society." A broader coverage of bibliographical materials about haciendas and related economic themes can be found in

Florescano, "Perspectivas," pp. 317–38, and *La historia*, 1: 163–206; 2: 66–77, 225–46. Florescano compiled a collection of papers dealing with recent hacienda research presented in 1972 at the Rome Congreso Internacional de Americanistas (*Haciendas*). The topic received even greater attention at the same congress's meetings in Mexico City (1974), with continuing emphasis at meetings in Paris (1976) and Vancouver (1979).

10. Works about Jesuit hacienda activities in Mexico have been produced by Benedict, Berthe, Ewald, J. Riley, and Tovar Pinzón. Regional studies have been presented by Brading, Chance, L. González, González Sánchez, Morin, Osborn, Patch, and Taylor. Case studies include those of Barrett, Bazant, Couturier, Harris, Lavrín, and M. Riley. For studies of a more topical nature, see Bakewell, Bishko, Brand, Chevalier, Dusenberry, Espejo-Ponce de Hunt, Florescano, García Bernal, González de Cossío, Katz, Keith, Ladd, Lavrín, Lockhart, Miranda, Moreno Toscano, Morrisey, Tutino, and Zavala.

11. Two series in particular: DBCJM, 10 vols., and MM, 5 vols.

12. Colmenares; Cushner; Macera, *Instrucciones*; Mörner, "Los jesuítas," "Los motivos," *Political and Economic Activities*; and Popescu.

13. Gemelli Carreri, 1: 141.

14. The comment was made by the viceroy responsible for taking over the Jesuit properties in New Spain, December 24, 1767, in a letter to his brother in Spain; BNM, Temporalidades, Libro 10.

15. Gibson, *Aztecs*, pp. 116, 150, 409.

16. This refers to a comment by the conquistador Ruy González to Philip II concerning Indigenous conflicts; *Epistolario*, 8: 33. In the case of the Jesuits, as will be shown throughout the study, conflicts over possession of properties were placed in the hands of lawyers armed with documents, whereas before and during the Conquest, disputes over the same properties had been settled by armed conflict.

17. For discussion of this point see Chapters 8, 11, and 12.

18. There has not yet been a systematic analysis of the use of the term *hacienda* in colonial Mexican society. Chevalier, *La formación*, pp. 209–10, traces the evolution of the term. He shows that in the sixteenth century it referred to any sort of real or movable property, but by the eighteenth century it was more closely associated with livestock estates. Lavrín, "El convento," p. 80, found the same properties being called *labores* early in the seventeenth century, but by 1667 being referred to as *haciendas*. Taylor, "Haciendas coloniales," pp. 292–93, sees a transition from a general to a specific meaning of the term *hacienda* taking place at the end of the sixteenth century for Hispanic America, and somewhat later (the 1660s) in the Valley of Oaxaca. Lockhart, "Encomienda and Hacienda," p. 423, finds seventeenth-century usage of *estancia* and *hacienda* to be almost interchangeable. Patch, pp. 35–39, points out that in Yucatán the term *estancia* dominated until the second half of the eighteenth century, when *hacienda* came to mean rural properties. In Yucatán, *hacienda* retained its general meaning of goods and property. In the 1780s Indian properties, for example, "small haciendas of not more than 4,000 trees," were thus called; see *Inventory*, p. 3. The hacienda-plantation distinctions have been most clearly articulated by Wolf and Mintz, based on nineteenth- and twentieth-century data. Dessaint, pp. 333–35, sees haciendas originating in the

sixteenth century but persisting until the present, whereas the plantations came into being after industrialization. Strickon and other writers have accepted the Wolf-Mintz typology as valid for both colonial and contemporary situations. Mörner, "Spanish American Hacienda," after surveying research on colonial haciendas, comes to the conclusion that characteristics assigned to *hacienda* and *plantation* are not clearly distinguishable in the colonial period.

19. For two representative inventories, see AGNAHH 307, 14, and 329, 6.

20. But not exclusively, since miners were still being referred to as hacendados in the eighteenth century; see Brading, *Miners*.

21. For details, see Chapters 2–4 and 8 on resource utilization, Chapters 9–11 on labor exploitation, and Chapters 5, 6, and 9 on administration.

22. For discussion of this issue, see Florescano, *Haciendas;* Gibson, "Writings"; Keith, "Encomienda, Hacienda" and *Haciendas;* Lockhart, "Encomienda and Hacienda"; and Taylor, "Landed Society."

Chapter 2

1. Sánchez Baquero, p. 111. According to the Roman Catholic religious calendar, this would be December 13, although the legal purchase took place on different dates.

2. LB, pp. 95–96. In 1583 the Jesuits began their official record book, containing the notarized copies of legal documents relating to the acquisition of the Colegio de San Pedro y San Pablo.

3. Sánchez Baquero, pp. 110–11; AGNAHH 258, 1: 27–28. Copies of the contract between the Jesuits and Villaseca are in AGNAHH 258, 2; LB, pp. 4–5; and MM 1: 229–36.

4. Sánchez Baquero, pp. 110–11.

5. AGNAHH 258, 1: 17–27.

6. Aug. 6, 1571, letter of Philip II to Viceroy Enríquez, MM 1: 18–21.

7. Don Vasco de Quiroga, Bishop of Michoacán (1538–1565), made the first of many such petitions; Alegre, 1: 100–2. See also F. Warren. Villaseca had also attempted to finance the coming of the Jesuits to Mexico and sent his brother in Spain 2,000 ducats to back up his petition; AGNAHH 258, 2; LB, p. 4.

8. MM 1: 5–6, 18–20. Pedro Sánchez had previously been provincial in the Spanish Jesuit province of Toledo, and Diego López had been rector of the Jesuit college in Córdoba; MM 1: 20–29.

9. AGNAHH 258, 1: 17–19; Alegre, 1: 107–14; Sánchez Baquero, pp. 34–39. The Jesuits crossed the Atlantic with the royal fleet (*flota*) during one of its regular departures. The normal trip between San Juan de Ulúa and Mexico City, by mule and carriage (in the Highlands) normally took twenty-two days, and during the rainy season up to thirty-five days; see Arcila Farías, p. 81. Details about offers of patronage made by leading members of New Spain society are also in ANCJM 264, 13.

10. Sánchez Baquero, p. 50.

11. Villaseca was usually careful to avoid public display in his works of charity. After his death documents were discovered showing that he had

donated over 400,000 pesos to religious and political causes; see Alegre 1: 275.

12. AGNAHH 258, 1: 19–20; LB, pp. 2–3; Alegre, 1: 122–23; Sánchez Baquero, pp. 49–50.

13. LB, p. 4; Alegre, 1: 123.

14. Don Alonso was one of three sons of Don Andrés de Villaseca and Doña Teresa Gutiérrez de Toranza, who lived in the small Spanish town of Aricola, in the diocese of Toledo. Francisco Cervantes de Salazar was Villaseca's cousin, and the letters he received provide insights about Villaseca's family; see *Cartas recibidas*, nos. 1, 4, 6, 51.

The exact date of Alonso de Villaseca's arrival in Mexico remains to be discovered. Earliest records of his business transactions in Mexico encountered were in 1542; AGNJ 3, 3. See also AGNAHH 258, 1: 19–20, 27–28; and Sánchez Baquero, pp. 49–50.

By 1580 Villaseca's haciendas reportedly produced annual incomes amounting to 150,000 ducados; AGNJ 3, 3: 259. For contemporary opinions about him, see *Cartas recibidas*, p. 22.

15. Alegre, 1: 274.

16. AGNAHH 258, 2 and 3; AGNJ 3, 3; Chevalier, *La formación*, pp. 96, 116–17.

17. Letter of Jesuit father general to Pedro Sánchez, March 8, 1573, MM 1: 65. Legal disputes between the Jesuits and the heirs of Alonso de Villaseca began the year after his death, in 1581, and continued over the next forty years; AGNAHH 258, 5; AGNJ 3, 3: 239–63.

18. Copies of these documents are in LB, pp. 3–4.

19. LB, p. 3.

20. Copies of the statutes of the society that applied to the Villaseca donation can be seen in AGNAHH 258, 6, and ANCJM 264, 13.

21. LB, p. 4.

22. Chevalier, *La formación*, Chap. 6, outlines the attempts made by the crown to provide safeguards against the usurpation of Indigenous properties. For a more general discussion of crown policy regarding the property rights of native communities, see Mörner, *La corona*.

23. Chevalier, *La formación*, p. 188, suggests that the Jesuits did not have clearly defined goals and objectives upon their arrival in New Spain. There is no documentary evidence to support this interpretation; see MM 1: 1–46.

24. Alegre, 1: 122–25, 128–29, 133–34, 138.

25. Sánchez Baquero, pp. 52–53.

26. Ibid., pp. 52–58; Villerías, fols. 20–22.

27. AGNAHH 258, 60; Alegre, 1: 152–56; Villerías, fols. 21–22.

28. Alegre, 1: 143–88, 37; Sánchez Baquero, pp. 168–92.

29. BNM 1087, 2–9; LB, pp. 1–80.

30. RCRVP 1, 478r–479v.

31. Sánchez Baquero, p. 90; Villerías, fol. 28.

32. AGNAHH 324, 1.

33. Alegre, 1: 191–192; Sánchez Baquero, pp. 110–11.

34. LB, p. 4.

35. These included, according to the Jesuit Constitutions, the necessity of the father general's passing judgment on any condition set by a found-

ing candidate when such conditions were not in accordance with set procedures; see Ganss, pp. 295, 329–30.

36. AGNAHH 258, 4 and 7; LB, p. 4.

37. Copies can be seen in the following sources: AGNAHH 258, 2; LB, p. 4; MM 1: 229–36.

38. November 1, 1573, letter of Mercurian (who replaced Borja in 1573) to Sánchez, MM 1: 87. The first visitador finally arrived in Mexico in 1579.

39. June 20, 1577, letter of Mercurian to Sánchez, MM 1: 278–82; instructions for Province, MM 1: 365–67; March 15, 1578, letter of Mercurian to Villaseca, MM 1: 372–73; MM 1: 363–65.

40. Representative panegyric treatments of Villaseca by Jesuit writers can be found in Alegre, 1: 273–74; Sánchez Baquero, pp. 160–62; and Villerías, fols. 27–28.

41. The owning of rural estates, although new to the Jesuits, was not an innovation for regular orders in New Spain. In the 1540s, the Dominicans in the Valley of Oaxaca owned rural estates; see Taylor, *Landlord*, p. 4.

42. LB, pp. 97–98.

43. On González, see PCRMR, 3 and 4, 12: 47; LB, pp. 431–39, 461–68. Crown ordinances formally forbade ecclesiastical purchase of rural properties. For a detailed discussion of such ordinances (1535–1579) and their application, see Chevalier, *La formación*, pp. 182–83. The purchase and donation dates are in LB, pp. 97–104.

44. Weights and measures were not standardized in New Spain immediately after the Conquest, or in Spain itself. Carrera Stampa, pp. 2–24, provides an overview of colonial developments. Royal instructions are surveyed in Galván Rivera. Chevalier, *La formación*, pp. 71–87, and Gibson, *Aztecs*, pp. 257–77, describe in detail the types and uses of units in New Spain.

45. LB, pp. 97–104.

46. The following overview is based on Gibson's studies, *Aztecs* and "Transformation," as well as the corpus of documentation relating to property titles surveyed in this study.

47. As Gibson succinctly summarized his data: "Direct Spanish influence was most pronounced at the upper levels of these hierarchies [of the municipal governments] . . . the titles and duties, the records kept, the legal forms, the *residencias*, the orders of procedure, were all of Spanish origin, and the office-holding Indian class adapted its political behavior to Spanish norms with regularity and persistence." "Transformation," pp. 588–89.

48. 18,851, according to Gerhard, GHGNS, p. 313, and 19,400 according to Gibson, *Aztecs*, p. 142.

49. GHGNS, pp. 210, 227, 298, 402; Gibson, *Aztecs*, p. 142.

50. Gibson, *Aztecs*, pp. 136 ff.

51. Ibid., p. 449. This epidemic affected all the Indian population but few Spaniards, and resulted in large numbers of deaths.

52. Gibson describes the Ponce de León encomienda of Tecama, ibid., pp. 426–27.

53. Gibson, ibid., pp. 257–99, provides a detailed overview of the Valley of Mexico land grants, and Chevalier, *La formación*, pp. 45–92, pro-

vides an overview for New Spain. Tepeatzingo, in Nahuatl, signifies location on a rocky hillock; *Nombres geográficos*, p. 159.

54. LB, p. 439.
55. See Chevalier, *La formación*, pp. 71–76, 95–109.
56. Gibson, *Aztecs*, p. 426.
57. LB, p. 440; Galván Rivera, and Chevalier, *La formación*, pp. 71–76, 95–109.

58. LB, pp. 440–41.   59. LB, pp. 441–55.
60. LB, pp. 95–104, 439–55.   61. *Nombres geográficos*, p. 136.
62. LB, pp. 456–57.   63. AGNM 9: 117; LB, pp. 459–60.
64. LB, pp. 459–64.   65. LB, p. 458.
66. AGNM 5: 196.   67. LB, pp. 67–68.
68. *Nombres geográficos*, pp. 97–98; LB, p. 427.
69. LB, pp. 427–29.
70. LB, pp. 431–39.
71. Rodríguez Camarra was a *teniente de alguacil mayor*, a law-enforcement officer.
72. LB, p. 433.
73. LB, 433–39.
74. Chevalier's analysis of Spanish acquisition of properties to create the haciendas in central and northern Mexico details procedures whereby crown officials took constant advantage of position to gain land for themselves and their friends (*La formación*, pp. 95–118), as does Gibson's analysis of events in the Valley of Mexico (*Aztecs*, pp. 270–99). The property titles of additional lands acquired by the Jesuits in the Valley of Mexico and elsewhere show the same pattern.
75. BNM 1087, 3: LB, pp. 95, 429, 465.
76. In this case González borrowed 2,000 pesos, with annual interest amounting to 143 pesos. As security for the loan he offered the six properties later sold to the Jesuits, plus all equipment and livestock associated with them; LB, pp. 468–70. For a discussion of the role of ecclesiastical bodies as money lenders see Lavrín, "Role."
77. Sánchez Baquero, p. 111.   78. LB, pp. 95–100.
79. LB, pp. 101–04, 468–70.   80. MM 2: 450 and 18–21.
81. In LB, pp. 95, 99, and 101, González is listed as a resident of Tecama. The reason given for the absence of his wife's name on the original document of sale was that she was at home in Tecama, whereas the documents were drawn up in Mexico City. LB, p. 438, lists González as a resident of Cuauhtitlán.
82. LB, pp. 95–104, 458.
83. LB, p. 95.
84. BNM 1087, 3; LB, p. 101.
85. González's brand was *un bozo por la cara y horcadas ambas orejas*; LB, p. 101.
86. Sánchez wrote about the purchase in two separate letters, dated in March and April 1577. Mercurian received the letters in early 1578 and responded in March of the same year. Copies of Sánchez's letters could not be located, but their contents are reflected in Mercurian's answers, MM 1: 368–70.

87. MM 1: 368, 370. The father general seems to have been aware of the clauses in the property titles that forbade sale to any ecclesiastical body. The procedures advised were in keeping with the Constitutions of the society; see Ganss, pp. 295–300, 324–28.

88. MM 1: 287–343; Alegre, 1: 512–28. These Provincial Congregations were held approximately every six years in Mexico. Between 1572 and 1763 thirty congregations were held by the Mexican province, the shortest time between meetings being twenty months, the longest nine years.

89. MM 1: 298–99.

90. MM 1: 324.

91. AGNAHH 324, 1, and MM 1: 324. Jesús del Monte remained under rental until 1583.

92. MM 1: 287–343, 414–16.

93. January 1579, MM 1: 415–16.

94. Mercurian apparently believed, or it had been reported to him, that Sánchez had gone into *compañía* with Villaseca—that is, had made a commercial contract equivalent to a company, a common practice in New Spain during the early colonial period. See Miranda, pp. 29–30, for an analysis of how such contracts functioned. The agreements between Villaseca and Sánchez involved nothing resembling economic partnership.

95. This conflict, which predated Jesuit ownership of Tepeatzingo, is thoroughly documented in PCRVP 1: 1–225.

96. AGNAHH 324, 1. For a more detailed discussion of the issue, see Chapters 3 and 7.

97. MM 1: 412–14, 414–16, 392–93, 363–65, 446–47.

98. MM 1: 447.

99. AGNAHH 258, 3; Alegre, 1: 273; LB, p. 7. Despite Villaseca's insistence on anonymity and his personal austerity, he made provisions for visible and auspicious remembrances after his passing. According to the contract made with the Jesuits in late 1579, Don Alonso was to be buried in the center of the chapel of the Colegio Máximo, in a sepulcher of marble, jasper, or another very good stone, adorned with his coat of arms and covered perpetually with a black velvet cloth with a white and red cross. During the masses to be said in his honor, his sepulcher was to be surrounded by six large, lighted candles. The Jesuits were obligated to maintain the chapel, buy the materials, and provide the remembrance ceremonies; LB, p. 7. Villaseca's funeral, of which there are a number of accounts, was a lavish affair entirely out of keeping with his life-style. His embalmed body was accompanied with great ceremony from Ixmiquilpan and lay in state at the shrine of the Virgin of Guadalupe for three days while preparations were being completed in Mexico City. Besides the Jesuits, clerics from the other regular orders, the archbishop and his council, the Mexico City cabildo, the audiencia, the viceroy, and private citizens vied for the right to pay the greatest honor and carry the coffin to its final resting place in the Jesuit chapel. In the end the viceroy had to intercede with the audiencia, on behalf of the Jesuits, to allow them the privilege. Fittingly, Pedro Sánchez preached the funeral sermon. AGNAHH 258, 1: 27–28; Alegre, 1: 273–74; Sánchez Baquero, pp. 160–61; Villerías, fols. 37–40; and Pérez de Rivas, pp. 80–88.

100. Plaza had been named by the father general as the next provincial prior to his arrival in New Spain; Alegre, 1: 251; MM 1: 426–30.
101. LB, pp. 477–78.
102. LB, pp. 471–73. The pretext used to move the Indians was that this would aid in their Christian instruction. For an analysis of crown congregation policies in the area, see Gibson, *Aztecs*, pp. 282–86, and Cline, "Civil Congregations."
103. LB, pp. 472–77; AGNT 11: 135r; PCRMR, 3, 4.
104. MM 2: 130–49, 219–23, 71–89, 211–12.
105. MM 2: 446–54. The most efficient means for the father general in Rome to implement policy change in New Spain appears to have been through the change of provincials who had received previous instructions.
106. MM 2: 2–7, 270–80; Alegre, 1: 277–473, 2: 1–266.
107. MM 1: 446–47.   108. April 1584, MM 2: 331–33.
109. MM 2: 270–80.   110. October 1584, MM 2: 380–98.
111. January 1585, MM 2: 432–42.
112. *Estado de las haciendas Santa Lucía y Jesús del Monte*, January 1585, MM 2: 446–48.
113. MM 2: 448.
114. MM 1: 298–99, 448–49.
115. There are 8 reales per peso. The price given for beef prices was ½ ducat per yearling, here being calculated at 11 reales per ducat. MM 2: 448.
116. GHGNS provides jurisdictional coverage of population losses. The regional impact of the epidemic is discussed by Gibson, *Aztecs*, pp. 203, 231, 246, 279, 326, and 449.
117. The mayordomo's role was custodial and supervisory, usually with limited decision-making capacity apart from the owners' instructions. See Chapter 6 for a more extensive treatment of this role.
118. García's biography is in DBCJM 7: 153–59.
119. DBCJM 2: 83, 100–2. In one case the father general had to intervene because Father Francisco Majano complained bitterly about being sent to rural estates; DBCJM 9: 86, 90–97.
120. DBCJM 2: 81–85.
121. DBCJM 2: 36, 39, 49, 55–57; 6: 256–60; 7: 619–21; 10: 707–64.
122. MM 2: 450.
123. Among those consulted by Mendoza was the viceroy himself, the position then being filled by Archbishop Pedro Moya de Contreras, who maintained a close friendship with the Jesuits; MM 2: 450.
124. MM 2: 451–54.
125. May 1585, MM 2: 450–51. As rector of the Colegio Máximo, the administration of all college property, including the hacienda, came under his jurisdiction. Díaz later became provincial of the Jesuit province and held other important administrative posts in the order. For his biography see DBCJM 6: 207–22.
126. MM 2: 274, 450–54.
127. The Second Provincial Congregation (November 2–9, 1585), like the first, was held in Mexico City but was shorter—eight days in contrast to eleven days. The shorter period required, despite the time between congregations and the great amount of society activity in the province, sug-

gests less contentious issues and more efficient internal organization. For the congregation report see MM 2: 628–42.

128. Response to Mendoza's report, February 1586, MM 2: 668–82. Response to congregation report, MM 2: 604–60.

129. MM 2: 145–46.

130. MM 2: 656. For a more detailed discussion of the administrative roles within the order, colleges, and haciendas, see Chapter 5.

131. Sánchez Baquero, p. 111.

Chapter 3

1. The same pattern of investing in rural estates in order to provide long-term financing for their educational institutions was adopted by the Jesuits in the viceroyalties of New Granada, La Plata, and Peru. See Colmenares, Gracía, and Macera, *Instrucciones*, pp. 6–49.

2. MM 1: 324.

3. LB, pp. 472–77; MM 2: 688.

4. Chevalier, *La formación*, pp. 116, 121–22; LB, p. 470.

5. MM 2: 448–49.

6. For the construction of the hacienda residence the Jesuits apparently used *repartimiento* labor supplied by the crown, on request, for college residence construction. The Jesuit definition of college residence seems to have included the hacienda residence; MM 3: 164–65 and 216. Description of the constructions is based on hacienda documents (although no useful map or plan of the complex was found); on descriptions by later owners in Romero de Terreros, pp. 39–43; airphoto maps from the 1950s; personal inspection of what remained in 1971; and a later visit in 1976. Since the area is now a military airport, access to what remains of the original residence is severely restricted. Military engineers discovered, besides the subterranean chambers, a series of tunnels under the casco, including human skeletons still chained in cells. Local folklore associates such human remains with the Jesuit period of ownership, which seems to me unlikely. Permission to inspect the casco and perhaps investigate this element of intrigue was denied for reasons of "military security."

7. The skeletal remains of mammoths were discovered under 1.3 meters of sediment in April 1976, located 2 kilometers east of the residence. The nature of the remains suggests drowning and water levels much higher than at the time of the Spanish Conquest of the valley.

8. The central residence part of the hacienda was so well and securely constructed in the sixteenth century that military engineers, when building airbase facilities in the twentieth century, maintained and incorporated the old casco as control tower and operations center of the military airport.

9. PCRVP 1: 490r–501r; Chevalier, *La formación*, p. 235.

10. Chevalier, *La formación*, pp. 45–92, and Gibson, *Aztecs*, pp. 300–67, provide an overview of types of hacienda production for the Highlands and the Valley of Mexico. Barrett and Taylor, *Landlords*, also provide useful details.

11. For example, Herrera's donation given "en limosna por amor de Dios," LB, p. 60.

12. Chevalier, *La formación*, pp. 95–114.

13. LB, pp. 600–604.
14. BNM 1087, 3; PCRVP 1: 245–46.
15. AGNM 17: 68v.
16. BNM 1087, 2.
17. Ibid., GHGNS, p. 157; Alegre, 1: 308–18; Chevalier, *La formación*.
18. BNM 1087, 2; Chevalier, *La formación*, pp. 109–18.
19. BNM 1087, 2.
20. Ibid., DBCJM 5: 160–61; PCRVP 2, nos. 17, 33. See Chapter 7 for a more detailed discussion of the dispute.
21. AGNM 16: 115, 128; 18: 20; 24: 116, BNM 1087, 2.
22. BNM 1087, 2; LB, pp. 631–35; PCRMR 3 and 4: 1–229.
23. González's will is dated 1587. Neither his death date nor that of his wife is indicated, but it is clear that both had died by 1591; PCRMR 3 and 4: 48–58.
24. BNM 1087, 2; PCRMR 3 and 4: 203–14.
25. LB, pp. 631–35; PCRMR 3 and 4: 26–42, 48 ff.
26. PCRMR 3 and 4: 203–4, 212 ff.
27. PCRMR 3 and 4: 213 ff., 221–22.
28. PCRMR 3 and 4: 222.
29. AGNT 2033, 1: 31; BNM 1087, 2.
30. The actual size of the plot, given as 10 by 20 *brazas* (1 braza equaling 2 *varas* or slightly less than 2 meters) would be roughly one-eighth of a hectare. The normal calculation for half a fanega of maize was 1.78 hectares of farmland. If the seed and size figures were correct, this would seem to have been exceptionally fertile land. AGNT 2033, 1; BNM 1087, 2.
31. BNM 1087, 2.
32. Sánchez Baquero, p. 111, indicates size of flocks and income.
33. For an overview of agriculture and livestock developments in New Spain during the period, see Bishko, Brand, Chevalier, *La formación*; Dusenberry, *Mexican Mesta*; Matesanz; Morrisey, "Colonial Agriculture," "Northward Expansion"; and Zavala, *De encomiendas*.
34. The Jesuit records concerning the case are in AGNAHH 324, 1.
35. DBCJM 1: 488–90, 500–501. Pedro Díaz's trip was financed by Alonso Villaseca.
36. AGNAHH 324, 1.
37. See pp. 69–71 and Chapter 7 for further details regarding the diezmo issue.
38. PCRRP, fols. 39r–40v; Gibson, *Aztecs*, p. 449.
39. For a general discussion see Dusenberry, *Mexican Mesta*, pp. 97–127; Chevalier, *La formación*, pp. 78–81.
40. PCRRP, fols. 47r–48v.   41. PCRRP, fols. 49v–50r.
42. AGNAHH 314, 25.   43. PCRVP 3, 28.
44. PCRRP, fols. 42r–v.
45. Cline, "Civil Congregations." For copies of royal cédulas issued for implementation, see CDHH, 2, 1, nos. 33–35. For the Valley of Mexico, see Gibson, *Aztecs*, pp. 282–88, including his Table 22, which lists affected towns.
46. Gibson, *Aztecs*, and GHGNS.
47. AGNM 24: 193; BNM 1087, 2; DBCJM 6: 609; 7: 412; 8: 271; PCRVP 1: 226.

48. BNM 1087, 2; PCRVP 2: 156.

49. AGNM 13: 28; PCRVP 2: 156; Gibson, *Aztecs,* pp. 282–87.

50. San Juan still exists as a dairy farm with 700 head of Holstein cows as of April 1976. Part of the sixteenth- and seventeenth-century constructions—the chapel, part of the troje, and walls surrounding the original main patio—remain as part of a construction which has been considerably altered.

51. BNM 1087, 2; LB, pp. 635–36.

52. The main residence of San Xavier, as of May 1976, was being converted into a hotel for tourists. The basic external shell of the Jesuit structure constructed in the sixteenth through eighteenth centuries remains intact, as do the patios, chapel, and some walls. Post-Jesuit and contemporary alterations, however, have lightened its somber, monastic, Jesuit character.

53. See Gibson, *Aztecs,* Plate XII, for a reproduction of a map detailing such losses, and his description of futile legal attempts to regain lost land, pp. 295–96.

54. AGNM 26: 233v; BNM 1087, 2; DBCJM 3: 412.

55. AGNM 24: 90v, 181v, and 720; BNM, 1087, 2.

56. BNM 1087, 2.

57. Ibid.; PCRMR, 3 and 4: 127r–138v.

58. BNM 1087, 2.

59. AGNM 84: 339; BNM 1087, 2.

60. BNM 1087, 2; DBCJM 3: 411; 4: 741.

61. AGNM 12: 140; 13: 171v, 203–4; BNM 1087, 2. Hortigosa had held the position of *juez repartidor* in Tepotzotlán in 1585.

62. AGNT 2033, 1: 35; BNM 1087, 2.

63. BNM 1087, 2.

64. AGNT 2033, 1: 57; 2205, 1; PCRVP 1: 621–23. The Spaniards were Pedro de los Ríos, secretary of the Holy Office of the Inquisition, and Pedro de Salazar, who served as *alcalde mayor* in a number of jurisdictions in the 1590s.

65. AGNM 33: 228; AGNT 2033, 1; BNM 1087, 2; PCRVP 1; 603.

66. BNM 1087, 2.

67. The averages used are based on given prices for Jesuit purchases and are therefore a small sample that may not be accurate in terms of values per se.

68. BNM 1087, 2; DBCJM 3: 411–12.

69. PCRRP, fol. 75r.

70. AGNM 33: 228; BNM 1087, 2; PCRVP 1: 451v–453r.

71. BNM 1087, 2; PCRVP 1: 449v–453v, 474r–476v.

72. BNM 1087, 2; PCRVP 1: 449v–453v, 474r–476v; GHGNS, pp. 111–14, 170–72, 316–18.

73. See Chevalier, *La formación.*

74. PCRVP 3, 28.

75. Specific reference is made to the *jueces de estancias y labores.* The special order applying to Santa Lucía was a copy of a more general order applying to rural estates, first issued in October 1612, and reissued in June 1616 and again in November 1619. PCRRP, fols. 100r–v.

76. PCRRP, fol. 75r.

77. Mathes, pp. 431–35.

78. DBCJM 3: 248–49.

79. Davidson provides an analysis of the extent of the problem and the particular case. For the Jesuit description see Alegre, 2: 175–83.

80. Shiels.

81. Leonard.

82. BMNM, Papeles Jesuitas, Carpeta 8: 7–8.

83. BNM 1087, 2.

84. BMNM, Papeles Jesuitas. Chevalier, *La formación*, p. 181, goes so far as to make the claim that at the beginning of the seventeenth century most of the wills of nobles, wealthy miners, and merchants had provisions to leave funds to the Jesuits.

85. DBCJM 6: 286–88; Alegre, 2: 184–94.

86. For a less sympathetic description of the wealth of ecclesiastical establishments in New Spain during the time, see *Thomas Gage's Travels*.

87. PCRRP, fol. 75r.

88. This figure has been obtained by assuming an average cost of 150 pesos for 62 caballerías and 441.6 pesos for 27 *sitios de ganado menor* while making allowances for the sale of 1.5 sitios which resulted in a 1,000 peso reduction in total costs.

89. AGNM 9: 190v; DBCJM 3: 411.

90. PCRVP 1, 2: 279–83.

91. PCRVP 1, 2: 450r–452r, 275r–276v.

92. PCRMR 3 and 4: 79r–85v; AGNM 12: 1420; DBCJM 3: 411; 5: 160.

93. PCRVP 3: 1–22.

94. DBCJM 3: 411; 5: 160–61; PCRVP 2, 17.

95. PCRVP 1: 453v–454v, 477r–v.

96. For a broader discussion of property-regulation policies see Chevalier, *La formación*, pp. 265–77.

97. Jesuit copies of these cédulas are in PCRVP 1, 2: 312r–315v.

98. Two accounts of these proceedings have been located, in AGNM 51: 5–24 and PCRVP 1, 2: 308v–338r.

99. PCRVP 1, 2: 311r.

100. AGNM 51: 13. The consensus of the commission was based in part upon the state of legal order of the Jesuit papers, in part upon their special relationship with the crown. The officials representing royal authority included an *oidor* (judge) from the audiencia, a royal *fiscal* (attorney or prosecutor), a *contador* (accountant) from the *tribunal de cuentas* (tribunal of accounts), the treasurer of the *caja real* (royal funds), a *contador de reales alcabalas* (royal sales tax accountant), and an *alcalde del crimen* (justice of crimes) from the audiencia.

101. AGNM 51: 5–24; PCRVP 1, 2: 323–28.

102. For a recent attempt to evaluate the literature on this famous dispute, see Simmons.

103. For a breakdown of the Palafox figures, see DBCJM 4: 526–27.

104. ANCJM 264, 6. During the 1620s the Jesuits had bested the secular clergy in a drawn-out legal case on the diezmo issue; AGNAHH 297, 2.

105. See pp. 53–54 and AGNAHH 324, 1: 3.

106. Documents detailing the Jesuit reaction to Palafox's charges are summarized in Alegre, 3: 412–57; DBCJM 3: 415–18; 8: 116–64.

107. AGNAHH 322, 17.

108. A copy of the cédula is reproduced in Alegre, 3: 456–57.

109. The earliest Santa Lucía records referring to actual payment of tithe indicate a date of 1688 (AGNAHH 258, 20), although the Council of the Indies instructed diezmo payments as early as 1655 (AGNAHH 297, 2).

110. DBCJM 4: 526–27; provincial's report entitled *Estado económico de la provincia mexicana en 1644*, reproduced in Alegre, 3: 342–43.

111. J. Riley, "Management," p. 21, has additional information on internal financial matters of the Colegio Máximo.

112. Alegre, 3: 1–144, provides a chronological survey of Jesuit institutional growth in the Mexican province during the period.

113. Alegre, 3: 342–43.

Chapter 4

1. Chevalier, *La formación*, Gibson, *Aztecs*, pp. 257–99, and Simpson, *Exploitation*, provide insightful and useful sketches of the processes of takeover for New Spain as a whole and, in particular, the Valley of Mexico. For statistical breakdowns of populations see Cook and Borah, vol. 1, and GHGNS.

2. Gibson, *Aztecs*, pp. 136 ff., has a detailed breakdown for the Valley of Mexico; see his Figures 3–6 and Tables 10 and 11.

3. Gibson, *Aztecs*, pp. 173–99, demonstrates that pueblos in the valley were relatively helpless to withstand the Spanish takeover; whereas Taylor, *Landlord*, and Osborn, *Community*, demonstrate that, in the Valleys of Metztitlán and Oaxaca, native communities retained sizable areas. The question of land ownership, however, cannot be clarified by looking merely at the size of areas concerned. Of far greater importance were the type, location, and productivity of the land in question, and the ability to market the produce of the land.

4. Chevalier, *La formación*, pp. 145–78.

5. See also Chapter 7.

6. Borah, *New Spain's Century*.

7. AGNT 231 and 237; Chevalier, *La formación*, pp. 197–98; J. Riley, "Management," pp. 13–26.

8. DBCJM 4: 531.

9. November 1659, letter from father general to Mexican provincial, DBCJM 4: 212. For an analysis of the Xochimancas sugar hacienda, see Berthe.

10. See Appendix V, "Agricultural Conditions," in Gibson, *Aztecs*, pp. 454–55.

11. AGNAHH 299, 31 and 32.

12. *Inventariales de la hacienda de Santa Lucía y anexas. Recibos mensuales*, BNM 1058, 1: 1–22.

13. Ewald, pp. 103–09, surveys Tehuacán's early history.

14. AGNAHH 285, 33; 307, 14; 329, 6: 6r–v; BNM 1058, 1: 105, 112, 116, 123, 138, 149; PCRD, fol. 73r. Urban centers purchasing Tehuacán products were Tehuacán, Puebla, Córdoba, and Orizaba. See also Ewald, pp. 103–9.

15. Chevalier, *La formación*, pp. 117–18.

16. AGNT 2033, 1: 29–39; PCRMR 2, 1: 1–54v.

17. For information about the production of Altica see Chapter 9.

18. Activities of the Rivadeneira period of ownership are in AGNT 2033, 1: 29–39; PCRMR 2.

19. AGNAHH 285, 33 and 35.

20. These herds of mares, which varied from twenty-five to fifty-five animals per manada, usually were named, but sizes were not consistently given in the hacienda records. The average of forty has been derived from herds where numbers of animals were given. The average is used to calculate numbers of mares. What has not been determined is whether herd sizes differed in other parts of New Spain, since the sample used here is restricted to the northern perimeters of the Valley of Mexico. AGNAHH 285, 33.

21. Cf. Chevalier, *La formación,* pp. 76–84; Gibson, *Aztecs,* pp. 304 ff.

22. AGNAHH 285, 33; 307, 27.

23. These figures are based on figures given as *fanega de sembradura,* or the amount of land seeded by a fanega. The dimensions used are the following: for wheat and barley, 0.6 fanegas per hectare (1.5 per acre); for maize, 1 fanega per 3.57 hectares (8.8 acres); and for beans and peas, 1 fanega per 1.2–2 hectares (3–5 acres). For discussion of the *fanega de sembradura* see Carrera Stampa; Gibson, *Aztecs,* pp. 309–11, 323, 551–53, nn. 39 and 48; and Galván Rivera, pp. 105 ff.

24. Santa Lucía 1681 figures are in AGNAHH 285, 33.

25. AGNT 2033, 1: 10v–19v; PCRMR 1. See Appendix A.

26. PCRMR 1, 11: 1–42r.

27. PCRMR 1, 11: 7v–8r. Bartolomé and Diego Moreno sold the hacienda to Fuertes on February 28, 1685.

28. PCRMR 1, 11: 9v–12r.

29. PCRMR 1, 11: 24r–42r.

30. Concepción is still a functioning hacienda, in 1976 devoted largely to pulque production. Until recently it also had a dairy and still has roughly 100 residents (including workers and their families). Parts of the structures dating back to Jesuit ownership still remain, including surrounding walls, parts of the residence structure (patios, chapel), and a large water reservoir. The exterior dimensions of the enclosure are roughly 150 by 300 meters.

31. AGNAHH 286, 44, and 313, 17; Payno.

32. DMCJM 5: 433; 9: 538–39.

33. AGNAHH 313, 17.

34. Gemelli Carreri, 1: 141. See also Gibson, *Aztecs,* p. 280, and Romero de Terreros, pp. 41–43.

35. Gemelli Carreri 1: 141. According to Santa Lucía records, the number of sheep in 1697 was 66,509; AGNAHH 313, 17. At no point in its history did Santa Lucía have 10,000 cattle and oxen. Its maximum number of goats was 53,343; AGNAHH 285, 33. See Chapter 10 for a more detailed discussion of slave policies and practices.

36. For a discussion of regulations in Mexico, see Dusenberry, *Mexican Mesta.* Iberian practices are dealt with by Bishko.

37. AGNAHH 329, 6. This basic pattern was established early in the colonial epoch and changed hardly at all. Descriptions of the structure of

Alonso González's flocks in the 1560s are essentially the same as those for the Jesuit flocks of 1751; LB, p. 465, and AGNTe 20, 3. See Chapters 8 and 9 for more details about Santa Lucía sheep management.

38. AGNAHH 329, 6.

39. AGNAHH 314, 35; AGNTe 20, 3.

40. PCRD, fols. 70r–72r.

41. PCRD, fols. 77r–79r. The Cuautepec hacienda itself was never considered a part of Santa Lucía, but at times some of its pastures were used by sheep from Santa Lucía.

42. AGNT 2033, 1: 56v–62r.

43. PCRVP 1, 9: 290.

44. PCRVP 1: 543. Baltasar de la Cadena, in 1607, was corregidor of Coatepec and in 1614 was listed as a resident of Mexico City; AGNM 25: 222r–v and 436v.

45. The properties being included in this calculation consist of the *sitios de ganado menor* and *mayor* which were a part of Santa Lucía as of 1681. For the listing, see the Appendix.

46. The Jesuits also referred to this transaction as a donation on the part of Miranda Villaysan; DCBJM 5: 426. According to Chevalier, *La formación*, pp. 164–65, Miranda Villaysan used his position of power to become one of the largest landowners in northern Mexico. The Jesuit records of the case are in PCRVP 1, 2. Also see Appendix A.

47. PCRVP 1, 2: 260–62.

48. Colegio Máximo administrators described their sugar haciendas as nothing more than costly burdens at the time; AGNAHH 329, 6. For an overview of one of the largest Jesuit sugar estates in Mexico see Berthe; see Barrett for regional markets and conditions.

49. AGNAHH 329, 6: 6v.

50. AGNAHH 307, 8. J. Riley, "Management," p. 53, notes that this hacienda was heavily mortgaged when purchased by the Jesuits. Riley computes the total cost of the hacienda, by the time all debts were retired, as 230,000 pesos.

51. AGNAHH 286, 44, and 329, 6.

52. AGNAHH 307, 8. See Appendix A for a more detailed listing and description.

53. Post-purchase justifications are derived from reports of Joaquín Donazar (1735), AGNAHH 329, 6: 6r–v; (1739), AGNAHH 286, 44: 30v–31v. Santa Lucía administrative records show the goat ranch as part of Santa Lucía three years after the purchase of the new haciendas; BNM 1058, 1: 139. Negotiations for acquisition were made by Juan Nicolás, Donazar's predecessor.

54. A document outlining the pre-Jesuit legal history of these properties has much useful detail regarding the formation, assimilation, and repeated transfers of the properties; *Composición con S. M. de las haciendas de Chicavasco, Tepenene y la Florida*, PCRVP 3, 18: 63–92.

55. PCRVP 3, 18.

56. BNM 1058, 1: 144; AGNT 2033, 1: 39v–44r; AGNAHH 307, 8; PCRVP 3, 18.

57. BNM 1058, 1: 144–45. While attempting to visit the hacienda in April 1976, I was told it still existed but a road passable by motor vehicles

still needed to be constructed; a day's journey by horse or mule, from Actopan, is required to reach Florida.

58. AGNT, 2033, 1: 24 ff.; BNM 1058, 1: 144; PCRVP 3, 18.

59. Parts of the Tepenene casco were still extant in 1976, including the chapel, walls of the granary, and remnants of residence and corral constructions. The casco is now part of the pueblo of Tepenene, the chapel a Protestant church, the granary divided into the backyards of contemporary residences, and the colonial walls serving other than livestock functions. Outside the granary, built in the colonial era to store cereal crops (but within the former hacienda enclosure), rudimentary tree cribs for maize storage are still used—a silent comment on Indigenous reabsorption of colonial haciendas.

60. AGNT 2033, 1: 39v.

61. AGNAHH 307, 8; AGNT 2033, 1: 29r–v.

62. At Chicavasco, as in the case of most of the cascos of the anexas of Santa Lucía, former wooded slopes are no longer wooded except by shrubs, cacti, and the occasional recently planted tree.

63. AGNAHH 286, 44; BNM 1058, 1: 150–206. The outer shells of the Chicavasco casco still remain, of which the most impressive is the enormous roofless granary. The chapel and residence sections are completely in ruins, but many of the walls of corrals and of storage and processing facilities still stand, mostly without roofs. The old casco currently serves as a residence for a number of families and is separated accordingly into adjoining, separate units. The pueblo of Chicavasco has regained its status and is a town of considerable population.

64. Time proved the Jesuit judgment to be excellent, since the land values of parts of these, later devoted to maguey plantings, rose in the 1770s to values of 2,500 pesos per caballería. For a detailed breakdown of property values, maguey plantings, and later use, see *Testimonio de la escritura de venta de las haciendas de Santa Lucía y anexas que fueron del Colegio Máximo de San Pedro y San Pablo,* private library of the late Don Manuel Romero de Terreros, Mexico City.

65. AGNAHH 329, 6: 12.

66. Alegre, 4: 168–355, surveys the expansion and lists numerous people who wished to become Jesuit patrons, plus reasons for accepting or rejecting the offers. Jesuit lists of their rural estates and the colleges they pertained to, plus the missions they supported, are in AGNAHH 297, 2, and 329, 6.

67. AGNT 2033, 1: 44v–56v; PCRVP 1, 2: 294–95. Tulancalco originally was one of the native estancias of Ayacuba and lost its pueblo status during the implementation of congregation policies around 1600. It subsequently became the administrative center of the mayorazgo of Murilla, which the Jesuits later rebuilt into a substantial residence complex; GHGNS, p. 299. Tulancalco is now, again, a native pueblo.

68. AGNT 2033, 1: 44v–49v.

69. AGNAHH 286, 44; 307, 8; AGNT 2033, 1: 49v–56v.

70. AGNAHH 286, 44: 13v, 30v–39r; 329, 6: 6v–r; BNM 1058, 1: 154.

71. AGNT 2033, 1: 54v–55r.

72. AGNAHH 307, 8; see also Appendix A.

73. AGNAHH 286, 44; BNM 1058, 1.

74. These haciendas received greater attention from J. Riley, "Management," pp. 81–86, 351.

75. AGNAHH 293, 2; and 313, 17. These numbers refer to the young stock produced, which was tithed, not necessarily the animals that were sold in a given year. See Chapter 8 for additional details.

76. The sum is obtained by using values of the production at the time, provided in AGNAHH 293, 2.

77. AGNAHH 286, 44: 11.

78. AGNAHH 286, 44: 38r. These are figures provided by Joaquín Donazar for the father general in his futile attempt to justify his financial administration. The numbers must be treated with caution, since Donazar habitually exaggerated. Santa Lucía livestock, however, had reached new highs. My estimates for the year would show over 130,000 sheep, over 30,000 goats, 5,600–6,000 horses and mules, and 4,000–5,000 cattle—a total of almost 180,000 head of livestock. See Chapter 8 for details on sizes and production.

79. AGNAHH 286, 44; 297, 2; and 298, 1.

80. For a report from the Jesuit side of the controversy, see AGNAHH 297, 2.

81. One of the results was that Donazar lived in virtual exile from Mexico City for a number of years. In 1737 he was still complaining bitterly that his superiors were not pursuing his case with adequate vigor. A series of his letters in September and October 1737 deal with the diezmo conflict; AGNAHH 298, 1. He discusses other deals that created enemies in AGNAHH 286, 44.

82. AGNAHH 286, 44: 10v–11r.

83. AGNAHH 298, 1; and 307, 8. In another source, the purchase price is given as 50,219 pesos, which includes improvements and the value of livestock placed on it; AGNAHH 286, 44: 14r.

84. AGNAHH 286, 45.

85. AGNAHH 307, 8; BNM 1058, 1: 99–206.

86. AGNAHH 286, 44: 2v–3r.

87. Agustín Guerrero de Luna, son-in-law of Alonso de Villaseca, had owned the estate in the sixteenth century.

88. AGNT 1413, 2: 345, identifies the mayorazgo and the Rancho de Loreto. For San Nicolás, see AGNAHH 314, 35. For the rental of San Jerónimo y San Nicolás, see AGNAHH 286, 44: 36r–v. The Ixmiquilpan properties refer to Xante, AGNAHH 293, 2.

89. AGNAHH 297, 3.

90. The longest rental contract encountered was for nine years; two-year contracts appear to have been more common; AGNAHH 314, 35; PCRVP 3, 21. J. Riley, "Management," pp. 62–63, found rentals for Xoloc in 1729 and 1739, for Provincia in the 1730s, and for Santa Lucía (Tepeatzingo) in 1733.

91. AGNAHH 299, 4.

92. PCRVP 3, 21.

93. For a partial listing of these disputes see Appendix B and J. Riley, "Management," pp. 101–38.

94. Renter lists can be seen in AGNAHH 299, 4; PCRVP 1: 514–46.

95. See Chapter 7 for my discussion of the problem.

96. See Chapter 8 for a detailed breakdown of production.

97. Comprehensive documentation of this administration resulted during a prolonged legal dispute presented by Villaverde after the expulsion of the Jesuits; AGNTe 20, 83 and 205.

98. In a 1764 memorial, Fr. Diego González challenges the viceroy to examine his own conscience regarding moral questions related to pulque manufacture and sale. He does not mention the Jesuits directly, referring instead to those Jesuits who had been leading opponents of pulque, such as Francisco de Florencia, confessor of Philip II, and Bartolomé Castano, in the seventeenth century; BMNM, Fondo Franciscano, Carpeta 28, 81.

99. Payno provides an overview of pulque production in the *mesa central* for the colonial period.

100. Gibson, *Aztecs,* p. 396.

101. Payno, pp. 72–92, reproduces a copy of the Jesuit response, plus reactions from secular academic sectors. See also DBCJM 3: 410.

102. AGNAHH 299; BNM 1058, 1: 99–206; PCRVP 1: 514–45. For more details on pulque production see Chapter 8.

103. ANCJM 264, 32–38; AGNAHH 312.

104. In AGNT 2033, 1: 1134 ff., a breakdown of income and expenditures for Santa Lucía during 1769–1773 is listed in the accompanying table.

TABLE TO NOTE 104

Santa Lucía Income and Expenditures, 1769–1773

(Pesos and reales)

Year	Gross income	Expenses	Net income
1769	83,611.5	38,917.7	45,543.6
1770	79,459.3	37,144.3	42,315.0
1771	63,833.5	38,552.6	25,380.7
1772	58,830.4	34,930.2	23,900.2
1773	71,718.5	39,033.7	36,684.5

105. For a discussion of this point in detail, see Chapter 12.

106. Chevalier, *La formación;* Colmenares; Gracía; and Macera, *Instrucciones.*

107. The 1620 figures are based on Gibson's calculations, *Aztecs,* p. 277. The maximum dimension includes, here, an estimate of accessible pasture lands as well as property for which title was held.

108. Included in this figure are sums for buildings, livestock, and equipment, in some cases; but for others the amount paid for land has not been determined. See Appendix A.

109. Although the official designations of pasture versus agricultural lands were never respected, in practice they remain useful indices of land quality at the time of merced.

110. See Taylor, "Haciendas coloniales" and "Landed Society"; and González Sánchez.

111. See Harris, and Chevalier, "North Mexican Hacienda."
112. Harris, pp. 79–93; Taylor, "Haciendas coloniales," pp. 309–21.
113. The percentage of land area devoted to pulque production derives from a calculation of 120 square kilometers of maguey plantings in comparison to acquisitions totaling 2,725.1 square kilometers.
114. The reference here is to Toltec and Aztec explanations of the origin and significance of pulque, and the deities associated with it. See Gonçalves de Lima, and Payno, pp. 6–8.

Chapter 5

1. This theme permeates every section of the founding document of the Jesuit order, its Constitutions (CSJ).
2. Jesuit organizational structure has been the subject of much study. The best sources remain the primary documents published in the monumental 100-volume series, *Monumenta historica Societatis Jesu*, from which have been translated Loyola's autobiography (edited by Olin), containing the first sketch of Jesuit organization, and an annotated version of its Constitutions (translated by Ganss). Other useful sources are Espinosa Pólit, Brodrick, Foss, Ganss, Hughes, Jacobsen, and Popescu.
3. Olin.
4. CSJ, 326–27.
5. CSJ, 178.
6. The father general dealt with all points raised by the provincial congregations, and all matters concerning concessions and privileges involving the crown and papal offices; see MM.
7. See Chapters 3, 4, 8, and 9.
8. CSJ, 207.
9. See Chapter 9.
10. For details, see Chapters 6 and 9.
11. CSJ, 241, 66, 102. "To Request and to Command, each is good, nevertheless, . . . one is aided more by being commanded than by being requested."
12. CSJ, 128.
13. CSJ, 112.
14. Examples of this include Juan Turrado, whose good works and humility earned his entry into the society a few hours before he died; Marcos García, a Santa Lucía administrator who insisted upon lowly offices despite a father general's permit for him to choose higher offices; and Juan Nicolás, a Colegio Máximo procurador renowned for his devout piety. BMNM, Papeles Jesuitas, 8; 7–8 and 17r–v; AGNAHH 329, 12.

15. Olin, p. 109.   16. CSJ, 242.
17. CSJ, 324.   18. CSJ, 325.
19. AGNAHH 312, 13.   20. CSJ, 292–93.
21. CSJ, 293.   22. CSJ, 208.

23. CSJ, 208–9. "When these hours ought to be changed because of the seasons or other unusual reasons, the rector or the one in charge should consider the matter and what he orders should be observed."
24. Ayudantes and sobresalientes, when they functioned on behalf of or in place of mayordomos, kept accounts and made reports to the hacien-

da administrator. When they functioned under the supervision of the mayordomo they reported orally to him.

25. AGNAHH 258, 9. The published version was edited by Chevalier, *Instrucciones a los Hermanos* (IHAH).

26. For copies of actual accounts, see AGNAHH 258, 299, 313, and 329; BNM 1058, 1059, and 1087; LB; PCR.

27. IHAH, pp. 177–79. For copies of letters see AGNAHH 288, 298, and 312; for copies of receipts and other papers, AGNAHH 293, 307, and 324.

28. IHAH, pp. 178–79.

29. Berthe, pp. 107–17; AGNAHH 299, 4: 40–45.

30. Macera, *Instrucciones,* pp. 24–27, identifies numerous sets of instructions applying to Jesuit haciendas in Peru, as did Popescu, pp. 161 ff., for Paraguay.

31. Regarding the tithe issue, see also Chapters 3, 4, and 7.

32. CSJ, 313.

33. CSJ, 314.

34. Chevalier, *La formación,* and Dusenberry, *Mexican Mesta,* provide information regarding legislation concerning livestock regulations. Chapters 2–4 provide examples in the case of Santa Lucía. For discussion of general impact upon New Spain, see Zavala and Miranda.

35. See Chapter 2.

36. PCRVP 1: 449r–450v, 474r–475r.

37. For examples, see Chapters 2–4.

38. AGNAHH 314, 35.   39. AGNAHH 314, 35.

40. AGNAHH 314, 28.   41. See Chapter 7.

42. A copy of the contract between Villaverde and the Colegio Máximo is in AGNAHH 312, 13. The legal arguments upon which Villaverde based his case against the ex-Jesuit properties are in AGNTe 205, 5.

43. AGNAHH 299, 4: 7v.

44. Examples are evident in AGNAHH 297, 1–3.

45. AGNAHH 329, 1.

46. Espinosa Pólit, p. 29.

Chapter 6

1. Report of Ignacio Padilla, 1764, AGNAHH 286, 45.

2. Chevalier, *La formación.*

3. Taylor, *Landlord,* p. 122, and "Haciendas coloniales."

4. Gibson, *Aztecs,* pp. 57, 131, 181–82, 260.

5. During the seventeenth and eighteenth centuries, the estates were being operated by entrepreneurial, professional renters; Barrett, pp. 11–24.

6. Villaverde and his sons continued as administrators of Santa Lucía after its purchase by the Conde de Regla; AGNT 1560: 1–119.

7. See Table 3.

8. AGNAHH 298, 1, contains a sample of 115 letters, from 1746, written to the Colegio Máximo procurador from distant centers. The largest number, 31, were from the port of Veracruz.

9. The recommendations, in this case, were from a rector in León and

a procurador in Veracruz, and involved what must have been a year's supply of cacao—2,500 pesos worth—which was purchased from Guatemalan
rather than Caracas sources; AGNAHH 298, 1.

10. Nieto's biography can be found in DBCJM 10: 103–13.

11. For Turrado's biography, see BMNM, Papeles Jesuitas, 8: 7–8.

12. For their biographies, see BMNM, Papeles Jesuitas, 8: 16r–71v;
DBCJM 7: 153–59.

13. BMNM, Papeles Jesuitas, 8: 17r–v; DBCJM 7: 153–59.

14. BMNM, Papeles Jesuitas, 8: 16r–17r.

15. For their biographies see DBCJM 3: 248–52 and 254–62.

16. DBCJM 3: 249.

17. DBCJM 3: 248.

18. Although no copy of this document could be located, it must have
been one of the early, principal sources of the Instrucciones; see DBCJM 3:
248.

19. DBCJM 3: 254–62.

20. For his biography see DBCJM 7: 138; also Sánchez Baquero.

21. Mathes, pp. 431–32.

22. DBCJM 5: 159–61.

23. DBCJM 5: 160; PCRVP 2, 17. Types of authority delegated were
discussed in Chapter 5.

24. The training procedures were outlined in the Constitutions. The
career biographies of priests and hermanos confirms these trends. See
DBCJM, vols. 1–10.

25. These data come primarily from DBCJM, vols. 1–10.

26. Some coadjutores, despite their transgressions, managed to remain members of the society. The example of Hermano Juan Martín, who
worked on Colegio Máximo rural estates, indicates tolerance rather than
strict adherence to the rules. Brother Martín apparently had an affair with
a married woman *(mestiza casada)* from the Xalmolonga sugar hacienda.
About the same time he reported having witnessed a miracle in the hacienda chapel, having seen the statue of the Virgin Mary break out in a
sweat. The father general deliberated both aspects and instructed Brother
Martín's dismissal in 1652, but no immediate action was taken. Four years
later such instructions were repeated, and as late as 1668 the father general
commented in his correspondence to the Mexican provincial about the es-
capades *(salidas nocturnas)* of Brother Martín and two other members of the
society. DBCJM 9: 223–24.

27. DBCJM 8: 376, 405–6, 434, 586.

28. DBCJM 3: 782; 4: 332–33; 6: 256–60; 8: 397–98, 427–28, 452; 9: 511.

29. According to Palafox, in the 1640s the Jesuits in Mexico consisted
of 230 *hermanos coadjutores* and 312 others; *Carta*, p. 108.

30. *Carta*, pp. 112–14.

31. DBCJM, vols. 1–10, provides the information for the early period
and Zelis's catalogue, pp. 234–93, the data for the later period.

32. DBCJM 1: 523–29.

33. DBCJM 8: 744–51.

34. DBCJM 2: 207–15.

35. DBCJM 7: 347–52; PCRRP, fol. 47r.

36. Alegre, 1: 36, 250–53, 277, 283, 303, 513–14, 534–40.

37. This was the book of titles that became known as the *Libro becerro*, consisting of notarized copies of titles usable as legal evidence in case of disputes over property.

38. DBCJM 4: 741; PCRRP, fol. 100r; PCRVP 1: 450v–53v and 475r.

39. DBCJM 6: 47–57; 7: 284–94; 8: 270–73.

40. DBCJM 8: 270–73.

41. DBCJM 6: 47–57.

42. See pp. 73–75.

43. PCRMR 2, 1: 1–54; 3; and 4: 79r–85v.

44. AGNAHH 258, 11, and 285, 33; PCRMR 2, 1: 1–54; 3; and 4: 79r–85v.

45. AGNAHH 285, 33, 1.

46. AGNAHH 329, 12.

47. In 1723, college debts were 225,000 pesos; AGN, Historia 392, cited by J. Riley, "Management," p. 22.

48. Authorities listed as including the *consejo real, alcalde de crimen,* and *juez de provincia.*

49. In his introductory remarks to the Instrucciones, pp. 9–14, Chevalier attempts to date the original document, coming to the conclusion that its author's handwriting coincides with late seventeenth-century and early eighteenth-century script; that it includes no reference to published materials after 1712, and cites a litigation of 1722. All these pieces of evidence would support the authorship of Juan Nicolás.

50. AGNAHH 329, 12. *Breve apuntamiento . . . acerca del buen proceder del difunto Hermano Juan Nicolás de la Compañía de Jesús.* Xalmolongo was involved in serious land disputes with the pueblo of Malinalco and its dependent barrios. J. Riley, "Management," pp. 126–32, describes the conflict in detail.

51. PCRVP 2, 14.

52. The Florida, Chicavasco, and Tepenene purchases were initiated by Juan Nicolás but concluded by Donazar, who accelerated the expansionist trend started by his predecessor. See Chapter 4 for details.

53. Letter, July 23, 1737, AGNAHH 298, 1.

54. Letter, October 26, 1737, AGNAHH 298, 1.

55. Donazar refers to his own activities in twenty-eight letters written in 1737; AGNAHH 298, 1.

56. See Chapters 4 and 7 regarding expansion policies and conflicts; AGNAHH 286, 44 and 45; BMNM, Jesuitas 1566–1821, 332; PCRRP, fols. 101r–106v; and PCRVP 2: 214r–312v.

57. Letter, April 16, 1736, AGNAHH 286, 45.

58. Letter, September 1737, AGNAHH 298, 1.

59. PCRVP 1: 514 ff.

60. J. Riley, "Management," pp. 376–80, lists the administrators for the Colegio Máximo haciendas not associated with Santa Lucía. His reliance upon correspondence terminology rather than the province's formal membership lists results in classifying numerous *hermanos coadjutores* as padres. Although a common trend in the correspondence, such designations were frequently incorrect.

61. PCRVP 1: 514v–546v. Miers arrived at this figure by calculating the number of pulque renters under Lascano's control and comparing income received versus that called for in the formal contracts.

62. Miers produced a report in 1745 in which he listed the transgressions; PCRVP 1: 514v–546v.

63. Prior to Miers's administration, annual income was 5,882 pesos; PCRVP 1: 522v–524v.

64. AGNAHH 299, 4, 1: 4.

65. An attempt had even been made to sell San Juan, but no satisfactory agreement was reached regarding price; BNM 1058, 1: 180.

66. BNM 1058, 1: 180.

67. Letters, July 14 and 16, 1746, AGNAHH 298, 1. The Jesuits had audiencia authorization to impound any livestock damaging their crops or pastures, the owners of which were to be assessed a 500 peso fine.

68. IHAH, pp. 125–26.

69. AGNAHH 288, 1, and 312, 13; AGNTe 205, 5.

70. Villaverde's working arrangements are indicated in AGNTe 20, 2. For copies of the contracts see AGNAHH 312, 13.

71. Villaverde's will provides biographical information; AGNTe 205, 5. Don Pedro was born in Tlalpuxagua, the silver-mining center in Michoacán, 112 kilometers west of Valladolid. His father, Don Juan de Villaverde, had come from Spain (Rioja, Castile) late in the seventeenth century and married Doña Micaela de Muñoz, from Tlalpuxagua. Villaverde's regular residence was at his hacienda near Tetepango, called San Joseph de Batta. He also owned another hacienda called San Sebastián, but how he acquired these estates is not indicated. His wife, Doña Francesca Xaviera, died in 1753. Their children included one girl, Francesca Xaviera, and three boys, Francisco Antonio, Juan Ignacio, and Pedro Joseph.

72. BNM 1058, 1: 198. The furnishings of the room indicate it was a bedroom. Since Santa Lucía was one day's journey from Mexico City and the Jesuits normally had excellent relations with the viceroy, it would not be out of place for the royal official to stay there overnight during trips to and from his capital.

73. This special relationship can be noted in the correspondence, which includes frequent reference to domestic matters, such as the health of relatives and other nonbusiness comments.

74. Villaverde's correspondence between 1750 and 1764 is substantial, including 943 items in AGNAHH 288, 1, and 312, 12.

75. Thadeo Rosales, a *hermano coadjutor* who had been Miers's assistant at Santa Lucía (1743–1745), was the son of one of the mayordomos of San Xavier, Pedro Rosales.

76. AGNAHH 288, 1, and 312, 12.

77. See Chapter 8 for a more detailed description of hacienda production. Reported profits during the 1751–1763 period are in AGNT 1560, 4.

78. Letter, March 2, 1764, AGNAHH 312, 13.

79. Letter, April 14, 1764, AGNAHH 312, 13.

80. The dispute is well documented, providing additional information about general conditions of the period; AGNTe 20, 83 and 205.

81. Annual lists of Colegio Máximo personnel and positions occupied after 1746 are in AGNAHH 329, 3.

82. This is also reflected in the correspondence of the higher officials of the college during the period; AGNAHH, 297, 1–3.

83. Biographical data on individuals is included in Zelis's catalogue; pp. 231–93; BNMN, fondo Franciscano, carpeta 11.

Chapter 7

1. For example, the Yaqui missions, where the Jesuit mission impact resulted in a distinct Yaqui-Christian culture opposed to the rest of hispanized Mexican society; see Alegre, 2: 206 ff.; Pérez de Rivas; and Spicer. The most celebrated case was that of the Paraguayan *reducciones;* see Charlevoix, Graham, and Lugones.

2. GHGNS, pp. 10–17. Although the *eclesiástico* branch of government was filled by crown officials and by individuals holding other secular positions at the same time, here it is being dealt with separately. Santa Lucía did not involve the Jesuits with the *militar* branch, although much of their mission activity in the north did.

3. Instruction, dated March 14, 1579, directing the audiencia to carry out the royal will; PCRVP 1: 218v–219r.

4. PCRVP 1: 266; 2: 214r–312v; and PCRRP, fols. 101v–106v. The documentation clearly indicates Don Bernabé's willingness to use armed force to defend Zumpango interests but not to what extent his personal interests were involved.

5. In Madrid the Jesuits had founded the Colegio Imperial, which provided education for the elder sons of the higher nobility who later occupied important positions of power (see Lynch, 2: 131); in New Spain the Colegio Máximo served similar purposes (see Jacobsen).

6. A description of the facilities is in BNM 1058, 1: 198.

7. AGNM 51: 13.

8. Donazar provides the explanation, AGNAHH 286, 44: 14r, and lists a number of attempts to buy offices, AGNAHH 286, 44 and 45.

9. For example, Palafox and Juan Antonio de Vizarrón y Eguiarreta. The documentation covering Jesuit disputes over the diezmo issue is very extensive; see DBCJM 3: 414–21.

10. AGNAHH 329, 6.

11. AGNAHH 307, 18.

12. *Declaraciones de diezmo y apuntes para ellos tocante a la Hac.*^{da} *de Sta. Lucía y anexas,* AGNAHH, 293, 2.

13. AGNAHH 307, 18.   14. IHAH, pp. 216–17.

15. AGNAHH 293, 2.   16. IHAH, pp. 11–19.

17. Gibson, *Aztecs,* pp. 98–135, provides a detailed description of jurisdictions and disputes. Secular parishes of importance directly affecting Santa Lucía were Huehuetoca, Hueypoxtla, Tizayuca, Xaltocan, and Zumpango. For an analysis of Jesuit reasons for wanting to avoid taking over parishes see Shiels, pp. 253–76. GHGNS provides jurisdictional information for all of New Spain.

18. IHAH, pp. 227–40, 59–60.

19. *84 recibos de administración espiritual de la Hacienda de Santa Lucía, y anexas. Años de 1713 a 1739, 1726 a 1728, 1750 a 1757, 1763 a 1767,* AGNAHH 293, 2.

20. August 20, 1717, letter from González to Nicolás, AGNAHH 306, 5.
21. July 1745 correspondence between Miers and Terreros, AGNAHH 313, 18.
22. IHAH, pp. 211–19.
23. Alegre, 4: 237–42.
24. IHAH, pp. 248–51. Alms given out to *limosneros* (beggars) from a variety of religious orders in 1716, for example, totaled 19 pesos and involved eleven donations; AGNAHH 299, 4: 491. In 1735 a Jesuit spokesman claimed that the Colegio Máximo was spending 8,000 pesos a year in Mexico City and other places for alms, including gifts for the poor. This money was being spent for meat, bread, housing, or clothes, or distributed in cash; AGNAHH 329, 6.
25. AGNAHH 258, 12.
26. Donazar provides details, and his own interpretation of the events, in AGNAHH 286, 44: 31v–35v.
27. Zavala and Miranda provide a good discussion of the general context.
28. Gibson, *Aztecs,* provides a comprehensive portrait for the Valley of Mexico.
29. PCRVP 2: 78r–117r. Gibson, *Aztecs,* pp. 295–96, discusses the same case, and his Plate XII reproduces one of the maps used in the legal dispute. The map shows the pueblo entirely surrounded and choked off by the Jesuit properties.
30. Additional information on the dispute is in PCRVP 1: 244–55; 3: 161r–204v; and AGNT 238, 4. Donazar indicates Jesuit later use of pueblo crop land, AGNAHH 286, 44: 28r–30r.
31. AGNT 1504, 1: 85–97.
32. For example, Pando Terreros in 1712 (Appendix A, no. 37).
33. A court case still being fought by the Conde de Regla in 1808 provides details about over one hundred years of conflict between Santa Lucía and neighboring pueblos over access to pastures bordering Lake Xaltocan; AGNT 1672, 3: 1–28; PCRVP 1: 227 ff. Change in hacienda ownership was sufficient cause to bring forth renewed claims based on falsified documents, as was even a change in administrator.
34. For a Jesuit explanation of the problem, see AGNAHH 329, 6.
35. Indication of demographic trends can be seen in Table 1.
36. AGNAHH 314, 27.   37. AGNAHH 286, 44: 24r–v.
38. AGNAHH 286, 44.   39. AGNAHH 312, 13.
40. BMNM, Documentos Jesuitas, 332: 295r–334v.
41. *Arrendatarios de las Haciendas de Sta. Lucía . . . 1745,* PCRVP 1: 514r–546v.
42. PCRVP 1: 516r–545r.
43. PCRVP 3: 28r–160r.
44. The details of hacienda life are discussed in Part III.
45. AGNAHH 286, 44.

Chapter 8

1. There were periodic visits of inspection *(visitas)* by representatives of the provincial or the father general. Their reports were largely abstrac-

ted versions of the reports of local hacienda administrators; AGNAHH 285, 33.

2. Dusenberry, *Mexican Mesta;* J. Klein; Chevalier, *La formación.*

3. Problems over access to pasture and water, both essential commodities, resulted in many of the conflicts discussed in Chapter 7. Salt, however, could be bought, stored, or transported, and presented fewer problems. A major step in meeting salt needs was achieved in 1631, when the Jesuits inherited substantial funds from a Jerónimo del Campo. His heirs agreed to pay the Jesuits 4,350 pesos worth of salt annually to be delivered to storage barns in the pueblo of Tecomán, forty kilometers southwest of Colima; AGNAHH 258, 33. In the 1730s salt was still coming from the Colima source and was transported to other anexas; letter, Donazar, October 20, 1737, AGNAHH 288, 1.

4. Since droughts and diseases tended to affect all sheep ranches in a region, rather than only Santa Lucía flocks, the ability to make rapid size adjustments would allow the Jesuits to take quick advantage of improved prices in times and places of relative scarcity.

5. AGNAHH 313, 17.

6. Individual flocks were frequently also identified according to months of the year, the most common months being February–June and October–November. Within each ranch, individual flocks were identified with various months, suggesting that the month identification was associated with lambing. The months during which the sheep drives and shearing activities took place were not listed. If these were lambing-period associations, the shepherds were implementing carefully regulated breeding patterns, suggesting sophisticated stock control, but the evidence is not conclusive; AGNAHH 313, 17.

7. In 1737, for example, 76 Indian shearers cropped 13,000 sheep in 6 days, which works out to an average of 28.5 sheep per man per day; AGNAHH 298, 1. Records indicated two-thirds of the total flock being sheared; AGNTe 20, 3. Although the number of shearers and the percentage of the total flock being cropped are not usually listed, the starting and finishing dates frequently are; AGNAHH 313, 17. The available information indicates that both the size of the shearing work crew and the two-thirds ratio for animals cropped are reasonably accurate.

8. AGNTe 20, 3.

9. AGNAHH 313, 17.

10. MM 2: 450–51.

11. For sixteenth-century reproduction of flocks see Gibson, *Aztecs,* p. 280; AGNT 13, 5: 326r ff. The 1568 data refer to Pedro de Dueñas's flocks; BNM 1087, 2; PCRMR 3 and 4: 48–58 and 203–14.

12. AGNAHH 293, 2.

13. AGNAHH 313, 17.

14. Montejano reports this to have been the case during the 1740s through the 1760s; AGNTe 205, 1. Gemelli Carreri, 1: 141, reports the practices for 1696 in connection with Santa Lucía, and the Instrucciones include advice on how to avoid abuse of the system; IHAH, pp. 205–6. It is also discussed during Villaverde's legal suit over his administration during Jesuit times; AGNTe 83, 3.

15. AGNAHH 313, 17.

16. AGNAHH 313, 17, and 293, 2.

17. AGNAHH 293, 2.

18. AGNAHH 297, 2.

19. Brading, "Estructura," pp. 24–25. The 1.68 pounds per animal calculated for Santa Lucía during the eighteenth century corresponds very closely to 1.46 pounds per animal calculated for Jesuit flocks in Nueva Granada and Quito from data given by Colmenares, pp. 113–14.

20. These figures have been derived from flock sizes and sales of Santa Lucía; PCRMR 3 and 4: 221–22.

21. During 1596–1597, the Jesuits sold 7,000 arrobas valued at 7,875 pesos.

22. The tithe records covering 1702–1767 frequently list values assigned for wool by diezmo officials, to be paid either in cash or in kind; AGNAHH 293, 2. Wool prices fluctuated considerably during the course of a year. In 1751, for example, two prices were operational. The diezmo standard for black wool was 21 reales, and for white wool it was 20 reales. During the same year the Jesuits sold wool at 20 reales for black wool and 18 reales for white wool; AGNTe 83, 3.

23. This percentage is based on tithe records, using annual values assigned for both wool and sheep; AGNAHH 293, 2.

24. The high figure for 1738 represents two years rather than one, taking into consideration the adverse effects of the epidemic that started in 1736 and resulted in suspended accounting procedures for 1737.

25. Sánchez Baquero, p. 111.

26. Based on information on only two years (1678 and 1681); BNM 1058, 1: 99–115.

27. By 1684 the total had already declined to 42,178 goats; BNM 1058, 1: 116–22.

28. The ratio of annual production here refers to that portion of the goat population annually sold; AGNAHH 293, 3; AGNTe 83, 3.

29. AGNAHH 293, 2.

30. Using 2 reales as the value of a goatskin and 8 reales as the value of a goat carcass. These were the prices charged to the goatherds; AGNAHH 299, 11 and 14.

31. BNM 1058, 1: 197–206; AGNAHH 293, 2.

32. AGNAHH 288, 1.

33. Barrett, pp. 70–71, reports ratios of mule values versus horses and oxen, as well as the change from water power to animal power. See Table 8 for prices of animals according to age and function.

34. According to the report of an unidentified Jesuit spokesman writing in the 1730s; AGNAHH 329, 6.

35. Dusenberry, *Mexican Mesta*, p. 66.

36. AGNAHH 293, 2.

37. Assuming the unbroken horses to be three-year-old colts, worth 5 pesos each, and the unbroken mules to be three-year-olds worth 13.5 pesos each; AGNTe 83, 3.

38. AGNAHH 313, 21.

39. The Jesuits did go to the trouble of having part of Hueytepec legally defined as *ganado mayor*, in order to justify keeping horses there, but other than this did not possess land in the Valley of Mexico which was legally designated for raising cattle. The crown was reluctant to grant such

permission, having given only about ten grants for *ganado mayor* in the entire Valley of Mexico. See Gibson, *Aztecs,* pp. 275–79.

40. Bishko.

41. Dusenberry, *Mexican Mesta;* Gibson, *Aztecs,* pp. 275–79.

42. BNM 1058, 1: 99–123.

43. For example, in 1725 the Jesuits purchased ninety oxen for San Juan; BNM 1058, 1: 140.

44. Ox populations are listed for the following years: 249 in 1722; 347 in 1726; 378 in 1743; approximately 400 in 1746; 444 in 1751; 628 in 1764; 493 in 1767. BNM 1058, 1: 99–206.

45. PCRVP 1: 514v–546v.

46. Letter, Marcos de Echeverría to Pedro Villaverde, August 14, 1754, AGNAHH 288, 1. Many of the renters who pastured cattle in Santa Lucía marshlands near Lake Xaltocan were probably owners of dairy cattle (*vacas de ordeñar).* According to Santa Lucía officials, the proper type of grass for dairy cattle was only found in special locations. It was referred to as *pasto de nosciba;* AGNAHH 293, 6.

47. AGNAHH 299, 4: 67.

48. For numbers of hogs branded annually throughout the eighteenth century see AGNAHH 293, 2. Hacienda inventories give populations, BNM 1058, 1: 99–206.

49. Gibson, *Aztecs,* pp. 300–34, provides an overview of general conditions and maize production in the Valley of Mexico. Florescano, *Precios,* pp. 202–27, lists monthly and bimonthly prices for maize for the period 1708–1810. Moreno Toscano, pp. 59–96, attempted to correlate the penetration of European agricultural and livestock practices with cultural penetration of Indigenous communities. She found definite parallels between varying degrees of native cultural survival and retention of the cultivation of such crops as maíz, frijol, calabaza, and chile.

50. BNM 1058, 1: 113.

51. BNM 1058, 1: 117.

52. These figures are derived by adding up the rations of the number of workers employed in a given year, with allowances for seasonal fluctuations of the labor force; AGNAHH 299 and 313; AGNTe 20, 3.

53. The value of the maize is based on Florescano's data for 1747, *Precios,* p. 204. The volume of the rations for San Ignacio and the values of salaries for 1747 come from a *Cuaderno de los sirvientes en esta hacienda de San Ignacio,* AGNAHH 299, 17.

54. AGNAHH 313, 18 and 21.

55. AGNTe 83, 3. These were figures used in the Villaverde legal suit. Since the lawyers and accountants on both sides questioned almost all figures but did not question these assessments, they are being taken as representative.

56. For an elaboration on drunkenness as a response to cultural stress in the Valley of Mexico during the colonial period, see Gibson, *Aztecs,* pp. 116, 150, 409.

57. The data on pulque production are given by Payno, pp. 92–95.

58. Details about the pulque industry during the colonial period can be gleaned from a variety of sources. Payno provides greatest detail about hacienda production. Clavijero, Hough, pp. 577–92, Gonçalves de Lima, and

Montemayor are helpful. Sahagún is perhaps the best regarding pre-European times; Campo, Durán, and Motolinía are also helpful. Secondary sources for pre- and post-Conquest details about maguey and pulque include Madsen, Miller, Soustelle, Thompson, Vaillant, and Zabriskie.

59. Using a letter of Villaverde (April 1, 1754) to determine Santa Lucía production, AGNAHH 312, 13, and Payno, p. 93, for the Mexico City total.

60. Montemayor.

61. See also Gibson, *Aztecs*, pp. 7, 317–19.

62. Miers's detailed instructions regarding maguey planting and care are in AGNAHH 299, 4: 2–3.

63. *Testimonio de la escritura*, private papers, Don Manuel Romero de Terreros.

64. Such patterns developed early in the colonial period, as shown by Payno, and can still be observed on the properties that were formerly part of Santa Lucía. At Concepción, for example, in 1976, most of the extensive maguey plantings were widely spaced to allow cereal-crop production at the same time.

65. Miers reports having planted some 70,000 young plants in two years; BNM 1058, 1: 131–32.

66. ANCJM 264, 32–38. The 1775 evaluation of properties included at least twice the number of caballerías reported by Miers, indicating a continuing expansion till expropriation; *Testimonio de la escritura*, private papers, Don Manuel Romero de Terreros.

67. AGNAHH 299, 4: 2–3.

68. Letter, Villaverde to Gradilla, April 1, 1754, AGNAHH 312, 13.

69. PCRVP 1: 522v–523v.

70. BNM 1058, 1: 206. Villaverde's attempt to retain the pulque contract and his excuses for the lower incomes are found in his letters to the procurador's office after being given notice of his dismissal; AGNAHH 312, 13.

71. AGNT 1560, mapa no. 5.

72. *Recibos mensuales. Memorias inventariales de la Hacienda de Santa Lucía y anexas*, September 1646, to December 1648, BNM 1058, 1. Income from the frazadas, sayal, and paño during this period amounted to 4,220 pesos.

73. When the Colegio Máximo increased its sugar production and number of slaves, it was from Santa Lucía that woolen goods were acquired. The 1664 Xochimancas instructions indicate frazadas and sayal from Santa Lucía; Berthe, p. 115.

74. Boyd-Bowman, "Spanish and European Textiles," pp. 227–50, provides a list of the textiles common in Mexico during the early colonial period.

75. These jurisdictions being Mexico City, Oaxaca, Puebla, and Valladolid. For a review of crown legislation concerning obraje labor see Greenleaf, "Viceregal Power," pp. 365–79.

76. Gibson, *Aztecs*, pp. 143–46.

77. BNM 1058, 1: 99–206.

78. Attempts were made to grow cotton at San Juan during the 1750s; letter, Yañez to Villaverde, December 21, 1754, AGNAHH 288, 1.

79. Letter, Villaverde to Montejano, December 21, 1755, AGNAHH 288, 1.
80. AGNTe 242, 61.
81. IHAH, pp. 138–39.
82. AGNAHH 286, 31.
83. Donazar provides annual figures covering Colegio Máximo gross income and expenditures; AGNAHH 286, 44: 11r–v. For profits, see Table 16.
84. *Testimonio de la escritura*, private papers, Don Manuel Romero de Terreros.
85. Figure arrived at by ascertaining profit (40,000 pesos) as a percentage of assessed value (1,172,010 pesos).
86. AGNT 2033, 1. See also Gibson, *Aztecs*, p. 290.
87. For a more detailed discussion of similarities and differences with other haciendas, see Chapter 12.

Chapter 9

1. IHAH, Chapters 2 and 9. Gibson, *Aztecs*, pp. 248–56, has pointed out a distinction between resident and nonresident hacienda workers, referred to respectively as *gañanes radicados* or *gañanes*. Data from Santa Lucía suggest there was no standardized agreement in term usage by the middle of the eighteenth century.
2. IHAH, Chapter 2.
3. AGNAHH 329, 6.
4. A post-Jesuit inventory of the construction at Tepenene, in 1775, showed numerous residences for people previously employed by the Jesuits as sirvientes or goatherds; AGNAHH 299, 5 and 11; 313, 19; AGNT 1557: 38.
5. AGNAHH 299, 4: 133.
6. IHAH, p. 53.
7. AGNAHH 299, 4, contains an incomplete *Tabla de sirvientes de la hacienda*, for 1745. This partial list of hacienda residents includes the following: 4 widows and children; 3 single women with children, 3 bachelors; an oxherd and his family; a pasture guard and his family; a couple from Ixtlahuaca; and 102 renters from Ixtlahuaca. A 1732 list (AGNAHH 313, 18) shows 186 people, including occupations such as vacieros, atajeros, boyeros, milperos, herreros, arrieros, albañiles, and carpinteros.
8. Gibson, *Aztecs*, pp. 250 ff.
9. AGNAHH 299, 4 and 18; 313, 17 and 18.
10. AGNAHH 313, 5 and 18.   11. AGNAHH 299, 4: 181.
12. AGNAHH 299, 4: 188–90.   13. AGNAHH 313, 15.
14. IHAH, p. 164.   15. IHAH, pp. 128–29.
16. IHAH, pp. 128–31.   17. IHAH, pp. 55–58.
18. IHAH, pp. 126–28.   19. IHAH, pp. 53–57.
20. The account was settled on March 19, 1747; AGNAHH 299, 4: 65.
21. AGNAHH 299, 4: 8.   22. AGNAHH 299, 4: 79.
23. AGNAHH 299, 4: 451.   24. AGNAHH 299, 4: 452.
25. AGNAHH 299, 14, no. 2.   26. AGNAHH 299, 4: 472–73.

27. AGNAHH 313, 18.   28. AGNTe 83, 3.
29. AGNAHH 313, 18.   30. AGNAHH 299, 17.
31. AGNAHH 299, 6.   32. AGNAHH 313, 4, 12, and 17.
33. AGNAHH 299, 5 and 11; 313, 19.
34. AGNAHH 299, 15; 313, 11.
35. AGNAHH 299, 17. At Provincia the amount of the advances was related to the importance of occupations. For a *pastor,* the amount for a wedding was as low as 5.75 pesos; for the higher status of ranchero, the amount advanced for weddings was as high as 24.75 pesos. Funeral advances varied between 5.25 and 13.5 pesos, and baptism advances varied between 2.25 and 8 pesos. AGNTe 20, 3.
36. AGNTe 20, 3.
37. Ibid.
38. AGNAHH 299, 7 and 18; 313, 4, 17, and 18.
39. AGNAHH 313, 14.
40. AGNAHH 313, 6.
41. AGNAHH 299, 14.
42. AGNAHH 299, 5 and 11; 313, 19.
43. AGNAHH 299, 17.
44. The argument centered around whether Villaverde (as ex-administrator) should be held responsible for the unpaid debts of the sirvientes during his administration. The lawyers were quick to point out that such debts did not remain unpaid: "the *sirvientes* are perforce always in debt to the hacienda, and even when part was paid they always became indebted again. It was necessary that Villaverde, having received the *sirviente* accounts [with their debts], should be able to deliver them [to his successor] without having to show any omission; for although they appear to have been caused during his [administration], it was only because what the debtors paid in his time was credited [to them], as is proper and customary in cases of outstanding credit." AGNTe 205, 1.
45. AGNAHH 313, 17.
46. AGNTe 20, 3.
47. AGNAHH 313, 19.
48. Gemelli Carreri, 2: 198, comments on the dismal state of the Otomí inhabitants of San Jerónimo, near Mexico City, and cites the reasons: "The cause of much of their misery, without doubt, is their indolence; but much more because of the avarice of some *alcaldes* that take from them what they have earned over the whole year, forcing them to receive for their labor oxen, mules, horses, and textiles at prices three times what is fair, and, in contrast, get from them foodstuffs at whatever prices the *alcaldes* desire."
49. IHAH, pp. 53, 56, 71, 107, 124, 131, 136, 171, 205, and 206.
50. AGNAHH 299, 5, 7, 11, and 18; 313, 4, 17, and 19.
51. AGNAHH 313, 16.   52. AGNAHH 313, 7.
53. AGNAHH 299, 4: 474.   54. BNM 1058, 1: 197–206.
55. For a comprehensive treatment of such stratifications developed in Europe, see Bloch; for the Aztecs, see Gibson, *Aztecs;* for a more general view of the Mexican Highlands, see Vaillant.
56. PCRVP 3, 18.   57. AGNAHH 313, 17.
58. PCRVP 1: 546.   59. See Chapter 10.

Chapter 10

1. MM 2: 274 and 656.
2. This has been noted for New Spain by Dusenberry, *Mexican Mesta*; Vázquez de Espinosa, pp. 43, 177, 184; Chevalier, *La formación*; and Taylor, *Landlord*. Lockhart, *Spanish Peru*, reports that in sixteenth-century Peru most encomenderos used African "slaves to care for land and livestock" (p. 180). Slaves were accepted to such an extent that bills of sale for rural lands frequently included Negroes and mulattoes as part of the estates. See Acosta Saignes for Venezuela, Colmenares for Ecuador and Colombia, Gracía for Argentina, and Bowser and Macera for Peru. For additional data on Mexico see the works of Aguirre Beltrán; Boyd-Bowman, "Negro Slavery"; Chance; and Palmer.
3. Dusenberry, *Mexican Mesta*, pp. 145–47.
4. LB, pp. 94–96, 631–33.
5. AGN, Historia 406–8; AGNJ 2, 3, 6. For an analysis of general trends and specific cases see Aguirre Beltrán, *La población*.
6. AGNJ 2, 3, 6.
7. See King for bills of sale.
8. AGNJ 2, 3, 6.
9. Berthe analyzes the functioning of the estate.
10. Two inventories exist, AGNAHH 285, 48, and BNM 83. The latter has been used here because it provides greater detail.
11. This was the Cortés estate; see Barrett, p. 135.
12. AGN, Civil 1681: 111–14; see also Berthe.
13. AGN, Civil 1681.
14. See Chapter 6.
15. AGNAHH 285, 33.
16. Gemelli Carreri, 1: 141: "They multiply, which is of the greatest usefulness to the fathers, for they sell them for 300 and 400 pesos each."
17. BNM 1058, 1: 132 and 156.
18. BNM 1058, 1: 168.
19. AGNAHH 307, 9, and 329, 7–9.
20. AGNAHH 329, 7.
21. AGNAHH 307, 9.
22. On August 16, 1751, six slave herdsmen fled from Santa Lucía, and they were followed by another two families (with three and four children), plus a married female, on September 16. AGNAHH 312, 13, and 329, 1.
23. AGNAHH 329, 1.   24. BNM 1058, 1: 197.
25. AGNAHH 299, 4: 197–204. 26. IHAH, 78–81, 63–64.
27. AGNAHH 329, 1, 7–9.   28. AGNAHH 313, 7.
29. AGNTe 20, 3.   30. AGNAHH 299, 18, and 313, 18.
31. With a weekly ration of 12 quartillos of maize, valued at 16 reales per fanega (48 quartillos).
32. Using the same maize calculations and a monthly wage of 4 pesos.
33. Fridays, Saturdays, fast days, and the period of Lent were designated as days for withholding meat rations; IHAH, p. 71. The size of the meat rations is not indicated, preventing a more accurate assessment of food costs for slaves.

34. IHAH, pp. 61–83.
35. AGNAHH 329, 8.
36. Letter, Villaverde to Gradilla, October 25, 1751, AGNAHH 312, 13.
37. AGNAHH 329, 8.
38. Frequent mention is made in the records of burials of infants of slave and nonslave hacienda workers. Rates to be charged for burials in the bishopric of Mexico, in 1686, for slave infants were set at 4 pesos, whereas for Indians *(de cuadrilla* or *de los pueblos)* they were set at 2 pesos; AGNAHH 314, 25. In 1761 rates given for infants at the pueblo of Ixtlahuaca indicate 10 reales, claimed by the local cura to be too low; BMNM, Fondo Franciscano, 188: 269r ff.
39. Two such extended family units were found: the first included parents, two sons, and one daughter, with spouses, and four unmarried children, AGNAHH 299, 15; the second included parents plus eight children between the ages of two and twenty, plus two grandchildren, AGNAHH 329, 3.
40. See Mörner, *Race Mixture,* pp. 53–60.
41. AGNAHH 329, 7.
42. Pedro Villaverde, while administrator of Santa Lucía, bought twenty-two young slaves from the hacienda. What he paid for them and his use or resale of the eighteen males and four females are not indicated; AGNAHH 329, 1.
43. Letter, Villaverde to Gradilla, April 1, 1754, AGNAHH 312, 13.
44. IHAH, p. 73.
45. Letter, Donazar to Yarza, October 17, 1737, AGNAHH 298, 1. In 1744, when Manuel de Orruño was mayordomo at San Xavier, he requested permission to purchase two young female slaves, one of whom had recently given birth to an infant described as "un blanquito que lo hubo de un indio según dize" ("a white child which they say was of an Indian father"). The circumstances, however, give the impression that the mayordomo may have been the father of the child. Letter, Orruño to Miers, June 20, 1744, AGNAHH 313, 5.
46. AGNAHH 297, 3.
47. The guide had been written by a Jesuit, Juan de Steyneffer, and was published in Mexico in 1712. Cooper, p. 81, suggests that the use of this guide may not have been very effective since even literate persons using it made mistakes at every turn.
48. IHAH, pp. 74–76.
49. In 1717 the Santa Lucía administrator sent an injured young male slave to Mexico City, where better medical treatment could be obtained. Letter, González to Nicolás, August 20, 1717, AGNAHH 306, 5.
50. IHAH, pp. 61–83.
51. The author of the Instrucciones implies that contemporary punishment practices were tyrannical; IHAH, pp. 67–68.
52. IHAH, p. 66.
53. Letter, Montejano to Villaverde, February 8, 1752, AGNAHH 288, 1.
54. Letter, Villaverde to Gradilla, June 1, 1754, AGNAHH 312, 13.
55. DBCJM 8: 190; see Chapter 2.

56. Davidson, p. 250. For a description of the campaign by one of the Jesuit participants, see Alegre, 2: 176–81.

57. AGNT 167, 6.

Chapter 11

1. Chevalier, *La formación*, p. 311.

2. The person administering the punishment was referred to as a *fiscal;* IHAH, p. 53. The description of Santa Lucía presented is based on documentary references, a former owner's description (Romero de Terreros, pp. 39–43), and personal inspection of the remains of the complex. The latter included a number of visits between 1967 and 1976, airphotos from the 1950s, and information supplied by Mexican military engineers who converted the complex into the administrative center for an airport.

3. A 1678 inventory of chapel contents required seven folios. A series of such inventories covering 1678–1764 are in BNM 1058, 1: 99–206.

4. PCRVP 2, 24, contains a 1758 description of the chapel and its contents.

5. See Chapters 2 and 6.

6. IHAH, pp. 35 ff.

7. PCRVP 2, 24.

8. IHAH, pp. 25–46.

9. AGNAHH 288, 1; 298, 1; 312, 13.

10. "A chaplain father, from those who because of age, or lack of health, or for other reasons cannot work in the colleges, [goes to] serve to console the brothers in the solitude of the haciendas, and to provide them company, confess them and give them communion, and act as directors of their consciences, and resolvers of their doubts." IHAH, pp. 221–22.

11. IHAH, pp. 41, 51–52, 220–40.

12. PCRVP, 2, 24; IHAH, p. 236.

13. Letter, Donazar to Yarza, August 28, 1737, AGNAHH 298, 1.

14. IHAH, pp. 227–40.

15. Chapel structures at Santa Lucía, San Juan, San Xavier, Concepción, Tepenene, and Chicavasco were visited and carefully examined by the writer. Only two, at San Juan and Concepción, still serve as chapels for hacienda owners and managers. The Colegio Máximo chapel still serves as a church, and what is left of the colegio itself now functions as the Hemeroteca Nacional of Mexico.

16. For 1745 instructions to this effect, see AGNAHH 299, 4: 7v.

17. Early candidates for chaplain roles at Santa Lucía were fluent in both Nahuatl and Otomí; DBCJM, 8: 260–73.

18. The Instrucciones cite Indian obligations in home parishes to include confession and communion at least once a year, during Lent; IHAH, pp. 59–60. Gibson, *Aztecs,* p. 115, mentions only confession. In 1712 Santa Lucía workers were beaten while being questioned by officials from Zumpango—"they asked them the Christian doctrine, giving twelve lashes to some and to others eighteen"; PCRVP 2: 243r. In 1746 the Tolcayuca cura used similar tactics, administering the beatings with a *cuero ancho de seis ramales* ("a wide leather whip of six strands"); AGNAHH 314, 27.

19. For greater detail about secular clergy requirements, see Gibson, *Aztecs,* pp. 114 ff.

20. IHAH, pp. 58, 238.

21. For a detailed description of such visits in the seventeenth century, see DBCJM 3: 573–86.

22. Alegre, 4: 352.

23. PCRVP 2, 24.

24. AGNAHH 299, 15.

25. Chevalier, *La formación,* pp. 219–26; Wolf, *Sons,* pp. 202–11.

26. Instructions of the father general to the provincial in Mexico, DBCJM 1: 196.

27. August 28, 1754, AGNAHH 307, 10.

28. Letter, Donazar to Yarza, September 1737, AGNAHH 298, 1.

29. AGNAHH 329, 7 and 8.

30. IHAH, p. 57.

31. PCRVP 2, 24: 3r, includes a 1758 description of Santa Lucía as follows: "unfortunately, this hacienda, and this house have the misfortune of being situated in a small fixed plain . . . , which is surrounded on all sides by a vast marsh, with much water, which expands in the rainy season, closing the entrances and exits."

32. AGNTe 20, 3, includes examples, referring to Provincia shepherds during 1750–1751.

33. IHAH, p. 56.

34. AGNAHH 329, 7.

35. Santa Lucía use of chains is mentioned only during the administration of Villaverde, who used it for a variety of punishments; letter, Villaverde to Gradilla, June 10, 1754, AGNAHH 312, 13.

36. Letter, Antonio de los Angeles to Villaverde, October 2, 1754, AGNAHH 312, 13.

37. The tent used by the Provincia mayordomo was made up of 40 *varas de jerga.* His bed was described as "una cama de tablas ordinarias" ("a bed of ordinary boards"); AGNTe 20, 3.

38. Provincia patterns are based on documents in AGNTe 20, 3. For instructions to the administrator regarding the dismissal of shepherds who did not comply with Jesuit goals, see letter, Gradilla to Villaverde, November 23, 1761, AGNTe 205, 1.

39. The analysis of Negra operations comes from AGNAHH 299, 7 and 18; 313, 4, 12, 17, and 18.

40. Specific data on shepherds, including Joseph Antonio Rodríguez and Mathías de Buendía, come from AGNAHH 299, 7, and 18; 313, 4, 17, and 18.

41. The size of the Negra pastures is given in documents drawn up for the sale of Santa Lucía; private papers, Don Manuel Romero de Terreros, *Testimonio de la escritura,* pp. 61–64.

42. Joseph Serón records and those for San Ignacio are from AGNAHH 299, 17; 313, 4.

43. Tepenene accounts are from AGNAHH 299, 5 and 11; 313, 15, 19, and 22.

44. Manuel Felipe, Sebastián de la Cruz, and Zipriano Llano statements are in AGNAHH 299, 5 and 11; 313, 19.

45. Hueytepec operations and cowboy accounts, between 1740 and 1745, are in AGNAHH 313, 21.
46. San Pablo accounts are in AGNAHH 299, 8.
47. AGNAHH 299, 8.
48. IHAH, pp. 125–40.
49. The composite picture of the 1754 round of activities is based on 209 items of correspondence of the Santa Lucía administrator, its mayordomos, and the college administrators; AGNAHH 288, 1.
50. This is the picture indicated by Zorita for the late sixteenth century, by *Thomas Gage's Travels* for the early seventeenth century, and in Gibson, *Aztecs*, for the colonial period.
51. Wolf's *Sons* articulates the distinction between the hacienda communities and pueblo communities most clearly. The legislation of the Royal Council of the Indies expressed the royal intentions of separate pueblos; see Mörner, *La corona*. This matter will be discussed in greater depth in Chapter 13.
52. See Chapter 7.
53. The status of the Tolcayuca cura during 1740–1745 comes from AGNAHH 313, 18.
54. Zorita; Gibson, *Aztecs*; Zavala, *La encomienda*; and Zavala and Miranda.
55. PCRVP 1: 516r–546v.
56. PCRVP 1: 544r–545v. The vaciero income is being calculated as 6 pesos per month plus weekly rations of maize (12 quartillos) for a regular vaciero. For the good vaciero, the salary was up to 10 pesos a month. The value for horses and cattle used in the calculations is 5 pesos per head, for sheep the rate for the period was 5 reales per head, referring to total flocks.
57. PCRVP 1: 544r–545v.
58. PCRVP 1: 536r–538v.
59. PCRVP 1: 525r–527r. Only 1 renter planted up to 3 fanegas, the rest less than 2 fanegas, and the majority less than ½ fanega.
60. PCRVP 1: 530r–533v. At Florida the renters, on the average, planted less than 1 fanega, although one-third planted 1 fanega.
61. PCRVP 1: 540r–543v.
62. The comparison here is made between what vacieros, manaderos, or vaqueros would have earned in cash and the value of their maize and other rations, compared to what the livestock and milpas of the alcaldes and gobernadores might have produced during an average year.
63. AGNT 1557: 37–48.
64. ANCJM 264, 32.
65. Two lists of values of hacienda residence complexes have been located and used for the following descriptions. Both are in agreement as to the values of individual items or general categories. The AGNT 1557: 37–48 list is not as detailed as the ANCJM 264, 32 list.
66. The San Xavier facilities were added to and altered in various ways in the post-Jesuit period. Nevertheless, it is still possible to distinguish the old from the new by types of construction and materials. Most such evidence was being covered up by its conversion into a tourist hotel in 1976.
67. The Chicavasco troje still stands complete, but its roof has collapsed.

68. One of the surprises to me, during extended visits to Santa Lucía anexas and surrounding pueblos in April–May 1976, was the modest nature of the church structures in many of the pueblos. Except where there had been monasteries or convents, or the communities were regional centers of ecclesiastical administration, the churches were hardly larger than hacienda chapels built by the henequen hacendados of Yucatán in the early twentieth century. The churches the Franciscans had the Maya Indians build in the Yucatán pueblos, in comparison, are immense. Yet the population density at the time of construction, for the Valley of Mexico, was considerable and that of the Maya pueblos was not great. One of the explanations might be that the Franciscans in Yucatán managed to claim most of the available labor service of the pueblos, whereas in the Valley of Mexico this labor was expended on behalf of non-pueblo interests.

Chapter 12

1. Chevalier, *La formación,* identified the importance of Jesuit landholdings in Mexico as early as 1952, followed by Mörner's 1953 South American study, *The Political and Economic Activities of the Jesuits in the La Plata Region.* Popescu's *El sistema económico en las misiones jesuítas* provides a useful analysis of Jesuit economic principles. See also note 1, Chapter 7. Published materials derived from study of Jesuit estates are growing rapidly; see the works of Berthe, Colmenares, Ewald, Macera, Mörner, J. Riley, and Tovar Pinzón. None of these studies, however, fully explores the nature of individual estates or their impact.

2. Tovar Pinzón, p. 134.

3. AGNAHH 329, 6.

4. AGNAHH 286, 44; 307, 14.

5. It is difficult to ascertain total numbers because each Jesuit listing differs in its classification scheme. In one list a collection of estates is grouped as a single unit, whereas only a few years later the composition of the grouping changes; cf. AGNAHH 329, 6, with AGNAHH 307, 14. J. Riley names seventy-five estates for which there were land transactions between 1670 and 1767, a list that does not include all haciendas. His post expulsion list of estates includes eighty-two, but in different groupings. See "Wealth," pp. 260–62, 264–66.

6. Tovar Pinzón, pp. 150–51.

7. See Ewald, p. 134.

8. The timing of the acquisitions varies but not the patterns. Chicomocelo acquisitions started in the late 1500s, with major increases in the first decades of the seventeenth and eighteenth centuries; Tovar Pinzón, p. 143. The Colegio del Espíritu Santo acquisitions are few in the sixteenth century, increase substantially between 1600 and 1640, and continue until the 1740s—similar to the experience of Santa Lucía; see Tovar Pinzón, p. 141, and Chapters 2–4 in this study. In Nueva Granada, the Colegio de Latacunga began its acquisitions later, made significant increases during 1665–1680, then at a reduced pace, followed by significant increases during 1690–1710 and, after another slow period, increased acquisitions during 1755–1760; Colmenares, p. 55. For the Colegio Máximo at Córdoba (Argentina), acquisitions began in the 1620s and terminated shortly before

1700; Gracía, pp. 283–91. In all areas, the timing of purchases was related to expansion of the colleges and their activities.

9. See Gracía for Argentina, Macera for Peru, and Colmenares for northern South America.

10. Besides the works listed in notes 8 and 9, see Albo and Cushner, for Peru; and Berthe, Ewald, and J. Riley, "Management," for Mexico.

11. All references cited in notes 8–10, as well as Chapters 2–11, apply to the conclusions of this paragraph and the next.

12. The life histories of individuals provide many examples; see DBCJM, vols. 1–10; MM, vols. 1–5.

13. Chevalier, *La formación*, p. 242.

14. M. Riley, "El prototipo," pp. 49–69.

15. Simpson, *Encomienda*, pp. 164–67.

16. See Gibson, *Aztecs*, pp. 257–99; Simpson, *Exploitation*.

17. Gibson, *Aztecs*, p. 289. The Gibson figure of 160 is indicative of the number established but not of the actual number functioning as separate administrative entities at any given point.

18. For late eighteenth-century patterns see Ladd and Tutino.

19. Taylor ("Haciendas coloniales," "Landed Society," and *Landlord*) has studied the Oaxaca Valley in considerable detail.

20. Osborn, "Community" and "Indian Land."

21. AGNAHH 307, 8; 329, 6; AGNT 2033: 19v–56v; PCRVP 1, 9; 3, 18.

22. Couturier, pp. 1–92.

23. Morin, "Croissance," pp. 235–40.

24. Chevalier, *La formación*, pp. 119–44; Harris, pp. 3–27.

25. For San José de Coapa, see López Sarrelangue; for José Antonio Uría, see Semo and Pedrero; for Tehuacán, see Ewald; for La Parada y San Diego and Bledos, see Bazant, pp. 10–34, 73–84; and for the Sánchez Navarro estates see Harris, pp. 3–27.

26. See Chapters 2–4.

27. Couturier, who is currently preparing a family study of the Conde de Regla family.

28. Taylor, *Landlord*, pp. 214–20.

29. Brading, *Miners*, Harris, and Morin, "Croissance."

30. See Brading, *Miners*, pp. 116, 124–25, 178, 183, 191, 199, 263, 265, 296–98, 313, 317.

31. See Bauer, and Lavrín, "Role."

32. Brading, *Miners*, p. 91.

33. The percentage is derived from the values listed for the estates (493,222 pesos) and total value of funds committed for convents, capellanías, and pious works (113,690 pesos). See González Sánchez.

34. Figures taken from Brading, *Miners*, p. 215. Brading lists 4,680 pueblos and 6,680 ranchos oriented to subsistence production and 4,945 haciendas and ranchos producing for regional and other markets.

35. Brading, *Miners*, p. 215.   36. See Harris, pp. 27, 147–74.

37. Chevalier, *La formación*, pp. 59–60.

38. See Chapters 3 and 11 for description.

39. Data on Yucatán hacienda construction derives from personal inspection of numerous cascos during 1966–1976. For a survey, see Hartman.

40. J. Warren.

41. See M. Riley, "El prototipo," pp. 49–69; García Martínez; and Barrett.

42. For a discussion of continuity of roles, see Keith, "Encomienda, Hacienda," and Lockhart, "Encomienda and Hacienda."

43. See Barrett; Brading, *Miners;* Chevalier, *La formación;* Dusenberry, *Mexican Mesta;* Harris; López Sarrelangue; Morin, "Croissance"; Semo and Pedrero; and Taylor, *Landlord.*

44. See Chevalier, *La formación,* 119–44.

45. See Chapter 6 for a discussion of Jesuit practices.

46. Brading, *Miners,* p. 230.

47. For regional examples of rentals, see Chevalier, *La formación,* pp. 224–26; Couturier, p. 19; Morin, "Croissance," pp. 308–26.

48. J. Riley, "Wealth," and Tovar Pinzón provide overall data for the Jesuit colleges in Mexico. Riley notes that the smaller Jesuit colleges at greater distances from the large Spanish urban centers, such as Mexico City and Puebla, were less prosperous and their haciendas less productive. Tovar Pinzón suggests that an annual 5 percent profit on total worth of a hacienda was to be considered reasonable. He also shows a great range of variation within Jesuit haciendas, ranging from 1.57 percent to 21.92 percent (Cuadro 27).

49. Chevalier, *La formación,* p. 242, came to the conclusion that the Jesuit estates were constantly looking for ways to improve production but that secular hacendados frequently did not emphasize production; instead they scorned production and held their great estates for prestige. Such contentions have been unquestioningly repeated; see Dusenberry, *Mexican Mesta,* p. 179; González, pp. 51–63.

50. For a survey of Cortés's business activities, see Scholes, M. Riley, *Estate.*

51. See Chapter 2.

52. See Bakewell, Lang, Lynch, and MacLeod.

53. Brading, *Miners,* and Morin, "Croissance."

54. See Couturier; and Harris.

55. See Aguirre Beltrán, *La población.*

56. Lockhart, *Spanish Peru,* pp. 180–84.

57. For Argentina, see Gracía; for Colombia and Ecuador, see Colmenares; for Peru, see Macera, *Instrucciones;* for Mexico, see Chevalier, *La formación.*

58. Taylor, *Landlord.*

59. Vázquez de Espinosa, pp. 43, 177, 184, 304, 317, 341, 598, 729, 732.

60. Acosta Saignes, pp. 179–80.

61. Durham and Jones; Morrisey, "Northern Expansion," and MacEwan.

62. Mörner, *Race Mixture,* p. 119.

63. See Dusenberry, *Mexican Mesta,* pp. 67–70, 77–80, 85–86, 132–37, 146–47; also copies of royal ordinances in CDHH 2, 1, no. 86 (1607); no. 120 (1612); no. 203 (1628); no. 404 (1672); no. 494 (1681).

64. See Chapter 10; Aguirre Beltrán, *La población;* and Barrett.

65. For a survey of African slave conditions, see Aguirre Beltrán,

"Integration"; Bowser; Boyd-Bowman, "Negro Slavery"; Davidson; and Mellafe.

66. AGNAHH 307, 9, and 329, 7–9.

67. See Mörner, *La corona*, pp. 94–101, for a discussion of legal restraints directed against miscegenation.

68. For an overview of slave-importation practices and trends, see Aguirre Beltrán, *La población* and "Slave Trade."

69. Dusenberry, *Mexican Mesta*, pp. 77–80.

70. Of the free mulattoes in the Valley of Oaxaca in the late eighteenth century, 32 percent lived in rural areas; see Taylor, *Landlord*, pp. 21, 63, 144, 150–51, 156, 182.

71. For 1650, Davidson, p. 237, indicates significant numbers of Negroes and mulattoes on livestock estates. Harris, pp. 14 and 63, indicates conditions for the 1760s and 1770s for the Coahuila area, showing the majority working as domestics. See also Chevalier, *La formación*, pp. 220–22 and 229–30. For the Zacatecas region, see Bakewell, p. 122; and for the Bajío and Michoacán, see Morin, "Croissance," pp. 294–96. Gerhard (GHGNS) provides more systematic general coverage.

72. BNM 1058, 2: 131.

73. Chevalier, *La formación*, pp. 220–22 and 229–30.

74. Cf. BNM 1058, 2: 17, and Chevalier, *La formación*, p. 230.

75. Aguirre Beltrán, "Ethnohistory," p. 4.

76. The literature on hacienda labor management is rapidly expanding. For an excellent survey see Katz, "Labor Conditions." Details on areas and specific haciendas can be found in Barrett; Bazant; Brading, *Miners*; Couturier; Florescano, *Haciendas*; Gibson, *Aztecs*; Harris; Morin, "Croissance"; Patch; J. Riley, "Management"; Taylor, "Haciendas coloniales" and *Landlord*; and Tutino.

77. Bishko.

78. See Chapter 11 for a more detailed description.

79. The number of beds listed in the Santa Lucía inventories provides an indication of the number of residents within the bedrooms of the *casco principal*. In 1726 there were sixteen beds, in 1746, eleven, and in 1764, eighteen; see BNM 1058, 2: 129, 159, and 198.

80. See IHAH, which spells out the Jesuit policies.

81. See Chapters 9 and 11.

82. For example, see Chevalier, *La formación*, pp. 209–40; Wolf, *Sons*, pp. 202–32; and Willems, pp. 27–34.

83. López Sarrelangue, pp. 239–40. Tutino, pp. 518–24, shows similar conditions for haciendas in the Chalco region.

84. See Chapter 9 for an expanded discussion.

85. See Section III for a detailed discussion.

86. It is not being argued that all Jesuit haciendas were successful, or that only the Jesuit estates were successful. Recent studies indicate a wide range of success. See Ewald; J. Riley, "Wealth"; and Tovar Pinzón.

87. Katz, "Labor Conditions," p. 7.

88. AGNTe 20, 3.

89. AGNAHH 313, 4; 299, 14; 313, 17; 299, 11; 313, 6.

90. Morin, "Croissance," pp. 300–05.

91. Barrett, pp. 91–92; Taylor, "Haciendas Coloniales" and *Landlord*.
92. Chevalier, *La formación*, pp. 219–26.
93. Harris, p. 58. For additional details for the eighteenth and nineteenth centuries, see pp. 58–78 and 203–30.
94. See Harris, pp. 58 ff.
95. See Chapter 13 for a fuller discussion of pueblo reactions.

Chapter 13

1. Harris, for example, treats the Indian raids essentially as depredations, whereas Huerta and Palacios provide a more balanced picture.
2. See MacLeod, Patch, and López de Cogolludo.
3. For useful works covering this period, see Ricard; Simpson, *Exploitation* and *Studies*; Zavala, *Encomienda*; and Zavala and Miranda.
4. For a general survey, see Gibson, "Transformation."
5. Gibson, *Aztecs*, p. 78.
6. Ibid., pp. 78 and 409.
7. For a list of epidemics during the colonial period, see Gibson, *Aztecs*, pp. 448–51. The valley figures resulting in the percentages are those suggested by Gibson, ibid., p. 141, with 1.5 million at Conquest, 325,000 by 1570, and 70,000 by the mid-seventeenth century.
8. Clerical complaints and attempts to counteract Indigenous practices resulted in documents such as *Tratado*. For a discussion of the process of acculturation related to traditional medical practices, see Aguirre Beltrán, *Medicina*.
9. Wolf, in *Sons*, provides a Mesoamerican overview of rural developments. For more specialized studies see, Gibson, *Tlaxcala*; and Zorita.
10. See Chapters 9–12.
11. One of the early (and still one of the best) discussions of royal legislation is Solórzano y Pereira's; see also Zavala and Miranda.
12. See Chapter 7.
13. This interpretation has gained wide popularity since the publication of Wolf's *Sons*; see pp. 202–32. For an analysis of the concept see Góngora, pp. 98–119. Taylor, "Landed Society," applies the concept to southern Mexico.
14. See Vázquez. For a review of the legislation, see Konetzke (CDHH) and Mörner, *La corona*.
15. Peasant participation in markets and their relation to dominant economic systems have received a great deal of attention. See Barbosa-Ramírez; Geertz; J. Nash; M. Nash; Redfield, *Folk Culture* and *Peasant Culture*; Stavenhagen; and Wolf, *Peasants*.
16. See Gibson, *Aztecs* and "Transformation."
17. Gibson, *Aztecs*, p. 309.   18. Ibid., p. 335.
19. Ibid., p. 153.   20. Ibid., p. 163.
21. See Konetzke and Mörner, *La corona*; for a more general treatment, see Mörner, *Race Mixture*.
22. Gibson, *Aztecs*, pp. 155–65.
23. For a review of Mexican community studies as of the beginning of the 1950s see Cline, "Mexican Community Studies." For Middle America as a whole, see Wauchope. More extensive bibliographies covering Latin

America can be found in Heath, pp. 542–72, O'Leary, and Willems, pp. 395–410.

24. Wolf, "Types," p. 456.

25. Two recent general works about Latin America relying heavily upon the typology are Willems, pp. 125–45; Wolf and Hansen, pp. 71–117.

26. Zorita, pp. 112–22.

27. See Chapters 2–4.

28. See Chapters 7, 9, and 11.

29. Documentation of the cases is as follows: Jesús del Monte, BMNM, Documentos Jesuitas, 332: 295r–334v; Provincia, AGNAHH 297, 3, and PCRVP 3: 16v–24v; Xalmolonga, AGNT 2205–7; Tepenene, AGNAHH 312, 13, and 313, 13; San Xavier, AGNAHH 314, 27; Florida, AGNT 2033; Chicavasco, AGNAHH 312, 13; AGNT 1687, 1; PCRVP 1: 228–29; Ocuila, AGNAHH 329, 1; AGNT 2207, 1; PCRVP 1: 273 ff. and 543–44. See also Chapter 7.

30. AGNAHH 328, 1. Riley, "Management," pp. 114–38, also discusses these events.

31. Archer.

32. Huerta and Palacios, pp. 114–90; H. Klein.

33. For a recent interpretation, see González Navarro, "Las guerras," pp. 70–106. The Maya uprising has received considerable attention; see Canto López; González Navarro, *Raza;* and Reed.

34. Santa Lucía properties extended, to the west, as far north as Izatlán and as far south as Chilpancingo; to the east, to Tehuacán and into Vera Cruz Vieja. See Maps 2–3.

35. Following GHGNS. See Appendix A for the identification of the jurisdictions.

Glossary

Glossary

Adobero Adobe brick maker
Agostadero Seasonal summer pasture
Aguacate Avocado
Aguamiel Juice of the maguey; becomes *pulque* when fermented
Aguardiente Liquor made from sugarcane
Ahijador Lambing specialist
Ají Chile
Albañil Mason; construction laborer
Alcabala Sales tax
Alcalde Judge and *cabildo* member
Alcalde del crimen Criminal court judge
Alcalde mayor Spanish official in charge of a district
Alcalde ordinario Judge of a town council
Alcaldía Office and jurisdiction of an *alcalde*
Almud Unit of measure; one-twelfth of a *fanega*
Alobado *Lobo* slave with Indian features
Alumbre Alum dye
Alverjón Chickpeas
Anexas Annexes; separate property under administrative control of larger unit
Añil Indigo; an Indigenous dye
Arrendatario Renter of hacienda land
Arriero Muleteer
Arroba Unit of measure; about 25 pounds
Atajo Sheep flock of less than 1,000 animals
Atezado Negro slave with dark pigmentation
Audiencia High court of justice and governing body under the viceroy, or its jurisdiction
Avena Oats
Ayudante Assistant to the *mayordomo* or supervisor
Becerro Calf
Borrador Account book
Borrego Lamb
Boyero Oxherd

Bozal Slave newly arrived from Africa, without knowledge of hispanic culture
Bramante Hemp linen
Braza Unit of measure; commonly two *varas*
Brin Saffron linen
Buey Ox; *(de arada)* plow; *(de carreta)* cart
Bula Bull or papal indulgence
Caballerango Riding stock herdsman
Caballería Unit of farmland; about 105 acres
Caballo Horse; *(manso)* tame; *(cerrero)* untamed; *(quebrantado)* broken-in
Cabaña Hut
Cabildo Municipal council
Cabras Goats
Cacicazgo Estate or institution of *cacique* rule
Cacique Indian chief or local ruler
Caja real Royal treasury
Cajonero Box maker
Calabaza Squash
Caparrosa Copper and zinc sulfate dye
Capataz Crew foreman
Capellanía de misas Grant or fund to support special masses
Capitán Herd supervisor or labor-crew foreman; *(de la cuadrilla)* pueblo labor foreman
Capitanejo Labor-crew foreman
Caponero Castrator
Caporal Cowboy foreman or labor-crew foreman
Carga Load; generally 2 *fanegas*
Carnero Adult sheep
Carpintero Carpenter
Carretero Teamster
Carta de pago Promissory note; letter of credit
Casa principal Main hacienda residence; also *casco*
Casacalote Indigenous dye, used for textiles
Casos o censos Rents or annuities
Castas Genetically mixed groups, distinguishable (by law or social class)
Castizo Person with Spanish and *mestizo* parents
Cebada Barley
Cédula Royal order or instruction
Cerdo Hog; *(de sebada)* barley-fed; *(de sabana)* field-fed
Chía Sage
Chicharrón Fried pork skin
Chinampa Aquatic garden
Chinchorrito Sheep flock of less than 1,000 animals

Chivatos Kids or young goats of 6 to 12 months
Chivos Goats over 1 year of age
Ciénega Swamp or marshland
Cimarrón Fugitive or runaway slave
Coa Hoe
Coadjutor Co-helper; Jesuit brother who performed mostly secular tasks
Coche Type of carriage
Cofradía Sodality
Cojo Injured or maimed
Colecturía de diezmo Tithe collection center
Compadrazgo Relationship through godparents
Compadre Godparent
Compañía Partnership by means of contract
Composiciones de tierras Legalization of land titles
Consejo real Royal council
Contador Accountant
Cordero Lamb of less than 8 months
Corregidor Spanish official in charge of a district
Corregimiento Office or jurisdiction of a *corregidor*
Costal Sack or large bag
Coyote Light *mestizo* or person with *mestizo* and mulatto parents
Criada de casa Female domestic
Criollo Creole; person born in Spanish colonies; hispanized; *(de México)* from Mexico
Cuartillo Unit of measure; one-fourth of an *almud*
Cubero Cooper
Cura Parish priest; also *cura beneficiado*
Denuncia por realengas Claim against unappropriated or royal land
Desagüe Drainage
Diezmo Tithe
Doctrina Doctrine; parochial jurisdiction
Doctrinero Teacher of religion
Ducado Unit of gold currency; worth 375 *maravedís*
Eclesiástico Ecclesiastical; religious branch of colonial government
Encomendero Holder of an *encomienda*
Encomienda Right, by royal grant, of access to labor and tribute of Indians in specified area
Enfermero Nurse
Enfrenado In leg irons
Escribanía Office of a notary
Escribano Notary or clerical assistant
Estancia Ranch or rural property, frequently a subunit of a larger unit

Estanciero Cattleman; owner of an *estancia*
Estantes Livestock herds confined to local pastures
Fanega Unit of dry measure; about 1.5 bushels; *(de sembradura)* area planted with 1 *fanega* of seed
Fiador Bondsman
Fiscal Fiscal; prosecutor
Flautas Trinkets
Flota Fleet
Frailes Friar; member of a religious order
Frezada Blanket
Frijol Beans
Ganado Livestock; *(mayor)* horses, cattle, mules, donkeys; *(menor)* sheep, goats, hogs
Gañanes Laborers; *(radicado* or *rancheado)* resident hacienda workers
Garañón Stallion
Gobernador Governor
Gobierno Government; administrative branch of colonial government
Grillos Shackles or leg irons
Guarda Guard; *(milpa)* crop; *(pasto)* pasture; *(tierra)* property
Guarda mayor del real desagüe Royal drainage official
Habas Broad beans
Hacendado Owner of a hacienda
Hacienda Any revenue-producing business; government department of finance; landed estate
Hato Small ranch or herd of livestock
Herido de molino Mill site
Hermano coadjutor Lay brother in the Jesuit order
Herradero Branding specialist
Herrador Farrier
Herrero Smith
Huautli Amaranth
Huipiles Skirts or dresses; female garment
Intendencia District of an intendant
Indios principales Members of the Indian upper class
Ingenio Sugar estate with water-powered sugar mill
Invernadero Winter pasture
Jacal Rustic hut
Jaguey Water pond
Jerga Coarse woolen cloth
Juez Judge; *(de estancias y labores)* rural property judge; *(de provincia)* judge of a district or province
Juez repartidor Spanish official in charge of labor assignment
Juros Annuities assigned on crown revenue

Justicia Justice; judicial branch of colonial government
Labor Farm or cropland
Labrador Farmer
Ladrillero Tile maker
Latifundio System of large estates
Latifundista Owner of a large estate
Leña Firewood
Leñero Firewood supplier
Licencia License; formal permission
Limosna Alms
Limosnero Alms collector or beggar
Lobo Wolf; person with Indian and African parents
Lomo Loin
Macehualtin Indian commoners
Machos Male mules
Maderero Timber maker
Maestro Master craftsman; teacher; *(de muchachos)* teacher of boys in hacienda labor force
Maíz Maize
Manada Sheep flock of 1,500 to 3,000 animals
Manadero Supervisor of a *manada*
Manco Maimed or injured
Mandador Boss; instruction giver
Manso Tame
Maravedí Spanish coin; worth approximately one-sixth of a cent
Marca de fuga Brand on runaway slave
Marrón Runaway slave
Marrano Pig; hog
Matanza Slaughter; slaughterhouse
Mayorazgo Entailed estate
Mayaques Indians of subordinate class
Mayordomo Majordomo; custodian
Mechichile Black maguey; also *mechichitl*
Merced Royal grant of property; also *mercedes*
Mesta Stockmen's association
Mestizo Person of mixed European and Indian ancestry
Metate Grinding stone
Mexoxoctle Yellow maguey; also *metlcoztli*
Mexoxtle Plum maguey; also *mexocotl*
Militar Military; military branch of colonial government
Milpa Maize plantings
Milpero Maize grower
Misión circular Preaching tour commissioned by the Archbishop
Molendera Female tortilla maker
Molino Mill for grinding cereal grains

Mozo de mulas Mule caretaker
Muchacho Youth; young assistant herdsman or laborer
Mula Female mule; *(aparejo)* pack; *(de silla)* saddle; *(de volantera)* carriage
Mulato Mulatto; person with European and African ancestry; *(blanco)* light; *(prieto)* dark
Mulero Mulekeeper
Muleto Mule colt
Naguas Female petticoats
Naturales Indians
Negro Black; person of African ancestry; *(atezado)* very dark pigmentation
Nopal *(Cactus opuntia)* Cactus plant, source of *tuna*
Noriero Draw-well operator
Novillos Young bulls; also *toritos*
Obraje Workshop, especially for making textiles
Oidor Judge of the *audiencia*
Ordeñador Dairyman
Ovejas Ewes; frequently as a general reference to sheep
Ovejero Sheep owner; sheepherder
Padrino Godfather
Palmillas Blue woolen cloth
Panelas Sweets made from sugarcane; also *panochos*
Paño Fine woolen cloth
Pasto de nosciba Pasture grass for milk cows
Pastor Herdsman; *(de pie)* herdsman on foot
Pedazo Piece; small plot of land
Peón Unskilled day laborer
Peso Monetary unit; 8 *reales*
Petate Sleeping mat
Piedra y cal Stone and lime (mortar)
Piezas Slaves, as itemized on inventory lists
Pitas Trinkets
Potros Colts; *(de herradero)* branded (also *de marca*)
Preñadero Lambing specialist
Prieto Black
Procurador Attorney
Procurador (general) de la provincia Chief attorney or attorney general of a Jesuit province
Procuraduría Office of an attorney
Pueblo Village; small community in rural area
Pulque Liquor obtained from the maguey; fermented *aguamiel*
Quesero Cheesemaker
Rancheados Having residence status on a hacienda
Rancho Ranch; small community; usually a subunit of a hacienda

Real Royal; monetary unit; one-eighth of a *peso*
Reales Cash received as wages
Reales alcabalas Royal sales tax
Reata Leather rope used as a lasso
Recojero Roundup specialist
Reducciones Forced resettlement of Indians for purposes of religious conversion
Relator Court reporter
Repartimiento Distribution; forced sale; *encomienda;* usually labor draft
Residencia Court or trial held at the end of a term of office
Ropa Clothing
Ropas Textiles received in lieu of wages
Ruan Fine woolen cloth
Sacatlascale Indigenous dye used for textiles
Saleas Goat hides
Salitre Saltpeter; natural salt deposits; salt used for livestock
Sayal Coarse woolen sackcloth
Sillero Saddler
Sirviente Servant; livestock hacienda worker; *(de la tabla)* on hacienda lists
Sitio Location; property; *(de maguey)* maguey plantings; *(de venta)* for hostel or other business venture
Sobresaliente Substitute for *mayordomo;* supervisor
Soga Rope made of fiber
Soltero Unmarried person
Suplente Substitute supervisor
Tamal Stuffed maize-meal dumpling boiled in maize husks
Tarea Work quota or daily workload
Teniente Deputy or assistant
Tepetate Soil of marginal fertility
Ternera Heifer
Tienda de raya Hacienda store where worker debts were recorded
Tierra Soil; *(floja)* fertile; *(tepetate)* infertile
Tierras realengas Unappropriated or royal lands; *(baldías y sementeras)* vacant and seeded
Tlacotin Indian serf status
Tlatoani Indian ruler of a community
Tomatl Tomato
Tomín Monetary unit; one-eighth of a *peso*
Tortilla Thin pancake of maize meal
Transhumantes Livestock moved between summer and winter pastures
Trapiche Sugar estate with animal-powered sugar mill
Trasquilador Sheep shearer

Trigo Wheat
Troje Granary or storage bin
Tumulto Tumult; uprising
Tuna Prickly pear, a cactus fruit
Vaca Cow; *(de ordeñar)* milk; *(de vientre)* fertile
Vaciada Sheep flock of 3,000 to 5,900 animals
Vaciero Caretaker of a *vaciada*
Vales Bonds or promissory notes
Vaquero Cowboy
Vara Unit of measurement; usually about 33 inches
Visitador Inspector
Visitas Official inspection visits
Viuda Widow
Volante Type of carriage
Yeguas Mares; *(de trilla)* for threshing; *(de vientre)* for breeding
Zambo Person with African and Indian ancestry; also *lobo* or *alobado*
Zócalo Central square in city

Bibliography

Bibliography

My choice of Jesuit estates as a source for examining colonial society was based upon the probability that their documentation would be more copious and better preserved than that for privately owned haciendas. Jesuit bookkeeping practices, the Spanish crown's expropriation of the estates and documents pertaining to them, and the colonial bureaucrat's reluctance to destroy royal papers resulted in a research situation favoring a successful rather than a frustrated venture. However, over time, the wealth of documentation about a single hacienda complex such as Santa Lucía, located close to Mexico City, has been widely scattered. The most important corpus remains in the Archivo General de la Nación (AGN) in Mexico City, although many of the original property titles found their way to Washington State University, at Pullman, in a collection known as the Regla Papers (PCR). Some papers remained with the Regla family in Mexico City or came to be housed in the Biblioteca Nacional de México (BNM), the Museo Nacional de México (BMNM), or the Biblioteca Mariano Cuevas, and some found their way to the Archivo Nacional de Chile (ANC).

Since Santa Lucía was owned by a college pertaining to the Jesuit province of Mexico, but controlled by headquarters in Rome, Jesuit archives in Europe (Rome, Spain) and the Americas (Mexico, the United States, and Chile) have papers valuable for this type of study. As it was not feasible for me personally to examine all known Jesuit holdings, this study in no way exhausts the potential documentation of the topic. Publication of substantial materials related to Jesuit activities in Mexico by Francisco Zambrano (*Diccionario bio-bibliográfico de la Compañía de Jesús en México*), Félix Zubillaga (*Monumenta mexicana*), and the Jesuit Biblioteca Istituti Historici series (including Francisco Javier Alegre's *Historia de la provincia de la Compañía de Jesús de Nueva España*) provides a comprehensive, although selected, view of official correspondence and documents. Careful study of Jesuit collections such as the Archivo Histórico de la Provincia de México and the letters of the fathers general to the Mexican province (Jesuit archives in Rome) hold great potential for a fuller picture of overall Jesuit influences.

Letters, hacienda accounts, legal disputes, and colonial administrative records provided the primary resources for the preparation of this book. In the AGN, the Archivo Histórico de Hacienda (AGNAHH) houses the best single collection, especially legajos 258, 285–88, 293, 297–99, 306–7, 312–16, 322, 324, 328–29, and 862. Other ramos of the AGN found useful were Civil, Hospital de Jesús, Indios, Jesuitas, and Mercedes, legajos 20, 53, 83, 120, 167, 179, 180, 207, 228, 230–35, 238–40, 242, and 247; and Tierras, vols. 234, 238, 1058, 1413, 1476, 1482, 1504–6, 1556–60, 1580, 1634, 1661, 1672, 1687, 1691, 1784, 1803, 1849, 1915, 2033–35, 2054–55, 2080, 2085, 2089, 2200, 2205–7, 2328, 2356, and 2520. In the special manuscript section of BNM, vols. 680–84, 688, 1003–5, 1031–34, 1051, 1058–59, 1078, 1092, 1120, 1319, 1374, 1388, 1766, and 1772–83 were useful. In the Ramo de Jesuítas of the ANC (ANCJM), key volumes were 260, 264, 295, 301, 322, and 330–32. The private library of the late Don Manuel Romero de Terreros in Mexico City and nine volumes of the PCR at Pullman, Washington, were extensively consulted as well.

The bibliography lists articles, books, and published documents cited in the text and the notes.

Acosta Saignes, Miguel. *Vida de los esclavos negros en Venezuela.* Caracas, 1967.

Aguirre Beltrán, Gonzalo. "Ethnohistory in the Study of the Black Population in Mexico," *Contributions of the Latin American Anthropology Group,* 1 (1976): 3–6.

———. "The Integration of the Negro into the National Society of Mexico," in *Race and Class in Latin America,* ed. Magnus Mörner. New York, 1970, pp. 11–27.

———. *Medicina y magia: El proceso de aculturación en la estructura colonial.* Colección SEP/INI, no. 1, 1973. Mexico City, 1963.

———. *La población negra de México 1519–1810: Estudio etnohistórico.* Mexico City, 1946.

———. "The Slave Trade in Mexico," *Hispanic American Historical Review,* 24 (1944): 412–31.

Albo, Xavier. "Jesuítas y culturas indígenas, Perú 1568–1606. Su actitud, métodos y criterios de aculturación," *América indígena,* 26 (1966): 249–308, 395–445.

Alegre, Francisco Javier. *Historia de la provincia de la Compañía de Jesús de Nueva España;* ed. Ernest J. Burrus and Felix Zubillaga. 4 vols. Rome, 1956–1960.

Archer, Christon I. *The Army in Bourbon Mexico, 1760–1810.* Albuquerque, N.M., 1977.

Arcila Farías, Eduardo. *El siglo ilustrado en América: Reformas económicas del siglo XVIII en Nueva España.* Caracas, 1955.

Astrain, Antonio. *Historia de la Compañía de Jesús en la asistencia de España.* 7 vols. Madrid, 1902–1925.

Bakewell, P. J. *Silver Mining and Society in Colonial Mexico: Zacatecas 1546–1700.* Cambridge, 1971.

Barbosa-Ramírez, René A. *La estructura económica de la Nueva España, 1515–1810.* Mexico City, 1971.

Barrett, Ward J. *The Sugar Hacienda of the Marqueses del Valle.* Minneapolis, Minn., 1970.

Bauer, Arnold J. "The Church and Spanish American Agrarian Structure, 1765–1865," *The Americas,* 28 (1971–72): 78–98.

Bazant, Jan. *Cinco haciendas mexicanas: Tres siglos de vida rural en San Luis Potosí (1600–1910).* Centro de Estudios Históricos, n.s. 20. Mexico City, 1975.

Benedict, Harold S. "The Distribution of the Expropriated Jesuit Properties in Mexico, with Special Reference to Chihuahua (1767–1790)." Doctoral dissertation, University of Washington, 1970.

Berthe, Jean-Pierre. "Xochimancas: Les travaux et les jours dans une hacienda sucrière de la Nouvelle-Espagne au XVIIe siècle," *Jahrbuch für Geschichte von Staat, Wirtschaft und Gesellschaft Lateinamerikas*, 3 (1966): 88–117.

Bishko, Charles J. "The Peninsular Background of Latin American Cattle Ranching," *Hispanic American Historical Review*, 32 (1952): 491–515.

Bloch, Marc. *Feudal Society.* Translated by L. A. Manyon. Chicago, 1964.

Bolton, Herbert E. "The Mission as a Frontier Institution in the Spanish Colonies," *American Historical Review*, 23 (1917–18): 42–61.

———. *Rim of Christendom: A Biography of Eusebio Francisco Kino, Pacific Coast Pioneer.* New York, 1936.

Borah, Woodrow W. *New Spain's Century of Depression.* Berkeley, Calif., 1951.

———. "Tithe Collection in the Bishopric of Oaxaca, 1601–1867," *Hispanic American Historical Review*, 29 (1949): 498–517.

Bose, Walter B. *Los orígenes del correo marítimo español de las Indias Occidentales, 1500–1764, y los correos mayores de Indias residentes en España.* La Plata, 1940–41.

Bowser, Frederick P. *The African Slave in Colonial Peru, 1524–1650.* Stanford, Calif., 1974.

Boyd-Bowman, Peter. "Negro Slavery in Early Colonial Mexico," *The Americas*, 26 (1969–1970): 411–29.

———. "Spanish and European Textiles in Sixteenth Century Mexico," *The Americas*, 29 (1972–1973): 334–58.

Brading, David A. "La estructura de la producción agrícola en el Bajío de 1700 a 1850," *Historia mexicana*, 23 (1973): 197–237.

———. *Miners and Merchants in Bourbon Mexico, 1763–1810.* London, 1971.

Brand, Donald D. "The Early History of the Range Cattle Industry in Northern Mexico," *Agricultural History*, 35 (1961): 132–39.

Brodrick, James. *The Economic Morals of the Jesuits: An Answer to Dr. H. M. Robertson.* London, 1934.

———. *The Origins of the Jesuits.* London 1946.

Burrus, Ernest J. *Misiones norteñas mexicanas de la Compañía de Jesús, 1751–1757.* Biblioteca Histórica Mexicana de Obras Inéditas, no. 25. Mexico City, 1963.

Campo, Rafael M. del. "El pulque en el México precortesiano," *Anales del Instituto de Biología*, 9 (1938): 5–23.

Canto López, Antonio. *La guerra de castas en Yucatán.* Mérida, 1976.

Carrera Stampa, Manuel. "The Evolution of Weights and Measures in New Spain," *Hispanic American Historical Review*, 29 (1949): 2–24.

Carta del venerable siervo de Dios D. Juan de Palafox y Mendoza, al sumo pontífice Inocencio X. Translated by D. Salvador González. Mexico City, 1841.

Cartas recibidas de España por Francisco Cervantes de Salazar (1569–1575). Introduction and notes by Augustín Millares Carlo. Biblioteca Histórica Mexicana de Obras Inéditas, no. 20. Mexico City, 1946.

Chance, John K. *Race and Class in Colonial Oaxaca.* Stanford, Calif., 1978.

Charlevoix, Pierre. *The History of Paraguay.* London, 1769.

Chevalier, François. *La formación de los grandes latifundios en México (Tierra y sociedad en los siglos XVI y XVII)*. Translated by Antonio Alatorre. Problemas Agrícolas Industriales de México, vol. 8, no. 1. Mexico City, 1956.

———. "The North Mexican Hacienda: Eighteenth and Nineteenth Centuries," in *The New World Looks at Its History*, ed. Archibald Lewis and Thomas McGann. Austin, Texas, 1963, pp. 95–107.

Clavijero, Francisco Javier, S.J. *Historia antigua de México*, ed. Mariano Cuevas. 4 vols. Mexico City, 1945.

Cline, Howard F. "Civil Congregations of the Indians in New Spain, 1598–1606," *Hispanic American Historical Review*, 29 (1949): 349–69.

———. "Mexican Community Studies," *Hispanic American Historical Review*, 32 (1952): 212–42.

Colmenares, Gérman. *Las haciendas de los Jesuítas en el Nuevo Reino de Granada*. Bogota, 1969.

Cook, Sherburne F., and Woodrow Borah. *Essays in Population History: Mexico and the Caribbean*. 2 vols. Berkeley, Calif., 1971–1974.

Cooper, Donald B. *Epidemic Disease in Mexico City, 1761–1813: An Administrative, Social, and Medical Study*. Austin, Texas, 1965.

Couturier, Edith Boorstein. "Hacienda of Hueyapan: The History of a Mexican Social and Economic Institution, 1550–1940." Doctoral dissertation, Columbia University, 1965.

Crónicas de la Compañía de Jesús en la Nueva España, ed. Francisco González de Cossío. Biblioteca del Estudiante Universitario, no. 73. Mexico City, 1957.

Cuevas, Mariano. *Historia de la iglesia en México*. 5 vols. Mexico City, 1946–1947.

Cushner, Nicolas P. "Slave Mortality and Reproduction on Jesuit Haciendas in Colonial Peru," *Hispanic American Historical Review*, 55 (1975): 177–99.

Davidson, David M. "Negro Slave Control and Resistance in Colonial Mexico, 1519–1650," *Hispanic American Historical Review*, 46 (1966): 235–53.

Decorme, Gerard. *La obra de los Jesuítas mexicanos durante la época colonial, 1572–1767*. 2 vols. Mexico City, 1941.

Dessaint, Alain Y. "Effects of the Hacienda and Plantation Systems on Guatemala's Indians," *América indígena*, 22 (1962): 323–54.

Documentos para la historia de México. Vol. 7, *Don Juan de Palafox y Mendoza*, ed. Genaro García. Mexico City, 1906.

Documentos sobre la expulsión de los Jesuítas y ocupación de sus temporalidades en Nueva España, 1772–1783, ed. V. Rico González. Publicaciones del Instituto de Historia, 1st ser., no. 13. Mexico City, 1949.

Dunne, Peter M. *Early Jesuit Missions in Tarahumara*. Berkeley, Calif., 1948.

Durán, Diego. *Historia de las Indias de Nueva España e islas de la tierra firme*, ed. Angel Ma. Garibay K. 2 vols. Biblioteca Porrúa, nos. 36 and 37. Mexico City, 1967.

Durham, Philip, and Everett L. Jones. *The Negro Cowboys*. New York, 1965.

Dusenberry, William H. *The Mexican Mesta: The Administration of Ranching in Colonial Mexico*. Urbana, Ill., 1963.

———. "The Regulation of Meat Supply in Sixteenth-Century Mexico City," *Hispanic American Historical Review*, 28 (1948): 38–52.

————. "Woolen Manufacture in Sixteenth-Century New Spain," *The Americas*, 4 (1947–1948): 223–34.

Enggass, Peter M. "The Spanish League: A Geographical Conspiracy," *Journal of Geography*, 70 (1971): 407–10.

Epistolario de la Nueva España, 1505–1818, ed. Francisco del Paso y Troncoso. 16 vols. Biblioteca Histórica Mexicana de Obras Inéditas, 2nd ser. Mexico City, 1942.

Espejo-Ponce de Hunt, Marta. "Colonial Yucatán: Town and Region." Doctoral dissertation, University of California, Los Angeles, 1974.

Espinosa Pólit, Manuel María. *Perfect Obedience*. Westminster, Md., 1947.

Ewald, Ursula. *Estudios sobre la hacienda colonial en México: Las propiedades rurales del Colegio Espíritu Santo en Puebla*. Translated by Luis R. Cerna. Das Mexiko-Projekt der Deutschen Forschungsgemeinschaft, 9. Wiesbaden, 1976.

Florencia, Francisco. *Historia de la Compañía de Jesús en la Nueva España*. 2 vols. Mexico City, 1694.

Florescano, Enrique. "Perspectivas de la historia económica en México," *Investigaciones contemporáneas sobre historia de México*. Memorias de la Tercera Reunión de Historiadores Mexicanos y Norteamericanos, Oaxtepec, Morelos, November 4–7, 1969. Mexico City, 1971, pp. 317–38.

————. *Precios del maíz y crisis agrícolas en México (1708–1810)*. Mexico City, 1969.

————, ed. *Haciendas, latifundios y plantaciones en América Latina*. Mexico City, 1975.

————, ed. *La historia económica en América Latina*. 2 vols. Mexico City, 1972.

Foss, Michael. *The Founding of the Jesuits, 1540*. London, 1969.

Galván Rivera, Mariano. *Ordenanzas de tierras y aguas o sea formulario geométrico-judicial*. Paris, 1868.

Ganss, George E. *Saint Ignatius' Idea of a Jesuit University: A Study in the History of Catholic Education*. Milwaukee, Wis., 1956.

García, Genaro V. *Don Juan de Palafox y Mendoza, obispo de Puebla*. Mexico City, 1918.

García Bernal, Cristina. *La sociedad de Yucatán, 1700–1750*. Seville, 1972.

García Martínez, Bernardo. *El Marquesado del Valle: Tres siglos de régimen señorial en la Nueva España*. Mexico City, 1969.

Geertz, Clifford. *Agricultural Involution: The Processes of Ecological Change in Indonesia*. Berkeley, Calif., 1963.

Gemelli Carreri, Juan F. *Viaje a la Nueva España: México a fines del siglo XVII*. Translated by José María Agreda y Sánchez. 2 vols. Biblioteca Mínima Mexicana, vols. 13 and 14. Mexico City, 1955.

Gerhard, Peter. *A Guide to the Historical Geography of New Spain*. Cambridge Latin American Studies, no. 14. Cambridge, 1972.

————. *México en 1742*. Mexico City, 1962.

Gibson, Charles. *The Aztecs Under Spanish Rule: A History of the Indians of the Valley of Mexico, 1519–1810*. Stanford, Calif., 1964.

————. *Spain in America*. New York, 1966.

————. *Tlaxcala in the Sixteenth Century*. New Haven, Conn., 1952.

————. "The Transformation of the Indian Community in New Spain, 1500–1810," *Journal of World History*, 2 (1955): 581–607.

———. "Writings on Colonial Mexico," *Hispanic American Historical Review*, 55 (1975): 287–323.

Gonçalves de Lima, Oswaldo. *El maguey y el pulque en los códices mexicanos.* Mexico City, 1956.

Góngora, Mario. *Studies in the Colonial History of Spanish America.* Translated by Richard Southern. Cambridge, 1975.

González, Luis. *Pueblo en vilo: Microhistoria de San José de García.* Mexico City, 1968.

González de Cossío, Francisco, *Historia de la tenencia y explotación del campo desde la época precortesiana hasta las leyes del 6 de enero de 1915.* 2 vols. Mexico City, 1957.

González Navarro, Moisés. "Las guerras de castas," *Historia mexicana*, 26 (1976): 70–106.

———. *Raza y tierra: La guerra de castas y el henequén.* Mexico City, 1970.

González Sánchez, Isabel, ed. *Haciendas y ranchos de Tlaxcala en 1712.* Mexico City, 1969.

Gracía, Joaquín. *Los Jesuítas en Córdoba.* Buenos Aires and Mexico City, 1940.

Graham, Robert B. *A Vanished Arcadia; being some account of the Jesuits in Paraguay, 1607–1767.* London, 1901.

Greenleaf, Richard E. "The Inquisition and the Indians: A Study in Jurisdictional Confusion," *The Americas*, 2 (1965–66): 138–66.

———. "The Obraje in the Late Mexican Colony," *The Americas*, 23 (1966–67): 227–50.

———. "Viceregal Power and the Obrajes of the Cortés Estate, 1595–1708," *Hispanic American Historical Review*, 48 (1968): 365–79.

———, ed. *The Roman Catholic Church in Latin America.* New York, 1971.

Haring, Clarence H. *The Spanish Empire in America.* New York, 1947.

Harris, Charles H. *A Mexican Family Empire: The Latifundio of the Sánchez Navarros, 1765–1867.* Austin, Texas, 1975.

Hartman, Keith. "The Henequen Empire in Yucatán: 1870–1910." Master's thesis, University of Iowa, 1966.

Heath, Dwight B. *Contemporary Cultures and Societies of Latin America.* 2nd ed. New York, 1974.

Hough, Walter. "The Pulque of Mexico," *Proceedings of the United States National Museum*, 33 (1908): 577–92.

Huerta, María T., and Patricia Palacios. *Rebeliones indígenas de la época colonial.* Mexico City, 1976.

Hughes, Thomas A. *Loyola and the Educational System of the Jesuits.* New York, 1892.

Hurtado López, Flor de María. *Dolores Hidalgo: Estudio económico, 1740–1790.* SEP-INAH, Departamento de Investigaciones Históricas, no. 11. Mexico City, 1974.

Instrucciones a los hermanos jesuítas administradores de haciendas, ed. François Chevalier. Publicaciones del Instituto de Historia, 1st ser., no. 18. Mexico City, 1950.

An Inventory of the Collection of the Middle American Research Institute. No. 2. Calendar of the Yucatecan Letters. New Orleans, 1939.

Jacobsen, Jacob V. *Educational Foundations of the Jesuits in Sixteenth Century New Spain.* Berkeley, Calif., 1938.

Katz, Friedrich. *The Ancient American Civilisations.* Translated by George Weidenfeld. London, 1969.
——. "Labor Conditions on Haciendas in Porfirian Mexico: Some Trends and Tendencies," *Hispanic American Historical Review,* 54 (1974): 1–47.
Keith, Robert G. "Encomienda, Hacienda and Corregimiento in Spanish America," *Hispanic American Historical Review,* 51 (1971): 431–46.
——, ed. *Haciendas and Plantations in Latin American History.* New York, 1977.
King, James F. "Descriptive Data on Negro Slaves in Spanish Importation Records and Bills of Sale," *Journal of Negro History,* 28 (1943): 204–19.
Klein, Herbert S. "Peasant Communities in Revolt: The Tzeltal Republic of 1712," *Pacific Historical Review,* 35 (1966): 247–63.
Klein, Julius. *The Mesta: A Study in Spanish Economic History, 1273–1836.* Cambridge, Mass., 1920.
Konetzke, Richard, ed. *Colección de documentos para la historia de la formación social de Hispanoamérica, 1493–1810.* 3 vols. Madrid, 1953–1962.
Ladd, Doris. "The Mexican Nobility at Independence, 1780–1826." Doctoral dissertation, Stanford University, 1972.
Lang, James. *Conquest and Commerce: Spain and England in the Americas.* New York, 1975.
Lavrín, Asunción. "El convento de Santa Clara de Querétaro—La administración de sus propiedades en el siglo XVII," *Historia mexicana,* 25 (1975): 76–117.
——. "The Role of the Nunneries in the Economy of New Spain in the Eighteenth Century," *Hispanic American Historical Review,* 46 (1966): 371–93.
Leite, Serafim. *História da Companhia de Jesus no Brasil.* 10 vols. Lisbon and Rio de Janeiro, 1938–1950.
Leonard, Irving A. *Baroque Times in Old Mexico: Seventeenth-Century Persons, Places, and Practices.* Ann Arbor, Mich. 1959.
Lockhart, James. "Encomienda and Hacienda: The Evolution of the Great Estate in the Spanish Indies," *Hispanic American Historical Review,* 49 (1969): 411–29.
——. "The Social History of Colonial Spanish America: Evolution and Potential," *Latin American Research Review,* 7 (1972): 6–45.
——. *Spanish Peru, 1532–1560.* Madison, Wis., 1968.
López de Cogolludo, Diego. *Historia de Yucatán.* 3 vols. Campeche, 1955.
López Sarrelangue, Delfina E. "La hacienda de San José Coapa," in *Haciendas, latifundios y plantaciones en América latina,* ed. Enrique Florescano. Mexico City, 1975, pp. 223–41.
Lugones, Leopoldo. *El imperio jesuítico.* 3rd ed. Buenos Aires, 1945.
Lynch, John. *Spain Under the Hapsburgs.* Vol. 2, *Spain and America, 1598–1700.* Oxford, 1969.
Macera, Pablo. "Feudalismo colonial americano: El caso de las haciendas peruanas," *Studia latinamericana,* 35 (1971): 3–43.
——. *Instrucciones para el manejo de las haciendas jesuítas del Perú (ss. XVII–XVIII).* Nueva crónica, vol. 2. Lima, 1966.
MacEwan, J. W. Grant. *John Ware's Cow Country.* Edmonton, Alta, 1960.
MacLeod, Murdo J. *Spanish Central America: A Socio-Economic History, 1520–1720.* Berkeley, Calif., 1973.

Madsen, William. *The Virgin's Children: Life in an Aztec Village Today.* Austin, Texas, 1960.
Matesanz, José Antonio. "Introducción de la ganadería en Nueva España, 1521–1535," *Historica mexicana,* 14 (1965): 533–66.
Mathes, W. Michael. "To Save a City: The Desagüe of Mexico-Huehuetoca, 1607," *The Americas,* 26 (1969–1970): 419–38.
McBride, George M. *The Land Systems of Mexico.* New York, 1923.
Mellafe, Rolando. *Breve historia de la esclavitud negra en América Latina.* Mexico City, 1973.
Miller, Frank, *Old Villages and a New Town: Industrialization in Mexico.* Menlo Park, Calif., 1973.
Miranda, José. *La función económica del encomendero en los orígenes del régimen colonial (Nueva España, 1525–1531).* 2nd ed. Mexico City, 1965.
Montemayor, Loyola. *La industria del pulque.* Mexico City, 1956.
Moreno Toscano, Alejandra. *Geografía económica de México (siglo XVI).* Mexico City, 1968.
Morin, Claude. "Croissance et disparités sociales dans une économie coloniale: Le Centre-Ouest mexicain au XVIII siècle." Doctorat de 3ᵉ cycle, Université de Paris X—Nanterre, 1974.
———. *Santa Inés Zacatelco (1646–1812): Contribución a la demografía histórica del México colonial.* Mexico City, 1973.
Mörner, Magnus. *La corona española y los foráneos en los pueblos de indios de América.* Instituto de Estudios Ibero-Américanos, ser. A, no. 1. Stockholm, 1970.
———. "Los Jesuítas y la esclavitud de los negros," *Revista chilena de historia y geografía,* 135 (1967): 92–109.
———. "Los motivos de la expulsión de los Jesuítas del imperio español," *Historia mexicana,* 16 (1966): 1–14.
———. *The Political and Economic Activities of the Jesuits in the La Plata Region.* Stockholm, 1953.
———. *Race Mixture in the History of Latin America.* Boston, 1967.
———. "The Spanish American Hacienda: A Survey of Recent Research and Debate," *Hispanic American Historical Review,* 53 (1973): 183–216.
———, ed. *The Expulsion of the Jesuits from Latin America.* New York, 1965.
Morrisey, Richard J. "Colonial Agriculture in New Spain," *Agricultural History,* 31 (1957): 24–29.
———. "The Northward Expansion of Cattle Ranching in New Spain," *Agricultural History,* 25 (1951): 115–21.
Motolinía (Toribio de Benavente). *History of the Indians of New Spain.* Translated by Elizabeth A. Foster, Berkeley, Calif. 1950.
Nash, June. "Social Resources of a Latin American Peasantry: The Case of a Maya Indian Community," *Social and Economic Studies,* 15 (1966): 353–67.
Nash, Manning. *Primitive and Peasant Economic Systems.* Scranton, Pa., 1966.
Nombres geográficos indígenas del estado de México, ed. Mario Colin. Mexico City, 1966.
O'Leary, Timothy J. *Ethnographic Bibliography of South America.* New Haven, Conn., 1963.
Olin, John C., ed. *The Autobiography of St. Ignatius Loyola, with Related Documents.* Translated by Joseph O'Callaghan. New York, 1974.

Osborn, Wayne S. "A Community Study of Metztitlán, New Spain, 1520–1810." Doctoral dissertation, University of Iowa, 1970.

——. "Indian Land Retention in Colonial Metztitlán," *Hispanic American Historical Review*, 53 (1973): 218–38.

Palmer, Colin A. *Slaves of the White God: Blacks in Mexico, 1570–1650.* Cambridge, Mass., 1976.

Parry, John H. *The Spanish Seaborne Empire.* London, 1966.

Patch, Robert. "La formación de estancias y haciendas en Yucatán durante la colonia," *Boletín de la Escuela de Ciencias Antropológicas de la Universidad de Yucatán*, 4 (1976): 21–61.

Payno, Manuel. *Memorias sobre el maguey mexicano y sus diversos productos.* Mexico City, 1864.

Pérez de Rivas, Andrés. *Crónica e historia religiosa de la Compañía de Jesús en la Nueva España.* 2 vols. Mexico City, 1896.

Popescu, Oreste. *El sistema económico en las misiones jesuítas: Un vasto experimento de desarrollo indoamericano.* 2nd ed. Barcelona, 1967.

Redfield, Robert. *The Folk Culture of Yucatán.* Chicago, 1941.

——. *Peasant Culture and Society.* Chicago, 1956.

Reed, Nelson. *The Caste War of Yucatán.* Stanford, Calif., 1964.

Ricard, Robert. *La conquista espiritual de México.* Mexico City, 1947.

Riley, James D. *Hacendados jesuítas en México: El Colegio Máximo de San Pedro y San Pablo, 1685–1767.* Mexico City, 1976.

——. "The Management of the Estates of the Jesuit Colegio Máximo de San Pedro y San Pablo of Mexico City in the Eighteenth Century." Doctoral dissertation, Tulane University, 1971.

——. "The Wealth of the Jesuits in Mexico, 1670–1767," *The Americas*, 33 (1976–77): 226–66.

Riley, Michael G. *The Estate of Fernando Cortés in the Cuernavaca Area of Mexico, 1522–1547.* Albuquerque, N.M., 1972.

——. "El prototipo de la hacienda en el centro de México: Un caso del siglo XVI," in *Haciendas, latifundios y plantaciones en América latina*, ed. Enrique Florescano. Mexico City, 1975, pp. 49–70.

Romero de Terreros, Manuel. *Antiguas haciendas de México.* Mexico City, 1956.

Sahagún, Bernardino de. *General History of the Things of New Spain: Florentine Codex.* Translated by Arthur J. O. Anderson and Charles E. Dibble. Monographs of the School of American Research, no. 14. Santa Fe, N.M., 1950–.

Saint Ignatius of Loyola: The Constitutions of the Society of Jesus. Translated, with an introduction and a commentary, by George E. Ganss. St. Louis, Mo., 1970.

Sánchez Baquero, Juan. *Fundación de la Compañía de Jesús en la Nueva España, 1571–1580.* Mexico City, 1945.

Scholes, France V. "The Spanish Conqueror as a Business Man," *New Mexico Quarterly*, 28 (1958): 1–29.

Semo, Enrique, and Gloria Pedrero. "La vida en una hacienda-aserradero mexicana a principios del siglo XIX," in *Haciendas, latifundios y plantaciones en América latina*, ed. Enrique Florescano, Mexico City, 1975, pp. 273–305.

Shiels, W. Eugene. "The Legal Crisis in the Jesuit Missions of Hispanic America," *Mid-America*, 21 (1939): 253–76.

Simmons, Charles E. P. "Palafox and His Critics: Reappraising a Controversy," *Hispanic American Historical Review,* 46 (1966): 394–408.
Simpson, Lesley B. *The Encomienda in New Spain: The Beginning of Spanish Mexico.* Berkeley, Calif., 1950.
———. *Exploitation of Land in Central Mexico in the Sixteenth Century.* Ibero-Americano, no. 36. Berkeley, Calif., 1952.
———. "Mexico's Forgotten Century," *The Pacific Historical Review,* 22 (1953): 113–21.
———. *Studies in the Administration of the Indians in New Spain.* 3 vols. Ibero-Americano, nos. 7, 13, and 16. Berkeley, Calif., 1934–1940.
Solórzano y Pereira, Juan de. *Política indiana.* Amberes, 1703.
Soustelle, Jacques. *Daily Life of the Aztecs on the Eve of the Spanish Conquest.* Stanford, Calif., 1961.
Spicer, Edward H. *Potam, A Yaqui Village in Sonora.* American Anthropological Association Memoir, no. 77. Menasha, Wis., 1954.
Stavenhagen, Rodolfo. *Las clases sociales en las sociedades agrarias.* 8th ed. Mexico City, 1976.
Strickon, Arnold. "Hacienda and Plantation in Yucatán: An Historical-Ecological Consideration of the Folk-Urban Continuum in Yucatán," *América indígena,* 25 (1965): 35–63.
Super, John C. "Querétaro Obrajes: Industry and Society in Provincial Mexico, 1600–1810," *Hispanic American Historical Review,* 56 (1976): 197–216.
Tannenbaum, Frank. *Ten Keys to Latin America.* New York, 1960.
Taylor, William B. "Haciendas coloniales en el Valle de Oaxaca," *Historia mexicana,* 23 (1973): 284–329.
———. "Landed Society in New Spain: A View from the South," *Hispanic American Historical Review,* 54 (1974): 387–413.
———. *Landlord and Peasant in Colonial Oaxaca.* Stanford, Calif., 1972.
Thomas Gage's Travels in the New World. Translated by J. Eric S. Thompson. Norman, Okla., 1958.
Thompson, J. Eric S. *Mexico Before Cortés.* 2nd ed. New York, 1937.
Thwaite, R. G., ed. *Jesuit Relations and Allied Documents.* 73 vols. Cleveland, Ohio, 1894–1907.
Tovar Pinzón, H. "Elementos constitutivos de la empresa agraria jesuíta en la segunda mitad del siglo XVIII en México," in *Haciendas, latifundios y plantaciones en América latina,* ed. Enrique Florescano. Mexico City, 1975, pp. 132–222.
Tratado del las idolatrías, supersticiones, dioses, ritos, hechicerías y otras costumbres gentilicias de las razas aborígenes de México, ed. Francisco del Paso y Troncoso. 2nd ed. Mexico City, 1953.
Tutino, John. "Hacienda Social Relations in Mexico: The Chalco Region in the Era of Independence," *Hispanic American Historical Review,* 55 (1975): 496–528.
Vaillant, George C. *Aztecs of Mexico: Origin, Rise, and Fall of the Aztec Nation.* Garden City, N.Y., 1944.
Vásquez, Genaro V., ed. *Doctrinas y realidades en la legislación para los indios.* Mexico City, 1940.
Vázquez de Espinosa, Antonio. *Compendium and Description of the West Indies.* Translated by Charles U. Clark. Smithsonian Miscellaneous Collections, vol. 102. Washington, D.C., 1942.

Villerías, Gaspar de. *Relación breve de la venida de los de la Compañía de Jesús en la Nueva España,* ed. Francisco de Cossío. Mexico City, 1952.

Villoslada, García R. *Manual de historia de la Compañía de Jesús.* Madrid, 1954.

Warren, Fintan B. *Vasco de Quiroga and His Pueblo-Hospitals of Santa Fe.* Washington, D.C., 1963.

Warren, J. Benedict. "Managing an Encomendero's Business in Michoacán," paper presented at 23rd Annual Rocky Mountain Council for Latin American Studies Conference, Glendale, Ariz., 1975.

Wauchope, Robert, ed. *Handbook of Middle American Indians.* 16 vols. Austin, Texas, 1964–1976.

Wentworth, Edward N. "Trailing Sheep from California to Idaho in 1865: The Journal of Gorham Gates Kimball," *Agricultural History,* 28 (1954): 49–83.

Willems, Emilio. *Latin American Culture: An Anthropological Synthesis.* New York, 1975.

Wolf, Eric. *Peasants.* Englewood Cliffs, N.J., 1966.

———. *Sons of the Shaking Earth.* Chicago, 1959.

———. "Types of Latin American Peasantry," *American Anthropologist,* 57 (1955): 452–71.

Wolf, Eric, and Edward Hansen. *The Human Condition in Latin America.* New York, 1972.

Wolf, Eric, and Sidney Mintz. "Haciendas and Plantations in Middle America and the Antilles," *Social and Economic Studies,* 6 (1957): 380–412.

Zabriskie, Luther K. "Pulque and Other Maguey Products," *Bulletin of the Pan American Union,* 48 (1919): 275–88.

Zambrano, Francisco, ed. *Diccionario bio-bibliográfico de la Compañía de Jesús en México.* 10 vols. Mexico City, 1961–1970.

Zavala, Silvio. *La encomienda indiana.* 2nd ed. Biblioteca Porrúa, no. 53. Mexico City, 1973.

———. *De encomiendas y propiedad territorial en algunas regiones de la América Española.* Mexico City, 1940.

———. "Erígenes coloniales del peonaje en México," *Trimestre económico,* 10 (1943–1944): 711–48.

Zavala, Silvio, and José Miranda. "Instituciones indígenas en la colonia," in Alfonso Caso et al., *La política indigenista en México: Métodos y resultados.* 2nd ed. SEP/INI Colección no. 20. Mexico City, 1973.

Zelis, Rafael de. "Catálogo de los sujetos de la Compañía de Jesús que formaban la provincia de México el día del arresto, 25 de junio de 1767," in *Tesoros documentales de México, siglo XVIII,* ed. [Antonio López de] Priego, [Rafael de] Zelis, and [Francisco Javier] Clavijero. Mexico City, 1944, pp. 231–93.

Zorita, Alonso de. *Life and Labor in Ancient Mexico: The Brief and Summary Relations of the Lords of New Spain.* Translated by Benjamin Keen. New Brunswick, N.J., 1963.

Zubillaga, Félix, S. J., comp. *Monumenta mexicana.* 5 vols. Rome, 1956–1973. *Monumenta historica Societatis Jesu,* vols. 77, 84, 97, 104, 106.

Index

Index

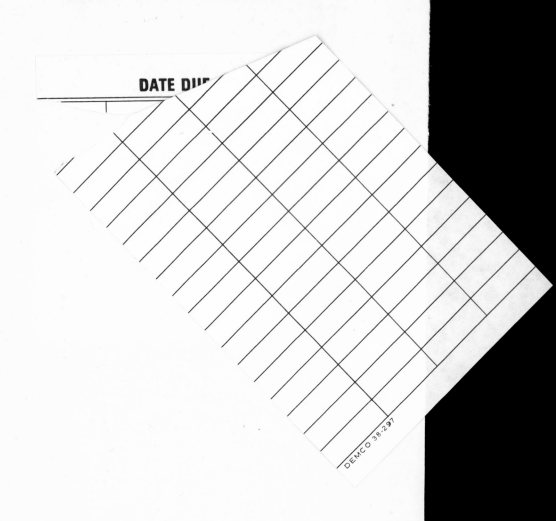

DATE DUE

DEMCO 38-297